The Mysteries of All Nations

Rise and Progress of Superstition, Laws Against and Trials of Witches, Ancient and Modern Delusions Together With Strange Customs, Fables, and Tales

James Grant

Contents

PREFACE. 7

THE RISE AND PROGRESS OF SUPERSTITION. 9

CHAPTER I. 9

CHAPTER II. 15

CHAPTER III. 18

CHAPTER IV. 21

CHAPTER V. 25

CHAPTER VI. 30

CHAPTER VII. 33

CHAPTER VIII. 38

THE GODS AND GODDESSES OF HEATHEN NATIONS. 44

CHAPTER IX. 44

CHAPTER X. 48

CHAPTER XI. 52

MYTHOLOGY OF GERMANY, GREAT BRITAIN, SCANDINAVIA, ETC. 60

CHAPTER XII. 60

NAMES OF DAYS, WHENCE DERIVED. 68

CHAPTER XIII. 68

NAMES OF MONTHS, WHENCE DERIVED. 74

CHAPTER XIV. 74

MIRACLES PERFORMED BY SAINTS AND OTHER HOLY ....

PERSONS, AND THE INFLUENCE OF SACRED RELICS. 85

CHAPTER XV. 85

HOW THE POETS HAVE FANNED THE FLAME OF SUPERSTITION. 96

CHAPTER XVI. 96

CHAPTER XVII. 106

CHAPTER XVIII. 115

CHAPTER XIX. 131

CHAPTER XX. 138

CHAPTER XXI. 150

CHAPTER XXII. 156

MONARCHS, PRIESTS, PHILOSOPHERS, AND SUPERSTITION. 174

CHAPTER XXIII. 174

CHAPTER XXIV. 179

CHAPTER XXV. 187

THE DRUIDS. 192

CHAPTER XXVI. 192
CHAPTER XXVII. 196
DEMONOLOGY. 200
CHAPTER XXVIII. 200
CHAPTER XXIX. 204
CHAPTER XXX. 207
CHAPTER XXXI. 211
CHAPTER XXXII. 216
CHAPTER XXXIII. 220
CHAPTER XXXIV. 225
CHAPTER XXXV. 229
CHAPTER XXXVI. 232
MAGIC AND ASTROLOGY. 244
CHAPTER XXXVII. 244
CHAPTER XXXVIII. 250
CHAPTER XXXIX. 254
DIVINATION AND ORACLES. 258
CHAPTER XL. 258
SIGNS, OMENS, AND WARNINGS. 264
CHAPTER XLI. 264
CHAPTER XLII. 269
CHAPTER XLIII. 273
CHAPTER XLIV. 277
AMULETS AND CHARMS. 282
CHAPTER XLV. 282
CHAPTER XLVI. 290
CHAPTER XLVII. 294
CHAPTER XLVIII. 298
CHAPTER XLIX. 303
TRIALS BY ORDEAL. 309
CHAPTER L. 309
CHAPTER LI. 315
CURSES AND EVIL WISHES. 320
CHAPTER LII. 320
CHAPTER LIII. 328
DREAMS AND VISIONS OF THE NIGHT 332
CHAPTER LIV. 332
CHAPTER LV. 336
LAWS AGAINST AND TRIALS OF WITCHES. 340
CHAPTER LVI. 340
CHAPTER LVII. 349
CHAPTER LVIII. 355
CHAPTER LIX. 367
CHAPTER LX. 372
CHAPTER LXI. 376
CHAPTER LXII. 381
CHAPTER LXIII. 388
CHAPTER LXIV. 393
CHAPTER LXV. 397
CHAPTER LXVI. 401
CHAPTER LXVII. 408
SUPERSTITION IN THE NINETEENTH CENTURY. 413
CHAPTER LXVIII. 413
CHAPTER LXIX. 420
CHAPTER LXX. 428
CHAPTER LXXI. 435
CHAPTER LXXII. 443
CHAPTER LXXIII. 447

THE MYSTERIES OF ALL NATIONS

RISE AND PROGRESS OF SUPERSTITION, LAWS AGAINST AND TRIALS OF WITCHES, ANCIENT AND MODERN DELUSIONS TOGETHER WITH STRANGE CUSTOMS, FABLES, AND TALES

by

James Grant

PREFACE.

In whatever light this work may be regarded by archaeologists and general readers, the writer submits it to the public, chiefly as the result of antiquarian research, and actual observation during a period of nearly forty years. The writer does not attempt to define what superstition is, either in its broadest or most literal sense; but, as he desires the expression to be understood, it may be considered to imply a fear of the Evil One and his emissaries, a trust in benign spirits and saints, a faith in occult science, and a belief that a conjunction of certain planets or other inanimate bodies is capable of producing supernatural effects, either beneficial or prejudicial to man. Superstition, generally so called, has run through a course of ages from sire to son, leaving it still deeply rooted in the minds of many of the present generation.

Not a few seeming repetitions in this work are not such in reality, but are instances brought forward to mark the resemblance between the opinions prevalent in past and present times, and to illustrate the similarity of perverted views in various parts of the world.

The examples of superstition herein given are taken from an almost unlimited number, yet the writer confesses to have omitted many interesting particulars. In proof of this it may be stated, that while the last sheet of these pages was being revised, an esteemed friend wrote, saying: "I can quite corroborate what you say of Ireland; for lately, on my way from Macroom to Glengariff, at a weird mountain pass, the coach stopped to enable us to visit the hermitage of St. Finbar. There, beside a lonely lake, I saw a number of devotees, afflicted with various ailments, expecting to be healed through the good offices of the departed saint."

In spite of a determination to omit unimportant matter and to be concise, this volume has swelled out far beyond what was originally intended. The more the subject of superstition is studied, the more interesting it becomes. One judges of a nation's strength by its victories, of its industry by its products, of its wealth by its mines and cultivated fields, of its domestic condition by its diet and dress, of its moral condition by its laws, of its religion and intelligence by its literature; but before obtaining full knowledge of a people's convictions, it is necessary to search into their superstitions. In these are discovered the secrets of man's inner life, and by these also have been forged strong fetters, which have kept his soul in thraldom for ages.

If the author has succeeded in pointing out, that, notwithstanding the progress of science and the advancement of civilisation and Christianity, some of the darker shadows that have disfigured past ages are still floating over a portion of our social horizon, he feels his labour will not have been altogether in vain. Like many of the ghosts alluded to in the following pages, that of superstition needs only the continued light of day to shine upon it, in order to make it vanish for ever.

January 1880.

THE RISE AND PROGRESS OF SUPERSTITION.

CHAPTER I.

Rise and Progress of Superstition--The Serpent--Cain's Departure from the true Worship--Worship of the Sun, Moon, and Stars--Strange Story of Abraham--The Gods of Antiquity--Ether, Air, Land, and Water filled with living Souls--Guardian Angel--Cause of the Flood--Magic--How the Jews deceived the Devil--A Witch   not permitted to live--Diviners, Enchanters, Consulters with familiar Spirits and Necromancers proved a Snare to Nations--Charms worn by the Jews--Singular Customs and Belief--Prognostication--Allegorical Emblems--Marriage   Customs--Divers Ceremonies at Death and Burials--Divination among all Nations--Observers of Times--Opinion concerning the Celestial Bodies--Power of Witches--Wizards--Necromancers' Power to call up the Dead.

Superstition has prevailed in every generation and country in the world. There are people who think that even Adam and Eve were tainted with this hateful delusion, and that their offspring of the second generation entertained opinions opposed to true religion. That man, soon after the Creation, became acquainted with and yielded to the doctrine of devils, scarcely admits of doubt. Those who conversed with our first parents must have learned from them the circumstances connected with the temptation, fall, and expulsion from the Garden of Eden. It is not unreasonable, then, to suppose that the serpent was looked upon at an early period as something more than an ordinary earthly reptile. One can imagine Adam and Eve, when wandering in perplexity and fear, after their first great sin, starting at the sight of a serpent,--not being certain whether they beheld a reptile of flesh merely, or looked upon their old enemy that had betrayed them in their days of innocence. If they looked with suspicion on the serpent, it is natural to suppose that their children would learn to view this creeping animal as a creature endowed with supernatural powers, by which it could bring about evil, and perhaps good.

Cain, there is reason to conclude, departed from the true worship of the Most High before his offering was refused, and ere he dipped his hands in his brother's blood. In Genesis iv. 26 there is an implication that man had forsaken the right and holy religion prior to the days of Seth. There is an opinion that men soon began to worship the sun, moon, and stars, and that subsequently they paid homage to objects which contributed to their preservation and to things that might do them injury. The wandering Jew, Benjamin, one of the greatest travellers in the East, gives an interesting account of solar worship in early times. The posterity of Cush, he tells us, were addicted to the contemplation of the stars, and worshipped the sun as a god. Their towns were filled with altars dedicated to this orb. At early morn the people rose, and ran out of the cities to await the rising sun, to which on every altar there was a consecrated image, not in the likeness of a man, but after the fashion of the solar orb, formed by magic art. These artificial orbs, as soon as the sun rose, took fire, and resounded with a great noise, to the joy of the deluded devotees.

Many Jewish doctors have condescended upon the precise time when man began to commit idolatry, and they name Enos as the first star-worshipper. Arabian divines tell a story of Abraham being brought up in a dark cave, and at his first coming forth he was so much struck with the appearance of the sun, moon, and stars, that he worshipped them; and there are people who imagine that in the Book of Job they discover evidence of the heavenly host being adored in the time of the old patriarch of Uz.

Some suppose that all the gods of antiquity were Egyptian kings, others that they were Thessalian princes, others that they were Jewish patriarchs; while not a few are of opinion that they were kings of the several countries where they were worshipped. It has been supposed that Saturn represented Adam; Rhea, Eve; Jupiter, Cain; Prometheus, Abel; Apollo, Lamech; Mercury, Jabal; Bacchus, Noah; and Phaeton, Elias. Others imagine that Saturn came in place of Noah; Pluto, of Sem; Neptune, of Japheth; Bacchus, of Nimrod; and Apollo, of Phut. A third class of thinkers maintain that all the heathen gods centre in Moses, and the goddesses in Zipporah his wife, or in Miriam his sister. A fourth class hold that Saturn was Abraham; Rhea, Sarah; Ceres, Keturah; Pallas, Hagar; Jupiter, Isaac; Juno, Rebecca; Pluto, Ishmael; Typhon, Jacob; and Venus, Rachel. Such are examples of imaginary resemblances between real and fictitious persons or gods that never had any existence except in the minds of fanatical romancers and a deluded people, whose faith was kept alive by deception and artifice.

It was an early belief that ether, air, land, and water were full of living spirits; and people believed, soon after man was created, that the souls of just men, subsequent to death, had part of the universe committed to them. This opinion being once established, assistance was sought from the spirits of departed men and women, and efforts were made in various ways to secure their favour. In course of time altars were set up, temples consecrated, and sometimes victims offered to obtain favour from spirits and false gods. Some rabbis affirmed that the angel Raziel was Adam's master, and taught him the Cabbala; and that Shem, Abraham, Isaac, Jacob, Joseph, Moses, Elias, etc. had each his guardian angel, who directed his thoughts and actions. Jewish doctors assign to magic great antiquity; they assert that it was known to those who lived before the Flood. There is a tradition that one of the causes of the Flood was the intercourse men had with demons. Though it has been stated by ancient historians that Abraham was given to magic, and that he taught it to his children, Josephus (obviously overlooking what had been written prior to his time, and forgetting what Moses had seen performed by the Egyptian priests before Pharaoh) thinks Solomon was the first who practised this art. The Jewish historian gives credit to the "wisest man" for inventing and transmitting to posterity certain incantations for the cure of diseases, and for the expulsion of evil spirits from the bodies of those possessed with such demons. According to Josephus, the expulsion was brought about by the use of a certain root sealed up in a wrapper, and held under the afflicted person's nose while the name of Solomon and words prescribed by him were pronounced. The learned historian does not seem to doubt the wonderful power of Solomon, but rather advances statements corroborative of what he had heard, for he asserts that he himself was an eye-witness to a like cure effected, by equally mysterious means, on a person named Eleazar in presence of the Emperor Vespasian. Descendants of Abraham believed that their great ancestor wore round his neck a precious stone, the sight of which cured every kind of disease.

Suppose we set aside these assertions as fables, we cannot deny that the Jews were at an early period addicted to magical arts. This propensity, there can be no doubt, whenever first manifested, was increased through the Hebrews' intercourse with the inhabitants of Egypt, Syria, and Chaldea.

Jews, who professed to work wonders by enchantments, gave directions how to select and combine passages and proper names of Scripture that would render supernatural beings visible, and bring about many surprising results. The sacred word Jehovah, they said, when read with points, multiplied by or added to a given number of letters, and composed into certain words, produced miraculous effects. By that sacred name and strange arrangements, their prophets, they thought, performed miracles. The devil was supposed to have the power of accusing mortal man at the great day of propitiation, so the Jews endeavoured to appease him with presents. They believed that on that day only he had the power to bring a charge against them, and therefore, to deceive him, they had recourse to a singular stratagem. In reading the accustomed portion of the law, they left out the beginning and the end,--an omission which was expected to cause Satan to overlook the important time. Those versed in magic could tell that the five Hebrew letters of which the devil's name was composed constituted the number 364, during which number of days he could not accuse them; and in some way or other unknown to us, in addition to the plan of mutilating the law, they kept his mouth shut year after year.

We find from the Holy Scriptures, that a witch was not permitted to live,--that there should not be found among the Hebrews any that used divination, an enchanter, a charmer, a consulter with familiar spirits, nor a necromancer, because the abominations of these mischievous people proved a snare to the nations that were driven out before the Israelites. Various opinions have been expressed regarding the witch of Endor. Parties are not agreed as to whether she did or did not bring up Samuel before Saul; but into their disputes it is unnecessary for us to enter. All that we mean to draw from the narrative is, that if the King of Israel had recourse to a witch in his hour of perplexity, superstition must have been general in the nation.

Religiously disposed Jews wore upon their arms and foreheads two pieces of parchment containing the ten commandments. These charms, or emblems of sanctity, or whatever they were called, were not allowed to be worn by women or by men when they went to a funeral or approached a dead body.

The Jews confessed their sins to their rabbis, and the penance or punishment was commensurate with their guilt. It was not uncommon for Jewish devotees to lash themselves, but the number of stripes did not at any time exceed thirty-nine. During the flagellation the penitent lay on the ground with his head to the north and his feet to the south, and it would have been considered profane to look to the east or west while the chastisement was being inflicted. A Jew would as soon have eaten swine's flesh as look to the east or west while he was in a bath. Offenders were sometimes cursed in addition to their other punishments; hence, it is presumed, the more modern recourse to curses or denunciations. A doomed or cursed individual was consigned to the power of evil angels, and prayers were offered up that he might be tormented in life with every disease, and afterwards cast into eternal darkness.

At the commencement of the Jewish Sabbath, half an hour before sunset on Friday, every Jew was bound to have his lamp lighted, though he should beg the oil. The women were required to light the lamps in memory of Eve, who by her disobedience extinguished the light of the world. Every Hebrew was obliged to pare his nails on Friday, beginning with the little finger of the left hand, and then going to the middle finger, after which he returned to the fourth finger, and then to the thumb and fore finger. In cutting the nails of the fingers of the right hand, he began with the middle finger, then proceeded to the thumb, and after that took the fore finger, the middle and fourth fingers, in the order stated. The parings were either buried or burned. The Hebrews believed that the sounding of a consecrated horn drove away the devil.

A curious custom prevailed among them in early times. The father of a family took a white cock, and each of his wives selected a hen, but such of them as were expectant mothers took both a cock and a hen. With these fowls they struck their heads twice, and at every blow the head of the family said, "Let this cock stand in my room; he shall die, but I shall live." Having said this, the neck of the fowl was drawn and its throat cut; and either the dead fowl, or its value in money, was given to the poor. In the evening previous to the feast of expiation, a man wishing to pry into futurity carried a lighted candle to the synagogue, and from particular appearances of the flame he prognosticated whether good was to follow him and his, or whether he and his family were to be overtaken by evil.

At their great feasts of tents or tabernacles (observed in memory of their living in tents in the wilderness) the Israelites went from their tents to the synagogue every day during the feast, bearing in their right hands branches of palms, myrtle, and willows, and in their left hands branches of citron. When they reached the synagogue, they turned the branches first to the east, then to the south, next to the west, and lastly to the north. These ceremonies were allegorical: the palm was an emblem of hypocrisy, the myrtle pointed to good works, the willow represented the wicked, and the citron the righteous. At marriages, while the young persons present held torches in their hands and sang the marriage song, the bride walked three times round the bridegroom, and he in turn walked thrice round her. In some countries--Germany and Holland, for instance--the guests threw handfuls of corn at the young wedded pair, telling them to "increase and multiply." The newly married people drank a little wine, and then emptied the cup on the floor. At the wedding repast a roasted hen and an egg were presented to the bride, who, after partaking of them, distributed the remainder to the guests. The hen had reference to the fruitfulness of the bride, and her delivery in childbirth.

The thumbs of a dead Jew were tied down close to the palms of his hands, to preserve the deceased from the devil's clutches. While the body was being washed, an egg was put into a glass of wine, and the deceased's head anointed with the mixture. Those who were not reconciled to the departed, before his death, kissed his great toe and asked pardon, lest he should accuse them at the great tribunal before the Most High. When the body was carried away for interment, a person, who remained behind, threw a brick after it, as a sign that all sorrow was past. The nearest friends or relations walked seven times round the grave, after each of them had driven a nail into the coffin. Hence the saying in our own time, when one signifies his willingness to do a friend a favour or kindness, "I will drive a nail into your coffin." When the body was put into the grave, every person present threw a handful of earth in after it.

On important occasions the Hebrews, like Pagans, consulted diviners, who had recourse to various ways of divination. In the days of Joseph there was divination by cups, one particular manner of proceeding being to observe how their wine sparkled when poured out. Casting or drawing of lots was a favourite method of divination, not only among the Jews, but among all nations. Mention is made of divination by means of household gods or images in human shape, prepared by astrologers under particular constellations, and made capable of the heavenly influences. The rabbis, in making some of these images, killed a man who was a first-born son, wrung off his head, seasoned it with salt, spices, etc., and then put a gold plate, bearing the name of an unclean spirit, under the head, which was fixed to a wall, and had candles burning beside it. The images were consulted as oracles concerning things accomplished but unknown, and regarding events in the future.

Among the Jews there were observers of times who laid great stress on certain seasons and critical moments, which they supposed depended on particular positions of the heavenly bodies. A learned rabbi expressed the opinion that the celestial bodies rewarded persons who put confidence in them, and that consequently men acted wisely to reverence the stars and implore their assistance. Guesses at futurities were made from the falling of a crumb of bread out of one's mouth or a staff from a man's hand, from a person sneezing, or the breaking of a shoe-latchet.

The Hebrew witches were supposed to possess the power of doing mischief to man and beast by their occult science, and of changing the form of things. Witches used their wicked skill to allure maidens. Through magical operations, a Jew endeavoured long ago to procure the love of a Christian woman, but she was preserved from the power of his craft by sealing herself with the sign of the cross. It was an ancient way of enchantment, to bring, by the power of magic, various kinds of beasts together into one place, which were designated as the "great congregation" and the "little congregation." The great congregation consisted of many of the larger animals, and the lesser was made up of numerous smaller creatures, such as serpents, scorpions, and the like. Wizards were famous fortune tellers; they pretended to be the interpreters of all the most important occurrences of the world. According to the Hebrew laws, the deceivers, and those who consulted them, were liable to be stoned. Necromancers obtained a footing among the Jews. Such wicked people were accustomed to fast, go to burying-places, and there lie down, fall asleep, and pretend that the dead appeared to them in dreams or otherwise, and told them what was desired. They also pretended to call up the dead by means of certain fumes and particular words. In cases where the spirits of dead men were obstinate and refused to appear or answer when summoned in the more simple form, recourse was had to the burning of portions of black cats, or the still more cruel method of cutting up young boys and virgins.

CHAPTER II.

Men endowed with Prophetic Spirits--The Jews forbidden to consult the Oracles of the Heathen--Succession and Schools of Prophets--Burial of Prophets--Influence of Music--The Prophetic Mantle--Way through which Revelations were made--Bath Kol--Urim and Thummim--False Prophets Strangled or Stoned--How False Prophets were discovered--Recourse to Diabolical Art--Moloch--Seething a Kid in its Mother's Milk--The Smooth Stones mentioned by Isaiah--Oil and Candles supposed to possess peculiar Virtues--The Saint entombed near the Barbary shore--Sheep-head and Sheep-head Broth--Casting Sins into the Sea--Custom of Fasting among the Pharisees--Dust of Heathen Countries--The number 10--Angels that had the care of Men--Souls of Dead Persons whispered with a feeble Voice--Hebrew Women who predicted when one would die--Punishment in the Grave by the Devil.

Every person who has read the Old Testament, knows that the Hebrews had among them extraordinary men really endowed with prophetic spirits. The Jews were forbidden to consult the oracles of the heathen nations round about them, but they were permitted to consult their own true prophets concerning that which was concealed from ordinary persons. There was a constant succession of prophets, and there were schools where young persons aspiring to the office of a seer were instructed. Over each of these institutions a venerable prophet presided. At first the scholars were not inspired, but received prophecies from the mouth of their master or president. At Jerusalem there was one of these schools within the second wall of the city. So great respect was paid to the prophetic character, that none were suffered to be buried in Jerusalem but kings, descendants of David, and prophets. Though old prophets could not inspire their young students, they improved their natural faculties, and taught them how to subdue irregular emotions that hindered inspiration. That the minds of the prophets might be the better disposed to receive the proper impulses, instrumental music was used in their devotions; and it is reported that at certain of their musical meetings the young men became so elated, that they manifested poetical genius as well as a prophetic spirit. When a young prophet gave unequivocal evidence of being inspired, he was installed into office by having the prophetic mantle (made of lamb's skin) thrown over his shoulders. Subsequent to inauguration, a prophet wore hair-cloth next his skin, and had a leather girdle round his loins.

The general way through which revelations were made to them was in dreams and visions, or by immediate inspiration. Their dreams were sometimes, indeed generally, sent for instruction or admonition; and in the prophetic dreams a clear and distinct impression was left through a real or imaginary communication with an apparition. At times the prophets had overpowering visions when awake, during which mighty revelations were made to them. When prophetic revelations ceased, the Jews had recourse to Bath Kol, that is, the Daughter of Voice, or the Daughter of a Voice, because it succeeded, they say, the Oracular Voice delivered from the Mercy Seat when Urim and Thummim was consulted.

The prophetic spirit being so common among the Hebrews, it became necessary to adopt a method to prevent false prophets from deceiving the people. To deter men from pretending they possessed a prophetic spirit, a severe punishment for every such pretence was appointed,--strangling or stoning to death. The manner of trying a false prophet was this: the judgments threatened by a prophet, and the good things predicted by him, were observed. If the judgments declared were not fulfilled, it was not regarded as conclusive evidence against him, because it might be that the punishments were for some wise reason averted; but if the promised good did not come to pass, the predictor was condemned as a deceiver and false prophet. If the words of a prophet were fulfilled in one or more particulars, but not in all, he was not deemed worthy of credence. When once one was condemned as a false prophet, no interest was powerful enough to save him from death.

The trial of prophets prescribed by the Mosaic law was intended to prevent impostors pretending to be prophets, and to save the people from being enticed by wicked deceivers into idolatry. In the time of Moses there were many who had recourse to diabolical arts. The oblation of children to Moloch being frequently mentioned, together with other diabolical and divinatory arts, reasons appear for supposing there was something magical in such superstitious rites, and that thereby people consulted demons about things future or secret. Moloch was the principal idol of the Ammonites, but other nations took the same idol for their chief god; for it appears from Pagan records, that the different nations were so very accommodating with their gods that they lent them to one another. Moloch seems to have been the same as Baal, both names signifying dominion, or more particularly the sun, the prince of the heavenly bodies.

There can be no doubt but the passage in the Old Testament, "Thou shalt not seethe a kid in his mother's milk," was a warning to the Hebrews not to follow the example of the heathen in connection with the payment by the latter of their first fruits. Dr. Cudworth, writing on this subject, says that he learned from the comments of an ancient Karaite upon the Pentateuch, that a superstitious rite prevailed among the ancient idolators, of seething a kid in his mother's milk when they had gathered in all their first fruits, and sprinkling the trees and fields with the broth, after a magical manner, to make them more fruitful in the following year. Spencer also observes that the Zabii used this kind of magical broth to sprinkle their trees and gardens, in hope of obtaining a plentiful crop.

The smooth stones mentioned by Isaiah, to which meat offerings were offered and drink offerings poured out, were anointed stones in the streets, on which passengers poured on them oil from phials; but what advantages were to result from the custom we are not fully informed. Oil and candles were believed by the ancients to possess peculiar virtues. Oil was often burned in honour of the dead; and the Algerines, when on the water, tied bundles of wax candles together, and, with a pot of oil, threw them overboard as a present to the saint, entombed near the Barbary shore, whom they regarded as their protector. We believe few who partake of sheep-head or sheep-head broth know that it is, or was, a custom with the Jews to serve up sheep-head on New Year's Day at their chief entertainment, as a mystical representation of the ram offered in sacrifice instead of Isaac. When a family or company sat down to this repast, each person took a piece of bread, and, dipping it in honey, said, "May this year be sweet and fruitful." The Jews, to cast their sins into the depth of the sea, sometimes went after dinner to the brink of a pond, if not near the sea, and threw into the water a live fish, in the hope that it would carry away all their iniquities, never more to be found.

It was customary among the Pharisees not only to fast twice a week (on Monday and Thursday), but at periods of perplexity to fast thirteen days consecutively. Sometimes, on account of such small trifles as dreams, they would abstain from food; but severe drought, pestilence, famine, war, and inundations were sure to make them fast until nature was nearly exhausted. The Hebrews held certain views and followed particular customs with respect to the dust of heathen countries. Dust that came from Gentile lands was reckoned so defiling, that the Jewish rulers would not permit vegetables to be brought from heathen countries into the land of Israel, lest the detested particles should be brought along with them. The number 10 was much noticed and used by the Jews. The blessing of the bridegroom, which consisted of seven blessings, was of no avail unless delivered in the presence of ten persons. Angels, which were believed to have the care of men, were supposed to ride unseen, on white horses, beside the objects of their attention.

Among the Jews there was a popular notion that the spirits of dead persons whispered in a feeble and peculiar way out of the dust; and it was a common belief that the soul had no rest unless the body was interred. There were women among the Hebrews who predicted how long one would live, and pretended to know when he was to die. One of a Jew's solemn prayers on the day of expiation was that he might be delivered from the punishment of the devil in his grave,--a punishment supposed to be inflicted by causing the soul to return to the body, breaking the deceased's bones, and tormenting both soul and body for a season. A similar form of prayer was used by the Mohammedans.

CHAPTER III.

Egypt steeped in Superstition--Power of Magicians--Way of obtaining Visions--Demons--Deification of Departed Heroes--Gods and Demi-gods--Altars or Living Stones--Sacred Animals--Isis searching for Osiris--Leeks and Onions--Priests were Physicians and Interpreters of Oracles--Sacrificing Human Victims--Wax Figures--Magic--Teaching of the Egyptian Priests--Transmigration--Character of Men judged of after Death.

E gypt was a country steeped in superstition. The people believed in sorcery, magic, and enchantments; and there is the fullest evidence in the sacred pages that the Egyptian magicians were able to perform dexterous feats that were truly surprising. Astronomy was studied with a view to success in astrology, as the latter was a science much esteemed, and very lucrative. Public or state astrologers were consulted in cases of emergencies. None dared to practise astrology, magic, sorcery, or any of the various modes of divination unless authorised by a master in the art, before whom he had "spread the carpet" for prayer. To procure sublime visions, seers shut themselves up for a long time, without food or water, in a dark place, and prayed aloud until they fainted. While in a swoon, strange visions appeared to them, and revelations made which sometimes filled the nation with gladness, and at other times spread mourning over the country. In advanced ages, as well as in early times, men believed there were a multitude of subordinate spirits, as ministers, to execute the behests of the supreme sovereign. To these spirits were committed the superintendence of all the different parts of nature, and their bodies were imagined to be composed of that particular element in which they resided. Altars were built in the midst of groves, where the spirits were supposed to assemble. Gratitude and admiration tended to the deification of departed heroes and other eminent persons. This probably gave rise to the belief of national and tutelar gods, as well as the practice of worshipping gods through the medium of statues cut into human form. At one time demi-gods gradually rose in the scale of divinities until they occupied the places of the heavenly bodies. Thus, following ancient hyperbole, a king, for his beneficence, was called the sun, and a queen, for her beauty, was styled the moon. As this adulation advanced into an established worship, the compliment was reversed by calling planets or luminaries after heroes. And to render the subject more reconcilable to reason, the Eastern priests taught that the early founders of states and inventors of arts were divine intelligences, clothed with human bodies. When celestial divinities disappeared or were obscured from observation, men had recourse to symbols of a temporary nature that produced fire. Altars of stone were built and consecrated in the name of the divinity whom it was intended to represent. Such altars were called animated or living stones, from a belief that a portion of divine spirit resided in them, and the prayers and praises offered up before them were thought to be as acceptable as if addressed to the gods themselves. That those altars or stones might be as near as possible to the objects of worship represented, they were generally placed on the tops of mountains, or, in flat countries like Egypt, on high structures, the works of men's hands. Many have attributed the building of the pyramids to the worship of gods; but whether that was the purpose to which those majestic structures, that have puzzled learned men, were devoted, we shall not venture to say. This, however, is certain that, throughout the East, altars, statues, and pillars were erected for superstitious purposes upon mountains and other high places.

Herodotus informs us that the ancient Egyptians were the first people who gave names to their gods. Of Osiris, Isis, and the many other gods and sacred animals that were worshipped in Egypt, we shall say little at this part of our subject. The bull, it is well known, was one of the most sacred animals. The priests affirmed that Apis was of divine origin, the cow that produced him having been impregnated with holy fire. Dogs, the Egyptians said, deserved homage because they guided Isis when she searched for the body of Osiris. She, it may be remembered, sought for the precious remains with true pertinacity till she found them. To accomplish her purpose, she found it necessary to transform herself into a swallow, to dry up the river Ph[oe]drus, and to kill with her glances the eldest son of a king. Her tears were supposed to cause the inundation of the Nile. At times she had the head of a cow, which identified her with the cow of whom the sun was born. The hawk was deified because one of these birds brought to the priests of Thebes a book, tied round with a scarlet thread, containing the rites and ceremonies to be observed in the worship of the gods. The wolf was adored because Osiris arose in the shape of that animal from the infernal regions, and assisted Isis and her son Horus to battle against Typhon. The cat was revered as an emblem of the moon, for its various spots, fruitfulness, and activity in the night. The goat (which, by the by, is said to be absent from the earth and present with Satan a part of every twenty-four hours of the day, and can never be seen from sunrise to sunrise without being lost sight of for a longer or shorter time) was honoured as the representation of manhood in full vigour, and was worshipped, from gratitude to the gods, for multiplying the people of the country. The crocodile was also advanced to the dignity of a god. If one killed any of the sacred animals designedly, he was put to death,--if involuntarily, his punishment was referred to the priests; but if a man killed a hawk, a cat, or an ibis, whether designedly or not, he died without mercy. During a severe famine, when the Egyptians became cannibals, not one of them was known to have tasted the sacred animals.

All revered animals were kept at great expense, and when they died costly funerals took place. When the Apis died at Memphis, in the reign of Ptolemy the son of Lagus, his funeral cost not less than L13,000 sterling. When a cat died, the family it belonged to expressed great grief, and prayed and fasted several days. In cases of fire, more care was taken to preserve the feline animals than the most valuable property in the house. Dead cats, which were almost invariably embalmed, were sometimes carried from remote parts to be interred in the city of Bubastis, and hawks and moles were buried with great solemnity at Butos, even though they should have died in foreign countries. Juvenal mentions that leeks and onions were objects of worship, and others say that the lotus was also sacred in various parts of the East. The priests were both physicians and interpreters of oracles; they carefully observed the phenomena of nature, and registered every uncommon occurrence. From such observations, they calculated the results of other events of similar nature. Hence arose the practice of divination, and afterwards that of dispensing oracles. Oracles were erected in every part of Egypt. Even the sacred animals had their several oracles. The Apis was consulted by observing into which of his chambers he entered. By a certain principle understood, the omen was regarded as foretelling good or evil.

The barbarous custom of sacrificing human victims was long in force in Egypt, and prevailed down to the reign of Amasis, by whom it was abolished. Not to give too severe a shock to the superstitious feelings of the people, wax figures, representing human beings, were permitted to be substituted for the living mortals. These customs were, no doubt, what sorcerers and witches imitated at their midnight feasts in after ages, and which led old women to imagine that, by making wax images of those whom they intended to injure, and sticking sharp instruments into them at one time, and at another time exposing them to a scorching heat before a fire, they would wreak their vengeance upon the individuals whom the figures represented. We have it from more than one learned writer, that the cruel and gloomy worship of Egypt arose from a belief that Typhon was labouring incessantly to counteract the happiness of mankind. He was considered to be greedy and voracious, and that it was necessary to glut his altars with blood in order to appease his anger.

Magic was a science in which the Egyptians excelled. Its attainment was esteemed the highest exertion of human intellect. Some imagined that the invention of magic exceeded human invention, and they pretended that the angel who fell in love with the antediluvian women taught it, and that the principles thereof were preserved by Ham after the Deluge, and that he communicated them to his son Mizraim; but others ascribed the invention to Hermes. Without either admitting or denying these assertions, we can have no hesitation in stating that much of our superstition may be traced back to Egyptian religion and customs, and that the singular belief of the Egyptians was general, and long anterior to the time Jacob and his sons went down to that country.

The Egyptian priests, taking advantage of the people's credulity, taught that the sun, moon, and whole host of heaven were endowed with intelligence, and exerted an influence over the destinies of men; and they (the priests) pretended to work miracles, and obtain oracles and omens. They also laid claim to the power of interpreting dreams.

The Egyptians believed that the souls of men went into other bodies at death,--such as had been virtuous going into exalted bodies, but the vicious passing into mean reptiles and other contemptible creatures. After remaining in a state of punishment for a certain number of years, they were supposed to pass into more exalted beings. Praise was not bestowed indiscriminately upon every person who died, however exalted his position. Characters were given by judges, after inquiry into the life and conduct of the deceased. The judges sat on the opposite side of a lake; and while they crossed the lake, he who sat at the helm was called Charon, which gave rise to the fable among the Greeks, that Charon conducted the souls of deceased persons into the infernal regions.

CHAPTER IV.

Babylon--The Chaldeans were Priests, Philosophers, Astronomers, Astrologers, and Soothsayers--Downfall of Babylon predicted--Worship of the Medes and Persians--Devils confined in an Egg--Sacred Fire--The Gaures--Births and Deaths in Early Times--A narrow Bridge--An immense Tree--Creation of Prophets--A Stone to which Abraham tied his Camel--Adam and Eve's Trysting Place--Black Art--Ways of discovering whether a supposed Criminal was Guilty or Innocent--Looking into Futurity--Canaanites, Syrians, and Arabians--Strange Fables--Abraham breaking Heathen Idols--Worship of the Egyptian Thorn--Altars--Religion of the Carthagenians and Tyrians--Supremacy of the Gods.

The great city of Babylon owed its origin to the ambition of the proud people who built the tower of Babel. In course of time Babylon rose to great grandeur, but superstition became so prevalent that it proved a snare to the inhabitants. Like the heathen around, they worshipped fire and images. The Babylonians pretended to great skill in astrology, soothsaying, and magic. The Chaldeans, so called in a strict sense, were a society of pretenders to learning, priests, philosophers, astrologers, and soothsayers, who, it is said, dwelt in a region by themselves, and the rest of the people were called Babylonians. While Babylon was in its glory, prophets predicted that dreadful judgments would befall it. And so it happened. On the very night the destruction came, the king, alarmed by the mysterious handwriting on the wall, consulted his magicians; and Daniel, who had been made master of the magicians, astrologers, Chaldeans, and soothsayers, made known the sad end of Belshazzar and his kingdom.

The Medes and Persians worshipped the sun, fire, water, the earth, the winds, and deities without number. Human sacrifices, as in other idolatrous countries, were offered by them, and they burned their children in fiery furnaces appropriated to their idols. At first the gods they worshipped were Arimanius, the god of evil, and Oromasdes, the giver of all good. Plutarch says that Oromasdes created several inferior gods or genii, and that Arimanius created many devils. The former also created twenty-four devils, and enclosed them in an egg; but the latter broke the egg, and by that means let out the demons, and created a mixture of good and evil. The religion of the Persians underwent a variety of revolutions. Temples were built for the worship of fire, prior to which Magian priests kept the sacred fire burning on mountain tops under considerable difficulties. They fed it with wood stripped of the bark; they were prohibited from blowing the fire with their breath or with bellows, lest it should be polluted. Had one done either, he would have been punished with death. The Jews had the real fire from heaven, and the Magi pretended to have received theirs from the upper regions likewise.

The Gaures held that the earth was inhabited at first by two persons. They had a tradition that Eve brought twins into the world every day, and that for one thousand years death had no power over her seed. They believed that a select company of angels were appointed guardians of mankind, but that, notwithstanding this, evil increased: men grew wicked and perverse in their ways, and therefore the deluge was sent to sweep them away. The Gaures had their guardian angels for every month and day throughout the year, and to them they devoted their prayers. New Year's Day was a high day with them, and they had a great many lucky and unlucky days.

The Persians hold that at the last judgment every man must pass along a bridge no wider than a razor's edge; that the unbelievers and the wicked will certainly in their passage fall into hell, there to be for ever and ever tormented; but that the faithful shall be so guided and supported that they shall pass the bridge swifter than a bird can fly through the air, and enter into paradise, and seat themselves on the banks of the river of delight, which, they say, is shaded by a tree of such immense size, that if a man were to ride forty thousand years, he would not pass the extent of one of its leaves. In Persia it was a common belief that there were many prophets living between the days of Adam and Mohammed, who were created before the world was made. Their prophets, according to history, were possessed of the power of working miracles; and charms and amulets were common in the country.

Pilgrims who went to Mecca invariably kissed a black stone, regarding which there is a curious legend: Abraham, we are informed, tied his camel to this stone when he went to sacrifice Ishmael, for the Mohammedans represent Hagar as Abraham's lawful wife, and Ishmael his heir. There is another tradition, that when Abraham was about to build the Kaaba, held in great veneration, the stones marched thither of themselves ready hewn and polished, and that the black stone, being left out when the building was completed, demanded of Abraham why it had not been used in the sacred structure. The prophet told the stone not to be disappointed, for he would cause it to be more honoured than any stone in the building, by commanding all the faithful to kiss it as they went in procession. The faithful people were wont to meet at the place which they supposed was Adam and Eve's trysting place after the expulsion, for it is related in one of their legends that the first man and woman wandered about the world, separately, hundreds of years after the Fall.

The Persians were extremely addicted to the study and practice of the black art and all magical incantations, supposing that by such mysterious operations they could influence the elements and all the products of nature. When any one was suspected to have died an unnatural death, the surviving relatives consulted spirits, with the view of discovering the cause of it. Sometimes the relatives alleged that a spell had been cast on the spirits consulted, which prevented their giving answers to interrogatories. In that case, magicians were employed to remove the fascination. A suspected murderer was submitted to a severe ordeal:--A particular liquid was poured upon the arm or thigh of the unfortunate person; but before the fluid was used it was boiled, while the supposed criminal's name was repeatedly mentioned. The moment the liquid began to boil, they commenced to address their imaginary spirits in the following terms: "Is the party on whom I pour this water guilty or not? If he is, may it scald him and shrivel up his skin." If the application of the boiling liquid did not injure the suspected person he was declared innocent, but if it burned him he was pronounced guilty. People anxious to know the result of approaching warlike engagements put a vessel full of water, mixed with particular ingredients, over a fire. As soon as the water commenced to boil they performed magical incantations, which, as they imagined, irresistibly attracted the titular genius of their enemies, and obliged the spirit or god to plunge himself into it. In this painful situation they confined him for a considerable time. When he had endured sufficient penance to humble him, he was questioned relative to the success of the war. The information sought was delivered, as the people thought, through the appearance of the scum on the water. By turning a red-hot pot upside down, attended with magical incantations, they imagined the courage of their soldiers exposed to its heat could be raised.

Canaanites, Syrians, and Arabians were all superstitious, and given to idolatry. These people had various idols, regarding which there are strange fables. An idol worshipped by the Philistines and Syrians, called Derceto, has an interesting history. Near Askelon there was a deep lake, abounding with fish. Not far from the lake stood the temple of this famous goddess, the mother of Semiramis, who had the face of a woman, and the rest of her body resembling part of a fish, for which the Syrians assigned the following reason:--Venus having conceived a hatred against Derceto, caused her to fall in love with a young Syrian, whom she subsequently murdered, and then threw herself into the lake, where she was transformed into the shape of a fish with a woman's face; for which reason the Syrians did not eat any fish, but worshipped them as gods. There is a legend of Abraham, before he left Ur of the Chaldeans, which exhibits the contempt he had of idols. It is said he took an opportunity of breaking in pieces all the idols he could reach, except Baal, and that he suspended about the neck of this idol the axe with which he had performed the destruction. The people coming to see what had been done, supposed that Baal was the author of the mischief. Some say that Abraham accomplished the exploit in his father's shop during his absence, and that Terah, returning home, inquired how the work of destruction had taken place. Abraham told him that the idols had quarrelled about an offering of flour that an old woman had brought them, and that Baal had proved the strongest, and broke all the rest to pieces.

The Arabians, Ishmael's offspring, were equally guilty of idolatry. So far did they carry this sin, that they actually worshipped idols under the shape of Egyptian thorns. In early times the thorns were adored in the open fields, but subsequently altars and temples were erected for their worship. The Arabians worshipped Assaf under the shape of a calf; and they had a goddess named Beltha, supposed to be the Venus of the Greeks. The Sabeans were the principal worshippers of this goddess; and such was their devotion to her, that they regularly presented to her a portion of their plunder.

The religion of the Carthaginians and Tyrians was horrid and barbarous. Nothing of moment was undertaken without consulting the gods, which was done in various ridiculous ways. Hercules was the god in whom the people placed most confidence. He was invoked before they went on any important expedition; and when their armies were victorious, sacrifices were offered to him. One of the chief deities that they worshipped was Urania, or the moon, to whom they appealed when over-taken by calamities, such as drought, excessive rain, destructive hail, thunder, and dangerous storms. Urania was the queen of heaven mentioned in the Scriptures, to whom even the Jewish women offered cakes, etc. Carthaginians, in worshipping Saturn, offered up human sacrifices to him. Even princes and other great men were wont, in times of distress, to sacrifice their most beloved children to this deity. People who had not any children of their own, purchased infants that they might offer them as victims to this idol, with the view of inducing him to fulfil their desires. Diodorus relates that when Agathocles was going to besiege Carthage, the people imputed all their misfortunes to the anger of Saturn, because, that instead of offering up to him children nobly born, he had been fraudulently put off with the offspring of slaves and foreigners. To atone for past shortcomings, two hundred children of the best families in Carthage were sacrificed, and further, to obtain the god's favour, three hundred adult citizens immolated themselves.

Nimrod, the great-grandson of Noah, was an idolator, as were also his descendants. Nineveh was the seat of his empire. As the sun and moon became early objects of worship among the As-syrians, so in later days they adored the fire as their substitute,--a form of worship that was com-mon among the ancients in many lands. The Assyrians published abroad that the gods of other na-tions could not stand before their fire-gods. A competition took place. A vast number of idols were brought from foreign nations, but as they were composed of wood, the god Ur (or fire) consumed them. After many contests, an Egyptian priest discovered a plan of destroying the reputation of this idol, which had become the terror of alien people. He caused the hollow figure of an image to be made of perforated earth, with the holes stuffed with wax, and the large internal cavity filled with water. He then challenged the god Ur to oppose his god Canopus,--a challenge which was accepted by the Chaldean priests. No sooner did the heat that was expected to devour the Egyptian idol begin to take effect, than, the wax being melted, the water gushed out and extinguished the fire. Before the Assyrian empire was joined to that of Babylon, Nisroch was the god worshipped in Nineveh, and it was in the temple of this idol that the great Sennacherib was murdered. This idol was in the shape of a bird--a dove or an eagle--made, if we can believe the Jewish rabbis, from a plank of Noah's ark. The people repented at the preaching of Jonah, but it was not long before they relapsed into their former idolatry and general wickedness.

CHAPTER V.

Greek Religion and Superstition--Whence the Greeks derived their Religion--Jupiter regarded as the President of the Law and Protector of Cities--Entertainment of Strangers--Dreams and Charms--Sacred Stones--Omens of Evil--Sacrificing the Hair--Flight of Birds--Compassing the Altar to the Right--Methods of discovering whether a Person was in Love--Love secured by Magic--Marriage Ceremonies--Most lucky time for Marriage--Way of protecting a Child from Evil Spirits--Divers magical Ceremonies--Strange Laws as to Dead Bodies--Fingers and Toes of Dead Men worn as Charms to frighten away Ghosts--Preparing a Body for Burial--Superstitious Customs--Swine and Swine's Flesh--Drinking Toasts--How Strangers were expected to behave in a Strange Land--Prophets consulted before Armies marched to Battle--Certain words avoided--Sneezing--Evil Omens--Throwing a Person overboard to save a Ship.

Herodotus was of opinion that the Greeks derived their religion and superstition from the Egyptians; Plutarch arrived at another conclusion; while many maintained that Orpheus brought the mysteries of religion into Greece. Whoever is right, this we know, that the Greeks became so prone to worship ancient deities, and so anxious to do homage to all the divinities, that they erected altars to unknown gods, for fear they would fail in their duty to any power that could assist them in time of need. Above all gods, Jupiter was held in the highest esteem. He was regarded as the president of law and justice, as the protector of cities, as governor and director of their councils, and as chief of their societies. To him they ascribed thunder, and supposed it was he who delivered them from the Persians, and who assisted them to buy and sell to advantage. They erected altars to him in the courts of their houses and before their gates. Regarding him as the god of strangers, they received and entertained visitors with great ceremony. As a sign of fidelity, the right hand of fellowship was given to a stranger, to whom salt was presented, in token that his person would be safe under the entertainer's roof. A stranger's bottle was kept, and when a visitor arrived at the door the head of the family and he joined feet together on the threshold. A cup of wine was drunk to an unknown person before his name was asked. To return respect to those in the house, the stranger did reverence to the genius of the place, and saluted the ground with a kiss. When one sojourned in a strange land, he was expected to conform to the recognised customs thereof; and on taking his departure he not only bade farewell to those with whom he had become acquainted, but took leave of their deities. When an important agreement was entered into, Jupiter was sacrificed to, and called to witness the covenant.

The Greeks purified themselves after frightful dreams; they wore charmed rings to protect themselves from witchcraft; they were accustomed to spit three times on seeing a madman; and they spat every time the devil's name was mentioned in their hearing. Stones were cast at every cat and weasel met by one when commencing a journey, and the meeting of a bitch with whelps was carefully avoided. The crowing of hens and the whistling of maidens were listened to with as great fear as the hissing of a serpent.

If a rat or a mouse ate a hole in one's clothes, evil, it was thought, was about to befall the luckless owner. The people had days of good luck and of bad omen. They cut their hair, and sacrificed it to rivers. They marked the flight of birds, particularly that of the owl. On seeing this night bird flying overhead at the battle of Salamis, the soldiers considered it a good sign, took courage, and won the fight. When one was going round an altar, he took care to keep his right hand towards it. People anointed sacred stones in token of thankfulness, as Jacob poured oil on the stone he took for a pillow at Bethel.

To know if one was in love, special notice was taken of his garland at a feast, and from its appearance the wearer's feelings were supposed to be known, though it might be thought there was no necessity for such observation; for, according to an old proverb, "Love and the cough can never be concealed."

If one could not secure a lady's affections in the usual way of courting, he endeavoured to get something of hers into his possession in order to bewitch her. Having received a glove, a ring, or any other article, he operated on it in a magical way, and thus obtained his desire. If a lady's girdle was properly tied into a true-lover's knot, she could not resist loving him who performed the charming trick. Another way of softening a woman's heart was by throwing a bitten apple into her lap. If she received it and ate the fruit, her affections were won. All the tokens and charms did not come from the gentleman's side, for it was not unusual for a lady, when she wanted to control a lover's affections, to send him charmed garlands, roses, or bitten apples.

On the wedding day, a bride, on coming to the house of her husband, found the doors hung with garlands made of herbs, flowers, and plants consecrated to certain gods and goddesses, which possessed peculiar virtues suitable for the occasion. Cakes were bestowed on the bride on her marriage day; and there was a custom among the Greeks and Romans of combing her hair with a spear which had belonged to a man that lost his life in a fight, or with a weapon that had been used in killing a man. If this was done, she was sure to have brave sons. As the bride rose to leave her father's house, she was carried over the threshold; and as she entered her husband's house, a practice similar to that observed among other nations was followed,--throwing figs and other fruit at her head, as an omen of fruitfulness. It was also the custom for a servant, on first coming into his new home, to have palm branches and various ornaments placed on his head, to secure prosperity. As the bride was led into her chamber, there was a sieve carried along with her, and a pestle hung at the door, implying that afterwards she was to assist in the household duties. When the bride and bridegroom

were together in the house, they ate an apple between them, to signify the pleasantness and harmony they were to enjoy in after life. Recourse was had to augury, the day before the wedding, to
ascertain whether the married life was to be prosperous. Before the bride retired for the night, she
was bathed with water drawn from nine different springs. The time of the year the Grecians deemed
most lucky for marriage was the first month of winter. This was contrary to the views of the Persians, who considered spring the proper season for entering into the matrimonial state. The Greeks
thought it better to get married in the first or second quarter of the moon rather than when it was
waning. General rules were at times departed from, for occasionally astrologers were consulted as to
the most auspicious day and hour for the happy lovers being united.

Through magical influence, a husband could have been made to hate his wife; but, to regain
his affections, a spider caught in early morn was confined in a box, protected by charms, prepared
for its reception. When a child came into the world, three men kept watch all night to keep away
evil spirits. One of those on guard was armed with an axe, another with a pestle, and the third with a
broom. Each protector kept his implement swinging through the air, to prevent the approach of the
dreaded beings. As soon as a child was born it was washed in water or wine, and wrapped in a cloth
worn by the mother when she was a virgin. In the cloth were wrought the image of the Gorgon and
the snakes of that monster's head, together with the likenesses of two dragons. When the child was
five days old, it was carried about the hearth to introduce it to the Penates. Arrangements were then
made for naming the child. A feast was prepared, at which there were doves, thrushes, coleworts,
and toasted cheese, besides many other things. The feast was kept up for seven days. The mother, in
gratitude for her child, sacrificed to Diana, and the father returned thanks to the nymphs for giving
him a fruitful wife.

If the little stranger died in infancy, it had only a cold funeral without fire, or any burial service or mourning. Sons, as soon as they were three years old, were registered in the tribe. A feast
was then prepared, called "the shearing feast," because at that time the youngster's hair was cut, and
consecrated to one of their gods.

The Athenians had a law, that if any one happened to discover a dead body, whether of a friend
or a stranger, he should cast earth on it three times; and the Romans had a similar law. If a Greek
omitted this duty, he was bound to make satisfaction by sacrificing a sow-pig. But some went farther,
and insisted that whoever saw a dead body and did not cast dust upon it, was both a law-breaker
and an accursed person. The people feared that the gods underground were angry if the dead were
left uncovered with their kindred dust. No greater imprecation could have been cast at an enemy
than that he might not be covered with the earth. Hence it was that the ancients stood in great fear
of death on the ocean, for there their bodies could not be interred. When one went to sea, it was
not uncommon for him to tie a reward to his body, that in case he should be drowned and his body
found, the finder would see it buried, and so become entitled to the treasure. Next to the happiness
of being assured that the body would be buried, was that of being interred in one's own country, and
not among strangers. When a man died far from home, frequent solemn invocations were made for
his soul, which, it was thought, could hear and understand what was said by friends even in distant
lands. At the burial of one that was slain in battle, his comrades marched three times round the

burning pile or grave, shaking their arms, and throwing swords, bridles, belts, and other articles into the fire or grave after the body. When a soldier fell fighting in the field, and his body could not be found, he was honoured with the carriage of an empty bier, and funeral ceremonies as if his remains were present.

If a man killed himself, the hand with which the deed was committed was cut off, and buried in another place to that in which the other part of the body was interred. If one man killed another in a righteous cause, the slayer washed his hands and held up the weapon that had been used towards the sun, with the blood on it, to show that he feared not though the heavens as well as the earth knew what he had done. The ancients were of opinion that if one were slain by a relative, the blood could never be thoroughly wiped off the blade that had cut down the individual. And for fear the Furies would avenge the death of one killed by a relation, amulets and spells were provided to prevent untoward events. The most powerful charms were supposed to be parts of the slain individual. Therefore the fingers, toes, and other extreme parts of the body were cut off and worn under the arm-pits, to prevent the murdered person's ghost taking revenge for the unlawful deed. In preparing a body for burial, the Greeks took a piece of money and put it into the mouth, to give to the ferryman Charon. With the money a small quantity of pudding or cheese was put in for Cerberus, to propitiate him. As a corpse was being carried out to be interred, the deceased was commended to the protection of the infernal gods. To burn a body was considered more honourable than to lay it in the cold grave, for the Greeks thought that the divine and purer part of man was carried by fire to the abode of the gods above. This belief induced fanatical persons, when tired of life below, to burn themselves, that they might all the sooner take their flight to the regions of bliss. If a high wind sprang up when a body was being consumed by flames, it was regarded as a favourable omen. On the body being consumed, the fire was extinguished with red wine.

After a funeral, the people fumigated the house with brimstone, and cleansed themselves by passing over a fire. They then kept a feast, or rather feasts, at which they sacrificed to Mercury, that he might carry the soul of the deceased to the realms of happiness. At the same time the ghosts of relations were sacrificed to. Those who petitioned the gods had garlands about their necks, or green boughs in their hands. The branches were either laurel or olive, because the former signified triumph, and the latter peace and goodwill.

Swine and swine's flesh were held in high esteem by the Greeks and Romans, for various reasons--one of which was that Jupiter was nursed by a sow. It was the custom to drink healths or toasts, and the last one before going to bed was to Mercury, that he might give sound sleep and pleasant dreams. Great men would, on a high occasion, drink to a favourite, and hand him the cup to keep. When a person drank to the health of one he loved, he partook of part of the liquor, and poured the remainder of the wine on the ground. Drinking cups in remote times were made from bulls' horns. The Greeks consecrated their horses to the sun, and before engaging in war they consulted their prophets and diviners. In particular, they paid great attention to the utterances of Egyptian priestesses kept by them. Then, similar to the manner of the Jews, Persians, and others, the Greeks consecrated to the gods, in the event of obtaining victory, portions of goods secured from the vanquished; and even relations were offered in sacrifice to the gods supposed to have given triumph to the victorious armies. A Greek general did not think it lucky to march his forces before full moon, or until the seventh day of the month. Sacrifices were offered to the water when an army came to a river,--a custom observed by other nations.

Certain words were never pronounced by the Greeks. For instance, they carefully withheld their lips from uttering "prison;" and if they happened to hear what they thought an unlucky speech, they replied, "Let it return to thine own head." So far did they carry their superstition, that if one heard an unfavourable expression when he was about to drink, he would throw the liquor on the floor and call for another cup. Sneezing was so superstitiously regarded, that it came to be counted among the number of gods. It was deemed inauspicious if a host sent his guests away from a feast without giving each of them a piece of cake, or such like, to take home. The cracking of a table and the spilling of wine or salt were regarded as evil omens. When a Greek ship was in danger in a storm, one of the crew or a passenger was chosen by lot, and thrown overboard, like Jonah, to appease the spirit that ruled the winds and the waves.

CHAPTER VI.

Roman Delusions and Customs--Augury--Election to the Magistracy; Omens relative thereto--Tokens of Futurity--Dire Misfortunes followed the Contempt of Augurs--Drawing of Lots--Events foretold by reading the first passage that turned up on opening a Book--Lucky and Unlucky Stars--Fortune Tellers--Dreams--Omens drawn from Appearance of parts of Animals offered in Sacrifice--Sibylline Books, Charms, and Incantations--Spirits going about to observe Men's Actions--Unlucky Days--Dress of a Bride--Marriage Ceremonies--Anointing Door-posts with the Fat of Swine or of Wolves, and crossing the Threshold--Fire and Water--Bridal Feast and Nuptial Songs--Funeral Rites--Souls of Unburied Persons--The Expiring Breath--Customs at a Deathbed; the Cypress exhibited at Houses in which were Dead Bodies and Funeral Observances--Hobgoblins and Lares--Purifying with Water and Fire--Ghosts partial to Beans, etc.--Offerings made to appease the Manes--Persons reported to be Dead--Dead Bodies used for Magical purposes.

The old Roman delusions and customs were as extraordinary as those of any nation with which history has made us acquainted. The augurs pretended to foretell future events from the flight of birds and the chirping and feeding of fowls, and also from other appearances. "Augurium" and "auspicium" were generally used promiscuously. Auspicium was properly the foretelling of future events from the inspection of birds; augurium from any omen or prodigy whatever. The augurs are supposed to have derived tokens of futurity chiefly from five sources--appearances in the heavens (such as thunder or lightning), from the singing or flight of birds, from the feeding of fowls, from the movements of quadrupeds, and from uncommon accidents. The birds which chiefly gave omens by sound were ravens, crows, owls, and cocks,--and those by flight, eagles and vultures. Contempt of the augurs, and neglect of their intimations, were said to be followed by dire misfortunes. Omens coming from the left were generally supposed by the Romans to be lucky. Thunder on the left was regarded as a good sign, and so was the cawing of a crow on the same side; but it was considered more fortunate to hear the croaking of a raven on the right than on the left. The Romans, as the Greeks had done before them, took omens from quadrupeds crossing their path or appearing in unaccustomed places. The augurs taught the people how to draw conclusions from sneezing, spilling salt, and other accidents, called dira.

Drawing of lots was frequently resorted to by the Romans wishing to pry into futurity. The lots were dice, or articles resembling those instruments of chance. They were thrown into an urn filled with water, or cast as dice in the ordinary way. If there was any difficulty in ascertaining the import of the dice throwing, the priests were employed to interpret. Future events were frequently inquired into by an inquisitive person cutting the branch of a tree into small pieces, and distinguishing them by certain marks, and then scattering them at random on a white cloth. The searcher after knowledge having prayed to the gods, took up the slips three times, and interpreted according to the marks. Future events were often inquired into by reading the first line or passage which happened to turn up on opening a book, or by observing the stars. It was supposed to be lucky to be born under a certain star, and unlucky to come into the world under another. Astrologers were consulted regarding one's natal hour. Fortune-tellers and books of fate were consulted on the most trivial occasions; and persons aspiring to the magistracy, after saying their prayers in the open air, had recourse to augury with the view of ascertaining whether the gods favoured their cause.

Great attention was paid by the Romans to dreams, and persons of disordered minds were supposed to possess the faculty of presaging future events. Omens of futurity were also drawn from the appearance of the entrails of animals offered in sacrifice to the gods. The flame and smoke from the altar were noticed, and so were the circumstances attending the driving, felling, and bleeding of the victim. Sibylline books were inspected by appointment of the senate at perilous times, as they were supposed to contain the fate of the Roman Empire. There was something mysterious about the origin of the sibylline books. It is reported that a woman called Amalthaea, from a foreign country, came to Tarquin the Proud to sell nine sibylline books. Upon Tarquin refusing to give her the price asked, she went away and burned three of them. Returning soon after, she sought the same price for the remaining six. Still the price was refused, and she went away and burned other three books. She again came to the king, and demanded the same price for the three unconsumed volumes as she had asked for the nine. Tarquin, who first regarded the woman as a senseless old creature, became surprised at her strange behaviour, and inquired at the augurs what he should do. They advised him to give the woman the price she demanded. The woman delivered the books, and, after desiring that they should be carefully kept, disappeared, and was never seen again.

The use of charms and incantations originated in the worship of the heathen gods. As people in this country believe that spirits, good and bad, go about at night, so did the Romans suppose that their gods went up and down the earth during the night to observe the actions of men. The priests and others, when engaged in acts of piety or important business, took care, when turning, to move to the right. Every Roman avoided repeating words of bad omen. Certain days were reckoned unfortunate for the celebration of marriages. The month of May was thought an unlucky time for marriages being solemnized. The most fortunate time for weddings taking place was in the middle of June. The dress of a bride on her marriage day was a long white robe and her face was covered with a veil, in token of her modesty; her hair was divided with the point of a spear into six locks, and she was crowned with flowers. No marriage was celebrated before recourse to auspices. The nuptial ceremony was performed in the bride's father's house, or in the residence of the nearest relation. In the evening the bride was conducted to her husband's house, taken thither apparently by force from the arms of her mother or other relative, in memory of the violence used to the Sabine women. Three boys, whose parents were alive, attended her; two of them supported her by the arms, while the third walked before, bearing a flambeau of pine or thorn. Maid-servants followed with a distaff and wool, intimating that she was to spin as matrons formerly did. Many relations and friends attended the nuptial procession. The young men repeated jests and made sport as she passed along. The bride bound the door-posts of her new home with woollen fillets, and anointed them with the fat of swine or wolves, to prevent enchantments. She was lifted over the threshold, or lightly leaped over it, as it was thought ominous to put her foot upon it, because the threshold was sacred to Vesta, the goddess of virgins. Both she and her husband touched fire and water, as all things were supposed to be produced from these two elements. With the water their feet were bathed. The husband gave a feast, and musicians attended and sang the nuptial song. After supper the bride was conducted to her bed-chamber by matrons who had been only once married, and laid on her couch, which was covered with flowers; songs were then sung by young women before the chamber door till midnight. Next day another entertainment was given by the husband, when presents were sent to the bride by her friends and relations; and she began her family duties by performing sacred rites. Great attention was paid to funeral ceremonies. Many people believed that the souls of the unburied were not admitted into the abodes of the dead before they had wandered about the Styx at least a hundred years. If one happened to discover an unburied body and did not throw earth on it, he was compelled to expiate his crime by sacrificing a hog to Ceres. When persons were at the point of death, their nearest relation present endeavoured to catch the expiring breath with their mouth, as they believed the soul or living principle went out by the mouth. The nearest relation among the Romans closed the eyes and mouth of the deceased, after putting money into the mouth for the ferryman who was to take the soul of the dead over the lake it had to cross. A branch of cypress placed at the door where the deceased lay, indicated that there was a dead body within. People were invited to public funerals by a herald. Magistrates and priests were supposed to be violated by seeing a corpse, and therefore the dead were generally buried at night with torch-light. At funeral processions pipers and other musicians attended, and women sang the funeral song or the praises of the deceased to the sound of the flute. By the law of the twelve tables, the number of flute players was restricted to ten. Next followed actors and buffoons, who danced and sang, while one of them imitated the deceased's words and actions when alive. Before the corpse there were carried the images of the deceased and of his ancestors. The ancients buried their dead at their own houses, whence arose the fear of hobgoblins, and a belief in lares, supposed to be the souls of the deceased. When the body was laid in the tomb, the people present were sprinkled three times with pure water by the priest, and when the friends returned home they were again sprinkled. Beans, lettuces, bread, eggs, etc. were laid in the tombs, in the belief that the ghosts would come and eat them. Offerings were made to appease the manes. If a person, falsely reported to have been dead, returned home, he did not enter his house by the door, but went into it through the roof. Dead bodies were often violated for magical purposes, by stripping them of valuable articles, or cutting off fingers, toes, or arms. Wax images of deceased persons were made, and, after a variety of ridiculous ceremonies, burned on piles, from the tops of which eagles were let loose to convey to heaven the souls set free from the body.

CHAPTER VII.

Ethiopian Superstition--Sacred Bread--Customs of   Ethiopian Monks--Heathen Indian Gods--Paraxacti and   her three Sons--Thirty thousand millions of Gods--Fate   of a Child written on its Forehead--Transmigration of   Souls--Seven Seas--Mountain of Gold--Adder of   monstrous size with a Hundred Heads--Vixnu--Dispute   between Bruma, Vixnu, and Rutrem--Curse pronounced against the Thistle--Iranien the   Giant--Transformation--Morning Star--Vixnu's different   Forms--A King's Head kicked into the lowest   Abyss--Prediction by Soothsayers--A Tyrant's   Intentions frustrated--Vixnu's Guilt and Punishment; his Marriages and supposed future   Appearance--Rutrem--A Son with Seven Heads--The Seven   Stars as Nurses--Parvardi's Loss of her Husband and   Birth of a Son--Rutrem's Revenge and its   Consequences--The Indians' Offering to the Sun--The   Ganges--The Giant Piamejuran--Superstitious   Observances at Marriages--Disposal of Dead   Bodies--Different degrees of Glory after   Death--Reverence for the Cow--Ways of detecting   Criminals--Addressing Oracles--Astronomy--Eclipse of   the Moon--Magic--John Gondalez.

I n Ethiopia, superstition was general over the entire empire. The Ethiopians used a sacred bread, called the corban. While this bread was being made, the baker was obliged to repeat seven psalms. Upon every loaf there were twelve impressions of the cross, and each cross was within a square. Ethiopian monks slept on a mat spread on the ground, and before lying down they stretched out their hands one hundred and fifty times in the form of a cross. Baptism was understood by the people of this empire to be a solemn ceremony that washed away all impurities; but the rite was observed by nearly all the ancient nations, in memory of the Deluge.

In an account of the empire of the Great Mogul, we find no end of superstitious observances. Each heathen Indian tribe had a separate god. Some tribes even worshipped boiled rice; after the same manner the Egyptians paid homage to leeks. Indian writers say that, in the beginning, a woman, whose name was Paraxacti (brought into existence by the great Creator), had three sons,--the first named Bruma, who came into life with five heads. He was endowed with the power of creating all inferior beings. The name of the second was Vixnu, appointed lord of providence and preserver of all things formed by Bruma. The third was named Rutrem, whose function or inclination was to destroy all things his other two brothers had made and preserved. Rutrem, like his brother Bruma, had five heads. Bruma assumed the form of a stag; and, to punish him for a serious crime he committed when in that shape, his brothers and thirty thousand millions of gods punished him by cutting off one of his heads.

According to the notions of Indian heathens, Bruma writes upon the forehead of every child an account of all that shall happen to him in the world. It is reported of Vixnu that he metamorphosed himself at pleasure. He first took the form and nature of a fish, and the second form assumed was that of a tortoise. The Indians believed there were seven seas in the world,--one of milk, of so delicious a nature that the gods ate butter made of it. One day, when the gods wanted to feast on the butter according to custom, they brought to the shore of the milk sea a high mountain of gold, which supported fourteen worlds that composed the universe. The uppermost part of the mountain served for a resting place, and over it was brought an adder of monstrous size, having a hundred heads. The gods made use of this adder as a rope, in order to get at the butter more easily; but while they were attempting to procure the butter, the giants, who had a continual hatred against the gods, drew the adder on the other side with so much violence that it shook the whole universe, and sunk it so low, that Vixnu, in his tortoise form, placed himself under it and supported it. Meanwhile the hundred-headed adder, being unable any longer to endure the pain the gods and giants inflicted on him, vomited poison upon the giants, which killed many of them on the spot. Vixnu afterwards assumed the form of a beautiful woman, and such of the giants as remained alive fell in love with the fair being. In this guise, he amused the giants till the gods had eaten all the butter.

In his third incarnation, Vixnu changed himself into the form of a hog, in consequence of the following circumstance:--One day a contest arose between the three gods, Bruma, Vixnu, and Rutrem, regarding the extent of their power. Rutrem undertook to go and hide himself, and at the same time promised to submit himself to him who should first discover his head and feet; but if they could not find these parts, then the baffled gods were to acknowledge him their superior. Bruma and Vixnu having agreed to this proposal, Rutrem vanished, and hid his head and feet in places a great distance from each other, where he imagined they could not be found. Bruma, in the likeness of a swan, commenced to search for the head, but, finding he could not obtain any trace of it, he resolved to return home. Just, however, as he was going to give up the search, he met the thistle flower, which came and saluted him, and showed the place where Rutrem had hid his head. Rutrem, exasperated, cursed the flower, and forbade it ever to enter his presence. For this reason, his followers prevented thistles being brought into their temples in any part of the East Indies.

For the purpose of finding the feet, Vixnu transformed himself into a hog, and went from place to place digging into the earth, but without success. For cogent reasons, Vixnu next assumed the form of a man and lion at the same time. Rutrem, it appears, conceived a strong friendship for one Iranien, a mighty giant, and granted him the privilege that no one should kill him either by day or by night. Instead of the giant proving grateful, he became proud and overbearing, and even insisted on being worshipped as a god. To punish the giant, Vixnu suddenly appeared before him in the form of a cloud, and then, taking the monster shape of a being half-man half-lion, resolved to take vengeance on the ungrateful wretch. In the evening, when Iranien was standing at the threshold of his door, Vixnu sprang at him, tore him to pieces, and drank his blood. But the blood affected Vixnu so much that he became stupid. Vixnu's fifth transformation was into a dwarf. At that time a cruel king's subjects appealed to Vixnu to relieve them of their oppressor, and, to carry out the people's desire, he, in the form of a dwarf, went to the city where the tyrant kept court. The dwarf begged from the king a grant of three feet of ground whereon to build himself a house. The tyrant was about to comply with the request, when the morning star, which attended the king in the character of secretary of state, suspected there was treason in the case. It was common, when requests were granted, for the king to take water into his mouth and pour some of it into the hand of the suppliant, and therefore the secretary, by the assistance of magic, slipped imperceptibly down the prince's throat, in order to prevent the water being thrown out. The magic had not the desired effect; for the king, finding something in his throat, forced a sharp instrument into it, which put out one of the secretary's eyes, and the water gushed out, ratifying the agreement. Vixnu changed himself into a monster so large that the whole earth was not sufficient to afford room for his feet. He then said to the king, "You have given me three feet of earth, and yet the whole world can scarcely contain one of my feet: where am I to place the other?" The tyrant, seeing deserved wrath awaiting him, laid his head down before Vixnu, who with one kick tossed it into the lowest abyss of hell. The wretched king, finding himself condemned to such a place of torment, begged pardon and mercy of Vixnu, but all the favour he received was one day's respite every year, to enable him to take part at a particular ceremony, to be observed in commemoration of his own downfall and punishment.

Vixnu's sixth form was that of a white man. He subdued many tyrants, and washed his hands in their blood. In this form he destroyed many giants, and compelled all the apes in the country to attend him. The last form Vixnu assumed was that of a black man, in which likeness his cunning and success were not less marked than when he was disguised in several of his former shapes. Here is another story told of him:--There was a great tyrant named Campsen, a violent persecutor of good men, who had a sister called Exudi. It happened that the soothsayers, of whom there were many in the country, having consulted the stars, told the king that Exudi would have eight children, and that the youngest of them would kill him. This enraged the monarch so much that he destroyed seven of her children as soon as they were born. Notwithstanding the natural affliction of the princess, she became pregnant for the eighth time, but, wonderful to relate, of no less a personage than the god Vixnu, who, unknown to her, succeeded in finding a place in her womb. Fearing the child would be conveyed beyond his reach as soon as it was born, the king placed spies everywhere to prevent the young prince's escape. The supposed father of the child succeeded in carrying him away, and placing him under the care of shepherds far up the mountains. Every effort was made by the baffled monarch to discover the young prince, and at last he found him. Desiring to be the executioner himself, he went and laid hold of the child to murder him. Just as the hand was raised to inflict the fatal blow, the prince vanished, and in his room appeared a little girl, whom the tyrant also attempted to kill; but she too, after mocking the king, disappeared uninjured. Vixnu grew from boyhood to manhood, when he raised an army against Campsen, whom he defeated and slew with his own hands, fulfilling the prediction of the soothsayers. Vixnu married two wives, but, neither of them pleasing him, he divorced them and espoused sixteen thousand shepherdesses. The people imagined that he would appear some time or another in the form of a horse, but thought that until that metamorphosis took place he would wallow in a sea of milk, with his head supported by a beautiful snake.

We are informed that Rutrem, the third son of Paraxacti, was much respected by the people, though, judging from the accounts transmitted to us, the wonder is that he was not detested. He married Parvardi, daughter of a king, whose dominion was in the mountains, with whom he lived a thousand years; but his two brothers, Bruma and Vixnu, having disapproved of the match, gathered together the thirty thousand millions of gods, and went in search of him. Accordingly he was found and dragged away from his wife, which caused him to wander up and down the earth in search of forbidden pleasures. One day the earth gave him a son with seven heads; but as a nurse could not be got to bring up the child, the seven stars undertook the task. Parvardi, disconsolate at the loss of her husband, went in search of him, but could not discover his place of abode. In her lonely state, she begged the gods would give her a son,--a request that was complied with, for a man-child dropped out of the sweat of her forehead. In the meantime Rutrem returned to his house, and, finding the child, became exceedingly enraged. His anger, however, turned into love on being informed of the miraculous manner in which he was born. The king of the mountains made a feast, to which the gods were invited, but Rutrem, his son-in-law, was not asked. This want of respect provoked him so much that he went to the banquet, and, laying hold of one of the gods, tore off a handful of hair from his head. From the hair a giant of enormous size started up, whose head reached to the firmament, and struck the sun with so great violence that all its teeth were knocked out. For this reason, the Indians refused to offer anything to the sun but what could be eaten without teeth. Not satisfied with knocking out the teeth of the sun, he bruised the moon so severely that the marks remain to the present day. He then killed several of the guests, among whom was his step-son, created from the sweat of his mother's forehead. Vinayaguien (that was the youth's name) lost his head, and had it replaced with that of an elephant. In the disfigured state into which he was turned, his father dispatched him in search of a wife as beautiful as his mother,--a task that proved endless, because there could not be found a woman equal in beauty to his maternal parent.

Rutrem married the River Ganges, which was represented under the form of a blooming woman. At that time there was a giant named Piamejuran, who had for several years undergone a severe penance for having offended Rutrem, but, becoming sensible of his offence, desired to be absolved. The favour was granted him, with the privilege of reducing to ashes everything he laid his hands upon. The power with which he was endowed proved his death. One day he went to the Ganges to bathe, and, lifting his hand to his forehead, it reduced him to dust.

At their marriages, the Indians were very superstitious, and paid great regard to omens. The consent of the parents being obtained, and a fortunate day appointed, the parties met with the relations, when the bridegroom threw three handfuls of rice on the head of the bride, and she cast an equal quantity at him. Part of the marriage ceremony consisted of the fathers of both bridegroom and bride putting a piece of money and a small quantity of water into the bride's hand. This being done, the bridegroom hung a ribbon, with a coin attached to it, round her neck.

As soon as a man died, his beard was shaved, his body washed, lime put into his mouth, and women rubbed his face with rice. When the body was burned, the deceased's ashes were thrown into the Ganges, for the water of that river was supposed to have a virtuous and holy influence on whatever it touched. The Brahmins believed that there were five different degrees of glory after death. Bruma, with his wife Sarassuadi, was in the fourth state attended by a large swan, on which he rode abroad, this god being supposed to be exceedingly fond of travelling. None but the most innocent were exalted to the fifth seat of glory.

Cows' dung was spread over the floors of Indian temples; and such was the people's reverence for the cow, that when sacrificing they poured milk on their altars. Their priests pretended that their gods had oracles, by which they could foretell future events. When several persons were suspected of stealing anything, and the guilty one could not be discovered by ordinary means, the priests wrote the names of the suspected persons on different pieces of paper, and laid them down before the altar, and invoked their oracle, after which they locked the doors, so that no person could get in. When they returned and found any paper removed, the person whose name was on it was declared to be the criminal. On the priests addressing their oracles, they became so excited that they remained for hours seemingly in great agony. After recovering, they explained to the people the sayings of the oracles. The Indians had tables of astronomy which they consulted. When the moon was eclipsed, they believed she was fighting with a black devil.

The Indians supposed that by means of magic a man could change himself into the form of a lion or any other animal he chose. We have heard of one John Gondalez, who changed himself into the shape of a lion, and in that form was shot by a Spaniard. The day on which Gondalez was fired at he was reported to be sick. A clergyman was called in to take his confession. The pious man, in giving an account of what he saw and heard, said, "I saw Gondalez's face and nose all bruised, and asked him how he had received the injuries. He told me that he had fallen from a tree and nearly killed himself. After this he accused the Spaniard of shooting at him. The affair was inquired into by a Spanish justice of the peace. My evidence was taken, and I told what Gondalez had said to me regarding his fall. The Spaniard swore that he had shot at a lion in a thick wood, where an Indian was not likely to be."

Gondalez was examined as to how he was not seen by the Spaniard when he went to look for the lion; to which he replied that he ran away lest the Spaniard should kill him. As Gondalez's dealings with the devil were well known to all in the neighbourhood, it was held that he had received his injuries when roaming as a four-footed beast; and therefore the justice discharged the Spaniard.

CHAPTER VIII.

John Gomez the Wizard and Man-tiger--Lopez the Man-lion--Vermilion Marks rendered the Devil powerless--Sacrificing Children--Offerings to the Ganges--A Rajah offering himself as a Sacrifice--Preventatives against Disease--Various Superstitious Ceremonies--Sacrificing to the Gods of the Four Winds--How the Devil was kept away--King's Wives and Retainers going with the Dead Monarch into the other World--An eternal Succession of Worlds--Apes supposed to have Human Souls--Worshipping Demons--Drinking Blood--Prognosticating from the Cries of Beasts--Witchcraft and Magic--Singular Opinions and Customs--Watching Graves, and providing for the Dead--Foretelling Future Events at the New Moon--Method of discovering a False Swearer--Offerings to the Sea and Winds--Superstition in China--Chinese Genealogy and Worship--Opinion of their Gods and Goddesses--Sacrifices--Beggars--Magical Arts--False Worship--Comfort of the Dead provided for--Superstition in Japan--Fortune-telling--Idols--Gods and Goddesses--Five Hundred Children hatched from Eggs--Human Souls supposed to reside in Inferior Animals--Beasts held in great esteem--Statues of Witches and Magicians placed in Temples in Japan--Charms sold by Priests--Value of Charms--Fortunate and Unfortunate Days--A Fairy in the likeness of a Fox--A valuable Charm.

The gentleman (a clergyman) who told the story of John Gondalez, gives another tale equally interesting. John Gomez, the chief of an Indian town, was nearly eighty years of age, and reputed to be possessed of more than ordinary shrewdness. His advice was preferred to that of all other chiefs. He seemed to be a very godly Indian, and very seldom missed morning and evening prayers in the church. "He was suddenly taken ill," proceeds the clergyman; "and one of his friends, fearing that he might die without making confession, called me up at midnight, desiring me to go presently to John Gomez to help him to die. I therefore visited Gomez, who lay with his face muffled. He confessed, wept, and showed a willingness to die. I comforted him, after which I returned home to refresh myself. Scarcely had I crossed the threshold of my house than I was called on to visit the sick man a second time, and give him extreme unction. As I anointed him on his nose, lips, hands, eyes, and feet, I perceived he was swollen black and blue. I went home again, and after

I had rested a little, an Indian called to buy candles to offer up for the soul of John Gomez, who, he told me, had departed. I went to the church, and found the grave being prepared for the deceased. Two Spaniards, to whom I spoke, told me of a great stir being made in the town concerning the death of Gomez. Amused at the information received, I desired a full and particular account of the whole circumstances. They told me that Gomez was the chief wizard of the town--that he was often changed into a tiger, and in that form walked about the mountains. Wondering at this statement, I went straight to the prison, where, I was told, I might obtain information on the subject. At the stronghold the officers communicated to me the whole matter. There were witnesses, they said, who saw a lion and a tiger fighting, and presently lost sight of them, but saw in their places Gomez and a man named Lopez. Gomez returned home much bruised, and on his deathbed declared to his friends that Lopez had killed him. Lopez was therefore taken into custody, and put in irons. The crown officers investigated the case with great care, and found that the body of Gomez was all bruised and torn in various places. Lopez, upon this, was taken to Guatemala, and there hanged, the evidence against him, in the estimation of the judges and people, being conclusive that he had fatally injured Gomez while the former was in the shape of a tiger, and the latter in the likeness of a lion."

The inhabitants of Bisnagar, Deccan, and elsewhere believed that the moment a priest marked any one on the forehead with vermilion, the devil had no power over the person thus distinguished. At Samorin there was a statue to which children were sacrificed. It was of brass, and, when heated by a furnace underneath it, the children were thrown into its mouth and consumed. Flowers were scattered upon the altars during the sacrifices, and herbs, steeped in the blood of a cock, perfumed the idol. The cock's throat was cut with a silver knife dipped in the blood of a hen. At the conclusion of the barbarous ceremony, the priest walked backwards from the altar to the middle of the chapel, where he threw a handful of corn over his head.

The Ganges, as is well known, was, and still is, worshipped by a large number of people. Vast numbers of pilgrims continually visit this great river. Formerly, if not now, they bathed in it in a peculiar fashion, holding short straws in their hands while they were performing their ablutions. Gold and silver were often thrown into the stream, in testimony of admiration.

At Quailacara a remarkable ceremony took place once every twelve years. On the morning of the important day, the rajah, who was both high priest and sovereign, offered himself a sacrifice to the gods. He first delivered an oration, and then with a sharp instrument cut off his nose, lips, and ears, and concluded the tragical event by cutting his throat. Similar ceremonies were performed in the same district by scores of deluded devotees, who bent their steps to the most celebrated temples, where they cut off their flesh, piece by piece, and then stabbed themselves to death. Their bodies were burned, and the ashes sold by the priests at high sums, as preservatives against disease. When the people came to bathe in the Ganges in the month of May, they erected piles of cows' dung, on which were placed baskets of rice, roots, and every description of vegetables. These were surrounded with wood besmeared with butter, and set on fire. From the appearance of the smoke and flame, those present pretended to discover whether the harvest was to be abundant or otherwise. At seed-time the priests took branches from trees, and walked in procession with them, going three times round the temples. A hole was then dug in the ground, and water from the Ganges poured into it. In this hole cows' dung and the branches were put and set on fire, and from the appearance of the flames the arch-priest was enabled to foretell what was to happen during the year. When a person was dying, he was carried to a river and dipped into it, that his soul and body might be purified. Happy was the individual who could be conveyed to the Ganges, because its waters were supposed to be possessed of virtues that did not exist in other rivers. Sometimes the hands of the dying person were tied to a cow's tail, and the invalid dragged through the water. If the cow emitted urine upon the person, it was considered a most salutary purification. If the fluid fell plentifully upon the expiring man, his friends testified their joy by loud acclamation, believing he was about to be numbered among the blessed. But when the cow did not supply the purifying liquid, the relatives showed their grief, for they thought their dying friend was going to a place of punishment.

At Assam and elsewhere, when a person was sick, sacrifices were offered to the god of the four winds. If the patient died, servants were kept beating on instruments of copper to keep away evil spirits, supposed to be hovering round the corpse. There was a belief that if an evil spirit passed over a dead body, the soul would return to the inanimate remains. At a funeral procession, men surrounded the coffin with drawn scimitars, to drive the devil away and help to confine him to his home of darkness. At a king's death, all his wives, ministers of state, and retainers surrounded the grave, and poisoned themselves, in order to accompany him into the other world. Horses, camels, elephants, and hounds were also interred along with his majesty, to be useful to him in the world of bliss.

In Pegu, the people believed in an eternal succession of worlds, and imagined that, as soon as one would be burned, another would spring out of its ashes. They thought that people devoured by crocodiles went to a place of perpetual happiness. The people believed that asses had human souls, and, reversing the theory of Darwin that human beings were the offspring of inferior animals, thought they were formerly men; but, to punish them for crimes they had been guilty of, the gods transformed them into their present shape. White elephants were much esteemed by the people. As the devil was worshipped, altars were erected in honour of him, and sacrifices were daily offered to appease his wrath and obtain his favour. Devout persons refused to taste food, before throwing part of it behind them for the dogs or devils to eat; for they imagined that every dog was possessed with evil spirits, if the animal was not Satan himself. It sometimes happened that a man left his house, swept clean and genteelly furnished, for the devil to take possession of it for a whole month.

On entering into a solemn agreement, the natives of Siam drank each other's blood. They attentively listened to the groans and cries of wild beasts, and prognosticated from them, and believed in witchcraft. They imagined, as spiritualists of the present time do, that answers were received from deceased friends or relations. Natives of the Philippine Islands had a notion that they could know, from seeing the first objects that presented themselves to them in the morning, whether they would be successful or unsuccessful in their undertakings during the day. If one of them happened to tread upon an insect when setting out on a journey, he would proceed no further. The islanders of the Moluccas watched the graves of their deceased relations seven nights, for fear the devil would steal the body away, and during that time the bed of the deceased was made as if he were alive. Further, victuals were prepared for him, lest he should return to earth and require nourishment. Many of the people wore bracelets, and on the appearance of the new moon a hen's neck was cut, and the bracelets dipped into the blood. From the appearance of the ornaments after being taken out, future events were brought to light. When the people of Ceylon were called upon to make oath, they wrapped their right hands in a cloth the previous night, and when they appeared in court, a caldron, containing a mixture of cows' dung and water, kept boiling over a strong fire, was in readiness for the deponents, subsequent to removing the bandages, to immerse their hands therein. This being done, their hands were again wrapped up until next day, when the fingers were rubbed with a linen cloth. He whose skin peeled off first, was declared to have spoken falsehoods; and he not only lost his cause, but was compelled to pay a penalty to the king. At the Maldive Islands, offerings were made to the sea when a voyage was about to be undertaken. Sacrifices were also offered to the winds, which was done by setting fire to a new boat, and consuming it to ashes. But if one was too poor to offer a boat, he threw into the ocean several cocks and hens; for it was the opinion that there was in the water a god that ate such things as were offered in sacrifice. One was warned not to spit against the wind when at sea. The ships and other vessels belonging to the people of these islands were consecrated to the gods of the sea and the winds.

Superstition in China was, and still is, both general and absurd in the extreme. The Chinese profess to have an uninterrupted genealogy of their kings for a period of twenty-four thousand years; but, notwithstanding their pretensions to antiquity, learned men suppose that these people are descendants of the Egyptians. On this difficult question, however, we do not propose to enter, and therefore proceed to notice a few of their ridiculous customs and notions. They have been idolaters for ages, and pay divine honours to numerous gods--particularly to Fo, who was deified and worshipped for more than a thousand years before the Christian era. The Chinese say that Fo was a king's son. As soon as the infant god was born, he could speak and walk. When young, he had four philosophers to instruct him, and at the age of thirty he began to work miracles. Report has it that he was born eight thousand times, and that his soul had passed through the bodies of many different animals. The doctrine of transmigration of souls was part of the people's creed, and this doctrine is still believed in by the people generally. Cang-y was the god of the lower heavens, and had power over life and death. He had three spirits constantly attending him, the first of whom sent rain to refresh and nourish the earth; the second was the god of the sea, to whom all their navigators made vows before going away with ships, and performed them on their return home; and the third presided over births and war. The great Chinese reformer, Confucius, was born four hundred and fifty years before Christianity was preached. As soon as he was born, two dragomans came to guard him against harm, and the stars bowed themselves before him. He married a wife, but, finding that she hindered him in his pursuit of knowledge, he put her away. He lived to the age of seventy years, when he died of a broken heart at beholding the evils around him. The highest honours were paid to him after death.

Hogs were offered in sacrifice to the gods. Wine was poured on the animals' ears, and if they shook their heads at this operation they were deemed proper objects to be offered, but if they remained motionless they were rejected.

On the 14th August of every year sacrifices were offered by the people to their ancestors, and all who assisted them at the solemn ceremonies were assured that they would receive particular favours from their dead relatives. Vast numbers of beggars constantly went about the country. If those mendicants were refused alms, they told the people that their souls would pass into the bodies of rats, mice, snakes, toads, and such other creatures as they knew the Chinese abhorred. Those mendicants told fortunes, and, if report speaks true, could raise the wind by striking the earth with a hammer of magical virtue. A ship captain, on going to sea, might have a fair wind and a prosperous voyage for a moderate sum. Divination was practised by means of household gods, of which there were many in the empire.

Conjurers and fortune-tellers were by law forbidden to frequent the houses of civil or military officers under the pretence of prophesying impending national calamities or successes, but the prohibition was not understood to prevent them telling fortunes and casting nativities by the stars in the usual manner. Whenever signs of calamity were observed in the heavens by the officers of the astronomical board, and they failed to give faithful notice thereof; they were punished with one hundred and twenty blows and two years' banishment. In later times a law was passed against sorcerers and magicians, prohibiting them, under pain of death, from employing spells and incantations, calculated to agitate and influence the minds of the people. Killing by magic was by statute placed among the most serious classes of offences. Magicians who raised evil spirits by means of magical books and dire imprecations, or who burned incense in honour of the images of their worship when they assembled by night to instruct their followers, were strangled.

It was enacted by the Chinese laws, that if any members of a private family performed the ceremony of the adoration of heaven and of the north star, and lighted the lamps of the sky and of that star, they were guilty of profanation, and liable to be punished with eighty blows. When a dead body was laid in the coffin, the mouth of the deceased was filled with corn, rice, silver, and gold; and scissors, tied up in purses, were put into the coffin, that the departed person might cut his nails as often as he pleased.

There was a sect in Japan called Jammabugi, who studied magic chiefly among the rocks and mountains. They procured a subsistence by pretending to tell fortunes. They possessed an almost incredible number of idols, one of which was Abbuto, noted for curing inveterate diseases, and for procuring a favourable wind at sea. To secure a quick passage, sailors and passengers were wont to throw money into the ocean as an offering to this idol.

The Japanese had gods for almost everything. A most ridiculous account is given of their goddess of riches. When a mortal, she had no children by her husband, which caused her to supplicate the gods to give her offspring. Her prayers were heard, and she produced five hundred eggs. Being afraid that if the eggs were hatched they would bring forth monsters, she packed them up in a box bearing a particular mark, and threw them into a river. An old fisherman found the box, and, seeing it full of eggs, carried it home to his wife. Not having a sufficient number of hens to hatch so many eggs, she put them into an oven, and, to the surprise of the aged couple, every egg produced a child. The two old people succeeded in bringing up the strange progeny to manhood, for they were all sons. They became robbers and beggars by turn; and it happened, one day during their rambles, that they came to their mother's house. From inquiries she made, it became clear that the young ruffians were her own children. She kept them, and reared them up to be virtuous and useful. She was afterwards taken up from the earth to be among the gods, where she remains, attended by her five hundred sons.

Apes and monkeys, as well as other creatures, were worshipped in Japan. So great faith did the people of that country put in the transmigration of souls, that they had hospitals for the reception of animals in whose bodies souls were supposed to reside. In a wood near Jeddo there were many sacred animals, daily fed by priests. These animals, the priests said, were animated by the souls of the most noble and illustrious heroes that ever lived. The people had such a profound veneration for stags, that they were to be seen in every street as numerous as the dogs in our country. If one killed a stag, not only was he condemned to die, but the houses where the deed was committed were razed to the ground. Dogs were held in great esteem. The inhabitants of every street were obliged to support a fixed number of them, they being quartered on the people like so many soldiers. When a dog died, it was buried among human remains. A man who killed a canine creature was punished with death. Fish were looked upon as sacred. Near the capital was a river that was so plentifully stocked with fish, that they thrust one another ashore, yet not one of them was injured. The people believed that if they touched one of the finny tribe, they would be smitten with leprosy, and it was considered an unpardonable sin to eat any of them. A belief prevailed, that fish possessed the souls of naval officers. Statues of witches, magicians, and devils find places in the Japan temples.

Charms were sold by the priests, which were represented to possess the virtue of curing diseases and driving away the devil. Money was sometimes borrowed on security of charms, not to be repaid in this world. A note was given, authorizing payment of the money in the land of spirits; and when the holder of the document died, his relations put it into his hand, believing that the debt would be duly paid to the deceased. The Japanese thought certain days were more fortunate than others. A table of their fortunate and unfortunate days was hung up in the passage of every house, for the guidance of the family when they went out. This table of days was prepared by a celebrated astrologer of universal knowledge in all mysteries, whether relating to the stars, dreams, or omens. Like other men of note in the East, he was born in a miraculous manner. His father was a prince, and his mother a fox. It appears that the lady fox being pursued by huntsmen, ran to and obtained protection from his highness. The creature discovered herself to be a fairy, and, throwing off her false appearance, became a beautiful princess. The prince being enamoured with her charms, married her, and had by her the celebrated astrologer spoken of. When he grew up he invented a set of mysterious terms, which he comprised within the compass of one verse, as a charm or protection for such persons as were compelled to work on unlucky days; and every one who repeated the verse reverently on the morning of an unlucky day, was preserved from all the evils that would have otherwise befallen him.

THE GODS AND GODDESSES OF HEATHEN NATIONS.
CHAPTER IX.

The Classification of Gods and Goddesses--Primeval	Parent Chaos--Creation--Influence of Ether--The Human	Race in danger of Perishing--Celestial Fire--Birth of	Cupid--Banishment of Cupid from the Blest	Abodes--Cupid's Armour--Fate--Eternal Decrees--Throne	of Jove--Fortune and Happiness--Misfortune and	Misery--Twofold Nature--Rewards and Punishments--First Man and Woman--Pan the Emblem of all Things--Power of	Heathen Gods--Descriptions of Juno--Venus the Goddess	of Love and Beauty--Rustics turned into	Frogs--Vulcan--AEolus--Momus the Jester--The Carping	God's Fault-finding--Improper Position of the Bull's	Horns--Minerva as a House--Window in Man's Breast.

We do not intend to notice at great length the ancient opinions and writings concerning the deities which heathen nations thought presided over the world and the heavens, and influenced the affairs of the spheres above and below; but as much of comparatively modern superstition has been traced to mythology, generally so called, we cannot pass without observation the history of the gods, nor avoid giving such extracts therefrom as bear particularly on our subject, "The Collected Mysteries of all Nations."

The gods and goddesses of heathen nations were classified as follows:--1st, the celestial gods and goddesses; 2nd, the terrestrial deities; 3rd, the marine and river gods and goddesses; 4th, the infernal gods; 5th, the subordinate and miscellaneous deities; 6th, the ascriptious gods, demigods, and heroes; and 7th, the modal deities. Ancient writers speak thus:

"When the primeval parent Chaos, hoary with unnumbered ages, was first moved by the breath of Erebus, she brought forth her enormous first-born Hyle, and at the same portentous birth the amiable almighty Eros, chief of the immortals. They had no sooner come to light than they produced the terrible Titans."

Again we are informed that--"Ere the universe appeared; ere the sun mounted on high, or the moon gave her pale light; ere the vales were stretched out below, or the mountains reared their towering heads; ere the winds began to blow, or the rivers to flow, or plants or trees had sprung from the earth; while the heavens lay hid in the mighty mass, and the stars were unknown, the various parts of which the wondrous creation consists lay jumbled without form in the Abyss of Being." There, it is said, they had lain for ever and ever if the breath of the terrible Erebus, the spirit that dwelt in eternal darkness, had not gone forth and put the mass into vital agitation.

From another source we learn that, first of all, Chaos existed; next in order the broad Earth; and then Love appeared, the most beautiful of all things. Of Chaos sprang Erebus and dusty Night, and of Erebus and Night came Ether and smiling Day.

The Earth conceived by the influence of Ether, and brought forth man and every description of animal. The human race was in danger of perishing from the face of earth. Naked, needy, and ignorant, they passed their dreary days, living in caves and lurking in woods like wild beasts. They were alike destitute of laws and arts. Their food consisted of herbs. Often were they compelled to fly before the mountain tigers and bears of the forest, while they were nearly frozen to death. Thus they lived in wretchedness until Prometheus came to their relief. He called Pallas, the goddess of wisdom, to his aid. By her assistance he mounted to heaven, where he secretly held the reed he carried in his hand to the wheel of the sun's chariot. In this way he obtained the celestial fire, and conveyed it to Earth, where he presented it to man. Prometheus did not stop here: he instructed man in arts and industry of almost every description.

There is an interesting account of Cupid. The goddess of beauty, we are informed, brought forth a delicate infant, whom she gave to the Graces to nurse. Unhappily, the child neither throve in person, nor put forth feathers to cover the wings which he had. Under this affliction, Cupid's mother and nurses had recourse to the most ancient and infallible Themis, who gave this answer: That love came, for the most part, single into the world, but that the child would not thrive until his mother brought forth another son. Then the one would thrive in virtue of the other; but if the one died, the other could not long survive. Venus brought forth another son, Anteros. He no sooner came into being, than his elder brother Cupid grew, and his wings were soon fledged. So strong did the little urchin become, that he flew to heaven. There he associated with the Muses, became intimate with Mercury, kept company with Hymen, and grew in favour with every one except the implacable Momus. Unfortunately, Cupid became insolent and vain, behaving with arrogance to the superior powers. He made enmity reign where peace and concord should have been found. Feuds raged among the gods and goddesses on his account. To rid themselves of a pest, the rulers of heaven called an assembly of the gods, to consider how peace could be restored. Cupid was accused of being a public incendiary, a disturber of good order; and the fomenter of discord being found guilty, he was banished from the blest abodes; ordered to be a retainer of Ceres and Bacchus on earth; and doomed to have his wings stripped of their feathers, that he might not again infest the confines of heaven.

Cupid is now armed with two bows, one of which he bends with the aid of the Graces, to secure a happy smiling lot, and he with the other, blind-folded, lets fly his arrows, to the confusion and misery of many in life. Like his mother, he is constantly in want. He is eager, ravenous, and wandering about bare-footed, without home or habitation, sleeping before doors or by the wayside, under the open sky. But at the same time he is ever forming designs upon all that is beautiful, is forward, cunning, and fond of new tricks.

Fate mysteriously clings round this earth, the heavens, and the creatures in the regions above and below. When Jupiter heard of the death of his son Sarpedon, in great grief he called on Mercury to go instantly to the Fates, and bring from them the strong box in which the eternal decrees are laid up. Mercury went to the Fatal Sisters, and delivered his message. The Sisters smiled, and told him that the other end of the golden chain which secured the box with the unalterable decrees was so fixed to the throne of Jove, that were it to be unfastened, the master's seat itself might be shaken.

Jupiter holds in his hands the unerring balance of fate. Close to his throne stand the two in-exhaustible urns--the one filled with good fortune and happiness, the other with misfortune and misery. Out of these is mixed a dose of life to every mortal man; and as the draught is, so are one's days embittered with disasters, or made pleasant with serenity, ease, and prosperity. To every star is allotted a mind, and all things have their fixed irrevocable laws. The human nature is twofold; and man, who lives well on earth, returns after death to the habitations of his congenial star, and there leads a blessed life; but, failing in his duties, he is doomed to live a thousand years in a degraded state. Sometimes a human soul is destined to animate a wild beast, never to be relieved until it reattain the purest of its first and best existence.

The Goths and Vandals entertained the opinion that the first man and woman were made of an ash-tree. Odin, it is said, gave them breath, Hener endowed them with reason, and Lodur injected blood into their veins, and provided them with beautiful faces.

Pan has been represented as the emblem of all things, and among the learned of early times he passed for the first and oldest of the divinities. His person is composed of various and opposite parts--a man and a goat. According to the most ancient Egyptians and Greeks, he had neither father nor mother, but sprang of Demogorgon at the same instant with the Fatal Sisters, the Parcae.

The power of the heathen gods and goddesses is reported as truly wonderful. Apollo turned Daphne, whom he loved, into a laurel, and his boy Hyacinth into a violet. Mars was the son of Jupiter and Juno, or, according to Ovid, of Juno alone, who conceived him at the smell of a flower shown her by the goddess Flora.

Juno is esteemed the goddess of kingdoms and riches. She is represented as a majestic beautiful woman, riding in a golden chariot drawn by peacocks, waving a sceptre in her hand, and wearing a crown set about with roses and lilies, and encircled with fair Iris, or the rainbow. She is also supposed to preside over matrimony and births, and is the guardian angel of woman.

Venus is the goddess of love and beauty; she sprang from the foam of the sea. As soon as she was born she was cast upon the island of Cyprus, where she was educated, and afterwards being carried to heaven, was married to Vulcan. Her image is fair and beautiful; she is clothed with purple, glittering with diamonds. There are two Cupids on her side, while around her are the Graces. Her chariot is of ivory, drawn by swans, doves, or swallows.

Whilst Latona was wandering through the fields of Lycia, she desired to drink from a spring at the bottom of a valley, but the country rustics drove her away. In spite of her entreaties, they refused to allow her to slake her thirst, whereupon, in wrath, she, cursing them, said, "May ye always live in this water!" Immediately they were turned into frogs, and leaped into the streams and pools, where they continued to exist.

Vulcan, notwithstanding his noble descent, is obliged to follow the trade of a blacksmith. On account of his deformity, he was cast down from heaven into the isle of Lemnos. His leg was broken by the fall. He erected a forge, where he makes thunderbolts for his father Jupiter and armour for the other gods. His servants are called Cyclops, because they have but one eye. Though Vulcan is unpleasant in the sight of others, Venus thinks him the most beautiful of all the divinities.

AEolus keeps the winds under his power in a cave in the AEolian Islands, where he dwells. He can raise storms and hurricanes, and restrain their rage at pleasure.

Momus is a jester, mocker, or mimic. His life is spent in idleness, merely observing the sayings and doings of the gods, and then censuring and deriding them. For instance, when Neptune was made a bull, Minerva a house, and Vulcan a man, Momus was appointed to judge as to whom the greatest skill was manifested in creation. The carping god disapproved of all. He found fault with the bull for not having his horns before his eyes in his forehead, that he might be enabled to push the surer. He condemned the house, because it was fixed and could not be carried away in case it was placed in a bad neighbourhood. But the god, he said, who made man, was most imprudent because he did not make a window in the human breast, that the thoughts might be seen.

CHAPTER X.

Satyrs described--Diana's Retirement--Pallas, the Goddess of Shepherds and Pasture--The vile Flora--Pomona deceived--Celestial Nymphs--Terrestrial Nymphs--River Gods and Goddesses--Sirens--Witch Circe--Infernal Deities--Passage to Tartarus--Palace of Pluto--Judges of Hell--Goddesses of Destiny--Furies--Night, Death, and Sleep: by whom presided over--Names of Monsters condemned in the place of Punishment--Tartarian Regions--Delights of the Elysian Fields--Food and Drink of Pagan Gods--Festivals of Heathens--Colour of Gods--Sacrifices to Deities--Things sacred to Gods.

Satyrs are partly of human likeness and partly of bestial shape. They have heads of human form, with horns and brutish ears; they have crooked hands, rough hairy bodies, goats' legs and feet and tails. The chief of these monsters is the god Pan, the inventor of the musical pipe.

Diana, out of love to Chastity, avoids consort with men, retires into the woods, and there diverts herself with hunting, whence she is reckoned the goddess of the woods and the chase. Pallas is esteemed the goddess of shepherds and pasture, and is the reputed inventress of corn, and is thought by some to be Ceres or Vesta. Flora is the goddess of flowers. By a vile trade, she accumulated a vast amount of money, and made the people of Rome her heirs, who, in return, placed her among the divinities.

Ferona and Pomona are two goddesses of trees and fruits. The latter was advised by the god Vertumnus to enter the matrimonial state in the guise of a hagged old woman; but without success, till he appeared to her as a fair young man, and then she felt the power of love, and yielded to his wishes. The Nymphs are a company of neat charming virgins, living near the gardens of Pomona. They are of three classes:--1st the Celestial Nymphs, called Genii, who guide the spheres and dispense the influences of the stars to things on earth. 2nd, the Terrestrial Nymphs, as Dryades, who preside over the woods and live in the oaks; and Hamadryades, who are born and die with the oaks; the Oreades, who preside over the mountains; the Napaeae, who preside over the groves and valleys; the Limnatides, who look after the meadows and fields. 3rd, Marine Nymphs.

As the chief of the marine and river gods and goddesses, Neptune stands at the head. He is represented with black hair and blue eyes, arrayed in a mantle of azure, holding a trident in his right hand, and embracing his queen with his left arm. He stands upright in his chariot, drawn by sea horses, and is attended by nymphs. Proteus is the son of Neptune, but some say he is the offspring of Oceanus and Tethys. His business is to tend the sea-calves. He can turn himself into any shape. Triton, the son and trumpeter of Neptune, is a man to the middle and a dolphin below; he has two fore feet, like those of horses, and is provided with two tails. Oceanus is the son of C[oe]lum and Vesta, husband to Tethys, god of the sea, and father of the rivers and springs. Nereus, also the son of Oceanus and Tethys, is father of fifty daughters, called Nereides or Sea Nymphs. Palaemon and his mother Ino, together with the fisherman Glaucus, are reckoned among the sea deities. The Sirens resemble mermaids, having the faces of women, but bodies of flying fish. They are reported to be excellent songsters, that play on the Sicilian coasts, and tempt passengers on shore, where they sing them asleep and kill them. Scylla and Charybdis are two other sea monsters. Scylla is the daughter of Phorcys, and beloved by Glaucus, whom therefore the witch Circe by her enchantments turned into a rock, with dogs around her. Charybdis is a very ravenous woman, who stole Hercules's oxen, for which crime Jupiter struck her dead with a thunder-bolt, and then turned her into a gulf or whirl-pool in the Sicilian Sea. The Sea Nymphs are the Nereides already referred to. The Naides or Naiades preside over fountains and springs; the Potameides preside over rivers, and Limniades over lakes.

In noticing the Infernal Deities, we shall describe the dismal regions, where wicked spirits dwell, and over which they are reported to preside. The name commonly given to these regions is Hades or Tartarus, understood to signify hell. The passage leading thereto is a wide dark cave, through which one has to pass by a steep rocky descent till he arrives at a gloomy grove and an un-navigable lake called Avernus, from which such poisonous vapours rise as to kill birds flying over it. Yet over this lake the souls of the dead must pass. To assist them, an old decrepit, long-bearded fellow, the oft-heard of Charon, attends with a ferry-boat to carry them to the other side, at a fare not less than a halfpenny.

After this there are four rivers to be passed over--Acheron, whose waters are very bitter; the Styx, a lake rather than a river, and so sacred to the gods, that if any of them swore by it and broke his oath, he was deprived of his godhead, and was prohibited from drinking nectar for a hundred years; the river Cocytus, which flows out of Styx with a lamentable groaning, resembling the painful sounds and exclamations of the damned; the river Phlegethon, so called because it swells with waves of fire and streams of flames.

The souls having passed these rivers, are conducted to the palace of Pluto, king of the infernal regions, where the gate is guarded by Cerberus, a dog with three heads, whose body is covered with snakes in place of hair. This dog is the porter of hell.

Pluto initiated funeral obsequies for the dead: he sits on a throne covered with darkness, hold-ing a key in his hand, and crowned with ebony. Beside him is his queen Proserpina, whom he stole from Ceres.

Minos, AEacus, and Rhadamanthus are judges in hell. The first two are sons of Jupiter by Eu-ropa, and the last is his son by AEgina. These are believed to judge the souls of the dead.

The Fates are named Clotho, Lachesis, and Atropos, and are the goddesses of destiny. They order and manage the fatal thread of life. Clotho draws the thread, Lachesis turns the wheel, and Atropos cuts the string asunder when spun to a due length.

The Furies, called sometimes Eumenides, Dirae, and Manes, are the daughters of Nox and Acheron: their names are Alecto, Tisiphone, and Megaera, and are known by the common name of Erinnys. They have faces like women, their looks are full of terror, they hold lighted torches in their hands, and snakes and serpents cling to their necks and shoulders. Their office is to punish the crimes of wicked men, and to torment and frighten them by following them with ghastly looks and burning material.

Erebus and Nox preside over darkness and the night; Mors over death; and Somnus is the god of sleep, who, by his servant Morpheus, sends dreams to men while asleep.

Besides others, there are in the infernal regions the following monsters:--The Centaurs, whose upper parts are human, but whose bodies and legs are those of a horse. They were begotten of a cloud by Ixion. Gorgon is a monster with three heads. The Harpies, born of Oceanus and Terra, have the faces of virgins, and the bodies of birds with claws. Their names are Ocypete, Aello, and Celeno. The Gorgons are Medusa, Stheno, and Euryale, daughters of Phorcys and Cete. They have heads covered with snakes instead of hair, which so terrifies beholders that they immediately turn into stones. The Lamiae and Empusae have each only one eye and one tooth. They have faces, necks, and breasts like women, but their bodies are covered with scales, and they have the tails of serpents. The Chim[oe]ra is a monster that vomits fire, and has the head and breast of a lion, the belly of a goat, and the tail of a dragon. The Sphinx, begotten of Typhon and Echidna, has the head and face of a virgin, the wings of a bird, and the body of a dog. A riddle she put forth being explained by [OE]dipus, so enraged her that she threw herself from a rock and was killed.

The most famous of the condemned in the place of punishment are the Giants; they are great in stature, and have horrible feet, like dragons. They make war against the celestial gods, but never prevail, and are struck down to hell by Jupiter's thunder-bolts and the arms of the gods. The principal offenders are Typhon, AEgaeon, Al[oe]us, and Tityus; and, to prevent them rising again, the Island of Sicily is fixed on Typhon, and Mount AEtna on AEgaeon, and Tityus is doomed to have a vulture always gnawing his liver, which grows afresh every month. Phlegias fired Apollo's temple at Delphi, for which he was sentenced to have a great stone hung over his head, ready every moment to fall and crush him to pieces. Ixion, for an assault on Juno, was struck down to hell, and tied to a wheel, which kept continually turning. Sisyphus is a notorious robber, condemned to roll a stone up to the top of a hill, which is made to roll down again immediately; and as he has to begin and roll it up again as soon as it comes down, his labour is perpetual. The Danaides are fifty virgins (sisters), who all but one, by the command of their father Danaus, slew their husbands on their wedding night. For this they were condemned to draw water out of a deep well, to fill a tub whose bottom was full of holes like a sieve. Tantalus invited the gods to a feast, and, to improve their divinity, he killed, boiled, and served up Pelops on the table before them to eat. They refused to partake of this horrid dish, and condemned Tantalus to stand in water which he could not drink, and to have meat placed before him which he could not taste, though suffering the pangs of hunger and thirst--a punishment he was to endure for ever.

In the Tartarian regions there is a place supposed to abound with all kinds of pleasures and delights, called Elysium, because thither the souls of good men are conveyed after being freed from the body. This is the heathen paradise, consisting of pleasant plains, the most verdant fields, the shadiest groves, and the finest and most temperate air that can be found. After the souls of the pious have spent many ages in these Elysian fields, they drink the water of the river Lethe, which makes them forget all things past; and then they return to the world and pass into new bodies.

The Pagan deities have ambrosia for their food, and nectar for their drink, both of which have the property of giving immortality to those who partake of them.

The festivals of the heathens were many, as almost every deity was allowed sacred honours. In sacrificing, the animals offered to the celestial deities were white, and those to the infernal gods were black. To Jupiter a white ox was sacrificed; to Neptune, Mars, and Apollo a bull, ram, and boar; to Ceres, milk, honey, and a sow-pig were offered; to AEsculapius, goats and poultry; to the Lares, a cock; to the Sun, a horse; to Juno, a she-lamb; to Venus, a dove; to Diana, a crow; to Pan and Minerva, she-goats; and to the Fauns, kids.

The fir and vine were sacred to Bacchus, the cypress to Pluto, the cedar to the Furies, the ash to Mars, the oak to Jove, the laurel to Apollo, the myrtle to Venus, the olive to Minerva, the poplar to Hercules, the pine to Cybele, and the rose to Venus.

CHAPTER XI.

Achilles's Mother--Prediction concerning the taking of Troy--Bravery, Armour, Love, and Death of Achilles--Acrisius's Daughter--Danae and her son Perseus--Ardea changed into a Bird--Pluto's Invisible Helmet--Minerva's Buckler--Mercury's Wings--Medusa deprived of Life--Sea Monster--A Gorgon's Head and its Virtues--Stheno and Euryale not subject to Old Age or Death--Minerva's Revenge against Medusa--Serpents in Africa and Pegasus produced by Medusa's Blood--Tales by the Daughters of Minyas--Punishment by Bacchus--The Search of Cadmus for his sister Europa--Halcyon's Sorrow--Transmigration--Strength and Exploits of Hercules--Love Potion--Hymen--Jason's Adventures--Power and Cruelty of Medea--How a Favourable Wind was procured--Manner in which Orion came into Existence--False Swearer punished--Palladium--The Life and Deeds of Paris--Golden Apple--Marriage of Peleus and Thetis--Impiety of Pentheus--Rhea and her Sons--Scylla turned into a Sea Monster.

Achilles's mother being endowed with a prophetic spirit, knew that her son would lose his life at Troy. She dipped him in the river Styx, by which he was rendered invulnerable, except in the heel, by which he was held during the operation. The seer Calchas announced that, without Achilles, Troy could not be taken. His mother, to keep him from danger, concealed him among King Lycomedes's daughters, disguised as a girl; but being discovered by Ulysses, he joined his countrymen, and sailed for the Trojan coast. After giving many proofs of his bravery and military prowess, he quarrelled with Agamemnon, commander-in-chief of the Grecian army, and in disgust withdrew from the contest. During the absence of Achilles, the Trojans were victorious; but his friend Patroclus, clad in his armour, having rashly encountered Hector, fell by the hand of that hero. Achilles, to revenge his death, resolved instantly to take the field. For this purpose, Vulcan, at the request of Thetis, made her son a complete suit of armour and weapons. With these celestial arms, many of the Trojans were put to death. Achilles, falling in love with Polyxena, a daughter of the Trojan king, whilst soliciting her hand in the temple of Minerva, was wounded by her brother Paris in the heel, which caused his death.

Acrisius, the son of Abas, king of Argos and Ocalea, being informed by an oracle that he would be put to death by his daughter Danae's son, confined her in a tower, to prevent her having children;

but without effect, for Jupiter, in a golden shower, entered the chamber of Danae, and she became the mother of Perseus. She and her infant son were then, by order of Acrisius, exposed to the sea in a slender bark, which the wind drifted to Seriphus, where both were taken ashore by some fishermen and carried to Polydectes, the king of the island. The king conceived a violent attachment to the mother, but sought the destruction of the son. Danae and her son left Seriphus and went to Larissa. Danae built Ardea; and on its being burned, the inhabitants said it was changed into a bird. Perseus, by the aid of Pluto's invisible helmet, Minerva's buckler, and Mercury's wings (the Talaria), and short dagger made of diamonds (called Herpe), deprived Medusa, one of the Gorgons, of life, and carried off her head in triumph. He killed the sea monster to which Andromeda was exposed, and then married her. A memorable battle ensued at their nuptials. Phineus, the uncle of Andromeda, who passionately loved her, entered with a band of armed men, and attempted to carry her off by violence. But Perseus made a brave resistance; and at last, finding himself on the point of being overpowered, presented the Gorgon's head, which instantly turned all his enemies to stone in the posture in which they were then standing. Immediately after this he returned to Seriphus, in time to protect his mother from the insult of Polydectes, to whom Perseus showed the Gorgon's head, which converted him into stone also. Medusa, it will be remembered, was the only one of the three Gorgons who was mortal. Her sisters, Stheno and Euryale, were neither subject to old age nor death. She greatly surpassed the other two in elegance of figure and comeliness of face; but in nothing was her superiority more remarkable than in the beauty of her locks. Minerva, provoked either because her temple had been profaned, or because her personal charms had been slighted by Medusa, who had preferred her own beauty to that of the goddess, turned her fine hair, of which she boasted greatly, into serpents, and gave to her eyes the power of converting to stone all at whom she looked. The blood which fell from Medusa's head when Perseus carried it over Africa in his flight, was supposed to produce the numerous serpents which infest that country, and also the winged horse Pegasus.

But to return to Acrisius. Let us see whether the prediction of the Oracle, that foretold he would be put to death by his daughter's son, was fulfilled. The fame of his grandson, after his remarkable adventures, having reached the ears of Acrisius, he went to Larissa to see him, at the time Teutamis was celebrating funereal games in honour of his father. To this city Perseus had repaired with the view of distinguishing himself among the combatants. Here he accidentally killed, with a quoit, an old man, who was found to be his grandfather Acrisius, and thus verified the oracular prediction.

Alcithoe and her sisters denied the divinity of Bacchus, and refused to join in his worship. Whilst the Theban women were employed celebrating the orgies of that god, the daughters of Minyas (for that was their father's name) continued at their looms. To enliven their hours of labour, one of them proposed that each in her turn should relate some amusing tale, to which, the other sisters agreeing, she with whom the idea originated was requested to begin. After hesitating for some time which of her numerous collections would be most agreeable--whether Babylonian Dercetis changed to a fish or her daughter to a dove, or Naias, who by magic transformed young men to fishes, or the tree the berries of which were formerly white, but turned to purple by being stained with blood--she preferred the last in consequence of its being little known. She then narrates the simple but beautiful and affecting fable of Pyramus and Thisbe. Leuconoe next, after mentioning the exposure of Mars and Venus, relates the history of Leucothoe, with whom Apollo fell in love, and afterwards turned into a rod of frankincense. To this she adds the fiction of Clytie, whom the same god changed into a sunflower. Alcithoe being then requested by her sisters to tell a story--despising as too common the fables of Daphnis, a shepherd on Mount Ida, who, for violating his marriage promise, was transformed to stone; of Scython, who changed his sex; of Celemis, a nurse of Jupiter, converted to adamant; and of the nymph Similax, and her lover Crocus, turned into flowers--prefers the history of the fountain Salmacis, who conceived a violent attachment for Hermaphroditus, the son of Mercury and Venus. These sisters, having discontinued their narrating, remained still obstinate in their contempt of Bacchus, who, in revenge, changed their implements into vines and ivy, and themselves into bats.

Cadmus, a son of Agenor, king of Ph[oe]nicia, and Telephassa or Agriope, was ordered by his father to go in search of his sister Europa, whom Jupiter had carried away, and not to return unless he found her. His search being unsuccessful, he is said to have consulted the oracle of Apollo, by which he was commanded to build a city where he saw a heifer standing on the grass, and call the country B[oe]otia. Having found the heifer, he sent his men to a fountain for water, which was at no great distance, that he might offer a sacrifice in gratitude to the god. But the spring being sacred to Mars, a dragon guarded it, which devoured all his men. By the art of Minerva, he overcame the dragon, and sowed its teeth, which grew up armed men, who, on his throwing a stone amongst them, began to fight, and all were killed except five, who assisted him in building Thebes. Hence Pentheus, in addressing the Thebans, calls them Anguigenae, serpent or snake-descended. The ferocity of the petty tribes who inhabit that part of Greece, and Cadmus's plan of subduing the natives by artfully exciting them to fight against each other until the strength and resources of the contending parties were quite exhausted, satisfactorily explain the tale of the dragon, the armed men that sprang from his teeth, and the stone which he threw among them. He afterwards married Harmonia or Harmonie, the daughter of Mars and Venus, by whom he had one son and four daughters. In advanced life, oppressed with sorrow at the fate of his daughter Ino and her two sons, he fled from Thebes to Illyricum, where he was changed into a dragon.

Halcyone's husband, Ceyx, a king of Trachinia, was drowned while attempting to cross to Claros to consult the Oracle. Disconsolate in consequence of his departure, she incessantly implored the gods for his safe return. Juno, moved by her constant prayers for her husband after his death, and compassionating the violence of her sorrow, entreated Somnus to send Morpheus, who, assuming the form and voice of Ceyx, appeared in a dream, and informed her of his fate. Frantic with grief, she ran to the beach, and, according to her dream, found the body of Ceyx floating lifeless to the shore. The queen of Trachinia was changed into a bird, in her attempt to reach by a bound the body of her husband, which she no sooner touched than it underwent the same transformation. Their mutual attachments remaining, they continue to live together as birds, distinguished by the same tenderness and affection which had marked their conjugal state when in the human form.

Hercules was possessed of the greatest physical strength. He had a great enemy in Hera, who, knowing that the child who should be born that day was fated to rule over all the descendants of

Perseus, contrived to delay the birth of Hercules and hasten that of Eurystheus. Eurystheus thus, by decree of fate, became chief of the Perseidae. While yet in the cradle, Hercules showed his divine origin by strangling two serpents sent by Hera to destroy him. In course of time Eurystheus summoned Hercules to appear before him, and ordered him to perform the labours which, by priority of birth, he was empowered to impose on him. Hercules, unwilling to obey, went to Delphi to consult the Oracle, and was informed that he must perform ten labours imposed on him by Eurystheus, after which he should attain to immortality. The first labour imposed on him was to destroy the lion that haunted the forests of Nemea and Cleonae, and could not be wounded by the arrows of a mortal. Hercules boldly attacked the lion and strangled him. The second was to destroy the Learnaean hydra, which he accomplished with the aid of Iolaus; but because he obtained assistance in his work, Eurystheus refused to reckon it. Hercules's third labour was to catch the hind of Diana, famous for its swiftness, its golden horns, and brazen feet. The fourth was to bring alive to Eurystheus a wild boar, which ravaged the neighbourhood of Erymanthus. The fifth was to cleanse the stables of Augeas, king of Elis, where three thousand oxen had been confined for many years; which task he accomplished in one day, by turning the rivers Alpheus and Peneus through the stables. For certain reasons this exploit was not counted. His sixth was to destroy the carnivorous birds, with brazen wings, beaks, and claws, which ravaged the country near the lake Stymphalis, in Arcadia. The seventh was to bring alive to Peloponnesus a bull, remarkable for its beauty and strength, which Poseidon had given to Minos, king of Crete, in order that he might sacrifice it; which Minos refusing to do, Poseidon made the bull mad, and it laid waste the island. Hercules brought the bull on his shoulders to Eurystheus, who set it at liberty. The eighth labour was to obtain the mares of Diomedes, king of the Bistones, in Thrace, which fed upon human flesh. The ninth was to bring the girdle of Hippolyta, queen of the Amazons. The tenth was to kill the monster Geryon, and bring his herds to Argos. These were all the labours originally imposed on Hercules; but as Eurystheus acknowledged only eight of them, Hercules was commanded to perform two more. The eleventh labour was to obtain the golden apples from the garden of the Hesperides. Atlas, who knew where to find the apples, brought them to Hercules, who meantime supported the vault of heaven. The last labour was to bring from the infernal regions the three-headed dog Cerberus. When Hercules brought the dog to Eurystheus, the latter, pale with fright, ordered him to be set at liberty, whereupon Cerberus immediately sank into the earth. Hercules's servitude was now ended, but his great performances were not. He fought with the centaurs and giants. When his period of slavery had ended, he married Dejanira; with her he went to Trachinia. At the river Evenus he encountered the centaur Nessus. Nessus, under pretence of carrying Dejanira over, attempted to offer her violence, which caused Hercules to slay him with a poisoned arrow. Nessus, before expiring, instructed Dejanira how to prepare a love potion for Hercules. He erected an altar to Zeus Kenaeos. In order to celebrate the rite with due solemnity, he sent Lichas to Trachis for a white garment. Dejanira, being jealous, anointed the robe with the philter she had received from Nessus. Hercules put it on, and immediately the poison penetrated his bones. Maddened by the pain, he seized Lichas by the feet and flung him into the sea. He tore off the dress, but it stuck to his flesh, which was thus torn from his bones. Dejanira, being informed of what had taken place, destroyed herself. Hercules repaired to Mount [OE]ta, where he erected a funeral pile, and, ascending it, commanded that it should be set on fire. The pile was suddenly surrounded by a dark cloud, in which, amid thunder and lightning, he was carried up to heaven.

Hymen, the god of marriage, attended the celebration of marriage, and the ancients believed the parties would be miserable during the remainder of their lives unless he attended.

Jason was a famous hero of antiquity. No sooner had he finished his education under the centaur Chiron, than he went boldly to Pelias, who had banished him, and mounted the throne, and demanded the kingdom. Pelias, for various reasons, durst not appeal to arms, but, to accomplish the warlike youth's ruin, advised him to undertake an expedition against AEetes, king of Colchis, who had murdered their relation Phryxus, and, on his return, promised to resign to him the crown. To this proposal Jason agreed, and undertook the voyage to obtain the golden fleece, so celebrated in history under the name of the Argonautic Expedition. After a series of wonderful adventures he arrived at Colchis; and by the assistance of Medea, the king's daughter, whom he promised to marry, he fulfilled the hard terms on which he was to accomplish the object of his voyage. By her aid and directions, he was enabled to tame the bulls with horns and feet of brass, which breathed nothing but fire, and to plough with them a certain field; to kill a huge serpent, from whose teeth sprang up armed men; to destroy a dreadful dragon, which watched continually at the foot of the tree on which the golden fleece was suspended; and then to carry off the prize in the presence of all the Colchians, who were equally confounded at his intrepidity and success. He returned to Thessaly in great triumph, but his future life was rendered miserable by his infidelity, and the barbarous mode of revenge adopted by Medea, whom he married according to promise and carried to Greece. After many years' happiness, it may be remembered, he most iniquitously divorced her. But she severely revenged his ingratitude by causing the death of his favourite Glauce, and the ruin of her family. Not satisfied with these acts of cruelty, she put two of Jason's sons to death before his eyes, and then fled through the air in a chariot drawn by winged dragons. Having visited Corinth, she settled at Athens. Other barbarous actions again forced her to have recourse to her chariot. She returned to Colchis, where a reconciliation took place between her and Jason.

When the princes of Greece had, in fulfilment of their oaths, taken up arms to revenge the criminal conduct of Paris, Agamemnon, on account of his military talents, and being the brother of Menelaus, was appointed commander-in-chief of the combined forces. After the army had assembled in the port of Aulis, Diana, provoked at his having killed one of her favourite stags, prevented by contrary winds their sailing for Troy. On consulting the Oracle, the Greeks were informed that Iphigenia, daughter of Agamemnon, must be sacrificed to appease the enraged goddess, otherwise they must remain in harbour. Struck with horror at this awful response, Agamemnon sternly refused to give up his daughter, and ordered the princes to return home with their troops. But the winning eloquence of Ulysses and the urgent remonstrances of the other chiefs at last prevailed, and paternal affection yielded to military fame. Ulysses was then sent to Mycenae, to carry the beautiful Iphigenia to bleed on the altar of Diana. The innocent victim's blood procured a favourable wind to the Grecian fleet.

Orion sprang from Jupiter and Mercury. These gods promised to Hyricus, a B[oe]otian peasant, who had entertained them hospitably, whatever he would ask. Having no child, his wife being dead, and he being bound by promise not to marry again, requested a son. The gods then put water into the hide of a bull, which Hyricus had offered to them in sacrifice on discovering their divinity, and ordered him to bury it in the earth for nine months. At the end of that time, taking it out, he found a lively boy.

Palici, twin brothers, were sons of Jupiter and Thalia or AEtna, a daughter of Vulcan, who during her pregnancy prayed to be saved from the fury of Juno, by being concealed in the bowels of the earth. Her request was granted, and Tellus at the proper time brought to light the two boys. They were worshipped with great solemnity by the Sicilians. Their temple stood near the lakes or springs, strongly impregnated with sulphur, to which those who wished to put an end to quarrels by oath used to repair. False swearers were punished there in a miraculous manner, whilst the innocent escaped without injury. Some suppose that the perjured persons were destroyed by secret fire, while others think they were drowned.

Palladium was a statue of the goddess Pallas or Minerva, said to have fallen from heaven, near the tent of the king of Troy, when he was building the Citadel. An ancient oracle declared that, so long as the Palladium remained within the walls, Troy could not be taken. On that account it was kept with great care. The Greeks, aware of this prediction, sent Diomedes and Ulysses to carry it away during the night--a feat which they accomplished.

Paris was a son of Priam, king of Troy. His father ordered him to be put to death at his birth, in consequence of his mother having dreamt that she was delivered of a firebrand which reduced the city to ashes, and the augurs interpreting the dream to portend that the child would occasion the destruction of Troy. The persons appointed to despatch the child, contented themselves with exposing him on Mount Ida, where he was brought up by the shepherds. On account of his extraordinary strength and courage in defending the flocks from ravenous beasts and repelling the attacks of robbers, he was called Alexander. There he passed the early part of his life, and, whilst engaged tending his flock, gave judgment in the appeal of the three goddesses, Venus, Juno, and Minerva, who contended for the golden apple. Each endeavoured to bribe him: Juno promised him a kingdom, Minerva military glory, and Venus the most beautiful woman in the world for his wife. Upon the mind of the noble shepherd the promise made by Venus produced the deepest impression, and he adjudged the golden apple to her. The decision of Paris, which gave great offence to the other two goddesses, provoked their wrath against the empire and nation, and caused the Trojan War, and all the evils and calamities to which that memorable struggle gave rise. His father subsequently received him at court, and treated him as his son. After spending some time in his native city among the Trojan princes, Paris set out for the court of Menelaus, king of Sparta, with a view to carry off his wife Helena, the most beautiful woman in the world, as the reward of the judgment which he had pronounced in favour of Venus. The young Trojan met with a most welcome reception at the Spartan court; but he abused the laws of hospitality by prevailing on the queen to elope with him. Though demanded back by all the princes who had sworn to protect her, and threatened with the vengeance of the combined forces of Greece, he persisted in refusing their request. His father, on account of Ajax carrying off his sister Hesione, encouraged him in his obstinacy and guilt. In consequence of this outrage, the Greeks immediately commenced hostilities, which ended in the total destruction of the city and kingdom of Troy.

To bring out more fully the story of the apple adjudged by Paris to Venus, it is necessary to notice what happened at the marriage of Peleus and Thetis. At the celebration of the nuptials, all the gods and goddesses were present except the goddess of discord, who, exasperated at not being invited, threw into the assembly a golden apple with the inscription, "Detur Pulchriori." At first all the female deities asserted their right to the apple; but subsequently it was claimed by Juno, Minerva, and Venus only. These three agreed to refer the matter to Jupiter. But the sovereign of Olympus, knowing that it could not justly be given to Juno, and dreading the effects of her anger were it awarded to either of the other goddesses, advised them to plead their cause before Paris. The decision of Paris, and the serious results thereof; are already known.

Pentheus foolishly refused to acknowledge the divinity of Bacchus. To complete his impiety, the Theban king sent his servants to bring the god in chains before him. Assuming the appearance of one of his attendants, Bacchus allowed himself to be taken prisoner, and to be carried into the presence of the king, to whom, under the character of Ac[oe]tes, he related the transformation of the Tuscan sailors. Despising the narrative, Pentheus ordered him to be put to death. Loaded with fetters, the attendants of that prince shut him up in prison, from which he miraculously escaped. Pentheus then went out to see the Bacchanals, and to learn their mysteries; but, approaching too near, he was torn in pieces.

Quirinus, son of Rhea Sylvia, sometimes called Ilia, a vestal virgin, the daughter of Numitor, king of Alba Longa, was the twin brother of Remus. This princess, to extenuate her guilt, and to give divinity to her sons, declared that Mars, the god of war, was their father. Amulius, who had dispossessed his brother Numitor, killed the sons of the latter, and made Rhea a vestal, and, to secure the crown to himself and his descendants, ordered his niece to be burnt alive, and her infants thrown into the Tiber. The river at that time being swollen above its banks, the persons appointed to dispose of the children could not reach the main current. The cradle in which the twins were exposed floated to a place of safety on dry ground; and the infants were suckled by a wolf until found by Faustulus, the king's shepherd, who carried them to his house, where they were brought up as his own children. Their youthful years were spent in feeding cattle. After they were grown up, Remus being taken prisoner by the servants of Amulius, Faustulus, anxious to preserve the captive, disclosed to Romulus the truth respecting their birth. He, with the assistance of a few daring and resolute young men, killed Amulius, delivered his brother, and restored their grandfather to the throne.

After this event, the two brothers formed a design of building a city on the mountains where they had spent the early part of their life. From its being unknown which of them was the elder, they had recourse to augury to decide which of them should have the honour of founding and governing the new city. To Remus six ravens appeared, and to Romulus twelve. The former claimed the sovereignty from the priority of his omen, and the latter from the greater number of the birds. Each being saluted king by his own party, a battle ensued, in which Remus was killed. Others say that he was killed by Romulus, because he had, in contempt, leapt over the wall the latter was building when founding the city of Rome. The measures which Romulus adopted to increase the number of his subjects, the plans he formed for the regulations of the city, and the laws he enacted, discovered a surprising degree of political knowledge. His military talents were still more remarkable. He conquered every nation which declared war against him. The Sabines and Romans having for a considerable time fought with great ferocity, and victory inclining to neither side, they coalesced, and Tatius, the king, was appointed joint sovereign of Rome with Romulus. After the death of Tatius, Romulus found himself sole master of the city. His prosperity rendered him insolent and tyrannical. When reviewing his army, the senators, taking advantage of a storm that suddenly arose, tore him in pieces, and reported that he had been translated to heaven. The Romans, believing the story, deemed Romulus worthy of divine honours, and accordingly ranked him among their gods under the name of Quirinus.

Scylla, a daughter of Phorcys, was turned by Circe into a sea-monster of a most hideous form, either from jealousy, because she was a greater favourite with Glaucus, or at the request of that deity. According to some, she retained her original form and beauty down to the waist; but others say she had six heads and as many throats, and instead of hands had two claws. Her middle was compassed by dogs, which never ceased barking. The lower part of her body terminated in a large fish with a forked tail.

There was another Scylla, the daughter of Nisus, king of Megara, who conceived a violent passion for Minos when he was besieging her father's capital. To ensure the fall of the city, she cut off from her father's head, whilst he slept, a hair of purple colour, on which his good fortune depended, and presented it to her lover. Possessed of this charm, Minos soon carried the place, but he punished the perfidy of Scylla: she was thrown into the sea, and changed, according to one account, into a fish, and, if we can believe another narrative, her form became that of a bird.

MYTHOLOGY OF GERMANY, GREAT BRITAIN, SCANDINAVIA, ETC.
CHAPTER XII.

Mythology of Germany, Great Britain, and Scandinavia--Scandinavian Gods, Giants, and Elves--The world Niflheim--The world Muspelheim--How Ymir was created--The cow Aedhumla--Ymir's Offspring--Odin, the chief God--Odin's Seat and Ravens--Valhalla--Queen Frigga--How the Seas, Waters, Mountains, and Heavens were made--Chariots and Horses in Heaven--Night and Day--What a Wolf is to do--Three beautiful but evil-disposed Maidens--Creation of New Beings--Bridge between Midgard and Asgard--Sacred Fountain--Roots of the ash Yggdrasil--Baldur's Dreams and sad End--Loki, the Evil Spirit--Hel and her Brothers--Ignorance of Giants, and Cunning of Dwarfs--Worship of Scandinavian Gods--Norsemen and their Ancient Gods and Goddesses--The Volsung Tale--Odin, Loki, and Haenir's Wanderings--The Sword Gram--Sigurd's Exploits--What the Worshippers of Odin believed--Frodi's Maidens and Quern--Thor, and Subordinate Gods of the Laplanders--Belief and Worship of the Laplanders--Drums as Implements of Superstition--Sale of Winds--Power of Demons--Lucky and Unlucky Days--Other Superstitions.

The mythology of Germany, Great Britain, Scandinavia, and the other northern nations is as extraordinary as that of Greece and Rome. Every race and nation under the heavens were at one time steeped in superstition to such an extent as to make people, living in enlightened ages, wonder that creatures endowed with reasoning powers should ever have given themselves over to such vile delusions as some of our forefathers seem to have done. The adventures of the Scandinavian gods, giants, and elves were not behind those of the gods and supernatural beings in the south and east. In the beginning of time, we are informed, a world existed in the north called Niflheim, in the centre of which was a well from which sprang twelve rivers. In the south was another world, Muspelheim--a light, warm, radiant world, the boundary of which was guarded by Surt with a flaming sword. From Niflheim flowed cold streams called Elivaager, which, hardening into ice, formed one icy layer upon the other, within the abyss of abysses that faced the north. From the south there streamed forth the sparkling heat of Muspelheim; and as the heat and cold met, the melting ice-drops became possessed of life, and produced, through the power of him who had sent forth heat, Ymir, the sire of the frost giants. Ymir obtained his nourishment from four milky streams that escaped from the udders of the cow Aedhumla--a creature formed from the melting frost. From Ymir there came forth offspring while he slept, viz. a man and woman, who emerged from under his left arm, and sons from his feet. Thus was produced the race of the frost giants. Meantime, as the cow Aedhumla licked the frost-covered stones, there came forth the first day a man's hair, a head the second day, and a man, complete in all his parts, the third day. This man, Buri, had a son named Bor, who married Beltsa, one of the giant race, by whom he had three sons, Odin, Vili, and Ve.

Odin became the chief god, and ruled heaven and earth, and was omniscient. As ruler of heaven, his seat was Valaskjalf, from whence he sent two black ravens, daily, to gather tidings of all that was being done throughout the world. As god of war, he held his court in Valhalla, whither brave warriors went after death to revel in the tumultuous joys in which they took pleasure when on earth. Odin had different names and characters, as many of the gods had. By drinking from Mimir's fountain, he became the wisest of gods and men. He was the greatest of sorcerers, and imparted a knowledge of his wondrous art to his favourites. Frigga was his queen, and the mother of Baldur, the Scandinavian Apollo; but he had other wives and favourites, and a numerous progeny of sons and daughters. All over Scandinavian lands, but particularly in Denmark, the people imagine that they hear his voice in the storm.

The other two brothers were less famous, but they were gods, and assisted Odin to slay Ymir, and carry his body into the middle of Ginnungagap, and formed from it the earth and heavens. Of his blood the brothers made all the seas and waters, taking the gore that flowed from his body to form the impassable ocean which is supposed to encircle the earth. Of his bones they made the mountains, using the broken splinters and his teeth for the stones and pebbles. From his skull they made the heavens, at each of the four corners of which was stationed a dwarf, of whom we shall hear more by-and-bye. Of Ymir's brains clouds were formed, of his hair plants and herbs, and of his eyebrows a wall of defence was made against the giants round Midgard, the central garden or place of abode of the sons of men. The work of the celebrated brothers was not ended by these achievements; for they took the sparks that were cast out of the world Muspelheim, and, throwing them over the face of the heavens, produced the sun, moon, stars, and fiery meteors, and so arranged them in their places and courses, that days, months, and years followed. Allfader placed chariots and horses in heaven, where Night rode round the earth with her horse Hrimfaxi, from whose bit fell the rime-drops that every morning bedewed the earth. After her course followed her son Day, with his horse Skinfaxi, from whose shining mane light beamed. Mani directed the course of the moon, and Sol drove the chariot of the sun. They were followed by a wolf, which was of the giant race, and that will in the end of time swallow, or assist to swallow, up the moon, darken the sun's brightness, let loose the boisterous winds, and drink the blood of every dying man.

Three beautiful but evil-disposed maidens arrived at Asgard from the giants' world, Jotunheim, by whom confusion and ill-will were spread over the world. Then the gods determined to create new beings to people the universe. They gave human bodies and understanding to dwarfs, who had been generated within the dead body of Ymir, and who took up their abodes in the bowels of the earth, in rocks, in stones, and in trees and flowers. Then Odin, with two companions, went forth on an excursion to the earth, and created a man and woman; and from this pair, whose abode was at Midgard, the human race sprang. A bridge of various colours, known to men as the rainbow, connected Midgard with Asgard, and over this the gods rode daily to a sacred fountain. This fountain lay at one of the three roots of the ash Yggdrasil, whose branches spread over the whole earth and reached above the heavens. Under one of these roots was the abode of Hel, the goddess of the dead, under another that of the frost giants, and under the third was the dwelling of human beings.

Baldur dreamt evil dreams of threatened danger to his life. He related them to the gods, who endeavoured to protect him from injury. Frigga made fire, water, iron, and all metals, stones, earth, plants, beasts, birds, serpents, poison, and all diseases, swear that they would not hurt Baldur. Loki was displeased at this. He changed himself into the form of an old woman, and, inquiring the cause of Baldur's invulnerability, was told by Frigga that all things, animate and inanimate, had sworn not to harm him, with the exception of one little shrub, the misletoe. Loki, rejoicing at the information he had received, procured this little shrub, and hastened with it to an assembly of the gods, where he placed it in the hands of the blind Hoder, the god of war, who cast it at Baldur, and pierced him to the heart. Hermoder, the son of Odin, offered to proceed to Hel to release Baldur; and Hel, on hearing the request made, consented to let him go, on condition that all things would weep for Baldur. All men, all living beings, and all things wept except the witch Thock, who refused to mourn for the departed god. Baldur was therefore compelled to remain in Hel, where he will be to the end of the world.

Loki was beautiful, and possessed of great knowledge and cunning. He often brought the gods into trouble, from which, however, through his craft he extricated them. Hence he was regarded as the Evil Spirit. Sometimes he was called Asa-Loki, to distinguish him from Utgarda-Loki, a king of the giants, whose kingdom lay at the uttermost limits of the earth.

Hel, who dwelt under one of the three roots of the sacred ash Yggdrasil, was the daughter of the wicked Loki. Hel, together with her brother, the wolf Fenrir, and the serpent Jormundgand, was brought up in the giants' home of Jotunheim, where she remained until, at the request of the gods, Allfader sent for her and her brothers to destroy them, as it was known that by their origin they would prove the instruments of calamity. After casting the serpent that surrounded all lands into the deep ocean, he hurled Hel into Niflheim, and gave her authority over nine worlds, in which she was to assign places to all who died of sickness and old age. Her abode was surrounded by a high enclosure and massive gates. She was of fierce aspect, was inexorable, and would set no one at liberty who had once entered her domain. Her dish was hunger, her knife starvation, her servants slow-moving, her bed sickness, and her curtains wide-spread misery.

With Ymir perished all the giants except Bergelmir. It was a popular belief that, through the power of giants, mountains and islands were raised, and that, by these monsters, mountains and rocks were hurled from their original sites. Notwithstanding the huge bulk and the number of heads and arms that many of the giants had, they were supposed to be ignorant monsters, unable to cope with ordinary human beings.

The Dwarfs, of whom an account is given in the *Eddas*, were cunning and crafty elves, and skilled in magic. Some gave them a place between men and giants. It was believed that the dwarfs appeared under the forms of elves, brownies, and fairies. They used charms, and possessed all the skill of witches. It was in their power to raise storms, kill people by their diabolical art, fly away with children, and even with grown-up persons, through the air, or imprison them in caverns within the earth. They assisted men to discover the precious metals, of which they (the dwarfs) were very fond. Occasionally they were seen through an aperture of a hill, in their underground retreat, in palaces with jasper columns, surrounded with vast treasures of gold and silver.

The Scandinavian gods were worshipped in spacious temples, or on stone heaps or altars. These sacred places were always near a consecrated grove or tree and a sacred fountain. Human sacrifices were not uncommon at times of public calamities, such as war, disease, or famine. Three great festivals were held every year, the first of which was celebrated at the new year, in the Yule-month. On these occasions offerings were made to Odin for success in war, and to Freyr for a peaceful year. The chief victim was a hog, which was sacrificed to the latter god, on account of swine having first instructed man to plough the soil. Feasting and games occupied the whole month, therefore it was called the Merry Month. Yule continues to be observed in several places at the present time, and points to the custom of sun worship and the adoration of the early gods of the north. The frumenty eaten on Christmas eve or morning in England, and the sowans in Scotland, seem to be imitations of the offerings paid to Hulda or Berchta, to whom the people looked for new stores of grain. The second festival was in mid-winter, and the third in spring, when Odin was chiefly invoked for prosperity and victory.

The mythology of the Scandinavians and our ancestors was in many respects similar. It was from the principal gods of the northern nations that the names of the days of our week were taken, as will appear under the observations we shall make on the Calendar. But in addition to the chief gods there were inferior deities, who were supposed to have been translated to heaven for their great deeds, and whose greatest happiness consisted in drinking ale out of the skulls of their enemies in the hall of Wodin. The Norsemen delight to recount the exploits of their ancient gods and goddesses and celebrated mythical persons. The Volsung Tale is often referred to with pleasure. Volsung, a descendant of Odin, was taken from his mother's womb by a surgical operation, after six years' bearing. In his hall grew an oak, whose branches spread out in every direction. In that hall, when Volsung's daughter was to be given away to Siggeir, king of Gothland, in came an old guest with one eye. In his hand he held a sword, which at one stroke he drove up to the hilt in the oak. "Let him," said he, "of this company who can pull it out, bear it, and none shall say he bore a better blade." Having said this, he disappeared, and was seen no more. Many tried to possess himself of the sword, but none could draw it from the oak, till Sigmund, the bravest of Volsung's sons, laid his hand upon its hilt. At his touch, it freed itself from the mighty oak; and the sword turned out to be the celebrated blade Gram, of which every Norseman has heard. Sigmund was armed with this weapon when he went out to battle against his brother-in-law, who quarrelled with him about this very sword; for every one who knew its virtues was anxious to become its possessor. All perished in the fight except Sigmund, who was saved by his sister Signy. Sigmund, after taking vengeance against his brother-in-law, took possession of the kingdom, which was his by inheritance. When Sigmund was stricken in years, he went out to fight against the sons of King Hunding. Just as he was about to prove victorious, a one-eyed warrior, of more than mortal might, rushed at him with spear in hand. At the outstretched spear Sigmund struck with his hitherto trusty blade, when it snapped in two. In the one-eyed warrior's features he discovered the giver of the sword, who was no less famous a personage than Odin. Sigmund then knew that his good fortune had departed from him, and he sank down on the battle-field and died.

There is a legend of Odin, Loki, and Haenir in one of their many wanderings coming to a river side, where they saw an otter with a salmon in its mouth. Loki killed the otter with a stone. Then the Æsir passed on, and came at night to Reidmar's house to seek shelter. They showed the otter and salmon to him, on which he cried to his sons to seize and bind them, for they had slain their brother, Otter. To make compensation for what they had done, they agreed to pay any sum Reidmar might name. Otter was flayed, and Reidmar commanded the Æsir to fill the skin with gold, and cover it without that not a hair could be seen. Odin sent Loki down to the dwellings of the black elves to obtain the precious metal. The cunning god caught Andvari, the dwarf, and compelled him to surrender all the gold he had accumulated. The dwarf begged and prayed that he might be permitted to retain one ring, for it was the source of all his wealth, as ring after ring dropped from it. Loki was inexorable; not a penny-worth would he leave with the dwarf. Seeing he could not retain the ring, the dwarf laid a curse on it, and said it would prove a bane to every one into whose possession it might pass. Reidmar having all the gold except the ring laid at his feet, filled the skin with the yellow ore, and set it up on end. Odin poured gold over it until it was covered up. Reidmar carefully looked at the skin, and declared that he saw a grey hair, and desired them to cover it also. Odin reluctantly drew out the ring, which he would fain have kept for himself, and laid it over the grey hair. Before the Æsir departed, Loki repeated the curse which Andvari had laid upon the ring. The curse began to take effect. Regin, one of Reidmar's sons, asked for a share of the gold, but his father refused to give him any. This undutiful son and his brother Fafnir conspired against their sire, slew him, and took possession of the gold. Fafnir being the stronger brother, determined to keep the whole treasure to himself; and not only that, but he threatened that unless Regin went off he would share his father's fate. Regin fled for his life, and his brother assumed the form of a dragon, in which shape he lay on the Glistening Heath, coiled round his store of gold and precious things.

Sigurd requested Regin, who was the best of smiths, to forge him a sword. Two were made, but both broke at the first stroke. The broken pieces of Gram were then obtained, and out of them Regin forged a blade that clave the anvil in the smithy, and cut a lock of wool borne down to it by a stream. Armed with Gram, and mounted on Gran, his steed, which Odin had instructed him to choose, Sigurd rode to the Glistening Heath, dug a pit in the dragon's path, and slew him as he passed over him on his way to drink at the river. Sigurd roasted the heart of Fafnir; and while it was being cooked, he tried it with one of his fingers to see if it were soft. The hot roast burned his finger, which caused him to put it to his mouth. He tasted the dragon's blood, and instantly he understood the songs of birds. Sigurd slew Regin, ate the heart, rode on Gran to Fafnir's lair, took the spoil, and escaped with it.

On and on he rode, till on a lone fell he saw a flame; and when he reached it, it blazed all around a house. No horse but Gran could pass through that flame, and no man but Sigurd could guide him in his fiery path. Brynhildr, Atli's sister, who in consequence of giving victory on the wrong side had the thorn of sleep thrust into her cloak by Odin, lay in the house in a deep sleep. She was under a curse to slumber there until a man bold enough to ride through the fire came to liberate her, and win her for his bride. Dashing onward to where the fair maiden lay, his first touch wakened her from the long sleep to which the cruel god had consigned her. They swore with a mighty oath to love each other, and she taught him runes and wisdom.

Sigurd's mission was not yet accomplished; so on he rode to King Giuki's hall, king of Frankland, whose queen was Grimhildr, who had two sons named Gunnar and Hogni, and a step-son called Guttorm, and whose daughter was the lovely Gudrun. Sigurd, greatly attached to his lovely bride at the lone fell, purposed going back for her; but Grimhildr, who was skilled in the black arts, longed for the brave Volsung for her own daughter, and therefore prepared for him the philter of forgetfulness. He quaffed it off, forgot Brynhildr, fraternised with Gunnar and Hogni, and married Gudrun. Giuki now wanted a wife for Gunnar, and the brothers with their bosom friend set out to woo. They chose Brynhildr, whom they found still sitting on the fell, waiting for Sigurd to come back. She had made it known, that whoever could pass that flame should have her for his wife; so, when Gunnar and Hogni reached the spot, the former rode at the flame, but his horse swerved from the fierce fire; then, by Grimhildr's magic arts, Sigurd and Gunnar changed shapes and arms, and Sigurd mounted Gran, and the noble steed carried him through the flame. Thus Brynhildr was wooed and compelled to yield. That evening they were united in wedlock; but when they retired to rest Sigurd unsheathed Gram, and laid it between them. Next morning, when he arose, he took the ring which Andvari had laid under a curse, and which was among Fafnir's treasures, and gave it to Brynhildr as a gift, and she gave him another ring in return. Then Sigurd returned to his companions in his own shape; and Gunnar went and claimed Brynhildr as his bride, and carried her home. No sooner was Gunnar wedded than the power of the philter ceased to operate: he remembered all that had passed, and the oath he had sworn to the fair Brynhildr. When she discovered that she had been deceived, she engaged Gunnar to revenge her wrong. By charms and prayers the two brothers set on Guttorm, their half-brother, to take vengeance, and the hero was pierced through with a sword while he lay in Gudrun's white arms. Though Sigurd turned and writhed in agony, he had strength left to hurl Gram after the treacherous Guttorm as he fled. The keen blade cut him asunder, and his head rolled out of the room. Brynhildr's love returned; and when Sigurd, who expired of his wound, was laid upon the pile, her heart broke. She in song predicted woes that were to come, made them lay her side by side with Sigurd, with Gram between them, and so went to Valhalla with her old lover. Andvari's curse was thus fulfilled.

The worshippers of Odin believed that at certain times the gracious powers showed themselves in bodily shape, passing through the land, and bringing blessings with them. On other occasions the gods were supposed to ride through the air on clouds and storms, and speaking in awful voice as the tempest howled and the sea raged. They were also supposed to be present in battle, fighting for votaries, and defeating the wicked. The goddesses assisted women in times of peril; they taught the maids to spin, and punished them if the wool remained long on the spindles. It was supposed that Odin had a band of followers who accompanied him in the whirlwind. The wanderings of the gods are mentioned in the *Odyssey*, and the sanctity of the rites of hospitality, and the dread of turning a wanderer from the door, originated lest the stranger should be a disguised being of exalted character. Goddesses as well as gods were supposed to wander up and down among men, telling them what was to happen. Freyja, the goddess of love and plenty, who presided over marriages, was one of these, and the three moons, Urd, Verdandi, and Skuld, who determined the fate of gods and men, were also among the number.

We are informed that in Frodi's house were two maidens of the old giant race, whom he had bought as slaves, and he made them grind his quern Grotti, out of which peace and gold were produced. He kept them at the mill, not giving them any longer rest than the time the cuckoo's note lasted. That quern turned out anything that the grinder chose, though formerly it had ground nothing but peace and gold. The maidens ground and ground without ceasing. As Frodi was deaf to their cries for rest, they caused the quern to grind fire and war. While the quern went on making these evils, Mysing, the sea rover, came at night and slew Frodi and all his men, and carried away the hand-mill, maidens and all. When at sea, the rover caused the maidens to grind salt; and they performed their task until they ground as much as has kept the sea salt ever since that time.

Thor was the chief god of the Laplanders. They had also subordinate deities, one of which was Storjunkarr, their household god. Wirchu Archa was a female deity worshipped by them. She was the goddess of old women. These deities were represented under the figure of unsculptured stones. Spirits, angels, and devils were worshipped by those people. Souls of departed relations were also prayed to by the more superstitious of the people. Magic was a famous art among them. When sacrificing to Thor, they smeared the head of his image with the victim's blood; and when they made an offering to Storjunkarr, a thread was run through the right ear of the victim. When it was a reindeer that was sacrificed, the horns, head, and other parts were carried to a mountain devoted to Storjunkarr, and deposited there, the animal's tail being tied to one of the horns, and a red thread to the other.

The Laplanders used to sacrifice reindeers to the sun. In this ceremony a white thread was put through the victim's right ear. In sacrificing to the sun, willows were used, but in their other sacrifices birch trees were employed. Many of their superstitions were similar to those of the Greeks, Romans, and Tartars.

So much were the Laplanders given to superstition, that they worshipped the first object that presented itself in the morning. Every house and family had a deity. They had magical drums, which were consulted in a particular manner on important occasions; and when they engaged in battle, these drums were carried to the scene of action. In consequence of their supposed virtue, writers have said that drums were originally implements of superstition in our armies rather than instruments of music. Brass and copper rings, together with a hammer, were appended to a drum. A woman was not allowed to touch a sacred drum, nor was she permitted to go over the same road that it was carried, within three days of its removal.

Laplanders and Norwegians sold favourable winds to sailors and travellers. A rope with three knots was given to the buyer, who, when he wanted a gentle breeze, untied one of the knots; when he wished a fresh strong wind, he undid another; and when he desired storms and tempests, he unfastened the third. The first two descriptions of wind were generally obtained for good purposes, but the third through wicked motives. By the unloosing of the third knot, many a shipwreck was caused to bring about the death of a hated individual, and for the purpose of securing wreck cast ashore by the sea. Magicians could, the moment they were born, control the winds that blew. In this way one magician had power over the east wind, another of the south, a third of the west, and a fourth of the north. Magical shafts, which went through the air unseen, were thrown at enemies, and distempers were caused by charms. Gans or demons were enticed by secret art to perform acts of malice and deeds of revenge.

The Laplanders had their lucky and unlucky days. They thought it was unlucky to meet a woman when they were going out to hunt. When a Laplander died, the house was deserted by the family, because it was supposed the soul of the deceased remained near the inanimate body. When they buried their dead, they, like the ancient Danes, Saxons, and others, deposited a hatchet, war-like implements, a steel, flint, and tinder-box with each body, under the impression that they would be useful to the deceased in another world. Their witches--and they had many--who were born in winter, were supposed to be able to make that season cold, or comparatively mild, as they pleased.

NAMES OF DAYS, WHENCE DERIVED.
CHAPTER XIII.

The Calendar--Names of Days, whence derived--Worship   of Plants--Nature-Worship--The Power of   Jupiter--Influence of Zeus--The god Indra--Origin of the term "Hours"--Hours under Planetary   Control--Coronation of a Persian King--Evils   transferred to the Turks and Kafirs--The Moon's   Controlling Power--Time reckoned by Moons--A strange   Story--Discovery of Maize, Beans, and Tobacco--Sayings   of an Old Writer--Heathen Gods--Thor's Palace--Thor's Power--Frigga's Abilities--Description of Seater or   Crodo.

The Fates have apparently decreed that the Pagan religion and superstitions shall be kept in perpetual remembrance. If one examine heraldry, he will find traces of heathen mythology and superstition; if he look at the most famous of Great Britain's public buildings, he will see emblems of the ridiculous; if he glance at the Calendar, he will ascertain that months and days have been named after, or mentioned in connection with, mythological beings or objects of profane adoration; and if he read the pages of the greatest authors, he will discover much that has assisted to keep alive the embers of superstition. Passing over heraldry and ancient edifices, let us inquire whence the names of months and days are derived, and how certain seasons are observed.

The Saxons called the day D[oe]g; whence the term. It is thought they obtained it from the Roman Dies, a Diis, the names of the Roman days having been taken from the planets, which were called Dii, or gods.

In noticing the first day of the week, we need scarcely give the reason for its being denominated "Sabbath," as every Jew and Christian knows the reason why one day of the week is so called; but we shall, in carrying out the line of our narrative, take leave to make a few remarks as to the cause of that day being known as "Sunday." The Romans called it Dies Solis, because it was dedicated to the worship of the sun; and the Saxons gave it the name Sunnan-d[oe]g, or Sun's-day, for a similar heathenish cause. Whether the Saxons received their mythology from the Romans, or whether they had idols of their own, is a matter of doubt. The Romans worshipped the planets by the names of some of their favourite deities; and there is a resemblance in the Latin characteristics to certain of those of the Saxons, though they are in most instances different in their appellations. The names of the days of the week have no doubt been continued from the Saxons, whatever the origin may have been.

The luminous body which gives title to our first day of the week was regarded by the ancient heathen with superstitious reverence, as it was considered to be the superintending and governing power presiding over nature.

The adoration, therefore, that was paid to the sun was the most prevalent of all the errors of superstition. That this should have been the case among people ignorant of the existence of the great omnipotent Being, is not surprising; for how much more glorious were the shining lights in the heavens, but more particularly the sun, than the many objects worshipped by Pagans in our own and other lands! Nature-worship was the foundation of all polytheistic religions; and that the principal heathen deities were originally personifications of the great luminary that gives light and heat to the earth, or of certain influences thereof, admits of little doubt. The solar character of numerous deities is clearly discernible. Jupiter had power over the phenomena of the skies. The future was known to him; the destinies of human beings were in his hands. Strange appearances in the heavens, or wonderful events happening on the earth, were the signs by which he made his pleasure or displeasure known. On special occasions sacrifices were offered to Jupiter, and his favour implored.

Zeus's influence was like that of the sun; he had the rule of the heavens and air, he directed the lightning, and guided the stars in their courses, and controlled the seasons. Prophecy belonged to him, and it was from this god Ph[oe]bus received oracular gifts. Indra was a god of similar attributes; he was the great ruler of the firmament, and the upholder of the heaven and earth, and the god who created the dawn. He presided over the east, and was the god that sent rain and wielded the thunder-bolts. Many sacrifices were offered to him, and homage was also paid in numerous ways. Baal was originally the god of the sun, and ruler of nature. Some suppose that Baal was the same god as Moloch, to whom human sacrifices were offered, and whose worship also consisted principally of purifications, mutilations, perpetual virginity, and ordeals by fire. Bullocks, and even children, were sacrificed to Baal.

The origin of the term "hour" has been supposed by some authors to be derived from Hora, a surname given to the sun, the parent of time, and called by the Egyptians Horus. Hours are occasionally distinguished by the epithet of "planetary," from a supposition of the ancients that the Sun, Venus, Mercury, the Moon, Saturn, Jupiter, and Mars alternately presided over them. The first hour of the first day of the week was under the control of the Sun, the second under that of Venus, the third of Mercury, the fourth of the Moon, the fifth of Saturn, the sixth of Jupiter, and the seventh of Mars. After such rotation, the sun governed the eighth hour, Venus the ninth, and so on through the whole twenty-four hours.

The sun, moon, and stars have been considered by the people of nearly every nation on the face of the earth to affect the destiny of mortals here below. A story of the proceedings at the coronation of a Persian king is not without interest. The important ceremony of crowning could not be performed before the lord of the astrologers--an officer of great importance--declared the lucky moments that a happy constellation pointed out the time for placing the crown on the monarch's head. It was recorded that about ten o'clock at night the chief of the astrologers and his companions, having been long observing the position of the stars and conjunction of the planets, returned to give notice to the prince and company that the fortunate time for the coronation would be within twenty minutes. When the twenty minutes were nearly expired, everything being in readiness, the grand astrologer winked, and immediately the prince was made king.

For two years everything went well; but then the king's health began to decline. Sometimes he lay whole weeks together, languishing in his harem. In consequence of his majesty having indulged too freely in stimulants, the court physician applied his secret arts to counteract the effect of the baneful liquids, but without any good result; and the astrologers began to whisper that the monarch would not recover. They could not, they reported, find in his horoscope that he had more than six years to live after the date of his coronation; and they predicted that two of the years he had to survive would be spent in perpetual misery. The queen-mother quarrelled with the physician, asking him how it came to pass that her son was sick, and accused him of treason or ignorance. The man of healing art defended his own conduct, and blamed the stars or astrologers. He said that if the king lay in a languishing condition and could not recover, it was because the astrologers had failed to observe the happy hour, or the aspect of a fortunate constellation at the time of the coronation. This view of the case was taken by many at court, and even by some of the astrologers themselves. One of those wise men made it plain to those whom he addressed, that the moment fixed for the coronation was inauspicious; and afterwards, by arguments, satisfied the queen-mother and chief courtiers that the king's ill-health proceeded from his coronation, which had been solemnized under unfortunate aspects. The king, his wives, and others believed the physician, and therefore it was in vain the unlucky astrologer maintained the correctness of his calculations.

The question now arose, What was to be done to rectify the mistake which had been committed? And at length it was resolved that the king should change his name, and that a second coronation should take place. Long deliberations took place before the second coronation was fixed. The astrologers at length agreed that the happy hour would be about the time of the year that the sun was under the influence of a certain planet, which, according to account, was to be on Tuesday the twentieth of March, about nine in the morning. The new ceremony had the desired effect, for the king became well again.

No sooner had the king improved in health than another danger threatened the nation. A great and remarkable comet appeared, which filled the people's minds with terror. All the Persian astrologers declared that the alarming sign signified wars, murders, seditions, conflagrations, dangerous diseases, overturning of kingdoms and states, and all kinds of calamities; but, by means unknown to us, they transferred all these evils on the Turks, Kafirs, and Christians, and so Persia escaped danger.

Monday was dedicated by the Saxons to the adoration of the moon, whence it was called Monday, Moon-day, and Monan-d[oe]g. The Romans, as well as the Saxons, consecrated this day to the moon. They (the Romans) called it *Dies Lunae, feria secunda*; and anciently, on the first day of every lunar month, festivals were held in commemoration of the benefits bestowed during the former moon, and in gratitude for the return of that luminary. The worship that was paid to the moon as a deity, originated from causes similar to that assigned to the sun. In Europe all avowed sincere adoration of these orbs has ceased, but traces of sun and moon worship having been once common still remain. In several parts of England it is customary to bless the new moon, while in Scotland people not only do the same, but in mock adoration they bow to it at the same time.

Many superstitious beliefs remain as to the influence of the moon. It is unlucky for one to have his hands empty when he first sees the new moon, and it is regarded as a good sign if one has silver in his hand the first time he sees it. It has, or is supposed to have, a great effect on the weather and sea. One often hears it said in times of stormy weather, "We will not have a change before the new moon." It influences the affections of lovers to a very great extent. If a swain is halting between two opinions, viz. whether he will propose to such a lady, let him invite her to take a walk with him by moonlight, and the chances are ten to one, that if they go out together, they will be married. If one doubts this, he is advised to try it, and he will see how warm the affections will become. If one is going to enter into an important undertaking, he will be wise to do so when the moon is filling. People who are married in one of the first two quarters of the moon, are more happy than those who enter into the matrimonial state when it is on the wane; and, taking a sudden bound from the sublime to things that are common, we are compelled to say that not a few consider the effects of the moon so great, that they would not kill their pigs but when it was on the increase. Then every one has heard of the effects the moon has on the human mind; whence the term "lunacy." There are many tribes and nations that reckon time by moons, and not by years, as we now do. This reminds us of a story which shows the credulity of the savages of North America, and how they calculated time. It is this:--

A Swedish minister was preaching a sermon one day to the savages, and when he had finished, an Indian orator stood up to thank him for his discourse, which had reference to our first parents eating the forbidden fruit. "What you have told us," said the orator, "is very good. It is indeed bad to eat apples; it is better to make them all into cider. We are much obliged by your kindness in coming so far to tell us those things which you have heard from your mothers. In return, I will tell you some of those we have heard from ours. In the beginning, our fathers had only the flesh of animals to subsist on; and if they were unsuccessful in the hunt, they could get nothing to eat. Two of our young hunters having killed a deer, made a fire in the wood, to broil part of the flesh. When they were about to satisfy their hunger, they beheld a beautiful woman descend from the clouds, and seat herself near the young men. They said to each other, 'It is a spirit that has smelt our broiled venison, and perhaps wishes to eat of it: let us offer some to her.' They presented her with the tongue. She was pleased with the taste of it, and said, 'Your kindness shall be rewarded. Come,' said she, 'to this place after thirteen moons, and you will find something that will be of great benefit in nourishing you and your children to the latest generation.'

"The hunters, deeply impressed with what the fair one had said, watched with something like impatience the appearance and disappearance of moon after moon, till the thirteenth moon had come and gone, and then they repaired to the spot where they were to receive their reward. To their surprise, they found plants they did not know, but which have been constantly cultivated ever since, to the great advantage of man. Where the woman's right hand had rested, they found maize; where her left hand had touched the ground, they discovered beans; and where she had sat, tobacco grew luxuriantly."

We are accustomed to speak of the sun as "he," and of the moon as "she," but in many other countries the former is considered to be feminine, and the latter masculine. In Hindoo mythology the moon is a male deity, and is represented as the son of the patriarch Atri, who procreated him from his eyes; but by others it is said the moon arose from the milk sea when it was churned by the gods to procure the beverage of immortality. An old writer says that the sun supplies the moon, when reduced by the draughts of the gods to a single ray; and in the same proportion as the moon is exhausted by the celestials, it is replenished by the sun, for the gods drink the nectar accumulated in the moon during half the month; and from this being their food, they are immortal. When the remaining portion of the moon consists but of a fifteenth part, the Manes (infernal spirits, or inferior deities) approach it in the afternoon, and drink the remaining portion of nectar. And probably in this statement are to be found grounds for the superstitious belief that the time when the moon is increasing is more fortunate than when it is waning.

Tuesday was so called from Tiwes-d[oe]g, which signifies the day of Tiw, or Tiu, a name for the old Saxon war god Tyr. Other names were given to it by the Romans and Germans. It was called by the Romans *Dies Martis, feria tertia*, from its having been dedicated to Mars. Wormius, Marshall, and Sommes endeavour to prove that the day took its name from Thisa or Desa, the goddess of justice, the wife of Thor. Taking the views of any of the authors who have written on the subject, it is plain that the day was named in honour of some mythological deity. Tyr did not belong entirely to the Northern mythology, but was known to the Germans as Ziu or Zio, and to Anglo-Saxons as Tiv.

Tyr, it will be remembered, was single-handed. When the gods prevailed on the wolf Fenrir to allow himself to be bound with the bandage Gleipner, Tyr put his right hand into the wolf's mouth, as a pledge that he would be loosened. The gods refused to liberate the wolf, which in revenge bit off Tyr's hand. He and his enemy, the monster dog Garmr, met their death in the twilight battle of the gods.

The Roman divinity, Mars, was a war god, and seems to have been originally an agricultural deity. To him propitiatory offerings were presented, as the guardian of fields and flocks; but as the shepherds who founded the city of Rome were of a warlike disposition, it is easily understood how Mars became the god of war.

Wednesday signifies Wodin's-day or Odin's-day. Wodin or Odin, as is well known, was a great Northern god. He was believed to be the god of war, who gave victory, and revived courage in the conflict. He was also worshipped as the god of arts and artists; and to him magnificent temples were built, and sacrifices offered. He adopted as his children all those who were slain with swords in their hands; hence the hardihood and brilliant examples of courage displayed by Northern warriors. He had two black ravens, that flew forth daily to obtain tidings of all that was being done throughout the world. His greatest treasure consisted of his eight-footed steed Sleipner, his spear Gungner, and his ring Draupner, by which he performed many strange acts. Frigga was his queen, but he had other wives and favourites, and a numerous family of sons and daughters. By drinking at Mimir's sacred fountain, he became the wisest of gods and men. He is reputed to have possessed every power of witchcraft, prophecy, and transformation; and in the shape of a lion or other beast of prey, he, we are told, destroyed whole armies.

Thursday (Thors-d[oe]g) was dedicated to the adoration of Thor, the bravest of the sons of Odin. Thor was the god of thunder; he had a magnificent palace, which had five hundred and forty pillars, where he received and made happy the warriors who had fallen in battle. By the rolling of his chariot, thunder was produced. He had a smasher or mauler, made by cunning dwarfs, which, after being thrown at an enemy, had the property of returning to him. It was believed by the Pagans that he possessed marvellous power and might, and that all people in the world were subject to him. In the air he governed the winds and clouds; and when displeased, he caused thunder, lightning, and tempest, with excessive rain, hail, and bad weather. When pleased with his worshippers, he gave them favourable weather, and caused corn and fruit to grow abundantly, and kept away disease from man and beast.

The Laplanders represented Thor by the stump of a tree, rudely carved to represent a man; and they supplied him with flint and steel, that he might strike fire when he wanted it. Moreover, they placed a hammer near him, which they supposed he would use with force against evil spirits, for they thought he had sovereign authority over all the mischievous and malevolent spirits that inhabited the air, mountains, and lakes. High festivals were held in honour of this deity, as noticed elsewhere, to supplicate for a propitious year, and at these festivals every excess of extravagant and dissolute pleasure was not only permitted, but was considered requisite.

Friday derived its name from Frigga, the wife of Odin. She, as well as her husband, possessed wonderful abilities, and, like Juno, was held in the highest esteem and veneration for her power of procuring easy access into the world, and bestowing every felicity connected with the softer endearments of life. Frigga was thought to be the mother of all the Pagan divinities of the Northern nations begotten by Odin.

The Romans dedicated this day to Venus; whence its name, *Dies Veneris, feria sexta*. That goddess having possessed many of the attributes for which Frigga was celebrated, many authors have supposed them originally to have meant the same divinity.

Saturday has its name from Seater or Crodo, worshipped by the old Saxons. He was lean, had long hair and a long beard. In his left hand he held up a wheel, and in his right he carried a pail of water, wherein were flowers and fruits. He stood on the sharp fins of the perch, to signify that the Saxons, for serving him, should pass, without harm, in dangerous and difficult places.

The seventh day of the week was dedicated by the Romans to Saturn, and called, in honour of him, *Dies Saturni, feria septima*. Seater or Crodo, and the Roman Saturn, have been considered by many to be the same deity.

NAMES OF MONTHS, WHENCE DERIVED.
CHAPTER XIV.

Names of Months, whence derived--January--First of   January, how kept--Heathens and Christians--New Year   Gifts--February--Sacrifices for purging Souls--Second   of February, how kept--Virtue of Candles--Shrove   Tuesday--Eating Pancakes--Partaking of Brose--Choosing   a Valentine--March--Prognostications observed in this   Month--April dedicated to Venus--First of May--Roman   Floral Games--Queen of the May--May Poles and May   Fires--Dispute between Men and Gods--Superstitious   Customs in Scotland--Superstitious Ceremonies in   England--June regarded as the most favourable Month   for Fruitful   Marriages--July--August--September--October--Hallow-e'en   Ceremonies--November--All Hallows--Souls in   Purgatory--St. Leonard--St.   Britius--December--Christmas Trees and Gifts--The   Misletoe--Privileges in Leap Year--Yule Log--Christmas   Festivities.

January, it is generally admitted, derived that appellation from the Latin *Januarius*, in honour of Janus, one of the heathen divinities. Janus was supposed to preside over the gates of heaven. The Saxons originally called this month Wolf-monat, and afterwards it was called Aefter-Yule--After-Christmas. The first of January having been observed by the heathens as a day of great rejoicing, and offering up profane and superstitious sacrifices to Janus, the early Christians observed it as a fast to avoid the appearance of doing honour to a heathen deity. The Grecians, at the commencement of every year, held festive meetings to celebrate the completion of the sun's annual course. From that people the Romans borrowed the custom of observing the first of January; and from the Romans our forefathers received it. In giving New Year gifts, we follow the example of the ancients; and to receive such tokens of goodwill, was then, as now, considered propitious.

The name of February is taken from *Februa*, *Februta*, or *Februalis*, names of Juno, who presided over the purification of women; or, according to other authors, from *Februis expiatoriis*, sacrifices for purging souls, there having been a feast on the second day of this month, when sacrifices were offered to Pluto for the souls of the dead. This day was kept by certain Christians as a solemn festival, in memory of the humiliation of the Virgin Mary, who submitted to the injunction of the law under which she lived. They offered up thanksgiving on this day, and paraded about with flambeaux and candles--proceedings which some thought were too close imitations of the Pagan customs of *bren-ning*--in honour of Juno. There is in this instance a resemblance to the Pagan superstition; and from the burning of candles on the day we are referring to, they were, and are yet, lighted on occasions of danger, to avert evil. Persons in this country have been known to light candles, as a charm against thunder and lightning; and lighted candles, when once charmed (which it is supposed can be done), are considered by the ignorant at home and abroad, to possess virtue sufficiently powerful to frighten away evil spirits. Such candles are sometimes placed in the hands of persons while in the agonies of death, to protect them from the evil one.

Shrove Tuesday, or Fasten's Eve, is a day observed in many lands. In olden times, after the people had made confession at this season, they were permitted to indulge in festive amusements, although not allowed to partake of any repast beyond the usual substitutes for flesh; and hence arose the custom of eating pancakes and fritters, and partaking of brose, in Scotland, at this time. The brose was then made of oatmeal and butter, with a ring in it. The bicker of brose being set in the middle of a table, the unmarried members of the family, and invited friends who had not entered the matrimonial state, seated themselves around and partook of the repast. They took spoonful about till the ring was found, and then it was put into a second dish of brose, and again into a third, and he or she who found the ring twice left the table, assured of being married before another Fasten's Eve. At a later hour of the evening, pancakes, sometimes called "sauty bannocks," were made, and through their magical virtues future husbands and wives were discovered. A large cake or bannock was prepared, in which a ring or other small article was put, and the young person whose lot it was to secure the piece of cake or bannock with the concealed article was looked upon as being as lucky as the individual who picked the ring twice out of the brose. While all this was going on, unbounded mirth prevailed, and before the company broke up, dreaming cakes or bannocks were prepared, that every one might take one and place it under his or her pillow. To make the cakes of any avail, the baker had to remain mute when preparing them, and the receivers had, immediately after obtaining them, to slip off quietly to bed, when, if all the preliminaries had been duly observed, the sleeper's future companion in life appeared in a vision or dream of the night.

The practice of choosing a valentine on the 14th of February is well known. The first person of the opposite sex who was seen by an unmarried person on the morning of that day, was regarded as the valentine for the year. Another way of finding out a valentine was to cast into a receptacle small billets, with (if the consulters were young women) bachelors' names on them, and then to draw them out lottery-wise. The bachelor whose name appeared on a billet thus extracted at random, became the valentine of the spinster to whose lot it fell. In this way a bevy of young ladies ascertained, in a few minutes, secrets they were most anxious should be disclosed. When the gentlemen were anxious to discover their valentines, they proceeded in the same way, taking care, however, that the ladies for whom they had the greatest affection should be named on the billets. A lady's valentine was her knight for the year, and not unfrequently he became her husband. The amusements of Valentine's Day were very popular among all classes in the fifteenth century. It was customary at one time for both sexes to give each other presents, but the ladies, through modesty, or some other cause best known to themselves, have ceased to bestow gifts in their valentines. Many attempts have been made to abolish the heathen custom of young men drawing the names of young women, and *vice versa*, on this day, but without success.

March was called after Mars, the god of war; but the Anglo-Saxons knew it as *Hraed-monat*, signifying rugged month, and *Hlyd-monat*, meaning stormy month. Those who indulged in prognostications, carefully observed the state of the weather in this month. Dry weather at this time portended a plentiful season, while a rainy month indicated scarcity of food.

The fourth month of the year, it is generally believed, derived its name, April, in allusion to the buds then beginning to open; but the old Anglo-Saxons called it *Eoster-monat*, in honour, some think, of the goddess Easter. The Romans dedicated April to Venus, and frequently called it *Mensis Veneris* as well as *Aprilis*. The old and general custom of sending people useless errands on the first of April is so well known that we do not require to say anything more about it, than that it is thought to have originated in the acts of sending Christ backward and forward to various tribunals to secure His condemnation.

On the first day of May the Romans offered sacrifices to Maia, the mother of Mercury. Apollo was the tutelar deity of this month. This day is observed with mirth, in imitation of the old Roman celebration of the days when the goddess Flora was worshipped. The Roman floral games began on the 28th April, and continued a few days. At one time these celebrations were conducted with obscenity, but by degrees the amusements became more moral. It was customary during the middle ages for rich and poor to go out on May-day, with music and other signs of joy and merriment, to gather flowers, and sip the dew before sunrise. The people then decorated their houses with the flowers, conspicuous amongst which was the hawthorn blossom. The most beautiful maid of the district was chosen "Queen of the May," and crowned with flowers. So general was the custom of observing May-day in the reign of Henry VIII. that the Corporation of London went out a-Maying, and so did the king and queen. In England, France, Germany, and elsewhere, every village had its May-pole, till the May games were suppressed, or rather discouraged, on the ground that they were remnants of heathen superstition.

The Celts kindled their May-fires with much superstitious ceremony, a custom which had its origin in the worship of Baal. The principal festival of this worship was held in the beginning of May, but there were similar ceremonies in November. On these occasions all the fires in the district were extinguished, under the pain of death. Needfire was then obtained by friction, and all the fires were rekindled from what was regarded as the sacred flame. At times of public calamities and distress, the practice of kindling needfire was resorted to. It was supposed to counteract sorcery, and stay disease among cattle. These superstitious operations remind one of the story of Prometheus. The myth runs thus:--"During the reign of Zeus, men and gods, once upon a time, were disputing with one another. With the view of outwitting Zeus, Prometheus cut up a bull and divided it into two parts, hiding the meat and the intestines in the skin, and putting an inferior piece on the top, while he heaped the bones together and covered them with fat. Zeus was asked to choose either of the lots, and, suspecting that an attempt was made to deceive him, he selected the good portion; but, enraged at the stratagem, he took his revenge on the mortals by withholding from them the fire necessary for the cooking of meat. Prometheus by his cunning art obtained fire in a hollow staff, and brought it to them; and he took from man the gift of foreseeing future events, but gave him the better gifts of hope and of fire." Down to a recent date, people in the north of Scotland cut a trench in the ground; they then kindled a fire and dressed a repast of milk and eggs, something like a custard. This being done, they kneaded a cake of oatmeal, and toasted it before the fire. The custard was then eaten, and the cake was broken into pieces and thrown into a bag, not, however, before one of the pieces was burned black. Every one of the company in turn was blindfolded, and drew out a piece of the cake; and he who drew out the burned piece was dedicated to Baal, in order to render the year fruitful. The person supposed to be devoted was then compelled to leap three times over the fire, as symbolical of the sacrifices offered to this god in former ages.

In England there were Ram Feasts. At one of these a ram was roasted in its skin, and after it was cooked a great scramble took place for pieces thereof, it having been thought good fortune would attend those who secured a portion. Men and women partook of the feast.

The name of June was given in reverence to Juno, and was called *Sear-monat* by the Anglo-Saxons. Mercury was regarded by the Romans as the deity who presided over this month. June is considered in the present age as the most favourable period of the year for marriages.

July was originally called *Quintilis*, or fifth month, in honour of Julius Caesar; but the Anglo-Saxons came to know this month as *Maed-monat*, or mead month, in consequence of it being the usual season of the year for securing honey and making mead.

St. Swithin's Day (15th July) is observed in commemoration of this wet or rainy saint. He was of Saxon descent, and distinguished for his piety and learning. St. Swithin was buried in the church-yard of Winchester, and the consecrated spot where his remains rest has been, we are told, the scene of frequent miracles. In consequence of the virtues flowing from his body, it was resolved to convey his remains to the choir of the cathedral, but, on the day appointed for the removal of his sacred dust, violent rain commenced, which continued without ceasing for forty days. From this circumstance, it was inferred that the intended removal of his remains was displeasing to St. Swithin, and the intention was for a time abandoned. Subsequently his body was transferred to another resting place, without the elements or the saint manifesting any displeasure. It is unnecessary to do more than recall to memory the wide-spread opinion, that if it rain on St. Swithin's Day, forty days wet weather will follow. Absurd as this superstition may appear, it has been believed in from the time of his death, in 862.

St. Margaret, whose festival falls to be held on the 20th July, was the daughter of an idolatrous priest at Antioch. She became a convert to the Christian religion, from which she was sought to be seduced by Olybius, a ruler in the East who sought her hand in marriage. She refused to forsake the true religion, or to become his wife; and her refusal was fatal to her. The cruel monster put her to the most dreadful torments he could invent, and afterwards ordered her to be beheaded, about the year 275. St. Margaret has been worshipped by the Eastern and Western Churches, from her supposed power to assist females in childbirth. It is related that Satan, in the form of a dragon, swallowed her alive, but that she escaped unhurt from the monster. Her girdle was long preserved in the abbey of St. Germain, in Paris; and females were, it was generally believed, undoubtedly relieved in their hour of suffering by the application of the sacred relic.

August, formerly called *Sextilis*, was named August in honour of the Emperor Augustus. And September still retains its original Roman name--that of the seventh month, though now really the ninth month--in consequence of the change made by commencing the year in January instead of March; but the Anglo-Saxons knew it by the name of *Gerst-monat*, or barley month, because their barley crop was usually gathered in in this month.

October, known by the Saxons as *Wyn-monat*, or wine month, has long been regarded with peculiar interest, owing to the many superstitious customs observed in it. In Rome, a horse, called October, was sacrificed to Mars in this month; and the Greeks and Romans held many Bacchanalian festivals in it, at which the people had recourse to magic and divination. In the days of our ancestors the Hallow-e'en ceremonies were more generally followed than they are by the present generation, but still in various places, particularly in the north of Scotland, people observe them with mirth, mixed with superstitious fear of fairies, ghosts, and other supernatural beings, supposed to be then at large, performing good and evil deeds. At this season, however, the most diabolical fiends are supposed to be chained in their abodes of darkness, or at all events prevented from venting their full wrath against the human race. The worst thing that Satan, assisted by all his emissaries, can do on Hallow-e'en, is to allot to one an ill-looking, decrepit, or sour partner in life, or send him or her a great swarm of children; or perhaps do what is worse--prevent any offspring being given to loving married couples. Unmarried men and women are accustomed to meet at the house of a friend, to spend this evening in searching into futurity. Various are the charms and modes of divination they have recourse to. The first spell they try is pulling kail-stocks in the dark with their eyes closed. There must be no attempt to pick what is thought the best stocks, but each person should pull up the first plant that comes to hand. After every one has obtained a root, the company returns to the house to examine the stocks. A long straight plant denotes that the holder thereof is to get a fine-looking husband or wife, as the case may be; whereas one who has unfortunately pulled a crooked, ill-shaped stock, may expect that his or her conjugal companion will be deformed and uncouth. In proportion to the quantity of earth adhering to the root, so will the riches of the possessor be; and according to the sweet or sour taste of the stem's centre, so will the temper or disposition of the expected partner be. The ceremony of pulling and tasting being over, the stocks are deposited above the door, and careful notice is taken of the strangers who come in when they are there. Favourites are invited in, but those whose presence is not desired are prevented, if possible, from crossing the threshold.

Those in pursuit of pleasure and fortune next proceed to the stack-yard, and pull each a stalk of oats, and, by counting the grains upon the stem, the puller will ascertain the number of little branches that will shoot forth from the family tree. It is peculiarly fortunate if the top grain be found on the stalk.

If a young man or single woman go to the barn three times to winnow corn, an apparition resembling the future spouse will appear before the chaff is separated from the third sieveful of grain. The like result may be expected if one go unperceived to the peat-stack and sow a handful of hempseed, or travel three times round it. Another way of revealing one's husband or wife, is this:--Go to a ford through which a funeral has passed, dip the sleeve of the shirt or chemise, and the wearer, on returning home and going to bed, after hanging the garment before the bedroom fire, will see the apparition of his or her object of affection turn the sleeve to dry the other side. To find the name of one's future spouse, one has nothing more to do than to go on Hallow-e'en to a barn or kiln, throw into it a clew of blue thread, which the person begins to wind up into another clew, having of course kept hold of one end of the thread. Before the winding operation is completed, some one will take hold of the thread, and on the question being asked, "Who holds?" an answer will be returned, in which will appear the name of him or her the fates have destined to be the inquirer's partner in life.

These modes described of lifting the veil that conceals the future are easy, and the objects aimed at pleasant; but even Hallow-e'en has both its lights and shadows; and one has something more to do than to inquire into the affairs of affection and domestic bliss. From curiosity or some other cause, a person may wish to know whether he or any of his neighbours will be taken away by the cold hand of death before another year. If he has such a wish, let him repair to a public highway which branches off in three directions, and take his seat (a three-legged stool is thought the best) in the centre of the road, a little before twelve at night. Simultaneously with the nearest clock striking that hour, he will hear proclaimed the names of those who are to die in the parish before the next Hallow-e'en. The curious individual should not omit to take with him a good many articles of wearing apparel. If he hear pronounced the name of any one whose life he does not desire to prolong, he will do well to retain his property; but if the name of one dear to him is sounded, he may rescue the person from early doom by casting away one of the articles. The life of esteemed friends is precious in one's sight, but his own life is generally dearer, and therefore the listener should take care not to cast away every rag he has, lest his own name should be called after he has parted with his last garment.

Another way of discovering one's future partner:--Let a person take up a position before a mirror, eat an apple before it while combing his or her hair, and now and again holding out the apple, as if offering it to some one supposed to be standing on the right side. Before the hair is properly arranged and the apple eaten, the person whose presence is desired will appear in the attitude of accepting the apple.

By the burning of nuts, it may be discovered whether lovers are to prove true or false to each other. One nut is taken to represent the gentleman, and another is named after the lady. Both nuts are laid in the fire: if they consume quietly together, then it is learned that fortune has appointed the lady and gentleman to spend their lives in happy union; but if one of the nuts start away, or should they both fly off in different directions, the individuals appealing to the fates are to understand that they will never be united in wedlock.

November--gloomy November--was known as *Blot-monat* (blood month) by the Saxons, as it was the time when large numbers of sheep and cattle were killed for sacrifices and for provisions.

The first day of November--All Saints or All Hallows--is a day of general commemoration of all saints and martyrs in honour of whom no particular days have been expressly assigned. The origin of this festival is supposed to have been in 607, when Phocus, the emperor, wresting the Pantheon from the heathens, gave the splendid edifice to the Christians. Boniface IV. consecrated it to the Virgin Mary and all the saints of both sexes. The Pagan dedication of it was to Cybele and all the gods.

The second day of November is an important day in the eye of the Church of Rome. On this day there are particular services in that Church relative to the souls supposed to be in purgatory. Odilon, abbot of Cluny, enjoined, in the ninth century, the ceremony of praying for the dead. The practice became common after this, and the next century a general festival was established, having for its object the release of suffering souls. Persons dressed in black went round the towns, ringing bells on the streets, every Sunday evening during the month of November, calling upon the inhabitants to remember the deceased suffering the expiatory flames of purgatory, and to join in prayer for the repose of their souls. The practice is still continued in some places, but an edict for its abolition was passed in the reign of Elizabeth. Praying for the dead, and offering sacrifices at their tombs, were early resorted to. Ovid ascribes the origin of the ceremonies to AEneas; and Virgil favours this idea in his fifth book. Certain saints declared that they heard the howlings of devils, as they complained of the souls of men being taken away from them, through the alms and prayers of holy people.

The Romans held a festival which lasted eleven days, during which period they imagined that ghosts were not only relieved from punishment, but were suffered to wander round their tombs. In the Roman Catholic Church mass is performed for the repose of departed souls; but it is requisite that those who desire to aid their deceased friends should give substantial proof of sincerity. In the *Clavis Calendaria* we read, "When the Duke of Assuna was supplicated for charity by a mendicant friar, he said, 'Put a pistole in this plate, my lord, and you shall release that soul from purgatory, for which you design it.' The duke complying, was assured his charity had been effective. 'Say you so, holy man?' replied his grace; 'then I shall take back my money for a future occasion, as you cannot, nor would you, I am confident, if you were capable, again condemn the poor soul to its former endurance.'"

Frederick the Great of Prussia, desirous of recovering the revenues of one of his forests from a monastery, demanded of the prior by what title it was held. To this question he received the prompt reply, that the income had been given in consideration of the holy brotherhood daily saying mass for the repose of the soul of one of his Majesty's ancestors. "How much longer," said Frederick, "will that holy work continue requisite?" "Sire," said the prior, whose experience far surpassed that of the friar who had addressed the duke, "it is not possible for me to speak of the precise time; but when it shall have been effected, I shall instantly despatch a courier to inform your Majesty."

The 6th November is sacred to St. Leonard. He was the friend of captives and all others in distress. If monkish legends can be credited, the mere mention of his name by one bound in fetters was sufficient to break the chains wherewith he was secured, and cause the prison doors to open, seemingly of their own accord, that the captive might go free. St. Leonard died in the year 500.

On festive and holy days at this period of the year, people strewed the graves of their relatives and the churchyards with evergreens.

Martinmas, now regarded in Scotland as the winter term-day, is observed by Roman Catholics in honour of St. Martin, born in Pannonia in or about the year 316, who is reported to have performed many miracles. Formerly, St. Martin's Day was one of great festivity. Sports were entered into at the market cross and village green, and kept up till a late hour, when, by the ringing of a bell, the people were warned to retire to their homes. It has been supposed that the Martinmas feeing markets, for the engagement of agricultural and other servants, originated at these sports. At those merry gatherings there was invariably a large concourse of people, either taking part in or witnessing the games; consequently the opportunity was taken advantage of by masters requiring servants, and by servants seeking employment.

The 13th of November is St. Britius's Day. He was a pupil of St. Martin, who prophesied that his youthful scholar would be subjected to many severe afflictions, but that he would be appointed a bishop some day. The latter part of the prediction was fulfilled in 399, by the election of St. Britius to the see of Jaurs, on the death of his master. The other part of St. Martin's prophecy also came to pass. Grievous slanders were circulated concerning St. Britius; and among other offences he was accused of being the father of a child by his laundress. The people, enraged at the incontinence of their bishop, threatened to put him to death; and they would have carried their threat into execution, but for most extraordinary evidence coming from the lips of a child only one month old. Holy St. Britius adjured the infant, on the thirtieth day of its existence on earth, to tell who was its father. Whether the infant revealed the name of its paternal parent, we are not informed; but this we are told, that it clearly and audibly testified that it had not sprung from the bishop's loins. This miracle did not satisfy certain wicked people--they attributed the strange occurrence to sorcery; and to give another test of his innocence, St. Britius had recourse to the fiery ordeal. He, to show that he was free from guilt, carried burning coals on his head to the shrine of St. Martin, without the cap he wore being burned or a hair of his head singed. This second miracle was also attributed to his intimacy with Satan, and he was expelled from the city for seven years. At the end of that time he was restored to his dignities, which he enjoyed until his death, in the year 444.

St. Britius was among the first who submitted to a fiery ordeal, but others had been subjected to this mode of trial before him. The first appeal of this nature, we are informed, was that of Simplicius, a bishop of distinction, in the fourth century. Having been married before attaining his high ecclesiastical position, he was charged with continuing to partake of matrimonial indulgences. To prove his innocence, the bishop's wife not only held burning coals in her lap without injury, but applied the coals to her breast without receiving hurt. He, too, submitted to various forms of fiery ordeal, and came out scatheless; and as their innocence was in this way manifested, they were acquitted.

From the strange custom of ordeal by water originated the practice of ducking witches, but to the witch either sinking or swimming proved alike fatal. If she sank she was permitted to drown, and if she swam it was regarded as a proof of guilt, and was therefore forced below the water and drowned. Sometimes the ordeal was by hot water. The bare legs and arms were immersed in boiling liquid, and if they sustained no injury the accused was considered innocent.

Edmund, the king and martyr, to whose memory the 20th of November is sacred, was the last titular of the East Angles. When the Danes first landed in his district, in England, they defeated him, and when he fell into their hands they scourged him, bound him to a tree, pierced him with many arrows, and afterwards beheaded him. Before being captured, Edmund offered to surrender himself to the Danes, provided they would spare his subjects, and permit them to enjoy the privileges of Christians; but the invaders refused to listen to the proposition, hence the Church has regarded him as a martyr. His head was thrown into a thicket, and lay there for twelve months, at the end of which time the Christians found it in a perfect state, guarded by a wolf, which held the precious caput between its paws. Probably it never would have been seen, but for the departed saint being heard uttering the words, "Here, here, here!" Fifty years after the head was discovered, the body was found near the same spot. The remains of Edmund were buried in a remote place in the year 903, but in 1010 they were exhumed and translated to London. In 1012 this human dust was removed to the place whence it was taken.

The Danish invasion and murder of Edmund are ascribed to Bearn, a dissolute English nobleman. The story runs that Lodebrock, king of Denmark, having been alone in a boat, was driven by a tempest from the Danish coast to the Yare, in Suffolk. The inhabitants brought him to Edmund, who treated him with so much mildness and consideration, that his affections were alienated from his own country. Among other pastimes, the Dane was in the habit of hawking with Bearn, the king's huntsman, who at length murdered him. A favourite hound belonging to Lodebrock never quitted the body of its murdered master, except when compelled by hunger. This being noticed, and Bearn being found guilty of the murder, he was sentenced to be put in Lodebrock's boat, without food or instrument of navigation, and committed to the mercies of the sea. By a strange providence, he was carried to the very place in Denmark from which Lodebrock had been driven. The Danes, who knew the boat, and who had heard of the murder, examined Bearn on the rack as to his guilt. To avoid the just punishment of his crime, he affirmed that Edmund was the author of the horrid deed. On hearing the false declaration, wrung from Bearn by torture, Hinguar and Hubba, sons of Lodebrock, to avenge their father's death, sailed for East Anglia, where they killed Edmund.

St. Cecilia's Day is the 22d of November. She was a native of Rome, and suffered martyrdom in consequence of her embracing the Christian religion. Her story is a remarkable one. It is related that she made a vow of chastity, but that nevertheless her parents compelled her to marry a young nobleman named Valerianus, a heathen. On the evening of their wedding day, Cecilia told her husband that he must not enter her chamber, as she was nightly visited by an angel, who would destroy him were he found in it. Surprised at the statement, but not alarmed, he sought an interview with the spirit, but she told him that could not be unless he first became a Christian. He consented to change his religion, and he and his brother Tibertius were baptized. Shortly afterwards the husband found his wife at prayers in her closet with an angel, like a beautiful youth, clothed with brightness, by her side. The angel informed Valerianus that he and his brother would soon be beheaded, and that Cecilia would be thrown into a cauldron of boiling water, and scalded to death. All the predictions were fulfilled. Cecilia's martyrdom took place about the year 230, though some authorities suppose it happened earlier.

The 30th November is the anniversary of St. Andrew, the patron saint of Scotland. There is a wonderful legend regarding St. Andrew's Cross. The cross, we are informed, appeared in heaven to Achaius, king of Scots, and Hungus, king of the Picts, to encourage them to engage in battle with Athelstane, king of England. Achaius and Hungus led on their forces, and were victorious. In acknowledgment of this wonderful manifestation, they vowed to bear St. Andrew's Cross for ever on their ensigns and banners.

November was considered a good month for invalids being bled or physicked, but every day was not considered equally lucky for applying the lance or swallowing the draught. Almanacs were therefore sold, with directions how to avoid the inauspicious times.

December, it is generally believed, was consecrated to Saturn; others, however, think it was sacred to Vesta. In ancient times the Saxons called it *Midwinter-monat* and *Yule-monat*. This last-mentioned name points to the far-back period and high festivals held this month by the Northern nations in honour of the sun. The evergreens with which houses are decked, and Christmas trees with their gifts, are relics of the symbols by which our heathen ancestors exhibited their belief in the power of the sun to deck the earth anew with green, and to laden the trees with rich fruit. The misletoe, exhibited at Christmas and the New Year in almost every house, is looked upon as a semi-sacred thing, that possesses charms and confers privileges on people possessed of it, or who may come under the support from which it is suspended. In olden times the ancient Britons believed their gods were in the oaks. When the misletoe berries were ripe, the Druids invited the people to a great feast, and the oldest Druid, dressed in white, climbed up the trees where the misletoe grew, and with a golden sickle cut it down, while the other Druids sang and prayed. We have various accounts of the misletoe, and of the strange superstitious proceedings in gathering it. The misletoe is supposed to be the golden bough which AEneas made use of, to introduce himself to the Elysian regions. It is often worn about the neck of children, to prevent convulsions and pain when getting their teeth.

New Year's gifts and Christmas boxes were given by friends to friends in ancient times. Both the Greeks and Romans gave presents and entertainments during their annual superstitious meetings. Masses and prayers were offered for the safety of persons and ships, but more particularly for vessels that went on long voyages. A box, devoted to each ship, was kept by the priest, into which money might be dropped, in order to give efficacy to the supplications of the Church; and these boxes being opened at Christmas in each year, acquired the name of Christmas boxes. In course of time all presents given at this season of the year were familiarly called boxes. Poor people begged box money to enable them to supply the priest's box, that they might have the benefit of his prayers.

The old salutation of "a merry Christmas," like that of wishing "a happy New Year," adverted to the hospitality of the rich, whose spacious halls, crowded with tenants and neighbours, were scenes of boundless hospitality. Boar's-head is sometimes served on Christmas Day, to give expression of the abhorrence of Judaism. Plum-puddings are emblematical of the offerings of the wise men; and mince-pies, with their pieces of paste over them in the form of a hay rack, commemorate the manger in which the Saviour was first laid. Dancing and gambols have been among the Christmas amusements for a long series of years.

The wassail bowl was the vessel out of which our Saxon ancestors took such copious draughts, that legislative measures were adopted with the view of enforcing temperance. Wassail not only refers to a certain liquid preparation, but it is a term applied to drinking songs, which in the cider-producing counties were sung on the eve of the Epiphany, when libations were poured out to the apple-trees for a fruitful season--a custom evidently followed in example of the heathen sacrifices to Pomona, the goddess of fruit-trees and orchards.

Dunstan, to check the vicious habit of excessive indulgence in intoxicating liquors, introduced the custom of marking or pegging drinking-cups at certain places, to restrain the draught to a limited quantity. But the contrivance, instead of being attended with good effects, led to greater excess; for those who formerly strove to avoid intoxication, were now, they thought, obliged to drink to the "pegs," it being understood that it was imperative to drain the vessel to the pin.

From the use of peg or pin-cups or tankards, may be traced phrases yet repeated. When a person is in a cheerful mood, he is said to be in a merry pin. Speaking of bringing a man "down a peg," refers to a regulation which deprived a troublesome fellow of his turn of drinking. When a person is dull, he is described as being "a peg too low." "Getting on peg by peg," means that a man is gradually emptying his cup.

Anciently, confectionery was presented to the Fathers of Rome, made up in the forms of crosses, infants, etc., to which has been ascribed the origin of bakers presenting their customers with cakes, or, as they are sometimes called, "Yule dough." It is supposed that the New Year's ode composed by the Poet Laureate was originally regarded as a Yule song or Wassail song. For such verses Christmas carols were substituted, as being more appropriate for the season of the year, observed with joy in honour of Christ's birth in Bethlehem.

MIRACLES PERFORMED BY SAINTS AND OTHER HOLY PERSONS, AND THE INFLUENCE OF SACRED RELICS.

CHAPTER XV.

Introductory--St. Peter and Simon the Magician--Clement's Miracles and Death--St. Agnes the Innocent--A Miraculous Circumstance--St. Blase's Power over Men and Beasts--St. Agatha's Holy Life, Tortures, and Wonder-working Veil--St. Patrick's Missionary Labours, and Expulsion of Reptiles from Ireland--St. Germanus stilling the Raging of the Sea--St. David and the Welsh Leeks--The Stirrup Cup, and Origin of "Pledging"--Elfrida's Treachery and Remorse--St. Benedict's Power over the Elements--St. Dunstan cured by an Angel; his Encounter with Satan--The AEolian Harp--St. Columba's Prophecy concerning Iona--The Dream of Columba's Mother--Tragic Events--Prayer answered--Sacred Ducks of Ireland--St. Paul binding a Dragon--Saints and Frogs--Friars and Jesuits--Father Mark proof against Fire--Virtue of Holy Water--St. Noel's Imprecation--Men-wolves--Stories about Bees--Strange Story about the Host--Blood-stained Jews--Miracles--St. Boniface--Pope Silvester assisted by Satan--Necromancing Popes--St. Januarius's Blood--St. Anthony's Conflicts with the Devil--St. Anthony's Hog and Bees--A Tradition concerning Melrose--St. Cuthbert--Waves of Blood--Strange Narrative--A Princess swallowed up by the Earth--Monk Waldevus's inexhaustible Stores--Holy Relics--Rusticus and his Hog.

In laying down rules for our own guidance in carrying on this work, we resolved to make few allusions to the miracles and mysteries related in the Old Testament. We also determined to avoid reference to Christian rites, ceremonies, and performances, either in early or later times, when that could be accomplished without materially affecting the subject of superstition generally so called; but as an important link would be left out were we to refrain from giving a few examples of miracles wrought, or said to have been wrought, by holy persons connected with Christian churches, we are under the necessity (considering those persons have had numerous base imitators) of departing to a certain extent from our original plans, and of devoting this chapter to the

"Miracles performed by Saints and other Holy Persons" since the dawn of Christianity.

St. Peter, whom the Roman Catholics place at the head of the list of bishops of Rome, did undoubtedly perform miracles; but tradition tells us of so many strange circumstances concerning him, that at least a few of the relations must be regarded as nothing better than romance. We are informed that he went to Rome to oppose Simon, the celebrated magician; that at their first interview, at which Nero was present, the magician flew up into the air, but that the devil, who assisted him up, let him fall from a great height to the ground, by which his legs were broken. This tradition was long believed; and a reddish stone, supposed to be blood-stained, was pointed out as the stone on which Simon received his injuries.

We read that *Clement*, the third bishop of Rome, was banished by Trajan beyond the Euxine Sea; that there he caused a fountain to spring up miraculously for the benefit of Christians; and that he converted the whole country to the true faith. These acts provoked the Emperor so much that he ordered him to be thrown into the sea, with an anchor fastened to his neck. On the anniversary of his death, the sea ebbed to the place where he had been drowned, though three miles from the shore; that on its retiring there appeared a most magnificent temple of the finest marble, and in the temple a monument containing the saint's body; that the sea continued thus to retire every year on the same day, and did not return for a week, that worshippers might, without apprehension of danger, perform their devotions in honour of the holy martyr. In connection with these ceremonies, a most wonderful circumstance occurred, even more strange than what has been related of the temple. One year a mother left her young infant in the temple, and on her return next year she found her child not only alive, but in perfect health. Gregory of Tours and many others gave credit to this story.

St. Agnes was so great a favourite that her festivals were celebrated with more than ordinary pomp. She was descended from a Roman family of rank and opulence, and endowed by nature with great personal beauty. She was beheaded at the early age of thirteen, in the year 306. By the sentence of her judge, she was ordered to be treated in a most shameful manner, but through a providential interposition she was saved from the ignominy her persecutors intended for her. After that event the Roman women worshipped her. The parents of St. Agnes were blessed with a vision while praying at her tomb, in which she appeared to them in white raiment, with a lamb standing by her side, being the universally acknowledged emblem of innocence. On the fast held on St. Agnes's Day, two of the whitest lambs that could be procured were presented at her altar, and afterwards carefully reared until they were shorn. Their wool was then hallowed, and converted into white cloth for holy garments. Rural virgins were said to practise singular rites, in keeping St. Agnes's Fast, for the purpose of discovering their future husbands.

In the time of Liberius, a Roman of wealth and rank, named John, having no children, resolved to make a gift of his whole substance to the Holy Virgin. With the consent of his wife, the entire estate was therefore conveyed to Mary, whom they thenceforth jointly entreated in their prayers to let them know by some token in what manner she chose to dispose of it. Their prayers were heard. On the night of the 4th August, when the heat was great at Rome, there was a miraculous fall of snow, which covered part of the Esquiline Mount. The same night John and his wife were advised in their dreams to build a church on the ground which they should find covered with snow. Next morning they went to acquaint Pope Liberius with what had happened. Strange to say, the Pope had had a similar dream. A grand procession of the whole clergy, in which the Pope walked himself, attended by crowds of people, went to the above-mentioned mount, and having discovered the snow-covered spot, the Pope laid the foundation of a magnificent church there, long known as Saint Mary in the Snow.

St. Blase, who suffered martyrdom by decapitation in the year 289, after having been cruelly whipped and scourged, wrought numerous miracles of an extraordinary nature. Shortly before his decease, he prayed that whosoever sought his help in consequence of disease in the throat, or any sickness, he might have the assistance desired. After this, all who implored the aid of the saint were heard and healed. In his lifetime he saved from death a devout widow's son, who, without his assistance, would have been choked by a fish bone. Even the wild beasts of the field were under the saint's control. A wolf that had carried away a poor person's pig, was forced by the holy man to bring back another animal of equal value. In honour of St. Blase, candles were offered to him, which, through the very act of devotion, were rendered holy, and became serviceable for all pious uses.

St. Agatha performed many miracles. Quintianus, the governor of Catania, smitten with her beauty and extraordinary accomplishments, endeavoured to gain her affections, but was unsuccessful. Consequently his love turned into inveterate hatred, which ended in the fair Agatha being scourged and cast into a loathsome prison. The Pagan ruler commanded her to sacrifice to heathen deities, but she adhered to her Christian principles in spite of his wrath, which found vent in burning her with hot irons and cutting off her breasts. To manifest the displeasure of heaven, the walls of her prison were thrown down by some unseen power, and two of the governor's servants were deprived of life in a mysterious manner when torturing her. Her enemy had intended other and more fearful cruelties, but, in answer to her earnest prayers, death stepped in and relieved her from every trouble. In Catania a church was built and dedicated to St. Agatha, and her sacred veil, which she had often used to conceal her lovely features from the lustful Quintianus, was placed in it, to protect that city from the eruptions of Mount AEtna, and the earthquakes so frequent in Sicily. This valuable relic was long preserved by those who believed in its efficacy. It not only had power over the mountain and internal fires, but it conveyed virtue to everything it touched, similar to that which itself possessed. There were few Catanians who did not obtain, through this veil, sovereign protections from evil.

St. Patrick, the apostle and father of the Hibernian Church, and patron or tutelar saint of Ireland, was a Briton by birth, having been born at Kilpatrick, near Dumbarton, in the year 377. When about sixteen years of age he was taken prisoner and conveyed to Ireland, where he was sold as a slave. Escaping from his master, he returned to the place of his nativity. When in exile, he saw the evils arising from Paganism, and resolved to do what he could to convert the Irish Pagans to Christianity. In due time he entered into his missionary labours with indefatigable zeal, and proved to be the blessed means of converting the benighted Irish to the true faith. The miracles attributed to him are numerous, the most noted of which is the expulsion of reptiles from the Irish soil. It was he who made the shamrock--the Irish national emblem--so famous.

St. Germanus, bishop of Auxerre, and *St. Lupus*, bishop of Troyes, were sent to Britain by Celestine, the forty-second bishop of Rome, in the year 429, to preach Christianity. The two missionaries, on their way, passed through Paris; thence they pursued their journey to the sea-side, and embarked. On the ocean a storm was raised by the devil, when Germanus, who was asleep, awoke just as the vessel was on the point of sinking, and having rebuked the sea and poured a few drops of oil into it, the raging of the waves ceased. Germanus, after safely landing in Britain, restored to sight a blind girl by the application of certain relics he possessed.

St. David was a learned, elegant, and zealous saint, reported to have performed miracles. The Welsh regarded him as their tutelar saint, and annually held festivals in his honour. In answer to the saint's prayers in the year 640, the Britons, under King Cadwallader, gained a complete victory over the Saxons. From a garden near the battle-field, he caused leeks to be pulled and stuck in the caps of the British warriors, to enable them to distinguish each other, whereas the opposing parties, through want of a distinguishing badge, mistook friends for foes, and cut one another to pieces. From this circumstance sprang the custom of the Welsh wearing leeks in their hats on St. David's Day. Tradition says that the birth of this saint was predicted thirty years before the event took place; that a spirit constantly attended him, to minister to his wants; that the waters of Bath received their excellent qualities from his benediction; that he healed the sick; and that he even restored the dead to life.

Edward, the martyr, was crowned King of the West Saxons, when a youth, by Archbishop Dunstan, who had espoused his cause in opposition to the wishes of Elfrida, his step-mother, who desired to secure the throne for her own son Ethelred. Four years after his accession, Edward was hunting one day in Dorsetshire, near Elfrida's castle, and took the opportunity of paying her a visit, unattended by any of his retinue. After what was thought an agreeable interview, he mounted his horse to ride away, and when in the act of drinking the stirrup-cup, a servant, instigated by Elfrida, stabbed him behind. The youthful prince, finding himself wounded, put spurs to his steed, but, becoming faint from loss of blood, fell from the saddle and was killed. The foul deed struck the nation with so much dread, that subsequently every man secured the protection of a staunch friend before he would venture in public to drain the wassail-bowl. Hence arose the expression of "pledging," when partaking of the cheerful glass. Elfrida, seized with remorse, strove to atone for her guilt, but could not get rid of the heavy load that constantly weighed her down. At length she gave way to despair, her conscience causing her to imagine that a monstrous fiend was always on the watch to drag her down to the place of everlasting torment. When alone, in the still hours of the night, she imagined she felt the infernal being's grasp, and, to protect herself, she had recourse to charms.

St. Benedict possessed the power of performing miracles. Not only could he control the actions of man in a way that showed his supernatural ability, but he also set the elements at defiance. In the year 529, Benedict, with a few devotees selected from the many pious men around him, went to Monte Casino, where idolatry prevailed, and broke the images in Apollo's temple; they then founded a monastery there, and instituted the order after the saint's name. The manner of this Christian's death is not mentioned, but it is supposed to have been easy and natural. When the Goths invaded Italy, they attempted to burn him in his cell. Fiercely did the flames rage around him, but they could not burn so much as a hair of his head. This preservation still more enraged the heathen, who threw him into a close hot oven, and kept him there till next day. To their surprise, when the oven was opened, they found the saint safe--neither his body being scorched nor his clothes singed.

St. Dunstan was thought by the ignorant people to be in league with infernal spirits. When a boy, disease brought him to the point of death, but he was restored to health by medicine brought to him by a spirit riding in a storm. Feeling himself well again, Dunstan repaired to the church to return grateful thanks. Satan met him on the way, surrounded him with numerous fierce-looking black dogs, and endeavoured to defeat his pious intention. Nothing daunted, the holy saint pursued his way, and, by the assistance of an angel that came to his help, he defeated the devil and his black dogs. Dunstan found the church door shut; and to save time, lest Satan should overtake them before entering the sacred edifice, the angel carried him through the roof to the proper place of devotion. At another time, while St. Dunstan was working at his forge, the devil attempted to lead him into evil paths. The evil spirit appeared, not in a hideous form, but as a beautiful young lady, all smiles and endearments. Though the hook was skilfully concealed, the deception did not succeed: the saint knew the arch-fiend, and suddenly taking a pair of red-hot tongs from the fire, seized the fiend's nose with them, whereby the nasal organ was disfigured for ever. The AEolian harp is thought to have been invented by St. Dunstan, and he is said to have been able to play upon that instrument without touching a string thereof. At one time, in consequence of the high esteem in which harps were held, every person of rank was supposed to possess one of these instruments, and to be able to perform on it. Slaves were prohibited from performing on this sacred instrument. Creditors were prevented by law from seizing for debt a gentleman's harp, though everything else he possessed might be sold to discharge his obligations.

St. Columba was the apostle of the Highlands and Western Islands of Scotland, and founder of the famous cathedral of Iona, long regarded as the mother church of the Picts. Concerning this building he wrote the prophetic lines, which have been in part verified:

> "O sacred dome of my beloved abode!
> Whose walls now echo to the praise of God;
> The time shall come when lauding monks shall cease,
> And howling herds here occupy their place;
> But better ages shall hereafter come,
> And praise re-echo in this sacred dome."

Striking miracles were ascribed to him; his prophecies almost invariably came to pass, and he had marvellous visions. Columba's mother dreamed, one night before his birth, that a person of superhuman mien and figure presented her with a veil of the most beautiful texture; that in a short time the giver resumed possession of his gift, and, raising it up, it flew through the heavens. Gradually the veil extended itself on all sides, till it spread over mountains and plains. Grieved at the loss of such a valuable article, she expressed her sorrow; but he who had given and taken away, comforted her with the assurance that it was an emblem of the child soon to be born, who, he assured her, would prove a blessing to the nation. One day, while the saint was a youth, a young girl, pursued by a barbarian, came running to him for protection; but before he could lift his slender arm to save her, the monster pierced her through with a spear. One who witnessed the tragic deed exclaimed, "Ah! how long will this atrocious crime remain unpunished?" To this question Columba replied, "The soul of the murderer may yet be in hell as soon as that of the murdered is in heaven." Scarcely had he uttered these words, than the unhappy criminal fell a lifeless corpse. At another time the saint observed a man falling from a considerable height, and beseeched an angel to uphold him. The good man's prayer was heard: a heavenly messenger, with a speed swifter than that of lightning, came to the rescue, and the man escaped unhurt.

In olden times there were sixteen ducks that usually swam about a certain lake in Ireland; but when any injury was done to the church or clergy they flew away, and did not return until satisfaction was given and reparation made for the wrong perpetrated. During the absence of the ducks, the water of the lake, naturally clear, became corrupt and smelt so badly that man and beast refused to taste it. If any person injured one of those birds, condign punishment was sure to overtake him. A kite having caught one of them, flew to a tree with it, but immediately all the ravenous bird's members became so powerless that it could not devour its prey. At another time a fox caught a second bird of the flock, but he had better, we are told, have let it alone, for next day the greedy animal was found dead near the lake, with the innocent duck sticking in its throat.

St. Paul, bishop of Leon, was entreated by the inhabitants of a seaport in Ireland to deliver them from a dragon that had killed many people. The pious bishop assured them of help, provided they repented and renounced their superstitions. They promised to do all he required of them. An altar was prepared, whereon he said mass. Then he went out and, with a loud voice, commanded the dragon to come before him. Immediately it appeared with open mouth and rolling eyes, and cast itself at the saint's feet. St. Paul cast a stole round its neck, and, fixing his staff in the ground, bound the dangerous creature so that it could not hurt any one after that time.

A holy saint, being disturbed one day by the croaking of a number of frogs in a pool near the church, went and smote the waters with his staff. Presently the frogs ceased their noise, and never croaked again.

Once upon a time a rivalship existed between the Austin friars and the Jesuits. The father-general of the Austin friars was dining with the Jesuits, and, on the table-cloth being removed, he entered into a formal discourse touching the superiority of the monastic order, and charged the Jesuits with assuming the title of "Fratres," while they held not the three vows which other monks were obliged to consider sacred. The general was very eloquent and authoritative. On the contrary, the superior of the Jesuits being unlearned, though shrewd in many respects, preferred to see a miracle performed, to prove the superiority of his order, rather than enter into a controversy. He therefore proposed that one of his friars and an Austin friar should show which of them would most readily obey his superior. The Austin friar consented. The Jesuit then, turning to the holy friar Mark, who was waiting on them, said, "Brother Mark, our companions are cold; I command you, in virtue of the obedience you have sworn to me, to bring instantly, in your hands, some burning coals from the kitchen fire, that our friends may warm themselves over your hands." Father Mark obeyed, and, to the astonishment of the Austin friars, brought on his palms a supply of red burning coals, that whoever thought proper might warm himself. The father-general, with the rest of his brethren, stood amazed. He looked wistfully at one of his monks, as if he wished to command him to perform a similar exploit; but the Austin monk, who understood what was meant, said, "Reverend father, forbear; do not command me. I am ready to fetch fire in a chafing dish, but not in my bare hands." The triumph of the Jesuits was complete: the miracle was noised about to their advantage. But the Austin friars could never account for the miracle, nor could they imitate it.

A priest in Ireland, travelling in Ulster, was forced to pass a night in a forest. He, and a boy who accompanied him, lighted a fire under the branches of a tree. Scarcely had they seated themselves than a wolf came near, and spoke as follows:--"Fear nothing; I am of a race of men-wolves, from which every seven years, by force of an imprecation made by St. Noel, two from among us, a male and a female, are constrained to lay aside the outward shape of reasonable creatures, and live in the form of wolves for seven years. At the end of that period other two men-wolves are sent out, and the former two return, if they survive the dangers of wolf-life. Not far from this place, my wife, who is the female wolf, lies very unwell, and I beseech you to go and comfort her." So the priest, ever ready to perform a good act, went to see the sick wolf. She was in the hollow of a tree, suffering great pain. He administered comfort to the invalid, but possessed not the power of changing her into her natural shape. The male wolf conducted the priest back to the fire, remained on watch all night to keep the other wolves away, and in the morning directed the priest how to go.

A French peasant, whose bees were dying of disease, was advised to go to the communion, carry off the host, and blow it into one of his hives. He did as recommended, but the result proved different to what he expected. Some time afterwards he discovered that his bees were dead. On examining the hive, he was amazed to find that the host put among the honey-combs was turned into a beautiful infant--cold, however, in the arms of death. Intending to bury the child's body in the church, he was proceeding thither, when, on the way to the sacred edifice, the infant vanished. This unhallowed use of the host brought a curse on the neighbourhood. The people were so chastised by divers calamities, that the country was depopulated, and became like a wilderness.

Another peasant, having communicated on Easter Day, received the host into his mouth; but instead of using it according to sacred rules, he laid it among his bees, thinking that by doing so he would bring all the bees in the neighbourhood, with their honey, to his hives. So far did his project succeed; but the bees brought no fruit which the wicked peasant could desire. They hummed melodious music, and built a small wax church at the time the wicked wretch thought they should be collecting honey for him. One day, walking near the hive into which he had put the host, the bees came out, and stung him nearly to death. Remorse seized him, and in bitter anguish he went to the priest to confess his fault. As the case was an extraordinary one, the priest consulted the bishop, who advised that the parishioners, headed by the priest, should go in procession to the hives. On the people's arrival, the bees testified their joy by their melodious humming. In the hive into which the host had been put an altar of wax was found, and a sacred relic lying thereon.

In 1399 a woman and her daughter engaged to procure consecrated hosts for a band of wicked Jews, who intended to use them for unhallowed purposes. The woman went to a church and stole three hosts when the friars were at dinner. Having received the hosts, the Jews assembled in a cellar, threw them contemptuously on a table, and stabbed them with a dagger. Blood spurted out from the dagger holes, and covered the faces of the impious men. The marks could not be washed away, so that they, Cain-like, bore unmistakeable signs of guilt to the day of their death. Blood also ran on the cellar floor, and could not by any means be removed. The Jews being terrified, sent two men to bury the hosts in a field. As the men passed a pious youth, named Paul, who had charge of two oxen, the hosts flew up in the air, and became like beautiful butterflies. At the sight of these, the oxen kneeled down on the ground. Paul, on becoming acquainted with what had happened, hastened to a magistrate to give information against the wicked people. Instead of being believed, he was cast into prison as a base fellow. In answer to his prayers, the prison gates opened of themselves; so he went out, and again presented himself before the judge. This time Paul's word was taken. The case was reported to the bishop, who ordered the hosts to be collected for preservation. Proceedings were taken against the Jews: they were burned, and their goods confiscated. By order of the king, a church was built at the place where the hosts appeared to Paul as butterflies. Many miracles were afterwards wrought there. From that time to the year 1604 no fewer than 382 were performed, the most notable ones being the raising of thirty-six persons from the dead.

St. Boniface, the apostle of Germany, slept one night in a tent pitched in an open plain. In the still dark hours a bright light suddenly appeared, in which he saw St. Michael, who spoke words of encouragement to him. After devotional services in the forenoon, he ordered his steward to prepare dinner, but the servant told him he had nothing in that barren place to set on the table. "What!" replied the apostle, "has he that fed his people forty years in the wilderness nothing to give his servant and his attendants?" Having said this, he ordered the cloth to be spread on the table, and immediately a large bird came flying with a fish, sufficient to feed the whole company for a day.

Another good story is told of St. Boniface. When he was a child, he observed a fox running away with a hen belonging to his mother. He hastened to the church, and prayed that the hens and chickens, which his mother fed in her back-yard to maintain herself and little family, might be preserved. To his astonishment, on returning home, the fox appeared before him with the hen, unhurt, in its mouth. Crouching like a spaniel, the beast of prey laid the fowl at the child's feet, and fell down dead.

Pope Silvester II. is reported to have reached the Papal chair by Satan's assistance. In his youth Silvester was a monk, but he deserted the monastery, and became a follower of the devil. He went to Spain in search of magical instruction. Being introduced to a Saracen philosopher skilful in magic, he became his disciple. But his stay with the learned man was short; for seeing a valuable book of necromancy belonging to his instructor, he stole it. Fleeing to a place of safety, he studied the black art very closely. His intercourse with Satan was frequent. Through the devil's assistance, he became an archbishop, and subsequently a pope, upon condition that, after his death, he would become the absolute property of the black fiend. During his popedom he kept a brazen head, which he regularly consulted concerning diabolical subjects. Desirous to know how long he would reign, Silvester betook himself to the devil for information. In answer to a question, the wicked spirit informed him that if he stayed away from Jerusalem he would live to an old age. A few years after this information, Silvester imprudently went to the Holy City, where he was suddenly seized with fever. Before his senses left him he repented, and confessed his familiarity with Satan. He desired that, after death,

his hands and tongue might be cut off, because with them he had served the devil; that his mutilated body should be put into a cart, with horses having no driver, and that wherever they halted,
after being started, his body should be buried there. All being done as requested by the dying pope,
the horses stopped when they came to the church of Lateran, and there he was interred. Whatever
became of his soul, it is plain the devil did not let his body alone. Shortly before the death of many
popes who succeeded him, his bones were heard to rattle, and his tomb was seen to sweat. By these
signs people knew when the dissolution of a pope was nigh. This narration may seem strange to the
present generation, but to people living in olden times it was not considered very extraordinary. Report says that eighteen popes, who succeeded one another, were necromancers. Benedictus IX. was,
through his wickedness and sorcery, called Maledictus. He was killed, we are told, by the Devil in
a wood. After his death, a hermit met his body, in the form of a bear, with a mitre on his head. The
hermit, so the story goes, asked him how it happened that he was metamorphosed. "Because," said
he, "in my popedom I lived without law, and now I wander like a beast."

St. Januarius, the patron saint of Naples, suffered martyrdom about the end of the third century. When he was beheaded, a pious lady secured a small quantity of his blood, which, report says,
has been preserved in a bottle ever since, without losing a grain of its weight. The blood is usually
congealed, but when brought near the saint's carefully preserved head, it is miraculously liquified.
The experiment is, or at least was, made twice a year by the Neapolitans. When there is an eruption
of Mount Vesuvius, the saint's head is, or was, carried in procession, in order to render the outbreak
harmless.

St. Anthony had serious conflicts with the Devil in bodily shape, when victory was generally
declared in favour of the good man. The saint performed miracles, and was famed for curing the
disease called after his name. In youth he was a swine-herd, and afterwards became the patron saint
of swine-herds. To do him honour, the Romanists were wont to keep a hog at the public expense,
which was venerated, and designated St. Anthony's hog. A picture or an image of the saint, hung up
in a house, kept away the plague from the dwelling. As the relics of this saint were capable of curing
St. Anthony's fire, so were those of St. Lucia useful in removing toothache, and those of St. Apollonia
were infallible remedies in cases of hydrophobia.

The history of Melrose is made up in great part of romance and superstitious traditions. Melrose, Malerose, or Mull-ross, signifying a bare promontory, derived its name from a young princess,
who was obliged to fly from her home on an island of the Greek Archipelago, in consequence of her
too close intimacy with a lover to whom she was sincerely attached. In her country a breach of the
seventh commandment by a young female was visited by death. As soon as her guilt became known,
she, to save her life, fled in search of an asylum, where she might have time and opportunity to atone
for her guilt. Certain good priests whom she consulted, directed her to sail northwards to an island
called Hibernia; and, moreover, the priests offered to accompany her wherever she went, for the
good of her soul. They accordingly set sail, and landed at a port on the north-east coast of Scotland.
She and her companions went inland, and settled down at Melrose, on the banks of the Tweed,
where she erected an abbey. St. Cuthbert was an abbot at Melrose before he removed to Lindisfarne,
now called Holy Island, where he was appointed bishop of St. Peter's Church at the latter place. He

died at Holy Island in the year 687, and was buried in a stone coffin there. Eleven years after the interment he was taken out of the grave, when it was found that the body was free from corruption.

Three years afterwards, Abbot Edred stealthily removed the body, carrying it from town to town for seven years. Many of the inhabitants of Holy Island, on learning that the saint's body was taken away, left their property, and went south after it. In consequence of the persecution then raging in England, the body, it was resolved, should be conveyed to Ireland for its greater security. The bishop, abbot, and others engaged in transporting the body, went on board a ship with their sacred treasure, intending to cross the Channel. A storm was encountered, three waves were turned into blood, and the ship was driven ashore, and cast on its side. A volume, containing the Evangelists' writings, in letters of gold and having its boards set with precious stones, fell from the vessel into the sea, which caused the saint to appear in a vision to one of the monks, and commanded him to search the shore for the book. He searched and found it, and, to his surprise, it appeared more beautiful than before, seeming to have been polished with a heavenly hand. On attempting to remove the body again, it became heavy and difficult to carry, which greatly perplexed those bearing the burden; but their difficulty was of short duration, for they perceived a bridle on a tree, and a red horse running toward them, which, on its approach, offered to carry St. Cuthbert's body. Accepting the proffered service, the body was put on the mysterious animal's back, which carried it to Crake Minster. Thence it was conveyed to Chester, where it remained a hundred and ten years. At the termination of that time it was removed to Ripon, to be laid beside the body of St. Wilfrid; but it was not destined to remain there more than a few months. As war, which had devastated the country, had ceased, St. Cuthbert's body was lifted with the intention of bringing it back to Chester; but the bearers halting with it at Wardenlaw, could not remove it again, as it seemed to be fastened to the ground. This caused the monks to pray for three days, and instructions were asked as to how the body was to be disposed of. Their prayers were heard: it was revealed to Eadmer, one of the monks, that the body should be taken to Durham, as its last resting-place. The extraordinary heaviness of the remains was no longer felt; it was removed thither, and deposited in the abbey in the year 997, where it lies to the present day.

Another story of St. Cuthbert is related. He lived on the borders of the Pictish territory, where many people went to him for instructions. At this time the king's daughter was injured by a young man, whom the princess spoke of as "the solitary young man who dwelleth hard by." Greatly incensed, the king went to St. Cuthbert, thinking that he was the guilty person, and accused him of committing the crime. For unknown reasons, the princess stated, and persisted in saying, that the holy man was the offender. Knowing his innocence, the saint prayed that the work of iniquity should be laid open, and that by some token it would be made known that the accusation was false. A sign was soon given; for scarcely had the supplication been made than the earth on which the princess stood suddenly opened with a hissing noise, and swallowed her up. The king, struck with terror, and in great distress at the loss of his daughter, implored the saint to restore the princess. This petition the holy father granted, clogging it, however, with the condition, that thenceforward no woman should resort to him. From that time a woman was never seen approaching his place of seclusion; and more than that, the restriction was extended to all the Pictish churches dedicated to him.

In connection with the history of Melrose, there is a tale of a monk named Waldevus, who increased the corn in the granaries belonging to the monastery in the villages of Eildon and Gattonside, out of which were fed, in a time of scarcity, four thousand poor people for three months, without any diminution of the first quantity, until the fruits of harvest were gathered, and then the store began to diminish according to the quantities withdrawn from it. Waldevus's tomb was opened twelve years after his death, which took place about the middle of the twelfth century, when his body was found entire, and his garments undecayed. In the year 1240 Waldevus's place of sepulchre was again opened, but his remains were then decayed. Those who were present carried away some of the small bones, leaving the rest of the ashes to repose in peace. William, son of the Earl of Dunbar, was one of the company present: he secured one of the saint's teeth, which turned out to be a valuable prize, for by it many wonderful miracles were performed.

Waldevus and his corn reminds us of Rusticus and his hog. Two Christian pilgrims, we are informed, were travelling in Poland, when they were hospitably entertained by Rusticus, then a Pagan peasant, afterwards converted, and promoted to sovereignty. They arrived at his residence when he was preparing to give an entertainment on the occasion of the birth of a son. A hog was killed for the feast, to which the wearied travellers were invited; and rumour has it, that they did ample justice to the good things, particularly to the hog's flesh, set before them. To show their gratitude, they resolved to work a miracle for the everlasting benefit of their host and his family. Half of the hog remained uneaten, and over it they prayed earnestly that it might never be consumed, but become a constant source of supply to the family. Their prayers were heard; and the swine's flesh remained undiminished in weight, however freely slices were carved from it for hungry mortals. Such was the effect produced on Rusticus's mind by this miracle, that he forsook heathenism and became a Christian.

HOW THE POETS HAVE FANNED
THE FLAME OF SUPERSTITION.
CHAPTER XVI.

Prophetic Verse--Druids called Bardi--The Bardi as Instructors--Virtue of Serpents' Eggs--Bards maintained by Noblemen--Queen Elizabeth and the Bards--Effects of Prophetic Sayings, and of Pipe Music--Message, how conveyed to another World--Voices of Deceased Friends heard in the Gale--Human Forms in the Clouds--Evenings in the Highlands--Michael Scott--Constant Work for Evil Spirits--Stemming the Tweed--How the Eildon Hills were formed--Place of Torment--Ropes of Sand--Scott and his Magic Books buried at Melrose--Ossianic Poems--Stories by Bards.

Poets have done much to fan the flame of superstition. They have indulged in prophetic verse, and handed down to posterity the strange belief of our ancestors. Certain Druids, called Bardi, were well known to be versed in astrology. They are supposed to have been the same, in particular respects, among the Britons as the Sophi among the Greeks, or the Magi among the Persians. Having been chosen from the best families in the land, the Bardi were held in the highest esteem by the common people; and the children of the chiefs were instructed by them. Their practical verses were never written, but given to their pupils *viva voce*, that they might assist in conveying them orally to the people. The Bardi dealt in particular charms, such as serpents' eggs, gathered in a particular way, and under certain phases of the moon. These eggs were imagined to be effectual for the gaining of law-suits, and for the securing of the good graces of princes. The Vates (another class of Druids), if not the Bardi, sought for omens among the entrails of victims offered in sacrifice.

The Bards, at various periods, possessed uncommon privileges, but these were from time to time diminished or increased, according to the caprice of those under whose government they lived. Almost every nobleman of distinction maintained bards in his family, and treated them with great consideration. Queen Elizabeth, however, acted differently: she ordered bards and minstrels to be hanged as traitors, as she believed they instigated rebellion by their songs. Bards followed clans to the field, where they eulogized the chiefs, and sang in extravagant verse the deeds of the favourite warriors. Before a battle, they went from tribe to tribe, or from clan to clan, exhorting and encouraging by prophetic sayings, in which success to friends was foretold and the doom of enemies pronounced. In the tumult of fight, when the bards' voices could not be heard, they were succeeded by pipers, who with inspiring warlike strains kept alive the enthusiasm the composers of verse had kindled. After the contest was sounded, the bards were employed to honour the memory of the brave that had fallen in battle, to celebrate the deeds of those who survived, and to excite to future acts of heroism. The piper was called upon, in turn, to sound mournful lamentations for the slain. In poetical language, the people were told that the dead sympathized with the living left behind to maintain the honour of their clans or country. Messages were given to dying friends, that they might be delivered to the spirits of relatives in another world. Highlanders imagined they heard, in the passing gale, the voices of departed relatives, and in their solitude they beheld the forms of their fathers in the bright clouds. In cases of emergency, the spirit of the mountains gave friendly warnings, which enabled cautioned ones to avoid dangers, that otherwise could neither be foreseen nor prevented.

Traditional poetry is highly esteemed by the mountaineers. It is a favourite pastime with the Highlanders, when seated round the evening fire, to relate and listen to tales of witches, fairies, etc., and to sing the soul-stirring songs of their native bards. Formerly, those who could recount the deeds of Fingalian times were special favourites. To such persons every door was open, and every table free. Nothing but ignorance could lead inhabitants of towns to suppose that Highlanders spend their winter months in gloomy solitude. Except where poverty or sickness prevails, the winter evenings among the mountains have something bewitching about them. The day's toil being over, neighbours come in, and parents and children, masters and servants, friends and relations, hold social intercourse in the same apartment, where there blazes a hearty fire of peats and bog-fir. None of the young women remain idle; for while the joke and merry laugh go round, one knits, a second sews, a third spins, and a fourth handles a distaff. Once the happy conversation has commenced, the wind may blow, the tempest roar, without disturbing the friendly group. There may be now less highly-gifted bards in the Highlands, romance and chivalry may have yielded to other ideas and pursuits, but still much of the same characteristic spirit remains: the love of ancient tradition and song exists, and the superstitions of bygone ages are unforgotten. Those who do not venerate their poets, and have respect to the early history of their country, are a dull, besotted people.

Not unfrequently were poets and other men of genius regarded as wizards or magicians. As an instance, we refer to the history of Michael Scott, the celebrated philosopher and poet, who lived in the thirteenth century. He was a native of Fife, and in early life became versant in occult science. After studying in Scotland, he went to Oxford and Paris, where he attained wonderful proficiency in philology, mathematics, natural philosophy, and theology. He visited other foreign countries--in particular, Norway, Germany, and Spain. His fame spread over the whole of Europe. His knowledge of natural magic procured for him the appellations of enchanter, magician, wizard. His works recommended him to the favourable notice of Frederick II. of Germany, by whom he was appointed his royal astrologer. To Scott, it is reported, the heavens were as a great book, wherein was written not only the history of nations, but of individuals also. In the vaulted heavens, he declared, man might read his own fortune. He predicted when, where, and how the Emperor Frederick's death would take place. Scott returned to Scotland, when he had the honour of knighthood conferred on him. He performed almost innumerable miracles; and so thoroughly was he believed to be in league with the Devil, that he was tried for sorcery, but through his influence in high quarters, or his subtle arts, he escaped the fangs of the law. Tradition says that upon a certain occasion, being embarrassed by evil spirits, he undertook to find the wicked ones constant employment. Not a few strange feats were gone through, which Scott thought were impossible for Satan himself to perform. Neverthe-less, they were done. One day, the spirits demanded more work; and the wizard ordered that a dam-head should be built across the Tweed at Kelso, to prevent the flow of the river. Next morning the work was found completed. More work was demanded; and this time Scott requested that the Eildon Hill, which had only one cone, should be divided into three parts. Away went the infernal spirits in great glee to perform the task assigned them. On the sun rising the following day, the hill had three cones, as are to be seen at the present time. Back came the wicked beings to intimate that the task was accomplished. This Sir Michael well knew meant a determination to have more work, or to claim him in accordance with an agreement between him and Satan. Scott remembered he had sold himself to his Satanic Majesty, but did not forget that he was entitled to a respite so long as he could procure diabolical work for Satan's favourite imps. "What," Scott asked himself; "is next to be done? Am I to order the world to be turned upside down, and perhaps perish in the ruins? or am I to demand the evil spirits, which torment me night and day, to bring down the sun, moon, and stars, and leave the universe in perpetual darkness? No," replied he, mentally; "to do so, would be to make myself more of a fiend than they that take pleasure in gathering together into the place of torment those who have persistently disobeyed the dictates of reason. Shall I then at once surrender myself to the merciless tyrants, and thereby free the world from an instrument of unrighteousness? Ah!" exclaimed Scott, "life is sweet, and death bitter; let me prolong my days to the utmost limits allowed to man." Exhausted, Sir Michael leaned back on the seat whereon he sat. Long watching, deep study, and vexatious encounters with the evil ones so exhausted him that he fell into a disturbed sleep. In his dreams he beheld the place of torment with all its horrors. The fiery lake looked more dismal than anything he had heard described, or what he could have imagined. Within were many known faces; every one endeavoured to excel the other in his endeavour to make the place what it was in-tended to be--a place of torment. No one repented of his wicked deeds or expected mercy. The gates of the unholy place were thrown open, and in went the chief spirit that had so often communed with Scott. Like a furnace door, the gate was closed after him. What took place may be imagined. Again the red-hot gate turned on its hinges, and out came Satan, with a thousand of his swiftest messengers, to bring home Sir Michael, against whom a charge was pending of breach of bargain. Horror-stricken, the sleeper started to his feet, and to his great relief found none but his old familiar spirits before him. "Work, more work," said the spirits. "Yes, work, endless work," shouted Scott. "Go," said he, "and make the sea-sand into ropes." With a gloomy countenance the fiends departed, never to return to molest the enchanter. For aught that is known, says the legend, the spirits may still be endeavouring to perform the impossible task of making ropes out of sea-sand. All parties are not agreed as to how Sir Michael Scott died, nor where he was interred, but the general belief as to where his remains rest is, that he was buried, together with his magic books, at Melrose Abbey.

Assuming that the poems asserted to be those of Ossian are authentic, we see there was in his time a general belief that ghosts and spirits floated through the air, that the dead revisited the earth, that the destiny of man was under the control of supernatural beings, and that the astonishing power of witches was real, and not imaginary. This is abundantly proved (always assuming the authenticity of the Ossianic poems) by the work before us, from which we take the following quotations:--

> "Fingal advanced his steps wide through the bosom of
> night, to where the trees of Loda shook amid squally
> winds.... I beheld the dark moon descending behind thy
> resounding woods. On thy top dwells the misty Loda,
> the house of the spirits of men. I saw a deer at
> Crona's stream; a mossy bank he seemed through the
> gloom, but soon he bounded away. A meteor played round
> his branching horns; the awful faces of other times
> looked from the clouds of Crona. These are the signs
> of Fingal's death. The king of shields is fallen, and
> Caracul prevails. 'Rise, Comala, from thy rock;
> daughter of Sarno, rise in tears. The youth of thy
> love is low; his ghost is on our hills.'...

> "Autumn is dark on the mountains; grey mists rest on
> the hills. The whirlwind is heard on the heath. Dark
> rolls the river through the narrow plain. A tree
> stands alone on the hill, and marks the slumbering
> Connal. The leaves whirl round with the wind, and
> strew the grave of the dead. At times are seen here
> the ghosts of the departed, when the musing hunter
> alone stalks over the heath....

> "The deer of the mountain avoids the place, for he
> beholds a dim ghost standing there. The mighty lie, O
> Malvina! in the narrow plain of the rock.

> "Often did I turn my ship, but the winds of the east
> prevailed. Nor Clutha ever since I have seen, nor
> Moina of the dark-brown hair. She fell in Balclutha,
> for I have seen her ghost. I knew her as she came
> through the dusky night, along the murmur of Lora: she
> was like the new moon, seen through the gathered mist,
> when the sky pours down its flaky snow, and the world

is silent and dark. 'Raise, ye bards,' said the mighty
Fingal, 'the praise of unhappy Moina. Call her ghost,
with your songs, to our hills, that she may rest with
the fair of Morven, the sunbeams of other days, the
delight of heroes of old.'...

"The night passed away in song; morning returned in
joy. The mountains showed their grey heads; the blue
face of ocean smiled. The white wave is seen tumbling
round the distant rock; a mist rose slowly from the
lake. It came in the figure of an aged man along the
silent plain. Its large limbs did not move in steps,
for a ghost supported it in mid air. It came towards
Selma's hall, and dissolved in a shower of blood.

"The king alone beheld the sight; he foresaw the death
of the people....

"'My spirit, Connal, is on my hills: my corse on the
sands of Erin. Thou shalt never talk with Crugal, nor
find his lone steps in the heath. I am light as the
blast of Cromla. I move like the shadow of mist!
Connal, son of Colgar, I see a cloud of death: it
hovers dark over the plains of Lena. The sons of green
Erin must fall. Remove from the field of ghosts.' Like
the darkened moon, he retired in the midst of the
whistling blast. 'Stay,' said the mighty Connal,
'stay, my dark-red friend. Lay by that beam of heaven,
son of the windy Cromla! What cave is thy lonely
house? What green-headed hill the place of thy repose?
Shall we not hear thee in the storm? in the noise of
the mountain stream? when the feeble sons of the wind
come forth, and, scarcely seen, pass over the
desert.'...

"'Sons of Cona!' Fingal cried aloud, 'stop the hand of
death. Mighty was he that is low; much is he mourned
in Sora! The stranger will come towards his hill, and
wonder why it is so silent. The king is fallen, O
stranger! The joy of his house is ceased. Listen to

the sound of his woods. Perhaps the ghost is murmuring there! But he is far distant, on Morven, beneath the sword of foreign foe.'

"Lorma sat in Aldo's hall. She sat at the light of a flaming oak. The night came down, but he did not return. The soul of Lorma is sad. 'What detained thee, hunter of Cona? thou didst promise to return. Has the deer been distant far? Do the dark winds sigh round thee on the heath? I am in the land of strangers; who is my friend but Aldo? Come from the sounding hills, O my best beloved.'

"Her eyes are turned towards the gate. She listens to the rustling blast. She thinks it is Aldo's tread. Joy rises in her face! But storm returns again, like a thin cloud on the moon.... His thin ghost appeared on a rock, like a watery beam of feeble light, when the moon rushes sudden from between two clouds, and the midnight shower is on the field. She followed the empty form over the heath. She knew that her hero fell. I heard her approaching cries on the wind, like the mournful voice of the breeze, when it sighs on the grass of the cave!

"She came. She found her hero! Her voice was heard no more. Silent she rolled her eyes. She was pale, and wildly sad! Few her days on Cona. She sank into the tomb. Fingal commanded his bards; they sang over the death of Lorma. The daughters of Morven mourned her for one day in the year, when the dark winds of autumn returned."

In Ossianic times there were prophets and prophetesses, who were consulted by the chiefs of armies and by the common people on important occasions. Even a thousand years after the time of Ossian, the bards uttered their prophetic sayings. We have the story of five bards passing an October night in the house of a chief, who, like his guests, was a poet, entertaining their hearers with poetic descriptions of the night. The first bard delivered himself thus:

"Night is dull and dark. The clouds rest on the hills.
No star with green trembling beam; no moon looks from
the sky. I hear the blast in the wood, but I hear it
distant far. The stream of the valley murmurs, but its
murmur is sullen and sad. From the tree, at the grave
of the dead, the long-howling owl is heard. I see a
dim form on the plain! It is a ghost! it fades, it
flies. Some funeral shall pass this way: the meteor
marks the path. The distant dog is howling from the
hut of the hill. The stag lies on the mountain moss:
the hind is at his side. She hears the wind in his
branchy horns. She starts, but lies again. The roe is
in the cleft of the rock; the heath-cock's head is
beneath his wing. No beast nor bird is abroad, but the
owl and the howling fox. She on a leafless tree; he in
a cloud on the hill. Dark, panting, trembling, sad,
the traveller has lost his way. Through shrubs,
through thorns he goes, along the gurgling mill. He
fears the rock and the fen. He fears the ghost of
night. The old tree groans to the blast; the falling
branch resounds. The wind drives the weathered burs,
clung together, along the grass. It is the light tread
of a ghost! He trembles amidst the night. Dark,
dusky, howling night, cloudy, windy, and full of
ghosts! The dead are abroad! My friends, receive me
from the night."

The second bard says:

"The wind is up. The shower descends. The spirit of
the mountain shrieks. Woods fall from high. Windows
flap. The growing river roars. The traveller attempts
the ford. Hark! that shriek! He dies! The storm drives
the horse from the hill, the goat, the lowing cow.
They tremble as drives the shower, beside the
mouldering bank. The hunter starts from sleep, in his
lonely hut; he wakes, the fire decayed. His wet dogs
smoke around him. He fills the chinks with heath. Loud
roar two mountain streams, which meet beside his
booth. Sad on the side of the hill the wandering

shepherd sits. The tree resounds beside him. The stream roars down the rock. He waits for the rising moon to guide him to his home. Ghosts ride on the storm to-night. Sweet is their voice between the squalls of wind. Their songs are of other worlds. The rain is past. The dry wind blows. Streams roar and windows flap. Cold drops fall from the roof. I see the starry sky. But the shower gathers again. The west is gloomy and dark. Night is stormy and dismal. Receive me, my friends, from night."

The third bard sings:

"The wind still sounds between the hills, and whistles through the grass of the rock. The firs fall from their place. The turfy hut is torn. The clouds divided, fly over the sky, and show the burning stars. The meteor, token of death, flies sparkling through the gloom. It rests on the hill. I see the withered form, the dark-browed rock, the fallen oak. Who is that in his shroud beneath the tree by the stream? The waves dark tumble on the lake, and lash its rocky sides. A maid sits sad beside the rock, and eyes the rolling stream. Her lover promised to come. She saw his boat, when yet it was light, on the lake. Is this his broken boat on the shore? Are these his groans on the wind? Hark! the hail rattles around. The flaky snow descends. The tops of the hills are white. The stormy wind abates. Various is the night, and cold. Receive me, my friends, from night."

The fourth bard takes up the theme thus:

"Night is calm and fair; blue, starry, settled is night. The winds, with the clouds, are gone. They sink behind the hill. The moon is up on the mountain. Trees glister; streams shine on the rock. Bright rolls the settled lake; bright the stream of the vale. I see the trees overturned; the shocks of corn on the plain. The wakeful hind rebuilds the shocks, and whistles on

the distant field. Calm, settled, fair is night! Who
comes from the place of the dead? That form with the
robe of snow; white arms with dark-brown hair! It is
the daughter of the chief of the people--she that
lately fell! Come, let us view thee, O maid! thou that
hast been the delight of heroes! The blast drives the
phantom away; white, without form, it ascends the
hill. The breeze drives the blue mist slowly over the
narrow vale. It rises on the hill, and joins its head
to heaven. Night is settled, calm, blue, starry,
bright with the moon. Receive me not, my friends, for
lovely is the night."

The fifth bard chants:

"Night is calm, but dreary. The moon is in a cloud in
the west. Slow moves that pale beam along the shaded
hill. The distant wave is heard. The torrent murmurs
on the rock. The cock is heard from the booth. More
than half the night is past. The housewife, groping in
the gloom, rekindles the settled fire. The hunter
thinks the day approaches, and calls his bounding
dogs. He ascends the hill, and whistles on his way. A
blast removes the clouds. He sees the starry plough of
the north. Much of the night is to pass. He nods by
the mossy rock. Hark! the whirlwind is in the woods! A
low murmur in the vale! It is the mighty army of the
dead returning from the air. The moon rests behind the
hill. The beam is still on the lofty rock. Long are
the shadows of the trees. Now it is dark all over.
Night is dreary, silent, and dark. Receive me, my
friends, from the night."

The chief replies:

"Let clouds rest on the hills, spirits fly, and
travellers fear. Let the winds of the woods arise, the
sounding storms descend. Roar streams, and windows
flap, and green-winged meteors fly! Let the pale moon,
from behind the hills, enclose her head in clouds!

Night is alike to me, blue, stormy, or gloomy the sky.
Night flies before the beam when it is poured on the
hill. The young day returns from his clouds, but we
return no more.... Raise the song, and strike the
harp; send round the shells of joy. Suspend a hundred
tapers on high. Maids and youths, begin to dance. Let
some grey bard be near me to tell the deeds of other
times, of kings renowned in our land, of chiefs we
behold no more. Thus let the night pass until morning
shall appear on our hills. Then let the bow be at
hand, the dogs, the youths of the chase. We shall
ascend the hill with day, and awake the deer."

From the foregoing, we obtain a glimpse of the superstitions and customs of remote ages. Greek mythology is confessedly the creation of poets; and to the bards of our own country we are indebted for some of our strangest fictions. Fletcher of Saltoun must have been fully aware of the poetic influence; for he expressed himself as willing to let any one who pleased make the laws, if he were permitted to compose the national ballads.

CHAPTER XVII.

Shakspeare--An Outline of his Composition--"The   Tempest"--Ship at Sea
in a Storm--Miranda beseeching   Prospero to allay the Wild Waters--Ariel's
Readiness   to serve his Master--The Witch Sycorax--Ariel kept in   a Cloven
Pine twelve years--Caliban's Evil   Wish--Mischief by Ariel--Neptune chased-
-Charmed   Circle--Miracles--"Midsummer Night's Dream"--Exploits   of a
Fairy--Doings of Puck--Charmed Flower--Titania   and her Attendants--Ghosts
and   Spirits--Song--"Macbeth"--Weird Sisters--Hecate and   the Witches-
-Magic Arts--Macbeth's Doom--Witches'   Caldron--Macbeth admonished by
Spirits--Eight Kings   and Banquo's Spirit--Noblemen warned by a   Spirit--
"Antony and Cleopatra"--Dreadful   Apparition--King's Death avenged.

Shakspeare, the immortal English poet, born in the year 1564, has assisted in no small degree
to spread the knowledge of superstition. So opportunely do his works come to support our
statements, that we are induced to give, in prose and verse, an outline of certain portions of
his compositions touching the many mysterious subjects on which he wrote.

In the *Tempest* there is a ship at sea in a storm, with thunder and lightning. On board are the
master, boatswain, mariners, Alonso, Sebastian, Antonio, Ferdinand, Gonzalo, and others. The ship
is thought to be in danger; but Gonzalo tells his companions to take comfort, for he thought the
boatswain had no drowning mark upon him, his complexion being perfectly gallows-like. "If," said
Gonzalo, "he be not born to be hanged, our case is miserable." The mariners thought all was lost,
and went to prayers.

Miranda beseeched Prospero, whom she addressed as father, to allay the wild waters in their
roar, and not suffer a brave vessel that had noble creatures in her to sink. Prospero laid aside his
magic garment; and while Miranda slept, Ariel declared his readiness, at the request of Prospero, to
swim, to dive into the fire, to ride on the curled clouds. In answer to Prospero's inquiry whether the
spirit had directed the tempest according to instructions, Ariel answered that he had boarded the
ship, joined Jove's lightnings, and made Neptune's bold waves tremble. Ariel, who thought his services were most valuable to his master, craved his liberty; for Ariel was a bound servant of Prospero
for a specified time. Prospero reminded the spirit that he had freed him from torment; and asked
if he remembered the witch Sycorax, famed for her sorceries, and who had, by the aid of her most
potent ministers, put him (Ariel) into a cloven pine, within whose rift he remained imprisoned for

twelve years, tormented so greatly that his groans made the wolves howl, and penetrated the breast of every bear. Sycorax could not, proceeded Prospero, undo what she had done; it was his art alone that made the pine gape and set him free. Then he threatened the spirit that if he again murmured, he would send an oak, and peg him in its knotty trunk till he had howled away twelve winters. The spirit asked pardon, and declared his readiness to obey Prospero's commands. Prospero promised that if he did so, he would discharge him in two days. "Go," said Prospero, "make thyself like to the nymph o' the sea; be subject to no sight but mine; invisible to every eye-ball else. Go take this shape, and hither come in't: hence with diligence." Miranda having been awakened, was invited by Prospero to visit his slave Caliban, son of Sycorax, then dead. Ariel here came before his master, who was pleased with his appearance.

On Prospero calling to Caliban, "Thou poisonous slave, got by the Devil himself," to come forth, Caliban appeared and said, "As wicked dew as e'er my mother brush'd with raven's feather from unwholesome fen, drop on you both!" For this, replied Prospero, thou shalt be tortured this night.

Alonso, Sebastian, Antonio, Gonzalo, Adrian, and Francisco escaped to an island, which to them seemed to be a desert. Caliban found them; and a conspiracy was entered into to kill Prospero and secure the person of Miranda. Solemn and strange music was heard, and several strange shapes appeared at a banquet. Thunder rolled, and lightning flashed: Ariel, in the form of a harpy, clapped his wings upon the table, and the banquet vanished. Prospero gave Ferdinand a rich compensation to make amends for past austere punishments; and that compensation was nothing less than the hand of Miranda. He recommended them to be prudent before their nuptials, and told them that if they disregarded his injunctions in this respect, they would have hate and discord between them. Ariel, by an unseen power, induced Caliban and others whom Prospero desired to have in his cell, to repair thither; but before reaching it they were hunted by divers spirits in the shape of hounds, that chased them to the lime groves, where they were secured as prisoners.

Prospero, addressing the elves of hills, brooks, standing lakes, and groves, those that on the sands with printless foot chased the ebbing Neptune, the demi-puppets that by moonshine made the sour-green ringlets which ewes would not bite, those whose pastime was to make midnight mushrooms, reminded them that he had, among other mighty deeds, by their aid, rifted. Jove's stout oak, plucked up the pine and cedar, and roused sleepers in the grave. But this rough magic, he informed them, he would abjure, after working his airy charms. This being done, he would break his staff, bury it deep in the earth, and drown his book. Ariel re-entered, and after him Alonso, Gonzalo, Sebastian, Antonio, Adrian, and Francisco, and stood charmed within a circle which Prospero had made.

Gonzalo exclaimed, "All torment, trouble, wonder, and amazement inhabit here! Some heavenly power guide us out of this fearful country!" Prospero made himself known to the king as the wronged Duke of Milan. Pardon was sought, and the dukedom resigned. Alonso craved, that if he were Prospero, he should give them particulars of his preservation, and how he met them there, having, but three hours before, been wrecked upon the shore, where he had lost his dear son Ferdinand. A door was opened, and Ferdinand and Miranda were discovered playing at chess. Sebastian declared this to be a most high miracle. Ariel, who had been instructed by Prospero to go to the ship and bring the master and boatswain to him, entered with these worthies. In answer to the question, "What is the news?" the boatswain answered, "The best news is, that we have safely found our king and company; the next, our ship--which, but three glasses since, we gave out split--is tight and yare, and bravely rigged, as when we first put out to sea." The boatswain, in answer to another query how they came thither? replied, if he were awake, he would strive to tell. He remembered hearing strange noises--roaring, shrieking, howling, jingling chains, and more diversity of sounds, all horrible; and when they were wakened (for they had been asleep), they found themselves at liberty. Prospero, pointing out Caliban, told his friends, "This mis-shapen knave's mother was a witch; and one so strong that she could control the moon, make flows and ebbs." Prospero invited the king and his train to take rest in his cell, where he would tell the story of his life, and in the morning bring them to their ship and give them auspicious gales; then, addressing Ariel, he concluded, "Chick, that is thy charge; to the elements, be free, and fare thee well!"

In the *Midsummer Night's Dream* Shakspeare brings forward a fairy at a wood near Athens. The fairy, in answer to Puck's question whither it wandered, replied that it went over hill, over dale, through bush, through brier, over park, over pale, through flood, through fire. It wandered everywhere, swifter than the moon's sphere; it served the fairy queen to dew her orbs upon the green. Puck told the fairy that the king would keep revels there that night, and advised that the queen should not come within his sight; for Oberon was fell and wroth, because she, as her attendant, had a lovely boy, a sweet changeling, and that jealous Oberon would have the child to be a knight of his train to trace the forests.

The fairy asked Puck if he was not the knavish spirit that frightened the maidens of the villagery, that skimmed milk, and sometimes laboured in the green, and bootless made the housewife churn, and sometimes made the drink to bear no barm, and whether Puck did not mislead night wanderers, and then laugh at their harm, and do the work of hobgoblins? Puck acknowledged that the fairy spoke aright; said he was the merry wanderer of the night, playing pranks, and making people laugh. A smart angry discussion took place between Oberon and Titania as to which of them was to have the little changeling boy. They parted in rage, Oberon threatening to torment Titania. Oberon summoned Puck to attend him, and bring the herb he once showed him, the juice of which, laid on sleeping eyelids, made man or woman dote upon the next creature seen. Having this herb's juice, Oberon would watch Titania when she was asleep, and drop the liquor into her eyes, that when she wakened she might pursue the first object she cast eyes on with the soul of love, whether it should be lion, bear, wolf, or bull, or meddling monkey, or busy ape. The delusion accomplished, he would give her another herb to remove the charm, but not before she gave up the boy.

Puck found the charmed flower; and while Oberon was to streak Titania's eyes with some of the juice thereof, Puck was to anoint the eyes of the disdainful youth with another quantity of it, that he might be compelled to adore a sweet Athenian lady in love with him. Puck was then dismissed with instructions to meet Oberon before the first cock-crow. Titania, in another part of the wood, distributed her attendants, some to kill cankers in the musk-rose buds, some to war with bats for their leathern wings to make small elves' coats, and some to keep back the clamorous owl that nightly hooted at the quaint spirits. Having given her instructions, she fell asleep. This was Oberon's opportunity--and one he did not neglect. He squeezed the flower on Titania's eyelids, and disappeared.

Titania wakened with eyes fixed on Bottom, who, by Puck's art, had an ass's head. Nevertheless, she thought him wise and beautiful. She instructed her attendant fairies to be kind and courteous to the gentleman, and to feed him with apricots, dewberries, purple grapes, green figs, and mulberries. Then they were to steal the honey-bags from bumble bees for his service, and to crop their waxen thighs, and light them at the fiery glow-worm's eyes, to show her love to bed; and further, to pluck the wings from butterflies, to fan the moonbeams from his sleeping eyes. By Puck's mistake, the love juice was laid in absence of the fair Athenian lady, and so the object desired was not obtained. In consequence of this, much confusion and misunderstanding followed. To prevent a fight, Oberon, whom Puck addressed as "king of shadows," ordered the night to be overcast with drooping fog, that the rivals might be led astray. Other instructions were given, which Puck suggested should be done quickly, as in the distance shone Aurora's harbinger, at whose approach ghosts, wandering here and there, trooped home to churchyards. Damned spirits, he said, that had burial in cross-ways and floods, had already gone to their wormy beds, lest day should look on their shame. Oberon began to pity Titania, and, touching her eyes with an herb, her love for the loathsome visage she had admired for ever vanished.

The *Midsummer Night's Dream* concludes with the following song, if we except Puck's address:

> "Now, until the break of day,
> Through this house each fairy stray,
> To the best bride-bed will we,
> Which by us shall blessed be;
> And the issue, there create,
> Ever shall be fortunate.
> So shall all the couples three
> Ever true and loving be:
> And the blots of nature's hand
> Shall not in their issue stand;
> Never mole, hare-lip, nor scar,
> Nor mark prodigious such as are
> Despised in nativity,
> Shall upon their children be,--
> With this field-dew consecrate,
> Every fairy take his gait;
> And each several chamber bless,
> Through this palace with sweet peace:
> E'er shall it in safety rest,
> And the owner of it blest.

   Trip away,
   Make no stay;
  Meet me all by break of day."

In gleaning from *Macbeth*, we shall pass over the weird sisters' predictions as lightly as possible, without breaking the connecting links, though we are greatly tempted to incorporate a considerable part of this play into our collection of tales and traditions, seeing that, in our opinion, none of Shakspeare's works bring out more graphically the superstition of past ages than the poet's *Macbeth*.

The play is represented as beginning in an open place, where, in a thunder-storm, three witches appeared and disappeared without doing any important deed of darkness. They met again on a heath, in another thunder-storm. One of them told the other hags that she had been away killing swine. Another told tales of a sailor's wife who had gone to Aleppo, and threatened to sail thither in a sieve. Macbeth and Banquo discovered the witches and saluted them. Through the women's subtlety, the fiend entered Macbeth's heart, and induced him to form the bloody plans of removing all obstacles in the way of his obtaining the crown, and handing it down to his descendants. First one victim, and then another, fell under his treachery. He was sorely troubled: the ghost of Banquo haunted him.

Hecate joined the witches on the heath, and upbraided them for trading and trafficking with Macbeth without consulting her, the mistress of their charms. Away the witches were sent, with instructions to meet at the pit of Acheron in the morning. There Macbeth was to know his destiny. Vessels and spells the hags were to provide, while Hecate was to catch a vaporous drop that hung on the corner of the moon, before it touched the ground. That drop, distilled by magic sleights, would raise such sprites, that by the strength of their illusion would draw Macbeth to confusion. Such, Hecate declared, would be his doom for spurning fate, scorning death, and bearing his hopes above wisdom, grace, and fear.

The three witches met in a dark cave, and, while the thunder rolled without, they boiled a cauldron of hellish soup, the ingredients of which may be gathered from the following lines:--

  1 **Witch**. "Thrice the brindled cat hath mew'd.

  2 **Witch**. Thrice; and once the hedge-pig whined.

  3 **Witch**. Harper cries: 'Tis time, 'tis time.

  1 **Witch**. Round about the cauldron go;
      In the poison'd entrails throw.--
      Toad, that under coldest stone,
      Days and nights has thirty-one
      Swelter'd venom sleeping got,
      Boil thou first i' the charmed pot.

All.   Double, double toil and trouble;
         Fire, burn; and, cauldron, bubble.

2 *Witch*.   Fillet of a fenny snake,
         In the cauldron boil and bake;
         Eye of newt, and toe of frog,
         Wool of bat, and tongue of dog,
         Adder's fork, and blind-worm's sting,
         Lizard's leg, and owlet's wing,
         For a charm of powerful trouble,
         Like a hell-broth boil and bubble.

All.   Double, double toil and trouble;
         Fire, burn; and, cauldron, bubble.

3 *Witch*.   Scale of dragon; tooth of wolf;
         Witches' mummy; maw and gulf
         Of the ravin'd salt-sea shark;
         Root of hemlock, digg'd i' the dark;
         Liver of blaspheming Jew;
         Gall of goat; and slips of yew,
         Silver'd in the moon's eclipse;
         Nose of Turk, and Tartar's lips;
         Finger of birth-strangled babe,
         Ditch delivered by a drab,--
         Make the gruel thick and slab:
         Add thereto a tiger's chaudron,
         For the ingredients of our cauldron.

All.   Double, double toil and trouble;
         Fire, burn; and, cauldron, bubble.

2 *Witch*.   Cool it with a baboon's blood;
         Then the charm is firm and good.

Hecate.   O, well done! I commend your pains;
         And every one shall share i' the gains.
         And now about the cauldron sing,

Like elves and fairies in a ring,
Enchanting all that you put in.

SONG.

'Black spirits and white,
  Red spirits and grey;
Mingle, mingle, mingle,
  You that mingle may.'

2 **Witch**.   By the pricking of my thumbs,
          Something wicked this way comes:--
          Open, locks, whoever knocks."

Macbeth appeared and demanded what the midnight hags were about. The reply was, "A deed without a name." He entreated them, by that which they professed, to answer him. One of the witches asked whether he would rather have his answer from their mouths or from their masters'. On Macbeth desiring to see the masters, witch No. 1 directed that the blood of a sow that had eaten her nine farrow, and grease that had been sweaten from the murderer's gibbet, should be thrown into the flame. Accompanied by a clap of thunder, an armed head rose, and admonished Macbeth to beware of Macduff. Another demon, more potent, in the shape of a bloody child, rose and bade Macbeth be courageous; to laugh to scorn the power of man, for none born of woman could harm him. A second child, after the first had descended into the bowels of the earth, told the king that he would not be vanquished till great Birnam wood to high Dunsinane hill should come against him. The monarch was admonished to ask no more, but he disregarded the warning. "Why sinks that cauldron? and what noise is this?" he asked. Eight kings, and Banquo following, appeared to Macbeth's vision. The whole vision, if such it could be called, surprised him greatly; but no part of it so much as the spirit of Banquo, whom he had cruelly put to death with the intention of frustrating destiny, as revealed to him by the weird sisters, when he first met them on the heath. Seeing the king dejected, the witches, to cheer him, danced and sang for a time, and then suddenly disappeared.

Before Macbeth had time to recover from his reverie, a messenger arrived to inform him that Macduff, whom he dreaded, had fled to England. So greatly was he exasperated by the tidings, that he declared his intention of seizing Macduff's castle, giving to the sword his wife, babes, and all his other relations of whatever degree. This threat he partly carried into execution.

The day of vengeance was near. Macbeth, mad with fear and ambition, strove to avert the evil brooding over him, but he could not succeed. The fiat had gone forth: he was king, as the weird sisters had foretold he would be, but all his bloody deeds, and the scheming of his queen, unscrupulous like himself, could not change the decree. Birnam wood seemed to come to Dunsinane, and Banquo's seed came in due time to inherit the throne the fates had reserved for them.

In *King Henry the Sixth* more light is thrown on the doings of evil spirits. On a deep dark night, the time when owls cried, dogs howled, spirits walked, and ghosts broke up their graves, a spirit rose, in compliance with certain ceremonies for making demons appear. Bolingbroke inquired of the evil one what would become of the king? The reply was, "The duke yet lives that Henry shall depose. But him outlive, and die a violent death." In answer to the question, "What fate awaits the Duke of Suffolk?" came the reply, "By water shall he die." The Duke of Somerset was advised by the spirit to shun castles. Having thus delivered itself, the evil spirit descended to the burning lake. Farther on in the piece we are told of a witch that was condemned to be burned at Smithfield.

Passing from *Henry the Sixth*, we come to *Antony and Cleopatra*, and proceed to glean a few sentences bearing on superstition.

Charmian, addressing Alexas in a flattering manner, asked where was the soothsayer he praised so much. The soothsayer, who was immediately forthcoming, told those who listened to him that he knew "things" from nature's book of secrecy. A banquet was prepared, at which Charmian asked the soothsayer to give him good luck. "I make not, but foresee," was the response. Charmian, Alexas, and their companions seek to hear their fortunes told, but the soothsayer did not choose to reveal anything important at that time.

We shall take leave of Shakspeare by noticing, in a few sentences, the ghost of Hamlet's father.

Bernardo, Marcellus, and Horatio were met at a late hour to talk over a dreadful apparition that had disturbed the two former on the previous night, when they were startled by the same apparition--a ghost making its appearance. They observed it resembled the king who was dead. Horatio charged it to speak, but it stalked away without deigning a reply. It reappeared, but suddenly vanished on hearing the cock crow. How long elapsed we are not informed; but on a certain night, just after the clock had struck twelve, Hamlet, Horatio, and Marcellus were engaged in earnest conversation when they were alarmed. The first entreats the ghost to say wherefore it visited them. It beckoned to Hamlet to follow it; and he did so, despite those who were with him, and saw the spirit as well as he did. The ghost's tongue was unloosed, and thus it spake: "Lend thy serious hearing to what I shall unfold: My hour is almost come, when I must render up myself to sulphurous and tormenting flames. I am thy father's spirit; and, for the day, confined to fast in fires, till the foul crimes, done in my days of nature, are burnt and purged away. Were I not forbidden to tell the secrets of my prison-house, I could a tale unfold that would harrow up thy soul; freeze thy young blood; make thy eyes start; and make thy locks part like quills upon the fretful porcupine: but this eternal blazon must not be. If ever thou didst love thy father, revenge his foul and most unnatural murder." "Murder!" exclaimed Hamlet. "Murder," said the ghost, "most foul, as in the best it is." "Reveal it," gasped Hamlet, "that I may with swift wings sweep to my revenge." "Thou shouldst be duller than the fat weed that rots itself on Lethe's wharf, wert thou not to stir in this," ejaculated the spirit. The ghost continued: "It has been given out, that, when sleeping in mine orchard, a serpent stung me to death; but know thou that the serpent that did sting thy father now wears his crown.... Sleeping within my orchard, as my custom was in the afternoon, on my secure hour thy uncle stole with cursed juice of hebenon in a vial, and did pour the leprous distilment into mine ears, that curdled my blood. Thus was I, by a brother's hand, despatched from crown and queen; cut off in the blossoms of my sin, unprepared, disappointed, and, without extreme unction, sent to my account with all my imperfections on my head. O, horrible! most horrible! Let not the royal bed be a couch for luxury and damned incest. Farewell; the glow-worm shows the morning to be near, and begins to pale his ineffectual fire: Adieu! Remember me." The king's death was avenged. The treacherous queen, and he who murdered the monarch, drank a poisoned cup, and thus received measure for measure.

CHAPTER XVIII.

The Poet Gay--The "Spell"--Hobnelia--Lubberkin going   to Town--A
Maiden fine--Spells resorted to--Marking   the Ground, and turning three times
round--Hempseed as   a Charm--Valentine Day--A Snail used in   Divination--
Burning Nuts--Pea-cods as a   Spell--Ladybird sent on a Message of Love--Pippin
Parings--Virtue of United Garters--Love   Powder--Gipsies' Warnings--Knives
sever Love--Story of   Boccaccio--Apparition of a Deceased Lover--Poems by
Burns--"Address to the Deil"--"Tam o' Shanter."

John Gay, the old English poet, writes in his *Spell*:

"Hobnelia, seated in a dreary vale,
In pensive mood rehearsed her piteous tale;
Her piteous tale the winds in sighs bemoan,
And pining Echo answers groan for groan.
   I rue the day, a rueful day I trow,
   The woeful day, a day indeed of woe!
When Lubberkin to town his cattle drove,
A maiden fine bedight he kept in love;
The maiden fine bedight his love retains,
And for the village he forsakes the plains.
Return, my Lubberkin, these ditties hear,
Spells will I try, and spells shall ease my care.
   With my sharp heel I three times mark the ground,
   And turn me thrice around, around, around.
When first the year I heard the cuckoo sing,
And call with welcome note the budding spring,
I straightway set a-running with such haste,
Deb'rah that won the smock scarce ran so fast;
Till, spent for lack of breath, quite weary grown,
Upon a rising bank I sat adown,
Then doff'd my shoe, and, by my troth, I swear,

Therein I spy'd this yellow frizzled hair,
As like to Lubberkin's in curle and hue,
As if upon his comely pate it grew.
   With my sharp heel I three times mark the ground,
   And turn me thrice around, around, around.
At eve last summer no sleep I sought,
But to the field a bag of hempseed brought,
I scattered round the seed on every side,
And three times in a trembling accent cry'd:
This hempseed with my virgin hand I sow,
Who shall my true love be, the crop shall mow.
I straight look'd back, and if my eyes speak true,
With his keen scythe behind me came the youth.
   With my sharp heel I three times mark the ground,
   And turn me thrice around, around, around.
Last Valentine, the day when birds of kind
Their paramours with mutual chirping find,
I early rose, just at the break of day,
Before the sun had chas'd the stars away;
Afield I went, amid the morning dew,
To milk my kine (for so should housewives do).
The first I spy'd, and the first swain we see,
In spite of fortune shall our true love be;
See, Lubberkin, each bird his partner take,
And canst thou then thy sweetheart dear forsake?
   With my sharp heel I three times mark the ground,
   And turn me thrice around, around, around.
Last May-day fair I searched to find a snail
That might my secret lover's name reveal;
Upon a gooseberry bush a snail I found,
For always snails nearest sweetest fruit abound.
I seiz'd the vermin, home I quickly sped,
And on the hearth the milk-white embers spread.
Slow crawl'd the snail, and, if I right can spell,
In the soft ashes mark'd a curious L:
O may this wonderous omen luck prove!
For L is found in Lubberkin and love.
   With my sharp heel I three times mark the ground,
   And turn me thrice around, around, around.
Two hazel nuts I threw into the flame,

And to each nut I gave a sweetheart's name,
This with the loudest bounce me sore amaz'd,
That in a flame of brightest colour blaz'd.
As blaz'd the nut, so may thy passion grow,
For 'twas thy nut that did so brightly glow.
   With my sharp heel I three times mark the ground,
   And turn me thrice around, around, around.
As pea-cods once I pluck'd, I chanc'd to see
One that was closely fill'd with three times three,
Which, when I crop't, I safely home convey'd,
And o'er the door the spell in secret laid,
My wheel I turn'd, and sung a ballad new,
While from the spindle I the fleeces drew;
The latch mov'd up, when who should first come in,
But in his proper person--Lubberkin.
I broke my yarn, surpris'd the sight to see,
Sure sign that he would break his word with me.
Eftsoons I joined it with my wonted slight,
So may his love again with mine unite.
   With my sharp heel I three times mark the ground,
   And turn me thrice around, around, around.
This lady-fly I take from off the grass,
Whose spotted back might scarlet red surpass.
Fly, lady-bird, north, south, or east, or west,
Fly where the man is found that I love best.
He leaves my hand; see, to the west he's flown,
To call my true love from the faithless town.
   With my sharp heel I three times mark the ground,
   And turn me thrice around, around, around.
I pare my pippin round and round again,
My shepherd's name to flourish on the plain,
I fling th' unbroken paring o'er my head,
Upon the grass a perfect L I read;
Yet on my heart a fairer L is seen
Than what the paring marks upon the green.
   With my sharp heel I three times mark the ground,
   And turn me thrice around, around, around.
This pippin shall another trial make,
See from the core two kernels brown I take;
This on my cheek for Lubberkin is worn,

And Boobyclod on t' other side is borne.
But Boobyclod soon drops upon the ground,
A certain token that his love's unsound,
While Lubberkin sticks firmly to the last;
O were his lips to mine but joined so fast!
     With my sharp heel I three times mark the ground,
     And turn me thrice around, around, around.
As Lubberkin once slept beneath a tree,
I twitch'd his dangling garter from his knee;
He wist not when the hempen string I drew.
Now mine I quickly doff of inkle blue;
Together fast I tye the garters twain,
And while I knit the knot, repeat the strain:
Three times a true-love's knot I tye secure,
Firm be the knot, firm may his love endure.
     With my sharp heel I three times mark the ground,
     And turn me thrice around, around, around.
As I was wont, I trudged last market day
To town with new-laid eggs preserved in hay.
I made my market long before 'twas night,
My purse grew heavy, and my basket light.
Straight to the 'pothecary's shop I went,
And in love powder all my money spent;
Behap what will, next Sunday, after prayers,
When to the ale-house Lubberkin repairs,
The golden charm into his mug I'll throw,
And soon the swain with fervent love shall glow.
     With my sharp heel I three times mark the ground,
     And turn me thrice around, around, around.
But hold: our Lightfoot barks and cocks his ears,
O'er yonder stile see Lubberkin appears.
He comes, he comes, Hobnelia's not bewray'd,
Nor shall she, crown'd with willow, die a maid.
He vows, he swears he'll give me a green gown;
O dear! I fall adown, adown, adown."

Gay also writes:

"Last Friday's eve, when, as the sun was set,
I, near yon stile, three sallow gipsies met,

Upon my hand they cast a poring look,
Bid me beware, and thrice their heads they shook;
They said that many crosses I must prove,
Some in my worldly gain, but most in love.
Next morn I missed three hens and our old cock,
And off the hedge two pinners and a smock.
I bore these losses with a Christian mind,
And no mishap could feel while thou wert kind;
But since, alas! I grew my Colin's scorn,
I've known no pleasure, night, or noon, or morn.
Help me, ye gipsies, bring him home again,
And to a constant lass give back her swain.
Have I not sat with thee full many a night,
When dying embers were our only light,
When every creature did in slumber lie,
Besides our cat, my Colin Clout, and I?
No troublous thoughts the cat or Colin move,
While I alone am kept awake by love.
Remember, Colin, when at last year's wake
I bought the costly present for thy sake:
Could thou spell o'er the posy on thy knife,
And with another change thy state of life?
If thou forget'st, I wot I can repeat,
My memory can tell the verse so sweet:
'As this is grav'd upon this knife of thine,
So is thy image on this heart of mine.'
But woe is me! such presents luckless prove,
For knives, they tell me, always sever love."

In the story of *Isabella*, by Boccaccio, there are touching incidents
of the apparition of a deceased lover appearing to his mistress. The
tale is thus rendered by Keats:

"It was a vision. In the drowsy gloom,
  The dull of midnight, at her couch's foot
Lorenzo stood and wept: the forest tomb
  Had marr'd his glossy hair, which once could shoot
Lustre into the sun, and put cold doom
  Upon his lips, and taken the soft lute
From his lorn voice, and passt his loomed ears

Had made a miry channel for his tears.

Strange sound it was, when the pale shadow spoke;
  For there was striving in its piteous tongue,
To speak as when on earth it was awake,
  And Isabella on its music hung:
Languor there was in it, and tremulous shake,
  As in a palsied Druid's harp unstrung;
And through it moaned a ghostly under-song,
Like hoarse night gusts sepulchral biers among.

Its eyes, though wild, were still all dewy bright
  With love, and kept all phantom fear aloof
From the poor girl by magic of their bright,
  The while it did unthread the horrid woof
Of the late darkened time--the murd'rous spite
  Of pride and avarice--the dark pine roof
In the forest--and the sodden turfed dell,
When, without any word, from stabs it fell.

Saying moreover, 'Isabel, my sweet!
  Red whortle-berries droop above my head,
And a large flint-stone weighs upon my feet,
  Around me beeches and high chesnuts shed
Their leaves and prickly nuts; a sheep-fold bleat
  Comes from beyond the river to my bed:
Go shed one tear upon my heather-bloom,
And it shall comfort me within the tomb.

'I am a shadow now, alas! alas!
  Upon the skirts of human nature dwelling
Alone: I chaunt alone the holy mass,
  While little sounds of life around me knelling,
And glossy bees at noon do fieldward pass,
  And many a chapel bell the hour is telling,
Paining me through: these sounds grow strange to me,
And thou art distant in humanity.'"

Let us now see what Burns, the never-to-be-forgotten Scottish poet,
says in his **Address to the Deil** and **Tam o' Shanter**. In his own

felicitous way he brings out the belief the ancient inhabitants had of visible devils, water-kelpies, spunkies, witches, charms, spells, and many other forms of superstition.

ADDRESS TO THE DEIL.

"O thou! whatever title suit thee,
Auld Hornie, Satan, Nick, or Clootie,
Wha in yon cavern grim an' sootie,
        Closed under hatches,
Spairges about the brunstane cootie,
        To scaud poor wretches.

  Hear me, auld Hangie, for a wee,
An' let poor damned bodies be;
I'm sure sma' pleasure it can gie,
        E'en to a deil,
To skelp and scaud poor dogs like me,
        An' hear us squeel?

  Great is thy pow'r, and great thy fame;
Far kend and noted is thy name:
An' tho' yon lowin' heugh's thy hame,
        Thou travels far;
An' faith! thou's neither lag nor lame,
        Nor blate nor scaur.

  Whyles ranging like a roarin' lion
For prey, a' holes and corners tryin';
Whyles on the strong-winged tempest flyin',
        Tirling the kirks;
Whyles, in the human bosom pryin',
        Unseen thou lurks.

I've heard my reverend grannie say,
In lanely glens you like to stray;
Or where auld ruined castles grey
        Nod to the moon,
Ye fright the nightly wand'rer's way,
        Wi' eldritch croon.

When twilight did my grannie summon
To say her prayers, douce honest woman!
Aft yont the dyke she's heard you bummin'
      Wi' eerie drone;
Or, rustlin', thro' the boortrees comin',
      Wi' heavy groan.

  Ae dreary, windy, winter night,
The stars shot down wi' sklentin' light,
Wi' you, mysel', I got a fright,
      Ayont the lough;
Ye, like a rash-bush stood in sight,
      Wi' waving sough.

  The cudgel in my nieve did shake,
Each bristled hair stood like a stake,
When wi' an eldritch stour, quaick--quaick--
      Amang the springs,
Awa ye squatter'd like a drake,
      On whistling wings.

  Let warlocks grim, and wither'd hags,
Tell how wi' you on ragweed nags,
They skim the muirs, and dizzy crags,
      Wi' wicked speed;
And in kirk-yards renew their leagues
      Owre howkit dead.

  Thence countra wives, wi' toil an' pain,
May plunge an' plunge the kirn in vain;
For oh! the yellow treasure's ta'en
      By witching skill;
An' dawtet, twal-pint Hawkie's gaen
      As yell's the bill.

  Then mystic knots mak great abuse,
On young guidman, fond, keen, and crouse,
When the best wark-lume i' the house,
      By cantrip wit,

Is instant made no worth a louse,
      Just at the bit.

  When thaws dissolve the snawy hoord,
An' float the jinglin' icy-boord,
Then water-kelpies haunt the foord,
      By your direction,
An' 'nighted trav'llers are allured
      To their destruction.

  An' aft your moss-traversing spunkies
Decoy the wight that late and drunk is;
The bleezin', curst, mischievous monkeys
      Delude his eyes,
Till in some miry slough he sunk is,
      Ne'er mair to rise.

  When masons' mystic word an' grip
In storms an' tempests raise you up,
Some cock or cat your rage maun stop,
      Or, strange to tell,
The youngest brother ye wad whip
      Aff straught to hell!

  Lang syne, in Eden's bonnie yaird,
When youthfu' lovers first were pair'd,
An' a' the soul of love they shared,
      The raptured hour,
Sweet on the fragrant flowery swaird
      In shady bower!

  Then you, ye auld, sneck-drawing dog!
Ye came to Paradise *incog.*,
An' played on man a cursed brogue,
      (Black be your fa'!)
An' gied the infant world a shog,
      'Maist ruined a'.

  D'ye mind that day, when in a bizz,
Wi' reekit duds and reestit gizz,

Ye did present your smoutie phiz
    'Mang better folk,
An' sklented on the man of Uz
    Your spitefu' joke?

  An' how ye gat him in your thrall,
An' brak him out o' house an' hall,
While scabs and blotches did him gall
    Wi' bitter claw,
An' lowsed his ill-tongued wicked scaw,
    Was warst ava?

  But a' your doings to rehearse,
Your wily snares an' fechtin' fierce,
Sin' that day Michael did you pierce,
    Down to this time,
Wad ding a Lallan tongue, or Erse,
    In prose or rhyme.

  An' now, auld Cloots, I ken ye're thinkin'
A certain Bardie's rantin', drinkin',
Some luckless hour will send him linkin'
    To your black pit;
But faith, he'll turn a corner, jinkin',
    And cheat you yet.

  But, fare ye weel, auld Nickie-ben!
O wad ye tak a thought and men'!
Ye aiblins might--I dinna ken--
    Still hae a stake--
I'm wae to think upon yon den,
    Even for your sake!"

TAM O' SHANTER.

  "When chapman billies leave the street,
And drouthy neebors, neebors meet,
As market days are wearing late,
An' folk begin to tak the gate;

While we sit bousing at the nappy,
An' gettin' fou an' unco happy,
We think na on the lang Scots miles,
The mosses, waters, slaps, an' styles,
That lie between us and our hame,
Where sits our sulky sullen dame,
Gathering her brows like gathering storm,
Nursing her wrath to keep it warm.

 This truth fand honest Tam o' Shanter,
As he frae Ayr ae night did canter;
(Auld Ayr, wham ne'er a toun surpasses,
For honest men and bonny lasses.)

 O Tam! hadst thou but been sae wise,
As ta'en thy ain wife Kate's advice!
She tauld thee weel thou was a skellum,
A blethering, blustering, drunken blellum;
That frae November till October
Ae market-day thou was na sober;
That ilka melder, wi' the miller,
Thou sat as lang as thou had siller;
That ev'ry naig was ca'd a shoe on,
The smith and thee gat roaring fou on;
That at the L--d's house, even on Sunday,
Thou drank wi' Kirkton Jean till Monday.
She prophesy'd that, late or soon,
Thou would be found deep drown'd in Doon;
Or catch'd wi' warlocks in the mirk,
By Alloway's auld haunted kirk.

 Ah, gentle dames! it gars me greet,
To think how mony counsels sweet,
How mony lengthen'd sage advices,
The husband frae the wife despises!

 But to our tale: Ae market night
Tam had got planted unco right;
Fast by an ingle, bleezing finely,
Wi' reaming swats, that drank divinely:

And at his elbow, Souter Johnny,
His ancient, trusty, drouthy crony;
Tam lo'ed him like a vera brither;
They had been fou for weeks thegither.
The night drave on wi' sangs an' clatter;
And aye the ale was growing better:
The landlady and Tam grew gracious,
Wi' favours, secret, sweet, and precious;
The souter tauld his queerest stories;
The landlord's laugh was ready chorus:
The storm without might rair and rustle,
Tam did na mind the storm a whistle.

  Care, mad to see a man sae happy,
E'en drown'd himself amang the nappy;
As bees flee hame wi' lades o' treasure,
The minutes wing'd their way wi' pleasure:
Kings may be blest, but Tam was glorious,
O'er a' the ills o' life victorious!

  But pleasures are like poppies spread--
You seize the flow'r, its bloom is shed!
Or like the snow-fall in the river,
A moment white--then melts for ever;
Or like the borealis race,
That flit ere you can point their place;
Or like the rainbow's lovely form,
Evanishing amid the storm.--
Nae man can tether time nor tide:
The hour approaches Tam maun ride--
That hour, o' night's black arch the key-stane,
That dreary hour he mounts his beast in,
And sic a night he taks the road in,
As ne'er poor sinner was abroad in.

  The wind blew as 'twad blawn its last;
The rattlin' showers rose on the blast:
The speedy gleams the darkness swallow'd;
Loud, deep, and lang the thunder bellow'd;
That night a child might understand

The deil had business on his hand.

  Weel mounted on his grey mare, Meg--
A better never lifted leg--
Tam skelpit on through dub and mire,
Despising wind, and rain, and fire;
Whiles holding fast his guid blue bonnet;
Whiles crooning o'er some auld Scots sonnet;
Whiles glow'ring round wi' prudent cares,
Lest bogles catch him unawares;
Kirk-Alloway was drawing nigh,
Whare ghaists and houlets nightly cry.

  By this time he was 'cross the foord,
Whare in the snaw the chapman smoor'd;
And past the birks and meikle stane,
Whare drucken Charlie brak's neck bane;
And thro' the whins, and by the cairn,
Whare hunters fand the murder'd bairn;
And near the thorn, aboon the well,
Whare Mungo's mither hang'd hersel.--
Before him Doon pours all his floods!
The doubling storm roars thro' the woods;
The lightnings flash from pole to pole;
Near and more near the thunders roll;
When glimmering thro' the groaning trees,
Kirk-Alloway seem'd in a bleeze;
Thro' ilka bore the beams were glancing,
And loud resounded mirth and dancing.

  Inspiring bold John Barleycorn!
What dangers thou canst make us scorn!
Wi' tippenny we fear nae evil;
Wi' usquebae we'll face the devil.--
The swats sae ream'd in Tammie's noddle,
Fair play, he cared na deils a boddle.
But Maggie stood right sair astonish'd,
Till, by the heel and hand admonish'd,
She ventured forward on the light;
And, wow! Tam saw an unco sight!

Warlocks and witches in a dance;
Nae cotillon brent new frae France,
But hornpipes, jigs, strathspeys, and reels
Put life and mettle in their heels.
A winnock-bunker in the east,
There sat auld Nick in shape o' beast;
A towzie tyke, black, grim, and large,
To gie them music was his charge:
He screw'd his pipes and gart them skirl
Till roof and rafters a' did dirl.
Coffins stood round like open presses,
That shaw'd the dead in their last dresses;
And by some devilish cantrip sleight,
Each in its cauld hand held a light,
By which heroic Tam was able
To note upon the haly table,
A murderer's banes in gibbet airns;
Twa span-lang, wee unchristen'd bairns,
A thief, new cutted frae a rape,
Wi' his last gasp his gab did gape:
Five tomahawks, wi' blude red-rusted;
Five scimitars, wi' murder crusted;
A garter which a babe had strangled;
A knife a father's throat had mangled,
Whom his ain son o' life bereft,
The grey hairs yet stack to the heft
Wi' mair o' horrible and awfu'
Which ev'n to name wad be unlawfu'.

  As Tammie glowr'd, amaz'd and curious,
The mirth and fun grew fast and furious:
The piper loud and louder blew,
The dancers quick and quicker flew;
They reel'd, they set, they cross'd, they cleekit
Till ilka carlin swat and reekit,
And coost her duddies to the wark
And linket at it in her sark!

  Now Tam, O Tam! had they been queens
A' plump an' strapping, in their teens;

Their sarks, instead o' creeshie flannen,
Been snaw-white seventeen hunder linen!
Thir breeks o' mine, my only pair,
That ance were plush o' guid blue hair,
I wad hae gi'en them aff my hurdies,
For ae blink o' the bonnie burdies!

But wither'd beldames auld and droll,
Rigwoodie hags wad spean a foal,
Louping and flinging on a crummock,
I wonder didna turn thy stomach.

But Tam kenn'd what was what fu' brawlie,
There was a winsome wench and walie,
That night enlisted in the core,
(Lang after kenn'd on Carrick shore!
For monie a beast to dead she shot,
And perish'd monie a bonnie boat,
And shook baith meikle corn and bear,
And kept the country side in fear).
Her cutty sark o' Paisley harn,
That while a lassie she had worn,
In longitude though sorely scanty,
It was her best, and she was vauntie:
Ah! little kenn'd thy reverend grannie,
That sark she coft for her wee Nannie,
Wi' twa pund Scots ('twas a' her riches),
Wad ever graced a dance o' witches!

But here my muse her wing man cour:
Sic flights are far beyond her power:
To sing how Nannie lap and flang,
(A souple jade she was an' strang),
An' how Tam stood like ane bewitch'd,
An' thought his very een enrich'd:
Even Satan glowr'd and fidg'd fu' fain,
And hotch'd and blew wi' might and main:
Till first ae caper, syne anither,
Tam tint his reason a' thegither,
And roars out, 'Weel done, Cutty sark!'

And in an instant all was dark;
And scarcely had he Maggie rallied,
When out the hellish legion sallied.

  As bees bizz out wi' angry fyke,
When plundering herds assail their byke;
As open pussie's mortal foes,
When, pop! she starts before their nose;
As eager runs the market crowd,
When 'Catch the thief!' resounds aloud,--
So Maggie runs, the witches follow,
Wi' monie an eldritch screetch and hollow.

  Ah, Tam! Ah, Tam! thou'll get thy fairin'!
In hell they'll roast thee like a herrin'!
In vain thy Kate awaits thy comin'!
Kate soon will be a waefu' woman!
Now do thy speedy utmost, Meg,
And win the key-stane o' the brig;
There at them thou thy tail may toss,
A running stream they darena cross.
But ere the key-stane she could make,
The fient a tail she had to shake!
For Nannie, far before the rest,
Hard upon noble Maggie press'd,
And flew at Tam wi' furious ettle;
But little wist she Maggie's mettle--
Ae spring brought aff her master hale,
But left behind her ain grey tail:
The carlin caught her by the rump,
An' left poor Maggie scarce a stump.

  Now, wha this tale o' truth shall read,
Ilk man and mother's son take heed:
Whene'er to drink you are inclined,
Or cutty sarks run in your mind,
Think ye may buy the joys o'er dear,
Remember Tam o' Shanter's mare."

CHAPTER XIX.

Sir Walter Scott, the "Great Unknown"--His belief in   Superstition--How his Tales of Fiction are composed--A   Town-Clerk frightened by an Apparition--A Ghost that   did not understand Erse, but could communicate in   Latin--Lovel and Edie Ochiltree--Discovery of Hidden   Treasure by Occult Science--"Rob Roy"--Fairies'   Caverns--Supposed Apparition in the Trossachs--Elfin   People at the Firth of Forth--A Minister taken away by   Fairies--Dame Glendinning's Tale--Lines from   "Marmion"--A Fairy Knight--Mysterious Steed.

Sir Walter Scott, the "Great Unknown," was sensibly affected by his country's tales of witches, fairies, and ghosts. Whether the fear he entertained proceeded from early impressions, or whether an awe imperceptibly crept over him, through his frequent communings with old people (when he was in more advanced life) who had no doubt of the existence of witches and spirits, good and bad, visiting the earth, and performing acts of benevolence or malevolence, according to the inclination or caprice of the uncanny or unearthly agent, we cannot say; but of one thing there can be no doubt, that even in years of maturity he believed there were spirits that appeared to men, and assisted them to perform actions they could not have done without superhuman aid, and that by such beings future events were made known. Were it not for the dash of superstition he threw here and there into his tales, they would be comparatively of a commonplace description. Like other writers of fiction, or authors whose writings rest on a slender foundation of truth, Sir Walter Scott often brings forward a witch, wizard, gipsy, fairy, ghost, and other spirits. A haunted castle, a fortune-teller, and a good or evil genius are as indispensable in a good story as a cruel parent, a rich uncle, and a disappointed lover. None knew better than the great Scottish novelist how to work on his readers' feelings; and hence his success.

Sir Walter tells, in the *Antiquary*, a story of Rab Tull, the town-clerk, being in an old house searching for important documents, but who was obliged to go to bed without finding them. The bodie had got such a custom of tippling and tippling with his drunken cronies, that he could not sleep without his punch, and as usual he took his glass that evening. In the middle watches of night he had a fearful wakening--he was never himself after it--and was stricken with the dead palsy that very day four years. He thought he heard the bed curtains move, and out he looked. Before him appeared an old gentleman in a queer-fashioned dress. Rab, greatly frightened, asked the apparition (for it was a spirit that stood before him) what it wanted. The spirit answered in an unknown tongue. Rab replied in Erse, but the spirit did not seem to understand this language. In his strait, the clerk bethought him of two or three words of Latin he used in making out the town's deeds; and no sooner had he tried the strange object before him with these, than out came such a blatter of Latin, that Rab Tull--who with all his pretensions was no great scholar--was overwhelmed. It then made a sign to Rab to follow it. He followed up-stairs and down-stairs to a tower in a corner of the house. There the ghost pointed out a cabinet, and suddenly disappeared. In a drawer of that repository the missing deed was found.

Lovel, after shooting M'Intyre in a duel, fled from justice, under the guidance of old Edie Ochiltree. Exhausted by excitement and a long walk through a thicket, they reached a cave with narrow entrance, concealed by the boughs of an oak. Passing through the aperture, not much larger than a fox-hole, they reached the interior. Lovel was led to a narrow turnpike stair leading to a church above. In the evening they reached a spot which commanded a full view of the chancel in every direction. Ere long, Lovel was startled by the sound of human voices. Two persons, with a dark lantern, entered the chancel. After conversing together some time in whispers, Lovel recognised the voice of Dousterswivel, pronouncing in a smothered tone, "Indeed, mine goot sir, dere cannot be one finer hour nor season for dis great purpose.... I will show you all de secrets dat art can show--ay, de secret of de great Pymander." The other individual turned out to be Sir Arthur Wardour, and their business evidently had reference to the discovery of hidden treasure, by means of consulting the heavenly bodies or some friendly spirit. Before Sir Arthur and Dousterswivel left the ruins of St. Ruth, they found a casket containing gold and silver coins. These two worthies, along with Mr. Oldenbuck, set out, on another occasion to search for treasure at the ruins of St. Ruth. Arrived at the scene of operations, the Antiquary addressed the adept Dousterswivel: "Pray, Mr. Dousterswivel, shall we dig from east to west, or from west to east? or will you assist us with your triangular vial of May-dew, or with your divining-rod of witch-hazel?" This was said tauntingly, yet nevertheless they proceeded to dig, in the hope of finding treasure; and sure enough, a chest containing ingots of silver to the value of a thousand pounds was discovered. Dousterswivel claimed the credit of bringing about the discovery. Mr. Oldenbuck refused to give him any credit, telling him that he came without weapons, and did not use charms, lamen-sigel, talisman, spell-crystal, pentacle, magic-mirror, nor geomantic figure. "Where," asked the Antiquary, "be your periapts, and your abracadabras, man? your May-fern, your vervain--

> "Your toad, your crow, your dragon, and your panther,
>   Your sun, your moon, your firmament, your adrop,
> Your Lato, Azoch, Zernich, Chibrit, Heautarit,
>   With all your broths, your menstrues, your materials,
>   Would burst a man to name?"

Dousterswivel, like all others who resort to enchantments, believing in the existence of hobgoblins and divination, was not certain but his own art had really contributed to the success of his party. Chagrined at the treatment of Mr. Oldenbuck, and separated for a time from Sir Arthur, he was glad to enter into conversation with Edie Ochiltree, who witnessed the finding of the treasure with a keen eye to future operations. Edie had surreptitiously obtained possession of the treasure box-lid, and on it he and the conjurer were able to decipher, "Search number one." The old beggar, who knew many of the traditions of the country, told Dousterswivel that the remains of Malcolm the Misticot were, along with a large amount of gold and silver, buried somewhere at St. Ruth. Moreover, he recited the old prophecy:

"If Malcolm the Misticot's grave were fun',
The lands of Knockwinnock are lost and won."

They resolved to return to the ruins of St. Ruth at midnight to make another search, not on account of Sir Arthur or Mr. Oldenbuck, but for themselves. Neither gold nor silver were found; but those engaged in the search got a fright, one supposing he saw evil spirits rising from the earth's bowels, and the other that he was chased by a ghost on horseback. A series of interesting incidents connected with adventure, love, and crime follow. Dousterswivel was discovered to be an impostor; certain persons engaged in a dark plot were cut off by death, but the virtuous were rewarded.

Sir Walter Scott, in *Rob Roy*, makes mention of an eminence or mound near the upland hills, whence the Forth springs, supposed by the people in the neighbourhood to contain within its unseen caverns the palaces of fairies; and in his Notes to *Rob Roy* it is stated that the lakes and precipices, amidst which the river Forth has its birth, are still, according to popular tradition, haunted by elfin people. In one note the reader is informed that the Rev. Robert Kirk, who died at Aberfoyle in the year 1688, was supposed to have been taken away by fairies. Mr. Kirk was walking near his manse on a *Dun Shie*, or fairy mound, when he sank down apparently in a faint, and seemingly died. The body was supposed to be buried, but shortly afterwards he appeared in living form to a friend, to whom he told that he was not dead, but in fairyland, whither he was carried at the time he fell down in a swoon. The reverend captive gave directions how he might be rescued by him; but the person who was appointed to perform the prescribed ceremony failed to proceed as directed, and Mr. Kirk, who had been twice seen after his supposed death, never appeared again.

*   *   *   *   *

As we are writing of Rob Roy's country, and of an incident connected with the fate of a minister there, we suddenly break the thread of our narrative, to introduce the particulars of a most extraordinary circumstance connected with another clergyman in that quarter.

A few years ago, about 1870, a most respectable gentleman belonging to Edinburgh, devoid of superstitious fear, told the writer: "In the autumn I was enjoying the retirement and grandeur of the Trossachs and surrounding district. The lake, the hill, the dale, and, above all, the people, interested me. Often was I in the humble cot, and, although a sojourner, I became acquainted with families in the more exalted positions in society. Among others, I gained the friendship of a venerable clergyman, whose charity and piety were known far and near.

"While I had my residence in the Trossachs Hotel, the clergyman, I was told, one day was dangerously ill. Next morning, before starting with a few friends up Loch Katrine, I sent to inquire after the invalid's health. The answer returned conveyed the impression that he was fast sinking. We proceeded up the lake, and came back by the last boat for the day. We took outside seats on the coach, and while turning a corner of the road, about half-way between the lake and the hotel, I and several other passengers (including the captain of the Loch Katrine steamer and the driver) observed a gentleman passing us, whom we all declared was the clergyman. Trusting our sight, we thought it most extraordinary that a man, considered to be dying in the morning, should be seen in the evening on the highway, far from home.

"The steamboat being unusually late of arriving at her destination, the sun had gone down, and the shades of night were closing over us before half our journey by coach could be accomplished, still it was not so dark when the figure of the pious minister appeared but that one might not only see the figure of a man, but observe his every feature. The sight struck all, who recognised in the traveller the invalid minister with amazement, and some with fear. On the coach arriving at the hotel, a messenger was despatched to inquire after the reverend gentleman's health. The answer received disclosed the startling intelligence that the clergyman had expired shortly before the time we saw his figure walking with slow step and sad countenance towards Loch Katrine."

*　　*　　*　　*　　*

But we now return to Sir Walter Scott's works. Those who have read the *Monastery* (and who have not?) may recollect of Dame Glendinning telling Tibb what she had seen on a Hallowe'en in her youth--which was as follows:--

"Aweel, aweel, I had mair joes than ane, but I favoured nane o' them; and sae, at Hallowe'en, Father Nicolas the cellarer--he was cellarer before his father, Father Clement, that now is--was cracking his nuts and drinking his brown beer with us, and as blithe as might be, and they would have me try a cantrip to ken wha suld wed me; and the monk said there was nae ill in it, and if there was, he would assoil me for it. And awa' I went into the barn to winnow my three weights o' naething--sair, sair, my mind misgave me for fear of wrang-doing and wrang-suffering, baith; but I had aye a bauld spirit. I had not winnowed the last weight clear out, and the moon was shining bright upon the floor, when in stalked the presence of my dear Simon Glendinning, that is now happy. I never saw him plainer in my life than I did that moment; he held up an arrow as he passed me, and I swarf'd awa' wi' fright. Muckle wark there was to bring me to mysel' again, and sair they tried to make me believe it was a trick o' Father Nicolas and Simon between them, and that the arrow was to signify Cupid's shaft, as the Father called it; and mony a time Simon wad threep it to me after I was married--gude man, he liked not it suld be said that he was seen out o' the body!--But mark the end o' it, Tibb: we were married, and the grey-goose wing was the death o' him, after a'!"

The following lines appear in *Marmion* in reference to a combat with a goblin knight:--

"Soon as the midnight bell did ring,
 Alone, and armed, forth rode the King
 To that old camp's deserted round:
 Sir Knight, you well might mark the mound,
 Left hand the town,--the Pictish race
 The trench, long since, in blood did trace;
 The moor around is brown and bare,
 The space within is green and fair.
 The spot our village children know,
 For there the earliest wild flowers grow;
 But woe betide the wandering wight,
 That treads its circle in the night!
 The breadth across, a bowshot clear,
 Gives ample space for full career;
 Opposed to the four points of heaven,
 By four deep gaps is entrance given.
 The southernmost our monarch passed,
 Halted, and blew a gallant blast;
 And on the north, within the ring,
 Appeared the form of England's king,
 Who then a thousand leagues afar,
 In Palestine waged holy war:
 Yet arms like England's did he wield,
 Alike the leopards in the shield,
 Alike his Syrian courser's frame,
 The rider's length of limb the same:
 Long afterwards did Scotland know
 Fell Edward was her deadliest foe.

The vision made our monarch start,
 But soon he manned his noble heart,
 And in the first career they ran,
 The Elfin Knight fell horse and man;
 Yet did a splinter of his lance
 Through Alexander's visor glance,
 And razed the skin--a puny wound.
 The king, light leaping to the ground,
 With naked blade his phantom foe
 Compelled the future war to show.

Of Largs he saw the glorious plain,
Where still gigantic bones remain,
  Memorial of the Danish war;
Himself he saw amid the field,
 On high his brandished war-axe wield,
  And strike proud Haco from his car,
 While all around the shadowy kings,
  Denmark's grim ravens cowered their wings.
'Tis said that, in that awful night,
Remoter visions met his sight,
Foreshowing future conquests far,
When our sons' sons wage northern war;
A royal city, tower and spire,
Reddened the midnight sky with fire;
And shouting crews her navy bore,
Triumphant, to the victor shore.
Such signs may learned clerks explain,
They pass the wit of simple swain.

The joyful king turned home again,
Headed his host and quelled the Dane;
But yearly, when returned the night
Of his strange combat with the sprite,
 His wound must bleed and smart;
Lord Gifford then would gibing say,
'Bold as ye were, my liege, ye pay
 The penance of your start.'
Long since, beneath Dunfermline's nave,
King Alexander fills his grave,
 Our Lady give him rest!
Yet still the nightly spear and shield
The elfin warrior doth wield,
 Upon the brown hill's breast;
And many a knight hath proved his chance
In the charmed ring to break a lance,
 But have all foully sped;
Save two, as legends tell, and they
Were Wallace wight, and Gilbert Hay.--
 Gentles, my tale is said."

One of Sir Walter Scott's poetic effusions has reference to a popular story concerning a fairy knight:--

"Osbert, a bold and powerful baron, visited a noble family in the vicinity of Wandlebury, in the bishopric of Ely. Among other stories related in the social circle of his friends (who, according to custom, amused each other by repeating ancient tales and traditions), he was informed, that if any knight, unattended, entered an adjacent plain by moonlight, and challenged an adversary to appear, he would be immediately encountered by a spirit in the form of a knight. Osbert resolved to make the experiment, and set out, attended by a single squire, whom he ordered to remain without the limits of the plain, which was surrounded by an ancient entrenchment. On repeating the challenge, he was instantly assailed by an adversary, whom he quickly unhorsed, and seized the reins of his steed. During this operation, his ghostly opponent sprang up, and darting his spear like a javelin at Osbert, wounded him in the thigh. Osbert returned in triumph with the horse, which he committed to the care of his servants. The horse was of a sable colour, as well as his whole accoutrements, and apparently of great beauty and vigour. He remained with his keepers till cock-crowing, when, with eyes flashing fire, he reared, spurned the ground, and vanished. On disarming himself, Osbert perceived that he was wounded, and that one of his steel boots was full of blood. Gervase adds, that as long as he lived, the scar of his wound opened afresh on the anniversary of the eve on which he encountered the spirit."

CHAPTER XX.

Lord Byron taught Superstition by his Nurse and   others--Byron and the Maid in Green--The Maid's   Keepsake or Charm--Bridge of Balgonie--Byron's fear to   ride over it--His belief in Unlucky Days and   Presentiments--Socrates's Demon--Monk Lewis's   Monitor--Napoleon's Warnings--A Sorrowful Tale--A   Strange Story--Qualities of Mind descending from Sire   to Son--Byron's Fortune told by a Sybil--Hebrew   Camyo--Abracadabra--Loch-na-Garr--Oscar of   Alva--Byron's last Instructions.

Lord Byron, who was taught superstition by his nurse, became acquainted with the peculiar belief of the Highlanders while, in early life, he dwelt within sight of "dark Loch-na-Garr." When wandering about Pannanich, the shepherds told him many strange legends, and the old dames often enticed him into their huts to amuse him with fairy tales and witch stories. It was thought by the old crones that the wonderful boy had communings with more uncanny neighbours than these simple-minded people, who no more doubted the existence of witches and fairies than they doubted that the Dee flowed from the mountains to the sea. If report spoke true, he was often heard in conversation with intelligent beings, though to ordinary human eyes no other form but that of his own was seen. After his fame was wide-spread, an old woman, who lived in a little straw-thatched cottage by the roadside near Balmoral, declared that she expected that he would enlighten the world, for she had often seen him with those who could instruct him and tell him of past and future events. One of those persons, she said, was a little maid dressed in green, whose beautiful face, flowing hair, and agile figure were faultless. Frequently was she seen climbing steep precipices on which human foot was never known to rest, and bring him flowers, and even the eagles' nests were not beyond her reach. While the young and middle-aged would wonder who she was, the aged shook their heads. Whoever the fair little maid was, one thing in connection with her was exceedingly strange. Either Byron did not know her relations and home, or, for reasons he kept to himself, he chose to conceal them. Her merry laugh, clear as the sound of a silver bell, or her sweet voice in song, was generally what indicated her approach. At one time she would emerge from a thicket, and rise at another, like a spectre from behind a rock. Her disappearance was equally mysterious. At their last parting she gave him a keepsake or charm, which he long wore, suspended by a ribbon, round his neck, and it was not till he threw it aside that he became unfortunate and unhappy. We cannot vouch for the truth of this story; but if Byron did not hold intercourse with unearthly beings, he has, by his writings and speech, left room for simple-minded people who have read his works and history, to suppose that he did. His belief in presentiment was very strong, as also visionary warnings of imminent danger or impending calamities.

A school-fellow of Byron had a small pony, and one day they went to the Don to bathe. When they came to the bridge of Balgownie, the young poet remembered the old prophecy:

> "Brig o' Balgownie! wight is thy wa',
>   Wi' a wife's ae son, an' a mare's ae foal,
> Down shalt thou fa'."

He immediately stopped his companion, who was then riding, and asked him if he recollected the prophecy, saying, that as they were both only sons, and as the pony might be "a mare's ae foal," he would rather ride over first, because he had only a mother to lament him should the bridge fall, whereas he, his companion, had both a father and mother to grieve for him if he perished. Byron, however, was not the only one who put faith in such prophecies. Leslie says, "Persons have been known to dismount when they came to the brig o' Balgownie, and send their horses over before them."

Byron had a belief in unlucky days. He once refused to be introduced to a lady because the day was Friday; and on this day of the week he would not visit his friends. "Something," he said, "whispered to me at my wedding that I was signing my death warrant. I am a great believer in presentiments. Socrates's demon was no fiction; Monk Lewis had his monitor, and Napoleon many warnings. At the last moment I would have retreated if I could have done so."

The poet had a high opinion of Monk Lewis. Here are two stories told by Byron:

"Whilst Lewis was residing at Mannheim, every night at the same hour, he heard, or thought he heard, in his room, when he was lying in bed, a crackling noise like that produced by parchment or thick paper. This circumstance caused inquiry, when it was told him that the sounds were attributable to the following cause:--The house in which he lived had belonged to a widow who had an only son. In order to prevent him marrying a poor but amiable girl to whom he was attached, he was sent to sea. Years passed, and the mother heard no tidings of him nor of the ship in which he had sailed. It was supposed the vessel had been wrecked, and that all on board had perished. The reproaches of the girl, the upbraidings of her own conscience, and the loss of her child, crazed the old lady's mind. Her only pursuit was to turn over the gazettes for news. Hope at length left her: she did not live long, and continued her old occupation after death."

The other story runs thus:

"Two Florentine lovers, who had been attached to each other almost from childhood, made a vow of eternal fidelity. Mina was the name of the lady; her husband's I forget, but it is not material. They parted. He had been some time absent with his regiment, when, as his disconsolate lady was sitting alone in her chamber, she distinctly heard the well-known sound of his footsteps, and, starting up, beheld not her husband, but his spectre, with a deep ghastly wound across his forehead. She swooned with horror. When she recovered, the ghost told her that in future his visits should be announced by a passing bell, and the words distinctly whispered, 'Mina, I am here!' Their interviews became frequent, till the woman fancied herself as much in love with the ghost as she had been with the man. But it was soon to prove otherwise. One fatal night she went to a ball. She danced, and, what was worse, her partner was a young Florentine, so much the counterpart of her lover, that she became estranged from the ghost. Whilst the young gallant conducted her in the waltz, and her ear drank in the music of his voice and words, a passing bell tolled. She had been accustomed to the sound till it hardly excited her attention, and, now lost in the attractions of her fascinating partner, she heard, but regarded it not. A second peal!--she listened not to its warnings. A third time the bell, with its deep and iron tongue, startled the assembled company, and silenced the music. Mina turned her eyes from her partner, and saw, reflected in the mirror, a form, a shadow, a spectre: it was her husband. He was standing between her and the young Florentine, and whispered, in a solemn and melancholy tone, the accustomed accents, 'Mina, I am here!' She instantly fell down dead. The two ghosts walked out of the room arm in arm."

Byron believed that the quality of mind descended from sire to son, and contended that any passion might be worn out of a family by skilful culture. To his uncle, who was very superstitious, and fed crickets, he ascribed his superstition; to another of his ancestors, who died laughing, he ascribed his buoyant spirits. Two of his relations had such an affection for each other, that they both died at the same time. "There seems," he said, "to have been a flaw in my escutcheon there, or that that loving couple have monopolised all the connubial bliss of the family."

Byron's superstition was so great that it led him to have his fortune told by a sybil. It was prophesied that his twenty-seventh and thirty-seventh years would prove unlucky to him. Some people have thought that the prophecy was fulfilled: he was married in his twenty-seventh, and died in his thirty-seventh year.

He was convinced that the principal charms of the Scotch resembled those of other nations. He was not ignorant of the supposed virtue of the mountain ash as an antidote against witchcraft. Everything pertaining to superstition was interesting to him. He had stored up in his memory many curious anecdotes. On being told of a particular race of men skilled in Cabala, who by a single gaze of their "evil eye" could level an enemy to the earth and occasion instantaneous death, and of parents who had handsome children hanging cameos round their necks to protect them from the evil consequences of a wicked eye, his Lordship said, "I remember reading somewhere that Serenus Samonicus, preceptor to a young Gordian, recommended the Abracadabra or Abrasadabra as a charm or amulet in curing agues, and preventing other diseases."

A Hebrew Camyo, supposed to have been handed down from father to son since the building of the first temple, has a similar effect. Lucky is the circumcised Jew who has, in the time of need, the good fortune to have the Hebrew charm applied to his leprously-inclined body; and thrice fortunate is he, whoever he may be, that has it constantly at his command, and can claim it as his family relic.

The word Abracadabra or Abrasadabra must be written on parchment, or other suitable substance, in the manner below, omitting in every new line the last letter of the former line, so that the whole may form a kind of inverted cone:

```
Abracadabra
 Abracadabr
  Abracadab
   Abracada
    Abracad
     Abraca
      Abrac
       Abra
        Abr
         Ab
          A
```

Byron looked as if he had added greatly to his stock of knowledge when he learned that, which way soever the letters of the charms might be taken, beginning from the lower point and ascending from the left to the right, they make the same word.

To every one who has read *Loch-na-Garr*, it must be evident that Byron believed, or wished it to appear that he believed, like the Highlanders, that the voices of the dead were heard in the storm, that the souls of departed heroes rode on the wind, and that the dark clouds encircled the forms of chieftain sires that added lustre to their country's glory. But the poet shall speak for himself:--

"Away, ye gay landscapes, ye gardens of roses!
  In you let the minions of luxury rove;
Restore me the rocks where the snow-flake reposes,
  Though still they are sacred to freedom and love:
Yet, Caledonia, beloved are thy mountains,
  Round their white summits though elements war;
Though cataracts foam 'stead of smooth-flowing fountains,
  I sigh for the valley of dark Loch-na-Garr.

Ah! there my young footsteps in infancy wander'd;
  My cap was the bonnet, my cloak was the plaid:
On chieftains long perish'd my memory ponder'd,
  As daily I strode through the pine-cover'd glade;
I sought not my home till the day's dying glory
  Gave place to the rays of the bright polar star;
For fancy was cheer'd by traditional story,
  Disclosed by the natives of dark Loch-na-Garr.

'Shades of the dead! have I not heard your voices
  Rise on the night-rolling breath of the gale?'

Surely the soul of the hero rejoices,
  And rides on the wind, o'er his own Highland vale.
Round Loch-na-Garr, while the stormy mist gathers,
  Winter presides in his cold icy car:
Clouds there encircle the forms of my fathers;
  They dwell in the tempests of dark Loch-na-Garr.

'Ill-starr'd, though brave, did no visions foreboding
  Tell you that fate had forsaken your cause?'
Ah! were you destined to die at Culloden,
  Victory crown'd not your fall with applause:
Still were you happy in death's earthy slumber,
  You rest with your clans in the caves of Braemar;
The pibroch resounds to the piper's loud number,
  Your deeds on the echoes of dark Loch-na-Garr.

Years have roll'd on, Loch-na-Garr, since I left you,
  Years must elapse ere I tread you again:
Nature of verdure and flowers has bereft you,
  Yet still are you dearer than Albion's plain.
England! thy beauties are tame and domestic
  To one who has roved o'er the mountains afar:
O for the crags that are wild and majestic!
  The steep frowning glories of dark Loch-na-Garr!"

In *Oscar of Alva* will also be found something of popular
superstition. Passing over a part of the tale, Byron says:--

"From high Southannon's distant tower
  Arrived a young and noble dame;
With Kenneth's lands to form her dower,
  Glenalvon's blue-eyed daughter came.

And Oscar claimed the beauteous bride,
  And Angus on his Oscar smiled;
It soothed the father's feudal pride
  Thus to obtain Glenalvon's child.

Hark to the pibroch's pleasing note!
  Hark to the swelling nuptial song!

In joyous strains the voices float,
  And still the choral peal prolong.

        *   *   *   *   *

But where is Oscar? Sure 'tis late:
  Is this a bridegroom's ardent flame?
While thronging guests and ladies wait
  Nor Oscar nor his brother came.

At length young Allan join'd the bride;
  'Why comes not Oscar?' Angus said:
'Is he not here?' the youth replied;
  'With me he roved not o'er the glade.'

        *   *   *   *   *

'O search, ye chiefs! O search around!
  Allan, with these through Alva fly;
Till Oscar, till my son is found,
  Haste, haste, nor dare attempt reply.'

Three days, three sleepless nights, the chief
  For Oscar searched each mountain cave
Then hope is lost: in boundless grief
  His locks in grey torn ringlets wave.

        *   *   *   *   *

Days rolled along: the orb of light
  Again had run his destined race;
No Oscar bless'd his father's sight,
  And sorrow left a fainter trace.

For youthful Allan still remain'd,
  And now his father's only joy:
And Mora's heart was quickly gain'd,
  For beauty crown'd the fair-hair'd boy.

She thought that Oscar low was laid,

And Allan's face was wondrous fair:
If Oscar lived, some other maid
    Had claim'd his faithless bosom's care.

And Angus said, if one year more
    In fruitless hope was pass'd away,
His fondest scruples should be o'er,
    And he would name their nuptial day.

Slow roll'd the moons, but blest at last
    Arrived the dearly destined morn;
The year of anxious trembling past,
    What smiles the lovers' cheeks adorn!

Hark to the pibroch's pleasing note!
    Hark to the swelling nuptial song!
In joyous strains the voices float,
    And still the choral peal prolong.

Again the clan, in festive crowd,
    Throng through the gate of Alva's hall;
The sounds of mirth re-echo loud,
    And all their former joy recall.

But who is he whose darken'd brow
    Glooms in the midst of general mirth?
Before his eyes' far fiercer glow
    The blue flames curdle o'er the hearth.

Dark is the robe which wraps his form,
    And tall his plume of gory red;
His voice is like the rising storm,
    But light and trackless is his tread.

'Tis noon of night, the pledge goes round,
    The bridegroom's health is deeply quaff'd;
With shouts the vaulted roofs resound,
    And all combine to hail the draught.

Sudden the stranger chief arose,

And all the clamorous crowd are hush'd;
  And Angus' cheek with wonder glows,
  And Mora's tender bosom blush'd.

'Old man!' he cried, 'this pledge is done;
  Thou saw'st was duly drunk by me:
It hail'd the nuptials of thy son:
  Now will I claim, a pledge from thee.

While all around is mirth and joy,
  To bless thy Allan's happy lot,
Say, had'st thou ne'er another boy?
  Say, why should Oscar be forgot?'

'Alas!' the hapless sire replied,
  The big tear starting as he spoke;
When Oscar left my hall, or died,
  This aged heart was almost broke.

'Thrice has the earth revolved her course
  Since Oscar's form has bless'd my sight;
And Allan is my last resource,
  Since martial Oscar's death or flight.'

''Tis well,' replied the stranger stern,
  And fiercely flashed his rolling eye;
'Thy Oscar's fate I fain would learn:
  Perhaps the hero did not die.

'Perchance if those whom most he loved
  Would call, thy Oscar might return;
Perchance the chief has only roved;
  For him thy beltane yet may burn.

'Fill high the bowl the table round,
  We will not claim the pledge by stealth;
With wine let every cup be crown'd:
  Pledge me departed Oscar's health.'

'With all my soul,' old Angus said,

And fill'd his goblet to the brim;
'Here's to my boy! alive or dead,
I ne'er shall find a son like him.'

'Bravely, old man, this health hath sped;
But why does Allan trembling stand?
Come, drink remembrance of the dead,
And raise thy cup with firmer hand.'

The crimson glow of Allan's face
Was turn'd at once to ghastly hue;
The drops of death each other chase
Adown in agonizing dew.

Thrice did he raise the goblet high,
And thrice his lips refused to taste;
For thrice he caught the stranger's eye
On his with deadly fury placed.

'And is it thus a brother hails
A brother's fond remembrance here;
If thus affection's strength prevails,
What might we not expect from fear?'

Roused by the sneer, he raised the bowl,
'Would Oscar now could share our mirth!'
Internal fear appall'd his soul;
He said, and dash'd the cup to earth.

'Tis he! I hear my murderer's voice!'
Loud shrieks a darkly gleaming form;
'A murderer's voice!' the roof replies,
And deeply swells the bursting storm.

The tapers wink, the chieftains shrink,
The stranger's gone--amidst the crew
A form was seen in tartan green,
And tall the shade terrific grew.

His waist was bound with a broad belt round,

His plume of sable stream'd on high;
But his breast was bare, with the red wounds there
  And fixed was the glare of his glassy eye.

And thrice he smiled, with his eye so wild,
  On Angus bending low the knee:
And thrice he frown'd on a chief on the ground,
  Whom shivering crowds with horror see.

The bolts loud roll from pole to pole,
  The thunders through the welkin ring;
And the gleaming form, through the mist of the storm,
  Was borne on high by the whirlwind's wing.

Cold was the feast, the revel ceased,
  Who lies upon the stony floor?
Oblivion press'd old Angus' breast,
  At length his life-pulse throbs once more.

Away! away! let the leech assay
  To pour the light on Allan's eyes:
His sand is done--his race is run;
  O! never more shall Allan rise:

But Oscar's breast is cold as clay,
  His locks are lifted by the gale:
And Allan's barbed arrow lay
  With him in dark Glentanar's vale.

And whence the dreadful stranger came,
  Or who, no mortal wight can tell;
But no one doubts the form of flame,
  For Alva's sons knew Oscar well.

Ambition nerved young Allan's hand,
  Exulting demons wing'd his dart;
While Envy waved her burning brand,
  And pour'd her venom round his heart.

Swift is the shaft from Allan's bow;

Whose streaming life-blood stains his side?
Dark Oscar's sable crest is low,
  The dart has drunk his vital tide.

And Mora's eye could Allan move,
  She bade his wounded pride rebel;
Alas! that eyes which beam'd with love
  Should urge the soul to deeds of hell.

Lo! seest thou not a lonely tomb
  Which rises o'er a warrior dead?
It glimmers through the twilight gloom:
  O! that is Allan's nuptial bed.

Far, distant far, the noble grave
  Which held his clan's great ashes stood;
And o'er his corse no banners wave,
  For they were stain'd with kindred blood.

What minstrel grey, what hoary bard,
  Shall Allan's deeds on harp-strings raise?
The song is glory's chief reward,
  But who can strike a murderer's praise?

Unstrung, untouch'd the harp must stand,
  No minstrel dare the theme awake;
Guilt would benumb his palsied hand,
  His harp in shuddering chords would break.

No lyre of fame, no hallow'd verse,
  Shall sound his glories high in air:
A dying father's bitter curse,
  A brother's death-groan echoes there."

The incidents immediately preceding Byron's death show that, to his last moments, he entertained what is generally regarded as superstitious sentiments. He thought it possible for him to waken from the sleep of death, and torment those he desired to punish. Perceiving that he was seriously ill, he called his faithful attendant Fletcher, and gave him several directions. The servant expressed a hope that he (his master) would live many years. To this Byron replied, "No, it is now nearly over;" and then added, "I must tell you all, without losing a single moment. Now pay attention--You will be provided for--Oh, my poor dear child, my dear Ada!--could I but see her--give her my blessing--and my dear sister Augusta and her children--you will go to Lady Byron, and say--tell her everything." Here his Lordship seemed to be greatly affected; his voice failed him so much that it was difficult to understand what he said. After remaining silent for a short time, he raised his voice and said, "Fletcher: now if you do not execute every order which I have given you, I will torment you hereafter, if possible." These were nearly the last words he spoke, having very soon afterwards fallen into an easy sleep, from which he never awoke.

CHAPTER XXI.

Tale by Hogg, the Ettrick Shepherd--Aikwood   Castle--Black Pages in Livery--The Witch Henbane--Imps   demanding Work--Michael Scott--Curious Sport--Dreadful   Threat--Rats transformed into the form of   Men--Inventor of Gunpowder--Witches'   Operations--Summoning Evil Spirits to torture a Man--Latin the Language best understood by Satan and   his Emissaries--Holy Signs and Charms--Two   Captives--Effects of a Friar's Blessing--Magic   Lantern--Man blown into the Air--Michael Scott's   Sealed and Subscribed Conditions--Imps' Song--Spirits   in the forms of Crows--Dreadful Storm--Warlocks' Hymn--Eildon Hill.

Hogg, the Ettrick Shepherd, whose memory will long be remembered in Scotland, particularly in the Border counties, introduces, in his *Three Perils of Man*, a party of travellers approaching Aikwood Castle, about nine miles from Melrose. The edifice scarcely seemed to be the abode of man. "Is that now to be my residence, Yardbire?" said the beautiful Delany. "Will you go away, and leave Elias and me in that frightsome and desolate-looking mansion?" "Thou art in good hands," said the friar. "But thou art perhaps going into a place of danger, and evil things may await thee. Here, take thou this, and keep it in thy bosom; and, by the blessing of the Holy Virgin, it will shield thee from all malevolent spirits, all enchantments, and all dangers of the wicked one." As he said this, he put into her hand a small gilded copy of the four Evangelists, which she kissed and put into her bosom. All the rest of the company saw the small volume, and took it for a book of the black art. Close to the castle gate there appeared three pages in black livery, although a moment before there was no living creature there. They seemed to have risen out of the ground. All at once the horses and mules on which the travellers rode became restive; at this, the elves set up a shout, and skipped about with the swiftness of lightning. Hearing the noise, the great master asked his only attendant, Gourlay, "What is the meaning of the uproar?" "It is only Prim, Prig, and Pricker making sport," replied the servant.

As soon as the mighty master knew of the friar and his companions being in the castle, he ordered them to be treated as spies. The old witch Henbane, who acted as housekeeper, and the three pages, were called into the presence of the wizard, to receive instructions from him. First the imps threatened Gourlay, and then rushed on Michael himself, as if they would tear him to pieces, and cried out with one voice:

"Work, master, work; work we need;
Work for the living, or for the dead:
Since we are called, work we will have,
For the master, or for the slave.
Work, master, work. What work now?"

Michael Scott (no doubt the reader has by this time discovered that he was the master of the castle), to keep the restless beings at work, told them to give Gourlay three varieties of punishment, but no more. They soon began their wicked pranks, first changing the seneschal from one grotesque form to another. Quickly transforming him into a dog, they chased him up and down and round about with a pan at its tail. Next they made him assume the shape of a hare, while to all appearance they became collie dogs. An exciting chase followed over hill and dale, but the poor hare succeeded in eluding its pursuers, and returned to the master, who, by one touch of his divining rod, changed Gourlay into his own natural shape. As soon as the poor ill-used servant recovered speech, he threatened to cut his throat, that he might be freed from his severe bondage. Michael dared him to do such a thing, as he had him wholly in his power, dead or alive. "Were you to take away your life by a ghastly wound," said the wizard, "I would even make one of these fiendish spirits enter into your body, reanimate it, and cause you to go about with your gaping wound, unclosed and unpurified, as when death entered thereat." "Cursed be the day that I saw you, and ten times cursed the confession I made, that has thus subjected me to your tyranny!" exclaimed Gourlay.

Michael again asked what living creatures were in the castle. The servant replied, "I again repeat it, that there is no mortal thing in the castle but the old witch, and perhaps two or three hundred rats." "Call out those rats," said Michael; "marshal them up in the court, and receive the visitors according to their demerits." At the same time the master gave the servant a small piece of parchment, with red characters traced on it, and told him to put it above the lock-hole of the door. "It shall serve as a summons, and Prig, Prim, and Pricker shall marshal your forces," continued the wizard. The citation was effective: the running and screaming of rats were heard in every corner of the castle, and forthwith a whole column of armed men marched into the court, led by the three pages, and headed by the seneschal in grey mantle and cap. In walked the strangers, and passed between two ranks of men, or rather rats, the appearance of which raised a suspicion that they were spirits or elves.

The friar, it should be noticed, was the great philosopher and chemist who invented gunpowder, and made many other wonderful discoveries, for which he was in danger of being burnt as a wizard and necromancer.

The friar, followed by his companions, found entrance to a room, where they expected to meet the great enchanter Michael, but instead of him they beheld an old woman, so busily engaged with something on the fire, that she scarcely deigned to notice their entrance. She had a wooden tube, with which she blew up the fire, and then spoke through it, saying:

"Sotter, sotter, my wee pan,
   To the spirit gin ye can;
    When the scum turns blue,
    And the blood bells through,
    There's something aneath that will change the man."

The crone continued her orgies, one time blowing her fire, again stirring the liquid in the cal-dron, and then making it run from the end of a stick that she might note its gelidity. All her opera-tions were being gone through to call up certain familiar spirits whose presence she desired.

In another apartment sat Michael Scott. He wore a turban of crimson velvet, ornamented with mystic figures in gold, and on the front of it was a dazzling star. His eyes were bright and piercing, resembling those of a serpent. He was stout-made, and had a strong bushy beard, turning grey. On beholding Charlie Scott (he alone entered the wizard's *sanctum sanctorum*), the wizard stamped three times on the floor, and in a moment Prim, Prig, and Pricker stood beside him. "Work, master, work--what work now?" demanded they. "Take that burly housebreaker, bind him, and put him to the test," were the instructions they received. When the elves were about to seize Charlie, he drew his sword, and thrust out right and left, but his blade did nothing more than whistle through vacancy. In an instant he was thrown down and bound with cords. The master and his familiars then had a conversation in Latin (the language best understood by Satan and his emissaries) concerning the prisoner's baptism. They stripped him, and were about to begin a painful operation, when Charlie, bound though he was, succeeded in crossing himself and pronouncing a sacred name. That instant the pages started back trembling, and their weapons fell from their hands. Another of the company was thrown down and bound by the imps; but when they attempted to seize the friar, they could not so much as touch his frock. The fair Delany stood trembling behind the pious father; and on the fiends feeling their want of power over him, they rushed at the young virgin. But the moment they touched her garments, they retired in dismay. The friar, remembering that the maid had the blessed Gospel concealed in her bosom, concluded that in that precious book she found protection. As to his own personal safety he had no fear, as he possessed a charm, proof against Satan himself. "He drew his cross from below his frock--that cross which had been consecrated at the shrine of Saint Peter, bathed in holy water, and blessed with many blessings from the mouths of ancient martyrs--had done wondrous miracles in the hands of saints of former days--and lifting that reverently on high, he pronounced the words from holy writ, against which no demon or false spirit's power could prevail. In one moment the three imps fled yelling from the apartment." At the same time the countenance of the enchanter fell, and his whole body quaked. The friar then unloosed those that were bound.

"Great and magnificent Master of Arts," said the friar, addressing Michael Scott, "we are come to thee from the man that ruleth over the borders of the land, and leadeth forth his troops to battle. He sendeth unto thee greeting, and beseecheth to know of thee what shall befall unto his people and to his house in the latter days. It is thy counsel alone that he asketh, for thou art renowned for wisdom and foresight to the farthest corners of the earth. The two nations are engaged in a great and bloody contest, and high are the stakes for which they play. The man who sent us entreateth of thee to disclose unto thy servants who shall finally prevail, and whether it behoveth him to join himself to the captain of his people. He hath moreover sent unto thee, by our hand, these two beautiful captives, the one to be thine handmaiden, and the other to be thy servant, and run at thy bidding."

The wizard, highly flattered, listened with patience to the friar, and answered that the request made would take many days to consider, as he had to deal with those who were more capricious than the changing seasons, and more perverse than opposing winds and tides. Reluctantly the friar and his friends were prevailed on to remain at the goblin castle, and how it fared with them we shall soon see.

Gourlay was summoned into the presence of Scott, who instructed him to provide an entertainment for the strangers. In due time the steward appeared with his rod of office in his hand, and with great ceremony marshalled his guests upstairs to an apartment, where there was a table covered with rich viands in great abundance. A few graceless fellows in the company began to eat and drink before a blessing was asked, and seemingly fared well. But with the holy friar it was different. In conformity with a good old custom, he lifted up his hands, closed his eyes, and, leaning forward, repeated his oft-said stereotyped phrases. In his respectful attitude, he came in close contact with what appeared to be a beautiful smoking sirloin of beef. So near was he to it that he actually breathed upon it, and was nearly overcome by its savoury flavour. Never had blessing a more baneful effect on meat: when the friar opened his eyes the beef was gone--there was nothing left but an insignificant thing resembling the joint of a frog's leg, or that of a rat.

A contention arose between Michael Scott and the friar as to which of them could perform the most wonderful feats; and when the former discovered that he was in conversation with no less a personage than the Primate of Douay, author of the book of arts, he was much pleased. By means of a curious lantern, he made it appear that the mountain Cape-Law was rent and divided into three parts. This was only an optical delusion, but he in reality blew poor Gourlay into the air by an explosion of gunpowder, the composition and power of which were unknown to the wizard, or to any one except the friar. The master could not bear the idea of being outdone by any one. He strode the floor in gloomy indignation. "Look," he shouted, "at that mountain on the east. It is known to you all--the great hill of Eildon. You know and see that it is one round, smooth, and unbroken cone." He then gave three knocks with his heel on the floor, and called the names of his three pages, Prig, Prim, and Pricker. As at other times, these infernal spirits were before him, exclaiming, "Work, master, work; what work now?" "Look at that mountain yclept the hill of Eildon. Go and twist me it into three." The imps looked with Satanic glare. "The hill is granite," said one. "And five arrows' flight high," said another. "And seventy round the base," said the first. "All the power of earth and hell to boot are unmeet to the task," added the third. In an imperious manner, the master declared the thing must be done. "I know my conditions; they are sealed and subscribed, and I am not to be disobeyed," continued he. The three pages began singing:

> "Pick and spade
> To our aid!
> Flaught and flail,
> Fire and hail:
> Winds arise, and tempests brattle,
> And, if you will, the thunders rattle.
> Come away,
> Elfin grey,
> Much to do ere break of day!
> Come with spade, and sieve, and shovel;
> Come with roar, and rout, and revel;
> Come with crow, and come with crane,
> Strength of steed, and weight of wain.
> Crash of rock, and roar of river,
> And, if you will, with thunders shiver!
> Come away,
> Elfin grey;
> Much to do ere break of day."

As they sang the last line, they sped away, in the forms of three crows, toward Eildon Hill.

That night was a dreadful one. A storm burst forth in all its fury, sweeping over hill and dale. The woods roared and crashed before the blast, and a driving rain dashed with such violence on the earth, that it seemed as if a thousand cataracts poured from the western heaven to mix with the tempest below. Now and again eldritch shrieks, as of some one perishing, were heard, and then the voices of angry spirits, yelling through the tempest, reached the ear. One of the inmates of the castle was reminded, by the raging storm, of the warlocks' hymn:

> "Pother, pother,
> My master and brother,
> Who may endure thee,
> Thus failing in fury?
> King of the tempest that travels the plain
> King of the snow, and the hail, and the rain,
> Lend to thy lever yet seven times seven,
> Blow up the blue flame for bolt and for levin,
> The red forge of hell with the bellows of heaven!
> With hoop and with hammer!
> With yell and with yammer,

Hold them in play
Till the dawn of day!
Pother, pother!
My sovereign and brother.
O strain to thy lever,
This world to sever
In two or in three--
What joy it would be!
What toiling and mailing, and mighty commotions!
What rending of hills, and what roaring of oceans!
Ay, that is thy voice, I know it full well;
And that is thy whistle's majestic swell;
But why wilt thou ride thy furious race
Along the bounds of vacant space,
While there is tongue of flesh to scream,
And life to start, and blood to stream?
    Yet pother, pother!
    My sovereign and brother
And men shall see, ere the rising sun,
What deeds thy mighty arm hath done."

Michael Scott and his guests kept watch together during the eventful night; and when the friar and Charlie stepped out to the battlements in the morning, they beheld the great mountain of Eildon, which before then had but one cone, piled up in three hills, as described by us in chapter XVI.

CHAPTER XXII.

Allan Ramsay--"The Gentle Shepherd"--Bauldy the   Clown--Mause the reputed Witch--A Witch's   Crantraips--Praying Backwards--Sad Misfortunes attributed to Mause--Supposed Power of the Devil to   raise the Wind and send Rain and Thunder--Mause's   Reflections--Sir William disturbed--Symon's Announcement--Promise to gain a Lassie's Heart--Doings   of the supposed Witch--Witches' Tricks--Longfellow's   "Golden Legend"--"Song of Hiawatha." Allan Ramsay, who wrote in the first half of the eighteenth century, does not appear to have believed in witches or evil spirits. He, however, like other poets, found it convenient to introduce superstition into his poetical effusions. This will be seen from the following extracts from his *Gentle Shepherd*.

BAULDY.
"What's this?--I canna bear't!--'tis worse than hell,
To be sae burnt with love, yet daurna tell!
O Peggy! sweeter than the dawning day;
Sweeter than gowany glens or new-mawn hay;
Blyther than lambs that frisk out o'er the knows;
Straighter than aught that in the forest grows;
Her een the clearest blob of dew outshines;
The lily in her breast its beauty tines;
Her legs, her arms, her cheeks, her mouth, her een,
Will be my dead, that will be shortly seen!
For Pate looes her--waes me!--and she looes Pate
And I with Neps, by some unlucky fate,
Made a daft vow. O, but ane be a beast,
That makes rash aiths till he's afore the priest!
I darna speak my mind, else a' the three,
But doubt, wad prove ilk ane my enemy.
'Tis sair to thole;--I'll try some witchcraft art,
To break with ane, and win the other's heart.

Here Mausy lives, a witch that for sma' price
Can cast her cantraips, and gie me advice.
She can o'ercast the night, and cloud the moon,
And make the deils obedient to her crune;
At midnight hours, o'er the kirk-yard she raves,
And howks unchristen'd weans out of their graves;
Boils up their livers in a warlock's pow;
Rins withershins about the hemlock low;
And seven times does her prayers backwards pray,
Till Plotcock comes with lumps of Lapland clay,
Mixt with the venom of black taids and snakes:
Of this unsonsy pictures aft she makes
Of ony ane she hates,--and gars expire
With slow and racking pains afore a fire,
Stuck fu' of pins; the devilish pictures melt;
The pain by fowk they represent is felt.
And yonder's Mause: Ay, ay, she kens fu' weel,
When ane like me comes rinning to the deil!
She and her cat sit beeking in her yard:
To speak my errand, faith, amaist I'm fear'd!
But I maun do't, tho' I should never thrive:
They gallop fast that deils and lasses drive.

     *   *   *   *   *

 How does auld honest lucky of the glen?
Ye look baith hale end fair at threescore-ten.

       MAUSE.
 E'en twining out a thread with little din,
And beeking my cauld limbs afore the sun.
What brings my bairn this gate sae air at morn?
Is there nae muck to lead? to thresh nae corn?

       BAULDY.
 Enough of baith: but something that requires
Your helping hand employs now all my cares.

       MAUSE.
 My helping hand! alake, what can I do,

That underneith baith eild and poortith bow?

BAULDY.
Ay, but you're wise, and wiser far than we;
Or maist part of the parish tells a lie.

MAUSE.
Of what kind wisdom think ye I'm possest,
That lifts my character aboon the rest?

BAULDY.
The word that gangs, how ye're sae wise and fell,
Ye'll maybe tak it ill gif I should tell.

MAUSE.
What folk say of me, Bauldy, let me hear;
Keep naething up, ye naething have to fear.

BAULDY.
Well, since ye bid me, I shall tell ye a'
That ilk ane talks about you, but a flaw.
When last the wind made Glaud a roofless barn;
When last the burn bore down my mither's yarn;
When Brawny, elf-shot, never mair came hame;
When Tibby kirn'd, and there nae butter came;
When Bessy Freetock's chuffy-cheeked wean
To a fairy turn'd, and cou'dna stand its lane;
When Wattie wander'd ae night thro' the shaw
And tint himsell amaist amang the snaw;
When Mungo's mare stood still and swat wi' fright,
When he brought east the howdy under night;
When Bawsy shot to dead upon the green;
And Sara tint a snood was nae mair seen;--
You, lucky, gat the wyte of a' fell out;
And ilka ane here dreads ye round about,--
And say they may that mint to do ye skaith:
For me to wrang ye I'll be very laith;
But when I neist make groats, I'll strive to please
You with a firlot of them mixt with pease.

MAUSE.
 I thank ye, lad!--Now tell me your demand;
And, if I can, I'll lend my helping hand.

BAULDY.
 Then, I like Peggy; Neps is fond of me;
Peggy likes Pate; and Patie's bauld and slee,
And looes sweet Meg; but Neps I downa see.
Could ye turn Patie's love to Neps, and then
Peggy's to me, I'd be the happiest man.

MAUSE.
 I'll try my airt to gar the bowls row right;
Sae gang your ways and come again at night;
'Gainst that time I'll some simple things prepare,
Worth all your pease and groats, tak ye nae care.

BAULDY.
 Well, Mause, I'll come, gif I the road can find;
But if ye raise the deil, he'll raise the wind;
Syne rain and thunder, maybe, when 'tis late
Will make the night sae mirk, I'll tine the gate.
We're a' to rant in Symie's at a feast,--
O! will ye come, like badrans, for a jest?
And there you can our different haviours spy;
There's nane shall ken o't there but you and I.

MAUSE.
 'Tis like I may: But let na on what's past
'Tween you and me, else fear a kittle cast.

BAULDY.
 If I aught of your secrets e'er advance,
May ye ride on me ilka night to France!

MAUSE.
 This fool imagines--as do many sic--
That I'm a witch in compact with Auld Nick,
Because by education I was taught
To speak and act aboon their common thought:

Their gross mistake shall quickly now appear;
Soon shall they ken what brought, what keeps me here.
Now since the royal Charles, and right's restor'd,
A shepherdess is daughter to a lord.
The bonny foundling that's brought up by Glaud,
Wha has an uncle's care on her bestow'd,--
Her infant life I sav'd, when a false friend
Bow'd to the usurper, and her death design'd,
To establish him and his in all these plains
That by right heritage to her pertains.
She's now in her sweet bloom, has blood and charms
Of too much value for a shepherd's arms.
None know't but me!--And if the morn were come,
I'll tell them tales will gar them a' sing dumb.

* * * * *

SIR WILLIAM.
　How goes the night? does day-light yet appear
Symon, you're very timeously asteer.

SYMON.
　I'm sorry, sir, that we've disturb'd your rest;
But some strange thing has Bauldy's spirit opprest,
He's seen some witch, or wrestled with a ghaist.

BAULDY.
　O! ay; dear sir, in troth, 'tis very true;
And I am come to make my plaint to you.

SIR WILLIAM.
　I lang to hear 't.

BAULDY.
　　　Ah! sir, the witch ca'd Mause,
That wins aboon the mill amang the haws,
First promis'd that she'd help me with her art,
To gain a bonny thrawart lassie's heart.
As she had trysted, I met wi'er this night;
But may nae friend of mine get sic a fright!

For the curst hag, instead of doing me good--
The very thought o't's like to freeze my blood!
Rais'd up a ghaist, or deil, I kenna whilk,
Like a dead corse in sheet as white as milk;
Black hands it had, and face as wan as death.
Upon me fast the witch and it fell baith,
And gat me down, while I, like a great fool,
Was labour'd as I wont to be at school.
My heart out of its hool was like to loup;
I pithless grew with fear, and had nae hope;
Till, with an elritch laugh, they vanished quite.
Syne I half dead with anger, fear, and spite,
Crap up and fled straight frae them, sir, to you,
Hoping your help to gie the deil his due.
I'm sure my heart will ne'er gie o'er to dunt,
Till in a fat tar-barrel Mause be burnt!

       *   *   *   *   *

          SIR WILLIAM.
  Troth, Symon, Bauldy's more afraid than hurt;
The witch and ghaist have made themselves good sport.
What silly notions crowd the clouded mind,
That is through want of education blind!

          SYMON.
  But does your honour think there's nae sic thing
As witches raising deils up through a ring?
Syne playing tricks--a thousand I could tell--
Cou'd ne'er be contriv'd on this side hell.

          SIR WILLIAM.
  Such as the devil's dancing in a moor,
Amongst a few old women craz'd and poor,
Who were rejoiced to see him frisk and lowp
O'er braes and bogs with candles in * * *
Appearing sometimes like a black-horn'd cow,
Aft-times like Bawty, Badrans, or a sow;
Then with his train through airy paths to glide,
While they on carts, or clowns, or broomstaffs ride;

Or in an egg-shell skim out o'er the main,
To drink their leader's health in France or Spain;
Then aft by night bumbaze hare-hearted fools,
By tumbling down their cupboards, chairs, and stools.
Whate'er's in spells, or if there witches be,
Such whimsies seem the most absurd to me."

To glean from Cowper, Wordsworth, Tennyson, and the many other poets
who have contributed to superstitious lore, would swell this portion
of our work (**The Poets and Superstition**) to an undue proportion; and
therefore we take leave of the poets, after giving extracts from
Longfellow, whose talented effusions are not only read and appreciated
in America and England, but over the whole world.

FROM "THE GOLDEN LEGEND."

LUCIFER.
"Hasten! hasten!
O ye spirits!
From its station drag the ponderous
Cross of iron, that to mock us
Is uplifted high in air!

VOICES.
O, we cannot!
For around it
All the saints and guardian angels
Throng in legions to protect it;
They defeat us everywhere!

THE BELLS.
Laudo Deum verum!
Plebem voco!
Congrego clerum!

LUCIFER.
Lower! lower!
Hover downward!
Seize the loud, vociferous bells, and

Clashing, clanging, to the pavement
Hurl them from their windy tower!

       VOICES.
All thy thunders
Here are harmless!
For these bells have been anointed,
And baptised with holy water!
They defy our utmost power.

       THE BELLS.
   Defunctos ploro!
   Pestem fugo!
   Festa decoro!

       LUCIFER.
Shake the casements!
Break the painted
Panes, that flame with gold and crimson;
Scatter them like leaves of autumn,
Swept away before the blast!

       VOICES.
O, we cannot!
The archangel
Michael flames from every window,
With the sword of fire that drove us
Headlong out of heaven, aghast!

       THE BELLS.
   Funera plango!
   Fulgura frango!
   Sabbata pango!

       LUCIFER.
Aim your lightnings
At the oaken,
Massive, iron-studded portals!
Sack the house of God, and scatter
Wide the ashes of the dead!

VOICES.

O, we cannot!
The apostles
And the martyrs, wrapped in mantles,
Stand as warders at the entrance,
Stand as sentinels o'erhead!

THE BELLS.

Excito lentos!
Dissipo ventos!
Paco cruentos!

LUCIFER.

Baffled! baffled!
Inefficient,
Craven spirits! leave this labour
Unto Time, the great destroyer!
Come away, ere night is gone!

VOICES.

Onward! onward!
With the night wind,
Over field and farm and forest,
Lonely homestead, darksome hamlet,
Blighting all we breathe upon!"

THE SONG OF HIAWATHA.

"Should you ask me whence these stories?
Whence these legends and traditions,
With the odours of the forest,
With the dew and damp of meadows,
With the curling smoke of wigwams,
With the rushing of great rivers,
With their frequent repetitions,
And their wild reverberations,
As of thunder in the mountains?
  I should answer, I should tell you:

'From the forests and the prairies,
From the great lakes of the Northland,
From the land of the Ojibways,
From the land of the Dacotahs,
From the mountains, moors, and fenlands,
Where the heron, the Shuh-shuh-gah,
Feeds among the reeds and rushes.
I repeat them as I heard them
From the lips of Nawadaha,
The musician, the sweet singer.'

* * * * *

Can it be the sun descending
O'er the level plain of water?
Or the red swan floating, flying,
Wounded by the magic arrow,
Staining all the waves with crimson,
With the crimson of its life-blood,
Filling all the air with splendour,
With the splendour of its plumage?
 Yes, it is the sun descending,
Sinking down into the water;
All the sky is stained with purple,
All the water flushed with crimson!
No; it is the red swan floating,
Diving down beneath the water;
To the sky its wings are lifted,
With its blood the waves are reddened
 Over it the star of evening
Melts and trembles through the purple
Hangs suspended in the twilight.
No; it is a bead of wampum
On the robes of the Great Spirit,
As he passes through the twilight,
Walks in silence through the heavens!
 This with joy beheld Iagoo,
And he said in haste, 'Behold it!
See the sacred star of evening!
You shall hear a tale of wonder;

Hear the story of Osseo,
Son of the evening star Osseo.
  'Once, in days no more remembered,
Ages nearer the beginning,
When the heavens were closer to us,
And the gods were more familiar,
In the Northland lived a hunter,
With ten young and comely daughters,
Tall and lithe as wands of willow;
Only Oweenee, the youngest,
She the wilful and the wayward,
She the silent, dreamy maiden,
Was the fairest of the sisters.
  'All these women married warriors,
Married brave and haughty husbands;
Only Oweenee, the youngest,
Laughed and flouted all her lovers,
All her young and handsome suitors,
And then married old Osseo,
Old Osseo, poor and ugly,
Broken with age and weak with coughing,
Always coughing like a squirrel.
  'Ah, but beautiful within him
Was the spirit of Osseo,
From the evening star descended,
Star of evening, star of woman,
Star of tenderness and passion!
All its fire was in his bosom,
All its beauty in his spirit,
All its mystery in his being,
All its splendour in his language!
  'And her lovers, the rejected,
Handsome men with belts of wampum,
Handsome men with paint and feathers,
Pointed at her in derision,
Followed her with jest and laughter,
But she said, "I care not for you,
Care not for your belts of wampum,
Care not for your paint and feathers,
Care not for your jests and laughter:

I am happy with Osseo!"
 'Once to some great feast invited,
Through the damp and dusk of evening
Walked together the ten sisters,
Walked together with their husbands;
Slowly followed old Osseo,
With fair Oweenee beside him;
All the others chatted gaily,
These two only walked in silence.
 'At the western sky Osseo
Gazed intent, as if imploring,
Often stopped and gazed imploring
At the trembling star of evening,
At the tender star of woman;
And they heard him murmur softly,
"***Ah, showain nemeshin, Nosa!***
Pray, pity me, my father!"
 '"Listen!" said the elder sister,
"He is praying to his father!
What a pity that the old man
Does not stumble in the pathway,
Does not break his neck by falling!"
And they laughed till all the forest
Rang with their unseemly laughter.
 'On their pathway through the woodlands
Lay an oak by storms uprooted,
Lay the great trunk of an oak-tree
Buried half in leaves and mosses,
Mouldering, crumbling, huge and hollow.
And Osseo, when he saw it,
Gave a shout, a cry of anguish,
Leaped into its yawning cavern,
At one end went in an old man,
Wasted, wrinkled, old, and ugly;
From the other came a young man,
Tall and straight and strong and handsome.
 'Thus Osseo was transfigured,
Thus restored to youth and beauty;
But, alas for good Osseo,
And for Oweenee, the faithful!

Strangely, too, was she transfigured.
Changed into a weak old woman,
With a staff she tottered onward,
Wasted, wrinkled, old, and ugly!
And the sisters and their husbands
Laughed until the echoing forest
Rang with their unseemly laughter.
  'But Osseo turned not from her,
Walked with slower step beside her,
Took her hand, as brown and withered
As an oak-leaf is in winter,
Called her sweetheart, Nenemoosha,
Soothed her with soft words of kindness,
Till they reached the lodge of feasting,
Till they sat down in the wigwam,
Sacred to the star of evening,
To the tender star of woman.
  'Wrapt in visions, lost in dreaming,
At the banquet sat Osseo;
All were merry, all were happy,
All were joyous but Osseo.
Neither food nor drink he tasted,
Neither did he speak nor listen,
But as one bewildered sat he,
Looking dreamily and sadly,
First at Oweenee, then upward
At the gleaming sky above them.
  'Then a voice was heard, a whisper,
Coming from the starry distance,
Coming from the empty vastness,
Low and musical and tender;
And the voice said, "O Osseo!
O my son, my best beloved!
Broken are the spells that bound you,
All the charms of the magicians,
All the magic powers of evil;
Come to me; ascend, Osseo!
  '"Taste the food that stands before you;
It is blessed and enchanted,
It has magic virtues in it,

It will change you to a spirit.
All your bowls and all your kettles
Shall be wood and clay no longer;
But the bowls be changed to wampum,
And the kettles shall be silver;
They shall shine like shells of scarlet,
Like the fire shall gleam and glimmer.

'"And the women shall no longer
Bear the dreary doom of labour,
But be changed to birds, and glisten
With the beauty of the starlight,
Painted with the dusky splendours
Of the skies and clouds of evening!"

'What Osseo heard as whispers,
What as words he comprehended,
Was but music to the others,
Music as of birds afar off,
Of the whippoorwill afar off,
Of the lonely Wawonaissa
Singing in the darksome forest.

'Then the lodge began to tremble,
Straight began to shake and tremble,
And they felt it rising, rising,
Slowly through the air ascending,
From the darkness of the tree-tops
Forth into the dewy starlight,
Till it passed the topmost branches;
And behold! the wooden dishes
All were changed to shells of scarlet!
And behold! the earthen kettles
All were changed to bowls of silver!
And the roof-poles of the wigwam
Were as glittering rods of silver,
And the roof of bark upon them
As the shining shards of beetles.

'Then Osseo gazed around him,
And he saw the nine fair sisters,
All the sisters and their husbands,
Changed to birds of various plumage.
Some were jays, and some were magpies,

Others thrushes, others blackbirds;
And they hopped and sang and twittered,
Perked and fluttered all their feathers,
Strutted in their various plumage,
And their tails like fans unfolded.
  'Only Oweenee, the youngest,
Was not changed, but sat in silence,
Wasted, wrinkled, old, and ugly,
Looking sadly at the others;
Till Osseo, gazing upward,
Gave another cry of anguish,
Such a cry as he had uttered
By the oak-tree in the forest.
  'Then returned her youth and beauty,
And her soiled and tattered garments
Were transformed to robes of ermine,
And her staff became a feather,
Yes, a shining silver feather!
  'And again the wigwam trembled,
Swayed and rushed through airy currents,
Through transparent cloud and vapour,
And amid celestial splendours
On the evening star alighted,
As a snow-flake falls on snow-flake,
As a leaf drops on a river,
As the thistle-down on water.
  'Forth with cheerful words of welcome
Came the father of Osseo,
He with radiant locks of silver,
He with eyes serene and tender.
And he said, "My son, Osseo,
Hang the cage of birds you bring there,
Hang the cage with rods of silver,
And the birds with glistening feathers,
At the doorway of my wigwam."
  'At the door he hung the bird-cage,
And they entered in and gladly
Listened to Osseo's father,
Ruler of the star of evening,
As he said, "O my Osseo!

I have had compassion on you,
Given you back your youth and beauty,
Into birds of various plumage
Changed your sisters and their husbands;
Changed them thus because they mocked you
In the figure of the old man,
In that aspect sad and wrinkled,
Could not see your heart of passion,
Could not see your youth immortal;
Only Oweenee, the faithful,
Saw your naked heart and loved you.
  '"In the lodge that glimmers yonder,
In the little star that twinkles
Through the vapours, on the left hand,
Lives the envious Evil Spirit,
The Wabeno, the magician,
Who transformed you to an old man.
Take heed lest his beams fall on you,
For the rays he darts around him
Are the power of his enchantment,
Are the arrows that he uses."

  'Many years, in peace and quiet
On the peaceful star of evening
Dwelt Osseo with his father;
Many years in song and flutter,
At the doorway of the wigwam,
Hung the cage with rods of silver,
And fair Oweenee, the faithful,
Bore a son unto Osseo,
With the beauty of his mother,
With the courage of his father.
  'And the boy grew up and prospered,
And Osseo, to delight him,
Made him little bows and arrows,
Opened the great cage of silver,
And let loose his aunts and uncles,
All those birds with glossy feathers,
For his little son to shoot at.
  'Round and round they wheeled and darted,

Filled the evening star with music,
With their songs of joy and freedom;
Filled the evening star with splendour,
With the fluttering of their plumage;
Till the boy, the little hunter,
Bent his bow and shot an arrow,
Shot a swift and fatal arrow,
And a bird, with shining feathers,
At his feet fell wounded sorely.
    'But, O wondrous transformation!
'Twas no bird he saw before him,
'Twas a beautiful young woman,
With the arrow in her bosom!
    'When her blood fell on the planet,
On the sacred star of evening,
Broken was the spell of magic,
Powerless was the strange enchantment,
And the youth, the fearless bowman,
Suddenly felt himself descending,
Held by unseen hands, but sinking
Downward through the empty spaces,
Downward through the clouds and vapours,
Till he rested on an island,
On an island, green and grassy,
Yonder in the big sea-water.
    'After him he saw descending
All the birds with shining feathers,
Fluttering, falling, wafted downward,
Like the painted leaves of autumn;
And the lodge with poles of silver,
With its roof like wings of beetles,
Like the shining shards of beetles,
By the winds of heaven uplifted,
Slowly sank upon the island,
Bringing back the good Osseo,
Bringing Oweenee, the faithful.
    'Then the birds, again transfigured,
Resumed the shape of mortals,
Took their shape, but not their stature;
They remained as little people,

Like the pigmies, the Puk-Wudjies;
And on pleasant nights of summer,
When the evening star was shining,
Hand in hand they danced together
On the island's craggy headlands,
On the sand-beach low and level.
  'Still their glittering lodge is seen there,
On the tranquil summer evenings,
And upon the shore the fisher
Sometimes hears their happy voices,
Sees them dancing in the starlight!'"

MONARCHS, PRIESTS, PHILOSOPHERS, AND SUPERSTITION.
CHAPTER XXIII.

Generality of Superstition--Commencement of Monarchy   in Scotland--King Fergus I. crowned on the Fatal Stone   of Destiny--Signs, Assistance of Spirits, Magicians,   and Fortune-tellers--Natholocus sends a Friend to   consult a Cunning Woman--Her Prediction   verified--Constantine and Maxentius--A Heavenly Cross--A Famous Standard--Queen Guanora's Grave--Fear   of St. Martin--The Church's Belief in the Intercession   of Departed Saints--Relics venerated--King bewitched   by Witches of Forres--Evil Signs during Elthus   Alipes's Reign--Sea Monster in the Don--Kenneth III.   killed by an Infernal Machine--Virtue of Precious   Stones--Weird Sisters--Consulting a   Pythoness--Predictions by Druids--Domitian's Death   foretold by Astrologers--Simon Magus--A Platonic Philosopher charged with Sorcery--The Emperor Julian   instructed in Magic.

In speaking of superstition, it may be truly said, "As with the people, so with the priest; as with the subjects, so with the monarch." In the humble cot the peasant is deluded and overawed by superstition; in the church the priest lays claim to supernatural power; and crowned heads have played a not unimportant part among the believers in and performers of the occult science, which has so long held the souls of men in bondage. We have it on record that a monarch has been made to tremble by the sayings of an old woman, supposed to be in league with the prince of darkness. A king and his army have been kept from battle by the movements of a harmless quadruped, or by the flight of a bird, unaware that before sunset it would be the eagle's portion. Other sovereigns have supported their tyranny over a down-trodden people by an arrogant pretension to an authority derived in a mysterious manner from another world.

Ancient historians date the commencement of monarchy in Scotland from Fergus I., who was crowned according to the superstitious custom of the age in which he reigned. He was seated on the fatal stone of destiny, to be afterwards described. Both before and after the introduction of Christianity into Scotland, not a freebooting excursion was undertaken before seeking a sign; not a friend was to be gained without asking the assistance of a generous spirit or fairy; and not an enemy to be overcome till the magicians and fortune-tellers secured the aid of unearthly creatures, either good or bad. When Natholocus's cruelty and oppression excited an insurrection, he had recourse to cunning people, supposed to be in league with Satan. He sent one of his particular friends to a distant island to an old woman, said to be skilled in necromancy, to inquire whether any of his courtiers were seeking his destruction. The sorceress, having consulted her familiar spirits, answered that Natholocus would die a violent death by the hand of one of his most intimate friends. On being pressed to disclose by whose hand the blow would be struck, she replied, "By thine own." The messenger reproached the woman, and told her that he entertained the greatest friendship for his master. He was afraid to tell Natholocus what the fortune-teller had said, and therefore entertained him with such false predictions as he knew would inspire confidence. For what reason we are not informed, but this is certain that the servant's friendship turned into hatred, and before long he verified the witch's prophecy.

Constantine, the son of Constantius Chlorus, being proclaimed his father's successor, caused Maxentius to declare war against Constantine. The latter, although a heathen, implored the true Deity to assist him. His prayers were heard. As he was marching with his army, about mid-day, he, and all who were with him, beheld in the heavens a bright cross of light, with an inscription over it, "By this, conquer." Constantine was greatly surprised at the vision, and the troops were equally astonished. On the following night a holy being appeared to him, and ordered him to make a representation of what he had seen in the sky, and use it for an ensign in battle. Next morning he called workers of fine material, and instructed them to make a standard according to tracings he prepared. It was made, adorned with gold and sparkling precious stones; and we scarcely require to say that Constantine was victorious when he fought under such a famous standard.

Queen Guanora, widow of Arthur, was, after the king's fall, about the middle of the sixth century, taken prisoner, and kept as such during the remainder of her life at Dunbar. She was buried at Meigle; and, if tradition can be trusted, every female walking over her grave is doomed to perpetual sterility. Speaking of the grave reminds us of a son of Clotaire, who was desirous of executing vengeance against his enemy Bason. He was prevented from doing so by the latter fleeing to St. Martin's Church for sanctuary. The prince, fearing that an invasion of the church would displease the saint, wrote a letter, and placed it on the glorified individual's tomb, requesting to be informed if he would be guilty of an outrage against religion were he to drag Bason from the church. For reasons best known to the saint, he did not return an answer. This mode of obtaining information may now be considered ridiculous; but it was not considered so, even in the Church, in the eighth century. After due inquiry and consideration, the second Council of Nice, in the year 787, declared that the Church had always believed it lawful and useful to invoke the intercession of departed saints, and to venerate their relics.

Duff, the son of Malcolm, having established Culen, son of Indulph, Prince of Cumberland, set out for the Hebrides, where great predatory disorders prevailed. He summoned the thanes of the isles to appear before him, and swore that if any of them should oppress the poorer inhabitants, he would visit the actors with condign punishment. His threats not being enough to deter the depredators, active measures were taken to punish the offenders. Meantime the king fell into a languid sickness, which baffled the skill of his physicians. A rumour was circulated that he was suffering under the incantations of certain far-famed witches at Forres. The report reaching the king's ears, he caused certain confidential servants to investigate the case secretly. Donevald, master of the fort at Forres, having learned that the *bonne amie* of a soldier there was the daughter of a witch, apprehended the damsel, and learned from her the whole secret concerning a diabolical plot to torture his Majesty. Means were taken to secure the wretches concerned when engaged in their devilish art. So carefully were the faithful servants' plans laid, that they could tell what part each traitorous one performed. While one of them turned, upon a wooden spit before the fire, a wax image of the king, fashioned as was supposed by Satan, another of them sang her charms, and poured a liquid slowly upon the image. According to the interpretation of these wicked women, the vocal charm kept his Majesty awake; that while the effigy was exposed to the fire and moistened with the liquor, he would sweat and consume away; and that when the image dissolved away, the king would cease to exist. The women declared they had been hired by the nobles of Murray--who were highly displeased at their king for oppressing them and compelling them to betake themselves to labour unsuitable to their rank--to perform the cruel acts. The implements of enchantment were destroyed, the witches burned, and the king recovered. This was but a mere respite to his Majesty: the friends upon whom he relied turned their hands against him, and before long his mangled body lay buried in the bed of the river Findhorn.

Elthus Alipes, or Swiftfoot, being a worthless prince, was confined in prison to the day of his death. Historians record many evil signs seen during his short reign--two years. An ominous comet, and shoals of monstrous fishes resembling human beings, swimming with half their bodies above the water, and having black skin covering their heads and necks, were among the portentous appearances. Spalding, in his history of the troubles of Scotland in his own time, describes a sea monster seen in the river Don in the month of June 1635. It had, says the historian, a head like a great mastiff dog, hands, arms, and breast like a man, short legs and a tail. Spalding concluded that the appearance of such a monster did not come as a sign of good to Aberdeen.

Kenneth III. became a victim to revenge, an inordinate taste for magnificence, and superstition. Kenneth, it appears, for reasons well pleasing to the Church, visited the shrine of St. Palladius at Fordun; and on returning home he fell into a snare laid for him. Around the castle of Fettercairn were grounds well stocked with beasts of chase, and there the king intended to indulge in the manly exercise of hunting. The owner of that place, Lady Fenella, a relative of Constantine and Grime, having a long deep-rooted hatred against Kenneth, conceived the design of bringing him to an untimely end. With this object in view, she built a grand tower, containing an infernal machine for throwing javelins or sharp-pointed lances at any one who should handle a golden apple, set with precious stones, held in the hand of a bronze statue of Kenneth that stood in the centre of a room. She invited him to become her guest--an invitation he accepted. After dinner, the perfidious woman conducted him into the tower, professedly to see and admire the exquisite furnishings with which it was decorated. In his fondness for grandeur, he lingered to admire the elegant figures and flowers; the rich tapestry, interwoven with gold; and the statue with its golden apple. Just at the moment the king's eyes rested on the statue, Fenella stepped forward and said, "Sire, this is a statue of your Majesty; I have given it the most adorned place in my castle, that all may perceive in what veneration I hold you. The apple you behold is intended as a present to you, beloved monarch--unworthy indeed of your acceptance, yet an expression of the good-will of the donor. The inserted gems are an emerald, a hyacinth, a sapphire, a topaz, a ruby, an azure, emitting an antidote against pestilence and deadly poison." Having thus excited the king's curiosity, she abruptly left the apartment, seemingly with the intention of bringing some other strange article for his inspection. Meantime Kenneth, left alone and charmed with the apple, commenced handling it. In an instant the secret machinery, being set in motion, discharged a shower of deadly darts against the king, who fell mortally wounded on the floor. The traitorous Fenella, rejoicing at her bloody cruelty, mounted a swift steed and fled far away before her act of treachery became known. Had she remained in Scotland, a cruel death would have been her doom, but she escaped to Ireland, and was lost sight of.

Fenella is reported as pointing out to the king pretended special virtues, to be found in the gems that ornamented the golden apple. And no doubt the credulous monarch believed what she said, because we have it on record, that not only in the tenth century, but long before and after it, both pagans and professing Christians believed that precious stones possessed greater virtues than even that which she ascribed to the settings of her golden apple.

The story of Macbeth and the three witches, noticed in chapter XVII., does not require to be repeated. Greater men than Macbeth were wont to consult fortune-tellers. A Druid told Alexander Severus that he would be unhappy. Vopiscus relates that the prince, having consulted the Gaulish Druids whether the empire should remain in his family, received the answer, that no name would be more glorious in the empire than that of the descendants of Claudius.

Titus Flavius Domitian, who commanded himself to be called by the names by which the Most High is known, and who passed the greatest part of his time in catching flies and killing them with a bodkin, became suspicious of his best friends, and his fears were increased by the predictions of astrologers. He was so frightened, that, to prevent sudden surprise, he caused a wall of shining stones to be built round the terrace where he usually walked, that he might perceive, as in a looking-glass, whether any one was approaching him. His precautions were unavailing: he perished by the hand of an assassin, as was foretold.

It is reported that St. John was thrown into a cauldron of boiling oil, by order of the Emperor Domitian, but that he came out unhurt. He was then at Rome, and from thence he was banished to the Isle of Patmos.

Lucius Apuleius, a Platonic philosopher of the second century, having married a lady of fortune against the wish of her relatives, they pretended that he had made use of sorcery to gain her heart and money. He was dragged before Claudius Maximus, on the charge of being a magician. In his defence he said, "Do you wonder that a woman should marry again after living thirteen years a widow? It is much more wonderful that she did not marry sooner. You think that magic must have been employed to induce a widow of her age to marry a young man; on the contrary, this very circumstance shows how little occasion there was for magic." He continued: "She was neither handsome nor young, nor such as could in any way tempt him to have recourse to enchantments." He also took notice of many inconveniences which attended the marrying of widows, and spoke highly of the advantages of a maid over a widow. "A handsome virgin," said he, "let her be ever so poor, is abundantly portioned; she brings to her husband a heart quite new, together with the flowers and first fruits of her beauty. It was with great reason," he argued, "that husbands set so great value upon virginity; all the other goods which a woman brought her husband were of such a nature that he might return them if he had a mind, but the flowers of virginity could not be given back; they remained in the possession of the first husband." Through his eloquence he escaped punishment, and the odium of being branded a sorcerer.

Maximus, the celebrated cynic philosopher and magician of Ephesus, instructed the Emperor Julian in magic. Certain historians say it was through his teaching that the apostacy of Julian originated. When the emperor went in search of conquests, the magician promised him success, and even predicted that his triumphs would be more numerous and brilliant than those of Alexander. After the death of Julian, Maximus was nearly sacrificed by the soldiers, but his friends succeeded in saving his life. He retired to Constantinople. Subsequently he was accused of magical practices before the Emperor, and beheaded at Ephesus in the year 366.

CHAPTER XXIV.

Louis XI. and the Astrologer--A King's Enchanted   Cap--David I. and the Mysterious Stag--Merlin the   Magician--Prophecies concerning Queen Eliza-beth and   Mary--Merlin's Mother--His mysterious Birth--Dragon   Caverns--Predictions of Evil--Strange Sights and   Sounds in the Air--Changing a King's Love--The Holy   Maid of Kent--Nobles put to Death for keeping company with Sorcerers--James I. of England and the   Witches--His Queen in Danger--Marriage of the King and   Queen--Tranent Witches and Warlocks--Wise Wife of   Keith--Engagements to serve the Devil--Satan's Respect   of Persons--Two Hundred Witches sailing in   Sieves--Mischief at Sea--Raising Storms at Sea--Witch   and Warlock Convention at Newhaven--Meeting of Witches   at North Berwick--Dead Men's Joints used for Magical   Purposes--Witches tortured in Holyrood--The Devil's   Mark--Strange Confessions--Bothwell's Fortune   told--Witches and their Associates burned.

An astrologer told Louis XI. that a lady to whom he was fondly attached would die in a few days, and the prediction was fulfilled. The king caused the astrologer to be brought before him in an upper chamber, and commanded the royal servants to throw the prophet out of the window on a certain signal being given. As soon as the astrologer was dragged before the king, the latter said, "You who pretend to be a foreteller of events, and know so exactly the fate of others, tell me instantly when and in what way your end will come." "Sire," replied the astrologer, knowing he had much to fear, but without displaying alarm, "I shall die just three days before your Majesty." On hearing this the king's countenance changed from rage to concern, if not alarm; and instead of giving the signal of death, he dismissed the astrologer in peace, heaped honours on him, and took special care to prolong his life.

King Erricus of Sweden publicly confessed that he was a magician. He had an enchanted cap, which he pretended enabled him to control spirits, and to turn the wind into any direction he pleased. So firmly did his subjects believe in his supernatural powers, that when a storm arose they would exclaim, "Ah! the king has got on his magic cap."

David I. founded the abbey of Holyrood. By tradition we are informed that, in the year 1128, he, while out hunting in the royal forest near Edwinsburg, was miraculously delivered from a stag at bay by the interposition of an arm, wreathed in smoke, brandishing a cross of the most dazzling brilliancy. At the sight of it the stag fled. The cross remained as a celestial relic in the royal hand. In consideration of this deliverance, strengthened by a vision, the foundations of Holyrood were laid. The same tradition further tells us that the miraculous cross was enshrined in silver, and placed on the high altar, where it remained until the fatal battle of Durham, when David II. was captured with his cross and crown.

Merlin was a noted magician and astrologer, who prophesied many things that came to pass in England hundreds of years after his death. Prophesying of the reigns of Queen Elizabeth and Mary, he says:

> "Then shall the masculine sceptre cease to sway,
> And to a spinster the whole land obey;
> Who to the Papal monarchy shall restore
> All that the Ph[oe]nix had fetched thrice before.
> Then shall come in the faggot and the stake,
> And they of convert bodies bonfires make;
> Match shall this lioness with Caesar's son,
> From the Pontific sea a pool shall run,
> That wide shall spread its waters, and to a flood
> In time shall grow, made red with martyrs' blood.
> Men shall her short unprosp'rous reign deplore,
> By loss at sea, and damage to the shore;
> Whose heart being dissected, you in it
> May in large characters find Calice writ."

Those acquainted with the history of Queen Mary's time, can have no difficulty in discovering the circumstances to which the several prophetic sayings refer; nor can they fail to be satisfied that the following lines apply to Queen Elizabeth, and the state of England at the time she swayed the sceptre:

> "From th' other ashes shall a Ph[oe]nix rise,
> Whose birth is thus predicted by the wise;
> Her chief predominant star is Mercury,
> Jove shall with Venus in conjunction be.
> And Sol, with them, shine in his best aspect;
> With Ariadne's crown, Astrea deckt,
> Shall then descend upon this terrene stage:
> (Not seen before since the first golden age).
> Against whom all the Latian bulls shall roar,
> But at Jove's awful summons shall give o'er.
> Through many forges shall this metal glide,

Like gold by fire re-pured, and seven times try'd,
Her bright and glorious sunbeams shall expel
The vain clouds of the candle, book, and bell.
Domestic plots, and stratagems abroad,
French machines, and the Italianated god,
The Spanish engine, Portuguized Jew,
The Jesuitic mine, and politic crew
Of home-bred vipers: let their menaces come
By private pistol, or by hostile drum;
Though all these dogs chase her with open cry,
Live shall she, lov'd and fear'd, then sainted die."

Merlin's early history was as strange as his prophecies were singular. For reasons best known to herself, his mother refused to reveal his father's name. She was daughter of King Demetrius, who reigned about two hundred years after Christianity was introduced into England. King Vortigern was obliged to fly into Wales from the fury of Hengist, and, fearing that he would be pursued thither, commenced building a stronghold on the Welsh soil. Though the ground appeared to be firm, it turned out that every stone laid sank suddenly into the ground. With the intention of discovering the cause of this mystery, the king sent for his wizards and bards. After consultation, the wise men informed him that his castle could never be built until the stones were cemented with the blood of a male child begotten without a father. The king, believing what he was told, sent his servants to search for such a child. On their way the messengers arrived at Marlborough, where they observed two boys fighting. One of these was young Merlin, whom they heard taunted by his youthful antagonist of being an imp that never had a father. This was enough: Merlin and his mother were seized and carried before the king.

In answer to the king's inquiries, the mother, not knowing the danger to which she was exposing little Merlin, told him that her boy never had a father. Her tale was believed; but Vortigern had compassion on the youth, who was fair and comely, and not only spared his life, but took him into his house. When Merlin learned all the particulars regarding the mysterious disappearance of the foundation stones, and the charm proposed by the wizards and bards, he told the king that his wise men were alike destitute of learning and natural penetration. "Know," said he, "that under the ground where your Majesty intends to build your castle is a deep lake, which has swallowed up all your building materials, and that under the water there are two stone caverns which contain two dragons. Dig deep into the earth, and you will discover that what I have said is true," concluded Merlin. The king commanded that a search, such as the youth had recommended, should be commenced under his (Merlin's) directions. Means were taken to drain the lake, which was discovered without difficulty, and, true enough, two horrible dragons were found. On the caverns being opened, the monsters, one red and the other white, rushed at each other. A terrible conflict took place between them, ending in the red dragon's death.

Merlin, in reply to the king's inquiries as to what all this portended, informed his Majesty that evil days were drawing near--that the time was not far distant when the Britons would be compelled to fly before the Saxons, and seek refuge among the caves and mountains of the earth, and that many of them would perish, for the red dragon signified the Britons, and the white monster the Saxons. But he assured the king that the Saxons would not always triumph, as a boar would come from the forest and devour the white dragon. Merlin predicted for Vortigern disappointments, defeats, and at last a miserable death, all of which came to pass.

It is reported of Merlin, that after King Vortigern was driven from power, he sought to amuse him in his solitude by bringing strange sights before his eyes, and causing pleasant sounds to salute his ears. The king supposed he heard melodious music in the air, and imagined that shepherds and shepherdesses, in rustic costume, danced before him. At times eagles and falcons were seen pursuing their prey; and whatever bird the king wished for his dinner, fell down dead, as if shot by a fowler. Hares and hounds were also made to appear in the clouds, for the king's amusement. On his castle-tower he could stand and watch a stag hunt with all the vividness of an ordinary chase. Merlin professed to have the power of transforming a man into a beast, and of making a man or woman look like a wild animal.

In the year 1474 the Duchess of Bedford was charged with having, by the aid of an image of lead made like a maid, turned the love of King Edward IV. from Dame Elianor Butteler, daughter of the Earl of Shrewsbury, to whom he was affianced, and transferred the royal affections to her own daughter.

The Holy Maid of Kent, a nun of great sanctity, having, according to common belief in the time of Henry VIII., the gift of prophecy, and the power of working miracles, pronounced the doom of speedy death against that monarch for his marriage with Anne Boleyn. She was attainted in Parliament, and, along with several accomplices, executed. So extraordinary were her miracles, and her predictions so striking, that even Sir Thomas More believed in her.

In the year 1521 the Duke of Buckingham was put to death in consequence of certain actions he was guilty of in conjunction with a magician; and in 1541 Lord Hungerford was beheaded for inquiring at fortune-tellers how long Henry VIII. would be king. In 1562 the Earl and Countess of Lennox were found guilty of treason, and of holding intercourse with sorcerers.

The story of King James VI. of Scotland and I. of England, and the witches who attempted to drown him and his queen at sea, enables us to judge of the credulity of the age in which this Solomon lived. The king having resolved to marry, sought the hand of Princess Anne of Denmark. In the month of July 1589 the Earl Marischal was despatched to Copenhagen with a suitable retinue to conclude the match. He found the Court of Denmark ready to listen to his proposals, and the lady so willing to comply, that little time was lost in arranging the match. Hasty preparations were made, and the marriage was solemnised by proxy. A fleet of twelve sail was fitted out to convey the young queen to Scotland. Through unforeseen circumstances, the queen's departure was long after the time originally intended. At last the fleet sailed; and it encountered such a fearful storm, that the ships were driven back to the coast of Norway. Owing to the lateness of the season, and the disabled state of the vessels, it was resolved that the queen should not again expose herself to the dangers of an angry sea that season.

When news reached the king of his queen's unfortunate misadventure, he resolved to proceed on a voyage of discovery in search of her. On the 22nd of October he embarked at Leith, taking with him his chancellor, chaplain, and a few courtiers. After a stormy passage of five days the king landed at Upsal, where the queen was waiting. On the 23rd of November the king and princess were married in a more solemn manner than they had been some time previously by proxy, and they went to Copenhagen to spend the winter. In Denmark the king spoke learnedly to the great men of the state, whom he convinced of his superior knowledge: he disputed on predestination and other favourite topics. After six months delay, he departed for his kingdom, and on May-day 1590, he, his youthful bride, and splendid train arrived in Leith.

The coronation ceremony, performed with great solemnity, was gone through on the 17th of May at Holyrood House. After three sermons, the queen's shoulders and part of her breast were uncovered, and the holy oil poured thereon, subsequent to which the crown was put on her head. On the Tuesday following the queen made her public entrance into Edinburgh, where she was received with extraordinary marks of rejoicing. At the city gate a municipal orator greeted her Majesty with an address in Latin, and then from a gilded globe, resting over the gate, a little fellow, representing an angel, descended and delivered to the queen the keys of the city.

James was convinced that the storms which kept him and his queen so long from meeting were the results of diabolical agencies. After his return to Scotland, suspicion fell on a dangerous gang of witches and warlocks at Tranent, and the king resolved to inquire into the whole case, with the laudable design of getting rid of such wicked subjects should he find them guilty. A man named David Seytoun, who held the appointment of deputy bailiff of Tranent, had a young female servant named Geillis Duncan, celebrated among the town's people for her skill in curing diseases. Seytoun, becoming suspicious that she was in league with Satan, questioned her closely without receiving satisfactory answers. Not to be defeated, he first put her to the torture, which he thought he had a right to do in virtue of his office, and then searched her person for devil's marks. One of those sure tokens of witchcraft being found on her throat, she was committed to prison. There she made a full confession, in which many persons were implicated. She admitted that the cures effected by her were brought about by means of witchcraft.

Of those said to have been associated with this woman in her guilty deeds, the most noted were Dr. John Fian, sometimes called John Cunningham, and three women, named Agnes Sampsoun, Euphame Mackalzeane, and Barbara Napier. Fian was a schoolmaster at Tranent, a small town on the south side of the Firth of Forth, and about nine miles east of Edinburgh. He admitted that he was an agent of the evil one. One night, he said, the devil appeared to him, and induced him to become his servant, under the promise that he would never want if he served him faithfully and well. The offer being tempting, the unscrupulous doctor became an instrument of evil. That there might be no mistake about the bargain, the devil put his mark on Fian's person. From that time the doctor was a sorcerer: he was often carried away in the night to visit distant places of the world, and was present at, and took part in, all the nightly meetings of witches held in the Lothians. He rose so high in the devil's favour, that he was appointed registrar and secretary of the conventions. One night Fian was carried through the air to North Berwick, where he found a number of witches and sorcerers assembled listening to Satan preaching to them from a pulpit. He implored them to give up all slavish fears of him; promised them great rewards so long as they were his servants, and assured them, that so long as they had hairs on their bodies they would receive no injury. He exhorted them to do all the evil they could, and to eat and drink and be merry. One night when Fian was riding home along a dreary road, in danger of losing his way, Satan came to his assistance, and put four candles on the horse's ears, which enabled the traveller and his servant to see as well as if it were day.

The three women mentioned occupied good places in society. Agnes Sampsoun was known as the wise wife of Keith; she, too, had knowledge of the healing art. In her confession she said that, after her husband's death, the devil appeared to her and offered her great riches if she would abandon all that was good, and serve him, the lover of evil. At times Satan appeared as a man, but more frequently like a black dog. On one occasion, when she was attending Lady Edmestoune, who was unwell, the devil came to her at night in the shape of a dog, and informed her that the lady would die. He then inquired where the lady's daughters were, for he wanted to have one of them. The witch, however, protested against such an outrage as the carrying away of a dying lady's daughter, and the dog went away howling into a well in the garden. At a later hour that night, when the young ladies were walking in the orchard, the evil one, disguised as before, rushed at them, seized one of them, and attempted to drag her into the well. Agnes, seeing this, laid hold of the lady, and sent the dog away howling. On another occasion Agnes and other witches wanted assistance from Satan at the bridge of Faulstruther, and, to secure this, they threw a cord into the river while some magical words were being repeated. Presently the devil seized the end of the cord that was in the water, and they drew him to land. After an assurance from them that they had been good servants to him, he gave them a charm by which they could perform wonderful works.

Euphame Mackalzeane was the daughter of Lord Cliftounhall. It would appear that when this lady bore her first child, she consulted Agnes Sampsoun as to how she could best get rid of her pains, which she dreaded much. Agnes, willing to relieve the amiable lady of every pang nature was prone to, transferred the pains to a dog. Time passed on, and another child was about to be brought into the world by Euphame Mackalzeane. Agnes was again called in, and the pains were conveyed to a cat.

Barbara Napier was of a respectable family also, but nearly all the other associates in their guilt were in poverty. Satan, like human beings on earth, made more of the rich than of the poor; for while he assigned exalted places to Dr. Fian and the ladies of birth, he appointed a poor peasant, called Grey Meal, to be doorkeeper at the witches' meetings.

More than one of the witches said that on Hallow-eve upwards of two hundred witches went to sea in riddles or sieves, and that, notwithstanding their perforated vessels, they were quite dry and comfortable, faring on the best food, and drinking the richest wines. At another time, Dr. Fian, Agnes Sampsoun, one Robert Griersoun, and others, left Prestonpans in a boat, proceeded to a ship at sea, went on board and made merry on good wine, after which they sank the vessel with all her crew. Dr. Fian stated, on being put to the torture, that Satan had told him and others, before the event, that he would make a hole in the queen's ship on the way from Denmark, and force her to return to her own country. Having intelligence that the queen was at sea, they held a meeting at Broomhills, where it was resolved they should go out to the ocean and raise a storm, to endanger her Majesty's life. They took steps accordingly, and threw a dog into the water, whereby the wind became boisterous, the sea rose, and the ships were damaged. Other diabolical means were resorted to, to endanger the queen's fleet. A meeting of witches was held at Prestonpans, when the following ceremonies were gone through:--First, one of the witches held a finger on the one side of the chimney crook, and another witch put one of her fingers on the other side; then they put a cat three times through or under the links of the crook; they next tied four joints of dead men's fingers to the four feet of the cat; and then the animal was conveyed to Leith pier and thrown into the water. Cats were also thrown into the sea at other places on the Firth of Forth. By these means a dreadful storm was raised, which wrecked many ships--amongst them the ferry-boat sailing between Leith and Kinghorn, with all on board. The fiendish crew, disappointed at the safety of the queen, determined to endeavour to drown the king. More cats were cast into the sea during his Majesty's voyage to Denmark; but all infernal arts proved ineffectual, as the king had a charmed life. Prior to their Majesties' return, another convention was held, at which Satan himself was present. He promised to raise a mist when the royal ships were coming home, which would cause them to land in England. According to Dr. Fian, the devil threw something like a foot-ball into the sea. This caused a dense fog to rise; yet, in spite of all their plans, James and his queen arrived safe in Leith.

Not long afterwards, more plots were entered into with the view of doing harm to the king. On Lammas-eve a grand convention was held at the Fairyhills, Newhaven, at which were present thirty of the principal witches and sorcerers in the country. The devil, the presiding genius, expressed a fear that their designs would be frustrated unless unusual measures were resorted to. He promised to give them an image of wax; and directed them to hang up and roast a toad, and then to lay the drippings of the toad mixed with wine, an adder's skin, and a certain part of the forehead of a newly-foaled foal, in the way where the king was to pass, or to hang the preparation in a position where it might drop on his body. These plans again miscarried; for the king escaped the dangers of them all.

At Hallow-eve of the year 1590 there was a meeting of witches and sorcerers, including those already named, in the church of North Berwick. According to all accounts, three hundred women and a few men were present. They danced across the churchyard; and when they reached the church door the women first paid their homage, turning six times round widderschinnes, and, following them, the men performed the same ceremony nine times. The devil, it was seriously asserted, took his place in the pulpit, around which old-like men, holding black candles in their hands, stood. Satan appeared as a black man, with a beard like that of a goat and a nose resembling a hawk's beak, and having on a black gown, and a black skull-cap on his head, and he read from a black book the names of those summoned to the meeting. The names, however, were not the real or proper names of the persons, but nicknames, by which they were known in the gang. The devil exhorted his hearers to pursue a course of evil, and assured them that the more mischief they did to mankind, the better he would be pleased with them. After their master's address, loud revelling was indulged in. Graves were opened, and the joints of two dead men taken out for magical purposes.

When information reached the king's ears of the doings of this wicked crew, he resolved to inquire into the case himself. Dr. Fian and a good many witches were tortured in Holyrood House, in presence of James, who took great delight in listening to their forced false confessions. Agnes

Sampsoun was stripped naked, that the devil's mark might be discovered; but as it could not at first be seen, her body was shaved, that what was looked for might not pass unnoticed. Of course it was found, and the unfortunate woman confessed her guilt. She said that Bothwell had consulted her as to the length of time the king was to live. She had a spirit that regularly attended her in the form of a dog, and it told her that in consequence of his Majesty's piety and wisdom he was proof against incantations. The notorious sorcerer Richard Graham confessed that the Earl of Bothwell had asked him for supernatural assistance to hasten the king's death. He said Bothwell had informed him that it had been predicted by a necromancer in Italy that he (Bothwell) would become rich and powerful; that he would slay two men; and would be accused before the king for two capital crimes, but would be forgiven for the one, but not for the other. Bothwell was satisfied that up to the time he consulted Graham the prophecy was fulfilled; and now, he said, the time was come for either him or the king being despatched. Barbara Napier, a witch against whom James had a bitter feeling, was acquitted, on her trial, by the jury, very much to the king's annoyance. Dr. Fian, Agnes Sampsoun, Euphame Mackalzeane, and many of their associates in supposed guilt, after mock trials, were burned.

CHAPTER XXV.

Cromwell in league with the Devil--Cromwell   consulting Astrologers--
Memorable Days in the Life of   Cromwell--Singular Narrative--Duke of Hamil-
ton warned   of his Fate--Peden's Predictions--Traditions   concerning Peden-
-John Brown the Martyr--Linlithgow   Loch Swans--Hereford Children--Great
Comet--Conjunction of Saturn and Jupiter at Eventful   Periods--Solomon's
Power over Evil Spirits and over   the Beasts of the Field.

Fabulous relations are given in connection with the career of Cromwell. We are told he was in league with the devil, to whom he sold himself for a brief period of power among a people whom he ruled with a rod of iron, and trampled their rulers under his feet. That Cromwell used to consult astrologers, there can be little doubt. He was accustomed to obtain advice from Lilly, the wizard, before entering into any important engagement. In particular, he sought the assistance of Lilly before he entered Parliament, and when he besieged Dunkirk. The 3rd of September was a memorable day in the life of Cromwell, for on a 3rd of September he fought his two most famous battles, and on a 3rd of September he yielded up the ghost--circumstances that gave colour to the reports circulated concerning the help and protection he received from Satan. Colonel Lindsay was responsible for the extraordinary stories spread abroad affecting the character of the dictator. From the colonel's statement, it appears that on the morning of the 3rd September 1651, the day on which the battle of Worcester was fought and the forces of Charles II. were routed, Cromwell and Lindsay entered a dark wood near the battlefield. Lindsay, unaware of the object Cromwell had in view in being in such a gloomy place, and thinking he perceived something strange in the appearance of his leader, was seized with horror and trembling, which prevented him going farther. Cromwell proceeded a short distance alone. He was met by an old man with a roll of parchment in his hand, which he gave to Cromwell, who perused it carefully. An altercation took place between Cromwell and the old man or devil, during which Lindsay heard Cromwell say, "This is but for seven years; I was to get twenty-one." The being to whom he spoke, replied that only seven years could be given. Cromwell, modifying his demands, craved fourteen years, but the old man was inexorable. "Seven years, and no more," he sternly replied. And the document, whatever was its real meaning or tendency, was signed by the two parties, with the "seven years" undeleted. As soon as the signatures were adhibited, Cromwell hastily returned to Lindsay, standing in amazement, and said with great emotion, "Now the battle is ours!" Cromwell and Lindsay were soon at their posts in the field, the former resolute and hopeful, the latter dismayed and irresolute. To retain his proper place in the field was Lindsay's intention; but after the first charge his courage forsook him, and he fled as fast as his charger could carry him, although no man pursued. The king's troops were beaten, leaving Cromwell master of the position. Prior to the result of the day's engagement being communicated by mortal man to Lindsay, he made known to a clergyman what had taken place in the morning, finishing his statement in these words: "I am sure the king's forces are beaten, and I am certain Cromwell will die this day seven years, for he has sold himself to the devil, who will not fail to claim him then."

Ever after this memorable day, Cromwell regarded the 3rd of September auspicious to him, as well he might; for in addition to the events at Worcester, it was on the same day of that month, in 1650, that he gained the battle of Dunbar. Years rolled on, in the course of which Cromwell encountered numerous dangers, and escaped conspiracies and plots, provoked by serious crimes, yet he survived to breathe his last on downy pillows, on the anniversary of his great triumphs at Dunbar and Worcester. Neither the clang of swords nor the roar of guns disturbed his last moments, but a dreadful commotion raged all around. Nature seemed to have lashed itself into a rage: a high wind, such as had never been heard before by the oldest inhabitants, unroofed houses on land, and caused wrecks at sea. In the midst of the tempest were heard shrieks, not of men, but of spirits revelling in the gale, as it carried destruction and death over the country. Notwithstanding Cromwell's body being embalmed and put into a leaden coffin, the stench therefrom became so insufferable, that the remains had to be immediately consigned to the grave, and afterwards the funeral ceremonies were performed over an empty coffin,--so at least says Echard, on whose authority we give the foregoing particulars concerning the Lord Protector. Though Cromwell's dust was interred in Westminster, it was not permitted to rest there. In January 1661, on the anniversary of the death of Charles I., his decayed body was disinterred and conveyed to Tyburn, where it was hanged on a gallows, then cut down, and the trunk cast into a pit, while the head was set up on a pole at Westminster Hall.

The Duke of Hamilton, who was executed in the year 1649, was warned of his fate by a witch. She said the king would be put to death, and that he would be his successor. This prediction being delivered somewhat ambiguously, Hamilton misunderstood its meaning. His impression was that he was to obtain the crown (which led him to act treacherously towards his Majesty), whereas the beldam meant that he would succeed the king on the scaffold.

Peden, one of the celebrated Covenanters, who was persecuted for righteousness' sake, foretold many of the woes that Scotland would pass through before the Church could have peace. The good old man died a natural death in his bed, and his bones were decently interred by the Boswells of Auchinleck in their family vault, under the deep shadows of wide spreading plane-trees. This honour coming to the ears of the soldiers in the garrison of Sorn, forty days after the interment, they cruelly rifled the tomb of its dead. There is a tradition in the district to the present day, that when the soldiers burst open the coffin and tore off the shroud, there came a sudden blast like a whirlwind, though the day had previously been without a breath of stirring air, which caught up the shroud, and twisted it round a large projecting branch of one of the plane-trees. From that day the branch withered away, and remained, for ages like a black shrivelled arm uplifted to heaven, as a protest against the sacrilegious crime. This is only one of the many wondrous tales concerning Peden, who was known far and wide as "The Prophet." Peden's remains were carried to the hill above Cumnock, where the common gallows stood, and there, in spite of the remonstrances of the Boswells and the Countess of Dumfries, suspended on the gibbet. When cut down, the body was interred, like that of a felon, at the foot of the gallows-tree. At that time the churchyard of Cumnock was in the town, but the old residenters, generation after generation, on seeing their end approaching, desired to be buried beside the old prophet. Thus the gallows-hill of Cumnock became the ordinary burying-ground of the town. Two old thorn bushes mark the spot where the prophet's ashes rest, in the midst of the remains of those he loved while in the land that groaned under the despotic sway of relentless tyrants.

Though Peden died, as we have stated, a natural death, he suffered great persecution in his life on account of his religion. His persecutors, who often pursued him as a beast of prey, at last seized him, confined him a prisoner in Edinburgh Castle, immured him in a dungeon on the Bass Rock, and sentenced him, along with sixty others, to banishment in America, then a penal settlement. Chained together, Peden and his companions were marched to Leith, and conveyed on board a ship for London, from thence to be taken to Virginia. Seeing his companions in bonds dejected, Peden shouted out to them, in presence and hearing of their guard, "Fear not, brethren, the ship is not yet built that will take us either to Virginia or any foreign plantation." Uneasiness was felt on board the ship, in consequence of a report being spread among the prisoners that thumbkins and other instruments of torture were to be used to them as implements of punishment. Peden assured his fellow-passengers that their fears were groundless, for, said he, neither thumbkins nor bodkins would hurt them. A tedious voyage of a fortnight brought them to London. When they were about to be put on board the vessel that was to carry them to Virginia, the captain of the foreign ship, discovering the character of those intended to be banished, declared that no authority in the world would compel him to go to sea with them. As another ship could not be procured, the prisoners were set at liberty, as Peden predicted. Fortunately for the discharged persons, they were befriended by Lord Shaftesbury, an ancestor of the present Lord Shaftesbury, who, along with other friends, provided for their immediate wants.

One morning, while Peden was at his devotions, a young girl fourteen years old began to mock him. The good man, turning an eye of pity on her, said, "Poor thing, thou laughest and mockest, but a sudden and surprising judgment on thee will soon stay the laughter of many." This was when he was in confinement on the Bass Rock. Shortly afterwards a swift gust of wind swept her into the sea, where she was lost.

Alexander (this was his Christian name) Peden said to a brother and sister during his last illness, "You will all be displeased at the place where I shall be buried at last. I could have wished to lie in the grave of my beloved Richard Cameron; but I shall not be allowed to rest where you lay me, though my bones shall at last be glorified."

Peden foretold the early and violent death of the martyr John Brown. Addressing Mrs. Brown one day, he said, "Isabel, you have got a good man to be your husband, but you will not enjoy him long; prize his company, and keep linen beside you for his winding sheet, for you will need it when you are not looking for it, and it will be a bloody one." Brown had a presentiment, too, that his end would be a tragical one. The end did come early. Claverhouse, who had been searching for him as well as for several other Covenanters, suddenly surprised him one morning, and ordered the dragoons to bring him in front of his (Brown's) house, where stood his weeping wife and helpless children. "Go to your prayers," shouted Claverhouse, "for immediately you shall die." Mrs. Brown exclaimed, "This is the day I have expected;" and Brown, while addressing a few farewell words to his beloved spouse, said calmly, "Isabel, this is what I told you of before we were married." Mrs. Brown was dragged from the side of her husband, who stood resigned to his fate. "Fire!" cried Claverhouse, and instantly the martyr fell, pierced through by half a dozen bullets.

According to Wodrow, the Scottish historian, the swans which were on Linlithgow Loch when the English obtained the mastery in Scotland, disappeared. On the king's return, the swans came back. Their flight was considered to foreshadow evil to the royal family, and their reappearance was regarded as a happy omen.

So great was the consternation caused about the middle of the seventeenth century by prodigious apparitions, that lamentations were heard in every dwelling. Women who were with child brought forth prematurely. At Hereford the town-clerk's wife bore three children at a birth, who, we are told, had all teeth, and spoke immediately after they were born. One said, "The day is appointed that no man can shun;" another asked, "Who will be sufficient to bury the dead?" and a third predicted that "there will not be enough of corn to feed the hungry." Each having thus expressed himself, expired.

In the year 1680 a great comet appeared, striking every beholder with awe. The terror partly arose from the fact that Kepler, the astronomer, had calculated that the conjunction of Saturn and Jupiter in Leo, which happens only once in eight hundred years, and which took place at the time of the appearance of this comet, would have an evil influence on the Romish Church. The consternation was increased by mathematicians declaring that the comet was six times longer than that which portended the death of Pope Alexander VII. These conjunctions were believed to have been always attended with important circumstances on earth. Tycho Brahe reckoned them thus:--The first, he said, was under Enoch; the second under Noah; the third under Moses; the fourth under Solomon; the fifth under a greater than Solomon; the sixth under Charlemagne, when the Romans were subdued; and the seventh conjunction was at the time first mentioned. Those who have made themselves acquainted with the cruel persecutions in the year 1680 and subsequent years, will not refuse to admit that, whether Kepler did or did not know beforehand through astronomical calculations what dire calamities were to take place on account of truth, his words prepared many for coming danger, and emboldened them to struggle on until Protestantism triumphed over Papacy.

In the *Day of Rest* for September 1877 we find the following statement relative to Solomon:-- "Eastern traditions inform us that Solomon possessed the secret power of expelling demons; that he composed spells by which diseases were removed; and that he left behind him exorcisms by which devils were driven away, never to return. In wild exaggerated stories in the Talmud, Solomon is credited with having dominion over the wild beasts, and over the birds of heaven, and over the creeping beasts of earth, and over all devils and spirits of darkness. He understood the languages of them all, and they understood him. On one occasion, proceeds the legend, when the wise king's heart was influenced with wine, he commanded that all the wild beasts, birds, and creeping things of earth, and also the devils and spirits of darkness, should be gathered together, that they might dance before him. And what is most wonderful, if the Rabbis lie not, every one that was summoned appeared before Solomon, and took part in the great dance."

THE DRUIDS.
CHAPTER XXVI.

Druids laid claim to Supernatural Power--Functions exercised by Druids--Representations of the Sun and Moon--Belief of Druids--Beltane Feasts--Arkite and Sabian Superstition--Dancing to the Song of the Cuckoo--Holy Liquor--Initiation into the Druidical Mysteries--The Goodmane's Land and the Guidman's Fauld--Places frequented by Fairies--Good Manes gave Plentiful Crops--Offerings to Demi-gods--Propitiating Beasts of Prey--Sacred Cairns--Trees dedicated to Demons--Law forbidding Worship of the Sun, Moon, Fire, Rivers, Wells, Stones, or Forest Trees--Extracts from Kirk-Session Records--Land dedicated to Satan--Midsummer and Hallow Fires forbidden--Yule-day, how kept--Order of the General Assembly as to Druidical Customs at the Fires at Beltane, Midsummer, Hallow-e'en, and Yule--Old Customs ordered to be discontinued.

In our introduction to *The Poets and Superstition* we noticed briefly particular classes of Druids--the Bardi and Vates. We now proceed to give fuller details of the Druids, a class of people who played a not unimportant part among the nations in olden times. There were male and female Druids; the latter generally called Druides. Both the men and women laid claim to supernatural power and knowledge.

The Druids were expert at legerdemain, and, by their astonishing exploits, sustained among an ignorant people a reputation of being magicians. They devoted much time to the study of astrology, observing closely the heavenly bodies, through which they pretended they could predict events kept secret from ordinary mortals. The Druids exercised the functions of magistrates, priests, teachers, and physicians. As judges, their authority was unlimited; they desired the people to believe that not only had they the power of imposing punishment in this world, but that they might sentence offenders to torment in the world beyond the grave.

The Arch-Druid wore a gold chain round his neck, from which was suspended a gold plate, having engraved thereon, "The gods require sacrifice," and on the front of the Druid's cap was a golden representation of the sun, and a silver representation of a half moon.

They believed in one supreme being; supposed that the soul was immortal; and thought the spirit of man began to exist in the meanest insect, and that it proceeded through the lower orders of existence, rising at every new birth until it reached the human body. When the soul animated the human form, a knowledge of good and evil dawned upon the being, who then became responsible for the thoughts and actions of life. If one chose evil instead of good, the soul, it was asserted, went after death into an inferior grade of animal life, low in proportion to the sinfulness of that existence. Those who chose the better part became at last so exalted that evil had no power over them, and they were happy for ever and ever. It was also believed that the beatified soul retained the love of its country and relations, and that the spirits of the good sometimes returned to earth, and became prophets among mankind, that they might assist in teaching divine things, and oppose the evil one.

The Druids were worshippers of Bel, Beal, Bealan, from whence come the Beltane or Bealteine feasts, of which they observed four of considerable importance every year, viz. those of May-eve, Midsummer-eve, and of the eve of the 1st of November, and of the eve of the 10th of March. With Druidical religious rites were blended Arkite and Sabian superstition. Dancing round the May-pole, old authors say, took its rise from the Druidical custom of dancing on the green to the song of the cuckoo. Taliesin, the Druidical bard, informs us that those who joined in the mystical movements went according to the course of the sun, as they attached much importance to the ceremony of going three times round their sacred circle from the east to west. At the celebration of sacred mysteries there was a caldron for the preparation of a decoction from plants held in high esteem. This liquor being holy, possessed rare virtues, one of which was the power of inspiring those who partook thereof, or to whom it was applied. The caldron was kept boiling a year and a day. During this time, at certain hours and under particular planets, plants possessed of peculiar properties were collected and added to the caldron's contents.

Not only did the sacred liquor, properly applied, enable one to see into futurity, but it was supposed to confer immortality on those who bathed in it. Further, by its application, the dead might have been brought to life again. All the sacred utensils and the company assembled at mystical feasts were purified with the decoction.

Initiation into the Druidical mysteries was something dreadful. None but those of strong nerve could successfully pass through the ordeal, all of which took place at night. Every one admitted into the fraternity bound himself by a solemn oath, like a freemason, not to commit to writing or divulge the secrets revealed to him.

In various parts of the country there were "the goodmane's land and the guidman's fauld," to cultivate which it was supposed would be followed by dire calamities. These places were, according to popular opinion, frequented by fairies and other supernatural beings. Music was often heard, and dancing seen, at such places. There, too, people are reported to have been enticed into subterranean abodes, and retained for years. Places dedicated to gods and demi-gods lay uncultivated, though the surrounding ground bore good crops. For these acts of self-denial in permitting ground to remain waste which might have been producing good fruit, "the good neighbours" sent untold-of blessings. To secure prosperity, goodmanes attached themselves to deserving persons and families, making their crops plentiful, causing their cows to have calves, and giving milk in abundance. We have an account of how offerings were presented to those demi-gods at stated occasions. The people made a circle on the ground, in which they kindled a fire, and then cooked a mess, consisting of milk, butter, eggs, and meal, for the beings whose favour they desired to secure for the first time, or whose continued good service was wished. Cakes were baked and offered to the manes in this manner: piece after piece was broken off the cake or bannock and thrown over the left shoulder, while the desire was expressed aloud, that those to whom the offering was made would preserve the cattle, horses, and other animals and substance from the power of evil spirits. In the same way, or after a fashion somewhat similar, beasts of prey were propitiated.

Then there were sacred cairns, consisting of stones thrown together by passers by, every one adding his stone. If any one removed these cairns, or part thereof, superstitious people predicted evil to the spoiler. The late Rev. James Rust, in his *Druidism Exhumed*, mentions that circles stood on the spot where one of the extensive manufactories at Grandholm, near Aberdeen, has been built. The people, shocked at the removal of the Druidical works, predicted retributive justice to those who disturbed the sacred relics. For a long time every misadventure to the company, or to individuals connected therewith, was attributed to the sacrilegious action.

Trees were sometimes dedicated to demons. The people worshipped such trees, holding them in the highest esteem that any earthly thing could be regarded. It was a capital offence to cut off a branch or shoot from one of them. King Cnut passed a law forbidding the worship of the sun, moon, fire, rivers, wells, stones, or forest trees of any kind.

Mr. Rust gives the following extracts from the Kirk Session records of the parish of Slains, which bear upon Druidical superstitions:--

"18th November 1649.--The sd day the Minister and
Elderis being conveinit in Sessione ... the Minister
askit at ye Elderis for delationes, and desyrit them
to try if yer was aney hallowe fyres set on be aney of
the parochiners upon a hallarse evine. The sd day the
Minister requirit of the Elderis if they knew aney
peices of land within the paroche that was calit the
goodmane's land or fauld, or dedicated to Satane, or
lattine by unlabourit. They sed yer was ane peice land
in Brogane calit Garlet or guidman's fauld, within
Andrew Robes tak that was not labourit this manie
yeires, for quhat respect they knew not. The Minister
desyrit them to try qrfr it lay unlabourit."

"25th November 1649.--... Intimat that yr be no
Midsumer, no hallow fyres, under the paine of the
haveris of them to be condinglie punishit."

"Sessione the 30th December 1649.--The sd day the
Minister and Elderis being conveinit in Sessione ...

compeirit Thomas Patersone, and confessit that yr was
a peice land in his rowme calit the goodmane's fauld,
quhilk was this long time unlabourit. He is ordainit
to labour it, and promist to do so efter Whitsonday,
qn it was for faching. The sd day the Minister did
inquyr of the Elderis that knew of aney that
superstitiouslie keipit Yoolday. They did all report
that it was not keipit, that they did not yoke yr
pleuches, but yokt their work-horses."

In the same year (1649) the General Assembly of the Church of Scotland appointed a commission of their own number to report to the next General Assembly as to the Druidical customs observed at the fires at Beltane, Midsummer, Hallow-e'en, and Yule. All the old customs were ordered to be discontinued, and the people warned against kindling fires for superstitious purposes.

CHAPTER XXVII.

Dr. Stuart On the Druids--Their Deities--Augury--Human   Victims--Nature of the Gods--Gauls descendants of   Dis--Funeral Rites--Slaves and Clients burned--What   Pliny says--Tallies used in making known the Will of Heaven--Walking through the Fire--Barbarous mode of   discovering Future Events--Wonder-working   Eggs--Colours of Eggs, and by whom worn--Virtue of   Globule of Ink--Easter Eggs represent Druidical   Eggs--Origin of the Druids dated from the Dispersal of   Babel--Arch-Druid of the Mountains--Wise Men of the   East were probably Druids--Island of Iona--Druidical   Cairns--Stones of Judgment--Mr. Rust's   Opinion--Misletoe regarded as a Charm--Rings worn as   Preventatives against Witchcraft--Legend concerning   Stonehenge--A Famous General--Merlin the   Magician--Stones brought from Africa by Giants--Graves   of British Lords.

D r. Stuart, writing of the Druids, says their chief deity was Mercury, of whom they have many images. They also worship Apollo and Mars, and Jupiter and Minerva. They held a meeting at a certain time of the year in a consecrated spot. They used rites of augury from the slaughter of human victims. According to Strabo, three classes of persons were much venerated among the Gauls--the Bards, Druids, and Soothsayers.

Caesar, from whom Dr. Stuart largely borrows, tells us that the whole of the Gallic nation was exceedingly superstitious. People of distinction who laboured under the more fatal diseases, and those who engaged in battles and other dangerous undertakings, either immolated human beings, or vowed that they would immolate themselves. They employed the Druids as their ministers at those sacrifices. It was thought the divine nature of the immortal gods could not be propitiated but by human life being substituted for human life. There were, Caesar continues, effigies of immense magnitude, interwoven with osiers, filled with living men. Then these former being ignited, the latter perished in the flames. The people thought that the sacrifices of guilty human victims, apprehended in the act of theft, robbery, or any other crime, were more agreeable to the immortal gods than those of innocent persons; but when the supply of culprits failed, non-guilty victims were sacrificed. All the Gauls boasted that they were descended from Dis as their father--a tradition communicated to them by the Druids. Funeral rites, considering the culture of the Gauls, were magnificent and sumptuous. Everything dear to the deceased, when alive, was carried into the fire. Even the animals did not escape; and, to manifest high esteem for a person of note, his slaves and clients who were beloved by him, were cremated together after the obsequies demanded by justice had been performed.

Pliny writes that the Druids exhibited the herb vervain in the exercise of their rites. They had tallies, consisting of sprigs lopped from a fruit-bearing tree, marked in a particular manner, thrown into a garment or covered with a veil, and drawn out by chance, through which means, it was supposed, the will of heaven was made known.

From various sources of information we know that the Druids had recourse to sortilege by fire. It was customary for a nobleman to take the entrails of a sacrificed animal in his hands, to walk barefooted three times through the embers of an expiring fire, and then carry them to a Druid performing at the altar. If the nobleman escaped unhurt, it was reckoned a good omen, but if injured, it was deemed unlucky to the country and himself. When a victim was put to death by the sword, the Druids who investigated the deed, pretended to discover future events by the manner in which he fell, the flavouring of the reeking blood, and the quivering of the body in the agonies of death.

The wonder-working eggs possessed by the Druids were insignia of a sacred character, set in gold, and worn suspended from the neck.

The Rev. John B. Pratt, in his work on the Druids, says: "These eggs were wholly artificial. Some of them were blue, some white, a third sort green, and a fourth regularly variegated with all these colours. They are said to have been worn by different orders--the white by the Druids; the blue by the presiding bards; the green by the Vains; and those with the three colours blended were pendants of the disciples. That the secret of manufacturing these amulets was totally unknown in Britain, except to the Druids, is thought most probable; and the secret of discovering things by looking into a globule of ink, which, it is asserted by some, the Egyptian jugglers still possess, may be a remnant of the ancient sortilege by means of the Druid's egg." Probably the coloured eggs children play with at Easter were anciently intended to represent the Druidical eggs.

Mr. Pratt concludes, that if it be true that the Druids came from the East, and that the traces of their existence there run back, as some suppose, into the remotest antiquity, "it is not altogether preposterous," he continues, "to suppose that their origin is to be dated from the dispersion at Babel.... Balaam, the Eastern magician, was probably the Arch-Druid of the mountainous country in which he lived. The offerings he made were at the high places of Baal, and for the purpose of enchantments, although he was not ignorant of the Most High.... The magi, or wise men of the East, probably were Druids, who, from their knowledge of astronomy, at once detected the star which indicated the fulfilment of Balaam's prophecy."

The earliest name borne by the island of Iona, so far as known in modern times, was Innis-nan Druidneach, or Isle of the Druids. The Druids retained their power not only in Iona until the year 563 or 564, but also on the mainland and in the islands. Mullingar is supposed to have been the last place in Ireland where the Druids had a residence. In the beginning of the last century a number of gold coins, found on the hill Karn Bre, near Truro, were thought to be Druidical coins. Some of them, Mr. Davies thinks, were impressed with rude hieroglyphics, symbolical of Ceridiven. Objects of different kinds are combined in one compound figure. To an arc or half moon is added the head of a bird, probably symbolical of the mother of the mystical egg. On other coins found there, magical ceremonies are represented, and on others the mystical sow appears sketched out.

In Druidical times there were rocking stones, or stones of judgment. They were large, some of them weighing fifty tons, and having sharp edges, on which they stood nicely balanced. A rocking stone of judgment, says Mr. Rust, "had been intended to test difficult questions, which could not be proved, disproved, or solved in the ordinary way, or for want of evidence, or which required the divine interposition of some particular deity, likely a bloodthirsty one; for as they had different deities, different temples, and different altars, they had also different judgment stones attached to them, and different ordeals through which the tried individuals, whether devotees, criminals, or captives, had to pass. These judgment stones had been anciently very common." According to the number of times a stone oscillated or refused to oscillate, the Druids determined to convict or acquit the suspected person.

Of the misletoe, and the esteem in which it was held by the Druids, we have written in page 127. This parasitical plant was regarded as a charm of no ordinary virtue. But the misletoe was only one of many articles they had possessing occult virtue.

Glass rings, manufactured by Druidical priests, were worn by the ancient Britons, as preventatives against witchcraft and the machinations of evil spirits.

A ridiculous legend is told concerning Stonehenge, the supposed Druidical temple near Salisbury. Aurelianus Ambrosius, a famous general of the ancient Britons, of Roman extraction, was, at the request of the Britons, sent over with ten thousand men to assist them against the Saxons, whom Vortigern had invited into Britain. Ambrosius had such successes against the Saxons that the Britons chose him for their king, and compelled Vortigern to give up to him all the western parts of the kingdom divided by the Roman highway, called Watling Street. Ultimately Ambrosius became sole monarch of Britain. Geoffrey says that this monarch built Stonehenge. Ambrosius, we are told, coming to a monastery where lay buried three hundred British lords who had been massacred by Hengist, resolved to perpetuate the memory of this action by raising a monument over their remains.

By the advice of Tremounus, Archbishop of Caerleon, Ambrosius consulted Merlin, the celebrated magician, as to how he should proceed. Merlin recommended him to send to Ireland for certain great stones, called *chorea gigantum*, the giant's dance, placed in a circle on a hill called Killaci, which had been brought there by giants from the farthest borders of Africa. A strong force was, in accordance with this advice, sent to Ireland, but the king of that country derided the folly of the Britons in undertaking such a ridiculous expedition, and opposed them in battle. The Irish king was vanquished, and, by the direction and assistance of Merlin, who had accompanied the expedition, the wonderful stones were conveyed to Salisbury, and, by order of Ambrosius, placed over the graves of the British lords. These gravestones are what are now called Stonehenge. Such stories, as may be expected, are discredited by historians, but our best antiquaries disagree as to the origin of these monuments of antiquity.

Gale, Dickenson, and others say the Druids borrowed their philosophy and religion from the Jews and Eastern heathen nations. Our older antiquarians believe that cromlechs are Druidical altars, in imitation of older heathen altars--a theory supported by reference to the stones called Petroma, near the temple of Eleusinian Damater in Arcadia: The Philistines pointed to the Deluge in their hieroglyphics of the serpent and mundane egg, the history which the serpent is supposed to designate being that of Noah, and the egg being reckoned an emblem of the ark, from the circumstance of it containing the rudiments of future life. The serpent is not unfrequently represented when reference is made to the betrayal of Eve.

People making acknowledgment to the gods for continual benefits, surrendered part of their increase for the service of the altar. Egyptian offerings consisted of fruits and herbs, while shepherds offered firstlings of their flocks. For this cause the Egyptians disliked shepherds almost with the cruel hatred Cain bore his brother Abel.

As the oak and misletoe were sacred to the Druids, so were they to the Israelites in their days of declension. And in Greece we find the famous oracle of Jupiter at the oaks of Dodona. To the ancient inhabitants of Italy the misletoe was a sacred emblem; and the golden branches of Virgil were none other than those of the misletoe.

As the Druids studied the heavenly bodies as a book (so says Origen), the heathen learned through the discovery of a new star the birth of a great person. From Virgil, it appears, it was commonly imagined the gods sent stars to point the way to their favourites in perplexity. The Jews entertained similar opinions.

According to Suckford, the ancients believed that heroes and other great men were transferred at death to some bright planet. In consequence of such belief, eminent persons were deified. Julius Caesar was canonised, because it was thought he was translated to a new star, discovered at the hour of his death.

DEMONOLOGY.
CHAPTER XXVIII.

First Ideas of Demonology--Rabbinical Tradition--Adam's Marriage--The Wicked Lilith--Demons--Egyptian Tradition--Arabian Worship of Genii--Christians' Opinions of Demons--Forms assumed by Evil Spirits--Demoniacal King--Duty of Inferior Demons--Task of Benign Spirits--Schools of Magic--What was taught in them--Circassian Opinions--Belief of Indians--Situation of Hell--Men's Actions recorded--Rewards and Punishments--How to frighten Demons--Treatment of the Sick--Condemning Spirits to Everlasting Punishment--Attendant Angels--Worship of Gods--Foretelling Future Events--Small-pox propagated by an Evil Genius--Souls of Deceased Persons--Dread of Evil Spirits--Effect of Charms.

To the Chaldeans we are indebted for the first ideas of demonology. From Chaldea the notions of demonology spread to Persia, Egypt, and Greece; but, as stated in another part of these pages, a belief in spirits or genii and of witchcraft prevailed at an early period of man's existence. There is an ancient Rabbinical tradition, no doubt very absurd, but illustrative of early notions of superstition, that Adam was first married to a sorceress named Lilith, or the mother of devils. She refused submission to Adam, and disregarded commandments conveyed to her by angels. She persisted in her disobedience; and having one day, in a more than ordinary state of impiety, invoked the name of Jehovah, according to the rules of the Cabala, she ascended into the air and disappeared. Lilith was feared by divers nations. When children died of diseases not properly understood, their deaths were attributed to Lilith, who was supposed to carry out her wicked purposes as an aerial spectre. Newly married pairs were accustomed to inscribe the names of angels on the inside partitions of their houses, and the names of Adam and Eve and the words "Begone, Lilith," on the outside walls. The name Lilith was given to women suspected of holding intercourse with demons. The legends of Lilith were transmitted from people to people until they came down to the Jews, who believed them. This people were wont to inscribe on their bed-posts the words, "Et zelo Chuizlilith," that the sleepers might be delivered by Lilith from dreams.

Demon was a term applied by the Greeks and Romans to certain genii or spirits who made themselves visible to men, with the intention of doing them either good or harm. The Jews and early

Christians ascribed a malignant nature to demons, the former endeavouring to trace their origin to intercourse between man and supernatural beings, and the latter maintaining that they were the souls of departed human beings, permitted to visit the earth to assist those they favoured, and punish persons against whom they or their favourites had a grudge. Certain spirits were supposed to be celestial, others watery, some airy, and not a few of them fiery. Tertullian said: "Spirits flew through the air faster than any winged fowl. Unless commissioned to act, they remained passive, neither doing good nor evil; but the evil spirits went and came at the devil's command, and both classes of spirits were at man's service if he only knew how to summon them into his presence."

The ancient Egyptians had a tradition, that at a far past period men rebelled against the gods, and drove them away. Upon this taking place, the gods fled into Egypt, where they concealed themselves under the form of different animals; and this was the first reason assigned for the worship of inferior creatures. A leading principle in the religion of the ancient Arabians was their belief in fairies or genii. They thought that these genii attended people through life; that every man had two of these waiting on him, the one good and the other evil; that all evil actions were committed at the instigation of the evil spirit in the absence of the good genii, who sometimes went with messages to the celestial regions. The Arabians further believed these genii were continually at war with each other, which, the people considered, accounted for the contending passions in their minds. Their principal genius was Hafedhah, to whom the people, on setting out on a plundering expedition, prayed he would send them a strong genius to assist them.

In the middle ages conjuration was regularly practised in Europe, and devils were supposed to appear under decided forms. A devil would appear either as an angel of light, or as a monster in hideous shape. An anonymous writer, discussing the subject, says: "A devil would appear either like an angel seated in a fiery chariot, or riding on an infernal dragon, and carrying in his right hand a viper, or assuming a lion's head, a goose's feet, and a hare's tail, or putting on a raven's head, and mounted on a strong wolf. Other forms made use of by demons were those of fierce warriors, or old men riding upon crocodiles, with hooks in hand. A human figure would arise, having the wings of a griffin; or sporting three heads, one of them being like that of a toad, the other resembling that of a cat; or defended with huge teeth and horns, and adorned with a sword; or displaying a dog's teeth, and a large raven's head; or mounted upon a pale horse, and exhibiting a serpent's tail; or gloriously crowned, and riding upon a dromedary; or presenting the face of a lion; or bestriding a bear, and grasping a viper. There were also such shapes as those of archers or bowmen. A demoniacal king would ride on a pale horse, assume a leopard's face and griffin's wings; or put on three heads, one of a bull, another of a man, and a third of a ram, with a serpent's tail and the feet of a goose; and in this appearance sit on a dragon, and bear in his hand a lance and flag; or, instead of being thus employed, goad the flanks of a furious bear, and carry on his fist a hawk. Other forms were those of a goodly knight; or of one who bore lance, ensign, and even sceptre; or of a soldier, either riding on a black horse, and surrounded with a flame of fire; or wearing on his head a duke's crown, and mounted on a crocodile; or assuming a lion's face, and, with fiery eyes, spurring on a gigantic charger, or, with the same frightful aspect, appearing in all the pomp of family distinction, on a pale horse; or clad from head to foot in crimson raiment, wearing on his bold front a crown, and sallying forth on a red steed."

To inferior demons was assigned the duty of carrying away condemned souls, and superior benign spirits had the pleasing task of conveying from earth the souls of the blessed.

Toledo, Seville, and Salamanca were great schools of magic. The teachers taught that all knowledge might be obtained by the assistance of fallen angels. These teachers were skilled in the abstract sciences, in alchemy, in the various languages of mankind, and of the lower animals, divinity, magic, and prophecy. They professed to possess the power of controlling the winds and waters, and of influencing the stars. They also pretended to be able to cause earthquakes, spread diseases or cure them, release souls out of purgatory, to influence the passions of the mind, procure the reconciliation of friends or foes, engender discord, and induce mania and melancholy.

The Circassians sprinkled holy water over their friends' graves, and the priests tolled bells near them to keep evil spirits from the bodies. Affectionate relations visited the burying grounds from time to time, to repeat prayers for the repose of the dead, who, they thought, continued to be acquainted with the affairs of the world.

When an Indian became ill, the Brahmin prayed over him; for it was believed that two spirits, one good and the other bad, attended the dying at the hour of death. If the expiring person lived a commendable life, he was conveyed in a flying chariot to a place of happiness; but if he was wicked, the evil spirit carried him before a dread tribunal, to be judged according to his works. Deceased was then sent back to wander on the earth ten days, in the shape of a magpie. For this reason the people always fed a magpie for ten days after the death of a relation, imagining that the bird might possess their friend's soul.

Indians believed in former times, whatever they may do now, that hell was situated at a great distance below the world, and that there was a president in it called Yhamadar. Under him, a secretary named Xitragupten wrote down a man's good and bad actions, and presented his record to the president the instant the deceased's soul came before him. This infernal president was reported to have been very equitable, distributing rewards and punishments according to justice. Some souls were supposed to be sent back to inhabit inferior bodies in this world, while others were tormented in the most cruel manner in the infernal regions. If a dying person laid hold of a cow by the tail, and a Brahmin poured water over his hand, and put a sum of money into it (the hand), the soul would be protected from the power of demons.

In Pegu, copper vessels or bells were used to frighten demons that wanted to disturb the repose of the dead. There the priests pretended to know what was most agreeable and acceptable to evil spirits, and professed to be able to appease their anger. A grand entertainment was sometimes made for the devil, at which the friends of a sick man danced to the sound of vocal and instrumental music. These heathens believed devils had bodies as well as souls, and that, although immortal, they had the same passions as men. They believed, also, that the devils or demons had power to foretell future events, and that all dreams happened in consequence of their promptings. They therefore consulted such devils nearly after the manner the witches of Great Britain were accustomed to do.

When a person in Cochin-China was at the point of death, his male relations surrounded his bed, brandishing their sabres and other warlike weapons, to drive away the demons, which they supposed were hovering around him to seize his soul the instant it was liberated from the body. When a prince died, the priests held a consultation, in order to discover what demon it was that caused the sad event; and when they made the discovery, which they invariably did, they in a solemn manner condemned the evil spirit to everlasting punishment. The inhabitants of the Molucca Islands were under the impression, like other heathens and Christians too, that two angels attended on every person on earth, the one seeking his good, and the other his eternal hurt. The good angel prompted the individual to holy actions, while the malignant one was constantly instigating him to shun the right path. The people worshipped the air under the name of Lanitho, which was subject to another being or spirit named Lanthila, but they had many gods they consulted on all occasions of importance. If it was considered necessary to consult a Nito or god, the people assembled under cloud of night, with tapers burning, and, after pronouncing mysterious words, called on their god to appear. As soon as the prescribed forms were gone through, Nito entered with one of the people, who, while under the demoniacal influence, foretold future events. A few families in that island claimed to have the power of witchcraft vested in them from generation to generation.

Being often afflicted with small-pox, the people conjectured the disease was propagated by an evil genius; and, to frighten the demon from their homes, images were placed on the house-tops. If one accidentally met a funeral or saw a corpse on the road, he returned home in haste. If the unlucky person was a woman carrying a child in her arms, her consternation was great, for it was imagined the soul of the deceased hovered in the air near the corpse, and endeavoured to injure the living, particularly young children. To protect their children from demons, parents tied charmed beads round the infants' necks. Indeed the people lived in constant dread of evil spirits; and, to frustrate their evil intentions, they, in addition to the preventatives already mentioned, always kept consecrated articles under their pillows.

CHAPTER XXIX.

Heathen Devotion in Ceylon--Superstitious Customs among the Schismatic Greeks--Negro Belief in Fetishes or Genii--Charms and Sacred Rings and Belts--Magic taught by the Priests--Dead Persons metamorphosed into Serpents--How the Gaures disposed of their Dead--Modes of discovering whether Souls were Blessed or Damned--Orders of Genii in Madagascar--Devil Worship--Belief of the Caribbees--Brazilian Superstition--Peruvian Tradition--Devil Worship among the American Indians--Demons in the Sixteenth and Seventeenth Centuries--Satan in France--Manes, Anima, and Umbra among the Greeks and Romans.

In Ceylon, when the heathens' prayers were not answered, they repaired to the most gloomy parts of their sacred groves, and offered up red cocks to the devil, where they supposed he and his imps and attendants delighted to dwell. And when any of the people were sick, they devoted a red cock to one of their genii. The priest, in offering the cock, made it known that the fowl was given only on condition that the invalid would be cured. It was believed that all the sacrifices offered to these genii were carried by them to heaven, to be presented to Buddha. To discover whether a patient's sickness was caused by a good or evil spirit, a bow of the first little stick that could be found was prepared, and on the bow-string the operator hung a small chisel, and holding the bow by the two extremities, named all the gods and devils he thought of. As soon as the name of the good or evil spirit that caused the disease was pronounced, the bow turned round. By means of bows the natives of Ceylon were also enabled to foretell future events.

Among the schismatic Greeks, an infant, previous to its baptism, was crossed by the priest, who commanded the devil to come out of the child, for it was believed an unclean spirit resided in it before baptism. After baptism, the priest hung a cross of gold, silver, or tin about the child's neck, which, in accordance with usual custom, was worn till death. If at death one was found without his cross, his body was cast into the ground without sacred ceremonies.

The negroes had fetishes or genii similar to the Manitous of the North Americans, and the ancient Fauns or Sylvans of the Romans. To these fetishes the negroes paid great respect. Particular kinds of birds, fishes, and trees were looked upon as fetishes; and certain of them were accounted the guardians of hills, mountains, and streams. Negroes supposed that if one broke off a branch from a sacred tree, he would immediately cause the destruction of their crops. They had stones resembling the Roman terminal-stones. Fetishes were consulted by the people as oracles; and when they appeared in living form to return answers, it was generally as black dogs. Large fetishes were kept for the protection of houses; and the people carried small ones about them, sometimes suspended from their necks, and sometimes concealed under their arm-pits, for their protection. Negro women hung charms round their infants' necks, to protect them from harm. Children four years of age had sacred rings round their legs and arms, to protect them from evil spirits. This was not all: mothers went the length of making their children wear bandages adorned with fetishes, to strengthen the little ones and keep away demons. Thursday was set apart for the worship of fetishes. The priests studied magic, and instructed the people in the art thereof. It was a belief among the negroes, that at death they were metamorphosed into serpents, and for that reason they would not kill or injure one of these reptiles.

Because the Gaures thought decomposed bodies polluted the earth, they did not bury their dead. They had round towers as receptacles for their departed friends, whose bodies were let down to their final resting-place through an aperture in the roof. During the first three days after the body had been laid in the tower, it was thought to be in danger of being carried away by the devil. It therefore became necessary for the friends to keep watch, in order to prevent Satan having an opportunity to torment the soul as it winged its way to the celestial regions. On or before the fourth day the soul was in a place of torment or happiness. On this, the fourth day, the priests prognosticated the future state of the deceased. The discovery was made in this way: the dead body was laid on its back, with the eyes turned towards heaven, and the vultures being permitted to come and feast on the deceased, it was considered a certain sign that the soul had gone to bliss if the right eye was taken out first, but it was an equally sure omen that it had gone to a place of punishment if the left eye was the first devoured. Another mode of ascertaining the state of happiness or misery of a soul was by the movements of a dog near a corpse. If the animal went close to it, then were the relatives convinced the soul was in a state of bliss, but if the dog could not be tempted to go near the body, they despaired of their friend escaping everlasting torment.

The islanders of Madagascar entertained the opinion that there were divers orders of genii or spirits; that some of them directed the motions of the stars and planets, and that others had power over the air, the meteors, the sea, and men. Besides these genii there was another order of spirits, male and female, who married and had offspring. They made known future events to man, and performed superhuman actions, such as are done by Scotch fairies. The natives of Madagascar also believed in the existence of phantoms and ghosts. To protect themselves, their friends, and property from the power of Satan, they, at stated times, with javelins in hand, danced, to the beat of drum, to drive away evil spirits.

The Floridans worshipped the devil in various ways. In the Caribbee Islands the inhabitants had a great variety of omens and superstitions. They thought bats were supernatural creatures, whose duty it was to watch over mortal man during night. These people consulted relics of deceased friends as to things past and future. The Boias, the native medico-priests, had each his particular genii, whom he pretended to summon to his assistance by humming certain words and burning tobacco. These genii were conjured in the night time, at a place without fire or light. The Boias were reported to have possessed the power of killing enemies by means of charms. The Caribbees ascribed diseases to Maboia; and whenever they were desirous of knowing the result of any illness with which they were afflicted, they presented an offering to Maboia, and sent for a Boia in the night, who, on his arrival, ordered the fires to be extinguished. In presence of the patient, he smoked a quantity of tobacco, rubbed another portion of the weed into powder, and blew it up in the air. From certain appearances the priest discovered the cause of the disease, and ascertained what would be the result thereof. If the patient was to die, the priest gave his assurance that the spirits would receive the dying individual into their blessed abode.

The Brazilians had domestic gods, which they consulted; and their priests were fortune-tellers and interpreters of dreams. After a friend died, the relations carried provisions to the grave every day for a short time, under the impression that the nourishment brought would prevent the deceased's spirit from dying.

The Peruvians had a tradition that a man of extraordinary form and character, whose name was Choun, came from the north into their country; that he levelled mountains, filled up valleys, and opened passages for himself through places inaccessible to ordinary man. It is related that this being having been offended by the inhabitants of the plains, changed part of the ground which was fruitful into a sandy desert, forbade the rain to fall, and dried up the plants. Subsequently he had compassion on the erring people, and opened the springs, so that the rivers once more flowed. Choun was worshipped till the appearance of a more mighty god called Pachacamac, who, on his coming, metamorphosed into wild beasts the former inhabitants that had done homage to Choun. The people had superstitious opinions concerning comets and rainbows. They drew predictions from dreams, from signs on earth, and from appearances in the heavens.

In olden times there was a system of devil worship among the American Indians; and almost everywhere, in the sixteenth and seventeenth centuries, demons made themselves seen and felt in nearly every part of the earth. In France, Satan had his witches, imps, and other inferior demons, who carried out his wicked purposes. At Lyons the devil appeared in the shape of a little woman, and, by cunning stratagem, led many persons into serious crimes. In the year 1612 the evil one, in the appearance of a beautiful woman, allured some Paris gentlemen into paths of sin. As a good deal of scandal was the result, the justices and physicians of the city commenced an inquiry, which ended in it being discovered that the apparently beautiful lady was the evil spirit of a woman that had been hanged shortly before. Great excitement prevailed at St. Steven's Church, Mascon, through the devil opening graves, raising the dead, and destroying the vintage.

The Greeks and Romans affirmed that, after the dissolution of the body, every man possessed three different kinds of ghosts or spirits, distinguished by the names of Manes, Anima, and Umbra. The Manes, it was supposed, descended into the infernal regions, the Anima ascended to the skies, and Umbra hovered about the tomb, seemingly unwilling to depart from the body.

CHAPTER XXX.

Belief in the Existence of Visible   Ghosts--Superstition among the People dwelling on the   Baltic Shores--A German Legend--Demons in the West of   Europe--Love, how plighted in Orkney--The Monster   Ymor--Origin of Fairies--The Duergar or Dwarfs--More   about Fairies--Brownies in Ireland and the Highlands   of Scotland--Nine Classes of Evil   Spirits--Vampires--Man's Double or Fetch--Churchyard   Ghosts--Souls of Suicides--Burial of Suicides and Murderers at Cross Roads--Luther on Evil Spirits and   Witches.

A belief in the existence of visible ghosts on earth was general before and after the middle ages. An old divine of our own country says:--"I look upon it as a special piece of providence, that there are, ever and anon, such fresh examples of apparitions and witchcraft as may rub up and awaken their" [the people's] "benumbed and lethargic minds into a suspicion at least, if not assurance, that there are other intelligent beings besides those clothed in heavy earth or clay. In this, I say, methinks the divine providence does plainly interest the powers of the dark kingdom, permitting wicked men and women, and vagrant spirits of that kingdom, to make leagues or covenants one with another, and to make the confession of witches against their own lives, and the miraculous feats they play, palpable evidence that there are bad spirits" as well as good.

An author, who wrote on second sight, last century, under the name of Theophilus Insulanus, considered all persons were irreligious who entertained a doubt of the reality of apparitions of departed souls.

Another author thought ghosts were mere aerial beings without substance that could pass through walls and other solid bodies at pleasure. Ghosts commonly appeared in the same dress as the persons whose spirits they represented were accustomed to wear when alive, though the ghosts were sometimes clothed in white. The appearance of spirits was generally accompanied by an unaccountable light. Dogs and horses possess the faculty of seeing ghosts.

People living on the Baltic shores have a deity named Putseet, whom they encourage to remain with them, by placing in their barns, every night, tables with bread, butter, cheese, and ale thereon. If the provisions are taken away, good fortune is expected; if left untouched, bad luck is looked for. This spirit assists in thrashing, churning, grinding, and sweeping the house at midnight.

The Northern nations regard spirits of this description as the souls of men who gave themselves up, during life, to illicit pleasures, and therefore were doomed, as a punishment, to wander about the earth for a limited time, to assist mankind.

There is a legend in Germany of an extraordinary nature. Travellers were shown a pair of brass gates, one of which had a crack, caused by the following circumstance:--When a supreme monarch had given orders for the building of a church, the devil came one day and asked what he intended it for, to which the Emperor answered, "For a gaming-house," and Satan went away seemingly well pleased. A few days afterwards the fiend returned, and seeing altars erected, asked what they were for. The Emperor answered, "For gaming-tables," which encouraged the devil to lend his assistance in the completion of the sacred building. Next time Satan made his appearance he brought a pair of large brass gates for the edifice, but happening to see a crucifix, he flung them down with such force that one of the gates was damaged. For many years the gates were objects of curiosity.

In the west of Europe, where superstition prevailed, there were many formidable demons, whose history originated in Celtic, Teutonic, and Eastern fables. In Orkney, even during the last century, lovers met within the sacred circle of stones dedicated to Scandinavian deities, to plight their love. Through a hole in one of the pillars the hands of contracting parties were joined, and the vow made was called the promise of Odin. To violate this vow, rendered the false one infamous in all time coming.

In the body of the giant Ymir several maggots had been generated, which, by order of the gods, partook of both human shape and reason. These little beings, to which reference is also made in pages 88 and 90, possessed the most delicate figures, and always dwelt in subterranean caverns or clefts in the rocks. They were remarkable for their riches, activity, and malevolence, and were probably the modern fairies of the north and west, who are usually described as beings of small stature, and gaily dressed. These creatures, the offspring of worms, possessed the power of making themselves visible and invisible. They multiplied their species, and lived in a style of grandeur that could not be surpassed by the greatest monarch on earth. They were good friends to certain members of the human family, but bitter enemies to others of Adam's posterity. With their elf arrows they could kill or wound man and beast. They carried off children and domestic animals, generally leaving vile creatures resembling the children or animals carried away, so as to prevent the felony being discovered.

Opinions originally entertained in this country relative to the dwarfs have undergone considerable modifications, from the same attributes being assigned to them as to the Persian peris. Fairies were supposed to have brought many blessings to England, sending people pleasant dreams, giving money to them in a mysterious manner, and causing the nation to prosper. In remote times a brownie was attached to the home of every considerable family in Ireland and the Highlands of Scotland. Like men, some brownies were tall, and some of small stature. They were industrious and faithful, if well treated in the way the Samogitae did the Putseet. When a brownie once united himself to a family, he seldom deserted it, but continued to serve generation after generation. Burton speaks of nine classes of evil spirits:--First, the false gods of the Gentiles, adored as idols, who gave oracles at Delphos and elsewhere, whose prince was Beelzebub; second, the liars and equivocators, as Apollo, Pythias, and the like; third, the inventors of mischief, as Theutus, in Plato; fourth, malicious, revengeful devils, whose prince was Asmodeus; fifth, coseners, such as belong to magicians and witches, their prince being Satan; sixth, aerial spirits, that corrupted the air, and caused plagues, thunder, fires, and other calamities; seventh, a destroyer, causing wars, tumults, and combustions; eighth, an accusing or calumniating devil, that drove people to despair; and the ninth, tempters in divers shapes, having mammon for their prince. Burton goes further. He asserts that "no place is void, but all full of spirits, devils, or other inhabitants; not so much as a hairbreadth is empty in heaven, earth, or waters above or under the earth. The earth is not so full of flies in summer as it is at all times of invisible devils."

Psellus founded a system of demonology, which had for its basis the natural history and habitation of demons. His first class consisted of fiery devils, that wandered in the regions near the moon, but were prevented from entering that luminary. They displayed their power in blazing stars, in counterfeit suns, moons, and meteoric lights, and prevented foul weather. These demons, we are informed, occasionally resided in the furnaces of Hecla, Etna, or Vesuvius. His second class was made up of aerial devils, that inhabited the atmosphere, caused tempests, thunder, and lightning, rended asunder trees, burned down steeples and houses, struck men and beasts, showered stones, wool, and frogs from the skies; counterfeited in the clouds the battles of armies, raised whirlwinds, fires, and corrupted the air so as to spread disease. The third class was terrestrial devils, such as lares, genii, fauns, satyrs, wood-nymphs, foliots, robin-goodfellows, or trulli. The fourth class was aqueous devils, as the various descriptions of water nymphs. The fifth class consisted of subterranean devils, known by the name of Getuli or Cobals. They preserved treasure in the earth, and prevented it being suddenly revealed; they were also the cause of horrible earthquakes. Psellus's sixth class of devils was named lucifugi. They delighted in darkness, entered into the bowels of men, and tormented those whom they possessed with frenzy and the falling sickness. An opinion prevailed that devils possessed corporeal frames, capable of sensation; that they could feel and be felt; that they could injure and be hurt; that they were nourished with peculiar food; that they did not hurt cattle from malevolence, but through a desire to obtain natural temperate heat and moisture from the animals they killed; that they disliked the sun's rays; and that they attained a great age.

Of all the kinds of demons we have heard of, the most loathsome are the vampires. Horst speaks of a vampire as a "dead body which continues to live in the grave, which it leaves, however, by night for the purpose of sucking the blood of the living, whereby it is nourished and preserved in good condition, instead of becoming decomposed like other dead bodies." Fischer, who believed there were vampires, informs us that the bite of a vampire left no mark upon the person, but that the bite speedily proved fatal, unless counteracted by the injured person eating some of the earth from the vampire's grave, and smearing himself with his blood. These precautions had only a temporary effect, if at all successful; for the bitten victim, sooner or later, became a vampire himself--died and was buried, but continued to follow the examples of old vampires in nourishing themselves, infecting others, and propagating vampirism.

Down to the middle of the last century there was a belief in vampirism in the east of Europe. This form of superstition created much anxiety in the public mind, none knowing when he might be bitten by one of those hated demons, and be thereby transformed into a vampire. Men of science bore testimony in favour of vampirism with seeming truthfulness and ability, worthy of a better subject.

In England every man was supposed to have his "double" or "fetch." The appearance of a fetch created great uneasiness in the mind of the person witnessing the apparition. It was taken as foreboding death or serious calamity to the being represented.

There were also churchyard ghosts in England, whose duty it was to watch bodies over which church rites had not been performed after violent death. In Scotland and England there were peculiar superstitious views concerning the souls of suicides. Authoritative decrees prohibited graveyard gates being opened to permit the bodies of such persons being carried through them for interment. If relations persisted in depositing the remains of a friend who had committed suicide, it was necessary for them to take the dead body over the graveyard wall after sunset. But in most cases the bodies of suicides and murderers were buried at a "cross road," with a stake driven through the corpse, to prevent its ghost rising to frighten or harm innocent people.

The precaution of driving a stake through the body did not always prove effectual, if countless tales related of ghosts being seen in the vicinity of such unhallowed burying-grounds be true. Surprise need not be expressed at such superstition prevailing in a country where faith in witchcraft still lingers, and in which, at no very remote time, the statutes against witches were in full force. The State and the Church believed in the existence of demons and witches.

Luther's opinions on the subject of the agency and operations of evil spirits may be inferred from his *Colloquia*. "Many devils," he says, "are in woods, in waters, in wildernesses, and in dark poolly places, ready to hurt and prejudice people; some are in the thick black clouds, which cause hail, lightnings, and thunderings, and which poison the air, the pastures, and grounds."

In a conversation on witchcraft, Luther said he had no compassion on witches: he would burn every one of them. He reminded the people, that, according to the old law, the priests threw the first stones at such malefactors. Luther said his mother had undergone infinite annoyance from one of her neighbours who was a witch. This witch could throw a charm upon a child, which would make it cry itself to death. A pastor having punished the witch for some of her wicked tricks, she cast a spell on him by means of some earth he had walked upon. The good man fell sick of a malady, which no remedy could remove, and shortly thereafter died. Luther was satisfied the devil, through his prophets, could, and did, foretell future events; that he (the devil) was so skilled that he could cause death even by the leaf of a tree; that he had more boxes and pots full of poison, wherewith he destroyed men, than all the apothecaries in the world had of healing medicine. The devil, Luther thought, was so crafty that he could deceive our senses. He caused one to think he saw something he saw not, and to hear thunder or a trumpet he heard not. Men, he argued, were possessed by the devil, corporeally and spiritually. Those whom he possessed corporeally were mad people.

CHAPTER XXXI.

Belief and Teaching of the Roman Catholic Church--Instructions to Ecclesiastics in reference to Demons--Swedenborg's Intercourse with Spirits--Marcus Brutus and his Evil Genius--Cassius and Julius Caesar's Ghost at Philippi--Phantom Soldiers and Horses--Plutarch on Spectres--Socrates on the same subject--Archbishop Bruno and the Spectre--A Haunted House--A Child's Ghost--Spectre at Sea--Ghost of a Murdered Man in New South Wales--A Haunted House--A Spectre at Sea.

The belief and teaching of the Roman Catholic Church lead to a conviction that there are many evil spirits who act on men immediately by forming in the imagination representations and phantasies of an evil nature. The subjects of Satan, on whom his tyranny is chiefly exercised, are those who wilfully come under the empire of the prince of darkness, such as magicians, sorcerers, and persons who have renounced their baptism.

In a summary of instructions for the guidance of ecclesiastics, entitled *De Instructione Sacerdotum*, which appeared about the middle of the seventeenth century, we find in substance the following:--

"Magic is produced by the power of demons. In reality there is no power existing in the magician, for the effects are produced by the devil at the command of the magician. In the first place, demons produce effects by transferring bodies with great rapidity from one place to another. For they have power over all inferior things, natural and artificial, in this respect; and, moreover, they are endowed with wonderful agility, which enables them to pass in an instant from one place to another, however remote. Secondly, demons produce effects by the occult application of natural causes, and by accelerating their actions, for their knowledge is incredible. They understand the nature and properties of everything in

the mineral, vegetable, and animal worlds, and they
know where everything is. Hence they sometimes produce
trees, fruits, and animals in an incredibly short
space of time. They often effect cures by the occult
use of medicines, or by entering the body and
expelling evil humours. Thirdly, they perform
prodigies by acting on the senses. The compacts
between the demons and magicians are based upon
engagements mutually entered into. The magician
promises to obey the demon, and the demon, on his
part, promises to work for him and at his bidding. The
compact is sometimes entered into with great
solemnity, with the demon seated on a throne,
surrounded by a host of evil spirits, as attendants
and witnesses."

Swedenborg entertained the conviction that the world of spirits held communion with certain favoured persons in this life; and up to the period of his death, in the year 1772, he pretended to have intercourse with spirits of celestial origin and those of deceased men. Swedenborg frequently narrated the wonders of other worlds, and particularly those of the infernal regions.

There are endless accounts of spirits appearing to men on earth. Here are a few of them:-- Marcus Brutus, one of the murderers of Julius Caesar, being one night in his tent, saw a monstrous figure coming in about the third hour of night. Brutus immediately cried out, "What art thou, a man or a god? and why art thou come hither?" The spectre answered, "I am thy evil genius; thou shalt see me at Philippi." Brutus, with feigned calmness, answered, "I will meet thee there." Disordered, however, in body, and disturbed in mind, Brutus related the affair to Cassius, who, being of the sect of Epicurus, told Brutus that what he supposed he saw was nothing more than mere fancy; that there were no such things as genii or other spirits which could appear to man; that even if they should appear, they could not assume a human shape or voice, and had no power over men. Though Brutus was somewhat encouraged by what Cassius said, he could not entirely overcome his uneasiness. In the midst of the battle of Philippi, Brutus thought he saw Julius Caesar, whom he had assassinated, riding to him at full speed, which so terrified him that he fell upon his own sword. Cassius also fell there under the hand of his freedman Pindarus.

Pausanius writes that, four hundred years after the battle of Marathon, there were heard, in the place where it was fought, the neighing of horses, and the shouts of soldiers animating one another to the fight. Plutarch also speaks of spectres seen and dreadful howlings heard in the public baths, where several citizens of Ch[oe]ronea, his native town, had been murdered. He says that the inhabitants had been obliged to shut up these baths, but that, notwithstanding this precaution, great noises continued to be heard, and dreadful spectres were frequently seen by the neighbours. Plutarch frequently makes mention of spectres and apparitions; particularly he says, that, in the famous battle above alluded to, several soldiers saw the apparition of Theseus fighting for the Greeks and against the Persians.

It is recorded in Socrates, that after the defeat of the Athenian army under the praetor Laches, as he was flying in company with the Athenian general, and came to a place where several roads met, he refused to go the same road that the others took, and the reason being asked him, he answered that his genius, or familiar spirit, who frequently attended him, dissuaded him from it; and the event justified the precaution, for all those who went a different way from him were killed or made prisoners by the enemy's cavalry.

When Bruno, Archbishop of Wirtzburgh, a short time before his sudden death, was sailing with Henry III., he descried a terrific spectre standing upon a rock which overhung the foaming waters, by whom he was thus hailed; "Ho! bishop, I am thy evil genius. Go whither thou choosest, thou art and shalt be mine. I am not now sent for thee, but soon thou shalt see me again."

A house at Athens was haunted by a spirit which roamed through the apartments at night, seemingly dragging a heavy chain after it. Athenodorus, the philosopher, hired the house, with the intention of discovering the cause of so much alarm to the inmates. One night, while pursuing his studies, he was startled by hearing what seemed to be the rattling of chains. On looking up he beheld a spectre enter his apartment and make a sign to him to follow. The philosopher rose and followed the ghost, which went into the courtyard and disappeared. The philosopher marked the spot where the spectre vanished, and on the following day caused a search to be made. The result was that the skeleton of a man in chains was discovered. The bones were publicly burned, and the ghost never again appeared.

A lady, while going along a dreary path one evening to see a sick child, was frightened by a strange sight before her. The mysterious object represented her friend's child dead, and wrapt in its winding sheet, floating up in the air heavenwards. It is almost needless to say that just about that time the sick child died.

Many years ago, when a ship of war was one night off the African coast, the officer on watch became deeply affected in a manner he could not explain, and became partially insensible, and could not rouse himself before a cold hand touched him. He then beheld a white figure walking away. It turned round, and in the face he beheld the features of a brother in England. The spectre, after remaining a few seconds, vanished. On arriving in Great Britain, the officer discovered that his brother died on the very night he saw the apparition.

A ghost story was related for the first time about twenty years ago, of the ghost of a murdered man appearing in the colony of New South Wales. A farmer named Fisher, in the prime of life and unmarried, suddenly disappeared, leaving L4000 worth of property behind him. A neighbour called Smith reported that Fisher had gone to England, and that he was authorized to act for him in all business matters during his absence. The statement was received as a fact; but a strange circumstance changed public opinion. An old man named Ben Weir, who had a small farm near that of Fisher, was returning home one night from Sydney, when he beheld farmer Fisher with a severe wound on the forehead, and blood flowing from it. When Weir got within a few paces of the figure, it disappeared. He could not rightly comprehend the meaning of all this, and did not mention what he had seen, lest his neighbours would say he had been drunk. A few nights afterwards he had occasion to pass the spot where Fisher had appeared, and there again the farmer stood before him as before. Weir could not now remain silent. He went to a justice of the peace and told his tale. At first the justice would not credit his informant, but subsequently he instructed an inquiry to be made. Marks of blood were discovered at the spot where the ghost appeared, and in a pond, a little distance off, Fisher's dead body was found. Smith was consequently arrested, and tried before the late Sir Francis Forbes. His guilt was established, and he was sentenced to death. Before his execution he confessed that he alone had murdered Fisher at the very spot where Weir saw the murdered man's ghost.

An account is given of a house that was haunted at Bow last century. A young girl declared one morning that a cold hand had been laid on her about midnight. This proved to be the hand of death. She sickened, and before many suns went down she lay in her winding sheet. Then followed a series of strange annoyances, which gave rise to the report that the house was haunted. So dreadfully were the inmates frightened, that though the house contained many apartments upstairs and downstairs, they took refuge in a small room on the ground floor. Night and day strange noises were heard, and furniture and other articles were flung about by unseen hands. A gentleman, a friend of the family, hearing of what was going on, engaged to solve the mystery. Entering an apartment upstairs, he observed the furniture moving about the floor, although no living being could be seen. Stones and bricks were thrown through the window; a staff danced round the room; dishes were thrown at his head. He examined every hole and corner, but could not discover any person or thing by which the articles were made to move. Fearing the presence of evil spirits, he hastened out, closing the door after him. It was instantly opened, and chairs, stools, candlesticks, and dishes were hurled after him. The worst had not come. While all the family were standing in amazement, a small boiler with hot water moved from one side of the grate to the other, the poker and tongs stood up and exchanged places, the pots and pans clattered loudly, and a small table was lifted into the air. A witch residing in the neighbourhood being suspected of causing the mischief, a noted wizard undertook to solve the mystery. He ordered the dancing staff to be burned. When it was blazing up, a suspected witch entered in great agony. She asked for a drink of water to quench her burning thirst. Those cognisant of the facts concluded that the perpetrator of the mischief was discovered. She was apprehended, tried, and acquitted for want of sufficient evidence. As she left the court she was heard to mutter, "I shall be revenged." She kept her word. The following night, the annoyance, which had ceased during her incarceration, recommenced with double fury. The inmates of the house, who had previously escaped without bodily injury, were struck by invisible persons, who, as often as they dealt their blows, shouted, "Take that;" while at the same time the furniture was knocked against the walls and broken to pieces. The inmates fled for their lives, and the house was shut up for many years, none daring to occupy the haunted house.

A young man at sea was alarmed, one night, to see an apparition of his mother standing before him. She delivered a message concerning family business. So frightened was he that he could not reply or put any questions to the spirit, although he earnestly desired to speak. After delivering the message, the apparition slowly retired, went over the ship's bulwarks, dropped gently into the sea, and floated away. The last glimpse he had of the unearthly figure was on the crest of a wave near the vessel's stern. On his return home he learned that his mother had died at the time he had seen her ghost. What was more strange, she left a message for him similar to that which the apparition delivered. On his next voyage the young man told his companions that on the previous night he had seen his mother floating in the water like a mermaid, and that she had made a sign for him to come to her. Next night a storm arose; the ship was in great danger, the decks were swept, and the young man was washed away. His last words were, "Mother, I come."

CHAPTER XXXII.

Spiritualism Past and Present--Coffee-house   Keeper--Magic taught in Leipsic--Intercourse with and   Control over Spirits--Spirit of Marshal Saxe called   up--How Spirits were Invoked--Voices of Good and Evil   Spirits--A Terrified Company--Mysterious Death of a   Magician--Unearthly Huntsman---Prediction and its   Fulfilment--An Estate lost at the Gaming Table--A   Baron Shot--A Marriage prevented by an   Apparition--Strange Sights and   Sounds--Murder--Consulting a Witch--Raising the Spirit   of a Murdered Man--A Murderer's Fate.

Writers generally supposed to be well informed have said that spiritualism is a system of professed communication with the unseen world, which originated in America about the year 1848. Others have endeavoured to trace the origin of spiritualism to the writings of Swedenborg. Both parties are in error. Long before Swedenborg's time, and anterior to Columbus discovering America, spiritualism in various forms was believed in in Scotland, England, Ireland, all over Europe, and elsewhere. Reginald Scot, in the year 1584, wrote against witchcraft and demonology; but so general was the belief in spiritualism, and so abhorrent were the opinions of Scot, that his book was ordered to be burned by the common hangman. Let those who claim for America the discovery of spiritualism, real or feigned, read 1 Samuel., and they will perceive how much they have been deceived. We may return to spiritualism as looked upon in the present time; meanwhile we shall continue our own course, proving, step by step, the former belief in spiritualism, or what we prefer to call demonology.

A coffee-house keeper in Leipsic, named Schrepfer, studied and taught magic as an art. He boasted of his intercourse with and control over spirits, whose presence, he alleged, could be commanded at any time. Owing to a degrading insult offered him, he left Leipsic, none knew whither, but after a lapse of time he appeared at Dresden, where his magical skill attracted many followers. His reputation reached Prince Charles of Saxony, who had been instrumental in causing the magician to depart from Leipsic; he visited Schrepfer, apologised for what he had done, and requested him to give manifestations of his supernatural art. He accepted the apologies, and exhibited many difficult operations in the science of magic. The prince requested Schrepfer, who had the power of calling before him the ghost of any one, however long dead, to bring up the ghost of Marshal Saxe, Charles's uncle, in the hope that information would be obtained regarding a vast amount of hidden treasure the deceased was supposed to have concealed from his relatives. This was a few years after the Chevalier de Saxe died, yet the magician readily agreed to comply with the request. The place chosen for commanding the spirit to appear was Prince Charles's palace in Dresden. On the appointed night, the prince and a large company of friends assembled in the apartment named for the purpose. Everything being in readiness, the door and windows were secured, that none possessed of mere human strength could effect an entrance. Schrepfer retired into a corner of the room, knelt down, and, with many mysterious ceremonies, invoked the spirits to come to his aid. A considerable time elapsed before they obeyed. While waiting he was under great agitation, being wet with sweat, and bordering on convulsions. At length a loud noise was heard at the windows, followed by other noises of a peculiar description, not easily described. The second sounds Schrepfer announced as the voices of good spirits come to help him. A short time afterwards frightful yelling was heard, which came, he declared, from malignant spirits, whose presence, he affirmed, was also essential. By this time the prince and his friends were filled with horror, wishing that the scene was over; but their courage had to stand more severe tests. Schrepfer continuing his invocations, the door suddenly opened with violence, and something resembling a black globe rolled into the room. It was surrounded with smoke or cloud, in the midst of which appeared to be a human face like the countenance of the Chevalier de Saxe. In a loud and angry voice the form inquired why it was disturbed. Great consternation prevailed among the spectators at such a sight. Charles did not venture to say a word concerning the concealed treasure, neither did his uncle's ghost. Kneeling down, the terrified prince besought the magician to dismiss the apparition, a request easier asked than could be complied with. Nearly an hour elapsed before Schrepfer, by his invocations, succeeded in dismissing the spirit. Just at the moment all thought that it had vanished, the closed door was again burst open, and the hideous form presented itself again to view. General terror prevailed, every one thinking he was about to be snatched away to the place of everlasting torment. None but the magician remained firm. He continued reiterating exorcisms until the apparition finally disappeared. The spectators dispersed, filled with amazement, and satisfied of Schrepfer's supernatural powers. Schrepfer's fame became great: gentlemen resorted to his night meeting to be initiated in his mysteries. For this purpose they accompanied him into a grove near Leipsic; and one night, when he was about to exhibit something more wonderful than his followers had ever seen, his earthly career suddenly terminated. While his disciples waited in great expectation, he retired to a quiet spot to make the requisite invocations. In a few minutes the report of a pistol resounded through the forest; his admirers rushed to the spot, and found him shot through the heart. A few thought he had shot himself; the more superstitious ones however, came to the conclusion that the deed was done by the devil. Whether the unfortunate magician terminated his existence by his own hand remains doubtful, but one thing the most of old people believed--that, having sold himself to the evil spirit, his time was come to go down to the dark abode; and such being the case, it mattered little by what instrument the deed was perpetrated. The demon sent to call Schrepfer hence might have fired the shot, or caused the magician to be his own executioner; yea, the foul fiend could have caused an elf shot or the glance of an evil eye to effect the fatal catastrophe.

Ludovicus Adolisius, lord of Immola, sent one of his secretaries on important business to Ferrara. On the way the secretary met one on horseback, dressed like a huntsman, with a hawk upon his fist, who addressed him by name, and desired him to request his master to meet him (the huntsman) at the place they then were, at the same hour next day, when he would discover things of no mean importance, which concerned his master and his estate. In the apparent huntsman the secretary discovered the apparition of his master's father. The secretary returned and delivered the important message to his lord. His lordship being afraid that evil was intended, sent one of his subordinates to meet the apparition. At the time and place appointed, the spirit appeared in the likeness it had done the previous day. It lamented the son's absence, on account of the strange revelations that would have been made had he come himself. "Return to your master," said the apparition, "and tell him that in twenty-two years, one month, and one day, he will lose the governorship of the city." Like a small cloud the spirit vanished. At the very time predicted, Philip, Duke of Milan, besieged the city, and the water being frozen, he was enabled to pass the moat, and having scaled the walls, surprised the city, and took Ludovicus prisoner.

An Italian of mean birth, named Carlo Stella, ingratiated himself into the good favour of Baron Cattaneo, a nobleman, who unfortunately was over fond of wine and the gaming-table. The former induced the latter to play for no less a stake than the baron's whole estates. The unlucky nobleman lost, and in the moment of excitement made over all his property to the wicked Stella. Next day the baron, remembering what had taken place, went to Stella, and expressed the hope that the convey-ance he had given the previous day would be returned. Stella told him that he could not give up the document, for he had destroyed it, looking on the whole proceeding as a farce. A few days after-wards the baron was found shot through the brain, and then Stella produced the document which he pretended had been destroyed. In virtue of the conveyance, the holder of it came into possession of a large sum of money and many acres of land, together with two noble castles, pleasantly situated. Be-ing thus raised into an elevated position, he sought in marriage a lady of rank. He was accepted, and an early day was fixed for the nuptial ceremony. Bride and bridegroom, priest, and rejoicing friends were assembled at the appointed time in the church, and the service was about to begin, when a man stained with blood entered the sacred building. He looked Stella sternly in the face, and then retired. Every one was horror-stricken, but none appeared so much affected as the bridegroom. He fainted, and had to be carried out without the marriage taking place. Next day he seemed better, and arrangements were entered into for having the pair (we cannot say happy pair) united in wedlock in the evening. As formerly, all were assembled, and the priest was about to begin the ceremony, when the lights went out, leaving the company standing in consternation. A dark cloud, which had obscured the moon, passed away, and then her pale rays partially lighted up the edifice. At this in-stant the bloody figure appeared, walked forward to Stella, whispered in his ear, and then vanished. So disconcerted were all parties that the marriage was again delayed, and ultimately it was resolved, on the part of the lady and her father, that the engagement should be broken off. Stella became troubled, sleep forsook him, horrid sounds reached his ears in the night, and the bloody apparition that had frightened him in the church frequently appeared to his sight. The cause of the strange sights and sounds was known to himself; those around were ignorant whence they proceeded. All may be explained in a few words. Stella had murdered the baron, and the bloody figure was his ghost. Disappointed and humbled, Stella resolved to consult a noted witch, of whom he had heard much. Arriving at her cottage, he handed her a purse of gold, and promised her a greater reward if she would send to the lower world the spirit that disturbed him. The old hag complied, received the money, counted it, spat on it, put it into a weasel-skin purse, and then into her pocket. With much ceremony she put a powder into the fire, which caused a blue flame to arise. In its midst the living form of the murdered baron appeared. The witch tried to reduce the spirit to her power, but the task proved a difficult one, for more than once it was nigh breaking through the circle she had formed. At last her magic charms prevailed, and the spirit descended into the bowels of the earth, exclaiming, "Murderer, we shall soon meet again." Stella's mind was greatly disturbed; he drank deep to drown his care, but peace was far from him. In company he was the gayest of the gay, but when alone in the still hours of night he would groan and start in his sleep, as if endeavouring to escape from some one. Already he seemed to be enduring the torments of internal fire. Drink, drink, more drink, he would call for, and then, mounting his horse, would ride ten or twelve miles without knowing whither he was going. One day he rode farther than usual, all the time his horse going at full speed, while now and again he looked behind him as if pursued. Several people, who witnessed Stella's mad career, feared that evil would happen him before he went much farther. Their fears were not groundless, for before him, where the road took a sharp turn, was a bridge that spanned a deep flowing river; and unless the animal was carefully guided, there was danger of him plunging into the water instead of taking the bridge. Nearer and nearer he approached the dangerous spot, swifter and swifter the horse went, urged on by the spurs that pierced its sides. Excited and more excited the rider became. Both man and beast appeared to be doomed; and so it proved. Over the fence they went, and in a few minutes Stella's body was carried over a fall into a deep boiling pool, out of which it could never be recovered.

CHAPTER XXXIII.

Antonio the Rich--Soul sold to the Devil--Dreadful   Announcement from a Volcano's Mouth--Three Ghosts--A   Thrilling Story--Human Remains found behind a   Stove--Mozart apprehensive of Death--A Strange   Visitor--Mozart writing a Requiem for himself--The   Stranger's Return--Messenger from another   World--Mozart's Death--Ghost of a Lady--The White   Lady--A Haunted House--Terrified Servants--Iron   Cage--Youth starved to Death--Frightful Dreams and   Dreadful Sights--Dog frightened by a Spirit--Ghost   sinking into the Earth--Deserting a Disturbed   House--Duchess of Mazarin--Madam de Beauclair--Compact   between the Living and the Dead--A Lady's Death   foretold by a Spirit--The Prediction fulfilled.

In the reign of Henry VIII., Mr. Gresham, a London merchant, coming home from Palermo (wherein resided one Antonio, generally called the Rich, who at one time had two kingdoms mortgaged to him), heard a strange voice that filled him with alarm. Antonio had accumulated a vast amount of riches, in ways not altogether in accordance with the eighth commandment. His money was given in loan at shamefully high rates of interest, and both principal and interest were often recovered by oppression. In fact, gold seemed to be his god: for it he appeared to live; for it, his poor neighbours asserted, he had sold his soul to the devil. Mr. Gresham being detained at Strombuli by contrary winds, he, with eight sailors, ascended a burning mountain there. Approaching the crater as near is they could with safety, they heard a hideous noise proceeding from the volcano's mouth, and a voice crying aloud "Dispatch, dispatch, haste, the rich Antonio is coming!" Terrified, the company hastened down the mountain, which, before they reached the level country, vomited out fire. At Palermo Mr. Gresham inquired for Antonio, and was informed that he died at the very time the voice proclaimed from the scorching flames, "Antonio is coming." Mr. Gresham, on his return to England, reported the strange circumstances to the king, who had the facts confirmed by the mariners' oaths. So deeply was Mr. Gresham impressed with what he had heard, that he abandoned commerce, distributed nearly all his riches among his friends and the poor, and spent the remainder of his days in pious works.

A learned professor of moral philosophy in Koenigsberg, when a young man, was presented by William I. of Prussia with a small benefice in the interior of the country, at a considerable distance from Koenigsberg. On taking possession of the parsonage, he slept in the bedroom which had been occupied by his predecessor, then dead. While lying awake in bed one morning, the curtains of his bed being drawn aside, he beheld the figure of a man dressed in a loose gown, standing at a reading desk, whereon lay a large book, the leaves of which he appeared to turn over. On each side of the figure stood a little boy, on whom he now and again looked earnestly. His countenance, pale and disconsolate, indicated distress of mind. At length the figure closed the book, and taking the children, one in each hand, he walked slowly with them across the room, and disappeared behind an iron stove at the farthest end of the apartment. The young parson was deeply affected by the sight, but thought it prudent to divulge nothing at the time concerning the apparitions. In nearly all Lutheran churches of the Prussian dominion, it was customary to procure and hang up in some part of the church the portraits of the pastors who had held the living. On looking, soon after seeing the three figures, at the portraits suspended in one of the aisles, he was astonished to discover in the last-placed picture an exact likeness of the man he had beheld in his bed-chamber. The sexton, with whom he entered into conversation, told him that he remembered several incumbents. "The last one," said he, "we considered as one of the most learned and amiable men who had ever resided among us. His character and benevolence endeared him to all his parishioners; but he was carried off in the midst of his days by a lingering illness, the cause of which has given rise to many unpleasant reports. It is, however, commonly believed that he died of a broken heart." The new incumbent's curiosity being excited, he pressed the sexton to disclose what more he knew of the subject. "Nothing respecting it," answered he, "is absolutely known, but scandal has propagated a story of his having formed a criminal connection with a young woman in the neighbourhood, by whom, it is asserted, he had two sons. As confirmation of the report, I know that there were two children who were seen at the parsonage--boys of about four or five years of age; but they suddenly disappeared, some time before the decease of their supposed father, although to what place they were sent, or what became of them, all are ignorant. It is equally certain that the surmises and unfavourable opinions formed respecting them reached his ears, and precipitated the disorder of which he died." This information recalled to the new pastor's mind, and seemed to give proof, of the existence of all that he had seen. Soon after, when winter approached, it became necessary to light fires in various apartments in the parsonage. Some difficulty was experienced in heating the room in which the figures of the man and two boys had appeared, as the stove not only smoked, but emitted an offensive smell. Having procured the assistance of a tradesman to make an inspection, he discovered in the inside, at the farthest extremity, the bones of two small human bodies, corresponding exactly in size, as well as in other respects, with the description of the two boys who had been seen at the parsonage.

Mozart, the celebrated composer, was extremely apprehensive of death, and at all times he laboured under profound melancholy. The circumstances attending the composition of his last piece were remarkable. One day, when his spirits were unusually depressed, a stranger, of a tall dignified appearance, was introduced. His manners were grave and impressive. He told Mozart that he came to request he would compose a solemn mass, as the requiem for the soul of a friend recently lost, and whose memory he was desirous of commemorating by this solemn service. Mozart undertook the task, and engaged to have it completed in a month. The stranger immediately paid a hundred ducats for the piece, and departed. This visit, somehow, had a serious effect on the mind of Mozart. He brooded over it for some time, then, suddenly calling for writing materials, began to compose with extraordinary ardour. Severe application to his studies brought on fainting fits, and failing health compelled him to suspend his work. "I am writing this requiem for myself," said he abruptly; "it will serve for my funeral service." This impression never left him. At the expiration of the month the mysterious stranger appeared, and demanded the requiem. "I have found it impossible," said Mozart, "to keep my word; the work has interested me more than I had expected, besides I have extended it beyond my first design. I shall require another month to finish it." The stranger made no objection, but, observing that for this additional trouble it was but just to increase the price, laid down fifty ducats more, and promised to return at the time appointed. Astonished at the stranger's proceeding, Mozart ordered a servant to follow the singular person, to find out who he was. The servant, however, lost sight of him, and returned unable to communicate the desired information. Mozart, persuaded that the stranger was a messenger from the other world sent to warn him that his end was fast approaching, applied himself with fresh zeal to the requiem, and, in spite of the exhausted state of his body and mind, completed it before the expiration of the month. On the day named the stranger returned, but Mozart was no more.

The ghost of a lady who died in the fifteenth century from the effects of her husband's cruel treatment, long after her decease haunted the castles of the allied families of Brandenburg, Baden, and Darmstadt, and other places far distant. The ghost was generally called "the White Lady," in consequence of it appearing in white dress and in the veil, through the folds of which a faint light glimmered. She glided hither and thither along the corridors and apartments of castles and palaces. Her appearance gave certain indication that a member of the family at whose residence she showed herself was about to expire. At another part of the country a white lady invariably looked in at the window of a house where a person was dying; and, at a third place, a woman hovered in the air over the abode of one taking leave of earth.

At the commencement of the first French Revolution, Lady Pennyman and her daughters retired to Lisle, where they hired a large house at a small rent. During their residence in this abode, the lady received from her husband, Sir John Pennyman, a draft for a large sum, which she carried to a banker in the town, and requested to have it cashed. She received a considerable portion of the money in silver, and, as she had several calls to make, she requested the banker to send the money in a parcel to her house. The parcel was committed to the care of a porter; and on the lady inquiring whether he understood from her directions the place to which he was to proceed, the man replied that he was perfectly aware of the place described--that it was called the "Haunted House." She paid little attention to his remarks at the time, but a few weeks afterwards his words were recalled to her recollection in a manner that surprised her. The housekeeper came to Lady Pennyman, and said that two of the servants, who had accompanied her ladyship from England, had that morning given warning, and expressed a determination to quit her ladyship's service, on account of being terrified, night after night, by mysterious voices in their apartments. This caused her ladyship, who was a woman of strong nerve and an unbeliever in all that related to ghosts and haunted houses, to sleep in a room evacuated by one of the servants, hoping that, by so doing, her domestics would change their minds and remain. She was greatly surprised to see in the room a large iron cage, and much astonished to hear the legend respecting it. It was related that a late proprietor of the house, a young man of great property, had in his minority been confined in that apartment by an uncle, his guardian, until the privations and divers acts of cruelties he was exposed to ended fatally. Often had the youth been kept for days in the iron cage without food. The unfeeling relative inherited the nephew's wealth, but, like all ill-gotten gear, it did not bring happiness. Frightful dreams and dreadful sights compelled the uncle to leave the mansion, where he had murdered by inches a comely, docile young man, once the comfort of a fond mother and loving father. For a few nights nothing of an alarming nature occurred; she began to hope that confidence would be restored in her household, and that she would be enabled to return in peace to her own proper sleeping apartment. Her expectations were not fulfilled. One night she was awakened by the sound of footsteps in the haunted chamber, generally known as the "cage chamber," while her son, a young man, who had just returned from sea, was annoyed by loud knocking at his bedroom door, and strange figures appearing before him. A friend, hearing of the noises and apparitions, resolved to sleep in the "cage room," that he might ascertain, if possible, who or what it was that disturbed the family. Locking himself and a faithful dog into the "cage chamber," he retired to rest, confident that he was secure against every intruder, whether material or airy. His assurance was of short duration. He had not lain long before his dog leaped into the bed, howling and terrified. The chamber door slowly opened, and a pale, thin, sickly youth came in, walked to the iron cage in the centre of the room, leaned against the iron bars, and, after remaining a short time, retired by the way he entered. The gentleman rose quickly to follow the ghost. On reaching the door, it was fastened on the inside, as he had left it before going to bed. His courage, however, did not fail him, and he continued to watch the retiring figure. The youth descended the stair-case with slow measured steps to the ground floor, when the form sank into the earth. Every one was now convinced that the house was haunted: a panic ensued, which ended in Lady Pennyman and her family abruptly leaving the disturbed habitation.

It is well known that the celebrated Duchess of Mazarin was a favourite of King Charles II., and Madame de Beauclair was a lady admired and beloved by his brother and successor, James II. Between these ladies there was an uncommon friendship. The two beauties were allotted handsome apartments in Stable Yard, St. James's, but, for obvious reasons, they had little conversation with the outer world. It was agreed between the ladies, that she who should be first taken away by death, would return, if possible, and give the survivor an account of what was doing in the other world. This promise was often repeated; and the duchess happening to fall sick, and her life despaired of, Madame de Beauclair reminded her of their agreement. Her Grace replied she might depend upon her performing what she had promised. These last words passed between them not more than an hour before the lady's death. Years passed on, yet not a voice or sign came from the dead. Madame de Beauclair concluded that there was no such thing as existence after death. Probably her mind would have remained unchanged, had not the Duchess of Mazarin at last appeared to her. One evening Madame de Beauclair was sitting alone, when she happened to turn her eyes to a corner of the apartment, and lo! before her stood the form of the departed duchess. The figure moved through the room, approached near the lady, and, looking with great sweetness, said, "Beauclair, between the hours of twelve and one this night you will be with me." Having said this, the spirit vanished.

So convinced was Madame de Beauclair, though in excellent health and spirits, that her dissolution was at hand, that she sent for her friends, to whom she gave tokens of friendship, and summoned a clergyman to administer spiritual consolation. All who visited the lady endeavoured to dissuade her from giving way to thoughts which there seemed not the least probability of being verified. "Talk not to me," she said to those who imagined she was labouring under a singular delusion, "with the view of making me believe that my eyes and ears have deceived me: my time is short, and I would not have the small space allowed me to be with you wasted in vain delusion. I know I have seen the Duchess of Mazarin, and am convinced that her words will come true." Twelve o'clock was about to strike, yet, to all appearance, Madame de Beauclair continued in good health. Another attempt, to no purpose, was made to remove all apprehension of early dissolution. The only response that came was, "I am already sick at heart." Her countenance suddenly changed, and before half an hour expired she had entered the world of spirits.

CHAPTER XXXIV.

Sir George Villiers' Ghost warning his Son of Danger--Warnings Neglected--Duke of Buckingham Murdered--Apparitions do not lie--Lord Lyttelton and others profaning Christmas--A Troubled Mind--Apparition of a Suicide--Neglected Warning--Deception of Friends--Accusing a Ghost of Falsehood--Approach of the Ominous Hour--Alarm--Lord Lyttelton found Dead at the dreaded time--Death of an old Roman King--Alarming Prodigies--Tales from the *Eddas*--A Scandinavian Warrior's Ghost--An Icelandic Lady's Ghost--Spectral Appearance--Mysterious Death of a Herdsman--Fear of approaching Calamities--Man beaten to Death by a Ghost--Association of Ghosts--Demon in the shape of a Seal--Apparitions of Drowned Men--Christians not disturbed by Spectres--A Band of Demons thirty strong--Priest exorcising Evil Spirits--Spirits frightened away.

An officer in the king's service at Windsor Castle, in the beginning of the seventeenth century, when a boy, was taken much notice of by Sir George Villiers, the Duke of Buckingham's father. The officer, after he had reached manhood, was lying in bed one night, awake and in good health, when he perceived a venerable form draw near his bed. The apparition (for so it turned out to be) asked him if he knew who he was. The frightened gentleman told the apparition that the figure of the deceased Sir George Villiers stood before him. The apparition replied that he was right, and that he (the gentleman) must go and acquaint Sir George's son, that unless he ingratiated himself into the good opinion of the people, he would soon be cut off. Next morning the gentleman began to think his senses had deceived him, and therefore he did not deliver the message. Next night the apparition appeared in a terrible aspect, and told him that, unless he complied with his commands, he could not expect peace of mind. A promise to obey was promptly made. Again the gentleman tried to persuade himself that he had been dreaming, and a second time broke his word. A third night the spectre appeared, reproaching him with breach of promise, and, after again requesting him to deliver the message to the duke, uttered threats of fearful punishment in case of non-compliance. Delay seemed dangerous, so the gentleman hastened to London, where the Court then was, and entrusted Sir Ralph Freeman, who was married to a lady nearly allied to the duke, with the message. Sir Ralph communicated with the duke, who, however, could not receive the messenger, but sent him word that next day he was going to hunt with the king, and that he would meet him at Lambeth Bridge at five o'clock in the morning, where, if the gentleman attended, he would speak to him. Sir Ralph, being satisfied of the importance of having the message correctly delivered, accompanied the gentleman to the appointed place of meeting. The messenger and the duke spoke privately for nearly an hour. Neither Sir Ralph nor his servants could hear what was said, but they observed that several times the duke laboured under great emotion. The duke rode off to meet the king, and the gentleman and Sir Ralph returned together. The man told Sir Ralph that when he mentioned certain facts to the duke, he swore that he could not have come to the knowledge of them except through the devil, for the particulars he disclosed, as a token of him being sent by his deceased father, were profound secrets. The duke returned from the hunting-field before the morning was past, and retired with his mother to her private apartments for two or three hours. On coming out his countenance was troubled. He received other warnings, which were disregarded. The result may be anticipated. His Grace was stabbed on the 23d August 1628 by John Felton, a discontented lieutenant, at Portsmouth. When the news of the duke's murder was brought to his mother, she received it with grief, but without surprise. She had long foreseen what would happen. "Apparitions," she said, "did not lie."

Lord Lyttelton, in the winter of 1778, left the metropolis with a party of loose and dissipated companions to profane the Christmas by riotous debaucheries, at his country house, near Epsom. They had not long abandoned themselves to their desperate orgies, before a sudden gloom came over the party by their host becoming extraordinarily depressed in spirits and dejected of countenance. All his vivacity departed, and he fled from his guests. Urged to make known the cause of his uneasiness, he revealed the secret. He told them, that the previous night, after retiring to bed, and his light extinguished, he heard a noise resembling the fluttering of a bird at his window. Looking to the window, he saw the figure of an unhappy female whom he had betrayed, and who in consequence had committed suicide, standing in the window recess. The form approached the foot of his bed, and, pointing her finger to a dial which stood on the mantel-piece, announced that if he did not take warning and repent, his life and sins would be concluded at the same hour of the third day after the visitation. By a preternatural light in the chamber he observed distinctly everything around him. While the warning spirit was speaking, he saw the time was twelve o'clock. Darkness came, and the apparition disappeared. Lord Lyttelton's companions laughed at his superstitious fears, and endeavoured to convince him that he must have mistaken a dream for a real spiritual visitation. He felt somewhat relieved by what they said, but was not altogether convinced or reassured. The fatal night approached, and, with the connivance of Lord Lyttelton's attendants, the guests put all the clocks in the house an hour and a half too fast. They kept his lordship as lively as possible, but when ten o'clock struck he was silent and depressed; eleven struck, the depression deepened; twelve struck: "Thank God; I am safe!" exclaimed the nobleman: "the ghost was a liar, after all!--some wine--what a fool I was to be cast down by such a circumstance! But," continued he, "it is time for bed; we shall be up early, and out with the hounds to-morrow. By my faith, it is half-past twelve; so good night." He went to his chamber, ignorant that the ominous hour was not yet past. His guests, notwithstanding their avowed unbelief, remained together in fearful dread. They heard the valet descending from his master's room; it was just twelve o'clock. Lord Lyttelton's bell rang violently; the company ran to his apartment, and found the unhappy nobleman lying in bed lifeless, with his countenance terribly convulsed.

Shortly before the death of an old Roman king, several prodigies of an alarming nature appeared. When he first became sick there arose a violent tempest of wind, which blew down the cross from one of the churches. After this followed a terrible earthquake, which shook the whole city. Moreover an old eagle, a domestic of the royal palace, that had lived there many years, took wing the day before the king's sickness began, and flew away no one knew whither; then the bells of the imperial chapel rang thrice of their own accord in the space of twelve hours. Strange apparitions were seen at midnight, some of them hovering in the air, and others of them lurking about the palace court. In particular, a funeral procession, consisting of unearthly beings, was observed one night going along the principal thoroughfare from the palace to the place of sepulchre, where the royal remains were soon afterwards laid.

From the *Eddas* we learn that when these singular works were written or compiled, a belief must have prevailed of the existence of ghosts, spirits, and demons in various forms. We therefore propose giving a few examples of ghost stories from the *Eddas*:--After the death of Helge (a Scandinavian warrior), a maid witnessed, in the evening, his ghost, with a numerous train, riding into the cairn where Helge's remains were deposited. The brave damsel inquired whether it was an illusion she saw, to which the ghost replied that it was not. When the maid told Sigrum, Helge's widow, what she had seen, the faithful mourning wife hastened to the cairn, and, on searching it, sure enough there was the shade of her dead husband. It addressed her thus: "Thou, Sigrum, art the cause of Helge lying here, slain by the dew of sorrow. Thou weepest burning tears, maid of the sun-glowing south; but we will drink the precious mead together, though we have lost gladness and lands. Now are the brides closed in the cairns, and the princely maidens laid beside us." Sigrum made a couch in the cairn, and invited the spirit to rest there from all trouble, saying, "Son of the Ylfinga, I will sleep in thy arms as formerly, when my hero lived." To this the ghost replied, "No longer will I say thou art unfaithful, since thou consentest to sleep in the embrace of the dead. And yet thou livest, offspring of kings. Let the pale steed tramp the steeps of the air. In the west must we be, by the bridge Vindhjalen, ere the cock in Walhalla wakes the sons of victory."

Far back in the history of time, the ghost of a lady that died in Iceland, whose deathbed commands were disregarded, returned to punish the living for disregarding her injunctions. The lady's corpse was conveyed to a distant place of sepulchre. As the interment could not take place the first day, the bearers, with their dead burden, reposed in a house over night. At midnight an apparition of the lady glided through the kitchen, and, on the night when the conductors of the funeral returned home, a spectral appearance, resembling a half moon, moved round the mansion in a direction opposite to that of the sun, and continued its revolution until the domestics retired to rest. This apparition appeared every night for a week, and was pronounced by certain wise sages as a presage of pestilence and death. A herdsman at the mansion was, shortly after the lady's death, persecuted by demons, and one morning he was found dead in bed. One Thorer, who himself had predicted that the apparitions were come to give warning of approaching calamities, was the next victim. One evening he was set upon by the shepherd's ghost, and so fearfully beaten that he died in consequence thereof. Evils continued to multiply: Thorer and the herdman's ghost associated themselves together in persecuting the inhabitants, several of whom fell victims to their rage. At times unseen agents upset tables and chairs, flung kitchen utensils about in all directions, and on other occasions a demon in the shape of a seal rose from the earth, to the dismay of a whole household. Thorodd, the master of the family, in crossing a river in a boat, was, along with two of his servants, drowned. Apparitions of the drowned men walked about Thorodd's old residence, but the appearances did not much disturb the people, who were Christians, as they believed that the spectres of such persons as had been favourably received by the goddess Rana were accustomed to show themselves after death. So fast did the demons increase in number that they became a great band of thirty, the exact number of people supposed to have had a period put to their existence by demons. Many fled from the neighbourhood, fearing that, if they remained, they would ere long be dead men, and their spirits infernal demons. Possibly their fears would have been realized, had not a pious priest exorcised the evil spirits. By a plentiful application of holy water and celebration of a solemn mass, they were frightened away, to return no more.

CHAPTER XXXV.

A Mysterious Hunter--Man and Horse supposed to be   Devils--Extraordinary Talents of the suspected   Hunter--Signs of Uneasiness--Terrible Shrieks--Groans of Despair--Tortured Spirits--Severe   Flagellation--Disappearance of the Flagellant--Tales   of the Scotch Highlands--Witches in the shape of Hares   worried by Dogs--Croaking Raven--Death of a suspected   Witch--Resort of Witches and Evil Spirits--Spirits   hastening to a Church--Dogs in Pursuit--Black Man with Eyes like Fire--Horse breathing Smoke and   Flame--Witch's Ghost and Demons sinking into the   Earth.

A strange tale of a mysterious hunter is given in the *Letters* of Lord Lyttelton, the truth of which, it is said, was attested by gentlemen whose veracity was beyond question. We give an abridged version of the tale:--

In the early part of --------'s life he attended a hunting club at their sports, when a stranger of genteel appearance, and well mounted, joined the chase, and was observed to ride with a degree of courage and address that called forth the utmost astonishment of every one present. The beast he rode was of amazing power; nothing stopped them; the hounds could never escape them; and the huntsman, who was left far behind, swore that the man and his horse were *devils from hell*. When the sport was over, the company invited this extraordinary person to dinner: he accepted the invitation, and astonished the company as much by the powers of his conversation, and by his elegance of manners, as by his equestrian prowess. He was an orator, a poet, a painter, a musician, a lawyer, and a divine; in short, he was everything, and the magic of his discourse kept the drowsy sportsman awake long after his usual hour. At length, however, wearied nature could be charmed no more, and the company began to steal away by degrees to their repose. On his observing the society diminish, he discovered manifest signs of uneasiness; he therefore gave new force to his spirits, and new charms to his conversation, in order to detain the remaining few some time longer. This had some little effect; but the period could not be long delayed when he was to be conducted to his chamber. The remains of the company retired also; but they had scarce closed their eyes, when the house was alarmed by the most terrible shrieks that were ever heard; several persons were awakened by the noise; but, its continuance being short, they concluded it to proceed from a dog which might be accidentally confined in some part of the house; they very soon, therefore, composed themselves to sleep, but were again soon awakened by shrieks and cries of still greater terror than the former.

Alarmed at what they heard, several of them rang their bells, and when the servants came, they declared that the horrid sounds proceeded from the stranger's chamber. Some of the gentlemen immediately arose to inquire into this extraordinary disturbance; and while they were dressing themselves for that purpose, deeper groans of despair, and shriller shrieks of agony, again astonished and terrified them. After knocking some time at the stranger's chamber door, he answered them as one awakened from sleep, declared he had heard no noise, and, rather in an angry tone, desired he might not be again disturbed. Upon this, they returned to their chambers, and had scarce began to communicate their sentiments to each other, when their conversation was interrupted by a renewal of yells, screams, and shrieks, which, from the horror of them, seemed to issue from the throats of damned and tortured spirits. The gentlemen listened attentively, and traced the sounds to the stranger's room, the door of which they instantly burst open, and found him upon his knees in bed, in the act of scourging himself with the most unrelenting severity, his body streaming with blood. On their seizing his hands to stop the strokes, he begged them, in the most ringing tone of voice, as an act of mercy, that they would retire, assuring them that the cause of their disturbance was over, and that in the morning he would acquaint them with the reasons of the terrible cries they had heard, and the melancholy sight they saw. After a repetition of his entreaties, they retired; and in the morning two of them went to his chamber, but he was not there, and, on examining the bed, they found it to be one gore of blood. Upon further inquiry, the groom said that, as soon as it was light, the gentleman came to the stable, booted and spurred, and desired his horse might be immediately saddled, and appeared to be extremely impatient till it was done, when he vaulted into his saddle, and rode out of the yard at full speed. Servants were immediately sent into every part of the surrounding country, but not a single trace of him could be found; such a person had not been seen by any one, nor has he since been heard of.

Tales are related in the Scotch Highlands of witches being mortally worried by dogs while they (the witches) appeared in the likeness of a hare. They are so similar in all essential particulars, that one is inclined to think that they are different versions of the same story. Here, at all events, is one version:--A hunter, one early morning, observed an old woman prowling about a glen in a suspicious manner. Wishing to know what she was about, he watched her movements, and succeeded in getting so near her that he was able to recognise her features. She was a near neighbour of his own, held in good repute by all in the district. Observing him approaching, the old woman walked away quickly, to avoid him recognising her; but, as the hunter was likely to overtake her, she transformed herself into the likeness of a hare, and darted away at great speed. The hunter's dog gave chase, and, after a long run, seized her. At that instant a shriek arose that made the hills echo and re-echo. Hurrying forward to call off his dogs, the hunter came within a few paces of the spot where the struggle was going on, when a raven rose from the ground and flew away, croaking angrily. A pool of blood marked the place, and his two dogs lay dead. On returning home, he learned that the old woman whom he had seen transformed into a hare lay dangerously ill in her house. At night she died. The same night another neighbour of the woman was returning home, whistling to keep up his courage, for he had to pass the old parish church and burying-ground, and walk through a wood, the favourite resort of witches and evil spirits. As the deep shadows of the forest were beginning to conceal the moon from view, he was startled by the appearance of a woman running in the direction of the church. She asked if she could reach it by twelve o'clock. He answered that he thought she could if she ran fast. His impression was that the voice, face, and figure were those of the woman the hunter had surprised in the morning. A little farther on he met two hounds coursing along at great speed. In a few minutes he met a black man riding on a black horse. The horseman inquired whether the traveller had seen a woman, and two dogs pursuing her. On replying in the affirmative, the horseman asked a second question, whether he thought the dogs would overtake her before she went the length of the old church? With a faltering voice he said it was likely they would. The frightened traveller, more dead than alive, observed that the black man had eyes like balls of fire, and that his horse breathed smoke and flame. As swift as his feet could carry him, the pedestrian hastened homeward, trusting that the terrors of the night were past, yet fearing and trembling exceedingly. Having to pass the old woman's house, and seeing a light, he went in, and then learned that she was dead. He had no doubt that the human-like figure he saw running on foot towards the church was the spirit of the departed witch, and that the pursuers were demons. After condoling with the bereaved relations, he took his departure from an abode cursed with the presence of a witch's remains. Scarcely had he crossed the threshold before he observed the black horseman riding swiftly towards the house, with the woman lying across the saddle-bow, and the two dogs following close behind. In an instant, man, woman, horse, and dogs sank into the ground.

CHAPTER XXXVI.

Leading Churchmen subjected to the Onslaught of Demons--Warfare with the Devil in corporeal shape--Triumph of Churchmen--St. Maurus rebuking a Troop of Evil Spirits--St. Romualdus' Five Years' Conflict with Satan--The Faculty of St. Frances--St. Gregory's Detection of the Devil entering a Man--A Greedy Monk denied Christian Burial--Monk in Purgatory--Institution of the Thirty Masses for the Dead--An Excommunicated Gentleman of Rome hiring Pagan Witches and Sorcerers--What befell them--St. Benedict and the Blackbird's Song--A Monk restored to Life--St. Benedict's Sister ascending to Heaven like a White Dove--St. Francis' Dominion over Living Creatures and the Elements--St. Catherine's Power over Evil Spirits--St. Stanislaus' Miracles--A Dead Man giving Evidence in a Court of Justice--The Dead refusing a Renewal of Life--St. Philip Nerius and Evil Spirits--Spirits ministering to St. Erasmus--St. Norbert closing the Mouths of Evil Spirits--Story relating to Henry I.--St. Margaret's Triumph--St. Ignatius' Command over Devils--St. Stephen curing Persons possessed of Devils--Satan's Hatred of St. Dominick--St. Donatus endowing a Corpse with Speech--St. Cyriacus, St. Largus, and St. Smaragdus, the Martyrs--St. Clare--St. Bernard's Power--St. Caesarius' Wonder-working Crook--St. Giles and the Hind--St. Euphemia's Guardian Angels--St. Francis' Spirit in Chariot of Fire--Devils blowing the Fire of Discord--St. Bridget's Intercourse with Angels--St. Denis' Spirit--St. Teresa and the Angels--St. Hilarian a Match for Satan and his Sorcerers--Her Miracles--St. Martin's Wonderful Power--St. Catherine's Body carried by Angels to Mount Sinai--St. Francis Xaverius' Belief in Virtue of Bells--St. Nicholas' Piety and Powers--St. Ambrose's Power over Necromancers and Spirits--St. Lucy raising her Mother from the Dead--St. Anastasia sustained by Bread from Heaven--St. Thomas enduring Martyrdom in Life and after Death--Penance of Henry II.--Barbarous Conduct of Henry VIII.--A Hungarian Legend.

If reliance can be placed on tradition and the writings of biographers, good men (particularly those of them who took a leading part in the ancient Church) were subjected to dreadful onslaughts by Satan. Not only had they to contend with invisible spirits of darkness, but they were compelled to carry on a continual warfare with the devil, in corporeal shape, seeking to seduce them from their faith. None were more frequently or fiercely assailed than the canonised saints of the old Catholic Church. To their praise, however, be it remembered, that almost invariably the Churchmen, sooner or later, triumphed. Having good consciences, and being protected by wonder-working relics, the saints defied the enemy of mankind. Those seeking lengthened information on the subject should consult *The Lives of the Saints, and the Calendars*, published by learned men, who believed what they wrote, and spoke that which they thought to be true. The subjoined sketches, read in connection with chapter XV., bear out what is affirmed.

St. Maurus had an encounter with Satan and a whole squadron of his monsters in bodily shape. At Maurus' rebuke the troop vanished, but not before they made the monastery shake, and brought the affrighted monks to their knees.

St. Romualdus may be said to have had a five years' conflict with Satan in visible forms. St. Frances had the faculty of seeing evil spirits when people beside her perceived nothing but natural forms. St. Gregory witnessed the devil entering into a man who indulged in and loved lies. A monk who determined to throw off his habit and forsake the monastery, was set upon by the devil in the form of a black dog. Other monks who broke their vows shared no better. Because a monk had been guilty of hoarding up a large sum of money, contrary to the rules of his order, he was denied Christian burial, and his body was cast upon a dunghill. After mass was said for the miser thirty days, the deceased monk appeared to a brother of his order and told him that he had been in purgatory till that day. From this blessed liberation St. Gregory instituted the custom of saying thirty masses for the dead. A gentleman in Rome, who was excommunicated by St. Gregory for unlawfully putting away his wife, hired certain pagan witches and sorcerers to torment the holy Pope. They caused the devil to enter into the Pope's horse, that it might cast the rider and crush him to death. The holy father, becoming aware of the plot, cast out the devil, and struck the witches and sorcerers with blindness. St. Gregory was entreated to restore the witches and sorcerers to sight, but he refused to do so, lest they should be tempted to return to their wicked art, and read books of magic and necromancy.

St. Benedict had his encounters with the tempter. One day the devil transformed himself into a little blackbird, which fluttered about him, and sang so sweetly that he was nearly drawn away from his devotions and led into sin. By a higher power than his own he overcame the enemy. He stripped himself of his clothes, and, casting himself on a thicket of briars and thorns, mangled his body so severely that blood ran from him in streams. The devil on one occasion endeavoured to hinder the building of a monastery, and at another time he cast a stone at a young monk and killed him. St. Benedict, in his goodness, put the devil to flight, and restored the monk to life. This saint, while watching over the spiritual welfare of the monks with whom he was associated, observed the devil riding on a mule to the monastery, and entering into an aged monk possessed of a covetous heart. Penance and a trust in holy relics drove the evil spirit away, and brought the monk to a proper frame of mind. When a pious sister of St. Benedict died, he saw her spirit in the likeness of a white dove ascending to heaven.

St. Francis, a devout servant of great sanctity, had dominion over all creatures. Fire, air, water, and earth were also subject to him. He drove away wicked spirits; he gave sight to the blind, speech to the dumb, health to those in decay, and life to the dead. The elements could not affect him. He walked upon fire, held his hands in a burning hot oven without sustaining injury; and he and a companion passed over the sea upon his cloak spread on the waves.

St. Catherine resisted the devil in various guises. On one memorable occasion she witnessed two thieves being conveyed to the place of execution, and tortured, in a cart. Instead of lamenting their sins, they behaved like demons. Though no one else beheld anything unearthly near the culprits, St. Catherine saw a multitude of devils provoking them to blaspheme and curse. Having compassion on the unhappy men, she went into the cart beside them, drove the evil spirits away, and brought the condemned men to repentance before expiating their crimes.

St. Stanislaus performed miracles, and, as for evil spirits, he made them fly as chaff before the wind. He cured sickness, and even gave life to the dead. One instance of his supernatural power is worthy of remembrance. Stanislaus bought a piece of ground from a man named Peter, but received no receipt for the price paid. Peter died, and then his heirs, to please the king, who desired to do Stanislaus an injury, sought to have the land restored to them. An order of court was about to be issued for the restoration of the land to Peter's heirs, when the saint craved three days to bring forward proof of the money having been paid. Accordingly an adjournment took place. Meantime Stanislaus fasted, prayed, and watched. At the termination of the time appointed, the saint, having offered up the holy sacrifice of mass, went to Peter's grave and caused it to be opened; then, touching the body with his crosier, the dead man came to life, followed the saint to the court, testified, to the astonishment of all, that the land had been lawfully bought, and duly paid for. After this no one could dispute the ownership of the land, which, we ought not to omit saying, had been bought for the Church. St. Stanislaus offered Peter a renewal of life for many years, but he who had been dead chose to return to the grave rather than to live longer a life of trouble. He told the saint he was in purgatory, and that he had yet something more to suffer for his sins, but still he would prefer undergoing his deserved punishment, that at last he might be free. St. Stanislaus accompanied Peter to the grave. Peter laid himself down in the dust, and the ground was closed over him, in the presence of a multitude of people.

St. Philip Nerius encountered three infernal spirits while in the proper discharge of his Christian duties; and the ghosts of deceased persons were visible to him. After the saint's death he appeared to his favourite followers, environed with a glorious light. Spirits ministered to St. Erasmus, at one time breaking the fetters wherewith he was bound, and at another speaking comforting words to him when he was sad at heart. St. Norbert had the power of controlling devils, and casting them out of possessed persons. Evil spirits went about in his time revealing all the sins of professing Christians, until St. Norbert closed their mouths in reference to such shortcomings as had been confessed to a priest. After the saint's death, he appeared to divers persons who knew him in life.

The following story is told of Henry I.:--At the time he was dying, a hermit saw the devil, in human shape, running in the direction where the emperor lay. "Whither passest thou?" demanded the hermit. "I am going," said the fiend, "to be present at his Majesty's death." "Come again," said the hermit, "and tell me how far thou hast succeeded." Within a short time Satan returned, howling and crying out, "Woe, woe to us, we are cozened, and have lost our labour; all our slight and power have come to nought; the angels have confounded us and driven us away. As the works and merits of the soul were examined and weighed in the balance, in presence of us and the angels, and our scale began to sink down with the weight of his sins, there stepped in a burned man with a golden cup and put it into the other scale, which caused it to descend with great force. Seeing this, the angels cried out 'Victory,' and conveyed away the soul with them, leaving us nothing but shame, ignominy, and confusion." The renowned martyr St. Lawrence turned out to be the burned man the devil saw with the cup.

St. Margaret at one time had a severe encounter with a serpent that appeared with death in his looks. She triumphed then as well as at other times. The enemy wounded her sorely and often, but she was cured, and ever afterwards had peace.

St. Ignatius had a strange command over the devils, who abhorred and persecuted him as their great enemy. Both at Paris and Rome the devils appeared to him in ugly shapes. Before he prevailed they nearly choked him, and scourged him so sorely that he did not recover for some time. In St. Ignatius' life-time the arch-fiend seems to have had considerable power. At one time he possessed a child, a woman, and a soldier, and raised tempests and furious storms. How far the mischief would have been continued no one can tell, had not this saint withstood him to the face. It fell upon a time that the holy fathers, in a certain Loretto college, were greatly disturbed night and day by devils making a hideous noise, and appearing like black-a-moors, cats, bears, and other beasts. Recourse was had by saying holy mass, prayers, sprinkling holy water, using exorcisms, and applying relics of saints, without effect. Father Ignatius' assistance was ultimately solicited; and he, without much difficulty, drove away the tormentors as if they had been as many mice.

St. Stephen exercised great control over Satan. The saint cured no fewer than threescore and thirteen persons possessed of devils.

Satan had a deadly hatred against St. Dominick, and often endeavoured to destroy his soul and body. St. Donatus was another mark at which the devil shot his fiercest arrows; but a man who raised the dead, as this saint did, did not stand in fear of an evil spirit. St. Donatus raised to life a woman that died suddenly without informing her husband where she had concealed a sum of money be-longing to him. From the mouth of the grave the resuscitated woman told where the treasure lay. A dishonest creditor was proved to be a false swearer and cheat by a corpse endowed with speech by St. Donatus.

St. Cyriacus, St. Largus, and St. Smaragdus drove evil spirits not only out of afflicted persons, but out of the country. Cyriacus, in particular, was so famous for his power over evil spirits, that princes in distant lands solicited his assistance to banish the demons to their own peculiar place of torment.

The holy virgin, St. Clare, though a feeble woman, fought and prevailed over the devil that came to her in the form of a black man.

St. Bernard cured persons possessed of devils, and he performed miracles with a crook of St. Caesarius. The former used his staff as a miracle-working instrument.

St. Giles was miraculously preserved by a hind sustaining him with her milk in a cave; and such was the saint's care over the helpless animal, that on two occasions he drew a line on the ground over which a pack of hounds chasing the hind could not pass, although there was nothing visible to restrain them.

St. Euphemia had her guardian angels that protected her from the violence of her enemies, who sought to burn her in an oven full of pitch, brimstone, and tow. She came out of the oven unhurt, but two men who laid hands on her were consumed by the flames. Wild beasts refused to devour her in their dens, and iron lost its force on her. St. Euphemia's time came however, and she met her fate as a martyr with Christian fortitude.

St. Francis' spirit appeared in a chariot of fire, sweeping through the air. Over a city distracted by factions and civil broils, he saw the devils very jocund, blowing the fire of discord. With a loud voice he commanded the spirits to depart; they obeyed him, and the city was restored to peace and concord.

St. Bridget possessed the faculty of witnessing angels, and enjoyed the privilege of having them for her companions; nevertheless, she had to sustain many conflicts with the devil. One time she saw Satan in a dreadful shape, with a hundred hands and as many feet. Terrified, she fled from the horrid monster and took shelter near a holy relic, where she was safe. In a sad hour of affliction the spirit of St. Denis appeared to her, and told her he would be her protector ever afterwards. She certainly, if report be true, turned out to be a saint endowed with extraordinary power, which enabled her to give sight to the blind, hearing to the deaf, speech to the dumb, and health to the sick; and, moreover, we are informed that she raised ten dead persons to life. On account of these miracles, and for her most holy life, Pope Boniface IX. canonised her, and put her in the number of the saints.

St. Gregory of Tours recounts numerous miracles wrought by St. Denis in life, and after his death. St. Teresa had glorious visions; and after, in her walks and seclusions, had the company of angels with beautiful countenances and corporeal shapes. In particular, one angel of the order of the Seraphim attended her in times of danger with a flaming sword, to drive back her enemies. Among St. Teresa's other powers was one of no mean importance--the power of delivering souls out of purgatory. Her faith in holy water was great, for by its force she swept away devils as by a mighty river.

St. Hilarian was a match for Satan and his sorcerers. A young man, desperately in love with a lady of rare beauty and chastity, who rejected his advances, applied to certain sorcerers, ministers of the temple of Esculapius. By means of their evil devices the damsel began to love her admirer extravagantly; indeed, so much so, that her emotions savoured more of madness than of true affection. Her parents laid her at St. Hilarian's feet, and he immediately drove out a devil that had taken possession of the maiden, both bodily and mentally. At one time St. Hilarian did what at first seemed invaluable service to the neighbourhood in which he lived. The people besought him to send rain, as their crops were withering away, and their cattle dying of thirst. He sent what they desired, but the rain bred serpents and venomous creatures, which destroyed the fruits of the earth and injured the inhabitants. Like St. Patrick, he drove away the reptiles, and healed the people who had been wounded by them. St. Hilarian also consumed, as with fire, a dragon of enormous size which swallowed oxen, devoured men, and laid waste the country far and near.

St. Martin, like many other saints, possessed the wonderful power of bringing the dead to life.

It was said he had dominion over devils and men, over the heavens and the elements, over diseases, and over all birds and beasts of the field.

So holy was St. Catherine, that, when she died, angels carried her body to Mount Sinai and buried it there, that her persecutors might not discover where she was laid. From her place of sepulture a sweet smell long continued to pervade the neighbourhood.

Although it would appear that all saints had many gifts and graces, certain of them possessed peculiar talents denied to others. St. Francis Xaverius, for instance, held the elements in his power. He was almost constantly at war with the devil and the flesh. To frighten away the one he kept ringing a bell by night, and to subdue the other he wore a hair shirt, lived on spare diet, and slept on hard boards or lay on the cold ground.

St. Nicholas was so uncommonly good a Catholic, that, even when an infant at the breast, he would not suck his mother's breast but once on the Wednesdays and Fridays. He, too, controlled the winds and waves, and sent the evil spirit away howling through the tempest.

St. Ambrose, of ever blessed memory, controlled sorcerers and necromancers, and made even the evil spirits obedient to him. On the day of the saint's death the devils flew away, crying that they were tormented by St. Ambrose.

St. Lucy raised her mother from the dead, and conquered demons.

St. Anastasia had power over Satan, and was for two months sustained by bread from heaven. And what shall we say of St. Thomas and many of the other saints who triumphed so gloriously in their day? St. Thomas, Archbishop of Canterbury, we are told, endured martyrdom twice--once in life, and again after death. To subdue the flesh, he scourged himself until the blood ran down his body. He kept long night vigils, and wore a hair shirt. In a vision he was told that he would illustrate the Church with his blood--a prediction that was fulfilled. It being proved that Henry II. was implicated in the foul deed, he had to do penance in public and private before being absolved. Many years afterwards, Henry VIII. commanded the dead saint to be summoned before him, and having condemned him as a traitor, directed his name to be erased from the catalogue of saints; forbade, under pain of death, his day to be celebrated, or his name to be mentioned as a saint; and ordered that his name should be blotted out of every book and calendar in which it appeared. The revengeful king also commanded that the saint's relics should be burned, and the ashes thereof scattered to the winds.

With the following old tale in verse we close our collected information on Demonology--a tale founded upon one of the most extraordinary events recorded in the annals of the human mind. Not a century and a half ago all the circumstances which form the romance, with the addition of many others nearly as ridiculous, were not only firmly believed by the peasants of a few Sclavonian villages, among whom they were supposed to have happened, but were received as truths, and seriously commented upon by learned divines and physicians of the surrounding provinces. A superstition somewhat similar appears to have prevailed in Bohemia and Silesia previous to the days of Dr. Henry More, who details several of the stories to which it gave rise, in his *Philosophical Works*:--

"I left the chaulkie Cliftes of olde Englonde,
  And paced thro' many a Countrie faire to see,
Thorowe the Reaulme of Greece and Holie-Londe,
  Untill I journeied into sadde Hongrie.

I sawe olde Cecrops' Towne, and famous Rome;
  But Davyd's holie place I liked beste:
I sawe dire Sightes before I found my Home,
  But much the direst at the Towne of Peste.

It was a goodlie Citie, fayre to see;
  By its prowde Walles and towering Mosques it gave
A delicate Aspect to the Countree,
  With its Bridg of Boates acrosse the Danow's Wave.

Yet manie thinges with Woe I did surveie;
  The Stretes were overgrowne with spiery grasse;
And, though it was upon a Sabbath-daie,
  No Belles did ringe to calle the Folke to Masse.

The Churchyardes all with Barrs were closed fast,
  Like to a sinfulle and accursed place;
It shewd as though the Judgment-daie were past,
  And the Dedde exiled from the Seate of Grace.

At last I met an old sadde Man, and asked
  Where a tired Traveller maye finde repose.
The Old Man shook his Hed, and wold have passed;
  But I caught him by his Arme and held his Clothes.

'Straunger,' said he, 'in Marie's name departe!'
  (Soe saying, wold agen have passed me by);
His hollow Voyce sank depe into my Harte:
  Yet I wold not let him goe, but asked Why?

'It now is Morne,' quoth he, 'the Sun shines brighte,
  And the Springe is blithe, save in the Walles of Peste;
But, were it Winter wylde, and a stormie Nighte,
  Not here, O Straunger, sholdst thou seeke to reste;

'Though Rayne in Torrents powred and cold Winds blew,
  And thou with travelling tired and with Hunger pale.'
'Though the Sun,' sed I, 'shine brighte and the Daie be new,
  I will not goe, till I have herd thy Tale.'

This woefull Wight then took me by the Hande;
  (His, like a Skeletonne's; was bonie and cold).
He seemed as though he scarse cold goe nor stande,
  Like one o'er whom full fourscore years had rold.

We came together to the Market-Crosse,
  And the Wight all woe-begon spake not a Word.
No living thinge along our Waie did passe,
  (Though dolours Grones in evrie House I herd).

Save one poore Dogge that walked athwart a Court,
  Fearfullie howling with most pyteous Wayle.
The sadde Man whistled in a dismall sort,
  And the poore thinge slunk away, and hid his Tayle.

I felt my verie Bloud creepe in my vaynes;
  My Bones were icie-cold; my Hayr on ende.
I wishd myself agen uponn the Playnes,
  Yet cold not but that sadde old Man attende.

The sadde old Man sate down upon a Stone,
  And I sate on another by his Side;
He heaved mournfullie a pyteous Grone,
  And then, to ease my doubts, himself applied.

'Straunger!' quoth he, 'Behold my Visage welle,
  And graspe this bonie Hand so thinne agenn!
How manie Winters thinkest thou I telle?'
  I answered doubtinglie: 'Three-Score and Tenn.'

'Straunger! not fourty yeares agoe I lay
  A puling Infant in my Nurse's arms:
Not fourty daies agoe two Daughters gay
  Did blesse my Vision with their dawning Charms.

'Yet now I am an olde and worn-out Man,
  And evrie droppe of Bloud hath left my Vaynes;
Als' my fayr Daughters twaine lie cold and wan
  And bloudless, bound in Deathe's eternal Chaynes.

'Straunger! This Towne, so pleasant to our sightes,
  With goodlie Towers and running Streames so faire,
Whilom for tender Maydes and doughtie Knightes
  From all Hungaria's Londe the Prize did beare.

'But now, the verie fewe that here remayne
  Are sobbing out their Breath in sorie Guise;
All that might flie, have fled this mournfull playne
  But onlie I, who wishe to close mine eyes.

'Seaven Weekes are gon since owr Townesfolke beganne
  To wax both pale and sadd, yet none knewe why:
The ruddiest Visage yellowe seemed and wanne,
  Our stoutest Youthes for very cold did cry.

'Some Doctours sed the Lakes did Agewes breede,
  But Springe returning wold the same disperse;
Whyles others, contrarie to Nature's creede,
  Averred the Heate itself wold make us worse.

'And though we leugh at these, like Doaters fonde,
  Or Menn that love in Paradox to deale;
Yett, as the Sunn grew warme, throughout the Londe,
  All Menn the more did wintrie shiverings feele.

'One miserable Wight did pyne and wane,
  And on the seaventh Daie gave upp the Ghoste;
His Corse was oped by a Chirurgeon of fame
  Who found that evrie dropp of bloud was loste.

'Nathless, our People though they pined and pined,
  Yet never did our appetites decaye;
Whole Oxen scarse suffised when we dined,
  And we cold drinke whole hogsheds of Tokaye.

'Soone Hundereds evrie daye gave up the Ghoste,
  (Els' we a Famine in our Lande had bredde).
And, to repayr the Bloud that we had loste,
  Our Beastes we killd and ate, but never bledde.

'Thus, by the Eve, our Colour freshe arose,
  And we did look agen more briske and gay.
All Nighte deepe Slumbers did our Eye lidds close,
  But worse and worse we wax by Breake of Daie.

'There was a taylour, Vulvius by name,
  Who long had dwelt at Peste in honest pryde;
A Godlie Man he was esteemed by Fame,
  And since some twelvemonths of a Feaver dyde.

'Now when at last this straunge Disease had growne
  To suche a Highte as neer was heard afore,
Among the reste in our unhappie Towne
  My youngest Daughter was afflicted sore.

'One Nighte it happed, as she was slepyng laied,
  Her wayting Girle at Midnight left her roome
To fetch some possett, brothe, or gellie, made
  To quelle the plague that did her life consume.

'When, as she softly shut the Doore, she heard
  An heavie Thinge come lumbering upp the Stayres,
Whereon the buried Tailour soone appeard
  And She (poor Mayd) full loud 'gan saye her Prayres.

'Shrowded he was, as when his Corse was laied
  Under the Earthe, and buriall Service redde;
Nor yet was he a Ghoste, for his Footsteppes made
  A Noyse more hevie than a Tunne of Ledde.

'She sawe him ope my Daughter's chamber-Doore,
  And had no Spirit to persewe nor flie,
And Vulvius agen, in half an houre,
  Lumbered downe Stayres yett much more hevilie.

'This Storie herd, I cold not chuse, but smild
  To think the seelie Mayd such Feares cold shake,
Yet the next Nighte, to prove such Phan'sies wild,
  I kept myself untille Midnighte awake;

'Whenn as the Midnight-Houre was past, I heard
  An hevie thinge come lumbering upp the Stayre;
The Tailour Vulvius to my Sights appeard--
  I could not follow to my Daughter fayre.

'Next Day, untoe a Convent nighe I hied,
  And found a reverend Father at his prayer;
I told him of the Wonderres I had spied,
  And begged his ghostlie Counsel I may share.

'Together to Sainct Stevenn's Churche we went,
  And he a Prayer on evrie Gravestone made,
Till at the Tailour Vulvius' Monument
  We stopped--we broughte a Mattocke and a Spade;

'We digged the Earthe wherein the Tailour lay;
  Tille at the Tailour's Coffin we arrived,
Nor there, I weene, much Labour found that Day,
  For evrie Nayle was drawen and the Hinges rived.

'This Sighte was straunge--but straunger yet remaynd,
  When from the Corse the cered Clothes we tore;
The Veynes seemed full of Bloud, the Lipps distained,
  All dripping with my Daughter's new-suck'd gore.

'When through own Towne this Sighte we had proclaimed,
  A dismall Horrour chilled our Townsmen's hartes;
The Vampyre (So our Priest the Tailour nam'd)
  Their Midnight-sleeps disturbed with feaverish startes.

The Churchyardes straight were ransacked all throughout
  With Pick-ax, Shovell, Mattocke, and with Spade;
But evrie Corse that we did digge thereout,
  Did shewe like living Menn in Coffins laied.

'It was the Corses that our Churchyardes filled,
  That did at Midnight lumberr up our Stayres;
They suck'd our Bloud, the gorie Banquet swilled,
  And harrowed everie Soule with hydeous Feares.

'And nowe the Priestes burnd Incense in the Quire,
  And scattered Ave-Maries o'er the Graves,
And purified the Church with lustrall Fire,
  And cast all thinges prophane to Danowe's Waves.

'And they barr'd with Boltes of Iron the Churchyard-pale
  To keepe them out; but all this wold not doe;
For when a Dead-Man has learn'd to draw a naile,
  He can also burst an iron Bolte in two.'

The sadde old Man was silent--I arose,
  And felt great Grief and Horrour in my Breste.
I rode nine Leagues before I sought repose,
  And never agen drew nigh the Walles of Peste."

MAGIC AND ASTROLOGY.
CHAPTER XXXVII.

Magic a Study among the Learned--Plato and Pythagoras   travelled to learn the Art, and taught it--How to   subdue a Furious Bull--How to make a tough Fowl   tender--Eagles' Feathers--Power of a Small   Fish--Speakers made Eloquent by Magical Art--Virtue of   Gems--How Jewels should be set-- When they are to be   Graven--Various Magical Operations--Cures effected by Hippocrates--Democritus on Magic--Many Charms--Evil   Spirits--Magicians sacrificing to the Planets--Vessels   and other articles used for Magical purposes--Success   in Magic--Magician's Power to produce Monstrous   Creatures-- Egyptian Magicians--Horses' and Asses'   Heads--Magical Circles--Throwing Old Shoes--Figures on   Shoes--A Hangman's Soul--Directions for raising Ghosts and Spirits.

Magic was, in ancient times, a favourite study among the learned. Plato, Pythagoras, and other men of note, travelled over many countries to learn this art. After studying for a long time, they publicly communicated the knowledge of magic to students from every quarter of the globe. The knowledge acquired by magicians, if real, was wonderful. One discovered that, by tying a bull to a fig tree, the animal, though of a furious nature, instantly became subdued. The same authority states that, by hanging an old tough fowl on the same description of tree, it would become tender. Another professor of magic taught that the feathers of an eagle, mixed with those of other birds, would consume them, and that a small fish called Remora could stop the progress of a ship at sea. Magicians supplied precious stones to public speakers, the possession of which made them eloquent, and brought them into favour with princes. A certain gem carried in a husband's pocket made him love his wife, and enabled him to overcome his enemies. Coral was a preventative against witchcraft, hence the fashion of ladies and children wearing necklaces and bracelets of this material. Hyacinth brought down rain, obscured the sun, and preserved from lightning. One stone resisted drunkenness, so that the bearer could be able to drink freely without becoming intoxicated. A chalcedony made the wearer lucky at law, increased the vigour of one's body, and prevented illusions of the devil. Those acquainted with magical art concluded that all stones possessed virtues, infused into them by the influence of planets. Alexander, Hermes, Zoroaster, and several other ancients, entertained this opinion. Magicians were the first to set stones in rings--an invention which, if not beneficial to man and woman, has helped to adorn their persons.

Gems used for magical purposes required to be set in such metals as had affinity with the planets whereby they (the gems) were influenced. The image of Saturn should be made in lead; of Sol, in gold; of Luna, in silver; of Jupiter, in tin; of Mars, in iron; of Venus, in copper; of Mercury, in quicksilver. A proper time should be observed for the graving of magical figures. If love is to be procured, the graving must be done under proper and friendly aspects, as in the hour of Venus. Such signs as ascend in the day must be taken in the day. If they increase in the night, then the work must be done in the night. Wise men tell us that an olive planted by a virgin will thrive, but if by an unchaste woman it will wither. If a serpent be found in a hole, it may be safely pulled out by the left hand, but to attempt to do so with the right would be dangerous.

Learned writers on magic say that if one take a new knife, and cut a lemon with it while the operator is expressing words of hatred or dislike against a person he or she may wish evil to, the object of hatred will feel uneasy, and become unwell. If a live pigeon be cut through the heart while an evil wisher is venting curses against a friend or neighbour, the individual against whom the evil wishes are made will suffer in body and mind. A man will be put in great fear if his image, prepared according to the arts of magic, be suspended by a single hair or thread, however far distant he may be from the scene of operation. If a person suffering from toothache or asthma catch a live frog before sunrise, and spit into its mouth, immediate relief will be the result. If the plague or any epidemic disease threaten a village or town, the disorder will be stayed by a live toad being suspended for three or four days in a chimney. The dried body of a dead toad, worn in the breast, prevents the possessor of the charm from being injured by any infectious disease. Hippocrates had great honours conferred on him on account of the cures he effected by the application of certain parts of reptiles to disordered persons. The heart of a toad, suspended by a blue ribbon round the neck, will cure the king's evil. Rape seed, sown with cursing and imprecation, grows better, we are told, than when the seed is blessed. If one wear a girdle of civet-cat skin in battle, he will escape unhurt. Those skilled in such secrets say they can be easily explained. In their arguments they point to the antipathy of certain natural things, animate and inanimate, to other things in nature. The wing of a bat and the heart of a lapwing repel evil spirits and wicked passions; the bustard flies off when a horse comes in sight, and the hart bounds away at the sight of a ram or viper; a lion trembles at the crowing of a cock. If one swallow the heart of a lapwing, mole, or weasel, taken from the animal when alive, it will improve his understanding, and enable him to prophesy.

Democritus says that if one cut the tongue out of a live frog, and lay it on a woman's breast opposite her heart, she will be compelled to answer every question put to her. Dogs will never attack a person that has a weasel's tail in his pocket or breast, provided the appendage has been severed from the little animal when it was alive. If one has a chameleon's tongue, cut out before the creature's death, he may defy all the sharpers in the world. If the blood of a civet-cat be sprinkled on the doors and windows of a house, witches and sorcerers will be prevented from entering it or molesting the inmates thereof. If an enemy desire to render any one hateful to friends and neighbours, it may be done by the touch of an ointment composed of the ashes of a calcined ankle-bone of a man, oil extracted from the left foot of the same body, and the blood of a weasel. Civet-cat gut tied round a man's left arm, makes all the ladies look on him with favour; and civet-cat skin worn as a cap, protects the wearer against the art of witches. If a stone that has been in a mad dog's mouth be put into ale handed round at a feast, discord will take place. If a bone taken from a toad's left side be secretly put into any part of a woman's dress, it will kindle her love into a burning flame; but if the corresponding bone of the toad's right side be used, the most ardent love of the woman will be cooled. If the snaffle of a bridle be made of a sword that has killed a man, the rider may with ease control a horse, however wild the animal may be; and if a sword that has been used in beheading a person be dipped in wine, it will impart a medicinal virtue to the liquor.

Pliny is accountable for a few of the foregoing and many other similar stories, all of which were believed at one time.

Fires kindled with human fat or oil frightens away evil spirits. On the other hand, vapours exhaled from certain suffumigations induce spirits to appear. The lungs of an ass, when burned, drive evil spirits away. Magicians say that if gold or silver be hid when the moon is in conjunction with the sun, and the place be perfumed with saffron, henbane, and black poppy, the treasure will never be feloniously carried away, for spirits will constantly watch over it. The blood of doves, lapwings, and bats possesses peculiar virtues--attracting spirits to places where they may be required to appear, and exciting love passions.

Magicians, when sacrificing to the planets with the view of securing their diabolical ends, throw into the flames such things as raise a pleasant perfume when they wish to perform good actions; but when they desire to bring about wicked results, they raise disagreeable smells. When soliciting the aid of the sun, it was customary to take the brain of an eagle or the blood of a white cock; when appealing to the moon, the blood of a goose was supposed to be good; when sacrificing to Saturn, the brain of a cat and the blood of a bat were indispensable; when soliciting Jupiter's assistance, the blood of a swallow or stork and the brains of a hart were recommended; when sacrificing to Mars, the blood of a man or of a black cat was thought best; and when Mercury was sacrificed to, the brain of a fox or of a weasel and the blood of a magpie were burned on the altar.

All instruments, vessels, and other things used for magical purposes were recommended to be new; and when a magical missive was to be written, the parchment was prepared from the skin of a black kitten, the pen was a feather plucked from a live crow or raven, and the ink consisted of human blood, or a preparation of calcined cuttle-fish bones, nutgalls, and rain water, prepared in the day and hour of Saturn.

In order to secure success in the magical art, it was necessary for the operator to have his whole soul in his work, otherwise his labour was in vain. Ancient philosophers have informed us that when the human mind is intent upon magical work, it is joined with the mind and intelligence of the stars, and hence the wonderful result of secret art.

Magicians pretended to possess the power of producing monstrous creatures, even devils. They could, if their statements can be relied upon, create a cockatrice by artificially hatching an egg in a preparation of arsenic and the poison of serpents. The ashes of a burned duck, treated in a magical manner, produced a huge toad. Numerous writers conclude that there are two species of toads--the one produced by ordinary generation, and the other by devilish science. Plutarch and more modern writers say that frogs descend from the clouds in rain. Egyptian magicians produced proof of mice, frogs, and serpents growing out of earth and flowers. It was said that Damnatus Hispanus could make them in any number he pleased.

By certain charms, magicians could place a horse or an ass's head upon a man's shoulders, and change the head of an inferior animal into that of a human pate.

Magicians attached great importance to their circles. One of the fraternity, when about to proceed with his secret art, clothed himself with a black robe reaching to the knee, and under that a white garment of fine linen. He then took his position in the centre of the place where he intended to perform his conjurations, and, throwing his old shoes about ten yards from the circle, put on consecrated sandals with curious figures on each. (Here we may observe that not a few antiquarians are of opinion that from these practices arose the custom of persons throwing old shoes after newly-wedded pairs and others for luck, and of shoemakers making fanciful outlines on shoes by means of pegging and stitching.) With a magical wand of hazel the magician stretched forth his arm to the four winds, turning himself round to every wind, and beseeching his "master" to consecrate the circle. All these ceremonies being performed, he claimed the consecrated ground as a defence from all malignant spirits, that they might not have power over his soul or body.

The most suitable time for making circles was during bright moonlight, or when storms of wind or thunder were raging, because then the infernal spirits were nearer the earth than at other times, and could more easily hear the invocations of those who sought their assistance. Magical circles were recommended to be formed at dark lonely places--either in woods or deserts, or in places where three ways met, or among ruins of castles, abbeys, or monasteries, or on the sea-shore. But if the conjuration was to raise the ghost of one deceased, the fittest places for the purpose were spots where persons had been slain, woods in which suicides had been committed, churchyards, and burying-vaults. If any one doubts the correctness of what is here stated, perhaps he will change his mind after reading the following story:--

"A certain hangman, passing the image of our Lady, saluted her, and commended himself to her protection. Afterwards, while he prayed before her, he was called away to hang an offender, but his enemies slew him by the way. And lo! a certain priest, who walked nightly about every church in the city, rose that night to go to our Lady's church. In the churchyard he saw the ghosts of many dead men. On demanding what was the matter, he was told that the hangman was slain, and that the devil demanded his soul, but which our Lady said was hers, and that the judges were at hand to hear the cause. The priest having made up his mind to be at the trial, hid himself behind a tree. When the judges had taken their seats, the hangman was brought forward pinioned, and proof adduced that his soul belonged to the devil. On the other side it was pleaded by our Lady, that at the hour of death the hangman commended his soul to her. The judges gave sentence that the hangman's soul should return to his body until he made sufficient satisfaction. The priest was called from his hiding-place and sent to the Pope with a rose of rare beauty, and instructions to crave the prayers of his Holiness for the poor man." Although we are not made acquainted with the result of the application to the Pope, there can be little doubt but that, through our Lady and his Holiness, Satan lost his eagerly desired victim.

Directions are given by the learned how to raise ghosts and evil spirits. To raise the ghost of one who had hanged himself, the exorcist was to provide himself with a straight hazel wand, and bind the head of an owl with a bunch of St. John's-wort to the end thereof. This done, he was to repair to a place where a miserable wretch had strangled himself, and at twelve o'clock at night, while the body remained suspended, begin his conjurations. First, he was directed to stretch forth his wand towards the four corners of the world, saying, "I conjure and exorcise thee, thou distressed spirit, to present thyself here and reveal unto me the cause of thy calamity--why thou didst offer violence to thine own life, where thou art now in being, and where thou wilt hereafter be?" Then, gently striking the body nine times with the wand, he was to demand the spirit of the deceased to reveal unto him what secrets he wished made known, whether these referred to the past or future. The conjuration being thrice repeated, we are assured the spirit would rise and answer the exorcist's questions. Directions were next given for laying the spirit, and that might be done by burying the body naked with lime, salt, and sulphur. If the ghost which the exorcist consulted was of one who died a common death, and received the usual burial, it was essential to dig the body out of the grave at twelve o'clock at night; and while the exorcist held a torch in his left hand, he was to smite the corpse three times with his consecrated rod, held in the right hand, and demand answers to his questions. When the ceremonies were gone through in a regular way, the interrogatories were truly answered. A caution was offered to the practiser of this art. The magician of no great experience was told that if the constellation and position of the stars at his nativity were not favourable, it would be dangerous for him to encounter a ghost for fear of being slain, as the ghosts of men could easily destroy magicians not protected by the stars.

Magicians were instructed how to raise the spirits Paymon, Bathin, and Barma, and secure their assistance. These spirits, though of various ranks and orders, were of one power, ability, and nature, and the mode of raising them is the same. The magician who desired to consult with these spirits had to appoint a night in the waxing of the moon, when the planet Mercury reigned, at eleven o'clock at night. But for four days before the appointed night he was required to shave his beard every morning, change his linen, and put on a consecrated girdle made of a black cat's skin. When all was prepared for the summoning of the spirits, the magician was instructed to enter a dark parlour or cellar, to light seven candles, and draw a circle with his own blood. When the candles were lighted, it was essential for the magician to protect himself with two drawn swords, and consecrate the circle, so that all evil spirits might be expelled. Everything being ready, the conjuration commenced in these words: "I conjure and exorcise you, the three gentle and noble spirits of the power of the north, by the great and dreadful name of your king, and by the silence of the night, and by the holy rites of magic, and by the number of the infernal legions, I adjure and advocate you that without delay ye present yourselves here before the northern quarter of the circle, all of you, or any one of you, and answer my demands." This, we are informed, had to be repeated three times, and then the three spirits appeared, or one of them by lot, if the others were engaged elsewhere. Before their appearance, they sent in advance three swift hounds in pursuit of a hare, which ran round the circle for seven and a half minutes. After this chase more hounds came in, and after all a little ugly

Ethiopian, who snatched the hare from the hounds. Next was heard a hunter's horn, and a herald on horseback came galloping swiftly with three hunters behind him upon black horses. After riding round the circle seven times, they stood at the northern quarter. The magician then demanded the demons to be faithful and obedient, which they readily agreed to be. Valuable information was obtained from the spirits, who gave the magician the powerful girdle of victory, which, on being tied about him, enabled him to conquer armies, and all men, however powerful. The spirits also were compelled to bring, at the magician's bidding, the richest treasure earth could afford, and to reveal the positions of hidden gold and silver mines.

The spirits could bestow the gift of invisibility, and the foreknowledge of the change of the weather; they could teach the exorcist how to raise storms and tempests, and how to calm them again; they could bring news in an instant of the result of any battle or other important event, wherever it took place. They could also teach the language of birds, and how to fly unseen through the air.

CHAPTER XXXVIII.

Josephus' Account of Astrology--Antediluvians acquainted with Astrology--Astrology after the Flood--Magicians in various Nations--The Spirit Bokim--Compact and Confederation with Spirits--Long Life and Magical Power--Feats of Magicians--A French Priest in compact with the Devil--Married to Venus--Turning Leather into Gold--A Novice in Magic destroyed by a Spirit--Principles of Magic--Implements, Materials, and Doings of Magicians--Piercing Sight--Lilly the Astrologer--Lilly consulted by Royalists--Astrological Predictions concerning Fires, Plagues, Famine, War, and the Fortunes of Great Persons.

Josephus says that the antediluvians were well acquainted with astrology, and inscribed the principles thereof on pillars to preserve them to posterity from the Flood; for it was by this art, he believes, that they were enabled to foresee the coming Deluge. Subsequent to the Flood, the Assyrians were the first people who turned their attention to astrology. The Chaldeans, Egyptians, and Arabians soon became acquainted with the art, and by perseverance brought it to perfection and high estimation. In several nations none but those skilled in astrology were admitted to the administration of sacred rites or to the management of state affairs.

In China, by the sacrifice of blood and the repetitions of several superstitious invocations to the sun and moon, devils were brought up from their place of abode, if not repose. In Tartary the magicians offered to the ocean, the mountains, and the stars, divers sorts of incense, by which means the spirits were compelled to appear. In the East and West Indies the power of magic was equally powerful. Greek and Roman magicians invoked spirits by prayers to the moon, and sacrifices of milk, honey, and blood. In our own country, incantation and conjuration, as already observed, were by no means uncommon.

When Chiancungi and his sister Napala first attempted to call up spirits, they began with the spirit Bokim, in the twentieth degree. They commenced their operations in a vault hung round with black cloth. Having drawn their circle of the order of thrones and the seven planets, and stamped their magical characters in the centre thereof, they proceeded to the ceremonies of conjuration without anything appearing. This caused them to become so desperate that they left the circle and betook themselves to the most detestable branch of magic--compact, or confederacy; through which they obtained from Bokim 155 years of life, and almost unlimited magical power, on the condition that in return their bodies and souls should at last be given to him. They performed strange miracles in every country. By the assistance of these magicians, the Tartars destroyed above one hundred ships belonging to the Chinese. Many a loss did they bring upon those against whom they had a private grudge, or against whom they were hired. Kingdoms were ruined, children slain, fruits withered, corn blasted, silk destroyed, navigation impeded, and adult lives sacrificed. Chiancungi had numerous public contests with magicians of several countries in magical science, in which art he was said to excel them all.

Lewis Gawfridi, a French priest, was another famous magician, who had compact with the devil of a closer relationship than common men of his craft could pretend to have. He served Satan for fourteen years in performing detestable works--sacrificing children, worshipping the devil in various shapes, and tempting people to become magicians, and to take part in disgraceful nocturnal conventions.

A wonderful relation is given in support of the belief of magicians having power over spirits. The story is this:--A newly-married man was amusing himself with his companions, when, in case he should lose his wedding ring, he put it on the finger of a statue of Venus. Returning to take his ring, he found the finger so bent that the ornament intended for his bride could not be removed. At night the image of Venus appeared to him and said, "Thou hast espoused me, and shalt not enjoy the society of any other woman." Again returning to the statue in the morning he found the finger straight, and discovered that the ring was gone. So greatly was he troubled, that he consulted a magician, who put him on a plan of obtaining his ring and releasing him of his engagement with Venus. The magician wrote a letter to a principal spirit in the dominion to which Venus belonged, and, giving it to the unhappy young man, instructed him to watch at a certain time and place, when he would see a troop of spirits pass by him, one of which, he said, would be seated on a chariot; and he it was for whom the letter was written. The young man, on acting as directed, espied the spirits, and gave the letter to the one for which it was intended. As soon as the fiend read its contents he burst into a rage, exclaiming, "How long shall we be subject to this accursed magician?" With hesitation, he called on a most beautiful woman near the chariot, and commanded her to return the ring to its owner, an order she reluctantly obeyed.

Henry Cornelius Agrippa, who was born at Cologne in 1486, was an astrologer and magician. When travelling, he paid his hotel bills with pieces of horn, which appeared as gold to those to whom they were presented. A foolish fellow entered Agrippa's study, and raised the devil therein during the magician's absence. The novice, being unable to subdue the fiend, lost his life. On Agrippa coming home, he found several spirits dancing on the house-top. He ordered them to enter the dead body, which they did, and then he cast it into a pit. Though Agrippa seldom left his study or conversed with any one, he was well acquainted with everything going on at home and abroad. People were of opinion that a black dog he kept was an evil spirit, which duly informed him of what was taking place far and near.

Every magical charm had its first principles according to certain laws; and the garments worn by magicians were manufactured and stitched at stated hours. The time was generally in the hour of Luna or of Saturn, in the moon's increase. Their needles were made of hedgehog's prickles, or bones of animals, as iron or steel possessed virtues not always favourable to magic. Their ointments were of man's fat, blood, hog's grease, oil, etc. Their characters were ancient Hebrew, and their speech in the learned languages; their fires were kindled with sweet wood and oil or resin; and their candles, of the fat of men and children. Their vessels were earthenware; their candlesticks had three feet, of dead men's bones. Their capes were like pyramids, with lappets or ears on each side, and lined with fur. Their gowns were, for ordinary purposes, long, reaching to the ground, and lined with fox-skin. Their girdles were three inches broad, having cabalistical names, signs, and circles inscribed thereon.

Some magicians had such piercing sight that they could discover everything, however carefully concealed, and look into futurity with a certainty of making known what was to come to pass. Lilly the astrologer was a great authority in England. He was consulted by the Royalists, (with the king's privity) as to whether the king would escape from Hampton Court, and whether he would or should sign the propositions of Parliament. For giving his opinion on these and a few other subjects, the astrologer received L20. In Lilly's *Astrological Predictions* in 1648 occurs the following passage:--

"In the year 1656, the aphelium of Mars, who is the general signification of England, will be in Virgo, which is assuredly the ascendant of the English monarchy, but Aries of the kingdom. When this apsis, therefore, of Mars shall appear in Virgo, who shall expect less than a strange catastrophe of human affairs in the commonwealth, monarchy, and kingdom of England? There will then, either in or about these times, or near that year, appear in this kingdom so strange a revolution of fate, so grand a catastrophe and great mutation unto this monarchy and government, as never yet appeared; of which, as the time now stands, I have no liberty or encouragement to deliver my opinion--only, it will be ominous to London, unto her merchants at sea, to her traffic on land, to her poor, to her rich, to all sorts of people inhabiting in her or her liberties, by reason of consuming fires and devastating plagues."

Accomplished events, even those which happened in his own time, and information obtained from the writings of ancient astrologers, enabled Lilly to predict important results. We find in a work *On the Probable Effects of the Great Conjunction of Saturn and Jupiter*, that "the mean or second greatest conjunction that happened in 1603"--Lilly was born in 1602--"was in the eighth degree of Sagittarius, the opposite sign of the ascendant of London. They were nearly conjoined the greater part of the year in which Queen Elizabeth died; and there was a severe plague in London, whereof died, in 1603 and 1604, more than 68,000 persons; and the year after, or in 1605, the Gunpowder Plot was nearly being carried into execution.

"The next conjunction happened in the seventh degree of Leo, in 1623. Within two years after, King James I. died; and there was also a severe plague in London, which carried off 35,417 persons, in 1625; and, what was observable, in 1639 there was a great eclipse of the sun, in ten degrees of Gemini, in opposition to the place of the first conjunction, in 1603; and exactly when Mars arrived to ten degrees of Pisces, or in quartile to both places, the Long Parliament began; and near the same time the Scots and English disagreed; and when Charles I. applied to the citizens of London, they refused to lend him money to be employed against them. It is also remarkable that Leo, the sign where the conjunction happened, was the ascendant in King Charles's nativity; and how unfortunate he was afterwards till his death, is pretty well known.

"The next took place in 1643, in the sign of Pisces, which found the king and his subjects in open arms, and was followed by dreadful civil wars in England, that terminated in beheading the king."

Whether Lilly did really foresee what he pretended had been revealed to him, we shall not here affirm or deny, but, there can be no doubt, many strange circumstances following his predictions went far to support his claim to the prophetic mantle. Further quotations from the same work will supply additional matter for reflection:--

"The fourth conjunction in this trigon took place in 1663, in Sagittarius, again opposite to the ascendant of London. The year after followed a war with the Dutch, and in 1665 they took our valuable Hamburgh fleet; and in that year also was the great plague in London, that carried away 68,586 people. This was followed by the dreadful fire of London, in 1666, that destroyed 13,200 houses, and consumed nearly 400 streets.

"The next happened in Leo, in 1682, and was repeated in 1683, when Lord William Russell was beheaded; and, two years after, Charles II. died.

"The next was in seven degrees of Aries, the ascendant of England, in 1702. That year King William died, and war commenced with France. In short, whoever takes his ephemeris in one hand and history in the other, will have no difficulty in convincing himself of the efficacy of such configurations; and though, by changing the signs, they may vary the effects and also the places most subject to their influence, yet it will appear that the observations of different authors (wherein they all agree that England is most passive to the fiery trigon) are founded on truth.

"The conjunction under consideration happened in the earthy triplicity, to which Ptolemy refers to Europe in general; however, the places most particularly under the sign Virgo are France, and more especially Paris; and some authors say Lyons, and the principal port of the Turkish dominions. Indeed it is curious to observe that the Turks have got possession of nearly all the places said by Ptolemy to be under this sign, wherein the conjunction happened, and I have no doubt will most sensibly feel the effects of it; neither will Russia and some parts of Germany and Switzerland escape its influence.

"As the signs of Sagittarius and Pisces are also afflicted, and Jupiter so oppressed by the conjunction, Spain and Portugal will likewise be sensible of their effects; neither do I like the mischievous position of Mars in Taurus, the ascendant of Ireland, particularly as he is upon the mid-heaven, and so near the mundane quartile of Saturn and Mars.

"Most authors agree that evil configurations in Virgo are generally attended with bloodshed, and that configurations in earthly signs have more signification of feuds, dissatisfaction, and secret contrivances among the common people, than they have of wars and differences between kings and rulers, who are more properly denoted by princely or fiery signs."

CHAPTER XXXIX.

Judicial Astrology--Reading the Heavens--Lucky and   Unlucky Days discovered--Kings' and Queens' Unlucky   Days--Highland Superstitions--Climacterics--Priests   foretelling Children's Future Destiny--Astrologer and   Charles IX.--Influence of the Moon--Official   Air-gazers--Sacrificing to Planets--Children born   under different Phases of the Moon--Dryden's Faith in   Astrology--Dryden calculating the Nativity of his   Children--Predictions concerning his Son fulfilled.

Judicial astrology, it is supposed, was invented in Chaldaea, and thence transmitted to the Egyptians, Greeks, and Romans, but there are persons who think it commenced with the Arabs.

Astrologers, in reading the heavens, had recourse to a semicircle which they called Position, by which they represented the six great circles passing through the intersection of the meridian and horizon, and dividing the equator into twelve equal parts. The spaces included between these circles were styled the Twelve Houses, which referred to the twelve triangles marked in their theme, placing six of these houses above and six underneath the horizon. The first of the houses under the horizon towards the east they named the Horoscope, or House of Life; the second, the House of Wealth; the third, the House of Brothers; the fourth, the House of Parents; and so on to the twelfth house, each having reference to a particular subject. All matters relating to issue, diseases, wedlock, death, religion, honour, friendship, and woe could be foretold by astrologers.

In the time of the civil wars the royalists and the rebels had their astrologers as well as their soldiers; and the predictions of the former had great influence over the latter. By means of astrology, lucky and unlucky days were discovered. Thursday was the unlucky day of Henry VIII. He, his son Edward VI., Queen Mary, Queen Elizabeth, and many other illustrious persons, died on a Thursday, as had been foretold; and we have already pointed out that the 3d of September was a memorable day in the life of Cromwell.

The Highlanders of Scotland entertained many superstitions in regard to the moon as well as in reference to the sun. A Highlander would not willingly commence any serious undertaking in the waning of the moon--such as marrying, flitting, or going on a far journey. When the roth, rath, or circle of the moon was full, then was the lucky time for beginning serious or important matters.

Astrologers have employed all the rules of their art to show that the years of man's age, called climacterics, are dangerous, even threatening death. The first climacteric is in the seventh year of life, the rest are multiples of the first--as 21, 49, 56, 63, and 84, which two last are called the grand climacterics. Marc Ficinus accounts for the foundation of this opinion. He says there is a year assigned for each planet to rule over the body of a man, each in his turn; and that Saturn, being the most malignant planet of all, every seventh year (which falls to its lot) becomes very dangerous, especially those of 63 and 84, when the person is advanced in years.

There were those who pretended that the climacteric years were fatal to political bodies as well as to individuals. Pythagoras based his calculations very much on numbers. He thought considerable importance should be attached to the number 7.

In France the new-born child was often presented naked to the astrologer, who read the first lineaments in its forehead, and the transverse lines in its hands, and from these he wrote down its future destiny. Catherine de Medicis brought Henry IV., then a child, to old Nostradamus, to ascertain the youth's destiny. An astrologer having assured Charles IX. that he would live as many days as he would turn on his heels in one hour, his Majesty, putting faith in the prediction, performed the exercise of revolving, as directed, every morning during the prescribed period of an hour.

The Egyptian astronomers held that the moon influenced all sudden matters of importance, but others not less learned affirmed that portentous events were regulated by wandering stars. Seneca speaks of a custom which prevailed, of appointing official air-gazers to give notice of an approaching storm, similar to the practice at the present day, of having persons at meteorological stations throughout the country to forecast the state of the weather. When they observed a cloud which indicated a hail-shower, they warned the people in order that they might protect their crops. The peasants, to propitiate the planets, offered in sacrifice fat cocks and white lambs; and the poor, who had neither fowls nor four-footed beasts to offer, cut their thumbs, in the full expectation that this insignificant libation of a few drops of human blood would secure the favour of the heavenly bodies, and avert the threatened calamity.

A child born on the first day of the new moon is likely to live long and happy, if it survives infancy. The child born on the second day of the moon shall grow strong, and be noted for wisdom. This day is fortunate in many respects. If one wishes to inquire into secrets, let him begin before the clock strikes the midnight hour. The infant born on the third day will never want an influential friend to lend him a helping hand in time of need. The fourth day is not quite so lucky, and the infant who comes into the world will require to be honest and diligent, to support an honourable position in life. The child born on the fifth day of the moon will turn out to be fickle and capricious. It is a good day, however, for beginning any new undertaking--particularly for laying the foundation of a building. Promises made on the sixth day will be long of being fulfilled. On this day people ought to take good heed to their ways, for on it they are very liable to err. The parents of children born at this time had better nurse the little ones tenderly, for nothing but scrupulous attention will sustain them through the dangers of youth. Dreams of the seventh day of the moon must not be revealed. Long life is promised to the child born this day; and if a person be stricken with sickness on it, a speedy cure will be effected. Tricksters and all sorts of dishonest people will be disappointed on the eighth, ninth, and tenth days of the moon; and children born on any of these days will be blessed with long life and health, if they escape certain contingencies known to the wise. The child born on the eleventh day will go far from home, and may expect to die in a foreign country, unless he make a fortune and return home, or have an estate left him.

The child born on the twelfth day of the moon will be wise and long-lived; but the infant born on the following day will be of slow understanding--in fact, will be a stupid creature, unless the disadvantage can be overcome by hard study. Children born on the fourteenth will excel in everything they may apply their minds to, or which they may take in hand. Every girl who comes into the world on the fifteenth will be beautiful, and have many admirers. Those born on the sixteenth day may expect to have many enemies; and those who are born on the seventeenth day are not likely to become rich by their own industry, but they may look for money from rich friends. The man-child born on the eighteenth day of the moon is likely to rise to honour and distinction, after encountering much opposition in his upward career. He or she born on the nineteenth day will require to pray for grace to subdue the natural disposition. The individual born that day will be churlish, perverse, and combative; and the infant who first draws the breath of life on the following day will be covetous and parsimonious.

The infant born on the twenty-first day of the moon may possess a strong constitution, but it is not certain that the mind will be vigorous. If the child of the twenty-second day survive infancy, long life will be awarded it, though much grief will be met with in life's rough path. Fair promises, with certain drawbacks, are made to children of the twenty-third day; and infants of the twenty-fourth day will be good-tempered, perhaps sottish. One who has been born on the twenty-fifth day of the moon had better walk carefully, lest adversity and danger overtake him. The young lady who has been born on the twenty-sixth day will, in all probability, be courted and married by a rich gentleman, who will ardently love her. Those born on the twenty-seventh day must not expect to become famous; and children born on the twenty-eighth day are more likely to be pious than rich. The twenty-ninth day of the moon does not promise prosperity to the children born on it; if they rise in the world, it will be in spite of great opposition, even from those near, if not dear, to them.

Dryden put faith in judicial astrology, and used to calculate the nativity of his children. On the birth of his son Charles, he caused the exact minute of his coming into the world to be noted. He calculated the child's nativity, and observed with grief that he was born in an evil hour; for Jupiter, Venus, and the sun were all under the earth, and the lord of his ascendant afflicted with a hateful square of Mars and Saturn. Dryden told his friends that if the child lived to the eighth year, he would narrowly escape a violent death on his very birthday; but if he should then overleap danger, he would in his twenty-third year be under the same influence; and if he should escape the second time, the thirty-third or thirty-fourth year would prove fatal. The boy's eighth birthday was looked forward to with great anxiety by his parents. On the dreaded day, Dryden, with the view of keeping him indoors and away from danger, gave him a double exercise in Latin. Charles was complying with his father's command, when a stag pursued by hounds was seen making towards the house. The noise reached the servants' ears, and they rushed out to see the chase. A manservant seized Charles by the hand, and took him out with him. Just as they reached the gate, the stag, being at bay, made a bold rush and leaped over the court wall, which, being old and low, the dogs followed, threw down a part thereof, and the unfortunate boy was buried in the ruins. He was much bruised, so that he was six weeks in a dangerous state. In the twenty-third year of the son's age he was at Rome, where he fell from an old tower belonging to the Vatican, which so greatly injured his head that he never fully recovered the accident. In his thirty-fourth year he was bathing in the Thames with another gentleman, when he was seized with cramp while in the water, and drowned before assistance could reach him. Thus the father's astrological calculations proved correct.

DIVINATION AND ORACLES.
CHAPTER XL.

Divination--Heathen Gods giving Signs--Sortes   Pr[oe]nestinae--St. Augustine's View of   Divination--Sortes Sanctorum--Divination in the Greek   and Latin Churches--Ceremonies at the Consecration of   Bishops, etc.--Declarations of the Divine Will--How   St. Consortia became a Nun--Responses--Hieroglyphic   Texts--Oracles--Sorcery and Divination among the   Jews--Training of Rabbins--Bath-Kool--Death of a   Friend foretold--Recovery from Sickness made   known--Plutarch on Oracles--Malthus's Belief in   Oracles--A Missionary's Opinion--Sibylline   Oracles--Various Modes of   Divination--Alectoromantia--Belomancy--Divination by   means of Rods--Cleromancy--Napoleon's Belief in   Cleromancy--Questions and Answers.

Divination is an art of foretelling future events by supernatural means. The word is generally understood to denote fortune-telling or sorcery, performed in divers ways--such as by the inspection of planets, stars, clouds; consulting spirits, witches, magicians; watching the flight of birds, inspecting the entrails of beasts and human victims, and examining the lines of the hand. But it is not necessary to extend the list here, as the various methods of divination will be enumerated and explained as we proceed. It was a maxim with the heathen nations of antiquity, that, if there were gods, they cared for men; and if they had any regard for the human family, they would give signs of their will. The Sortes Pr[oe]nestinae were famous among the Greeks; and this superstition passed into Christian nations.

St. Augustine did not disapprove of divination being resorted to, provided it was not used for worldly purposes. Gilbert of Nogent says that in his time (about the beginning of the twelfth century) it was customary, at the consecration of bishops, to consult the Sortes Sanctorum, to ascertain the success, fate, and other particulars of their episcopate. Many divines held that the lot was conducted by Providence. Though several popes about the eighth century disapproved of divination, and classed it among Pagan superstitions, traces of this mode of searching into futurity were found in after ages in the Greek and Latin Churches.

Upon the consecration of a bishop, after laying the Bible upon his head, the book was opened, and the first verse that the eye fell on was supposed to throw light on the bishop's future career. A bishop of Rochester, at his consecration by Lanfranc, Archbishop of Canterbury, had a happy presage in these words: "Bring hither the best robe, and put it on him." But the answer of the Scriptures at the consecration of St. Lietbert, Bishop of Cambray, was still more propitious: "This is my beloved son." The death of Albert, Bishop of Liege, was reported to have been made known to him by these words, which the archbishop who consecrated him found on opening the New Testament: "And the king sent an executioner, and commanded his head to be brought; and he went and beheaded him in prison." The Primate, greatly moved, embraced the new bishop, and said: "My son, having given yourself up to the sacred office, carry yourself righteously and devoutly, and prepare yourself for the trial of martyrdom." The bishop was afterwards murdered by the treacherous connivance of Henry VI.

De Garlande, Bishop of Orleans, became so odious to his clergy that they sent a complaint against him to Pope Alexander III., concluding: "Let your apostolical hands put on strength to strip naked the iniquity of this man, that the curse prognosticated on the day of his consecration may overtake him; for, the gospel being opened according to custom, the first words that appeared were: 'And the young man, leaving his linen cloth, fled from them naked.'"

William of Malmesbury relates that Hugh de Montaigne, Bishop of Auxerre, was obliged to go to Rome to answer several charges brought against him by some of his chapter, touching his morals; but his friends urged as undoubted testimony of his chastity the prognostic on the day of his consecration: "Hail Mary, full of grace."

Piously-inclined people not unfrequently went to church with the intention of receiving a declaration of the divine will, by hearing words of Scripture read or sung at the moment of the person's entrance. St. Anthony, when irresolute about his retirement, went to a church, where on entering he heard the words: "Go, sell all thou hast, and give it to the poor, then come and follow me." These expressions terminated his wavering: he withdrew to his solitude, leaving wealth and friends behind, and took up his abode in an old ruin on the top of a hill, where he spent many years of rigorous seclusion. He became the mighty oracle of the valley of the Nile.

It is reported that Clovis, the first Christian king of France, marching against Alaric, king of the Visigoths, sent nobles with presents to be offered at the tomb of St. Martin, and with instructions to endeavour to bring him a favourable augury, while he himself prayed for supernatural help. His messengers had no sooner entered the sacred place than they heard the priest chanting: "Thou hast girded me with strength for war; thou hast subdued under me those that rose up against me." Encouraged by this favourable prognostic, Clovis girded on his armour, engaged in battle, and gained a complete victory.

Peter de Blois, who lived in the twelfth century, says in a letter to Reginald, whose election to the see of Bath had long been strenuously opposed, that he believed he would soon be established in his diocese, for he (De Blois) had dreamed two nights successively of being at Reginald's consecration; and also, that being anxious to know the certain meaning of his dreams by lots and the psalter, his dreams were confirmed by the words turning up to him: "Moses and Aaron among the priests."

St. Consortia, in her youth, was passionately courted by a young man of a very powerful family, though he knew she had formed the design of taking the veil. Knowing that a refusal would expose her parents to many inconveniences, if not to positive danger, she desired a week to determine whether she would become his wife. At the expiration of that time her lover came to know her answer. "I can neither accept you nor refuse the offer," said she; "but if you agree to it, let us go to the church and lay the holy gospel on the altar, and say a joint prayer, then we will open the book, to be informed of the divine will." He did as suggested, and the first words that met the eyes of both were: "Whosoever loveth father or mother more than me, is not worthy of me." This was enough: the lovers acquiesced in the decree, and she became a nun.

Responses were given in the heathen temples through certain objects, such as the tinkling of the caldrons at Dodona, the rustling of the sacred laurel, the murmuring of streams, or by the action of sacred animals. In the Egyptian hieroglyphic texts the gods speak in an oracular manner, and their consultation by the Pharaohs is mentioned. Oracles were used by the Hebrews. Their oracles were by word of mouth, dreams, visions, and prophetical sayings. They were also in use throughout Babylonia and Chaldaea; but the Grecian oracles possessed the highest reputation for truthfulness, the most renowned of which was the Delphic oracle. The precedence of consulting this oracle was determined by lots; and sacrifices were offered by the inquirers, who went, with laurel crowns on their heads, and delivered their questions carefully sealed. There was a secondary class of oracles or prophetic persons in Greece. One was situated at Oropus, in Attica, being the shrine of a deified magician. Those who consulted it fasted a whole day, abstained from wine, sacrificed a ram to Amphiaraus, and slept on the skin in the temple, where futurity was opened up to them through dreams. The oracle of Trophonius, which owed its origin to a deified seer, was given in a cave into which the votary entered, bathed, and anointed himself, while holding a honeyed cake. He obtained the desired knowledge by what he saw and heard. Written oracles existed of the prophecies of celebrated seers, and were preserved in the acropolis of Athens. Among the Arabs divination was, and is, greatly practised, and also among the Celtic people. Oracular answers were usually couched in dark ambiguous terms; and it was thought that at times the information was given by demons.

Lightfoot proved that the Jews, after their return from Babylon, gradually abandoned themselves to sorcery and divination. The Talmud abounds with directions for the due observance of superstitious rites. Many Jews were highly esteemed, after the destruction of their holy city, for their pretended skill in magic. Rabbins were trained in the school of Zoroaster; they interpreted dreams, cured the sick, healed wounds, and detected thefts, through their intercourse with superior beings.

Bath-Kool, daughter of the voice, was the name given by the Jews to an oracle in the second temple, which, according to report, was destined to supply the defect of the Urim and Thummim, the mysterious oracles of former and greater days. Of Bath-Kool many stories are related. When two Rabbins went to consult this oracle concerning the fate of another Rabbin, they passed before a school, in which they heard a boy reading: "And Samuel died." On inquiry they subsequently found that their friend was no longer a dweller among men. Two other Rabbins went to visit Acha in his sickness, and as they proceeded on their way they agreed to hear what Bath-Kool would pronounce on the fate of their brother. Immediately on their going to the sacred place appointed for inquirers, they heard a voice saying: "The candle is going out; let not the light be extinguished in Israel." By these words they were assured that the sickness was not unto death. Acha recovered.

Plutarch wrote a treatise on the ceasing of oracles; and Van Dale, a Dutch physician, published a volume to prove that they did not cease at the dawn of Christianity, as had been supposed by early Christians. Malthus laboured to prove that there were real oracles, such as could not be reasonably attributed to any artifices of priests or priestesses; but he thought several of the oracles became silent before the Church and the prayers of saints. A pious missionary in India gave it as his opinion that the devil gave oracles there, but that he became meek wherever the gospel was preached. This religious man was not singular in his opinion, for most of the Fathers of the Church believed it was the devil that gave oracles. Pagan priests went to sleep in their temples, that they might receive responses in their dreams, and that they might with greater certainty play the prophet. The sibylline oracles were held in so great veneration among the ancients, that nothing of importance was undertaken without consulting them.

That divination was used and believed in by the Hebrews, is proved by the Scripture injunctions against divinations. The Jews were told not to have among them any that used divination, or any observers of times, or enchanters, or witches, or charmers, or consulters with familiar spirits, or wizards, or necromancers, or star-gazers, or miracle-mongers, or seekers of oracles.

One species of divination was performed by laying an agate stone on a red-hot hatchet. This is known as Axinomancy. The agate was called sacred, as it was regarded as a preservative against the poison of reptiles. Pliny has written a whole chapter on the virtues of agates.

There was an art among the Greeks known as Alectoromantia, by which future events were made known by means of a cock's movements. A circle was made on the ground, and divided into twenty-four equal parts, in each of which spaces was written one of the letters of the alphabet, and upon each of these letters was laid a grain of wheat. This done, the fowl was turned loose, and watched to ascertain the order in which the grains were picked up. The letters corresponding to those grains were formed into words, and supplied an answer to important questions.

Belomancy was a kind of divination by arrows, practised among various nations in the East, but chiefly among the Arabians. It was performed in different ways. One was to mark a parcel of arrows, and put eleven or more of them into a case. These were drawn out, and according to their marks future events were judged. Another way was to have but three arrows, upon one of which was written an injunction to do a certain thing; upon another a warning against doing it; and upon the third there was no writing. These were put into a quiver, out of which one of the arrows was drawn at random. If it happened to be the one with the injunction, the thing regarding which there was a consultation was done; if it chanced to be the arrow with the warning, the matter was let alone; but if the arrow without an inscription, a second drawing took place. Kings going out to war frequently consulted with arrows and images, and according to the drawing or flight of an arrow was it determined which city or town should be first besieged. The king of Babylon resorted to Belomancy before assaulting Jerusalem. When he came to a place where two roads met, one led to the city of Rabbath, and the other to Jerusalem. There he wrote the names of the two cities upon several arrows which were mixed together promiscuously in a quiver, and a boy who was unacquainted with the matter drew out one, and the name Jerusalem being on it, the king determined to lead his army towards that city.

Divination by means of rods prevailed among the Magi, Chaldaeans, and Scythians, whence it passed to the Sclavonians, and thence to the Germans. The women among the Alani gathered straight rods or wands, and used them in their superstition. In Sheppard's *Epigrams* we find:

"Some sorcerers do boast they have a rod,   Gathered with vows and sacrifice,   And borne about will strangely nod   To hidden treasure where it lies;   Mankind is sure that rod divine, For to the wealthiest ever they incline."

The notion still prevails in England and elsewhere, that water and precious treasure could be discovered, though far below the surface of the earth, by carefully and skilfully handling the divining rod. Men of scientific knowledge have been believers in the occult power ascribed to the divining rod, while others, who have considered the subject, regard the supposed power of this rod as a delusion, and ascribe the whole phenomenon to the effect of a strong impression on the mind of the operator.

Cleromancy was performed by the throwing of dice. At Brura, a city of Achaia, there was a temple and a celebrated oracle of Hercules, where such as consulted the oracle threw four dice, the points whereof being observed by the priest, he was supposed to draw an answer from them. The great Napoleon was a firm believer in various modes of superstition, particularly in Cleromancy. A curious book on divination was found in Bonaparte's cabinet of curiosities at Leipsic, during the confusion that ensued there after the defeat of the French army. It was looked upon by him as a sacred work, and he was accustomed to consult it prior to his most hazardous undertakings. The book, which was upwards of five hundred years old, was written in German. It contained a table called the Oraculum, at the top of which was a column of dots or points similar to those on dice, but arranged in somewhat different order. The way of proceeding to inquire what was about to happen, was by asking questions, and the answer, whether good or bad, was according to the number and position of the dots opposite to the interrogatives. There was also a table containing the letters of the alphabet from A to Q, disposed of in a particular manner, the exact position of which had to be observed in prying into futurity. But as it is not our province to instruct any one in occult science, we shall not further explain the method of procuring answers to the questions propounded.

Information on almost every subject might be asked, if not obtained. Among the list of questions we find:--"Shall I obtain my wish? Shall I have success in my undertaking? Shall I gain or lose my cause? Shall I have to live in foreign parts? Shall I have to travel? Will the stranger return from abroad? Shall I recover my stolen property? Does the person love and regard me? Will the marriage be prosperous? Will my wife have a son or a daughter? Will the patient recover from his illness? Will the prisoner be released? Shall I be lucky or unlucky to-day? What does my dream signify?"

Among many answers and advices there are:--"What you wish for, you will shortly obtain. Be very cautious what you do this day, lest trouble befall you. If you marry this person, you will have enemies unlooked for. The patient should be prepared to leave this world. She will have a son, learned and wise. You had better decline this love, for it will neither be constant nor true. Your travels are in vain; you had better stay at home. You must not expect to regain that which you have lost. You will obtain a great fortune in another country. You may have many impediments in the accomplishment of your pursuits. Beware! an enemy is endeavouring to bring you into strife and misfortune. This day is unlucky, therefore alter your intentions. Your fortune will soon be changed into misfortune."

There were unlucky days, on which one was advised not to consult the Oraculum: for instance, January 1, 2, 4, 6, 11, 12, and 20 were looked on as particularly unpropitious. The 1st, 17th, and 18th February were lucky, and so were the 14th and 16th March. Besides those mentioned, there were unfortunate days in all the months of the year. If a person wished to avoid meeting with severe disappointment, he was not to inquire twice in one day regarding the same subject.

SIGNS, OMENS, AND WARNINGS.
CHAPTER XLI.

Crying in Youth--Image of Opis--New-born Babes--Man   born to Trouble-
-How Man's Time is spent--Bacon's   Belief in Presages--Dugdale's Foresight-
-Sir Thomas   More's Power to judge of Passing Events--Erasmus at   the
Tomb of Becket--Sir Walter Raleigh's   Predictions--What Tacitus foresaw--
Solon's   Predictions--Cicero's Predictions--Philosophers'   Observance of Signs
and Omens--Knox's   Predictions--Queen Mary and Darnley--Death of Thomas
Maitland and of Kirkaldy of Grange predicted--Regent   Murray warned against
going to Linlithgow--Belief in   Physiognomy--Natural Phenomena--The Hu-
man Body a   medium for discovering Future   Events--Phrenology--Hairy
People--The Finger   Nails--Unaccountable Sounds--Death   Warnings--
Appearance of Spirits.

If the Romans were right in considering that crying in youth portended ill-fortune in old age, there can be little doubt it has been decreed that man's existence shall be more embittered with disappointments than sweetened with unalloyed pleasures; for it is nearly as common for children to cry as it is for them to come into the world. Parents may pray to their favourite gods for wise, happy children; expectant mothers may wear suspended from their girdles the image of Opis, in the fond expectation that their offspring shall find a smooth passage through life; and nurses may bring new-born babes into contact with sacred things before defiled hands have touched their tender skins,--yet the sad experience of every man and woman is, that misfortunes overtake them sooner or later. True, some people are more fortunate than others, but none are exempted from grief and pain. Have we not the best authority for saying that "man is born to trouble, as the sparks fly upwards." This being so, every member of the human family must submit to his destiny, strive against it how he may.

Since the time the old serpent beguiled Eve, to the present day, the half of man's time has been spent in bringing about prosperity and averting evil. He watches the signs of the times; he seeks for tokens and omens, as these, he supposes, are often sent for his guidance. That warnings were given to our fathers and mothers of old in mysterious ways, they fully believed; and if sent to them, there is no good reason for supposing, say our aged relations, that they should not be sent to us. Lord Bacon believed in presages; and so did other learned men of his time. Dugdale anticipated the approaching scenes in 1641, when many ancient monuments were destroyed. So convinced was he of their early destruction, that he hurried on his itinerant labours of taking sketches and engraving inscriptions, to preserve their history and appearance for future times. Sir Thomas More was enabled to judge from passing events of what was to happen in after years. Erasmus, when looking at the tomb of Becket at Canterbury, wished that the jewels with which it was loaded had been given to the poor; "for," said he, "those who have heaped up all this mass of treasure will one day be plundered, and fall a prey to rapacious tyrants in power." His prediction was literally fulfilled twenty years after it was uttered. Sir Walter Raleigh regarded omens, and from these predicted truly. Tacitus foresaw the calamities which long desolated Europe on the fall of the Roman empire, and wrote concerning the future events five hundred years before they happened. Solon predicted many of the miseries that overtook the Athenians. Aristotle collected remarkable information concerning predictions. Cicero always judged of the affairs of the republic by prediction; and he not only told what was to happen in his own time, but he also foretold important things that came to pass long after his death. Philosophers, however, did not pretend to have the second sight, or to possess any superhuman powers; but the art of prediction, if art it could be called, was acquired, they confessed, by carefully observing signs and omens.

Few put more confidence in signs and omens than Knox, the great reformer, did; and he himself foresaw several events, and the fate of certain persons. When condemned to a galley in Rochelle, he predicted that within two or three years he would preach the gospel at St. Giles's, in Edinburgh, which, improbable though it was at the time, happened as he had foretold. Of Queen Mary and Darnley he said, that in justice she would be made an instrument of retribution, and that he (the king) would be overthrown. Knox predicted the death of Thomas Maitland, and of Kirkaldy of Grange; and he solemnly warned the Regent Murray against going to Linlithgow, where he was assassinated. The common people imagined that Knox was not only a preacher, but a prophet. A Spanish friar foretold the death of Henry IV. of France. The king's friends made known to him that his life was in danger, but he disregarded the prediction, and, before a year went round, the friar's words were verified.

None of the persons we have named laid claim to the prophetic gift. Their predictions rested chiefly or solely on the observation of what was passing around them. The augury to which they trusted was more physical than divine. Some believed in physiognomy, others relied on the appearance of the political horizon, and so on. The foolhardy mariner sees the barometer falling, and perceives the blackened heavens, yet he goes to sea with his frail craft: the storm overtakes him, and he, his crew, and ship are lost in the mighty deep. The prudent sailor takes warning: he observes the black clouds gathering over his head, and hears the distant thunder; he stays in port until the disturbed elements cease their raging, and he lives to go to sea again and again. If the weather be propitious, we may expect a plentiful harvest; if a horse is given to stumbling, he is likely to come down some day; if the lakes are frozen, skaters may be expected to be drowned; and if men and women will bathe, we may calculate with certainty that some of them will go beyond their depths and perish in the water. Then again, if a man be diligent in business, we may expect him to become rich; but if he be slothful, he has nothing to look for but poverty. If an individual persist in a course of crime, he will, to an almost absolute certainty, be punished. All this is easily understood by the dullest-headed person, but it is not every one who can comprehend the more secret science that enables the initiated in deep subjects to gain knowledge from such trifles as air-bubbles or spiders' webs.

Everything connected with the human body is a medium through which future events may be foretold. A pale complexion has its signification, and so has a ruddy face. The hands and veins are special objects of observation, and so are the nails of one's fingers. From the colour, shape, and marks on nails, there are, or at least were, people who could read a person's fortune from infancy to old age.

Phrenology is a favourite science among ourselves; and so was it with the ancients, who, however, understood the science in a somewhat different light to what people of the present time do, and therefore we shall give an outline of their observations and deductions. The ancients supposed that a moderately large head denoted a well-conditioned person, studious, and possessed of a good memory and understanding. Those with large heads were supposed to be dull and stupid, gluttonous, rough in their manners, frequently melancholy, and predisposed to madness.

One with a head too large for the body, and having a thick neck and extended veins, was generally strong and of a martial spirit. When the head was long and of conical shape, the person was generally impudent and rash; and, if sprightly in early life, was supposed to lose spirit and vivacity before reaching the age of thirty years. A well-proportioned head, but slightly compressed at the sides, denoted a person of good apprehension, proceeding from the spirits domiciled there. A spherical head denoted inconstancy, forgetfulness, and want of discretion. A small head was looked on as an evil sign. The person having such a head was supposed to be vicious and ill-conditioned in many respects, in consequence of the spirits being confined in a narrow compass, and unable to exercise their functions. A person with a spherical head seldom lived beyond middle age. A long oblique head denoted lust and intemperance, and a flat cranium caused one to have a similar disposition.

A large head and broad brow indicated slowness, but laboriousness. A little forehead denoted obstinacy, wickedness, and weakness of intellect, yet conceited and given to mischief. According to Aristotle, a square forehead denoted magnanimity and courage. A person with a forehead without wrinkles showed that he was honest, but at the same time contentious, fond of law, and void of devotion. A forehead pointed at the temples, signified shallow capacity, vanity, and want of courage.

Those with hanging eyebrows were thought to be fraudulent, bold, and unmerciful. A person with a depressed forehead was put down as servile, cowardly, and fearful. Of the lines of the forehead, those which were straight or bent towards the nose foretold good fortune. If they were very crooked or approaching the form of a semicircle, they foreboded evil. Simple and straight lines were the signs of simplicity, honesty, and truth. Many lines signified changes in life, and the fewness of lines spoke of evenness and simplicity. When the lines increased or decreased, they gave warning of approaching changes in person and fortune. If the lines on the forehead near the hair of the head were broad, long, and not winding, they denoted eventful changes in the person's life; for it was believed that the first line next the hair referred to Saturn, that below it to Jupiter, and the next below it to Mars. If the third line mentioned was longer than the others, and not broken or discontinued, and having a cross upon it, the person was looked upon as one courageous and ambitious, and who would be fortunate in war; but if the line was broken or discontinued, or had a semicircular form, dangers and misfortunes were supposed to be threatened. If there were no more than three lines that bended at the extremities, the person was marked to be a prattler; and if the individual was a woman, she was put down as a scold or abusive person. Hairy people were among those on whom fortune smiled; whereas smooth-faced, beardless men were numbered among the despicable and despised ones.

Fortune-telling by means of the finger nails was not uncommon. The ancient practice was to rub the nails with oil and soot or wax, and to hold up the nails, thus prepared, against the sun; and upon the transparent horny substance were supposed to appear figures or characters, which gave the answer required. In more recent times, people have been found predicting by means of nails of the hand, and telling the disposition of persons with certain descriptions of nails. However absurd it may appear, we shall give examples of this superstition:--A person with broad nails is of gentle nature, timid, and bashful. Those whose nails grow into the flesh at the points or sides are given to luxury. A white mark on the nail bespeaks misfortune. Persons with very pale nails are subject to much infirmity of the flesh, and persecution by neighbours and friends. People with narrow nails are ambitious and quarrelsome. Lovers of knowledge and liberal sentiment have round nails. Indolent people have generally fleshy nails. Small nails indicate littleness of mind, obstinacy, and conceit. Melancholy persons are distinguished by their pale or lead-coloured nails; and choleric martial men, delighting in war, have red and spotted nails.

Particular marks on the person were looked on as having reference to one's destiny. A mole on the chin told that the person thus adorned would be prosperous and esteemed. A mole on the right breast denoted sudden accidents and reverse of fortune; one on the left breast was a sign of success and of an amorous disposition. The mole on the right breast foretold that the issue would be girls; that on the left indicated that the children would be boys. A mole under the left breast of a man was a sign of him having an unsettled mind, fond of rambling, and light in his conduct. A similar mark under a lady's left breast showed her to be sincere in love. A mole on the right knee gave tokens of the person so marked being destined to trouble and misfortunes. A mole on the left knee portended a good spouse, with great riches, to the happy individual so marked. A mole on either foot foreboded sudden illness, or unexpected misfortune, and one on any part of the shoulders indicated imperceptible decline and gradual decay in health and fortune. There were many other ways of divining the fate and dispositions of man, such as by the hand, foot, hair, mouth, ears, tongue, eyes, chin, walk, conversation, and complexion; but as it would be unprofitable to treat all these separately, we pass them without further notice in this chapter.

Mysterious knockings and unaccountable noises were indicative of the death of a relative. Warnings of this description were common and believed in. Educated people, as well as the ignorant, were victims of this kind of superstition. In the beginning of the last century a highly respectable gentleman in England was one night surprised by a sudden knock at the street door, so loud that he thought an attempt was being made to break it open. Springing from bed, he seized a brace of pistols, and was hastening to the door, when a second knock, louder than the first, was heard. A third knock followed just as he was withdrawing the bolt, but on looking out not a single person was to be seen, though it was clear moonlight, and nothing to prevent him seeing a long way off. Next post brought a letter informing him that a near relation in London had died just at the time the knocking alarmed him and his family, for they too heard the startling sounds. The disturbed persons firmly believed that, in one way or another, the knockings had reference to their friend's death.

A few years afterwards, the same gentleman, sitting one night at twelve o'clock with a sick brother, heard a noise, as of the driving of nails into a coffin, in the workshop of an undertaker, who was a neighbour. The gentleman thought it was very unkind of the undertaker, an intimate acquaintance of the sick person, to disturb him. As soon as the noise of nail-driving ceased, other and more disagreeable sounds reached his ears. The street door was opened, and, as he thought, two or three men went upstairs with a coffin. He naturally suspected that all this was a forerunner of his brother's death; and so it turned out to be. The invalid died next day at noon. Those who live in our time may think that the gentleman was insane, and that what he heard resulted from him having a diseased brain. If he was labouring under delusions, others must have been deranged too; for it was not uncommon in those days for an undertaker and his family to be advised of an early order to make a coffin by the sound of planes and hammers at work in the workshop. Gravediggers were not without their early notices of funerals. Sometimes the church bell would toll at midnight, the graveyard gate would be thrown open by unseen hands, and a living form be seen to enter alone; or it might be that the whole funeral cortege which would appear in the flesh a few days later, could be observed in spirit in the dreary hours of night. If the deceased person had lived a good and holy life, his spectre appeared in a pleasant, comely form; but if his career was a wicked one, he passed in a hideous shape, probably attended by infernal spirits.

CHAPTER XLII.

Ornithomancy--Mohammed's Pigeons--A Gigantic   Fowl--Cock-crowing--
Sacred Geese saving a   City--Phenomenon at Rome before Caesar's Death--Young
Swallows--Virtue of a Goose's Tongue--Crows'   Hearts--Divination by means of
a Sieve--Detection   of Crime--Capnomancy--Catoptromancy--Dactyliomancy--
Cledonism--Onomancy--Names--Romans toasting their   Mistresses--How Suc-
cess in War was ascertained--Loss of   Ships' Colours--Importance attached to
Regimental   Standards--Consecrated Banners--Flag of the   Prophet--Battle of
the Standard--A Highland   Superstition.

Ornithomancy was a popular way of searching into futurity. Mohammed had holy pigeons, which came to his ears and conversed with him about things that were to happen. And the Prophet, it will be recollected, gave an account of a multitude of angels that appeared to him in all kinds of shapes, some of which were in the form of birds. One of the angel birds resembled a white cock, so prodigiously large that its height extended from the first to the second heavens--a distance of five hundred years' journey, according to the rate we usually travel on earth. Many Mohammedans will have it that the sacred bird was even larger than what we have stated. They assert that the fowl's head reached to the seventh heavens; and in describing him, they say his wings were decked with carbuncles and pearls, and that he extended his pinions from the east to the west to a distance proportionate to his height. This winged creature was represented as the chief angel of the cocks, and was said to crow so loud every morning that every living creature, except men and fairies, heard it. Following the example of this great bird, the smaller cocks, before sunrise, herald that bright luminary as he speeds to the west.

When the Gauls under Brennus had scaled the Capitol without arousing even the sentinels or the watch-dogs, the sacred geese, kept in the court of the temple in honour of Juno, heard the approach of the enemy and commenced cackling. The patrician, Manlius, struck with the noise, roused his fellow-soldiers--the Gauls were discovered, attacked, and driven back. Thenceforth Roman geese were fattened, but not eaten. A golden image of a goose was made to commemorate their vigilance, and upon a certain day in every year one was placed in a litter, and carried in state about the city, while a dog was impaled upon a stake, to denote the national contempt for that animal. A singular circumstance happened at Rome about twenty-four hours before Caesar's death. A little bird was observed to direct its flight towards the senate-house, consecrated by Pompey, whilst a flock of other birds was seen to follow in close pursuit, apparently to destroy the little bird, or to deprive it of a sprig of laurel it carried through the air. The bird was overtaken, and torn to pieces by its pursuers.

We are told that if one take young swallows and put them in a pot to cook them, he will, on taking off the lid, find two of the swallows kissing each other, and two turning one from the other. If the kissing birds be dissolved in oil of roses, they will prove effectual, when applied according to custom, in securing the affections of the most blooming young lady in the parish; but in making use of the birds found back to back, for creating sympathetic feelings, they require to be pounded into an ointment, and applied to the eyelids of him or her whose affections are sought. If the tongue of a goose be cut out when the fowl is alive, and laid on the breast of a man or woman when asleep, he or she will confess every sin of life. When a man carried the heart of a male crow, and his wife the heart of a female crow, they lived in peace and happiness. It was customary with the good house-wives of England, on placing eggs in a nest for incubation, to swing a lighted candle over them, as a charm to prevent hawks, crows, and other birds of prey, flying away with the young birds hatched from the eggs.

Divination by means of a sieve was often resorted to. The sieve was suspended after the operator had repeated a particular form of words, and, by certain manipulations, information was obtained concerning thefts, etc. The names of suspected parties were repeated while the implement was made to turn round; and on the guilty person being named, the sieve, instead of turning swiftly and steadily, began to oscillate and shake. This was a very ancient practice, in which great faith was put. Theocritus mentions a woman who was very skilful in her art. At times the sieve was suspended by a thread, or fixed at the point of a pair of scissors, giving it room to turn, and naming, as before, the suspected persons. Coscinomancy was practised in England at no distant date.

Divination by means of smoke (Capnomancy) was in use among the ancients in their sacrifices. It was a good sign when the smoke rose light and straight. If, on the contrary, the smoke ascended dark and dense, evil was foretold.

Catoptromancy was a species of divination performed by the aid of a mirror. This method of divination was common among the Achaians. The mode of procedure was, when one was sick and in danger of death, to let down a mirror into a fountain before the temple of Ceres, and, from the appearance of the glass, to judge what was to be the result--whether the sickness was to be removed, or death to take place. If a ghastly, disfigured face was seen, it was regarded as a certain evidence of death; but if the patient's face appeared fresh, healthy, and comely, it was a sign of recovery.

Dactyliomancy was divination performed by means of a ring. The ring was suspended by a thread above a round table, on the edge of which letters of the alphabet were marked. The ring, in shaking or vibrating over the table, stopped over certain of the letters, which, on being connected, supplied the answer asked. But the operation was preceded and accompanied by several superstitious ceremonies. In the first place, the ring had to be consecrated; the person from whose hand it was suspended required to be clothed in linen garments; his head had to be shaven all round; and he required to hold vervain in his hand.

Cledonism denoted divination drawn from words only occasionally uttered. Cicero observes that the Pythagoreans made observations not only of the words of gods, but those of men also. Accordingly the people thought it was unlucky to pronounce at meal-time such words as conveyed peril, evil consequences, sickness, death, estrangement of friends, or the displeasure of their deities. In another sense Cledonism seems to be divination drawn from the movements of birds, such as those noticed in another part of our work.

Onomancy, Onomamancy, or Onomatomancy, was the art of divining the good or bad fortune of man from the letters of his name. This mode of divination was popular among the ancients. The Pythagoreans taught that the mind, actions, and successes of mankind were according to their fate, genius, and name. Plato, who recommended parents to give their children happy names, was inclined to think they were right, and adduced grounds for maintaining his opinion. Some of the Bible worthies are referred to in support of Onomancy; and a certain profane writer calls attention to tippling Meroe, supposing she would drink her wine without water. Hippolitus was torn to pieces by his own coach-horses, as his name imported; Agamemnon signified that he should linger long before Troy; Priam, that he should be redeemed out of bondage in his childhood. The greatest empires and states have been founded and destroyed by men of the same name. Cyrus, the son of Cambyses, established the Persian monarchy; and Cyrus, the son of Darius, ruined it; Darius, son of Hystaspes, restored it; and again, Darius, son of Asamis, overthrew it. Philip, son of Amyntas, greatly enlarged the kingdom of Macedonia; and Philip, son of Antigonus, lost it. Augustus was the first emperor of Rome; Augustulus, the last. Constantine founded the empire of Constantinople, and Constantine lost it. Some names are unfortunate to princes: Caius, among the Romans; John and Henry of France, and John of England and Scotland. One of the principal rules of this kind of divination among the Pythagoreans was, that an even number of vowels in a name signified an imperfection in the left side of a man, and an odd number in the right side. Another rule was, that the persons were the most happy in whose names the numeral letters added together, made the greatest sum; for which reason, it was alleged, Achilles vanquished Hector, the numeral letters in the former name amounting to a greater number than in the latter. From a like idea, the young Romans toasted their mistresses at their meetings as often as their names contained letters. Theodotus, king of the Goths, being anxious to ascertain the success of his wars against the Romans, consulted a Jew, who ordered him to shut up a number of swine in styes, and to give some of them Roman and others Gothic names, and there to keep them until a certain day. The Jews' instructions were complied with; and, on inspecting the styes at the appointed time, it was discovered that the animals which had received the Gothic names were dead, and those to which the Roman names had been assigned were alive. From these circumstances, the fortune-teller truly predicted the defeat of the Goths.

There was an old superstition among seamen, which is supposed to linger among them still,--we mean the evil that was feared would follow the total loss or tearing of a ship's colours. Sailors would have been less grieved at all their sails being split, their spars carried away, and their masts gone by the board, than at being deprived of their colours. The loss or tearing of a flag was a sign of misfortune, both to the vessel and the crew.

Soldiers, particularly those in Highland and Irish regiments, were equally credulous. Vast importance was attached to the preservation of their standards, and hence in some instances the great bravery that has been displayed in preventing the enemy carrying away a standard. A brave High-lander, or courageous Irish soldier, would rather die than surrender the flag of his company. Not only did the loss of regimental colours bring disgrace for the time on those whose duty it was to defend them, but it portended future defeats and demoralisation.

Consecrated banners were common in times when almost every man was a soldier. "*Go, con-quer by this*" was the motto inscribed on ensigns of several nations. In the devices of standards were found the eagle, the wolf, the horse, the boar, the lion, and often a figure of Victory or Mars. The "Flag of the Prophet" was the sacred banner of the Mohammedans. It was composed of the turban of the Koreish, captured by Mohammed. A black flag was afterwards substituted in its place, consisting of a curtain that used to hang in front of the door of Ayeshah's (one of the Prophet's wives) tent. The Mohammedans regarded this flag as a most sacred relic. Subsequent to passing through several hands, it was brought to Europe by Amurath III. It was kept in a costly casket, and deposited in a chapel, guarded by emirs. The banner used to be unfolded when war broke out, and carefully laid aside, as stated, when peace was restored.

In the history of the "Battle of the Standard," which took place on Cutton Moor, near Northal-lerton, between the English and Scots, at which the Scots lost 10,000 men, the success of the English was reported to have been due to their having consecrated banners with them. The battle derived its name from the circumstance of a flag-staff being attached to a waggon in the army's centre, bear-ing at its top the consecrated host, and the banners of St. John of Beverley, St. Peter of York, and St. Wilfred of Ripon.

A superstition long lingered in the Scottish Highlands, that it was unlucky for a clansman to learn any handicraft engaged in by Lowlanders. If a Highland youth left his native mountains and engaged in mercantile or mechanical pursuits, his friends thought he turned effeminate. For warfare he became unsuited, either as a leader or follower. The prowess of his ancestors forsook him, he be-came incapable of handling the bow or spear skilfully, and, what was worse, he carried ill luck with himself and to his companions wherever he went. Powerful clans have been beaten in the open field by opposing clansmen of inferior numbers, solely through the circumstance of the former having in their ranks men who had imprudently, in an evil hour, apprenticed themselves to the vulgar callings of life. To be a soldier was honourable, to be a tiller of the ground was not a disgrace, to be a cattle reiver was not a crime, but for a clansman to condescend to earn his bread by ordinary industry in a workshop, could not fail to bring discredit and misfortune on himself and kindred, however remote the relationship might be. To this superstition the nation is indebted for the many stalwart Highlanders who have fought England's battles, and won them too, at home and abroad. Ask the decrepit old woman, leaning on her staff, far up yonder glen, the cause of the expiring zeal among the mountain youths to study the art of war, and she will tell you in effect what we have said; and will add, that through the intimacy that has long existed between Highlanders and Lowlanders, and the frequent evictions that have brought a scandal on our nation, her country no longer remains a recruiting ground for armies.

CHAPTER XLIII.

Caution of our Ancestors--A Magpie crossing one's   Path--What four Magpies betokened--The Poet and the   Magpies--More about Magpies--Flight of Birds--Swarming   of Bees--Howling of Dogs--Lowing of Cattle--Crowing of   Cocks--Dogs' Power of Sight--Stockings wrong side   out--Evil effect of Suspended Eggs--Burning Fish   Bones--Sign of a Letter coming--Sneezing of a Cat--Various Signs--The sight of a Fox foreboding   Evil--Owls and Ravens--Various Signs and Omens--How to   prevent Ill Luck--Reputed Witches crossing the Path--Highland Superstition--Print of a Caldron, what   it denoted--Unlucky to pass over a Balance--How to see   in the Dark--When not to pare your Nails--Touching a   Dead Body--Funeral Processions--Storks and Storks'   Hearts--How to Sit--Marriages--A Prophetic   Rhyme--Favourable and Unfavourable Times for   Marriages--Unfortunate to lose or break a Wedding   Ring--Rules to be observed in taking possession of a   House--Throwing Slippers, Besoms, Salt, and Rice after   Newly-married Persons--Charms for Bridegrooms and Brides--Mothers and Children--More about   Marriages--Rules to be observed at Baptisms--How to   treat Young Children.

Mark the caution of our ancestors: If a magpie crossed one's path when setting out on a journey, his mission, whatever it happened to be, was certain to prove unsuccessful, unless the traveller immediately crossed himself--a ceremony he invariably performed--and thus the unfavourable influence of the hateful bird ceased. In the south of England, people supposed that if a person saw four magpies at one time, he would soon lose by death a dear friend. But an old English poet, writing of magpies, says:

"One is a sign of sorrow; two are a sign of mirth;   Three are a sign of a wedding; and four a sign of birth."

The chattering of one of these birds in the morning bespeaks the arrival of a stranger before evening. It is thought unlucky to kill a magpie or a swallow. The congregating of magpies on a house-top precedes an important event, in which the inmates are interested. If a bird fly through a window, it is a sign that one of the inmates will soon die. If a pigeon, which does not belong to any one of the family, come into a house, it forebodes death to the occupant of the domicile. The alighting of a swarm of bees on a dead tree or on the withered bough of a living tree, signifies that the owner of the tree will soon pass through death's portal. The howling of dogs, the lowing of cattle, and the crowing of cocks at night, foretell the death of some person in the neighbourhood. Dogs are supposed by not a few people to see death as it enters a dwelling; and hence, in their opinion, the cause of that quadruped's frequent dismal howling.

When one, by mistake, puts on his stockings in the morning wrong side out, he secures good luck for that day at least. Birds' eggs hung up in a house, prevent good luck entering that dwelling. He who wishes to thrive should abstain from burning fish bones. A spark in the candle gives notice that a letter is coming. If the cat sneeze or cough, nothing is more certain than that one person, at least, in the house will soon have a cold. When one's ears tingle, lies are being told about him. When his cheeks burn, he is assured people are talking about him. If the right eye itches, good luck is expected; and when the left eye waters, misfortune is looked for. When the nose itches, vexation-probably the death of friends--is expected. The meeting of a fox, or the seeing of one crossing the path, presages the attempt of an impostor to commit a fraud at the expense of the traveller. Owls or ravens appearing on important occasions, portend unlucky events. If a weasel be met in the morning, it is necessary to turn three times on the heel and throw three stones, to prevent ill luck. It is more lucky to meet a man than a woman as a first-foot. Every person is advised to avoid meeting a cat, when going on an important mission. It is also unlucky to meet a pig; and it is thought prudent to return home when a hare or a reputed witch crosses the path ere the morning dew disappears before the sun. A man leading or riding on a mare with foal, is cautioned against allowing the animal to go in the track of a wolf; because, if she place a hoof on the spot where that ravenous beast's foot has been, she will cast her foal.

Time was, in Great Britain as in the East, when almost every one, whether walking, riding, or sailing in a boat, went with the sun, when setting out on a journey, or proceeding to sea. The Highlanders of Scotland invariably went *deiseal*, or to the right, at every meeting of importance. They went to the right, around the grave, with the corpse--to the right three times around the consecrated well before drinking. The company at a marriage went three times round the house before crossing the threshold. Companies, on taking their seats at table, were expected to turn to the right. Even at the present day, the loving-cup and decanters are handed to the right around the social board. When one lets salt fall on the floor or table, he should not omit to cast a small quantity of the condiment over his left shoulder. Beware of passing the salt at table unless it be asked for, and of placing your fork and knife cross-ways.

When one sneezed, he did not evoke Jupiter to save him, the same as the people of some other countries did, but he, or some of his friends present, said *Deiseal*. When an infant was born, the midwife encircled it three times right about with a burning candle. These customs were no doubt commenced by the Highlanders in honour of the sun, which they once worshipped; but in later times people did as their forefathers and foremothers had done, through a superstitious belief, thinking that by so doing they would prevent evil consequences, and secure good fortune.

It is unlucky to leave the print of a caldron in the ashes after taking the utensil off the fire. If people are wise, they will not pass over a balance, or take up fire with a sword. To enable a person to see in the dark, he is recommended to anoint his eyes with a salve prepared from the right eye of a hedgehog, boiled in oil, and preserved in a brazen vessel. A blackamoor is an unlucky first-foot. If the chickens do not come out readily to feed in the morning, the owner may make up his or her mind to meet with disappointments before night.

It was formerly, if not now, unlucky to pare your nails on Sunday or Friday. To prevent one dreaming about a dead person he has seen, it is necessary to touch the body. To secure money being always in one's pocket, he is advised to keep a bent sixpence, or a coin with a hole in it, in his purse; to take it out and spit on it at every new moon; and to return it to the pocket while wishing himself good luck.

It is unlucky to look at a funeral through a door or a window. Should one wish to gaze on the melancholy procession, he ought to take his position in the open air. The family will be fortunate on the roof of whose house a stork builds its nest; and if any one take the heart of a stork, and tie it up in the skin of a hawk or of a vulture, no enemy can conquer him so long as he carries the charm attached to his right arm. To sit with one's hands closed is bad, but to sit cross-legged secures good fortune. At a card-table, people occasionally sit in the latter position, with the view of bringing lucky deals.

A bride should not be married in a white satin dress. That a newly-married couple may have no obstacles in the way of prosperity, every one meeting them going to church to be united, or returning home after the hymeneal knot is tied, should retrace his steps with them a short distance. No small importance is attached to the old rhyme:

> "Blessed is the bride that the sun shines on;
> Blessed is the corpse that the rain rains on."

Marriages at the festival of St. Joseph are carefully avoided as unfortunate. All fast-days and vigils should also be avoided as marriage-days, they being considered inauspicious. The first day of May continues in many lands to be held in great esteem, and the 12th of that month is a high day among the witches. At that time they may be seen dancing on the surface of lakes, brushing the dew off the grass, milking cows in their folds, and flying through the air, or escaping from pursuers in the shape of hares.

If a married woman lose her wedding ring, she has reason to fear the estrangement of her husband's affections. If she break it, she thinks there is danger of the matrimonial tie being soon severed by death. If a newly-married couple go into a clean-swept house, they expect to be poor all their days; but if the house be but indifferently cleaned, and the precaution taken to throw salt and a small quantity of coals in at the door before any furniture or household goods are carried across the threshold, good luck is expected. As a warning, however, to persons who might wish to injure their neighbours, we think it right to say that, down to the time we write, it is considered that any one removing from a dwelling with clean-swept floors, has reason to expect grief and trouble in his new abode. Every one knows that slippers, besoms, salt, and rice should be thrown after a newly-wedded pair; and that a cake must be broken over a bride's head when she first enters the house of her husband; but it is not so well known that a bridegroom should have silver--say sixpences--and salt in his shoes, when he first approaches the marriage bed, and that the bride should avoid putting her bare feet on the floor when preparing to retire for the night with her future companion in life. If these precautions be neglected, there is danger of the wedded pair being deprived of little prattlers around their fire in the early days of their wedded life, and of having sons or daughters to comfort them in declining years. A mother should not enter a neighbour's house after having an infant before she is "kirked"; nor should she carry her child even to her nearest and dearest friend's abode before the little one has been baptized.

It is unlucky for a bridegroom to have for his "best-man" one who is not his blood relation. It is unlucky for a "best-man" to have on a black coat at a marriage; it is an omen of evil to the bride and bridegroom. If a bride slip her foot or her horse stumble when proceeding to church to be married, it is regarded as an evil sign; and if the bridegroom come down when on his way to meet his betrothed, before the hymeneal knot is tied, misfortunes are expected. If he has to cross a stream, and his bonnet or hat fall into the water, his death is not far distant. A bride's glove should not be taken off before the bridegroom's is removed, preparatory to their joining hands in wedlock before the clergyman. If any part of a dinner-set or tea-set be broken at a marriage or baptismal feast, it is a sign that misfortunes are coming.

If two children--a boy and a girl--are baptized in church on the same day, and the latter be sprinkled before the former, the girl's relations have reason to fear that in ripe years she will have a beard. If a mother or nurse do not give bread and cheese to the first person she meets when going to church with a child to be baptized, it is questionable whether the infant's career through life shall prove prosperous. The "first-foot," on receiving his bread and cheese, is expected to return a short distance with the child, to show his good will.

If a person, who is a stranger, leave a house wherein there is an unbaptized child, particularly if it be a girl, without eating or drinking, the infant's beauty is in danger of being taken away. It is unlucky to let a child see its face in a mirror before it is a year old. When an infant is suspended by the dress with its head downwards for a few seconds after being washed in the morning, it prevents an evil eye from affecting the little one that day.

CHAPTER XLIV.

Floors should not be swept at Night--Fires at New Year and Christmas--Presents at New Year and Christmas--Lucky and Unlucky "First-Foots"--Looking through a Ladder--Sneezing--Air Bubbles on Tea--Tea Stalks--Stepping out with the Left Foot--Left Shoe to be put on first--Weather Prognostications--How to secure Favourable Gales--Superstitious Customs at time of Death--Corpse of one guilty of *Felo-de-se*, how to be Buried--Finding of Persons who die unseen--Superstitious Belief of Russian Seamen--Ancient Customs of Scotland--Friday an Unlucky Day for commencing an Important Undertaking--Friday as a Marriage Day--Anecdote of a Ship called "Friday"--Loss of the Ship "Amazon"--Sunday a Favourable Day for commencing a Voyage--Lawyers and Clergymen, how looked upon by Sailors at Sea--It is Lucky to have Women and Children at Sea--Dogs and Cats at Sea--Rats deserting a Ship--Whistling to raise the Wind--Deceased Sailors' Clothes--Old Boats not to be Broken up--Reluctance to go to Sea in a Boat from which a Person has been Drowned--Sharks following a Ship--Unfavourable Sign to see a Hatch turned upside down--A Four-footed Beast not to be named at Sea--Legend of Vanderdecken or the Flying Dutchman--A Grandfather's Axe--Other Signs and Warnings.

If a housewife wish everything to prosper with her and her family, she will not permit the floors of her house to be swept at night. The sweeping not only prevents good fortune, but it disturbs the spirits of the dead, supposed to be constantly walking about in thousands. If the kitchen fire burn down on New Year's morning or Christmas eve, it is thought, some person belonging to the house will die before these seasons come round again. Old women, who wish to have a peep into futurity, are accustomed to cover over with ashes the smouldering embers of their fires on the last night of the year. If a death is to happen in the house before twelve months expire, the foot marks of the doomed individual will be imprinted in the ashes; but if no such event is to happen, the ashes will remain with a smooth surface, and the embers kindled below. It is thought lucky to receive a present on New Year's day or Christmas; but it is unlucky to borrow or lend on these days. The destiny of the members of a family is greatly affected for a whole year, if not for life, by the "first-foot" on New Year's and Christmas mornings. An unlucky "first-foot" brings misfortune with him or her, but a lucky "first-foot" introduces prosperity.

If one look through a ladder, he should spit three times to prevent evil consequences; and it is unlucky to hand anything through a ladder. Sneezing to the left hand is unlucky, but prosperous when to the right. Plutarch relates that, by the sneezing of a soldier towards his right hand, the soothsayer predicted the victory of the Greeks and the complete overthrow of the Persians in battle. Candles and lights burn dim when spirits are present. The stalk of the tea plant floating on the surface of a cup of tea, foretells the coming of a stranger. If the stalk be short, look for a female visitor; but if long, then a man may be expected. Air bubbles on tea denote kisses and money. It is thought lucky to step out with the left foot first; and no one who has attended to the recommendation of his grandmother, thinks of putting his right shoe on first in the morning. These precautions--stepping out with the left foot first, and putting the left shoe on before the right--keep one from stumbling.

With reference to prognosticating the state of the weather, our fathers, we may premise, carefully observed the winds, the clouds, the sky, and the seasons. If the wind blew from the west on New Year's night, it was considered lucky, and supposed to foretell a season of abundance.

In the north of Scotland, the people wished to see the first three days of winter dark and cloudy. A northern bard says:

> "The south wind, heat and plenty,
> The west wind, fish and milk,
> The north wind, cold and stormy,
> The east wind, fruit on trees."

People in Scotland also prognosticated the weather of the coming season, according to whether Candlemas was clear or foul. Every one can repeat the old rhyme, and some put faith in it:

> "If Candlemas is fair and clear,   Ther'll be twa winters in the year."

When this day passed without a shower of rain or a fall of snow, people imagined there would be severe weather before spring was past; and they expected heavy snow storms before the following Christmas. A showery and tempestuous Candlemas, on the other hand, raised the people's spirits, for by such omens they were to expect a favourable summer and an abundant harvest.

Though they may be well known to most readers, we subjoin a few poetical proverbs on the weather:

> "The evening red, and the morning grey,
> Are certain signs of a fair day."
> "If red the sun begins his race,
> Expect that rain will fall apace."
> "In the waning of the moon,
> A cloudy morn--fair afternoon."
> "If woolly fleeces spread the heavenly way,
> No rain, be sure, disturbs the summer's day."
> "When clouds appear like rocks and towers,

The earth's refreshed by frequent showers."

From rainbows, shepherds and sailors predicted the state of the weather.

"A rainbow in the morning is the shepherd's warning;
A rainbow at night is the sailor's delight."

When peacocks cry, be sure rain will early fall; and when the night owl screeches from the ruined tower, look for a storm; so also, if the cat is seen washing its face with its fore paws, expect a gale. When ocean birds flock on shore, a tempest is brewing on the sea.

Seamen and fishermen's wives can secure a favourable gale for their husbands by going to a chapel after mass, and blowing the dust on the door in the direction the vessels have gone.

When a person is dying, no one in the house, of whatever age, should be permitted to sleep. When one expires, the clock should be immediately stopped, and the dial plate covered with a towel, and mirrors and pictures should be concealed, or their faces turned to the wall. All the cats belonging to the house ought to be caught and confined till after the funeral. That a necessity prevails for putting the feline animals out of the way, will be understood by the existing generation, when they understand that if a cat cross a corpse, and afterwards pass over a living person in a recumbent posture, that individual will be deprived of sight. When a dead body is dressed and laid out, the relatives would do well to put a Bible below the head, and one plate with salt, and another plate with a piece of green turf, on the breast. The corpse of every one guilty of *felo-de-se* should be buried either in a remote spot not customarily used as a place of burial, or near to a cross road; but if the relatives of any such unhappy person insist on having the remains interred in the ordinary place of sepulchre, they are expected to carry the corpse over the burying-ground wall, and inter it after sunset. It is believed that if a person die unseen, they who first discover the body will meet his death in a similar manner. This superstitious belief often prevents seamen and fishermen picking up and taking ashore dead bodies discovered at sea. Seamen have not yet risen above these superstitious delusions. A few years ago a Russian ship was lying in Leith Docks, when one of the crew fell overboard and was drowned. As long as there was a chance of rescuing the man, his companions did everything they could to save him; but as soon as they discovered that their comrade was dead, they rushed into the forecastle of their vessel, and refused to search for the body, believing that they who first beheld the corpse after being brought to the surface, would, sooner or later, meet a watery grave.

No person who understands the ancient customs of Scotland will think of commencing to make a new garment at the end of the year, if it cannot be finished before the new year comes in; nor will any one commence to make an article of clothing on Saturday, unless it can be ready for wearing on the Sunday. Friday is also an unlucky day for commencing any important undertaking. Some people refuse to be bled or physicked on a Friday. In certain parts of the country, Friday is the usual day for young men and women being united in wedlock, but at other places it is supposed bad luck would cleave to them during the whole of their lives if they were married on that day. It is believed by old crones that children born on Friday are doomed to misfortune. Friday night's dreams are sure to come true. It is well known, seamen dislike going to sea on Friday. Mr. Fenimore Cooper relates a very extraordinary anecdote in reference to Friday. He says:

"A wealthy merchant of Connecticut devised a notable scheme to give a fatal blow to the superstition of Friday being an unlucky day. He caused the keel of a very large ship to be laid on a Friday; he named her the 'Friday'; he launched her on a Friday; he gave the command of her to a captain whose name was Friday; and she commenced her first voyage on a Friday, bound for China with a costly cargo; and in all respects she was one of the noblest and best-appointed ships that ever left the port. The result was, neither ship nor crew was ever heard of afterwards. Thus his well-meant plan," adds Mr. Cooper, "so far from showing the folly of superstition, only confirmed seamen in their absurd belief."

Another instance may be given of a splendid ship sailing on a Friday being lost, as was supposed by the superstitious, through the imprudence of sending her to sea on the sixth day of the week. We refer to the West India steamer "Amazon," whose sad fate is a matter of history. Other examples might be given of ships beginning their voyages on Friday being lost; and, to the present time, sailors will tell you that more misfortunes happen to vessels leaving port on Friday than to ships departing on any other day of the week. Sailors consider Sunday a favourable day for commencing a voyage. They are averse to proceed to sea if a lawyer or clergyman is on board. They think the presence of one of these gentlemen raises a tempest that puts their craft in peril. This superstition is probably founded on the biblical story of Jonah in his flight to Tarshish, when such a mighty tempest was raised as to endanger the lives of those who manned the vessel that conveyed him from Joppa. Sailors are of opinion that it is lucky to have women or children on board a ship. Time was when they objected to sail with a native of Finland as one of the crew, thinking that the Finns were leagued with Satan, and that if they were offended, they took their revenge by raising adverse winds and causing accidents to happen. Old sailors objected to have dogs on board, but cats were held sacred; and if all tales be true, Puss often secured favourable winds, and prevented shipwreck. When rats are seen deserting a ship ready for sea, it is regarded as an evil omen. In calm weather, sailors whistle to raise the wind; but in a gale they neither whistle themselves, nor permit others to do so. It is unlucky to wear the clothes of a fellow-sailor who dies at sea before the termination of the voyage. It is thought unlucky to break up an old boat--a fact which accounts for so many useless boats being seen at fishing villages. If a man be drowned in or from a boat, sailors and fishermen are reluctant to put to sea again with her. It is an evil sign to see sharks following a ship. Inadvertently turning a hatch upside down, is considered an unfavourable sign. A four-footed beast should not be named at sea. A child's caul hung in the cabin, prevents the ship from sinking. A legend of Vanderdecken, the Flying Dutchman, is believed by seamen. It runs thus:--

Three hundred years ago a large Dutch Indiaman, commanded by Mynheer Vanderdecken, attempted to round the Cape of Good Hope against a head wind. His vessel was frequently driven back, but he doggedly persevered, in spite of many signs and warnings of failure, and declared that he would double the Cape, though he sailed till the day of judgment. For this impious saying, and disregard of signs and warnings, the ship and wicked captain, with his crew, were doomed to sail continually in the latitude of the Cape, without doubling it. Sailors have asserted that, in the midnight gale, the ship may be seen, with her antique build and rig, and the figure of Vanderdecken, on the poop, giving orders to his ghostly crew, contending with the wind and waves, which they can never overcome.

One day in the Middle Ages, as a troop of Condottieri crossed the Roman country, a young peasant, named Attendole, stood under an oak to admire them. Some of the soldiers invited him to join their company. The peasant was inclined to follow them, but being undecided he said, "I will throw the axe I hold in my hand against this oak, and if it enter far enough into the bark to remain fixed, I will be a soldier." So saying, he threw the axe with so much violence that it entered the tree deep and stuck fast. From that moment all hesitation was over: tearing himself from his friends, he joined the troop. Because it was with all his force he decided what his vocation was to be, his comrades called him Sforza. He fought in more than one hundred battles, and, after having served in Rome and at Milan, he at an advanced age perished while endeavouring to save one of his own pages from drowning. He left a son, who, like his father, gained renown. He rose so high in Italy as to be considered a suitable match for Bianca Visconti, the heiress of Milan. Their son Galeazza, Duke of Milan, used to look on the fair city and say, "See what I owe to my grandfather's axe!"

Warnings of approaching death are given in various ways. There are ancient families to whom the ghosts of their ancestors appear before the death of the chiefs or heads of the families. In one instance we have heard that the ghost of an old murdered lady keeps wandering through the castle halls shortly before any of the family dies; and in another instance it is said that a mysterious light blazes from the lofty battlements before the noble proprietor is laid low in death.

The falling of his portrait or statue is a sure presage of a great man's death. Archbishop Laud, going into his study (which no one could enter without him being present, as he invariably locked the door and kept the key), found his portrait one day lying on its face on the floor. He was extremely perplexed, for to him it was as his death knell, and he commenced setting his house in order. The sad summons was not long of coming, and death took him for its own.

AMULETS AND CHARMS.
CHAPTER XLV.

Amulets and Charms among the Chaldaeans, Jews, and   Persians--Amulets among the Greeks and   Romans--Ecclesiastics forbidden to wear Amulets and   Phylacteries--Amulets and Charms very   numerous--Pericles' Amulet--Lord Bacon's Opinion of   Charms--Cramp Rings and Eel Skins--Moss off a Dead   Man's Skull--How to remove Warts--Cure for St. Vitus'   Dance--Effect of Music--Kittens and Pigeons used as   Cures--Yawning and Laughing, Fear and Shame--Diseases   cured by Charms--Surprise a Cure for Hooping-cough--A Mad Dog's Bite--Touch of a Torpedo--Philosophers'   Opinions of Amulets--Bane and Antidote--Mr. E.   Chambers on Amulets--Poets on Enchantments--A Dairymaid's Charm--A Charm sent by a Pope to an   Emperor.

Amulets and charms were in great variety among the Chaldaeans, Jews, and Persians. They were also held in estimation among the Greeks and Romans, chiefly on account of their supposed virtue in exciting or conquering the passion of love. The Council of Laodicea forbade ecclesiastics to wear amulets and phylacteries, on pain of degradation. St. Jerome was likewise opposed to their use. Nevertheless, although amulets and charms are not held in the same repute they once were, their efficacy is not supposed to be entirely gone. Among early Christians amulets and charms were acknowledged to possess peculiar virtues beneficial to man. Amulets and charms were, and are, so numerous that it would be a herculean task to give an account of one half of them. Where the inhabitants were destitute of medical resources, amulets and charms were employed for the alleviation of bodily suffering. Pericles wore an amulet about his neck, as such charms were supposed to be capable of preserving the wearers from misfortune and disease. Lord Bacon was of opinion that if a man wore a planet seal, it might aid him in obtaining the affection of his sweetheart, give him protection at sea and in battle, and make him more courageous. Cramp rings and eel skins were worn round the limbs, to prevent sickness; and people were sometimes cured by laying sticks across each other in front of their beds at night. Moreover, the sticks thus placed prevented demons approaching the couch of rest. The moss off a dead man's skull, says the great Mr. Boyle, is an effectual remedy against bleeding at the nose. We are told by Lord Verulam, that when he was at Paris he had above one hundred warts on his hands, and that they were removed by the

English ambassador's lady rubbing them with a piece of bacon, afterwards nailed to a post. In five weeks the bacon, being exposed to the sun, melted away, and the warts disappeared.

St. Vitus' dance was cured by the sufferer visiting the tomb of the saint, near Ulm, every May. The bites of certain reptiles are rendered harmless by music. Dr. Sydenham orders, in cases of iliac passion, a live kitten to be laid on the abdomen. Pigeons, split alive and applied to the soles of the feet, are efficacious in fevers and convulsions. Quincey says that yawning and laughing are infectious, and so are fear and shame; and from these, by a system of reasoning peculiarly his own, he endeavours to prove that amulets may be sufficient to counteract, if not to entirely hinder, infection. Throughout the Mohammedan dominions the people were convinced that charms were indispensable to their well-being. By charms they cured every kind of disease, provided predestination had not determined that the sick man's days were at an end. Surprise, it is urged, removes the hooping-cough; looking from a precipice, or seeing a wheel turn swiftly, causes giddiness. "Why then," asks a wise man, "may not amulets or charms, by their secret influence, produce the effects ascribed to them? Who can comprehend by what impenetrable means the bite of a mad dog produces hydrophobia? Why does the touch of a torpedo induce numbness? When these causes and effects are explained," he concludes, "so may the virtue of amulets be accounted for." Ancient philosophers laid it down, as a proof of ignorance, the condemnation of a science not easily understood. In this way the advocates of amulets and charms have been enabled to silence people who have had the hardihood to throw odium on their superstitions. Believers in amulets and charms remind us that it is a well-ascertained fact in nature, that for every bane there is an antidote. Wherever the stinging nettle grows, the slimy stem of the dock is near; whenever the wasp stings, honey gathered by the industrious bee may be had, without going far, to put on the injured part; when the cold is most intense without, the fire burns brightest within; and if there be evil spirits seeking man's hurt, there are good angels hovering round him for his protection.

Mr. E. Chambers, who published his *Cyclopaedia, or A Universal Dictionary of Arts and Sciences*, in 1728, says that an amulet (*amuletum*) is a kind of medicament hung about the neck or other part of the body to prevent or remove diseases. Amulets, he proceeds, are frequently nothing else than spells or charms, consisting of quaint words and characters, supposed to have the virtue of warding off ill. And Mr. Chambers informs his readers, under the word "charm," that a charm is a magic power or spell, by which, with the assistance of the devil, sorcerers and witches are supposed to do wondrous things, far surpassing the power of nature.

Ancient poets, who were of a superstitious turn of mind, attached no small importance to amulets and charms. One of them says:

"Enchantments pluck out of the sky,
The moon though she be plac'd on high;
Dame Circe with her charms so fine,
Ulysses' mates did turn to swine:
The snake with charms is burst in twain,
In meadows where she doth remain.

* * * * *

> These herbs did Meris give to me,
> And poysons pluckt at Pontos,
> For there they grow and multiply,
> And do not so amongst us.
> With these she made herself become
> A wolf, and hid her in the wood;
> She fetched up souls out of the tombe,
> Removing corn from where it stood."

The following is an old translation from Virgil:

> "From thence a virgin priest is come
> From out Massyla land,
> Sometimes the temple there she kept,
> And from her heavenly hand
> The dragon meat did take: she kept
> Also the fruit divine,
> With herbs and liquors sweet that still
> To sleep did men incline.
> The minds of men (she saith) from love
> With charms she can unbind,
> In whom she list: but others can
> She cast to cases unkind.
> The running streams do stand, and from
> Their course the stars do wreath,
> And souls she conjure can: then shalt
> See sister underneath
> The ground with roring gape and trees,
> And mountains turn upright."

Ovid is made to say:

> "The river I can make retire
> Into the fountains whence they flow,
> (Where at the banks themselves admire)
> I can make standing waters go;
> With charms I drive both sea and cloud,

I can make it calm and blow aloud,
The viper's jaws, the rocky stone,
With words and charms I break in twain;
The force of earth congeal'd in one,
I move, and shake both woods and plain;
I make the souls of men arise,
And pull the moon out of the skies.

       * * * * *

And thrice she spake the words that caus'd
Sweet sleep and quiet rest;
She staid the raging of the sea,
And mighty floods supprest."

Other poets, writing of charms, say:

"With charms the corn is spoiled so
As that it vades the barren grass;
With charms the springs are dried low,
That none can see where water was.
The grapes from vines, the mast from oaks,
And beats down fruit with charming strokes.

       * * * * *

She plucks each star out of his throne,
And turneth back the raging waves;
With charms she makes the earth to cone,
And raises souls out of their graves:
She burns men's bones as with fire,
And pulleth down the lights from heaven,
And makes it snow at her desire,
Even in the midst of summer season.

       * * * * *

The course of nature ceased quite,
The air obeyed not his law,
The day delayed by length of night,

Which made both day and night to yaw;
And all was through that charming gear,
Which caus'd the world to quake for fear.

* * * * *

They talked with tongues of birds,
Consulting with the salt sea coasts,
They burst the snake with witching words,
Soliciting the spiritual ghosts;
They turn the night into the day,
And also drive the light away:
And what is 't that cannot be made
By them that do apply this trade."

Sir Thomas Brown mentions that a chalked tile at each corner of a
field and one in the centre thereof were rural charms that prevented
weeds growing; and the three following charms are given in Herrick's
Hesperides:

"This I'le tell ye by the way,
Maidens when ye leavens lay,
Cross your dough, and your dispatch
Will be better for your batch.

In the morning when ye rise,
Wash your hands and cleanse your eyes,
Next be sure to have a care
To disperse the water farre,
For as farre as that doth light,
So farre keeps the evil spright.

If ye fear to be affrighted,
When ye are (by chance) benighted;
In your pocket for a trust
Carry nothing but a crust;
For that holy piece of bread
Charms the danger and the dread."

Here are older charms in metre:

"With blessynges of Saynt Germayne
I will me so determyne,
That neyther for nor vermyne
Shall do my chyckens harme.
For your gese seke Saynt Legearde,
And for your duckes Saynt Leonarde,
There is no better charme.

Take me a napkin folte
With the byas of a bolte,
For the healing of a colte
No better thynge can be;
For lampes and for bottes
Take me Saynt Thomas Lattes,
On my life I warrande ye."

In the **Hesperides** we also find the following spell:

"Holy water come and bring:
Cast in salt for seasoning:
Set the brush for sprinkling.

Sacred spittle bring ye hither:
Meale and it now mix together,
And a little oyle to either.

Give the tapers here their light;
Ring the saints' bell to affright
Far from hence the evil sprits.

And good Saynt Francis' gyrdle,
With the hamlet of a hyrdle,
Are wholesome for the pyppe.

Besides these charms afore
I have feates many more
That kepe still in store,
Whom I now over hyppe."

The same writer quaintly says:

> "A charm or an allay for love,
> If so be a toad be laid
> In a sheep-skin newly flaid,
> And that ty'd to man, 'twill sever
> Him and his affections ever."

Butler, in his **Hudibras**, describes the supposed power of a cunning man thus:

> "Not far from hence doth dwell
> A cunning man hight Sidrophel,
> That deals in destiny's dark counsels,
> And sage opinion of the moon sells;
> To whom all people, far and near,
> On deep importances repair;
> When brass and pewter hap to stray,
> And linen slinks out of the way;
> When geese and pullen are seduced,
> And sows of sucking pigs are chows'd;
> When cattle feel indisposition,
> And need the opinion of physician;
> When murrain reigns in hogs or sheep
> And chickens languish of the pip;
> When yeast and outward means do fail,
> And have no power to work on ale;
> When butter does refuse to come,
> And love proves cross and humoursome;
> To him with questions and with urine
> They for discovery flock, or curing."

In the seventeenth century, dairymaids, when churning, used a charm, said over the churn in the following lines:

> "Come, butter, come,
> Come, butter, come;
> Peter stands at the gate,
> Waiting for a buttered cake,
> Come, butter, come."

This having been said three times, the butter came straightway; and very good butter it was, on the good saint being invoked.

A holy Pope of the good old times sent the following lines to an exalted Emperor:

"Balme, Virgine-wax, and holy water,
    An Agnus Dei make,
A gift than which none can be greater,
    I send thee for to take.

From fountain clear the same hath issue
    In secret sanctified;
'Gainst lightning it hath soverain virtue,
    And thunder-cracks beside.

Each hainous sin it wears and wasteth,
    Even as holy precious blood;
And women while their travel lasteth
    It saves, it is so good.

It doth bestow great gifts and graces
    On such as well deserve;
And borne about in noisome places,
    From peril doth preserve.

The force of fire, whose heat destroyeth,
    It breaks and bringeth down;
And he or she that this enjoyeth
    No water shall them drown."

CHAPTER XLVI.

Ear-rings buried by Jacob--Solomon's Belief in Spells--Reginald Scot's Recipe for preserving Cattle--What Mr. Pennant says on Charms--Parts of the Chameleon as Charms--A Condemned Sorcerer's Charm--Virtue of Trees and Plants--Deities' Crowns--Virtue of May Dew--Images Powerful Charms--How the Romans regarded their Images--The Egyptians' Confidence in Amulets and Charms--Evil Eye--Effects of an Evil Eye, how counteracted--Charms for Horses and Children--Sixpence-piece an Excellent Charm--Mothers and Children protected from Fairies--Cold Iron--Holy Things used as Charms--Filings of St. Peter's Keys--Lustral Water--Curing Sick Children by weighing them--Uses of Snow--Transferring Diseases from one Body to another--Keys of a Consecrated Building--Effect of standing on one Foot--Virtue of Consecrated Bread--Virtue rewarded--Pricking the Image of a King--Various Methods of securing Love--Indian Charms--Cure for Corns--Simple Plan for getting rid of a Troublesome Person--Curing the Hooping-cough.

There are people in existence, of opinion that the ear-rings which Jacob buried under the oak of Sechem were charms, and that Solomon had recourse to spells after his strange wives led him away from the true faith. Reginald Scot gives a recipe for a charm to preserve cattle from witchcraft. Here it is: "At Easter you must take certain drops that lie uppermost of the holy paschal candle; and upon some Sunday morning, light and hold it so as it may drop upon and between the horns and ears of the beast, and burn the beast a little between the horns on the ears with the same wax, and that which is left thereof stick it cross-wise about the stable or stall, or upon the threshold, or over the door, where the cattle go in and out; and for all that year your cattle shall never be touched."

Mr. Pennant says: "The farmers of Scotland preserve their cattle against witchcraft by placing boughs of mountain-ash and honey-suckle in their cow-houses on the 2nd May. They hope to preserve the milk of their cows and of their wives by tying red threads about them." The ancients had several superstitious customs touching the chameleon,--as that its tongue, torn out when the animal was alive, would assist the possessor to gain his law-suits; burning its head and neck with oak-wood, or roasting its liver on a red tile, would bring thunder and rain; that its right eye, torn out before the animal was slain, and steeped in goat's milk, removed disease of the eye; that its tongue, worn as a charm by a married woman, eased her pains; that its right jaw dispelled fear; and that its tail prevented streams overflowing their banks. A famous sorcerer, when under sentence of death, gave directions how to prepare a potent charm. It consisted of a new earthen pot--not bought nor bargained for--with sheep's blood, wool, hair of several beasts, and certain herbs therein. The pot and its contents were to be placed in a secret part in the neighbourhood where its effects were intended to be felt, which might be either the poisoning or tormenting of enemies. The charm could not be taken away but by the person who secreted it or by a superior power.

Particular trees and plants possess peculiar virtues in consequence of crowns for deities having been made from them. Thus we find Jupiter's crown was composed of flowers, generally of laurel; Juno's of the vine; Bacchus' of the vine, with grapes, and branches of ivy, flowers, and berries; those of Castor, Pollux, and the river gods, of bulrushes; that of Apollo, sometimes of laurel, and sometimes rushes; that of Saturn, new figs; that of Hercules, poplar; that of Pan, pine or alder; that of Lucina, dictamnus; that of the Horae, the fruits proper to each season; that of the Graces, olive branches; that of Venus, roses; that of Ceres, ears of corn; and that of the Lares, myrtle or rosemary. Rue was detested by witches and evil spirits. There was a heathen ceremony, called Dendrophoria, which consisted of the carrying of one or more pine trees through a city, at times of sacrifice in honour of certain deities. The pine or pines were afterwards planted, and the branches thereof were supposed to possess virtues not to be found in non-sacred things.

There was a spirit drawn from May dew, which had striking virtues attributed to it. Images were considered the most powerful of all charms. They were held in great reverence by the Romans and other nations. The noble Romans preserved the images of their ancestors with great care, and had them carried in procession at their funerals and triumphs. They placed them in the vestibules of their houses, there to remain, even though the houses happened to be sold, it being considered impious to displace them. It was not, however, allowed for every one who had the images of their ancestors, to have them carried at funerals. The privilege was conferred on those only who had honourably discharged themselves in their various offices in life. Persons who failed in this respect, forfeited all right to bring their images before the public; and the images of persons who had committed serious crimes were broken in pieces.

The Egyptians had great confidence in the power of amulets and charms to prevent and deliver from mischief. There was a class of persons who gained their livelihood by writing billets, to secure the wearers from the power of enchantment and all kinds of accidents. Their most intrinsically valuable relic was the veil sent to the Sultan to cover the Kaaba of Mecca. It was cut in pieces, and distributed over the whole empire. Parts of it were worn by the faithful, as one of the means of grace, and an assurance of divine protection; and these charms were sometimes buried in the grave along with the individuals who had prized them when in life.

The belief of the baneful effect of the evil eye, and of envious commendations, was prevalent in the East. Virgil's shepherd attributed to the malicious glance of an enemy the diseased appearance of his flock. Pliny relates that the Thessalian sorcerers destroyed whole harvests by speaking well of the crops. In Egypt, everything which could possibly attract attention or excite jealousy was protected by some counteracting influence. The eye of the malicious observer was rendered harmless by a sacred sentence, written in conspicuous characters, and placed in a particular way that the wicked eye might see it. The horse, it was believed, carried his rider in safety if a charm of blue beads dangled from the animal's neck. But the anxious mother did not consider her darling child safe, though it had a charm about its person, unless she frequently spat in its face.

When a mother had reason to suppose an evil eye had been cast on her little helpless babe, her duty was to borrow a sixpence from a neighbour, put it into a basin of water, and then wash the child with the water so charmed. By these means the spell was removed. To pass a child over a table was unlucky. Great apprehensions were formerly entertained of the malignant influence and interference of fairies with mothers in child-bed and children unbaptized. A Bible under the pillow protected the mother, or a bottle of holy water at the bed-foot did equally well; and the sacrament of baptism rendered the infant secure from fairies and witches. If one meet or see anything unlucky, all he has to do to avert evil is to touch cold iron. To prevent evil in time of a thunder-storm, let a candle be kept burning until the warring elements have ceased raging. And surely it has not been left for us to tell the good Catholics, that, to extinguish a fire or stop an inundation, their forefathers threw a consecrated wafer into the midst of the flames or overflowing river. Every little Catholic maid, who can count her beads, knows that if she cannot secure the affections of the young man on whom she has set her affections, she should unsparingly besmear him with the holy oil of her Church. We are assured that, before Protestantism weakened the hands of priests and rent the Church asunder, consecrated oil was regarded as an infallible charm and love-philter.

It was the custom at one time for the Popes to send a golden key to faithful priests, wherein was enclosed a small quantity of the filings of St. Peter's keys, kept sacred at Rome. These charms were worn in the bosom, to protect the happy possessor from disease, misfortune, and evil spirits.

The ancients had their lustral water for sprinkling and purifying the people. From them the Romanists borrowed the holy water used in their churches. The ancients called *Dies Lustricus*, or Lustral Day, that whereon the lustrations were performed for a child, and its name given, which was the ninth day from the birth of a boy, and the eighth from that of a girl. Lustral water possessed something like magical virtue. On the great day of ceremony the nurses and domestics handed the child backwards and forwards around a fire on the altars of the gods; after this the infant was sprinkled with the precious water, mixed with saliva and dust. There were public lustrations for purifying cities, fields, and people defiled by crime or impurity. A custom prevailed in the East, of curing sick children by weighing them at the tomb of a saint. The counterpoising or balancing medium consisted of money to be given to the Church.

It was generally supposed that the first snow which fell in the year had particular virtues. Bartholin wrote a treatise on the uses of snow, wherein he endeavoured to show that early gathered snow preserved from the plague, cured fevers, toothache, and sore eyes. In Denmark the people kept snow water, obtained in March, as a medicine.

Transplantation in natural magic was a method resorted to for curing diseases by transferring them from one body to another. The transplantation was effected either by the use of a medium or by simple contact. If a gouty person desire to get rid of his troubles, he is recommended to bore a hole in an oak, and deposit the parings of his nails therein; and if one has whitlow in his finger, the pain might be transferred to the domestic cat by rubbing the sore finger with the ears of the animal.

The keys of a consecrated building, shaken over the heads of dogs, horses, and cattle, when they are ill, effect a cure; and a faithful worshipper finds relief from acute suffering by standing on one foot and holding a wax taper in his hand, during particular portions of the mass. It is common in some places to lay upon the altar, during mass, the nails of a shoe taken from a horse which has become lame, to restore the animal to soundness. Pieces of consecrated bread carried home and preserved is a preventative against the bite of a mad dog. The shepherd who first gives his offering will be rewarded by his ewes bringing forth the finest lambs in the neighbourhood; and the horses and cattle that are watered immediately after the owners or keepers return from mass, will be saved from illness.

In 1589 the people placed on the altars of many of their churches in Paris, wax effigies of King Henry III., and pricked them with pins and needles during mass, in the hope of obtaining a speedy termination to his existence.

The wearing of a ribbon which has been worn by a lady, or a lock of her hair, near the heart, is supposed to be capable of securing her affections. But if everything else fail, the proper application of dead men's bones, holy relics, and magic spells will soften the hard heart.

It is related by the Indians of Vixnu, that a ribbon tied round the neck or arm, with the name "Laximi" (who for many years was worshipped under the form of a cow, and sometimes of a horse) written thereon or attached thereto, is a certain cure for all diseases; and is likewise a preventative against accidents. Corns are cured by one stealing a small piece of beef and burying it in the ground. As the flesh rots, the corns disappear. Whenever either an enemy or friend becomes troublesome, and it is considered necessary to get rid of him, the desire can be accomplished by securing a garment belonging to him and burying it in the earth. Just as sure as the burying of the beef destroys corns, as certain will the concealment of the garment in the earth send the obnoxious person to his long home. Fond mothers endeavoured to cure hooping-cough by passing their afflicted children three times before breakfast under a blackberry bush the branches of which grew into the ground; other parents went out into the highways in search of a man riding on a piebald horse, to ask him what would restore to health their children affected with this painful cough. Whatever he recommended, was adopted as a remedy.

CHAPTER XLVII.

Horse Shoes used as Charms--Spitting on Money to   secure Luck--Fortunate Persons to deal with--Methods   of securing Cattle against Accidents--Effect of Herbs--Professor Playfair on Superstition--The Lee   Penny--How to prevent Toothache--Divers Charms--A   Seer's Prescription--Lating the Witches--Grose on   Sorcerers, Magicians, and Witches--Man carried away by   an Evil Spirit--Irish Shamrock--Praying to   Swords--Irish Superstition--Smugglers and Brigands   addicted to Superstition--Charm found on a   Smuggler--Superstition in the East--Arab   Charms--Ladies' Arts.

Horse shoes have long been regarded as most valuable charms. Such shoes, nailed on the back of doors, keep out witches and evil spirits. Horse shoes are also safe-guards on board of ships and boats. To secure good luck in a market, the vendor is in the habit of rubbing or spitting on the first money obtained for goods sold. The good or bad luck of cattle-salesmen and petty merchants, superstitious people think, depends very much on the first purchaser. In the early part of the day a reduced price is sometimes accepted from a person reputed to be lucky, while business will not be entered into under any conditions with uncanny people.

In Suffolk an abortive calf is buried under the path along which the cows go to the fields, to prevent them being accidentally injured. One description of herb given to a horse prevents the horse-shoer pricking the animal's feet; and another, put into a man's shoes, enables him to travel more than forty miles a day without becoming wearied. Moon-wort is a powerful charm that loosens locks, fetters, and shoes from horses' feet. In olden times it was a stratagem in warfare to lead the enemy's horsemen upon a heath where moon-wort grew plentiful, for, in passing over it, the horses were sure to lose their shoes. In Aristotle's time, rue hung about the neck as an amulet prevented witchcraft. Rue was called an herb of grace, because the Romanists used it on Sundays in their exorcisms.

Professor Playfair, in a letter to Mr. Brand, dated from St. Andrews, in 1804, says: "In private breweries a live coal was thrown into the vat, to prevent the interference of the fairies. A cow's milk no fairy could take away, if a burning coal was conducted across her back and under the belly immediately after she calved. Witches and evil spirits were prevented from entering a dwelling-house if the lower end of the crook or iron chain by which the pots were suspended over the kitchen fire was raised up a few links before the inmates retired to bed. It was a common opinion in Scotland

and England, that a woman may, by means of charms, convey her neighbour's cow's milk to her own dairy. When a cow's milk was charmed away, a small quantity of rennet was taken from all suspected persons and put into an egg-shell full of milk, and when that obtained from the charmer mingled with it, it presently curdled. Some women used the root of groundsel as a protection against the produce of their dairy being charmed, by putting it among their milk and cream."

The Lee Penny, the property of a Scotch gentleman, was a charm known far and wide. Many were the cures effected by it, *i.e.* if tradition speaks true. This charm, when applied externally to man or beast, proved better than all known healing medicine, and, when water in which it had been dipped was given to man or beast to drink, it produced an effectual cure. Nails driven into an oak tree prevented toothache. A halter that had been used in suspending a criminal, when tied round the head, prevented headache. A dead man's hand dissipated tumours of the glands, by stroking the affected part nine times with it; but the hand of a man who had been hanged was the most efficacious. Chips cut from a gallows, when carried in a bag suspended from the neck, cured the ague. A stone with a hole in it, tied to the key of a stable door, deterred witches stealing the horses and riding them over the country at night. If a man or woman were afflicted with fits, he or she might be cured by partaking of broth in which a human skull had been boiled. This last-mentioned cure was not uncommon in the beginning of the present century.

A young girl, about sixteen years of age, being seized with fits, a seer was consulted, and he prescribed brose made from oatmeal and the "broo of a dead man's skull." That a cranium might be obtained, a grave was violated, and a body mutilated. The brose was prepared according to directions, and given to the afflicted girl. As might be expected, the matter created no small excitement in Perthshire, in which county the superstitious acts were perpetrated; but though the whole affair was looked on with disapproval by the better educated classes, and proceedings were taken by the authorities against the guilty parties, the death knell of superstition was not rung; for in that county a belief in witches, spirits, and charms still exists.

At one time a custom prevailed in Lancashire, called "lating the witches." It was observed on the eve preceding the 1st November, when witches were supposed to be busier than usual. The ceremony of lating was gone through in this way:--The poorer neighbours called at the houses of the more opulent, and at the door demanded lighted candles to carry in procession. We say demanded them at the door, because it would have been unlucky for those receiving the candles to cross a threshold then, and it would have been equally unlucky for any one of them to enter a house that night from which his or her candle was received, if the light was extinguished before the lating was concluded. Candles were given out according to the number of inmates of a house--one for every person--but it was optional for one to carry his own candle, or to find a substitute who would sally out for him to frighten the witches. The custom originated in the belief that if a lighted candle were carried about from eleven to twelve o'clock at night without being extinguished, the person it represented would be proof against witches during the year, but if the candle went out it foreboded evil.

Grose, in describing the difference between a sorcerer, magician, and witch, speaks highly of the power of charms and invocations. "A witch," he tells us, "derives all her power from a compact with the devil, while a sorcerer commands him and the infernal spirits by his skill in charms and invocations, and also soothes and entices them by fumigations; for the devils," he continues, "are observed to have delicate nostrils, abominating and flying from some kinds of stinks. Witness the flight of the evil spirits into the remote parts of Egypt, driven by the smell of fishes' liver burned by Tobit. The devil and spirits," he tells us, "are, on the other hand, peculiarly fond of certain perfumes."

Lilly writes that one Evans, having raised a spirit, at the request of Lord Bothwell and Sir K. Digby, and forgotten a suffumigation, the spirit, enraged, snatched him out from his circle, and carried him from his house in the Minories into a field near Battersea.

The shamrock is held sacred by the Irish. It became a custom among Irish soldiers, when going to battle, to conceal about their persons bunches of shamrock, to say certain prayers to their swords, to make crosses upon the earth, and thrust the points of their weapons into the ground, under the impression that by so doing they would secure success in the field. The shamrock was highly esteemed by lovers. An exchange of this plant frequently took place between betrothed persons in the same way as engagement rings are exchanged in our time. In Ireland many people continue to put faith in incantations and spells. Women's hair is thought to be a precious amulet; hence the custom of wearing hair bracelets, guards, and other such like ornaments.

Smugglers and brigands are much addicted to superstition. On the apprehension of one Jackson, a smuggler, who died in Chichester, there was found in his possession a linen purse containing the following charm:

> "Ye three holy kings,
> Gaspar, Melchior, Balthasar,
> Pray for us now and at the hour of death."

The charm had actually touched the heads of three kings at Cologne, and was thought by the smuggler to be an effectual protection against accidents, headaches, falling sickness, witchcraft, and various kinds of mischief. Jackson died suddenly, but this did not prove the charm to be worthless, as he lost it before his end came.

Various nations in the East entertained superstitious opinions concerning serpents and reptiles. They attributed numberless powers of good and evil to these reptiles. A belief prevailed, that if one killed a snake, the whole race to which it belonged would persecute the cruel individual. When any one was bitten by a serpent, a sovereign remedy was found in a particular stone. Such valuable stones were rare, and consequently they were greatly prized, even, more so than gold.

Arabs believed that the smoke of burnt hair taken from a Christian's head would cure a patient, whatever the disease was under which he laboured. They also wore enchanted rings, and carried herbs to strengthen their arms in the day of battle.

A young lady thought she could discover the social position and character of her future husband, by pulling large flower and taking off the leaves and petals one by one, while she repeated,

"Rich man, poor man, farmer, ploughman, thief."

The one who happened to be named at plucking the last leaf or petal was, she supposed, to be her husband. Another way: pluck an even ash leaf, and keep it in the hand, saying,

"The even ash leaf in my hand,
The first I meet shall be my man;"

then put the leaf into the glove, and say,

"The even ash leaf in my glove,
The first I meet shall be my love;"

and then put it into the bosom, and repeat,

"The even ash leaf in my bosom,
The first I meet shall be my husband."

Immediately after this the future husband will make his appearance.

Another method: After nightfall the sighing maiden may walk through
the garden with a rake in her left hand, and throw hemp seed over her
right shoulder while she keeps repeating,

"Hemp seed I set, hemp seed I sow,
The man that is my true love come after me and mow."

Sure enough, we are assured, the future husband will appear beside the
fair sower with a scythe, ready to cut down the crop when it grows.

We are further assured that a lady would succeed quite as well, were
she, on going to bed, to place her shoes so as to form the letter T,
and say,

"Hoping this night my true love to see,
I place my shoes in the form of a T;"

or were she, on retiring for the night, to write the alphabet on small pieces of paper, and put
them into a basin of water, with the letters downwards,--in the former case she would in her dreams
perceive her future husband, and in the latter she might expect to find, in the morning, the first letter of his name turned upwards, and all the other letters downwards, as she had left them.

CHAPTER XLVIII.

Earl of Derby's Death--A Queen Enchanted--Image of a   young King made for Wicked Purposes--Belgrave on   Charms--Childebert's Device for detecting Witches--A   Pot of Ointment--Witch Burned--Witch   Ointment--Men-Wolves--Component Parts of Witch   Ointment--Church Authorities' Instructions to   Inquisitors--Killing by a Look or Wish--The King of   Sweden and his Witches--Witches' Help in War--Witches   causing a Plague--Cattle Poisoned--Various Charms--How   to make Hair grow Long and Yellow--Holy Vestments--An   Angel's Charm to Pope Leo--Physicians' Faith in   Charms--Illusions--Inescation--Insemination--Method of   discovering if one is Bewitched--Egyptian Laws--Curing   the King's Evil.

Andrews, in his continuation of Henry's *History of Great Britain*, speaking of Ferdinand, Earl of Derby, says his death was attributed to witchcraft. No doubt the disease appeared to be peculiar. After his death a wax image with hair, in colour like that of the earl, was found in his chamber, which confirmed the suspicions entertained as to the cause of his demise. Another alleged atrocious crime was that of the wife of Marshal D'Ancre. She was beheaded for witchcraft, in so far as she had enchanted the queen, and made an image of the young king in virgin wax, and melted away one of its legs that he might become a cripple. Old Belgrave, in his *Astrological Practice of Physic*, observes: "Under adverse planets, and by Satan's subtlety, witches injured man and beast by making images or models of them, and pricking the likenesses with thorns, pins, or needles."

Childebert's device for detecting witches who dealt in charms, was to torture them by putting sharp instruments betwixt every nail of their fingers and toes. Judges, before whom witches were tried, were cautioned not to allow them to come near their persons nor the seat of judgment. That they might be all the more secure from witchcraft, judges kept suspended from their necks conjured salt, palm, holy herbs, and wax hallowed by the Church. To compel witches to confess their guilt, officers of justice were wont to write the seven words spoken on the cross, and cause these, with relics of saints, to be hung round the culprits' necks. When these charms were thus applied, it was impossible for witches to refrain from confessing their guilt, if at the same time they were sufficiently racked and tortured.

An incredible story is told of a gentlewoman in Lyons, who possessed a pot of ointment of such rare virtue, that the application of it to one's body proved sufficient to transport the individual, in an instant, through the air to distant towns and countries. The lady being one evening in a room with her lover, anointing herself with part of the ointment, and repeating words in an under tone, was in the twinkling of an eye carried away through the air. Her companion, though astonished and somewhat alarmed, did as he had observed his fair friend do, and *presto* he was conveyed away many miles to an assembly of witches. Afraid at what he beheld, he uttered a holy ejaculation. In an instant the assembly vanished, leaving him alone. He returned on foot to Lyons, and brought an accusation of witchcraft against his lover. The charge being proven, the woman, with her ointment, was consigned to the flames.

Witches and warlocks, learned in the art of transubstantiation, could by means of witch ointment turn themselves into wolves. Peter Burget and Michael Worden, having by means of such ointment turned themselves into wolves, killed and ate a large number of people. One night, when the men-wolves were out on one of their murderous expeditions, an archer shot one of them with a charmed arrow. Tracing the wounded creature to Peter's residence, the pursuers found the luckless man in bed in his natural shape, with the arrow deep in his thigh. Another man-wolf was punished by having his feet amputated, and in a moment he became a man without hands or feet.

Mountain parsley, wolves-bane, leaves of the poplar, and soot were frequently used in the preparation of witch ointment; and so were yellow water-cresses, the blood of a mouse, night-shade, oil, etc. A witch, rubbed all over with a preparation of these, could skim through the air in a moonlight night, singing, dancing, and otherwise making merry with her companions.

So generally did the belief in witchcraft, incantations, and charms prevail in the time of Pope Innocent VIII. and of Pope Julius II., that the Church authorities sent to the inquisitors the following official notice and instructions:--"It has come to our ears that many lewd persons of both kinds, as well male as female, using the company of the devils *Incubus* and *Succubus*, with incantations, charms, conjurations, etc., to destroy the births of women with child, the young of all cattle, the corn of the field, the grapes of the vines, the fruit of the trees; also men, women, and cattle of all kinds, and beasts of the field; and with their said enchantments, etc., do utterly extinguish and spoil all vineyards, orchards, meadows, pastures, grass, green corn, and ripe corn: yea, men and women themselves are by their imprecations so afflicted with external and internal pains and diseases that the births of children are but few: Our pleasure therefore is, that all impediments that may hinder the inquisitors' office be utterly removed from among the people, lest this blot of heresy proceed to poison and defile them that may yet be innocent: And therefore we ordain, by virtue of the apostolical authority, that our inquisitors may execute the office of inquisition by all tortures and afflictions, in all places, and upon all persons, what and wheresoever, as well in every place and diocese as upon any person; and that as freely as though they were named, expressed, or cited in this our commission."

Witches have confessed their power to kill a neighbour by a word, a wish, or a look.

In the wars between the kings of Denmark and Sweden, in 1563, the Danes wrote that the King of Sweden carried about with him in camp four old witches, who with their charms so affected the Danes that they were thereby unable to annoy their enemies. One of the witches, on being taken prisoner, confessed her guilt.

The West Indians, Muscovites, and Huns sought the help of witches in time of war.

A band of witches in Italy, in 1536, renewed a plague, then almost ceased, by besmearing with an ointment and a powder the posts and doors of men's houses. One of the wicked old hags having been apprehended and examined, confessed the fact. The like villany was perpetrated elsewhere about the same time. Weeping and lamentation were heard in every dwelling for fathers stricken down by death; but, strange to say, the women escaped injury. Cattle were killed through wolves' dung being hidden in stalls and among the pasture where they fed. The stench caused the animals to refrain from eating, and made them run about as if they were mad.

Witches highly prized, and frequently used in their nefarious art, the hair growing on the end of a wolf's tail, the brain of a cat, the head of a lizard, the bone of a green frog from which the flesh had been eaten by ants. One bone of a frog engendered love, while another bone caused hatred.

Garments of the dead, candles that had burned before a stiffened corpse, and needles wherewith dead bodies had been sewn in sheets, were precious in the eyes of cunning persons.

Witches and magicians had power, by means of charms, to put into the minds and consciences of men such thoughts as they pleased; and, moreover, they could induce people to disclose their heart secrets.

Maids hung up a quantity of their hair before the image of St. Urbane, trusting that by so doing their hair would grow long and yellow.

A holy vest was at times given by the Pope to a faithful son of Mother Church, to protect him from violence of every description. The manner of making a charmed waistcoat is thus explained:--On Christmas night, flax thread was spun by a virgin girl, and afterwards woven by her. After the garment was sewn by the same little hands which had spun the thread and woven the cloth, two figures in needlework were wrought on it to resemble Beelzebub and the Cross. One of these vestments gave the wearer courage in the hour of danger: witches were unable to harm him, bullets could not hit him, the sword's edge was turned aside, and the pointed spear levelled against him proved harmless.

Leo, Pope of Rome, reported that an angel delivered to him the following holy writing--a charm of inestimable value, as we shall presently learn:--"+ Jesus, + Christus, + Messias, + Soter, + Emmanuel, + Sabbath, + Adonii, + Unigenitus, + Majestas, + Paracletus, + Salvator Noster, + Agiros Iskiros, + Agios, + Adonatos, + Gasper, + Melchior, + Mattheus, + Marcus, + Lucas, + Johannes." The angel, so said Leo, directed him to take it to King Charles when he went to the battle of Roncesvalles. Moreover, the holy messenger said that whatever man or woman carried a copy of this writing, and every day said three paternosters, three aves, and one creed, would not be overcome by enemies, either bodily or ghostly; nor would the person thus protected be robbed, or slain by thieves, pestilence, thunder, or lightning; neither would he be hurt by fire or water.

By the writings of various authors, we gather that both the physician and priest placed a high value on amulets, charms, and incantations. Argerius Ferrarius, a celebrated physician, expressed the opinion that physic might benefit a patient to a certain degree, but that, to complete a cure, the application of amulets, charms, and characters was desirable. He cited many cases that came under his own observation and that of other physicians. Galen expressed the opinion that charms prevented bones sticking in people's throats.

Physicians skilled in magic applied three seeds of three-leaved grass to tertian ague, and four to a quartian. Of Homerical medicines, Argerius Ferrarius writes there are four sorts, whereof amulets, characters, and charms are three; but he commends and prefers the fourth, which, he says, consists in illusions or stratagems. He tells how Philodotus put a cap of lead upon one's head who imagined he was headless, whereby the person was freed from his delusion. Another cured a woman, under the impression that a serpent continually gnawed her entrails, by giving her a vomit, and making her believe that she vomited a little serpent.

A man who imagined that he was always burning in a fire, had his illusion dispelled by seeing fire taken out from beneath his bed. Great stress is put on the alleged fact that hiccough is cured by sudden fear or startling news, and that agues and many other diseases may be removed by excitement.

Inescation is a curious method practised for the cure of certain diseases. The cure may be effected by impregnating a proper medium or vehicle with some of the mumia or vital spirit of the patient, and giving it to an inferior animal to swallow. It is pretended that the animal unites and assimilates the mumia with itself, and imbibes its vicious qualities, and by that means restores health to the person to whom the mumia belonged.

Insemination is a cure, in certain respects, not unlike to that of inescation. It is performed by mixing the medium, impregnated with the mumia taken from the patient, with earth wherein has been sown the seed of a plant appropriate to the disease; but care must be taken to sprinkle it from time to time with water wherein the part affected had been washed. The disease, we are told, becomes less virulent as the plant grows.

By pouring molten lead into water held above a sick man, it could be discovered whether he was bewitched. If his illness arose from wicked and cruel tormentors, his image appeared in the lead; but if the disease resulted from natural causes, no distinct impression remained on the lead.

Montaigne says that it was an Egyptian law that the physician should for the first three days take charge of his patient at the patient's own peril, but afterwards at his own. He mentions that, in his time, physicians gave their pills in odd numbers, appointed remarkable days in the year for taking medicine, and gathered their simples at certain hours.

The mode of curing the King's Evil, or scrofula, by royal touch, has been so often referred to by various writers that we might well pass it without notice, were it not that our object is to bring together in these pages the many varied particulars of ancient superstition. Consequently we shall briefly describe the ceremonies gone through when sick persons were brought before the king. Let us premise, in the first place, that all parties are neither agreed as to the time nor the sovereign who first applied his royal hand to this method of healing disease. The kings of England and France long pretended to possess the power of curing scrofula by touching the sore. The right or faculty, the French people say, existed originally in their monarch; but the English nation would not admit this, and claimed the power for their king. In support of England's claim, monkish writers assert that the virtue was inherent in our kings as early as the days of Edward the Confessor. Others will have it that King Robert first exhibited the miraculous gift. Charles VIII. of France touched several persons at Rome, and cured them. At whatever time the power first manifested itself is of little importance; and through whatever royal line it descended need not trouble those alive, seeing, we are assured, the virtue perished with the last British sovereign of the House of Stuart. But, to return to the manner of curing the king's evil, we shall give, as an instance, the method pursued by Charles II. of England, Scotland, and Ireland, when healing any of his subjects:--

On 14th May 1664 a notice was given that his sacred Majesty would continue the healing of his people for the evil during the remainder of that month, and then cease doing so until Michaelmas. His Majesty sat in state in the banqueting house, and the chirurgeons led the sick to the throne; there, the invalids kneeling, the monarch stroked their bodies with his hands. The ceremony being concluded, a chaplain in attendance said, "He put his hands upon them, and healed them." These words were repeated as every one was touched. After all the diseased persons were operated on, another chaplain, kneeling, delivered gold angels, attached to white ribbons, to his Majesty, who suspended one about the neck of every one to whom his healing virtue had gone forth. Prayers being said for the sick, the ceremony concluded by his Majesty washing his hands in a basin brought to him by the lord chamberlain and comptroller of the household.

If a monarch could not be found to cure the king's evil, it might have been effected by the touch of a seventh son, between whom and his eldest brother no daughter had come to swell the family circle. And the virtue of healing by laying on of hands existed in particular noble families of untainted blood.

CHAPTER XLIX.

Precious Stones regarded as Objects of uncommon   Virtue--Extravagance in Jewellery accounted   for--Significance in relation to Gems--Abraham's   Precious Stones--Altars called Living Stones--The Urim   and Thummim--Rod of Moses--Charmed Rings--Sacred Rings   and Belts--Sacred Cairns, etc.--Destiny and Fate--The   Month of one's Nativity has connection with one or   other of the Precious Stones--Examples adduced--Kings   of England hallowing Rings--Ring preserved in   Westminster Abbey--Cramp Rings--Various Stones of   great Virtue--Iona Relics--The Green Stone of Arran--A   Crystal kept by ancient Priests as a Charm--A   Conjuring Beryl--Prophetic Stones--The Coronation   Stone or Stone of Destiny.

From an early period of history man has regarded precious stones as objects of uncommon virtue. A belief in their excellence has prevailed among Pagans, Jews, and Christians down to the present period. Extravagance in jewellery originated not so much from a love of finery as from a belief that jewels possessed efficacy or power peculiar to themselves. When we consider that every gem is supposed to be an amulet, we cannot be surprised at hearing of people in distant lands wearing jewels on their fingers and toes, on their ankles and arms, in their noses and ears, and even in their lips; nor can we be astonished at seeing in modern times the weaker sex loaded with rings, bracelets, pendants and other such articles, studded with precious stones.

As a language of flowers is known among botanists, so there is a significance in relation to gems, understood by the credulous. Every stone has its virtue, at least so we are told, as surely as every light and shadow produces its own effects. Important events connected with the lives of great men and memorable circumstances desired to be kept in remembrance, help to lend importance to sparkling gems and less ornamental stones. This will be better understood as we proceed.

Descendants of Abraham believed, as will be found under "Rise and Progress of Superstition," that their great ancestor wore, suspended from his neck, a precious stone the sight of which cured every disease. An interesting legend is also given there concerning Abraham and the stones marching, ready hewn, to find a place in the Kaaba he was about to build; of the black stone left out, which afterwards became so famous; and of the stone to which Abraham tied the beast he rode on when going to sacrifice his son. In that part of our work it will also be ascertained that altars were called living stones, from a belief that a portion of divine spirit resided in them.

Josephus and others maintain that the precious stones of Aaron's breast-plate were the Urim and Thummim, and that they discovered or predicted the issue of events to those who consulted them; and the Rabbins held that the rod of Moses consisted partly of sapphire. At page 27 it will be seen that the Greeks wore charmed rings, and at pages 7 and 58 we have stated that priests sold charms to credulous persons. At page 280 we have noticed the custom of negro children being provided with sacred rings and belts, to protect them from evil spirits. Again, when treating of magic and astrology, we pointed out that magicians supplied people with precious stones, supposed to be of immense value as amulets.

From time immemorial an opinion has obtained that there are sacred edifices, piles, cairns, and separate stones, which possess peculiar virtue. Not a few instances of these have been adduced in preceding pages; but a few more examples, we venture to say, will not be considered void of interest, more particularly if they can be connected with the destiny of man.

Every individual is supposed to be born under a particular destiny or fate (as has been over and over again stated in these pages), which it is impossible to avoid. The month of his nativity has a mysterious connection with one or other of the precious stones. This was so well understood by the ancients, that when one wished to make the object of his affections an acceptable present, a ring was given, set with the jewel by which the fate of the receiver was determined and described. For instance, we are informed by an old author, that the ring of a woman born in January should have a jacinth or garnet in it, for these stones belong to that month, and express constancy and fidelity. A list of the months and stones therewith connected, and their respective significance, is as follows:--

> JANUARY--Jacinth, or Garnet--Constancy and fidelity in
> every engagement.
>
> FEBRUARY--Amethyst--This month and stone preserve
> mortals from strong passions, and ensure them peace of
> mind.
>
> MARCH--Bloodstone--Courage, and success in dangers and
> hazardous enterprises.
>
> APRIL--Sapphire or Diamond--Repentance and innocence.
>
> MAY--Emerald--Success in love.
>
> JUNE--Agate--Long life and health.
>
> JULY--Cornelian or Ruby--The forgetfulness or the cure
> of evils springing from friendship or love.

AUGUST--Sardonyx--Conjugal fidelity.

SEPTEMBER--Chrysolite--Preserves from or cures folly.

OCTOBER--Aquamarine or Opal--Misfortune and hope.

NOVEMBER--Topaz--Fidelity in friendship.

DECEMBER--Torquoise or Malachite--The most brilliant
success and happiness in every circumstance of life.
The torquoise has also the property of securing
friendly regards, as is verified by the old saying,
"He who possesses a torquoise will always be sure of
friends."

Anciently, the kings of England, on Good Friday, hallowed, with great ceremony, certain rings the wearing of which was believed to prevent the falling sickness. The custom originated from a ring, long preserved in Westminster Abbey, which is reported to have been brought to King Edward by persons from Jerusalem. The rings consecrated by the sovereigns were called "cramp rings." Andrew Boorde, speaking of the cramp, says, "The King's Majesty hath great help in this matter in hallowing 'cramp rings' without money or petition."

Writing of Fladda Chuan, Martin writes: "There is a chapel in the isle, dedicated to St. Columbus. It has an altar in the east end, and therein a blue stone of a round form on it, which is always moist. It is an ordinary custom, when any of the fishermen are detained in this isle by contrary winds, to wash the blue stone with water, all round, expecting thereby to procure a favourable wind. And so great is their regard for this stone that people swear decisive oaths upon it." Martin also says it was an ancient custom among the islanders to hang a he-goat's skin to the boat's mast, in the hope of securing a favourable wind.

There was a stone in Iona, over which, if a man stretched his arm three times, he would never err in steering a vessel. In the island of Bernera there was a stone in the form of a cross, near St. Mary's Church, about five feet high, which the natives called the water cross. The old inhabitants were in the practice of erecting it when they wished rain, and of laying it flat on the ground when they desired dry weather. Martin further mentions a green stone, about the size of goose's egg, in the island of Arran, which possessed rare virtue, and was consequently handed down to posterity for many ages. By laying it on the side of a person troubled with pains in that part of his body, the patient immediately recovered, unless doomed to die. If the latter event were to happen, the stone removed of its own accord from the side; but if the patient was to recover, it rested where placed until the cure became complete. Disputed cases between the islanders were settled by oath at this stone. It possessed another virtue--causing powerful enemies to run away when it was thrown at their front. The custody of this valuable relic long remained a privilege of the Chattans.

In the Highlands of Scotland a large oval crystal--probably a Cairngorm stone--was kept by the ancient priests by which to work charms. Water poured upon it was given to the cattle, to preserve them from disease. Such charms were common in Scotland, England, and Ireland. Lilly describes a conjuring beryl or crystal. It was, he tells us, as large as an orange, and set in silver with a cross at the top, and round about it were engraved the names of the angels Raphael, Gabriel, and Uriel. A delineation of another charm is engraved in the frontispiece to Aubrey's *Miscellanies*. A mode of making inquiry by charms is imputed to Dr. Dee, the celebrated mathematician. The stone used by him came into the possession of Horace Walpole, and was long, if not now, in the Strawberry Hill collection. Sorcerers or magicians, says Grose, did not always employ their art to do mischief, but, on the contrary, frequently exerted it to cure diseases inflicted by witches, to discover thieves, recover stolen goods, to foretell future events, and the state of absent friends. A favourite method of consultation was this: The conjuror having repeated the necessary adjuration, and applied the proper charms, with the litany or invocation peculiar to the spirits or angels whose assistance was to be asked, the seer looked into a crystal or beryl, wherein he saw, or pretended he saw, the answers to his interrogatories, represented either by types or figures. Sometimes the spirits or angels answered audibly.

This part of our subject would be incomplete without reference to the Coronation Stone, the history of which is as interesting as it is curious. We have made mention of a stone or stones, under various names--Jacob's Pillow, Lia-Fail, Stone of Destiny, Marble Chair, Coronation Stone, etc. Writers on archaeological subjects are not agreed as to whether all these are or are not different names for one and the same relic. On the whole, we are inclined to think that there was but one coronation stone, but we leave that point to be definitely settled by others. From the information before us, we assume there was but one stone, and therefore proceed on this assumption, which is supported by tradition.

The Stone of Destiny, we are told, formed Jacob's pillow on the plain of Luz, and consequently was regarded as a sacred relic by the Jews. It was carried to Egypt, thence to Spain, and from the latter country it was conveyed by Simon Breck to Ireland, where it became known as the "Lia-Fail" or "Stone of Destiny" of the Irish kings. Ireland is often, from this stone, called by the priests Innisphail. The ancient Irish supposed that, in whatsoever country this stone remained, there one of their blood would reign. They pretended to have authentic memoirs of the stone for a period extending backwards more than two thousand years. In the practical tales of Ossian we find:

> "Though the sun glitters upon the heath, I will not
> behold her golden rays; though the stag should start
> by me, Ossian will chase him no more. Although Manus
> should cross the ocean again to invade Albin, my sword
> is not victorious in the slaughter, and my fame is not
> celebrated by the bards. I am not invited to a feast.
> My kiss is scorned by the virgin. My esteem is not
> equal to a king's son; one day is like a year to me.

"It was the reverse in Innis-phail, also in Selma, the
mansions of my mighty father: Ossian was honoured
above the rest: behold the uncertainty of everything
under the sun."

After the enchanted stone--for it was regarded as such--had long been kept at Tarah, it was
sent to Fergus, the first actual king of Scots; and it remained in Argyle (the original seat of the Scots
in Britain) until about the year 842. Three hundred and thirty years before the Christian era, Fergus
was crowned and seated on the famous chair. Kenneth, the second son of Alpin, having enlarged
his dominions by the conquest of the Picts, transferred the stone to Scone. As the supreme kings
of Ireland and the kings of the Scots used to be inaugurated by being seated on the ancient chair
before it was carried to Scone, so were the kings at Perth installed into regal office down to the time
that Edward I. carried to England the sacred relic, highly prized by every Scotchman. As soon as
the news of the loss spread, great concern was manifested. The death of a beloved monarch, or the
loss of many battles, where brave sons and fathers had fallen, would have been as nothing compared
with the national loss sustained. In fact, many in the highest circles conceived that the glory of the
kingdom had departed.

It appears from a document found among the records of England, that King Edward treated the
relic with great veneration. With the intention of using it for the same purposes in England as it had
been used for in Scotland and Ireland, he proposed to make it a part of a throne or royal seat, and
ordered his goldsmith to prepare a copper case for it. He changed his mind, and gave instructions for
a wooden chair being made, and the stone inserted in the seat. Such was the estimation in which he
held the stone, that he placed it in the most sacred place in England--close to the altar and shrine
of St. Edward. There are reasons for concluding that Edward had intended to return the stone to
Scotland, and had made arrangements to that effect in a treaty; but the citizens of London, who were
anxious to retain the stone in England, remonstrated against its being restored to the legal owners,
and the king complied with their wishes. This famous "Stone of Destiny," long sacred in Ireland, and
on which the kings of Scotland were crowned for more than a thousand years, now forms part of the
coronation chair of the kings and queens of England.

When the supreme kings of Ireland were inaugurated, in the times of heathenism, on the hill
of Tarah, the stone, which was enclosed in a wooden chair, was supposed to emit a sound under
the rightful heir to the throne, but to be mute under a man seeking power under false pretences.
On Aidanus being elected by universal acclamation, and solemnly seated in the same chair, he was
crowned by St. Columba, who with his right hand placed the diadem on the king's head, while in
his left he held a trumpet or wooden tube, to announce to the assembled throng the completion of
the joyful event. This tube was long preserved with great care at Dunkeld. Some suppose that the
fatality long assigned to the stone was fully believed in by Kenneth, by whose orders the following
couplet was carved on the chair:--

"Where'er this marble's placed, there, sure as fate,

Shall be the Scottish monarch's regal seat."

Wintoun tells us that Fergus, the son of Ere,

"Braucht this stane wytht-in Scotland
Fyrst quhen he came and wane that land,
And fyrst it set in Ikkolmkil,
And Skune thare-eftir it was braucht tyle;
And there it wes syne mony day,
Qhyll Edward gert have it away."

Without endorsing the opinion that Scotland and Ireland have lost their wonted power, or suffered decline through the "Prophetic or Fatal Stone" being carried away, it is an indisputable fact that in neither of these countries is there, strictly speaking, a "monarch's regal seat." The "Enchanted Stone"--the "palladium of Scottish liberty"--is certainly, as the English well know, one of the most ancient and valuable relics in Westminster Abbey.

TRIALS BY ORDEAL.
CHAPTER L.

Trials by Ordeal resorted to in Modern and Ancient   Times--Ordeal by means of Hot Iron--Plunging the Arm   into Boiling Water or Oil--Walking Blindfold in Dangerous Places--Weighing a Witch--Extending the Arms   before a Cross--Swallowing Consecrated Bread--Ordeal   among the Hindoos--Touching a Dead Body--A Murdered   Traveller--An Inquest, how conducted long ago--Dead Henry's Wounds--Sir George M'Kenzie's Opinion of Trial   by Ordeal--Killing a Brother by Sorcery--Touching a   Dead Body--Sir K. Digby on Trial by Ordeal.

Trial by ordeal were resorted to by many people and nations both in ancient and modern times, with the view of establishing the criminality or innocence of suspected persons. Among the ordeals may be enumerated: holding in the hand a red-hot bar of iron, plunging the arm into boiling water or oil, walking blindfold amidst burning ploughshares, passing through fires, swallowing a morsel of consecrated bread, swimming or sinking in water (or, as it was occasionally termed, weighing a witch), stretching out the arms before the cross until the sorest wearied competitor dropped his arms, and so lost his cause, and therewith perhaps his life or his estate, or it might be both.

*   *   *   *   *

A dispute occurred between the Bishop of Paris and the Abbot of St. Denis about the patronage of a monastery; and Pepin, surnamed the Short, not being able to decide such an intricate question, decreed that the matter should be settled by ordeal. Each of the disputants chose a man, and both the men appeared in a chapel, where they extended their arms in the form of a cross. Numerous spectators were present to witness the trial, and betted on the feat. The bishop's representative dropped his arms first, and thereby ruined his employer.

Warren Hastings has found, from Asiatic researches, that trial by ordeal was common among the Hindoos. He says these trials are conducted in nine ways: first, by the balance; secondly, by fire; thirdly, by water; fourthly, by poison; fifthly, by the Cosha, or water in which an idol has been washed; sixthly, by rice; seventhly, by boiling oil; eighthly, by red-hot iron; ninthly, by images.

"I. Ordeal by the balance is thus performed:--The beam
having been previously adjusted, the cord fixed, and
both scales made perfectly even, the person accused
and a Pandit fast a whole day; then, after the accused
has been bathed in sacred water, the homa, or
oblation, presented to fire, and the deities
worshipped, he is carefully weighed; and, when he is
taken out of the scale, the Pandits prostrate
themselves, and pronounce a certain mentra or
incantation, agreeably to the Sastras, and having
written the substance of the accusation on a piece of
paper, bind it on his head. Six minutes after, they
place him again in the scale, and, if he weigh more
than before, he is held guilty; if less, innocent; if
exactly the same, he must be weighed a third time;
when, as it is written in the Mitacshera, there will
certainly be a difference in his weight. Should the
balance break down, it would be considered a proof of
guilt.

"II. For the fire ordeal, an excavation, nine hands
long, two spans broad, and one span deep, is made in
the ground, and filled with a fire of pippal wood:
into this the person accused must walk bare-footed,
and, if his foot be unhurt, they hold him blameless;
if burned, guilty.

"III. Water ordeal is performed by causing the person
accused to stand in a sufficient depth of water,
either flowing or stagnant, to reach his navel; but
care must be taken that no ravenous animal be in it,
and that it be not moved by much air: a Brahman is
then directed to go into the water, holding a staff in
his hand, and a soldier shoots three arrows on dry
ground from a bow of cane; a man is next despatched to
bring the arrow which has been shot farthest, and,
after he has taken it up, another is ordered to run
from the edge of the water; at which instant the
person accused is told to grasp the foot or the staff
of the Brahman, who stands near him in the water, and

immediately to dive into it. He must remain under
water till the two men who went to fetch the arrows
are returned; for, if he raise his head or body above
the surface before the arrows are brought back, his
guilt is considered as fully proved. In the villages
near Banares, it is the practice for the person who is
to be tried by this kind of ordeal to stand in water
up to his navel, and then, holding the foot of a
Brahman, to dive under it as long as a man can walk
fifty paces very gently; if before the man has walked
thus far the accused rise above the water, he is
condemned; if not, acquitted.

"IV. There are two sorts of trial by poison. First,
the Pandits having performed their homa, and the
person accused his ablution, two retti's and a half,
or seven barley-corns, of vishanaga, a poisonous root,
or of sanc'hya, that is, white arsenic, are mixed in
eight mashas, or sixty-four retti's of clarified
butter, which the accused must eat from the hand of a
Brahman: if the poison produce no visible effect, he
is absolved; otherwise, condemned. Secondly, the
hooded snake, called naga, is thrown into a deep
earthen pot, into which is dropped a ring, a seal, or
a coin; this the person accused is ordered to take out
with his hand; and, if the serpent bite him, he is
pronounced guilty; if not, innocent.

"V. Trial by the cosha is as follows: the accused is
made to drink three draughts of the water in which the
images of the sun, of Devi, and other deities have
been washed for that purpose; and if within fourteen
days he has any sickness or indisposition, his crime
is considered as proved.

"VI. When several persons are suspected of theft, some
dry rice is weighed with the sacred stone called
salcram; or certain slocas are read over it; after
which the suspected persons are severally ordered to
chew a quantity of it: as soon as they have chewed it,

they are to throw it on some leaves of the pippal, or,
if none be at hand, on some b'hurja patra, or bark of
a tree from Nepal or Cashmir. The man from whose mouth
the rice comes dry or stained with blood, is holden
guilty; the rest are acquitted.

"VII. The ordeal by hot oil is very simple: when it is
heated sufficiently, the accused thrusts his hand into
it; and, if he be not burned, is held innocent.

"VIII. In the same manner they make an iron ball, or
the head of a lance, red-hot, and place it in the
hands of the person accused; who, if it burn him not,
is judged guiltless.

"IX. To perform the ordeal by dharmarch, which is the
name of the sloca appropriated to this mode of trial,
either an image named Dharma, or the Genius of
Justice, is made of silver, and another, called
Adharma, of clay or iron, both of which are thrown
into a large earthen jar; and the accused, having
thrust his hand into it, is acquitted if he bring out
the silver image, but condemned if he draw forth the
iron; or the figure of a deity is painted on white
cloth, and another on black, the first of which they
name dharma, and the second adharma: these are
severally rolled up in cow-dung, and thrown into a
large jar without having ever been shown to the
accused; who must put his hand into the jar, and is
acquitted or convicted as he draws out the figure on
white or black cloth."

Touching the body of a murdered person was one way, in Scotland, England, and elsewhere, of discovering who the murderer was. The practice, we are informed, originated in Denmark. Certain gentlemen in that kingdom, being together in a house, one evening fell out among themselves, and from words came to blows. Unfortunately the candles went out during the fray, and before lights could be procured one of the gentlemen was stabbed. The murderer was unknown. Christernus II., then king, to find out the murderer, caused all who were present at the brawl to stand around the dead body, and commanded that one after the other should lay his right hand on the dead man's breast, and swear that he had not committed the foul deed. The gentlemen complied; and no sign appeared to indicate the guilt of any of them, until the king's pursuivant kissed the feet of the corpse, and laid his hand on the breast. As soon as he did so, the blood gushed out in great abundance from the wound and nostrils. Thus condemned, the pursuivant confessed his guilt. By the king's sentence, the criminal was beheaded. Hence arose the practice, which was long common in many places, of finding out unknown murders. In most cases the murderer was discovered by the corpse bleeding the instant the bloodstained hand was placed on the cold inanimate clay, but at times the sign was given by the dead man opening his eyes on the slayer approaching the corpse.

A traveller was found murdered on a highway in Denmark; and because the slayer was unknown, the magistrates of the place caused one of the hands of him that was slain to be cut off, and hung up by a string at the top of a room in the town prison. About ten years after the crime was committed, the murderer happened to enter the apartment; and as soon as he did so, the dry withered hand began to drop blood on a table below it. The gaoler, beholding this, detained the man and called in the magistrates, who extracted from him a confession of his guilt.

In Herefordshire, in the time of Charles I., Johan Norkett, wife of Arthur Norkett, was found dead. At first it was thought she had committed suicide, but afterwards circumstances transpired which led to the belief that the unfortunate woman did not lay violent hands upon herself. A jury was summoned, and, after deliberation, the coroner directed that the body, which had been buried for a month, should be exhumed, and four suspected persons brought to touch the corpse. The persons being afterwards brought to trial at the assizes, an old minister swore that, the body being taken out of the grave and laid on the grass, the accused were required to touch it. On laying their hands on the brow, which before was of a livid and carrion colour, it began to have a dew or gentle sweat upon it, which increased by degrees until the sweat ran down the face. The brow then turned to a lifelike and flesh colour, and the dead woman opened one of her eyes and shut it again, and this opening the eye was done three times. She likewise thrust out the ring or marriage finger three times, and the finger dropped blood on the grass. Another clergyman corroborated the statement of the first witness. Sir Nicholas Hyde threw doubt on the correctness of the evidence, but the jury found three of the prisoners guilty of murder, and two of them were executed; the third being a woman, escaped with her life.

> "Dead Henry's wounds
> Open their congealed mouths, and bleed afresh;"

And Dryden says:

> "If the vile actors of the heinous deed
> Near the dead body happily be brought,
> Oft hath been proved the breathless corpse will bleed."

That murder might be discovered in the way referred to, was generally believed in Scotland in the seventeenth century. Sir George Mackenzie, when conducting the prosecution in the trial of

Philip Stansfield, said: "That divine power which makes the blood circulate during life, has oft-times, in all nations, opened a passage to it after death upon such occasions, but most in this case; for after the wounds had been sewed up, and the body designedly shaken up and down, and, which is most wonderful, after the body had been buried for several days, which naturally occasions the blood to congeal, upon Philip touching it, the blood darted and sprang out, to the great astonishment of the chirurgeons themselves, who were desired to watch this event; whereupon Philip, astonished more than they, threw down the body, and became so faint that they were forced to give him a cordial."

In the middle of the seventeenth century, Christina Wilson was accused, in one of the supreme courts of Scotland, of having killed her brother by sorcery. On being suspected of the crime by the minister and others, she was brought in to touch the corpse. At the first sight of the dead body, she prayed that He who made the sun to shine on their house would bring the murder to light, and immediately thereafter she touched the corpse. It bled, though it did not do so before when touched by others. Of course this was held sufficient proof against the unfortunate woman, and she suffered according to her supposed guilt.

In another case a man was condemned on similar evidence for the murder of his father; but the prisoner insisted that the bleeding was owing to an incision made on the body, and not to his presence. The defence was disregarded; but this need not be a matter of surprise, when such men as Sir K. Digby and Sir George Mackenzie took it for granted that the corpse of a murdered person would bleed on being touched by the murderer. He (Sir K. Digby) says in his *Religio Medica*: "And to this cause, peradventure, may be ascribed the strange effect which is frequently seen in England, when, at the approach of the murderer, the slain body suddenly bleedeth afresh: for certainly the souls of them that are treacherously murdered by surprise leave their bodies with extreme unwillingness, and with vehement indignation against them that forced them to so unprovided and abhorred a passage. The soul then, to wreak its evil talent against the hated murderer, and to draw a just and desired revenge upon his head, would do all it can to manifest the author of the fact. To speak it cannot, for in itself it wanteth organs of voice, and those it is parted from are now grown too heavy, and are too benumbed for it to give motion unto; yet some change it desireth to make in the body, which it hath so vehement inclination to, and therefore it is the aptest for it to work upon. It must then endeavour to cause a motion in the sublimest and most fluid parts (and consequently the most moveable ones) of it. This can be nothing but the blood, which, being violently moved, must needs gush out at those places where it findeth issues."

The swallowing of a piece of barley bread, over which mass had been performed, was not unfrequent in trials of ordeal. If the suspected person swallowed the bread without injury, he was declared innocent; but if the bread choked him in the attempt to swallow it, then was he considered to be guilty. At times cheese was given with the bread; but when that was done, it was essential to supply ewe-milk cheese made in the month of May.

CHAPTER LI.

A Popular Story--Ordeal of Red-hot Iron--Ordeal by Boiling Water--Theatberge, wife of Lothaire, accused of Incest--Purgation by Cold Water--Forbes's Memoirs--Ordeals by Boiling Oil--Trial by Wager of Battle--When Trial by Wager of Battle ceased--Trial by Jury--Combats in Germany--Bier placed near the Combatants--Court of King's Bench deciding the Legality of Trial by Battle--Sir Walter Scott's Illustrations of Superstition and Trial by Battle in Olden Times.

A popular story is told of Emma, mother of Edward the Confessor, being accused of too great familiarity with the Bishop of Leicester. To justify herself, she demanded the ordeal of red-hot iron. Her demand was complied with, and she passed barefooted and blindfolded over nine red-hot ploughshares without touching them. Her innocence was thereby held to be proved.

Nobles and great persons who submitted to ordeal by water were purged by boiling water, but the populace had to undergo the cold-water test.

Theatberge, wife of Lothaire of France, having been accused of incest, certain bishops were consulted as to the manner of establishing her guilt or innocence; and they concluded that recourse should be had to proof by boiling water. She was ordered to plunge her hand into a basin of boiling water, and take out a ring put therein. In place of complying, she availed herself of a privilege the law allowed--to find a substitute. He whom she chose produced the ring without injuring his hand, in spite of the fire under the caldron being so intense that the water boiled over.

In the trial or purgation by cold water, the accused, after prayers and other ceremonies, was cast into deep water, swaddled or tied in such a manner as to make it impossible for him or her to swim. If the accused sank, he or she was held criminal, and allowed to drown. If the person floated, it was regarded as a proof of innocence, and the lucky one was drawn out of the water to be set free.

Mr. Forbes, in his *Oriental Memoirs*, says that, among the curious circumstances connected with his administration of justice at Dheeborg, he was sometimes obliged to determine causes by ordeal trial. In one instance a man was accused of stealing a child wearing many jewels. Circumstances were against him, on which he demanded trial by ordeal. Mr. Forbes was at first averse to adopt such a measure, but, at the request of the Hindoo arbitrators, who sat on the carpet of justice, and especially at the request of the child's parents, he consented. A vessel full of boiling oil was brought into the durbar, and, after a short ceremony by the Brahmins, the accused person, without showing any anxiety, plunged his hand to the bottom and took out a small silver coin. He did not appear to have sustained any hurt, or to suffer the least pain. The suspected person's innocence being thus established in the eyes of the arbitrators and parents, he was set free.

Another instance of trial by ordeal is mentioned by Mr. Forbes. The coolies of a village in the northern part of Guzerat were accused of having seized and imprisoned a Bohra, and, of extorting a bond from him for 450 rupees. The chief, a Khemaria coolie, named Wagajee, denied the charge, and, for proof of his innocence and that of his people, offered to submit to trial by any kind of ordeal. The Bohra agreed to this mode of proof, and it was determined that the coolie should immerse his hand in a vessel of boiling oil. A large copper-pot full of oil was put on a fire in the market place, and a pair of blacksmith's bellows applied to blow the fire until the oil became very hot. A rupee was then thrown into the pot. The accused, when requested, came forward, stripped himself, said his prayers, and protested his innocence. He resisted every attempt to dissuade him from the trial. A crowd of people, impressed with the awfulness of such an immediate appeal to the deity, prayed devoutly that, if he were not guilty, he might pass through the test unhurt. Wagajee walked up to the boiling oil, dipped his hand into it, and laid hold of the rupee. He then held up his hand, that the spectators might satisfy themselves of his veracity. His hand appeared as if it had been merely put into cold oil. All parties were satisfied, and Wagajee was dismissed with the present of a new turban.

Trial by ordeal was introduced into England by the Saxons. Under the English laws, a prisoner might choose whether he would be tried by ordeal or by jury. Trial by ordeal was abolished in this country in the year 1218.

Trial by or wager of battle may be mentioned as a form of superstition which remained as a legal way of deciding criminal cases down to the time of George III.

In 1817 a young man, charged with murdering his sweetheart in England, claimed the right to have his case decided by wager of battle: the court admitted the claim, but he whose right it was to accept the challenge refused to fight, and so the accused escaped punishment. This led to the law, which allowed trial by battle, being repealed in 1819.

Before commencing the fight, the combatants were compelled to swear that neither of them would resort to sorcery or witchcraft. If the accused were slain, the judges regarded the fatal deed as proof of his guilt. If overpowered, but not killed, he was adjudged guilty, and sentenced to be immediately executed. Women, priests, infants, men sixty years of age, or lame or blind, had it in their option to refuse wager of battle, and were entitled to demand trial by jury.

An old author says: "If two neighbours dispute respecting the boundaries of their possessions, let a piece of turf of the contested land be dug up by the judge, and brought by him into the court, and the two parties shall touch it with the points of their swords, calling on the Most High to witness their claims. After this let them combat, and let victory prove who is right and who is wrong."

Sir Walter Scott gives a good illustration of the superstition of olden times, and of trial by battle, in *Ivanhoe*. We are told that after Ivanhoe was wounded at the tournament, Rebecca, the Jewess, lost no time in causing the patient to be removed to her father's dwelling, and with her own hands bound up his wounds. The Jews, both male and female, possessed and practised the medical science; and the monarchs and powerful barons of the time, says the novelist, frequently, when wounded or in sickness, committed themselves as patients to the charge of an experienced person among the despised people. A general belief prevailed among Christians that the Jewish rabbins were acquainted with the occult sciences, and particularly with the cabalistical art. The rabbins did not disavow such acquaintance with supernatural arts. Rebecca's knowledge of the healing art had been acquired under an aged Jewess, the daughter of a celebrated doctor. Miriam fell a sacrifice to the fanaticism of the times, but her secrets had survived in her apt pupil. The wounded knight, as might be expected, recovered under the medical treatment of Rebecca. For this she was accused of working cures by words, sigils, and other cabalistical mysteries.

"Nay, reverend and brave knight," answered Isaac, Rebecca's father, in reply to Beaumanoir, who brought the charge against the Jewess, "but in chief measure by a balsam of marvellous virtue;" and in reply to another question, Isaac reluctantly told that Rebecca had obtained her secret from Miriam, whom the Grand Master designated a witch and enchantress, whose body had been burned at a stake, and her ashes scattered to the four winds. "The laws of England," exclaimed Beaumanoir, "permit and enjoin each judge to execute justice within his own jurisdiction. The most petty baron may arrest, try, and condemn a witch found within his own domain.... The witch shall be taken out of the land, and the wickedness thereof shall be forgiven. Prepare the castle-hall for the trial of the sorceress."

Poor Rebecca was brought before the Grand Master, charged with various crimes. "We have," said the Master, "summoned to our presence a Jewish woman, by name Rebecca, daughter of York--a woman infamous for sortileges and for witcheries; whereby she hath maddened the blood, and besotted the brain, not of a churl, but of a knight--not of a secular knight, but of one devoted to the service of the holy temple--not of a knight champion, but of a preceptor.... By means of charms and of spells, Satan had obtained dominion over the knight, perchance because he cast his eyes too lightly upon a damsel's beauty."

Witnesses being invited by the Grand Master, forward came a once bedridden man, whom the prisoner had restored to the perfect use of his limbs by a miraculous balsam. Unwillingly he testified to Rebecca curing him, giving him a pot of spicy smelling ointment, and supplying him with money to pay his expenses to his father's house, whither he wished to repair. Other witnesses deponed that Rebecca muttered to herself in an unknown tongue, that the songs she sang were peculiarly sweet, that her garments were of a strange mystic form, and that she had rings with cabalistic devices. A soldier testified that he had seen her cure a wounded man in a mysterious way. He said she made certain signs upon the wound, and repeated words he understood not. The result, he declared, was that the iron head of a cross-bow bolt disengaged itself from the wound, the bleeding was staunched, the wound closed, and the seemingly dying man was within a quarter of an hour walking upon the ramparts. Another soldier deponed that he had seen Rebecca perch herself upon a high turret, and there take the form of a white swan, under which appearance she flitted three times round the castle of Torquailstone. Again she settled on the turret, and once more assumed her womanly form. The evidence was considered more than enough to condemn the unhappy Jewess; and in a solemn tone the Grand Master demanded what she had to say against sentence of condemnation being pro-nounced against her. Rebecca knew the law; she maintained her innocence, claimed the privilege of trial by combat, and offered to appear by a champion.

Brian de Bois-Gilbert was appointed to do battle on behalf of himself and the order of knights to which he belonged; and the day came when the die would be cast that was to decide the fate of Rebecca. At the castle of Templestowe everything was prepared by the prosecutor for the combat, but for poor Rebecca no champion appeared. Near the lists was a pile of faggots so arranged around a stake as to leave a space for the accused to enter within the fatal circle, chained by fetters, in order to be ready for the fiery punishment. At the hour appointed for the champions to meet, the large bell of St. Michael tolled mournfully, the drawbridge fell, the gates opened, and a knight, bearing a great standard, sallied forth from the castle, preceded by six trumpeters, and followed by the knights preceptors, the Grand Master coming behind. Then came Brian de Bois-Gilbert, armed *cap-a-pie*, ac-companied by two godfathers and many squires and pages. After these followed a guard of warders, with the trembling Jewess, stripped of all her ornaments, lest there should be among them amulets, which Satan was supposed to bestow upon his victims, to deprive them of the power of confession, even when under torture. While the Grand Master took his exalted seat, the unfortunate culprit was conducted to the black chair, near the ready prepared pile. Everything being arranged, a loud and long flourish of trumpets announced that the proceedings of the court were to begin. Brian de Bois-Gilbert stood ready for the combat, but a champion was still wanting for the appellant. Lest Jew or Pagan should charge the court with injustice, the Grand Master declared his readiness to wait till the shadows were in the west, to see if a champion would appear for the culprit. But the general belief prevailed that no one would stand up for her; and the craven knights whispered to each other, when the day was far gone, that the time had come for declaring the pledge of Rebecca forfeited. At this instant, a knight, urging his horse forward, appeared on the plain advancing towards the lists. A hundred voices exclaimed, "A champion! a champion!" Yes, it was a champion, the renowned Wilfred of Ivanhoe. "Rebecca," said he, riding up to the black chair, "dost thou accept me for thy champion?" The answer was in the affirmative. Little time was now lost; the champions confronted each other. Trumpets sounded, and the knights charged in full career. The wearied horse of Ivanhoe, and its no less exhausted rider, went down, as all had expected, before the well-aimed lance and vigorous steed of the Templar. This result all had foreseen; but although the spear of Ivanhoe did but lightly touch the shield of Bois-Gilbert, that combatant reeled in his saddle, lost his stirrups, and fell in the lists. Ivanhoe, extricating himself from his fallen horse, was soon on foot, hastening to mend his fortune by the sword; but his antagonist rose not. Wilfred, placing his foot on his opponent's breast, and the sword's point to his throat, commanded him to yield, or die on the spot. Bois-Gilbert returned no answer. The fallen knight was unhelmed. His eyes were closed--he was dead, supposed to have died a victim to the violence of his own passions. When the first moments of surprise were over, the Grand Master pronounced the maiden free and guiltless.

The conclusion of this story is touching in the extreme. Soon after this Ivanhoe and the Lady Ravena were married. On the second morning after the nuptials, Rebecca waited on the Lady of Ivanhoe, and presented her with a small silver casket containing jewels of great value; and leaving a message to her champion, who never ceased to remember her, she hastened away to other lands, to tend the sick, feed the hungry, and relieve the distressed.

CURSES AND EVIL WISHES.
CHAPTER LII.

Curses, Excommunication, and Anathemas--Dirae, the   Executioners of Vengeance--Curses and Anathemas not   confined to the Vulgar--Excommunication generally   accompanied by Anathema--Excommunicated Persons lost   their Civil Rights--Heretics forfeited their   Lives--Interment of Excommunicated Persons--Excommunication among the Hebrews--Different   Degrees of Excommunication--Solemn Curses pronounced   against Impenitent Persons--Stone laid on an Accursed   Person's Coffin--Last Degree of Excommunication   sometimes followed by Banishment or Death--Form of   Excommunication used by Ezra and Nehemiah when they   cursed the Samaritans--Death upon the Cross, Sawing   asunder, and other Punishments--Mode of Punishment   among the Romans, Greeks, and Persians--The Greek   Church annually excommunicated Roman Catholics--The   Druids resorted to Excommunication--Whole Families   excommunicated with Horrible Ceremonies and Dreadful   Imprecations--Bishops excommunicating Rats, Mice,   Caterpillars, and other Insects and Vermin--The Pope's   Claim--Napoleon I. excommunicated--Victor Emmanuel excommunicated--Effects of Excommunication--The   Inquisition and its Terrible Doings--The Pope's   Fearful Curse--Mr. Donald Cargill excommunicating the   King and Nobles--Indulgences, Pardons, and Penance.

Curses, excommunication, and anathemas have often been followed by sad consequences; but whether arising directly or indirectly from the denunciations, we do not say. Ancient nations had their goddesses Dirae, who were supposed to be the executioners of vengeance. They were called Furies on earth, and Eumenides in hell. These goddesses were invoked with prayers and charms. Curses and anathemas were not in former ages confined to the vulgar classes of persons, such as in the present time. Imprecations were hurled out by the priest and prophet, by the educated and uneducated, by professed Christian laymen, by the heathen, by the wandering gipsies, and the croaking crones.

Excommunication is generally accompanied by anathema, or ecclesiastical curse, and punishment, whereby a heretic is not only cut off from the society of the faithful, but is consigned to Satan, that condign punishment may follow. Sixty penalties have been reckoned as accruing upon excommunication. Major excommunication separates or cuts off the delinquent from all communion and fellowship with society--disables him from defending his civil rights. In more than one kingdom, a person who is not absolved from his excommunication in a year's time is deemed a heretic; and we know the punishment dealt out to such persons. Even in our own country, before the time of Charles II., a heretic forfeited his life, and generally expiated his guilt at the stake.

By law, an excommunicated person was not allowed to be interred according to the ordinary form and rites of burial, but the body was flung into a pit, or covered with a heap of stones called *imblocare corpus*. There was a time when the people believed that the bodies of excommunicated persons not absolved did not rot, but remained entire for ages, a horrible spectacle to posterity. This is attested by Matthew Paris and other writers. The Greeks, till recently, entertained the same opinion.

In the Hebrew republic the punishment of excommunication was devised by courts of justice, and inflicted by public sentence upon the offenders. There were three degrees of excommunication among the Jews: the first was a casting out of the synagogue, and implied a separation from all commerce and society, either with man or woman, for the distance of four cubits; also from eating or drinking with any one; from shaving, washing, or the like, according to the pleasure of the judge and the seriousness of the offence. It was in force for thirty days, unless there was repentance expressed and forgiven.

If the sinner remained impenitent longer than thirty days, he was sentenced to more severe punishment, with the addition of a solemn curse. This is supposed to be the same as delivering over to Satan. The offence was published in the synagogue, and, at the time of the publication of the curse, candles were lighted, and when it was extended they were extinguished, as a sign that the excommunicate was deprived of the light of heaven. His goods were confiscated; his male children were not permitted to be circumcised. If he died without repentance, a stone, according to judicial sentence, was cast upon his coffin or bier, to show that he deserved to be stoned. He was not mourned for with solemn lamentation, nor followed to the grave, nor buried with common burial.

The last degree of excommunication was anathematising, which was inflicted when the offender had often refused to comply with the sentence of court, and was followed by corporal punishment, and often with banishment or death. Drusius gives a form of excommunication which, the Jews say, was used by Ezra and Nehemiah against the Samaritans, in this manner:--The whole congregation was assembled in the Temple, and there were brought three hundred priests, three hundred boys, three hundred trumpets, and three hundred books of the law, and the Levites, singing, cursed the Samaritans by all forms of excommunication, particularly with the curse of the superior house of judgment, and with the curse of the inferior house of judgment. At the same time it was commanded that no Israelite should partake of a Samaritan's food. Hence arose the saying in reference to the breaker of this commandment: "He who eats a Samaritan's bread is as he who eats swine's flesh." Moreover, it was decreed that the excommunicate should have no part in the resurrection of the dead.

There were other punishments introduced among the Hebrews in later times of their government, which were borrowed from other nations. These were principally, death upon the cross, sawing asunder, condemnation to fight with wild beasts, the wheel, drowning in the sea, beating to death with cudgels, and boating. The first and third punishments were properly Roman inflictions; the second was likewise used by the Romans, but whether it was originally taken from them is doubtful; the fourth and sixth were Grecian penalties; the fifth was, in substance, in use among the Hebrews, Greeks, and Romans, but in the manner of drowning they differed, for the Hebrews tied a mill-stone about the culprit's neck; the last punishment was derived from the Persians, and is thus described:--The condemned person was laid upon his back in a boat, with his hands tied to the sides thereof; another boat was put over him, covering all his body except the head. In this posture the unhappy person was fed with milk and honey till the worms ate his very bowels, and thereby ended his days in extreme pain.

Every year the Greek Church, at Constantinople, pronounces excommunication against the Roman Catholic Church. Heathens as well as Christians resorted to excommunication. The Druids made use of excommunication against rebels, and interdicted the communication of their mysteries to such as refused to submit to their judgments.

In the Christian Church, excommunication has been practised in all ages, and ecclesiastics have had continual recourse to it as one of their spiritual weapons. Not only have they excommunicated individuals, but whole families and provinces have come under their law, with horrible ceremonies and dreadful imprecations. Even kings have not escaped the Church's maledictions. Fevret, writing of excommunications in the Romish Church, says that lighted torches were at times thrown on the ground, with curses and anathemas, and then trampled out while bells were rung. This is somewhat similar to part of the ceremony of excommunication by bell, book, and candle, to be afterwards more particularly described.

There are instances of bishops excommunicating caterpillars and other insects; and Fevret gives instances of excommunications going out against rats and mice. It sometimes happened that popes and churches excommunicated one another, each cutting off the other from the communication of the faithful, and delivering over the anathematised person or church to the devil. In 850 the synod of Pavia resolved that all who refused to submit to the discipline of the Church should be anathematised, and cut off from every Christian hope and consolation.

For fifteen centuries the Pope has claimed the power of disposing of men's souls as seems best to him. Whom he blesses, he says, are blessed; and whom he curses, he would make us believe, are cursed. He arrogates to himself the authority of holding the keys of heaven and hell.

In 1809 the Pope excommunicated Napoleon I., and in 1860 his Holiness excommunicated Victor Emmanuel, king of Italy--sentences which implied spiritual condemnation, and deprivation of earthly power. The subjects of an excommunicated king were freed from allegiance to their sovereign. It is supposed the Pope's power extends so far that he may pronounce excommunication against the dead, even to the debarring of deceased persons from being cleansed from their sins in purgatory, and the consigning of them to the place of eternal punishment.

Terror and amazement followed the footsteps of the inquisitionists. They proceeded with the greatest secrecy and silence. When a heretic was seized, the world abandoned him; his nearest friends durst not say a word in his defence. The heretical criminals were generally arrested in the stillness of night, examined, tortured, and, unless they recanted, condemned and executed without seeing or knowing who were their accusers. Usually the accused persons were tortured until they condemned themselves; and although witnesses were sometimes examined, the form of procedure was a mockery of justice.

As a convincing proof of how dreadful the Romish Church's anathemas are, we give the Pope's fearful curse, taken from a form of excommunication copied from the "Leger Book" of the church of Rochester, long in the custody of the dean and chapter there:--

"By the authority of God Almighty, the Father, Son,
and Holy Ghost, and of the holy canons, and of the
undefiled Virgin Mary, the mother and patroness of our
Saviour, and of all the celestial virtues, angels,
archangels, thrones, dominions, powers, cherubims and
seraphims, and of the holy patriarchs, prophets, and
of all the apostles and evangelists, and of the holy
innocents who in the sight of the Holy Lamb are found
worthy to sing the new song, of the holy martyrs and
holy confessors, and of the holy virgins, and of all
the saints, and together with all the holy and elect
of God: we excommunicate and anathematise him or them,
malefactor or malefactors, and from the threshold of
the holy church of God Almighty we sequester them,
that he or they may be tormented, disposed and
delivered over with Dathan and Abiram, with those who
say to the Lord God, Depart from us, we desire not Thy
ways. And as fire is quenched with water, so let the
light of him or them be put out for evermore, unless
it shall repent him or them, and they make
satisfaction. Amen. May the Father who created man,
curse him or them. May the Son, who suffered for us,
curse him or them. May the Holy Ghost, who was given
to us in baptism, curse him or them. May the holy
cross of Christ, for our salvation triumphing over his
enemies, ascend and curse him or them. May the eternal
and holy Virgin Mary, mother of God, curse him or
them. May St. Michael, the advocate of holy souls,
curse him or them. May all the angels and archangels,
principalities and powers, and all the heavenly host,
curse him or them. May the laudable number of
patriarchs and prophets curse him or them. May St.

John, the chief forerunner and baptist of Christ,
curse him or them. May St. Peter and St. Paul, and St.
Andrew, and all other Christ's apostles, together with
the rest of his disciples and evangelists, who by
their preaching converted the universal world, curse
him or them. May the holy and wonderful company of
martyrs and confessors, who by their holy works are
found pleasing to God Almighty, curse him or them. May
the holy choir of the holy virgins, who for the honour
of Christ have despised the things of this world,
curse him or them. May all the saints, who from the
beginning of the world to everlasting ages are found
to be the beloved of God, curse him or them. May the
heavens and the earth, and all the holy things
remaining thereon, curse him or them. May he or they
be cursed wherever he or they be, whether in their
house, or in their field, or in the highway, or in the
path, or in the wood, or in the water, or in the
church. May he or they be cursed in living, in dying,
in eating, in drinking, in being hungry, in being
thirsty, in fasting, in sleeping, in slumbering, in
waking, in walking, in standing, in sitting, in lying,
in working, in resting, in * * * * in * * * * and in
blood-letting. May he or they be cursed in all the
faculties of their body. May he or they be cursed
inwardly and outwardly. May he or they be cursed in
the hair of his or their head. May he or they be
cursed in his or their brain. May he or they be cursed
in the top of his or their head, in their temples, in
their foreheads, in their ears, in their eyebrows, in
their cheeks, in their jaw-bones, in their nostrils,
in their teeth or grinders, in their lips, in their
throat, in their shoulders, in their wrists, in their
arms, in their hands, in their fingers, in their
breast, in their heart, and in the interior parts to
the very stomach, in their veins, in their groin, in
their thighs, in their genitals, in the hips, in the
knees, in the legs, in the feet, in the joints, and in
the nails. May he or they be cursed in all their
joints, from the top of the head to the sole of the

foot. May there not be any soundness in him or them.
May the Son of the Living God, with all the glory of
His Majesty, curse him or them; and may heaven, with
all the powers which move therein, rise against him or
them, to damn him or them, unless he or they shall
repent, or that he or they shall make satisfaction.
Amen, Amen. So be it."

The superstition connected with excommunication was not confined to the churches and nations already mentioned. It extended to the Reformed Churches, and indeed this form of superstition lingers among them still. A most enthusiastic Reformer (the Rev. Donald Cargill), eminent in his day for piety and learning, who suffered martyrdom in 1681, scrupled not, a year before his death, to excommunicate at Torwood, Stirlingshire, several of the most notable and violent persecutors of the time--the King, the Dukes of York, Monmouth, Lauderdale, and Rothes, Sir George Mackenzie, and Sir Thomas Dalzell. If Mr. Cargill did not curse others whom he thought had done him and the cause of truth wrong, he predicted that evil would befall them; and what he foretold came to pass. He told James Irvine of Bonshaw, who apprehended him shortly before his execution, that his persecutor would not long escape a just judgment, not far from the place the arrest was made. This prediction was verified; for soon after Irvine had received 5000 merks as a reward for apprehending Mr. Cargill, he was killed in a duel near Lanark. One John Nesbet mockingly said one day to Mr. Cargill, "Will you not give us a word?" The reverend divine looked on the man with concern, while he said, "Wicked, poor man, mock not; ere you die you shall desire one word, but shall not have it." Soon after, this man was struck dumb, and died in great terror. When Rothes, one of those whom Mr. Cargill excommunicated, threatened him with torture and a violent death, he said, "Forbear to threaten me; for, die what death I may, your eyes shall not see it." This prophecy also came to pass. Rothes died, as is well known, a few hours before the condemned divine and his fellow-martyrs suffered the last penalty of man's law--death temporal.

One can easily imagine the terror into which a weak-minded person would be cast by having the Pope's dire curses pronounced against him, were it not known that he who is authorised to fulminate the ecclesiastical censure and bans, may, for a moderate pecuniary consideration, or by a mortification of the flesh, or good works, have the woes pronounced against him mitigated, if not entirely removed. Indulgences have been purchasable since the early centuries for this world, and for the remission of suffering in purgatory as well. Those most acquainted with the holy places in Rome are best able to make known the facilities with which indulgences are obtained. There is scarcely a church or a station, a convent or a holy place, neither is there hardly a service or a ceremony, which has not its own peculiar indulgences. Indulgences for hundreds of years may be secured by the exercises of a single day. The holy stairs, wherever they are situated, said to have belonged to the palace of Pontius Pilate, consisting of twenty-eight steps, possess peculiar virtue. Leo IV. conceded nine years' indulgence for each step ascended by a devotee on his bare knees. Thus, he who reaches the highest step secures an indulgence of two hundred and fifty-two years, whether he remains here, or finds himself in purgatory. Whoever kisses a cross at one end of the Colosseum of Rome, acquires an indulgence of one year and forty days; and there is a wooden cross in the centre of the arena, which secures an indulgence of two hundred days to every one who kisses it.

Leo XII. conceded for ever an indulgence of forty years and one thousand six hundred days, applicable also to the dead, for every time a faithful believer visits, during Lent, the churches where there are prescribed stations. He also conceded a plenary indulgence to all who have made such visits three times in three distinct days. For the information of all good Catholics, a carefully prepared index has been drawn up, showing the churches and stations which should be visited, together with the most effectual times of repairing thither. In conclusion, we give the following examples, to illustrate the system of procuring indulgences by pilgrimage to sacred places:--

Thus a visit "on January 1 to a station at S. Marie, in Transtevere, secures an indulgence of 30 years and 1200 days."

"On Ash Wednesday, to S. Tabina, an indulgence of 15 years and 600 days.

"On the following Thursday, to S. Georgio, in Velabro, an indulgence of 10 years and 400 days.

"On the fourth Sunday in Lent, to S. Croce, an indulgence of 15 years and 600 days.

"On Palm Sunday, to S. Giovanni, in the Laterno, an indulgence of 25 years and 1000 days.

"On holy Thursday, to S. Giovanni, a plenary indulgence.

"On holy Friday, to S. Croce, an indulgence of 30 years and 1200 days.

"On Easter Sunday, to S. Marie Maggiore, a plenary indulgence.

"On Easter Monday, to S. Pietro, in Vaticano, an indulgence of 30 years and 1200 days.

"On Thursday, Ascension-day, to S. Pietro, a plenary

indulgence.

"On Wednesday, to Pietro Vaticano, an indulgence of 30 years and 1200 days."

CHAPTER LIII.

St. Adelbert's Curse a Charm against Thieves--Complexion of Blackamoors attributed to a Curse of Noah--False Accusation, and its Results--Preservation of Children--A Joyful Mother--Ancestors of the Whelphs and Guelphs of Germany--An Interesting Legend--A Curse turned into a Blessing--A Gipsy's Curse--A Cruel Father and Husband--Morrar-na-Shean's Despair--Bitter Grief--Restoration of Three Daughters--A Grateful Father--Ancestors of the Sinclairs of Caithness, and of the noble family of Keith--The Curse of Moy--A Cruel Chieftain of Clan Chattan--A Lady's Dilemma--A Father yielding up his Life--Swearing by the Hand of a Bride--Grant of Glenmorriston waiting his Doom--Death of a Father and Lover--An Imprisoned Maiden--Maledictions and Prediction--Lady leaping from a Lofty Tower into a Lake beneath--The Monroes of Foulis--Foraying Expedition--An Unreasonable Request--End of a Relentless Tyrant--Prediction fulfilled.

St. Adelbert's curse was a charm against thieves. It was full of cursing against dishonest persons, and prayers that they might have their share with Dathan and Abiram, whom the earth swallowed up, and have their part with Judas. Thieves were to be cursed in their houses, fields, and everywhere; they were to be denied Christian burial; yea, the very ground in which they rested was to be cursed. Their bodies, in all their separate parts, and their children, were damned; and as Lucifer was expelled out of heaven, and Adam and Eve driven from Paradise, so they were sought to be expelled from the light of day. The terrible curse was pronounced with bell, book, and candle; and concluded with this fearful denunciation: "And as the candle, which is thrown out of my hand here, is put out, so let their works and their souls be quenched in the stench of hell-fire, except they restore that which they have stolen; and let every one say, Amen."

Perhaps few are aware that the dark complexion of the blackamoors is attributed to a curse of Noah; but as that statement has been disputed, we shall pass it without further notice.

Irmentrude, a German countess, accused a noble lady of adultery because she had three children at one birth, saying that she deserved to be tied up in a sack and thrown into the sea. Next year the countess herself was delivered of more sons at a birth than the lady had brought forth. Touched with remorse for the hard saying she had uttered against her neighbour, she concluded it was a just punishment inflicted; but being anxious to conceal the most extraordinary result, she sent a maid to drown all the children except one--a son--to heir his father's estate. Fate so determined that her husband, the earl, met the young woman as she was going to consign the young inoffensive infants to a watery grave. On asking what was in her lap, she answered that she was going to drown some whelps. The earl being a great hunter, and consequently fond of dogs, demanded to see the whelps, that he might judge whether they should be destroyed. To his astonishment, he found children in place of young dogs, all living, well-proportioned, and beautiful, but small. From the maid he learned the whole truth; whereupon he enjoined her to silence, and caused the infants to be carried to one of his tenants to be brought up. When they became of age, they were sent for to his house, after being dressed like their brother, who had been cared for by the mother. As soon as the countess cast her eyes on her offspring she knew them, and wept in a state between shame and joy. From those children descended the family of the Whelphs or Guelphs, long renowned in Germany.

An interesting legend is current in the north of Scotland, of a curse being turned into a blessing. It is said that Lochmore Castle, in the parish of Halkirk and county of Caithness, was built and inhabited by a person called Morrar-na-Shean, which signifies, Lord of the Game or Venison, because he was a great sportsman. He was very anxious to have a son to inherit his estates, but his hopes in this respect were blasted by the curse of a wandering gipsy. It appears that the gipsy was one day near Lochmore Castle, with a pretty little dark-haired swarthy-complexioned boy, her son, when she encountered Morrar-na-Shean in a towering passion--a state of mind in which he was often to be found. He ordered her and her "beggar bastard brat" to be off, or he would shoot them. The woman, instead of running away with her child or imploring mercy, knelt down and cursed him, and praying at the same time that he might never have an heir to carry down his name to posterity. However far the fortunes of Morrar-na-Shean's family were affected by the gipsy's curses and prayers, it is impossible to say; but this much is true, he never had a son. His lady had a daughter, at which he was greatly disappointed; she had a second daughter, at which he exhibited marked signs of displeasure; and in course of time a third daughter was born to the churlish parent. Disappointed and enraged at not having a son, he abused the mother and daughters to such an extent that the unhappy lady, for the sake of peace, and to save the lives of her children, sent them away privately, to be brought up by friends. They grew up beautiful and accomplished young ladies, while at the time their cruel father thought they were dead. Morrar-na-Shean, after the lapse of years, despaired of having any children to survive him, and therefore gave himself up to grief. In bitterness of soul, he wished that he had now even one of the little girls he spurned as if she were not his own flesh and blood. His lady, finding his mind so much changed, embraced a favourable opportunity of presenting him with his three daughters. Immediately, on seeing them, he was overcome by tender affection, evoked by the charms of three blooming girls he was privileged to call daughters. He lived to be grateful that fortune had so willed it that his estates would not be in the possession of one child, but would be claimed by three children whom he dearly loved. The daughters were soon disposed of in marriage--the eldest to a gentleman named Sinclair, an ancestor of the well and favourably known Caithness-shire family of that name; the second to a gentleman named Keith, whose descendants have long borne an honourable name in Scotland; and the third, to a nobleman, the scions of whose house have carved out for themselves niches in the temple of fame.

"The curse of Moy" was a fearfully realised one. On the larger of two small islands at Loch Moy (a beautiful lake, twelve miles from Inverness), may be seen the ruins of an ancient castle. Centuries ago a noble edifice stood where those decayed buildings are, occupied by a cruel chieftain of Clan Chattan. He and his followers had an encounter with another Highland chieftain and his retainers from Glenmorriston, when the latter chief, his fair daughter Margaret, and her lover Allan, the young heir of Alvie, were taken prisoners, and carried to Castle Moy. While the captured chieftain and Allan were immured in the dungeon, Margaret was conveyed to a feast in the hall, thence she was transferred to an apartment in the tower, where the chief of Clan Chattan (who, it should be remarked, was a rejected suitor of Margaret) tried to induce her to become his bride. To all his entreaties she turned a deaf ear, preferring to remain true to her youthful Allan. She pleaded earnestly for her father and lover's lives, and, after many entreaties and tears, succeeded so far as to obtain a promise that only one of them would die. She was permitted to make choice of the one she wished liberated, but was warned that by so doing she sealed the doom of the other captive.

As might be expected, the lady sank fainting on the floor, where she lay, more like one dead than alive, until rude attendants, desirous to please their lord, raised her up and hurried her into the presence of her father and lover, for whose sakes she would have willingly laid down her life if it could have saved theirs. With sobbing and tears, she made known the resolution of the hard-hearted revengeful monster, into whose power destiny had placed them. While the broken-hearted Margaret's eyes were now fixed on her lover's manly figure, and then on the bowed form of her aged father, and before she could really understand the full extent of responsibility that rested on her, she was embraced by her father, who took her hand and that of Allan, and joined them together, beseeching them to live and remember him when he was no more. He then made Allan swear by the hand of his bride that he would avenge his death, and so leave no stain on their honour or names. Girding himself up like a man of courage, he sent this message to the tyrant chief: "The Grant of Glenmorriston waits his doom."

Enraged at the turn of events, the chieftain, in violation of his promise to the maiden, determined that Allan should not survive to stand between him and the union of Margaret. Sad forebodings filled her mind during the succeeding night. Silent and alone she sat until break of day, when she was aroused by the shrill pibroch, heavy footsteps, and the clank of arms. A silent prayer went up for the soul of her parent, who, she rightly judged, was suffering the last pangs of death. How it was she could not tell, but something whispered to her that Allan too was passing into the land of spirits.

She had not long to wait, though the time seemed to her like an age, before the chieftain of Moy appeared before her, and commanded her to come forth to see the youth of her choice. More dead than alive, she staggered into the open air, to behold the lifeless forms of both her father and Allan. In derision, the monster asked what she thought now of her beardless boy, and said, "That is the way I tame haughty maids." Again she was conveyed to her lonely room in the castle tower to spend the night in solitude, and again the daylight broke in through the small window of her strongly-guarded prison. She heeded not the sun, nor the singing of birds as they warbled their matin songs--no, sorrow lay too heavy near her heart. None can ever tell the grief she endured in the dark watches of the lonely night, or when relief came; but come it did. Nature took its own way of causing the unhappy lady to forget her sadness of heart--reason left its seat, and the orphaned Margaret, instead of griev- ing over the past, was found singing as sweetly as if she were a bride in a peaceful bower. Now and again the shrill clear voice in song ceased, and then she talked (so the attendants said) to the unseen spirits of those dear to her, whose bodies were still suspended over the castle gate.

The fierce chieftain approached her again with overtures of love, offering her his hand, titles, and estates. To avoid his unholy embrace, she, without waiting to deign a reply, sprang past him with an agility which appeared superhuman, and rushed to the ramparts, that were skirted by the blue waters beneath; then, turning round to the chief of Clan Chattan, she uttered dreadful male- dictions against him, ending with the prediction that he would die a bloody death, leaving neither wife nor child behind. Having said this, she leaped from the giddy height into the lake below, in whose waves she preferred to take refuge rather than yield to the tyrant's solicitations. As far as can be ascertained, the wicked Macintosh repented not of his deeds, but continued to conduct himself in a tyrannical manner to all weaker than himself. At last a day of reckoning came--the day when Lady Margaret's curse was to alight upon the head of the murderer of her father and lover. In the summer of 1378, a short time after these deeds of darkness happened, the Monroes of Foulis were returning from a foraying expedition, and asked permission from the chief of Clan Chattan to pass through his country for half the booty they had with them. Macintosh demanded the whole spoil; but, his unreasonable request being refused, a sanguinary conflict ensued, in which the Clan Chattan chief was slain. The victorious Monroes then hastened to the castle of Moy, and put the whole of the inmates to the sword. Thus perished a relentless tyrant, leaving no fond wife to mourn his fate, nor any offspring to carry his name down to posterity. Thereby was fulfilled the prediction of Lady Margaret, whose bones still rest at the bottom of Loch Moy.

DREAMS AND VISIONS OF THE NIGHT.
CHAPTER LIV.

The Gift or Art of interpreting Dreams--Official   Interpreters of Dreams--Sleep, how portrayed--Goddess   of Dreams--Greeks soliciting the Inspiration of Dreams--Xenophon on Sleep--Prophetic Power of the   Dying--AEsculapius's Discoveries in Dreams--Code of   Menu--The Soma-drink--Josephus as a Seer--Dreadful   Proposal by Josephus--His Fortunate Escape--An Eastern   Conjurer--Reading a Sealed Letter--A Sultan warned of   his Death in a Dream--Alexander's Death foretold in a   Dream--Records of Dreams in Westminster Abbey--Lord Falkland's Dream--Rev. John Brown's Opinions--Early   Christian Faith in Visions and Dreams--Death of a   Friend foretold--The Devil's Sonata--Marriage of Queen   Mary--Fatality of the Stuart Family--Death of Henry   IV. of France.

The gift or art of interpreting dreams originated, at least so it is said, among the Chaldeans and Egyptians. From them it spread to other nations; and in course of time official or public interpreters of dreams were appointed. The sacred pages supply instances of good and bad men having glimpses of futurity through dreams; and profane history makes us acquainted with innumerable cases of curious revelations being made to men while they slept.

Among the ancients sleep was portrayed as a female with black unfolded wings, having in her left hand a white child, the image of sleep, and in her right hand a black child, the image of death. An author has described sleep as the "rest of the spirits, dreaming their tremulous motion;" another writer speaks of sleep as "the reality of another existence;" while a third says, "all men, whilst awake, are in one common world, but that each, when asleep, is in a world of his own." It is of dreams, however, we are writing, and therefore cannot enter into the deep philosophy of sleep.

The Romans worshiped Brizo, the goddess of dreams, and the Greeks were accustomed, in cases of great emergency, to solicit the inspiration of dreams, by performing religious rites, and lying on the reeking skins of oxen or goats offered in sacrifice. Pliny and others attached great importance to dreams. Xenophon remarks that in sleep the souls of men appear to be more unfettered and divine than when the eyes are not closed in slumber, and are enabled to look into futurity. Another writer observes that in sleep the soul holds converse with the Deity, and perceives future events. Socrates, Cicero, and Arian express belief in the prophetic powers occasionally manifested by the dying. Posidonius relates the story of a dying Rhodian predicting which out of six persons would die first, second, etc.; and the prophecy was verified. Hippocrates and Galen put faith in the prophetic character of dreams. Origen tells us that AEsculapius discovered means of cure through dreams, probably brought about by artificial means.

In the code of Menu there are passages showing various modes of producing the ecstatic states, such as through the influence of the sun and moon, by sacrifice, music, liquids, and solid ingredients. The Soma-drink was taken as a sacrament. In connection with human sacrifices, this beverage was sometimes prepared with magical ceremonies and incantations. It was supposed to be capable of producing visions in sleep, when revelations were made of what was passing in the inferior and superior worlds.

Josephus, like many other eminent men, possessed the faculty of predicting future events. Josephus, having fought with great courage against the Romans, refused to surrender to them until after the capture of Jatapat, when he began to reflect on the dreams he had had. In these, both the misfortunes of the Jews and the triumph of the Romans were revealed. When the determination of Josephus to yield became known, his companions in misfortune declared they would rather die than surrender. So exasperated were they, that they proposed to immolate him, and then destroy themselves. Their swords were drawn to kill their leader, when he suggested that they should terminate their lives by a reciprocal death--that the lot should determine successively who should give and who should receive death, until all were slain, and thus avoid the reproach of having laid violent hands on themselves. This suggestion was agreed to. The lots were drawn, and all perished except Josephus and one of his companions. Josephus predicted the good fortune of Vespasian and Titus, and the short life of their predecessors.

In an Eastern tale we are informed of a conjurer who had the reputation of possessing the faculty of reading the contents of sealed letters. Being called into the presence of his prince, he was asked whether he would undertake to inform him of the contents of a despatch he had received by a courier. "Yes," replied the conjuror, "to-morrow morning." The despatch remained sealed in the prince's possession until the following morning, when the conjuror gave the correct contents of the despatch. In explanation, the cunning man said, on going to bed, he excited in himself a strong desire to read the letter, that he then fell asleep, and in a dream he became acquainted with the whole document.

We are told of an old Sultan who was warned of his death in a dream. He thought he saw the great prophet Mohammed snatching the Alcoran out of his hand and taking his coat-of-arms from him by force, and striking him down with so great violence that he could not rise. The astrologers also foretold him that he would never see the feast of Ramazan, because the star that presided at his birth was much obscured in its conjunction with the planet that was then predominant. They affirmed that he would die soon. His dream, and the astrologers' predictions, were not long of being verified. The Sultan's death was accompanied with great ignominy.

From Aristotle we learn that the death of Alexander was foretold in a dream; and so was that of Caesar. In Westminster Abbey are singular records of the dreams of Edward the Confessor, and of instances of faith in visions.

Lord Falkland's dream, the night before the battle of Newbury, in which he was slain, in the year 1643, has often been referred to by persons who believe in dreams. James Montgomery, the poet, has in touching lines assisted to keep the dream from being forgotten.

In more modern times, good men, whom we might suppose to be free from the trammels of superstition, have to some extent directed their course in life according to the interpretation of their dreams. The Rev. John Brown, author of the *Dictionary of the Holy Bible*, writing of dreams, says: "It is like they often begin from some outward sensation of the body, in which spirits, good and bad, have no inconsiderable influence."

In visions and dreams the persecution of the early Christians was made known to many believers. Other important events were also predicted, and preceded by strange phenomena. But for dreams, not a few celebrated men who played important parts in national affairs would have been entrapped, and turned aside from their purposes.

A gentleman holding a good position in society was awakened by his wife one night, who told him she had had a most unpleasant dream. She thought that a friend, who was in the East India Company's service, had been killed in a duel. She described the place where the duel was fought, and where the dead body lay. Her husband endeavoured to quiet her fears, and characterised the dream as an absurdity, produced by a disturbed imagination. A few months after, the melancholy news reached this country that the Indian friend had fought a duel, been killed on the spot, and his body carried to a shed such as the lady had seen in her dream.

Fastini, a celebrated musician, dreamed one night that he had made a compact with the devil, who promised to be at his service on all occasions. He imagined that he presented the devil with his violin, in order to discover what kind of a musician he was. To Fastini's great astonishment, Satan, as he thought, played a solo of singular beauty, which he executed with such superior taste and precision, that it surpassed all the music he had ever heard or conceived. Fastini awoke greatly excited, and, taking his violin, composed a piece that excelled all his other works. He called it the "Devil's Sonata."

Before the marriage of the young Queen of Scotland with the Dauphin of France, many had strange dreams and visions. Prodigious signs were also observed in her native country. A comet shone for three months; rivers dried up in winter, and in summer swelled so high that cattle were carried away, and villages suddenly destroyed. Whales of enormous size were cast ashore in the Firth of Forth; hailstones as large as pigeons' eggs fell in various parts, destroying the crops; and, still more strange and alarming, a fiery dragon was seen flying low over the earth, vomiting forth fire, which endangered houses and farmyards.

The dire fatality that attended the Royal Stuarts did not surprise those who attended to warnings through dreams, signs, and omens. Few royal families were more unhappy than the Stuarts. James I., after having been eighteen years a prisoner in England, was, together with his queen, assassinated by his subjects; James II. was, in the twenty-ninth year of his age, killed while fighting against England; James III. was imprisoned by his subjects, and afterwards killed in battle by rebels; James IV. perished in a battle which was lost; Mary Stuart was driven from her throne, became a fugitive in Scotland, and, after languishing for years in prison, was condemned by English judges and beheaded; James VI. of Scotland and I. of England, her son, died at his palace at Theobalds, not without strong suspicion of being poisoned; Charles I. was betrayed by his own subjects, and, in terms of a sentence by English judges, lost his life on the scaffold; James VII. of Scotland and II. of England was driven from his kingdoms, and, to fill the cup of bitterness to the brim, the birth of his son, as legitimate heir, was disputed. The misfortunes of Prince Charles are too well known to require us to do anything more than refer to them. In his attempt to regain the throne of his ancestors, he was driven to such a strait that he was compelled, after many of his supporters had been put to death, to escape for his life under the guidance of a woman--Flora Macdonald, renowned in history.

A few days before the death of Henry IV. of France, his queen had two strange dreams. She thought all the jewels in her crown were changed into pearls--a dream that much disturbed her, as pearls were understood to signify tears. On the following night she had another dream which caused her greater uneasiness--that the king was stabbed in one of his sides. The king, as well as the queen, had presentiments that a sad calamity was about to happen them. On the day before his Majesty was killed he was very uneasy, and said something sat heavy on his heart. Before entering the coach in which he was assassinated, he took a tender farewell of the queen, kissing her thrice, and pressing her close to his breast. For a time he hesitated whether he would go out or not; but all at once he resumed his wonted courage, forbade the guards to follow him out of the Louvre, and drove away in an open carriage. The fates were against his Majesty: the fiat had gone forth, and that day the hand of a regicide plunged a knife into the sovereign's body, exactly as the queen had seen in her midnight vision.

CHAPTER LV.

Dreaming Dictionaries--Dreaming of an Anchor--Sick   Persons' Dreams--
Coloured and Rich Raiment--Dreaming   of Fruit--Funerals, Hearses, Graves--
Dreams sometimes   to be read contrariwise--Seeing Candles in the Visions   of
Night, what they foretell--Darkness and   Gloom--Jewellery, Gold, and Silver-
-Losing and finding   Property--Dreaming of Fowls and   Eggs--Flying--Bag-
pipes, Dancing, and Banquets--Dogs,   Cocks, Cattle, Horses, and Sheep--Cakes,
Corn, Milk,   and Cream--Dreams of Carrying and of being   Carried--Being
hurt by Cats or by any description of   Vermin--Angels, Spirits, and Children--
Clergymen and   Churches--A Broken Watch or Clock--Clouds--Falling   from
a High Place--Flowers and Fruit--Sailors'   Dreams--Running Streams and Still
Water--Swimming--Ploughed Ground and Green   Fields--Presents--Glass--
Dreaming of Hair--Fire, Cold,   a Tooth, Kisses, and Knives--Leaping, Climbing
a Hill,   and Writing--Clean and Dirty Linen--The Sun, Moon, and   Stars,
Rainbow, Snow, Thunder, and Lightning.

If dreaming dictionaries can be relied on, people may discover by their thoughts in sleep when they are to be prosperous or unlucky; when they are to have joy or sorrow; when they are to be successful in love and war; and when they may expect friends to guard them against enemies. To dream of an anchor is good; it gives hope of good fortune. If a sick person dream of white clothing, he may look for protracted indisposition, if not death; but black apparel denotes speedy recovery. It is not good to dream of raiment of many colours. To dream of being richly arrayed is good, but to see tattered clothing in the visions of the night forebodes evil. It is good to dream of good ripe fruit, but sour fruit signifies encounters with bitter enemies. Sweet apples indicate faithfulness in a sweetheart, whereas unripe cherries foretell vexation and disappointment to lovers. Good figs are signs of prosperity. Gooseberries indicate to husband or wife many children. Grapes foretell to the spinster a cheerful husband, and much happiness in all her life. Dreaming of melons, mulberries, or nuts, gives promise of riches, success in love, and harmony. It is also good to dream of peaches, pears, raspberries, and strawberries; but if oranges, plums, tamarinds, or walnuts are seen in the visions of night, losses and crosses may be looked for.

To dream of a funeral denotes marriage, good fortune, and happiness. If a maiden see a hearse in her sleep, she may expect a rich husband. If a grave appear to one in his dreams, sickness and disappointment may be expected, unless the dreamer imagines he is rising out of it. In that case, success may be looked for. On the other hand, to dream of being married is anything but favourable. Such a dream is indicative of approaching disappointments, loss of property, and death. The force of this seeming contradiction is to be explained by the acknowledged fact that dreams are in many instances to be read contrariwise. To dream of being burned is a sure sign of coming danger. To see a candle extinguished foretells sickness; but the appearance of a bright burning one betokens rejoicing. To the unmarried, burning candles show speedy marriage. Dreams of darkness foreshadow loss of property and friends; but if the dreamer in his sleep emerge from the gloom into light, he may expect that he will rise above his difficulties, and become richer and happier. To dream that a friend is dead betokens hasty news, but not of an unpleasant nature. It is fortunate to dream of jewellery. If a young lady see herself decked with chains of gold and precious stones, she may be certain a suitable husband will soon be hers. Precious stones give promise of many children to the married. If pure gold be dreamed of, success in business may be expected; but it is unlucky to dream of silver. To dream of the latter metal denotes attacks by bitter enemies and false friends. Small silver coins indicate poverty, and large ones give warning of early misery. It is more lucky to dream of receiving than of giving away money. If one dream of losing money, he will undoubtedly meet with disappointment before he goes much further in his journey of life. To dream of losing a purse has the same meaning attached to it as the loss of money has; and the finding of a purse may be read as the picking up of cash. To dream of having a ring on one's finger is good; but to dream of losing a ring is unfavourable. If a married woman lose her marriage ring, or dream that she has lost it, she may expect her husband will die soon. If a betrothed maiden lose or dream of losing her engagement ring, she may look for her lover deserting her and marrying another.

Dreams of hens and chickens are warnings of coming dangers. If one see in his or her dream an eagle soaring high, prosperity and honour are near. To lovers this bird is one of good omen, foretelling rich and good mates. To dream of geese is also favourable; but the person who sees in a vision an owl, had better prepare for sickness and poverty, and look for attacks from enemies. A young man who dreams of a peacock may be sure of getting a beautiful wife; and a maid who fancies in her sleep that this beautiful bird is coming towards her, may be certain that the fates are to provide her with a rich good-looking husband. To dream of swans denotes success to the business man, lovers to the unmarried, and peace and plenty to the married. If swallows are dreamt of, good news may be expected from afar, and prosperity looked for. To dream of selling eggs for gold is good, but to dream of selling them for silver betokens indifferent success in business, love, and war. To dream of buying eggs indicates the gathering of great riches. If a dreamer supposes that he is flying, he should prepare himself for a long journey. This dream indicates to lovers a happy termination to all their wishes, and to the married it denotes abundance and many children.

To dream of bagpipes signifies contention and trouble. To dream of dancing or of being at a ball or banquet, foretells preferment, joyful news; and, in particular, such a dream foretells prosperity in love.

Barking dogs, crowing cocks, bellowing bulls, are unlucky to dream of; but it indicates coming prosperity and happiness to dream of faithful dogs, horses, cows, and fleecy sheep. But look out for loss of goods if you see shorn sheep, and make up your mind to encounter danger if you suppose in your sleep that you are falling off a horse.

Cakes signify joy and plenty, corn in great store, riches and contentment, but grain in small quantities denotes scarcity. Milk or cream thrown or spilt on one's garments is favourable. To dream of selling milk denotes crosses in love; to dream of drinking milk betokens joyful news; and to dream of milking kine shows success in love to the faithful milk-maids. If a maid dream that she is engaged in a dairy, she may be certain that her lover will turn out to be an industrious, prudent husband. But if the farmer dream that he is assisting in the dairy, he may look out for bad crops, and disease among his cattle. If one dream he is being carried, he may expect to require early help of some kind or other. If he dream of carrying another, he may depend upon it, that before many days pass he will be called upon to give the loan of money, sign a bill, or give away property that will not be returned. If one dream of being hurt by a cat, or by any description of vermin, he has good reason to fear he will be overcome by enemies; but if he suppose in sleep that he drove away or killed the creature, he will triumph over his foes. If a squirrel be seen in a dream, the dreamer may rest satisfied some one is endeavouring to injure his reputation; and to a lover it is a warning of a busy and dangerous rival. To dream of angels speaking to you is of good signification; and to think that you see them flying above your head intimates joy. To dream of the devil or of evil spirits, denotes danger from secret and open enemies. If a lover dream of one of these evil beings, it indicates the existence of a powerful rival.

If a poor person dream of children, he or she may expect to become rich. If a childless spouse see in a dream children running round the fireside, there is reason to fear the little prattlers will never be there in reality. It is unlucky to dream that a girl has a beard, or that a boy is grey-headed. It is unlucky to dream of a minister, but it is not an evil sign for one to suppose he is worshipping in church. If you dream that a watch or clock falls or is broken, be sure danger is near.

Black clouds, seen in dreams, presage evil; white clouds denote prosperity; clouds drifting high in air indicate that the dreamer is going to travel, or that long absent friends are to return. To dream of red clouds foretells contention and strife. To dream of fighting or quarrelling should put one on his guard against the deceitfulness of his own heart and the hatred of enemies. If the dreamer suppose himself injured in a quarrel, he will be unable to escape humiliation and shame. To dream of falling from a high place betokens loss of substance and reputation. To dream of withered lilies, damaged violets, and crosses, betokens evil. It is not good for sick people to dream of withered roses; parsley foreshadows death to the sick. It is lucky to dream you see yourself gathering flowers fresh in colour and sweet in perfume. To dream of walking in a flower garden portends elevation in fortune and success in love; and to dream of being in an orchard where there is abundance of sweet and ripe fruit, gives true promise of riches.

If a sailor dream of seeing a dolphin, he will be sure to lose his lady-love; but if he dream that he is drowning, he may expect good luck to attend him. It indicates success in love and business for one to dream of catching fish. To dream of a rapid stream, is a certain warning of coming opposition in every business and undertaking. If one in sleep see a clear sheet of water, good fortune will certainly follow. This dream promises good alike to lovers and men of business. It indicates a smooth passage for one to dream of a calm bright sea; but disappointments and trouble are foreshadowed when a stormy ocean appears to the sleeper. Floating with the head under water foretells great affliction, but swimming buoyantly in clean water shows that the dreamer will rise above difficulties. If a person in business dream of drinking water, loss of goods may be expected; and if a lover dream of tasting water, whether from the sluggish river or from the clear gushing stream, he or she may look for grief and loss of friends.

To dream of ploughed ground forebodes death of a near relative, and to dream of green fields betokens happiness and prosperity. If a person dream of receiving a present, you may be sure fortune is about to show her favours in a peculiarly marked manner. To dream of glass is a sign of danger and the inconstancy of friends. The lady who dreams of combing her hair, has reason to believe her lover will prove true. If one's hair appear long in the dreams of the night, friends full of affection will cling round the dreamer; but if the hair be short and seem to be falling off, it is unlucky. If one dream of seeing a house on fire, he may be sure of receiving hasty news.

When one dreams of being cold or naked, he is threatened with sickness and poverty. It is good to dream of seeing the portraits of friends. One who dreams of losing a tooth, may look for death among his friends. It is good to dream of giving or receiving kisses--it denotes friendship, good health, and earthly prosperity. If one dream of knives or any other description of sharp weapons, he may look for strife. Difficulties await every one who dreams of leaping over a fence or of climbing a hill. It is lucky to dream of writing or receiving letters. Clean linen seen in sleep foretells gladness of heart and faithfulness of friends; but dirty linen denotes disappointment and distress. None could wish a better dream than that in which is seen the clear sun, the rising moon, or the bright stars, for each and all of these denote riches, joy, good news, and constant friends; but it is ominous to dream of a clouded sun, a waning moon, or a pale star.

The rainbow denotes early news of a pleasant nature: probably requiring the dreamer to travel. If an unmarried man dream of snow, he may depend upon it that he will before long lead a bride to the hymeneal altar; and to a young woman it promises an honourable husband and great riches. To the business man, snow seen in a dream foretells success in his undertakings. It is good to dream of thunder and lightning, in whatever state one is placed. He who dreams of these may expect good news from afar, and increase of goods.

LAWS AGAINST AND TRIALS OF WITCHES.
CHAPTER LVI.

Witchcraft treated with great Severity--Cutting out the Tongue--Laws of AEthelstane--Witchcraft in England--Royal Writers--Sir Edward Cole's Opinion--Statute of Elizabeth against Sorcerers--Law of Mary Queen of Scotland against Witches--Law against Witches abolished--Sir George Mackenzie on Witchcraft--William Forbes on the same--Extracts from Forbes's *Institute of the Law of Scotland*--Sir Matthew Hale a Believer in Witchcraft--Trial of Rose Cullender and Ann Duny--General Belief in the Existence of Witches--Punishment of Witches, by whom first countenanced--Pope John's Bull--Bishop Jewell--Lord Bacon and the Law against Witches--Fearful Slaughter of supposed Witches--*Malleus Maleficarum*, or Hammer for Witches--The last Persons executed in Scotland and England for Witchcraft--First German Printers condemned to be burned as Sorcerers--Reginald Scot on the Fables of Witchcraft--Mr. E. Chambers's Views on Witchcraft.

Witchcraft--the nature and theory of which will appear as we proceed--was treated with great severity in early times. In 840 a law was enacted in Scotland, making the punishment of witchcraft no less than the cutting out of the tongue; and, by the laws of AEthelstane in 928, witchcraft in England was made a capital crime. Witches were punished in the reign of Edward III.; and it suited the sanguinary temperament of Henry VIII., as well as the pedantry of other royal writers, to give written descriptions of this crime. Edicts were promulgated against prophets, sorcerers, feeders of evil spirits, charmers, and provokers of unlawful love. Sir Edward Cole thought it would have been "a great defect in government to have suffered such devilish abominations to pass with impunity."

By a statute of Elizabeth, passed in 1562, against sorcerers, it was ordained that for a first offence the punishment was to be restricted to standing in the pillory; for second and subsequent offences, severer inflictions were to follow. Barrington estimates that in the two hundred years during which the greatest severity against supposed witches prevailed in England, thirty thousand judicial murders were committed, under the guise of legal punishments for such imaginary crimes.

A year later (1563) it was considered advisable by Queen Mary of Scotland and her Parliament to pass an Act, having for its object the punishment of persons guilty of any of the crimes under consideration. The Act sets forth:--

"For-sa-meikle as the Queenis Majestie and the three
Estaites of this present parliament being informed of
the heavie and abominable superstition used be divers
of the lieges of this realm, be using of witchcraft,
sorcerie, and necromancie, and credence given thereto
in times by-gane, against the laws of God: And for
avoyding and away putting of all sik vaine
superstition in times to cum: It is statute and
ordained by the Queen's Majestie, and the three
Estaites foresaid, that na maner of person nor persons
of quhat-sum-ever estaite, degree, or condition they
be of, take upon hand in onie times hereafter to use
onie maner of witch-craftes, sorcerie, or necromancie,
nor give themselves furth to have onie sik craft or
knawledge thereof, their-throw abusand the people: Nor
that na persoun seik onie helpe, response, or
consultation at onie sik users or abusers foresaidis
of witch-craftes, sorceries, or necromancie, under the
paine of death, alsweill to be execute against the
user, abuser, as the seiker of the response or
consultation. And this to be put to execution be the
justice, schireffis, stewards, baillies, lords of
regalities, and royalties, their deputes, and uthers
or ordinar judges competent within this realme, with
all rigour, having power to execute the samin."

James VI. of Scotland and I. of England decreed that any one who should use, practise, or exercise any invocation, or consult or covenant with, entertain or employ, feed, or reward any evil or wicked spirit, to or for any purpose, or take up any dead body, should, on being convicted thereof, suffer death.

The laws against witchcraft remained in force, and were executed with severity, for a long time. During the continuance of the Long Parliament alone, three thousand unhappy persons were sacrificed because of their supposed connection with witchcraft. But by the Act 9 George II. cap. 5 it is ordained that no prosecution, suit, or proceeding shall be commenced or carried on against any person for witchcraft, sorcery, enchantment, or conjuration, nor shall any one charge another with any such offence, in any court whatever. But if any person shall pretend to exercise or use any kind of witchcraft, sorcery, enchantment, or conjuration, or undertake to tell fortunes; or pretend, from his skill or knowledge in any occult or crafty science, to discover where or in what manner any goods supposed to have been stolen or lost may be found: every person so offending, being convicted on indictment or information, shall suffer imprisonment for a year, and once in every quarter of the said year, in some market town of the county, upon the market day there, stand openly in the pillory for one hour, and also (if the court by which such judgment shall be given shall think fit) be obliged to give sureties for his good behaviour, in such sum, and for such time, as the said court shall judge proper, according to the circumstances of the offence, and in such case shall be further imprisoned until such sureties shall be given.

Sir George M'Kenzie, the distinguished Scotch lawyer, thought there was such a craft as witch-craft; and so did William Forbes, a member of the Faculty of Advocates, a professor of law in the University of Glasgow, and author of several works of considerable merit. The following extracts from Forbes's *Institute of the Law of Scotland* prove to some extent what was the legal creed in Scotland last century in regard to witches:--

> "Witchcraft is that black art whereby strange and wonderful things are wrought by a power derived from the devil. It goes under several names, taken from particular effects and ways of its operation: As those of magic, because it is a knowledge of more than is lawful to be known; divination, from a revealing of things past, present, or to come; enchantment, from a working by charms or ceremonious rites; sorcery, from the casting of lots to bring hidden things to light; necromancy, from the calling up and consulting the devil, in form of some dead person; fascination, from the hurting creatures by envious looks, and eye-biting, or by words, etc. Those who practise this art are, in like manner, termed witches, magicians, diviners, enchanters, sorcerers, necromancers, fascinaters. Which names, given for different causes to the devil's disciples, are, for the most part, promiscuously used to signify any person who, by covenant with Satan, and his assistance, doth work strange things, because of the affinity of all their operations, which have the same general foundation and tendency.

> "An express covenant is entered into betwixt a witch and the devil appearing in some visible shape, whereby the former renounces his God and baptism, engaging to

serve the devil, and do all the mischief he can, as
occasion offers, and leaves soul and body to his
disposal after death. The devil, on his part, articles
with such proselytes concerning the shape he is to
appear to them in, and the services they are to expect
from him, upon the performance of certain charms or
ceremonious rites. To some he gives certain spirits or
imps to correspond with, and serve them as their
familiars, known by them by some odd names, to which
they answer when called. These imps are said to be
kept in pots or other vessels that stink detestably.
This league is made verbally if the party cannot
write; and such as can write sign a written covenant
with their blood. On the meaner proselytes the devil
fixes, in some secret part of their bodies, a mark, as
his seal to know his own by, which is like a flea-bite
or blue spot, and sometimes resembles a little teat;
and the part so stamped doth ever after remain
insensible, and doth not bleed, though never so much
nipped, or pricked, by thrusting a pin, awl, or bodkin
into it. But if the covenanter be one of the better
rank, the devil only draws blood of the party, or
touches him or her in some part of the body, without
any visible mark remaining.

"A tacit covenant with Satan is understood to be
entered into by those who knowingly use the
superstitious rites or ceremonies observed by witches,
or unlawful means to bring anything about which they
know to be ineffectual in themselves without the
devil's concurrence.

"Witches used to be distinguished into good and bad
witches. The bad witch, commonly called the black
witch, or binding witch, is one who, by a league with
the devil, is assisted by him to work mischief. The
good witch is he or she who useth diabolical means to
do good--as to heal persons, loose or undo
enchantments, and to discover who are bewitched, and
by whom. But this term of a good witch is very

improper, for all who have commerce with Satan are
certainly bad.

"Some works of witches are really what they seem to
be; others are mere diabolical juggling, or a delusion
of the eyes of spectators with some strange sleight of
Satan. (To which last I may refer their imaginary
passing through shut doors, and transforming
themselves and others into the shape of cats, dogs,
hares, and other creatures.) Some of their actions
respect themselves, and their behaviour towards their
infernal master; such as their coming to appointed
meetings called their Sabbaths, where they pay homage
to him, and are taught to act all manner of
wickedness, and give an account of their horrid past
proceedings. Witches are chiefly employed in plain
mischief, by hurting persons or their goods, or by
bringing some actual evil or calamity upon them. But
they sometimes work mischief under a pretence or
colour of doing good--as when they cure diseases,
loose enchantments, and discover other witches. All
their designs are brought about by charms, or
ceremonious rites instituted by the devil, which are
in themselves of no efficacy, and serve only as
signals and watchwords to admonish Satan, as it were,
when, where, and upon whom to do mischief, or perform
cures, according to his compact with the witches."

"Under necromancy," says Mr. Forbes, "are comprehended
chiromancy, predictions, and responses by the sieve
and the shear, and all other hellish arts of
divination. It hath been sustained to bring in a
woman guilty of witchcraft, that she threatened to
do some mischief to a person who immediately or not
long after suffered a grievous harm in his body or
goods, by sorcery or witchcraft, without any apparent
or natural cause, though the manner or enchantment
used to work such mischief was not particularly
expressed, and the threat was only general, and did
not specify the ill turn to be done, in respect the

means used by witches are best known to themselves.
Some relevant articles of witchcraft are founded upon
events having no necessary dependence on the means
used by the person accused: as that a man on whom
a woman had laid a grievous sickness by her sorcery
was relieved thereof by her taking him by the hand,
and the moving of her lips; or that a woman came
several times into a house when the doors and
windows were all fast locked and shut at night,
combed her hair the last night, and laid her hand
upon a nurse's breast, upon which a child then
sucking her died within half-an-hour--because
injuries done by witches are not occasioned by
any inherent virtue or efficacy in the means used
by them, but only by the devil's influence; and that
there is no natural cause for the mischief done, is
the reason of ascribing it to witchcraft. Where one
is indicted for being in league with the devil, and
exercising acts of witchcraft, it sufficeth to prove
that the indictee was in confederacy with that evil
spirit, and did such things; but in the trial of one
indicted for bewitching any person, two things are to
be proved, viz. that such a person is bewitched, and
that the indictee is the witch."

Mr. Forbes says that symptoms of witchcraft are: "When
learned and skilful physicians find the patient's
trouble doth not proceed from any bodily distemper or
natural causes; when he is exceedingly tormented at
the saying of prayers and graces, or reading of the
Bible; when in his fits he tells truly many things
past and future, which in an ordinary way he could not
know; and when things are done with respect to him by
some invisible hand working in a manner that cannot be
understood. Other proofs are such as when one cannot
shed tears, and cannot say the Lord's Prayer. And
other presumptions," he proceeds, "are inferred from
the drawing of blood of the suspected person, or the
putting of something under a threshold where he or she
goes in, or under a stool where the suspected person

sits, or causes him or her to come into a room where
those afflicted with witchcraft are, and touch them;
or trying if the suspected person will sink or swim
when put tied into the water; the burning of cakes
wherein are the afflicted persons' urine, or the
burning of clothes in which such persons lie."

The learned professor thought that witchcraft might be proved by witnesses who have heard
the accused person invoking the devil for help, or seen the suspected party entertaining a familiar
spirit and feeding it in any form or likeness, conjuring to raise storms, showing in a glass or show-
stone the faces of absent persons. His opinion was that it was competent to receive as evidence
the dying testimonies of penitent witches concerning others informed against by them, as proof of
witchcraft was difficult to obtain; and the more secret acts--meeting of witches in the night-time to
adore their infernal master, and hatch their mischievous projects when other people are asleep, or
when they themselves are invisible--cannot be otherwise proved than by such as are privy thereto.

Sir Matthew Hale, the astute lawyer and judge, was a believer in witchcraft, and entertained
views on this subject similar to those of Mr. Forbes, as will appear from the following particulars of
the trial of Rose Cullender and Ann Duny in 1664. These women were accused before Sir Matthew
Hale of various acts of witchcraft--such as tormenting children by means of devilish devices, upset-
ting carts, killing horses, breeding vermin, etc., through diabolical means. At the trial, evidence was
given by Anne Durent, that William Durent, her son (one of the children bewitched) had strange
and sad fits, caused by Duny giving the child suck. A wise man (Dr. Jacob) advised her to hang up the
child's blanket in the chimney corner all day, and at night, when she went to put the child to bed,
if she found anything in the blanket, to throw the thing, whether apparently animate or inanimate,
into the fire. The blanket was hung up and shaken according to instructions, when, behold, a large
toad fell on the hearth-stone. The creature was thrown into the fire, and exploded like a gun. Next
day a friend of Duny's told deponent that a certain old woman was severely burned. On hearing this,
deponent went to the old woman's house, and found her grievously scorched. Duny (for it was she
who was in this sad condition) told the witness, that because of the evil she did to her, she (Duny)
would see much evil befall the Durent family. Deponent further stated that her daughter, Elizabeth
Durent, about ten years of age, was afflicted like her other child, and in her fits complained of Ann
Duny tormenting her. Duny had (so said the witness) predicted that the child named would not live
long, and within three days the child died. Deponent also testified that Duny had, while in a rage,
said that she (the witness) would yet be going with crutches--a prophecy followed by deponent becoming so lame in both her legs, that she could not walk without being supported by sticks. "And,
indeed," said she, exhibiting a pair of crutches in the witness-box, "I could not come into court
without them."

After lengthened and curious evidence touching the charges against the prisoners for bewitching the children, named in the indictment, Dr. Brown, a gentleman of great learning, expressed his
opinion that the children were bewitched. He said that in Denmark there had been a great discovery

of witches, who used the very same way of afflicting people, viz. by conveying pins and nails into them in a mysterious way. His opinion was that the devil, in witchcraft, did work upon the bodies of men and women, and afflict them with such distempers as their bodies were most subject to.

John Sloan testified that, while bringing home three carts of hay, one of the carts accidentally damaged the window of Rose Cullender's house, and that she, in consequence of this mishap, uttered violent threats against him. The other two carts passed her house safely several times that day, but the cart which damaged the window was two or three times overturned. Once, when taking the un-lucky vehicle through a gate, it stuck fast, though nothing could be seen that prevented it from being drawn along easily. After great trouble, the cart was brought home, but, there again, fresh difficul-ties had to be encountered: the vehicle could not be taken to the place where it was intended to be unloaded; and, what most frightened the witness and those aiding him was, that every one who ap-proached the cart to render any assistance on that eventful day, came away with his nose bleeding.

Robert Sherringhame swore that Rose Cullender, taking offence at him, threatened him and his horses with injury, and in a short time many of his horses and cattle died. Following these mis-fortunes, he became lame, and was so tormented with lice that he could not get them removed until he burned two suits of clothes.

Richard Spencer testified that he had heard Ann Duny say that the devil would not let her rest until she took her revenge upon Cornelius Sandswell.

The judge told the jury that they were to inquire, first, whether the several acts of witchcraft mentioned in the indictment had been committed; and, secondly, if they had, it was for them to say whether the prisoners were the guilty persons. The jurors, he said, could not doubt that there were such creatures as witches; for history affirmed it, and the wisdom of all nations had provided laws against such persons. He prayed that the hearts of the jury might be directed in the mighty thing they had in hand; for to condemn the innocent and let the guilty go free were alike an abomination. The jury brought in a verdict of guilty. The judge then passed sentence of death against the culprits, and they were executed.

A general belief in the existence of witches prevailed in every country, and stringent measures were adopted for their extirpation. If the punishment of witchcraft was not at first countenanced by the Church, the clergy subsequently, and for centuries, played a prominent part in the detection and condemnation of the so-called witches. Pope John stated in a bull of 1317 that several of his courtiers and his physician had given themselves up to superstition, and that their rings and mirrors contained evil spirits. Pope Innocent VIII. issued a bull against witchcraft in 1484. Thousands of innocent per-sons were burned, and others killed by the tests applied to them. Twenty-seven articles were issued in France in the fourteenth century against sorcery, the use of images, and the invocation of evil spirits. Many Templars were burned in Paris for witchcraft in 1309.

Referring to witches and sorcerers, Bishop Jewell, when preaching before his sovereign in 1598, said: "Witches and sorcerers, within the last four years, are marvellously increased within your Grace's realm. Your Grace's subjects pine away, even unto the death; their colour fadeth--their flesh rotteth--their speech is benumbed--their senses are bereft. I pray they may never practise fur-ther than upon your Majesty's subjects." Mr. Glanvil, chaplain to Charles II., was of opinion that "the disbeliever in witchcraft must believe the devil gratis;" and Wesley said that "giving up witchcraft was, in fact, giving up the Bible." The learned Lord Bacon, Lord Coke, and twelve bishops had a voice in the legislation of the country when the act of James I. of England against witchcraft became law.

Five hundred witches were burned at Geneva during three months of 1515. In the diocese of Como, one thousand were burned within one year. Nine hundred were burned in Lorraine in a period of fifteen years. Hundreds perished at Wurzburg in a few years; and upwards of one hundred thousand were executed in Germany, for which country the *malleus maleficarum*, or hammer for witches (drawn out by a clergyman and two inquisitors appointed by Innocent VIII.), was principally intended. In Poland and America, witches, or supposed witches, were also put to death by fire and water. Persecutions against witches raged with great fury in America in 1648-49. In New England, in 1692, nine persons were hanged by the Puritans for witchcraft. Under pressure, fifty persons there confessed themselves to be witches. Italy, Spain, and Portugal had their victims too. At one period the execution of witches exceeded those in England, though the number put to death in the latter country was truly appalling. In 1646 two hundred persons were tried and executed for witchcraft at the Sussex and Essex assizes. The last persons put to death for witchcraft in England were, some say, in 1664, while others assert the last victims suffered in 1682. The latest instance of a witch being executed in Scotland was in 1722, when the supposed offender was burned at Loth, or Dornoch, Sutherlandshire, by order of the sheriff of that county. In more recent times than several of the dates to which we have referred, discoveries, which might have been easily understood, gave rise to the supposition that the actors were in compact with the devil. On the first occasion of the German printers carrying their books to France, the ingenious inventors of printing were condemned to be burned alive as sorcerers--a sentence that would have been executed had those discoverers of a useful art not saved themselves by flight.

Reginald Scot, taking an enlightened view of superstition, says, "The fables of witchcraft have taken so fast hold of and deep root in the heart of man, that few endure the hand of correction without attributing the chastisement to the influence of witches. Such superstitious people," he says, "are persuaded that neither hail nor snow, thunder nor lightning, rain nor tempestuous winds, come from the higher powers, but are raised by the power of witches and conjurors. If a clap of thunder or a gale of wind be heard, the timid people ring bells, cry out to burn the witches, or else they burn consecrated things, hoping thereby to drive the devil out of the air."

Mr. E. Chambers did not think the art of witchcraft was carried on by or through intercourse with the devil or spirits (though he did not dispute there were such beings), but by or through philosophical means, altogether different from the operations supposed necessary to enable witches and wizards to perform actions not easily comprehended by the uninitiated.

CHAPTER LVII.

Witch-finders--Disasters ascribed to Witches--Witch-marks--Witches Familiars--Preparing a Witch for Judicial Examination--John Kinnaird--Patrick Watson and his Wife pricked--Confession of Guilt--The Devil's Sabbaths--Sumptuous Entertainments and Grandeur at Satan's Feasts--Repulsive Acts there also--Feasts ended at Cock-crowing--Transformation--A Woman weighing only Four Ounces--A Witch-finder sent from Scotland to Newcastle at the request of the Authorities--Complaints against Witches demanded--Deception discovered--Trying Witches in Northumberland County--Escape of the Witch-finder from Justice--Hopkins's Methods of detecting Witches--Zeal of the Clergy in Scotland in condemning Witches--Witch burned within the Sea-mark--Extracts from Kirk-session Records of Perth relative to Witchcraft--Witches at Kirkcaldy--A Clerical Witch-finder.

Every town and county had its witch-finder, whose duty it was to detect and bring to trial all those tainted with witchcraft or sorcery. Considering that almost every accident which happened was attributed to sorcery, the duties of the witch-finder were most important. According to his diligence so was the safety of persons and property. Hail-storms, destructive floods, dangerous fires, disease among cattle, and domestic afflictions were all ascribed to witchcraft. A mole or wart discovered on any part of an old woman's body was thought to be a witch-mark. If a suspected witch did not shed tears, it was presumptive evidence of guilt; if she kept a black cat, it was taken for a familiar; and all these circumstances together were regarded as infallible signs of her evil nature. An expert witch-finder knew all the wiles and arts of his profession. To prepare the suspected witch for judicial examination, a particular diet was sometimes given her, to counteract the unguents she had anointed herself with, to make non-effective the preparations of belladonna, aconite, parsley, and other ingredients she had swallowed, and to render of no effect the charmed cocks' combs and rams' kidneys partaken of by her.

John Kinnaird, a witch-finder, some hundreds of years past, brought many witches to justice in his time. In 1649 he pricked Patrick Watson, of West Fenton, and Minie Haliburton his wife, and found the devil's mark on the husband's back, and the same evil one's impress on the wife's neck. Though the operator thrust his sharp instrument deep into the spots, no pain was felt, nor did blood flow. These results proved that the accused husband and wife were in league with Satan; and Minie, seeing it was useless to deny her guilt, admitted the crime.

Under judicial examination, witches have confessed to having met the devil at his Sabbaths, the meetings always taking place near a cross road, upon a dreary moor, or beside a lake or stagnant pool, on Wednesday and Friday nights. At the meetings children were presented, so they said, to Satan. At these gatherings sorcerers were supplied with exquisite meat and drink, served in vessels of gold and silver; and at other times with cooked toads, unbaptised children, and the flesh of malefactors cut down from gibbets. Toads, having the rank of witches' familiars, appeared at the meetings, dressed in gay attire, and wearing small silver bells round their necks, or attached to their feet. At cock-crow Satan disappeared under the earth, and the witches flew through the air to their respective homes. That witches could transform themselves into hares, wolves, and other animals, nearly all the accused women readily admitted.

In the year 1728 a witch-finder discovered that a stout tall woman, suspected of sorcery, did not weigh more than four ounces. This was enough to make out a case against her; and not only against her, but against several confederates, and they were all burned in terms of law.

On account of a petition presented by the inhabitants of Newcastle to the authorities, in the year 1649, concerning the evil consequences of witchcraft, the magistrates sent two of their officers to Scotland to secure the services of a celebrated witch-finder, famous for detecting witches by means of pricking them with sharp instruments. The cunning man agreed to go with them to Newcastle to try such suspected persons as might be brought to him, at the rate of twenty shillings for every woman found guilty. When the officers brought the witch-finder to town, the magistrates sent their bellman through the streets to invite the inhabitants who had complaints to make against witches to make them without delay, that they (the witches) might be tried by the person appointed. Thirty women were brought to the town hall, and had pins thrust into their flesh, and most of them were found guilty. The witch-finder informed Lieutenant-Colonel Hobson that he knew whether women were witches or no by their looks. On a good-looking woman being brought to the finder, the gallant colonel thought it was unnecessary to try her, but the canny Scotchman knew better, and therefore submitted her to his infallible test. Having put a pin into her side, he marked her down a witch of the devil. The colonel, not satisfied that the woman was guilty, remonstrated, and then the witch-finder confessed he was in error. The highly-favoured damsel was therefore liberated; but as no champion appeared for the poor old withered hags, they suffered the pains of law.

Having rid Newcastle of witches, the witch-finder was summoned to Northumberland county to try women there for sixty shillings each. For some fault or crime connected with the discharge of his official duties, he was apprehended, and put under bond to appear at the sessions to answer such charges as might be brought against him. He escaped to Scotland, where he was made prisoner, indicted, and condemned for villany, exercised on the north side of the Tweed, in connection with witch-finding. He confessed that he had been instrumental in bringing to an untimely end above two hundred and twenty women in England and Scotland.

Matthew Hopkins, who regularly went on circuit in England to detect witches for a long period subsequent to the year 1644, applied the usual tests, such as finding witch-marks, thrusting sharp instruments into the bodies of suspected persons, dragging them through deep water while they were wrapped in sheets, with their great toes and thumbs tied together, keeping his victims awake sometimes as long as forty-eight hours to make them confess, ascertaining whether they could repeat the Lord's Prayer, or shed tears.

The clergy of Scotland lent themselves to witch-finding with a zeal truly marvellous. They, in General Assembly, passed five condemnatory acts against witchcraft between the years 1640 and 1649. Kirk-sessions throughout the land outvied each other in their efforts to bring suspected witches to trial, and to counteract the dark deeds of Satan.

The Rev. John Scott, one of the Established Church ministers of Perth from 1762 to 1806, author of the *History of the Earls of Gowrie* and other works, left several folio manuscript volumes of extracts from the kirk-session records of Perth; and from these we make the following abbreviated selections in support of what is here stated:--

"On 16th April 1582 the kirk-session (which for some time was designated the 'Assembly') ordained their box-master to give the witch in the Tolbooth eight doits (eight twelfths of a penny sterling) in the day."

"In November 1589 a day was assigned to certain honest neighbours of Tirseppie to be present and to declare whether it was true that Guddal, spouse to Richard Watson, was a witch, as John Watson alleged, or what evil likelihood they saw in her. Walter Watson, John Watson, George Scott, and James Scott, on being severally examined by the kirk-session, declared that they never saw such things of her whereby they might suspect her of witchcraft, but that she was an honest poor woman, who wrought honestly for her living, without whose help her husband, Richard Watson, would have been dead, as he was an aged man. Therefore the minister and elders ordained the act of slander to be put in execution against John Watson, and Helen Watson his daughter."

"In November 1597 the kirk-session ordained the magistrates of Perth to travel with his Majesty to obtain a commission to execute Janet Robertson, sorceress, who had long been detained in ward."

"The kirk-session, on 30th May 1615, requested the

bailies to ward Marion Murdoch, complained upon for
witchcraft, ay and until she was tried thereanent."

"On the 4th day of May 1618, conform to citation,
Isabella Garry, servitrix, and Margaret Lamb,
daughter-in-law to George Thompson, appeared before
the session, and were asked if they had been at the
well in the bank of Huntingtower the previous Sabbath,
and if they drank thereof, and if they had left
anything at it. They answered that they had been at it
and drank thereof, and that each of them had left a
pin thereat. This was found to be a point of idolatry.
Their case was continued until some other young women,
who were with them, should be summoned to appear
before the church court." [Though it does not clearly
appear what object the young women had in view in
drinking the Huntingtower well water, and putting pins
therein, we presume they simply did what maidens of
the present time do, namely, go to a spring supposed
to possess peculiar charms (as the Ruthven or
Huntingtower well was believed to have), drink of its
water, and each throw a pin into the well, under the
conviction that every one would get the wish uppermost
in her heart fulfilled--generally the securing of a
husband before the year was ended.]

"On the 3rd August 1619, Alexander Peebles, a burgess
of Perth, appeared before the session, and took
exception to the doctrine delivered by Mr. John
Guthrie, minister, on the previous Sabbath afternoon;
and alleged that the minister had slandered him and
his house by accusing him of sorcery, and turning the
riddle. The minister and session certified in one
voice that the doctrine was general, and necessarily
followed on the text from which Mr. Guthrie was
preaching. Peebles would have been censured had not
Mr. Guthrie interceded for him. Mr. Guthrie, however,
brought upon himself further annoyance, in consequence
of accusing other members of his congregation of
witchcraft and sorcery. On the 13th of the next month

Mr. Guthrie complained to his session, of Thomas Young
uttering speeches against him and his ministry, and of
refusing to discharge the civil duty of saluting him
when they met on the causeway. The members of session
were highly offended that any member of the church
should have so far misregarded his pastor and provoked
him to ire, and therefore ordered him to be cited to
appear before them the following day. Conform to
citation, Thomas Young appeared, who being accused of
uttering speeches against and misbehaving himself
towards Mr. Guthrie, the delinquent boldly answered
that it was not the duty of the pastor to charge his
people with witchcraft, sorcery, and turning of the
riddle. Witnesses were examined against Thomas, who,
before the court rose, confessed his error, and said
he was extremely sorry for offending his minister in
word or deed. Mr. Guthrie then admonished Thomas, and
craved the magistrates (who were present) and the
session to inflict no punishment on the said Thomas,
but to pass over his offences--a request that was
granted."

"On 10th May 1626 Bessie Wright was accused before the
presbytery of Perth of witchcraft, curing sick folks,
and frequenting the town of Perth after having been
banished from the burgh, and forbidden to exercise her
healing art. The moderator and brethren ordained that
she should be prohibited from performing any cure,
under pain of incarceration. It was likewise ordained
that the minister of Perth should make intimation on
the following Sabbath, that because the said Bessie
was under suspicion of witchcraft in curing diseased
persons by unlawful means, none would resort to her
for advice, under pain of the kirk's censures."

"Conform to citation, Robert Thomson, maltman,
compeared before the kirk-session on 30th December
1634, for causing a bairn of his to be taken to the
mill of Balhousie and put into the flappers thereof,
when the mill was going, to be charmed, which, it was

alleged, was a lesson of Satan. He answered that he knew not of the circumstance until the child was brought home." [The offence being considered an odious one, the session resolved to take the advice of the presbytery how to proceed, but we are not informed how the matter terminated.]

Lilias Adie, a Fife witch, obtained power from Satan to assist her and her friends, and to ruin her enemies. Like many other witches, she regularly attended the witch Sabbaths. How long she might have remained alive to strike terror into the hearts of the Torryburn people, none can tell, had not their worthy pastor, the Rev. Allan Logan, come to the rescue. Mr. Logan, report says, knew as well as any living man how to detect a witch. When "fencing" the sacramental table, he would look around him with his keen piercing eye, and call aloud, "You witch, begone from the holy communion table." The searching look and commanding voice made more than one woman retire from among the worthy communicants. Mr. Logan was well supported by a zealous kirk-session. This being so, Lilias Adie had little chance of escape. She and other suspected witches were submitted to a series of examinations and tests, which ended in her being burned within the sea-mark on the Fife coast.

From the ancient records of the kirk-session of Kirkcaldy, it seems that numerous reputed witches were burned in that town in the seventeenth century. In the year 1633 two witches were burned; the cost of their execution, including the price of tar barrels, and tow for tying the unfortunate beings at the stake, amounted to L2, 17s. 6d. Scots. One half of the sum was borne by the kirk-session, and the other half by the town. In the year 1649 a woman was burned on the estate of Burncastle, and the cost of watching her thirty days and of supplying fuel amounted to L92, 14s. Scots, a goodly sum in those days; but as L27, found in the possession of the reputed witch, was taken to assist in defraying the expenses of her judicial murder, the burden did not fall very heavy, after all, on the public.

CHAPTER LVIII.

Hiring a Witch to detect a Witch--Clerical Witch-finders--Agnew, the sturdy Beggar--His Diabolical Doings--Missiles thrown by Unseen Hands--Working Instruments destroyed--A Distressed Family--Minister's Remonstrance and Advice--Fresh Afflictions--House set on Fire--Prayer and Fasting resorted to--Meeting of Presbytery for Prayer on account of the Evil Doings of Satan and his Wicked Emissaries--Spirits Speaking--Minister's Reply--Fiend not put to Silence by Prayer--Application to the Synod for Advice--Solemn Humiliation ordained by the Synod--Annoyance continued--Beggar suspected, and hanged for Blasphemy--Bargarran Witches--An Esquire's Daughter bewitched--Physicians puzzled--Great Consternation in the Country--Parish Minister praying for the Afflicted Child--Other Ministers' Visits to Bargarran--Presbytery ordering Days of Humiliation--Effect of Fasting and Prayer--Recourse to the Law--Catherine Campbell imprisoned--Girl's continued Affliction--Representation to His Majesty's Privy Council--Commission appointed to inquire into the case--Proceedings of the Commission--Trial of Witches--Specious Pleading--Condemnation and Execution.

In the middle of the seventeenth century the mania against witches and warlocks became so prevalent, that almost every individual was affected therewith. If a child was sick, if a family became unfortunate, if cattle died, if boats were upset or ships lost, or if accidents of any description, even to the breaking of a plough, happened, the evils were attributed to witches or warlocks. If in any such misfortune the assistance of a professional witch-finder could not be secured, one witch was hired to detect the other witch, or more probably the gang of witches, who had occasioned the mischief. Again, in the event of the hired witch (it was seldom the professional witch-finder, provided with his instruments of torture, failed) not succeeding, the clergyman's assistance was sought; and if the witches and devil proved too many or strong for him, the presbytery, synod, and even the assembly, had to be appealed to. The following is a case in point:--

In October 1654 Alexander Agnew, a sturdy beggar, threatened hurt to Gilbert Campbell's household because he did not receive so good an alms as he demanded. The vagabond, by diabolical means, brought about a variety of annoyances and losses that came nigh to ruin the family. Gilbert Campbell was often hindered in business, through his working instruments being destroyed in a way he could not account for. In November, matters became extremely dangerous. At that time the devil, we are informed, came with new and extraordinary assaults, by throwing stones in through the doors and windows and chimney-head of this devil-besetted dwelling. Providentially no one was injured in person. Next, chests and trunks were opened, and the contents thrown about in all directions. Working implements were secretly carried away, and concealed in holes or other places where they were not likely to be found. Wearing apparel, blankets, sheets, curtains, and other soft goods were cut in pieces. To so great a strait was the family reduced, that the members thereof were compelled to leave their house. Nor was this all: Campbell himself was forced to abandon his employment.

The minister, hearing that the house was shut up, remonstrated against such a proceeding. He recommended that the devil should be withstood to the face. Acting on the good clergyman's advice, all the members of that afflicted household returned. Fresh disturbances broke out. The house was set on fire, and would have been reduced to ashes had not willing neighbours extinguished the flames. As the evil went on, prayer and fasting were resorted to, apparently unmixed with faith, for again the house was set on fire. The presbytery met at the house for solemn devotion, but their prayers were as ineffectual as those of the people who had conducted the religious services on previous occasions. Indeed things became worse. Not only were petty acts of mischief perpetrated, but strange voices were heard, without it being known whence they proceeded. The minister, accompanied by gentlemen of good position, went again to the house to pray with and for Mr. Campbell and his family. After prayer, they all heard a voice speaking out of the ground, asking if they desired to know anything of certain witches who were named. Gilbert Campbell informed the company that one of the witches mentioned was dead. The devil then answered, "It is true she is dead, yet her spirit is living in this world." The minister replied, "We are not to receive any information from thee, Satan; thou art but seeking to seduce this family."

All the people went again to pray, still the devil was not put to silence; the foul fiend demanded a spade to dig a grave, in which he might rest in peace. Advised by the clergyman, Mr. Campbell answered, "Not so much as a straw shall be given thee, though that would put thee to rest." A loud noise was heard, and a naked hand and an arm from the elbow were seen beating on the floor so terribly that the house shook, during which the voice called several times, "I will send my father among you." Night being now far spent, all the strangers went home except the minister, who stayed with the family to protect them. Notwithstanding his presence, and many prayers, the devil roared frightfully, his voice sounding like that of a lion. The very food the family partook of was bewitched: it did not supply them with nourishment, nor satisfy their hunger, even for a moment.

Mr. Campbell resolved to apply to the synod for advice as to whether he should remain in his house. When the subject came before that reverend body, the fathers and brethren thought fit to ordain a solemn humiliation to be observed through all the synodic bounds, with the view of turning away the affliction that distressed the poor family. Notwithstanding everything that could be done, the annoyance continued for a whole year. It was never discovered who was the instigator of the mischief, although strong suspicion rested on the sturdy beggar, who, we may observe in conclusion, was hanged, some time afterwards, for blasphemy.

Tales of the Bargarran witches are widely known in Scotland. In their time they created no small stir and alarm among laymen, in the church, and at the law courts. In the year 1696, Christina Shaw, eleven years of age, daughter of John Shaw, Esquire, of Bargarran, Renfrewshire, gave offence to a servant maid named Catherine Campbell, who wished the girl's soul might soon be in the place of torment. It was feared the offended damsel would seek revenge, and what followed convinced those cognisant of the facts that their fears were well founded.

Soon after this the girl had severe fits and strange visions; and, in a most unaccountable manner, she vomited or put out of her mouth unclean hay, wild fowls' feathers, gravel stones, nut-galls, candle-grease, egg-shells, and other substances, which she nor any other person could tell whence they had come. For a long time she was afflicted in a most mysterious manner. Her parents were distressed, and her physicians perplexed. Change of air did her good, but as soon as she returned to Bargarran her trouble recommenced. By-and-bye it became evident her affliction did not proceed from ordinary infirmity, but from the diabolical machinations of Satan and his emissaries--certain well-known witches in the neighbourhood, one being the offended Catherine Campbell. So convinced was the unfortunate sufferer of her ills being caused by human beings acting in a mysterious manner, that she frequently exclaimed that Catherine Campbell and others, whom she named, were cutting her sides and other parts of her body.

Great consternation prevailed in the country. The parish minister, like a good pious pastor, prayed with and for the child. Clergymen from adjoining parishes visited Bargarran, and witnessed Catherine Shaw's sufferings. The presbytery appointed days of humiliation on account of what left no doubt in the minds of divines that the girl was bewitched. Fasting and prayer seemed to have an alleviating tendency, yet they did not prevent the evil continuing in a mitigated form. Recourse was therefore had to the law. Mr. Shaw, the girl's father, applied to the sheriff-depute; and that officer, in what he considered a proper discharge of his duty, imprisoned Catherine Campbell.

This judicial proceeding had the effect of securing relief for the afflicted girl for a time, but her enemies were not all confined nor rendered harmless, for she declared she heard now and again tormentors, whom she repeatedly named, whispering among themselves that they were, by desire of the devil, to carry her away. And it was supposed she would have been conveyed away from her friends, had not the minister prayed for her at the time the witches were about to carry their diabolical intentions into operation.

The lamentable case of the afflicted family being represented to his Majesty's Privy Council, a commission was, worthily and piously it is said, appointed to inquire into the case. By warrant of this commission, certain suspected persons were apprehended. Alexander Anderson, represented as an ignorant irreligious fellow; Elizabeth Anderson, his daughter; and Jean Fulton, grandmother of the said Elizabeth Anderson, were secured. Elizabeth Anderson, on being severely interrogated, declared she had frequently seen the devil, in the likeness of a little black man, in the company of her grandmother. She also confessed that she herself had been at several meetings with the devil and witches; and she declared her father and a Highlandman in the neighbourhood, along with others, were active agents in tormenting Christina Shaw.

A quorum of the commissioners met at Bargarran; and the persons accused by Elizabeth Anderson to have been at the meetings with the devil, and to have been active instruments of Christina Shaw's trouble--viz. Alexander Anderson, Agnes Naismith, Margaret Fulton, James Lindsay, John Lindsay, and Catherine Campbell--were (except John Lindsay, not then in custody) confronted with the afflicted damsel before Lord Blantyre and other commissioners, together with ministers of the gospel and non-clerical gentlemen of note, and charged by her as her tormentors; and they (the persons in custody) having severally touched her, she was at each of their touches seized with grievous fits.

About this time Thomas Lindsay, a boy twelve years of age, was apprehended on presumption of complicity in witchcraft, he having said, before credible witnesses, that the devil was his father, and that if he pleased he could fly like a crow. Sometimes, he said, he could cause a plough to stand, and the horses break the yoke, on his pronouncing a few strange words and turning himself withershinns. Though at first he denied his guilt, yet he afterwards confessed he had a compact with the devil, and that he had been at several meetings with Satan and witches. His brother James, he said, was also present. James Lindsay was therefore apprehended, and identified by Christina Shaw as one of her tormentors. He too confessed to be guilty of Satanic acts.

Next day Margaret Lang, and her daughter Martha Semple, being accused by Christina Shaw of having been also active in tormenting her, came of their own accord to Bargarran House, and before they approached the girl she said she was now bound up, and could not accuse Margaret Lang to her face. Subsequently she named Lang and her daughter as two of her tormentors.

The commissioners had several conferences, and in their presence many suspected witches were shown to the girl at Bargarran. At these conferences strange things transpired, all tending to prove a most diabolical plot to punish the girl for her insult to Catherine Campbell. This was not all: the inquiry brought to light various other acts of witchcraft, mischief, and even murder, perpetrated by the devil and those in league with him. In due course the suspected persons were arraigned before the judges and jury; and able arguments, according to the light of those times, were entered into. An outline of the specious pleading of the advocate who conducted the prosecution is given, as an example of the manner in which convictions against suspected witches were obtained two hundred years ago.

> "Good men of inquest," he said, "you having sitten above twenty hours in overhearing the probation, we shall not detain you with summing up in particular, but shall only suggest some things, whereof it is fit you take special notice. 1st, The nature of your own power, and the management thereof. 2dly, The object of this power which lies before you, wherein you are to consider, in the first place, whether or not there has been witchcraft in the malefices libelled? and, in the next case, whether or not these panels are the witches?

"As to your power, it is certain that you are both
judges and witnesses, by the opinion of our lawyers
and custom; therefore you are called out of the
neighbourhood, as presumed best to know the quality of
the panels, and the notoriety of their guilt or
innocence....

"We are not to press you with the ordinary severity of
threatening an assize of error, in case you should
absolve; but wholly leave you to the conduct of God
and your own conscience....

"As to the probation itself, you see that it is
divided in three parts, viz. the extraordinariness of
the malefices; the probability of the concurring
adminicles; and the clearness of the positive
probation.

"As to the first part, the malefices, or corpora
delicti, are proven by unexceptionable witnesses to
have fallen out in such an odd and extraordinary
manner, that it points out some other causes than the
ordinary course of nature to have produced these
effects.

"For clearing of this, particularly in relation to the
torments of Bargarran's daughter, you may consider not
only the extraordinary things that could not proceed
from a natural disease, which lie proven before you,
but also several other matters of fact, which is
notour, have been seen by some of yourselves, and lie
here in a journal of her sufferings; every article
whereof is attested by the subscriptions of persons of
entire credit, before the honourable commissioners
appointed by his Majesty's Privy Council, for making
inquiry thereanent.

"This girl's throwing out of hairs, pins, and coals of
greater heat than that of her body or blood; as also

so dry that they appeared not to have come out of her stomach; nor had she any press of vomiting at the time; that she declared the same to have been put into her mouth by her tormentors--is deponed by Dr. Brisbane, in his opinion, not to proceed from a natural cause....

"She told that her tormentors were giving her a glass of sack, an orange peel, etc., and accordingly she was seen to move her lips, and to have an orange peel betwixt her teeth, though there was no visible hand that could have done it.

"She advertised beforehand that one of her tormentors was to be at the door at a particular hour, and that another of them was in the kitchen before any did tell her thereof; which accordingly fell out....

"When her glove fell down from her, at a time when several persons were about her, it was lifted again by a hand invisible to them.

"She was not only transported through the hall and down stairs without perceiving her feet to touch the ground, but also was hurried in a flight up stairs; and when a minister endeavoured to retain her, he found a sensible weight, besides her own strength, drawing her from him.

"She was most vehemently distorted upon attempting to tell, or even write, the names of her tormentors....

"She foretold that her tormentors had concerted to throw her into a fit (whereof they did premonish, of design to fright her to renounce her baptism by the terror) at a certain hour, and had left one of their number to execute it; according whereunto there was a woman with a red coat seen under a tree in the orchard, and the torment was brought on at the time appointed....

"She cried out at a time that her thigh was hurt; and one of the company having searched her pocket, found a knife, but unfolded; however, having folded up the same, and put it in a second time, she cries of new; and, upon the second search, it (though secured by the spring) is found open, to the great wonder of beholders; since they did watch that no visible thing could have possibly opened it.

"She told of a charm under the bed; and accordingly it was found in the shape of an egg, which melted away on being put in the fire....

"The story anent her telling that the commissioners, though at three miles distance, had granted a warrant to the sheriff to apprehend one of her tormentors; her telling so perfect an account of the sheriff and of Mr. Guthrie, who was with him, while her eyes were tied and fast; her being in excessive torments (as she foretold) till that person was apprehended, and immediately thereupon, though at many miles distance, her telling that her tormentors were now taken, betwixt twelve and one o'clock in the morning; and the sheriff, when he returned, did declare the seizure to have been made about that time--is so notour, and so well attested, that we need only to put you in mind thereof.

"Her falling into fits upon the sight or touch of her tormentors, was no effect of imagination; for she was fully hoodwinked with a cloak, so as she saw nobody whatsoever; yet, upon the approach of her tormentor, she immediately fell down as dead, whereas she remained no ways startled upon the touch of any other: which experiments were tried for ascertaining this means of discovery.

"Finally, she is naturally sagacious and observant, and discovered her integrity in face of court.... She

showed her firmness against the temptations of
becoming a witch; particularly against the last
assault of Satan; wherein he persuaded her at least to
go to their meetings, and she answered that she would
not follow such a base fallen creature; and he
rejoining that she would go to hell, however, for her
other sins; and she answering that he was a liar from
the beginning, and the blood of Jesus would cleanse
her from all iniquity: whereupon he disappeared, and
she perfectly recovered upon the Sabbath thereafter;
was a happy end put to this fearful tragedy of
witchcraft, and confirms to conviction the reality of
it.

"As to the murdering of the children, and the minister
libelled: you may observe several extraordinary things
appearing in them; particularly, the witnesses depone,
the minister to have been in excessive torments, and
of an unusual colour, to have been of sound judgment;
and yet he did tell of several women being about him,
and that he heard the noise of the door opening, when
none else did hear it. The children were well at
night, and found dead in the morning, with a little
blood on their noses, and blaes at the roots of their
ears; which were obvious symptoms of strangling....

"The second part of the probation consists of several
adminicles, proven by unsuspected witnesses, which
lead us to suspect those panels to be witches, as so
many lines drawn from a circumference to a centre, and
as an avenue to the positive probation thereafter
adduced; and these either strike at the whole panels
in general, or some of them in particular....

"You see that none of them doth shed tears; nor were
they ever discovered to do it since their
imprisonment, notwithstanding their frequent
howlings....

"In particular, you see how Katharine Campbell was

provoked by this girl's discovering her theft;
whereupon she has brought in the rest of her
confederates to act the mischiefs; how Campbell did
curse and imprecate in a terrible manner; how she
staid out of her bed at night, and was frequently
drowsy in the morning....

"Margaret Lang, that great impostor, has been a great
masterpiece of the devil: she has confessed unnatural
lust, which is known to some of your number; she sat
near the door where the charm of hair was found, which
the girl declared did keep up her tongue; and upon
burning thereof, it was loosed. The girl fell in fits
upon her approach; she has notable marks; particularly
one, which the confessants declared she lately
received; and, by inspection, it appears to be recent.
When she came from her private conversation (no doubt
with the devil) she raged as if she had been
possessed, and could not but declare that she expected
a violent death. She looked in the face of James
Millar's child, and asked her age, whereupon that
child sickened the same night, and named Margaret Lang
on her death-bed. It appears she was ready to show to
Janet Laird a sight of her mother, who had been three
years dead....

"Margaret Fulton was reputed a witch, has the mark of
it, and acknowledged, in presence of her husband, that
she made use of a charm, which appeared full of small
stones and blood; that her husband had brought her
back from the fairies....

"As to the Lindsays, they all have the mark, and were
all of a long time reputed to be witches. John
Lindsay, in Barlock, was accidentally discovered by
the girl's taking a fit upon his coming to the house.
John and James Lindsay were dilated by a confessing
witch in anno 1687, which confession is publicly read
before you, and there was money given to the
sheriff-depute for delaying of the pursuit. James

Lindsay appeared to William Semple suddenly, and flew
about like a fowl for an opportunity to strike him....

"It is true, some of these indications may be in one,
and others of them in another, either from nature or
accident, and yet that person not be a witch; but it
was never heard nor read that all these indications,
which are so many discoveries by providence, of a
crime that might otherwise remain in the dark, did
ever concur in one and the same individual person that
was innocent....

"As to the third part of the probation, we remit the
positive depositions of the confessants, and against
whom they do concur, wholly to your own perusal or
examination; only you would be pleased to notice, 1st,
Something which do very much sustain the credibility
of their testimonies, arising from their examination
in court. 2dly, We shall explain to you the import of
the word *Nota*, which is added to the interlocutor of
the judges admitting these last witnesses.

"First, Elizabeth Anderson is of sufficient age, being
seventeen; but so young and pointed, that her
deposition appears not affected by melancholy: she
accused her father to his face, when he was a-dying in
the prison, as now there are two of her aunts in the
panel, which certainly must proceed from the strength
of truth, since even Dives retained a natural
affection to his relations; she went on foot to the
meetings with her father, except only that the devil
transported them over the water Clyde; which was easy
to the prince of the air, who does far greater things
by his hurricanes....

"James Lindsay, it is true, is of less import; yet, by
his weeping when he came in, and was admonished of the
greatness of his guilt, it appears that he had a sense
of it.... He does not file the panels all at random,
but tells what occurred to his senses.

"Janet and Margaret Rodgers are instances of a singular providence; for they did confess, the same morning that the court did last sit, of their own proper motive, their being neither ministers nor judges beside them at the time....

"It is true, there are some few of the adminicles that are proven only by one witness; but as to this you may consider, 1st, That a witness deponing *de facto proprio*, is in law more credited than any other single witness. And this is the present case as to some of the adminicles. 2dly, The antecedent concomitant, and subsequent circumstances of fact, do sustain the testimony and make the *semi-plenary* probation to become full. But 3dly, The other adminicles, undoubtedly proven by concurring witnesses, are *per se* sufficient; and therefore you saw us, at the desire of the judges, forbear to call the far greatest part of our witnesses....

"We shall therefore leave you with this conclusion, that as you ought to beware of condemning the innocent, and ought to incline to the safest side; so, if these panels be proven legally guilty, then *quoad* bygones, your eye ought not to spare them, nor ought you to suffer a witch to live; and as to the future, you in doing otherwise would be accessory to all the blasphemies, apostasies, murders, tortures, and seductions whereof these enemies of heaven and earth shall thereafter be guilty, when they have got out. So that the question seems simply to come to this, Whether, upon your oath *de fideli*, you can swear that the panels, notwithstanding of all that is proven against them, are not guilty of witchcraft; in the determination whereof, we pray God may direct you in the right course."

The jury, after being enclosed nearly six hours, found the libel proven.

It only remains to be stated that the accused suffered the extreme penalty of the law, not for crimes committed, but on account of the superstition and ferocity of the period.

CHAPTER LIX.

Victims of Superstition--History of Lady Glammis--Her   Trial for causing the Death of her Husband and   attempting to poison the King--Found Guilty, and   Burned--Lady Fowlis an intended Victim--Hector Munro   tried for Sorcery--Making an Image of the young Lady   of Balnagowan--Elf Arrows--Consulting Egyptians--Trial   and Acquittal of Lady Fowlis--Her Accomplices not so   Fortunate--Hector Munro's connection with   Witches--Charge against Sir John Colquhoun and Thomas   Carlips for consulting with Necromancers--Love Philters and Enchanted Tokens--Eloping with a   Sister-in-law--Bewitching Sir George Maxwell--A Dumb   Girl detecting Witches--Witch-marks discovered before   the Sheriff of Renfrewshire--Strange   Confessions--Commission appointed by the Privy Council   to try Witches--Witches ordered to be Burned--Alison   Pearson's Intercourse with Fairies--Another Witch   Story.

After witchcraft became unpopular, persons of youth, beauty, and rank, as well as people of old age, poverty, and deformity, often fell victims to superstition. The history of Lady Glammis is a painful one, exhibiting the gross darkness and ferocity of her time. Being beautiful, and in good position, her hand was sought by noblemen whose name and fame did, in some respects, honour to their country. As Lady Glammis could have only one husband at a time, she was compelled to reject proposals made to her by members of first-class families--a necessity that was not looked at in its proper light; for her refusals, both when she was a maid and widow, to enter into matrimonial alliance with the heads of noble houses, raised formidable enemies against her. Her influence at court was great; but this did not save her from being accused of witchcraft. The fair popular lady was tried in a criminal court for procuring the death of her husband by intoxication, or unholy drugging; for a design to poison the king; and for notorious witchcraft. She was found guilty, and burned.

Lady Fowlis was another intended noble victim. She and her step-son, Hector Munro, were tried, in 1590, for witchcraft, incantation, sorcery, and poisoning. The charges against the lady were the diabolical acts of making two images of clay, the one representing the young lady of Balnagowan, and the other personating Robert Munro (both of whom, it was alleged, stood in her way of advancement in life), which figures two notorious witches put up in a room, and shot at with elf arrows. As these operations did not terminate the existence of the intended victims, an attempt was made to poison them; but for a time this also proved unsuccessful. At length the young lady of Balnagowan tasted her sister-in-law's infernal potion, whereby she contracted an incurable disease. Disappointed at the draught not immediately proving fatal, Lady Fowlis sent far and wide for gipsies and witches, to consult with them as to what was best to be done. More clay images were made, and shot at with elf arrows. She was tried by a jury, composed chiefly of the Fowlis dependants, who acquitted her.

Several of her witch accomplices were not so fortunate; they suffered the extreme penalty of the law. It was proved on trial, that Hector Munro had communed with three witches, in 1588, for the recovery of his eldest brother, Robert, who was dangerously ill. The witches "pollit the hair of Robert Munro, and plet the naillis of his fingers and taes;" but the charms were ineffectual, and Robert died. Hector, the panel, was unwell, and pronounced by women of skill to be incurable unless the chief man of his blood, George Munro of Abisdale, Lady Catherine's eldest son, should die for him. All things being ready, George was sent for to see his sick friend. When he came, a spell was applied, according to the directions of his foster-mother and certain witches. A grave was made between two manors, and at night the sick man was laid in the grave, where he rested until one of the witches consulted the devil as to what should be done next. The invalid was covered over with turf, while another witch, with a young boy in her hand, ran the breadth of nine rigs, coming back to the grave and asking who was her choice? The response came that Hector was to live and George to die for him. The ceremony being gone through three times, all the parties present, except the devil in bodily shape, returned home. Hector, like his step-mother, escaped punishment, though the evidence against him was lengthy and weighty.

In 1633 Sir John Colquhoun of Luss, and Thomas Carlips, a German servant in his employment, were charged with consulting necromancers and sorcerers, and with incest, contrary to the Act of Parliament 9 Queen Mary, and of an Act of James VI. Colquhoun was married to Lady Lilias Grahame, the Earl of Montrose's eldest daughter. The Earl being dead, Lady Colquhoun brought home Lady Catherine, her second sister (a beautiful young woman), to reside with her and Sir John. Colquhoun, fascinated with his sister-in-law's charms, made love to her, but, meeting with no encouragement from the young lady, he consulted with Carlips (a necromancer) and with several witches and sorcerers as to the best way of making her return his affection. They gave her philters and enchanted love tokens, including a jewel of gold set with rubies and diamonds. The enchanted jewel proved effectual: Lady Catherine's scruples were overcome, and she and Sir John eloped, making their way to London, whither they were accompanied by Carlips. Sir John and Carlips, though indicted, failed to answer the charge, and they were therefore declared rebels, and "put to the horn."

A singular account is given of the bewitching of Sir George Maxwell, who died in 1677. The story is founded on information supplied by his son. It appears that Sir George Maxwell, being in Glasgow on the 14th October 1676, was suddenly seized at night with a hot and fiery disease. He hastened home, fearing the worst; and it was well he did so, for he was long confined to bed of a painful disorder, that would not yield to his skilful physician's treatment. It happened about this time that a young dumb girl, a stranger, appeared in Polloktown. She came occasionally to Sir George's house, soliciting assistance. Observing the gentleman's state, she seemed much troubled, and, by signs, signified to his daughters that a woman had pricked Sir George's sides. The girl subsequently pointed out Janet Mathie as the person who had done the mischief. As suggested by the girl, Mathie's house was searched for a wax image, supposed to have been used as an instrument to torture the unfortunate gentleman. True enough, a wax image was found, with two pins stuck in it. Mathie was therefore apprehended, and committed to prison. In presence of the Sheriff of Renfrewshire, she was searched for insensible marks by competent inspectors, who found many devil's marks.

Sir George recovered slightly, but on the 4th January he became so poorly that his friends despaired of his life. Meantime, again acting on the dumb girl's suggestion, the house in which John Stewart (Janet Mathie's eldest son) resided was searched, and a clay image, having three pins stuck in it, lay in the bed where he slept. Stewart, and one of his little sisters, aged fourteen years, were instantly arrested. Being pressed to tell the truth, the girl apprehended told that the image had been made by her brother, Bessie Weir, Margery Craig, and Margaret Jackson, in presence of a black man, whom she understood to be the devil. Sir George, curiously enough, recovered after the second discovery of an image, the same as he had done at the finding of the former figure. John Stewart remained obstinate until his body was searched for insensible marks. These being discovered in great numbers, so confounded the man that he admitted his compact with Satan. In a judicial declaration he confessed his accomplices were his sister and the other women named. On further examination the girl admitted that she, as well as her mother and brother, had a paction with Satan.

Lord Ross and the Earl of Dundonald granted a warrant for the apprehension of Bessie Weir, Margaret Jackson, and Margery Craig. Margaret Jackson, who had reached the age of eighty years, like her accomplices, had many devil's marks on her person. She confessed being accessory to the making of images, with the intention of depriving Sir George Maxwell of life.

On the 17th January a third image was found under Janet Mathie's prison bed in Paisley, concerning which the dumb girl had given information; but it appeared to be the picture of a woman. The supposition seemed to be that it represented a lady belonging to the Pollok family; for against the whole household Mathie had taken an inveterate grudge.

The Lords of His Majesty's Privy Council, being informed of what had been done, granted a commission to Sir Patrick Gauston of Gauston, James Brisbane of Bishopton, Sir John Shaw, younger, of Greenock, John Anderson, younger, of Dovehill, and John Preston, advocate, with Lord George Ross as assessor, to try the persons in custody. The Commission held its first court in Paisley on 27th January 1677. Annabil Stewart, the girl of fourteen years, when brought before the court for the crime of witchcraft, stated that, in the previous harvest, the devil, like a black man, came to her mother's house and requested the declarant to give herself up to him, under pretence that if she did so she would never want. Enticed by her mother and Bessie Weir, she put her hand to the crown of her head, and the other to the sole of her foot, and swore that she yielded herself up to his Satanic majesty. She declared that she had a spirit that attended her, known to herself and the other witches by the name of Enippa. Declared further, that all the other witches had wicked spirits that assisted them in their evil deeds. She told who were present when the several images were made. One of the figures was put on a spit, and turned before the fire. As it went round, each and all of them kept repeating Sir George Maxwell, Sir George Maxwell. One night, she said, she saw her brother John

Stewart with a black man with cloven feet.

In a second declaration John Stewart confessed that he, Bessie Weir, Margaret Jackson, and Margery Craig had a meeting with the devil on the night of 3rd January, when he, at the request of Satan, renounced his baptism. He was induced, he said, to do this, by the devil promising that he should not want any pleasure, or fail to see revenge on those who did him wrong. That evening, effigies of clay were made for taking away the life of Sir George Maxwell. John observed, when the devil was moulding the image, that his hands were bluish, and that there were handcuffs on his wrists.

Margaret Jackson, in her confession, admitted she was present at the making of an effigy and of a picture formed in Janet Mathie's house, and that they were made as instruments for taking away Sir George Maxwell's life. Admitted further, that, forty years before her apprehension, she had given herself from the crown of the head to the sole of the feet to the devil. These declarations were subscribed by Robert Park, notary-public.

All the accused persons, except Annabil, were found guilty, and ordered, together with effigies they had prepared for Sir George's destruction, to be burned. Annabil seriously admonished her mother to confess before she suffered; but nothing, we are informed, would move the obdurate and hardened old witch--so she perished, denying her guilt.

In the case of Alison Pearson, who suffered for witchcraft in Scotland in 1586, several strange revelations were made. She had had a stroke of paralysis, which so affected her that at times she suffered severely. She was a reputed witch, averred to have done serious mischief to her neighbours. For this reason, she was indicted for holding communication with demons. She admitted having intercourse with the Queen of Elfland and the good neighbours. When she fell into a trance, which happened often, she saw her cousin, William Sympsoune, of Stirling (who had been conveyed away to the hills by the fairies), from whom she received a salve that could cure every disease; and from this ointment the Archbishop of St. Andrews confessed he derived benefit. In an indictment framed against her, it was set forth that she, being in Grangemuir, lay down sick, and that there came a man to her, clad in green, who said, if she would be faithful to him, he would do her much good; but she, being afraid, cried out, and he went away; that he appeared to her another time, accompanied by many men and women, making merry with good cheer and music; that she was carried away by them; and that, when she revealed anything, one of the folk chastised her so unmercifully as to leave ugly marks and take away the power from one of her sides. In her declaration she stated she saw the good neighbours (fairies) making their salves, with pans and fires, from herbs gathered under certain planets, and on particular days before the sun rose. Among other revelations, she stated that her cousin, William Sympsoune, appeared to her in the shape of a fairy, and bade her sign herself with the cross, to prevent her being carried to Elfland; for it was dangerous to go there, as one-tenth of the witches were annually conveyed thence to the place of everlasting torment.

Another witch story. One night a gentleman in the west, riding home, was suddenly stopped by an unseen hand seizing his horse's bridle rein. Having a sword, he first struck at one side of his horse's head, and then at the other. The animal, now unrestrained, galloped home, when, on putting the horse into the stable, the gentleman found a hand cut off at the wrist, hanging to the bridle reins. Suspecting he had been waylaid by Janet Wood (a reputed witch in the neighbourhood), he called on her next day, and found her in bed. She complained of being ill. After conversing with her for a short time, he rose to take his leave, and held out his hand to shake hands with her. She offered him her left hand; but he refused to take it, saying it was unfriendly to use the left hand for such a friendly purpose. After a good deal of hesitation, she admitted that she had lost her right hand in an encounter she had the previous night when out on witch business. The gentleman produced the hand, and, on it being compared with her stump, it fitted exactly. The question then came to be, how the stroke took effect, for no ordinary sword could have injured the witch; and it turned out that it had been charmed by the owner's grandmother, a sensible old woman.

CHAPTER LX.

Edinburgh and Leith Witches--Black Catalogue--Witches Burned and Drowned--James VI. and the Witches--Complaint to the Scottish Privy Council of Barbarous Conduct--Relics of Superstition--Images found at Arthur Seat--Witch-finders in Edinburgh and Leith--Royal Commission to Magistrates and Ministers to search for and put Witches to Death--Wife of a Judge in Edinburgh meeting a Witch's Fate--Repeal of the Laws against Witchcraft--Opposition to Acts being Repealed--Judge of the Supreme Courts of Scotland against a Change of the Law--Witches in Edinburgh and Leith in the Sixteenth Century--James Reid--Agnes Finnie, the Potter-row Witch--Alexander Hamilton, the Warlock--The Devil and Hamilton burning a Provost's Mill--Janet Barker curing a Bewitched Man--Margaret Hutchison, a habit-and-repute Witch--Young Laird of Duddingston--Major Weir and his Magical Staff--A Magical Distaff--Agnes Williamson, a Haddingtonshire Witch--Elizabeth Bathgate of Eyemouth--Isabella Young of Eastbarns burned at the Castlehill.

A gainst Edinburgh and Leith stands a black catalogue of judicial murders of supposed witches and warlocks. At the Cross, Gallow Lee, between Edinburgh and Leith, and on the sands of the latter town, unknown numbers of unhappy creatures, male and female, were executed in a most barbarous manner, for the imaginary crime of witchcraft. Nearly all the victims were first tortured to make them confess, and afterwards some of them were worried, and then burned; others were hanged at the Cross, Gallow Lee; and not a few supposed witches were fastened to a stake on South Leith sands, and allowed to remain there until the tide terminated their miseries.

Of James VI., and the witches who persecuted him, we have treated in chapter XXIV.; but it may be further mentioned that in his time an unprecedented number of reputed witches were put to death in Edinburgh. His brutish judges displayed unwonted activity in bringing men and women to an untimely end, because they knew their zeal brought them into royal favour. A time, however, came when the nation could no longer suffer the barbarities of bygone periods to be continued. Accordingly, in 1608 a complaint was made to the Scottish Privy Council against persons in power for so torturing the hapless women that they died amid smoke and flame, blaspheming the Most High, and uttering imprecations against their fellow-creatures.

In the Antiquarian Museum of Edinburgh are a few relics of superstitious times. They consist of small figures, representing human beings, which were found in the crevice of a rock at Arthur Seat, and are, no doubt, figures formed for magical purposes. In the Museum are also to be seen implements of torture, to be more particularly noticed in chapter LXIII. Edinburgh and Leith, like every large town, had professional witch-finders. Royal commissions were issued to magistrates and ministers of the Church, giving them power to search for, torture, and put to death, either by fire or water, every one guilty of witchcraft. Rich and poor were suspected. Even nobles were accused of witchcraft; and the wife of a senator of the College of Justice, in Edinburgh, did not escape a witch's fate. As indicative of the belief in witchcraft in high quarters about the middle of last century, we find that, when the Bill for the repeal of the Act against witches was introduced into Parliament, in 1735, it was opposed by persons from whom better sense might have been expected. Notably among them is named a judge of our Supreme Law Court in Scotland. Let us look back, however, to years antecedent to 1735, and see how it fared with witches in Edinburgh and elsewhere.

Near the latter end of the sixteenth century, Janet Stewart, belonging to Edinburgh, Christian Levingstone, Bessie Aitken, residing in Leith, and Christina Sadler of Blackhouse, were noted witches, who did much mischief to persons and property.

James Reid was instructed by the devil how to heal infirm people by the application of silk-laces, south-running water, and grease. He cured Sarah Borthwick by giving her south-running water from the Schriff-breyis well, and casting salt and wheat about her.

Agnes Finnie, an indweller in the Potter-row, Edinburgh, was indicted before a judge and a jury, on twenty articles of indictment, charging her with witchcraft and sorcery. The libel set forth that she had been guilty of laying on and taking off grievous sickness and diseases from people. Under one count it was set forth that Finnie having had a difference in June preceding with Christina Dickson, the accused, in great wrath, uttered these words, "The devil ride about the town with you and yours," and that shortly thereafter the said Christina's daughter, in her return from Dalkeith to Edinburgh, fell and broke her leg, which was caused, if the libel was truly drawn up, by the devilish threats and sorceries of the said Agnes Finnie. By way of aggravation of her crimes, it was stated she had confessed, at her first examination before the South-west Kirk-session of Edinburgh, that she had been commonly called a rank witch. She was convicted of nearly all the charges brought against her, and suffered accordingly.

Alexander Hamilton, a warlock, was indicted for sorcery. He was enticed away by the devil (so the complainant made it appear), in the likeness of a black man, to Kingstoun Hills, East Lothian. In consideration of the poor man renouncing his baptism, and promising to obey his Satanic master, that grim contractor, on his part, engaged that the accused should never want. The panel thereafter often called Satan up by means of beating the ground three times with a fir-stick; and he answered to the summons, sometimes like a corbie, and sometimes like a cat or dog. By the devil's assistance, Hamilton injured those who hurt him. In particular, he burned Provost Cockburn's mill, full of corn, by pulling out three stalks of corn from the Provost's stacks, and burning them at Gairnetoune Hill. From the indictment it would appear the devil instructed him how to prepare an ointment from the oil of spikenard and heart's grease, to cure diseases. A lady of rank having offended him, he and two witches, in Salton Wood, raised the devil, who appearing, gave him the "bottom of blue due," and bade him lay it at the lady's door, and that the panel, having disposed of the "bottom of blue due," as directed, the lady and her eldest daughter died soon thereafter. All the charges being solemnly admitted by the criminal, he was worried at a stake and burned.

Janet Barker, a servant, confessed to the magistrates and ministers of Edinburgh that she had cured a young man who had been bewitched, by giving him a waistcoat she had received from the devil; and by placing under a door a black card which she had also obtained from Satan.

Margaret Hutchison was found guilty, in 1661, of being habit-and-repute a witch--a supposed fact spoken to by the young laird of Duddingston; and of putting a disease on her servant maid, and thereafter removing it to a cat, soon after found dead near the servant's bed.

Major Weir, who ended this life, or rather whose existence was ended, in Edinburgh in the year 1670, was an enchanter who performed many unaccountable actions in his day. According to the statement of his sister, his whole magical power proceeded from a staff he possessed. The major's sister had at the same time a distaff which often spun yarn for her without any one handling it. At night she left the distaff empty, and in the morning it was full.

In the year 1662 Agnes Williamson, residing at Samuelston, Haddingtonshire, was indicted for witchcraft. She was charged, *inter alia*, with taking the strength out of her neighbour's meal by her enchantments; with raising a whirlwind, and thereby throwing her neighbour Carfrae into the water, where he saw her and other witches swimming about; with telling a neighbour that Carfrae would lose five hundred merks, and, by her sorcery, setting fire to his malt kiln; with renouncing her baptism, and taking the new name of "Nannie Luckfoot." The jury brought in a verdict of guilty as to her being habit-and-repute a witch, but they acquitted her of all the other charges.

In the beginning of the seventeenth century Elizabeth Bathgate, spouse of Alexander Pae, maltman in Eyemouth, was prosecuted at the instance of the Lord Advocate for sorcery. The charges exhibited against her were eighteen in number, from which the following are selected:--

"Causing the death of George Sprot's child by giving it an enchanted egg. Throwing the said George Sprot into extreme poverty by her sorcery. Making a horse sweat to death through the same means, and killing an ox by dancing on the rigging of the byre in which the animal stood. Using conjurations and running withershinns in the mill of Eyemouth. Standing bare-legged in her 'sark-vallie-coat,' at twelve o'clock at night, conferring with the devil, who was dressed in green clothes. Receiving a horse shoe from the devil, and laying it in a secret part of the door, that all her business in-doors might prosper. Casting away and sinking George Huldie's ship with several persons therein."

After a long trial, she was acquitted.

In the year 1629 Isabella Young, spouse of George Smith, portioner, Eastbarns, was indicted for witchcraft and sorcery. There were many acts of witchcraft and sorcery libelled against her, extending over a period of many years. The Lords of Justiciary, before whom the trial took place, found her guilty, and sentenced her to be worried at a stake, and thereafter burned to ashes on the Castle Hill.

CHAPTER LXI.

The Demon of Jedburgh--Recruiting Sergeant--Captain   Douglas--An Apparition--Witch Shot in the form of a   Cat--Isobel Gowdie, an Auldearne Witch--Sabbath   Meetings with Satan--Poor Farmer   Breadley--Disinterring Unbaptised Children--Strange   Mixture--Singularly-constructed Plough--An equally   singular Team--Attempt to shoot a Minister--Bessie   Hay's Attempt to slay Harie Forbes--The   Borrowstounness Witches--Their Trial and Sentence--A   Pittenweem Witch--An Unearthly Horse--Merciful View of   a Witch's Case--A Perthshire Witch--Water of Ruthven   Well--A Changeling.

The demon of Jedburgh" caused considerable annoyance in 1752. In that year Captain Archibald Douglas was on recruiting service in the town of Jedburgh. He had a sergeant under him, who asked permission to change his quarters, on account of the house in which he resided being haunted by a spirit of frightful form. The captain laughed at the inferior officer, and ordered him to stay in the lodgings appointed him.

At their next meeting the sergeant declared he had again seen an apparition, which threatened his life. Moved by a dream and the sergeant's statements, Captain Douglas resolved to inquire into the matters that so disturbed the non-commissioned officer. The latter told his superior that during the night a frightful spectre stood by his bed-side, that it changed into the shape of a black cat, jumped out at the window, and flew over the church steeple. Moreover, the sergeant informed the captain that he had learned the landlady was a witch, and the landlord possessed the faculty of second sight.

At night Captain Douglas accompanied the sergeant, and lay down beside him, leaving his sword and firearms near them. At midnight the captain was wakened by a noise, and, on looking up, observed a large black cat flying through the window. Presently the captain fired his pistol at the creature, and shot away one of its ears. Next morning the commissioned officer stepped into the kitchen to see what was going on there, when in came the landlady, and swooned away in a pool of blood. On removing her head-dress, he discovered a pistol-shot wound on one side of her face, and observed that one of her ears was gone. The officer swore he would bring her before the magistrates to have her tried as a witch. She and her husband entreated him to refrain from giving information to the authorities, and he, like a generous man, promised to keep silence, on the condition that they would abandon their wicked ways.

Isobel Gowdie, one of the Auldearne witches, was baptised by the devil, with whom she had many "Sabbath meetings." She and other witches appropriated Farmer Breadley's corn to themselves, and left him nothing but weeds. To secure the grain, they at one time disinterred an unbaptised infant, which, together with parings of their nails, ears of corn, and colewort leaves, they chopped and mixed together. At another time, to accomplish a similar object, a plough, having a colter and sock of rams' horns, was prepared, and a yoke of toads, instead of oxen, with dog-grass traces, made to draw it twice round the farmer's fields. The agricultural implement was held by the devil, and John Young, a warlock, goaded the team, while a band of witches followed, beseeching the ploughman to do his work effectually.

An attempt was made by the gang of witches to which Isobel Gowdie belonged, to shoot Harie Forbes, the minister of Auldearne, with elf arrows, shaped by the devil, and sharpened by his imps. Notwithstanding all this, the arrows missed the mark. Charms and incantations were next resorted to with the view of depriving the parish of a good useful parson, who had been instrumental, both in and out of the pulpit, in making Satan tremble. The flesh and gall of a toad, a hare's liver, barley grains, nail parings, mashed in water, were put into a bag. Bessie Hay, a celebrated witch, being intimate with Mr. Forbes, went into his room to slay him with the compound, but the good man was proof against infernal acts, and so escaped injury.

Certain witches--Annaple Thomson, Margaret Pringle, Margaret Hamiltown, relict of James Pollwart, William Craw, Bessie Wicker, and Margaret Hamilton, relict of Thomas Mitchell, sadly tormented Borrowstounness and other parts of Linlithgowshire, in the seventeenth century. Having entered into a paction with Satan, they did divers acts of wickedness, for which they were tried before Commissioners of Justiciary, specially appointed for the purpose by the Lords of His Majesty's Council. The indictment charged that:

> "Ye, and ilk ane of you, are indytted and accused,
> that where, notwithstanding, be the law of God,
> particularly sett down in the 20 chapter of Leviticus,
> and eighteen chap. of Dewtronomie, and be the lawes
> and actes of parliament of this kingdome, and constant
> practiq thereof; particularlie be 73 act, 9
> parliament, Q. Marie, the cryme of witchcraft is
> declared to be ane horreid, abominable, and capitall
> cryme, punishable with the paines of death and
> confiscatiown of moveables; never the less it is of
> veritie, that you have committed, and ar gwyltie of
> the said cryme of witchcraft, in swa far ye have
> entered in pactiown with the devill, the enemie of
> your salvatiown, and have renownced your baptizme, and
> have given your selffes, both soulles and bodies, to
> the devill, and have bein severall meetings with the

devill, and wyth swndrie witches in diverse places:
and particularlie, ye the said Annaple Thomsone had a
metting with the devill the tyme of your weidowhood,
before yow was married to your last husband, in your
cwming betwixt Linlithgow and Borrowstownes, where the
devill, in the lykness of ane black man, told yow that
yow wis ane poore puddled bodie, and had ane evill
lyiff, and difficultie to win throw the world; and
promesed, iff ye wald followe him, and go alongst with
him, yow should never want, but have ane better lyiff:
and, abowt fyve wekes therefter, the devill appeired
to yow when yow wis goeing to the coal-hill abowt
sevin o'clock in the morning. Having renewed his
former tentatiown, yow did condeschend thereto, and
declared yowrselff content to follow him, and becwm
his servant: and ye, and each persone of yow, wis at
several mettings with the devill in the linkes of
Borrowstownes, and in the howss of yow Bessie Vickar,
and ye did eatt and drink with the devill, and with
ane another, and with witches in hir howss in the
night tyme; and the devill and the said Wm. Craw
browght the ale which ye drank, extending to abowt
sevin gallons, from the howss of Elizabeth Hamilton;
and yow the said Annaple had ane other metting abowt
fyve wekes ago, when yow wis goeing to the coal-hill
of Grange, and he invitted yow to go alongest, and
drink with him in the Grange pannes. And yow the said
Margaret Pringil have bein ane witch thir many yeeres
bygane; hath renownced yowr baptizme, and becwm the
devill's servant, and promised to follow him; and he
tuik you by the right hand, whereby it was, for eight
days, grevowslie pained; but having it twitched of new
againe, it imediatelie becam haill. And yow the said
Margaret Hamiltown has bein the devill's servant these
eight or nyne yeeres bygane; and he appered and
conversed with yow at the toun-well at Borrowstownes,
and several tymes in yowr awin howss, and drank
several choppens of ale with yow; and the devill gave
yow ane fyve merk piece of gold, whilk a lyttill efter
becam ane sklaitt stane. And yow the said Margaret

Hamiltown, relict of James Pullwart, has bein ane
witch, and the devill's servant thertie yeeres since,
hath renwncid yowr baptizme, as said is. And ye, and
ilk ane of yow, wis at ane metting with the devill and
wther witches at the croce of Murestaine, above
Kinneil, upon the threttin of October last, where yow
all danced, and the devill acted the pyiper, and where
yow endeavored to have destroyed Andrew Mitchell, sone
to John Mitchell, elder in Dean of Kinneil."

Then followed the order and warrant for burning the witches named in
the indictment, couched and signed as follows:--

"Forsameikle as Annabil Thomson widdow in
Borrowstownes, Margaret Prinkle relict of John
Campbell ther, Margaret Hamiltown relict of James
Pollwart ther, William Craw indweller ther, Bessie
Wicker relict of James Pennie ther, and Margaret
Hamiltown relict of Thomas Mitchell ther, prisoners in
the tolbuith of Borrowstownes, are found guiltie be
ane assyse, of the abominable cryme of witchcraft
committed be them in manner mentioned in their
dittayes, and are decerned and adjudged be us under
subscryvers (commissioners of justiciary speciallie
appoynted to this effect) to be taken to the west end
of Borrowstownes, the ordinar place of execution ther,
upon Tuesday the twentie-third day of December
current, betwixt two and four o'cloack in the
efternoon, and there be wirried at a steack till they
be dead, and thereafter to have their bodies burnt to
ashes. These therefoir require and command the baylie
principal off the regalitie of Borrowstownes, and his
deputts, to see the said sentence and doom put to dew
execution in all poynts, as yes will be answerable.
Given under our hands at Borrowstownes the nynteenth
day of December 1679 years,

"W. DUNDAS.
"RICH. ELPHENSTONE.
"WA. SANDILANDS.

"J. CORNWALL.
"J. HAMILTON."

Beatrix Laing, a Pittenweem witch, became a most resentful woman. Because a young lad refused to give her a few nails, she, by means of putting burning coals and water into a wooden vessel, cast a grievous sickness on the young man, which made him swell prodigiously. For this she was cast into prison, pricked, and kept without sleep for five nights and days, to make her confess her dealings in charms and witchcraft generally. After considerable delay, a confession of guilt was extracted from the woman. Among other things, she told of a big black horse that had come to her with five packs of wool. Beatrix gave the animal to her husband, but the good man soon desired to get rid of the beast. It did not look like any other horse he had ever seen; neither whip nor stick would drive it away. Under the peculiar circumstances, the poor man consulted his wife as to what was best to be done. Long deliberation was uncalled for. "Go," said Beatrix, "cast his bridle on his neck, and you will get rid of him." The docile and alarmed husband did as instructed; and lo, the black horse flew off with a great noise. Repeated attempts were made by the magistrates of Pittenweem to induce the Privy Council to bring Beatrix to trial. The Earl of Balcarres and Lord Anstruther, members of the Council, looked on her as a dreamer, and obtained her discharge after five months incarceration. This act of clemency filled the Pittenweem people with rage: they drove her from home and habitation. Hungry and cold, she wandered about for many days, till death ended her sufferings.

A Perthshire witch cured little children by various charms. A cake made of meal obtained from nine several women was an infallible medicine, when eaten by a little sufferer; and a decoction of certain herbs, infused in water from the well of Ruthven, carried by one going to and returning from the spring, silently and alone, was an invaluable preparation. A neighbour, named John Gow, had a changeling left in his house in place of a beautiful infant, belonging to him, stolen by the fairies. The sickly-looking creature proved a source of great annoyance to him and his spouse, but, thanks to a witch, it was got rid of: a dose of her medicine administered to the disguised fairy proved sufficient to despatch it to fairyland, or to some other unknown place.

CHAPTER LXII.

Witchcraft in Aberdeen--Dean of Guild rewarded for his   Diligence in burning Witches--Trial of Thomas Leyis   for Witchcraft--Found Guilty--Expense of burning   Thomas Leyis--Expense of burning Janet Wischert and   Isobel Cocker--The Marquis of Huntly's Desire to   punish Witches--Action of the Presbytery anent   Witches--Helen Fraser--Man under the Protection of the Fairy Queen--Janet Wischert causing a Man to melt away   like a Candle--Ruining a Man and his Wife--Margaret   Clark's Power--Strathdown Witches--Merry   Wives--Transforming Besoms into the Likeness of   Women--Riding on Brooms--Crossing the Spey in   Riddles--Disappearance of Witches--Madge M'Donald of   Tomintoul--Witches' Pool--A Mountain Tale--Girl   controlling the Elements--Witch Burned--Caithness   Witches--Margaret Olson, one of the Evil   Sisterhood--Investigation by the Sheriff--Margaret   Nin-Gilbert--Helen Andrew--Shetland Witches--An Orkney   Lady--Mary Lamont of Innerkip.

Judging from the number of persons burned for alleged supernatural acts in Aberdeen--sometimes as many as twenty-three in a year--that city must have been a hotbed of witches. To hunt down witches there, and to bring them to the stake, met with general approval. Men in public office, noble lords, ecclesiastics, and the common people joined in the hunt, with results truly appalling. Under date 21st September 1597, the provost, bailies, and council showed their appreciation of the diligence of William Dunn in the discharge of his duties as dean of guild; and "besides, of his extraordinary pains in the burning of a great number of witches, and four pirates, and bigging of the port on the brig of Dee."

They "theirfor, in recompens of his extraordinarie panis, and in satisfaction theirof (not to induce any preparative to deanes of guild to crave a recompence heirafter), but to incurage ithers to travel also diligentlie in the discharge of thair office, grantit and assignit to him the sum of L47, 3s. 4d. owin be him of the rest of his account of the unlawis of the persons convict for slaying of black fische, and dischargit him theirof be their presentis for ever."

Thomas Leyis, a stabler in Aberdeen, fell a victim to the over-zeal of his fellow-citizens at this time, the chief of whom was, no doubt, the indefatigable dean of guild. Leyis appeared before the Court of Justiciary held in the tolbooth of Aberdeen, to answer to the undermentioned charges:--

"Imprimis, upon Hallowein last bypast, at twelff
houris at even or thairby, thow, the said Thomas
Leyis, accompaneit with umquhil Janett Wischert,
Isobel Coker, Isobel Monteithe, Kathren Mitchell,
relict of umquhil Charles Dun, litster, sorceraris and
witches, with ane gryt number of ither witches, cam to
the mercat and fish cross of Aberdene, under the
conduct and gyding of the dewill, present with you all
in company, playing before you on his kynd of
instruments. Ye all dansit about baythe the said
crosse and the meill mercate ane lang space of tym; in
the quhilk dewill's dans thow, the said Thomas, was
foremost and led the ring, and dang the said Kathren
Mitchell, because she spoilt your dans, and ran nocht
sa fast about as the rest. Testifeit be the said
Kathren Mitchell, quha was present with thee at the
tym foresaid, dansin with the dewill.

"Secundus, the said Thomas Leyis is accusit as a
common notorious witche, in using of witchcraft and
sorcerie these dyvers years bygane.

"The haill assis, in ane voce for the maist pairt
(except thrie), convicts and fyllis Thomas Leyis in
the first poynt, that he was the ringleader of the
dans on Hallowein last night about the croce, and in
either speciall poynts, and as a notorious witche be
oppen voce and common fame." [Thomas was burned.]

The following figures show the expenses incurred in burning the said unfortunate man:

"Item, for peattis, tar barrellis, fir, and coallis, to
burn the said Thomas, and to Jon Justice for

his fie in executing him   L2 13 4"

EXPENSES OF BURNING JANET WISCHERT AND ISOBEL COCKER IN ABERDEEN:

"Item, for twenty loads of peattis to burn them   L2 0 0
Item, for ane boll of coillis   1 4 0
Item, for four tar barrellis   1 6 8
Item, for fir and win barrellis   0 16 8
Item, for a staik, and dressing of it   0 16 0
Item, for four fadomes of towis   4 0 0
Item, for careing the peattis, coallis, and barrellis
  to the hill   0 13 4
Item, to Jon Justice for their execution   0 13 4"

Another instance of the Aberdonian zeal for the punishment of witches appears on 6th January 1603. A minute of the presbytery says:

"The quhilk day, anent the desyre of the Marques of
Huntlie desyring the presbyterie to tak tryell of the
witches, and consultares with them, and to send to his
Lordship the delatioun, with the names of sic as were
maist meitt to pass upon the assyse and tryell of
them. The presbyterie, for obedience heirto, ordanit
every minister within their precinct to tak ane
subtill and privie inquisition therein--viz. ilk
minister, with tua of his elderis that fearis God and
are maist zealous of his glorie, at ilk particular
kirk respective, tak the aithes of the inhabitants
within their charge, quhat they know of witches and
consultaris with them, and wreitt their depositions,
and return the same to the presbyterie, with the names
of sic as are metest to be assyssours to them, that
the same may be sent to the Marques with all hastie
expedition, conform to the desyre of his Lordship's
lettre, and his Lordship may charge them."

Helen Fraser, an Aberdeen witch, caused Robert Merchant, a married man, to fall in love with Isobel Bruce, a widow--an unholy affection that continued to the day Fraser was burned.

Andrew Man, an old Aberdonian, considered himself under the protection of the fairy queen, who imparted to him a knowledge of all things, and gave him the gift of healing every disease except one--the "stand deid"--the nature of which is unknown to us. By putting a patient nine times through a hank of unwashed yarn, and a cat as often through it in the opposite direction, he cast the disease on the cat, and thereby cured the invalid.

Janet Wischert, the expense of whose execution has been given, was a prominent witch in the north. She caused a man to melt away like a burning candle; she ruined a husband and his wife, by causing them to put nine grains of wheat in the corners of their house; she raised a wind, by putting a piece of live coal at two doors, whereby she was enabled to winnow some corn for herself, when none of her neighbours could winnow for want of wind.

Margaret Clark had the power of transferring pains from one person to another. She gave a valuable charm to a widow in search of a second husband. It was to be worn round her neck until she saw the man she loved best. When she met him she was to rub her face with the enchanted ornament, which would prove sufficient to induce the loved one to return the affection. Of the success of this scheme there is not sufficient proof; but there can be no doubt that, by means of charms, she (Clark) made a cruel husband leave off beating his wife. Clark was accustomed to attend a convention of twenty thousand witches, presided over by Satan, at Athole.

Strathdown, a wild romantic place in the north Highlands of Scotland, has long been celebrated for its witches, warlocks, ghosts, and fairies. An excellent story is told of two witches in that strath, who performed extraordinary feats through Satanic power.

An honest hard-working farmer there was constantly in great poverty. His cattle died, his sheep were worried, his ploughs broken, and his carts often overturned. Everything he did proved unprofitable. His cows' milk was bewitched; the cream would not turn into butter, the hens laid few eggs, and the chickens never throve. These misfortunes happened because he and his wife disregarded the traditions of their native country. How could they and theirs thrive? There was not an old horse-shoe nailed to one of their doors; no rowan tree lay above either door or window lintel; and the cattle were permitted to feed on the hill-side, without red thread tied round their tails. In short, the married couple lived as if no witches nor evil beings were among the glens and mountains, and as if they did not require to evoke the aid of the wise men and women in their parish.

The farmer had two neighbours, by no means noted for industry; still they throve. Their wives were comely happy creatures, beloved by close companions and friends. On one occasion, when the unfortunate farmer's wife was complaining to the other two farmers' wives, they told her that if she would take their advice she would become prosperous like them. She consented to follow their counsel. The first thing the witches did (for, as the sequel will show, they were witches deeply learned in Satan's wicked ways) was to impose on the novice a vow of secrecy; then to direct her, when going to bed, to take with her the besom, and, when her husband was asleep, to rise and come to them, leaving the besom beside him, and it would assume her appearance, so that he could not miss her.

The poor man's wife, having done as directed, hurried out to join her companions, whom she found ready to start on a journey. They had torches to light them on their way, brooms to ride on through the air, and riddles to ferry them over the rapid running Spey; for they had a meeting that night, on the north side of this river, with kindred spirits and the ruler of darkness. Every one of the three women bestrode a broom, and away they went over mountain and glen. A few minutes brought them to the Spey, where they alighted in safety. The experienced witches at once launched their riddles to cross the water; but the third woman hesitated to trust herself in the open agricultural implement. Impatient at delay, her companions urged her to follow them. Never did lover seem more anxious to meet lover than those two witches were to join the beings on the other side, engaged in mirth and revelry. At the foot of a mountain near by (on the top of which the ancient inhabitants of the north used to worship the sun and fire) orgies were being carried on, while the top seemed to be in flames. Sweet music saluted the ear, and a savoury smell arose from a huge table, on which were spread a thousand dishes. A tall man with swarthy complexion, as if he had come from a warm clime, stood to welcome all comers; and truly there were many hastening to the revel. Women flew as swiftly as if they were crows, and crossed the river as readily in their riddles as if they were mermaids. The novice became greatly alarmed, and crossed herself repeatedly. Just as the wicked witches reached the middle of the stream, she exclaimed, "Holy Mother, confound them!" The words had scarcely escaped from her lips, before the lights were extinguished and horrid yells of despair sounded far and near.

Left alone in such a fearful place, the poor woman began to think what she could do. Remembering her distance from home, she felt at first inclined to bestride a broom and fly back; but second thoughts brought to mind the fate of her two unfortunate companions, whom she believed were drowned. Resolved to walk, or rather run, back to her abode before morning dawn, she went forward over moorland wilds, staying not, nor even looking behind, until she entered her own house and barred the door. Husband and besom occupied the bed as on the previous night. Removing the latter, she quietly took its place, but not to sleep; for her nervous system had received a severe shock-
-indeed so much so, that for more than a week she did not rise.

Meantime the two lost women were missed; and the inhabitants far and near turned out to search for them. Every effort to discover them, dead or alive, proved unsuccessful.

When ordinary efforts to find the women failed, the disconsolate husbands sought the advice of Madge Macdonald, the wise woman of Tomintoul. This important person told the husbands there was a person not far away who could tell about the women's disappearance, and that if she did not speak out, she (Madge Macdonald) would see what could be done. Madge commenced muttering to herself, "East, west, south, north; east, west, south, north." This she said several times, and then followed a long pause. A new idea seemed to strike her; and she abruptly asked the farmers if either or both missed any of their besoms or riddles. They had not; but, search being made, sure enough, each husband missed a besom and a riddle. "So I thought," said Madge at their next interview; and then added, "Look for your wives in the Spey." No time was lost in following the woman's advice. A search was made from the source of the Spey to the ocean, without any trace of the bodies being obtained; but, most extraordinary, the riddles were found near the "Witches' Pool," a deep part of the river, known by this name to the present day.

A startling mountain tale is given of a girl who could control the elements by means of magical power. The story runs thus:--A little girl, walking with her father on his land, heard him complain of drought and want of rain. "Why, father," said the child, "I can make it rain or hail when and where I list." He asked from whom she had obtained such power. She replied, from her mother, who had forbidden her to divulge the secret. In violation, however, of a solemn promise, she said her mother had committed her to a master that did everything she desired. "Why, then," said her father, "make it rain, but only on one field." So she went to a stream, threw up water in her master's name, and presently it rained. Proceeding further, she made it hail on another field, when no hail fell elsewhere. Hereupon the father accused his wife of witchcraft, caused her to be burned, and of new had his child christened.

Witchcraft continued in all its phases in the first quarter of the eighteenth century. In the year 1718 the Caithness witches were particularly active. Margaret Olson, one of the evil sisterhood, tormented William Montgomerie, a mason at Scrabster, and his family. She became displeased at him in consequence of his coming into possession of a property from which she had been expelled. To work out her evil design, she and certain associates transformed themselves into the form of cats. One night there appeared in Montgomerie's house no fewer than eight cats, not mewing nor caterwauling, but speaking with human voices. As this kind of annoyance could not be endured, the mason boldly attacked them with a sword, and so seriously cut one of the feline crew that it appeared to be dead. Mangled, and seemingly lifeless, the carcass was cast into the open air. Next morning it could not be seen. A few nights afterwards the cats or fiends appeared again in full force, less one, and attacked a servant-man as he lay in bed. Montgomerie rushed to the rescue, thrust a dirk through the body of one of the intruders, beat it on the head with an axe, and threw the dead-like cat out before the door, as he had done with its former companion. Next day it could not be found. Rumour, with its thousand tongues, spread the report that Margaret Nin-Gilbert, a confederate of Olson, was one of the cats which had been seemingly killed. Proof was adduced that one of Margaret's neighbours saw her at her own door drop one of her legs, black and putrefied. The Sheriff-depute of Caithness-shire ordered her to be apprehended, and, when judicially interrogated, she confessed being the devil's servant. She also admitted it was she who, in the similitude of a cat, had been thrust through with a dirk and smashed by William Montgomerie. She did not attempt to deny that the neighbour who saw her leg falling off spoke the truth. She delated four women of evil repute, two of whom were Margaret Olson and Helen Andrew, the latter being the witch cut with a sword when appearing like a cat to Montgomerie. Poor Helen's injuries proved fatal; for she died, when thrown out, like a lifeless quadruped; and Nin-Gilbert soon followed her companion in sin to the grave, her broken gangrened leg having brought about her demise. Several years afterwards (1722), as seen in page 491, or, as Sheriff Barclay says, in 1727, the law was for the last time put into execution against a reputed witch in Great Britain, viz. in the county of Sutherland, a northern shire of Scotland.

Dunrossness had a witch in the middle of the seventeenth century that plagued the Shetlanders. A boat's crew having given her offence, she determined to procure their untimely end. To accomplish her diabolical purpose, she put a wooden cap into a tub of water, and then began to sing (presumably to the devil), in order that a storm might be raised, and the fishermen at sea drowned. As she sang, the water in the tub became greatly troubled, and ultimately it was so exceedingly agitated that the cap turned upside down. As the cap toppled over she exclaimed, "The turn's done." A few hours afterwards, word reached Dunrossness that the fishermen against whom she entertained the grudge were drowned.

In the beginning of the seventeenth century a cunning woman in Shetland succeeded, through diabolical art, in transferring a sore disease, which afflicted her husband, to the body of a neighbour.

An old Orkney lady removed diseases by pulling mill-foil in a particular way, repeating a few Latin words--sometimes benedictions, but more frequently maledictions--and performing certain mysterious operations at the marches of two estates.

Mary Lamont, eighteen years of age, residing at Innerkip in the year 1662, had power, like the girl mentioned in page 535, to control the elements. She could raise storms, and, if a tempest was desired in the Clyde or at sea, she only required to throw small charmed stones into the flowing tide. Then there were plenty of ships lost and men drowned. She and her diabolical companions not unfrequently made their power felt at Campbeltown, now famous for its whisky, and at the Mull of Kintyre, where many a sailor has perished on its dangerous shore, amidst the raging of the sea and roaring of the storm.

CHAPTER LXIII.

Neither Police nor Medical Men much required in Olden   Times--Instruments of Torture--Torture declared   Illegal--Case of John Felton--Berkly Witch--Attempt on   the Life of Edward II.--Master John of   Nottingham--Escape of Coventry Necromancers from   Justice--Ursley Kempe *alias* Gray--Annis Herd's Imps--Paying Blackmail to Witches--The Rutland Family   bewitched--Witchcraft of a Mother and her two   Daughters--A Pendle Witch--Strange Narrative-- Essex   Witches--Witches of Northamptonshire--Bullet-proof   Witch--Drawing Blood above the Temples--Anne Bodenham   foretelling how a Law-plea would be decided--Strange   Proceedings--Discovering Concealed Poison--Performing Spirits--Ride to London through the Air--Anne Bodenham   dying Impenitent.

Our forefathers did not so much require a detective police force nor medical men as we do. If thefts were committed, or persons became sick, cunning men or uncanny women were sent for. As rule, the offences or diseases were traced to witches or other missionaries of Satan. A suspected person received neither justice nor mercy at the hands of judges and juries. Instruments of torture were applied to wring out false self-accusations against the unhappy individual under trial. Thumbkins, or thumb-screws, were tightened on the hands; boots with wedges were put on the feet; and the flesh was torn with red-hot pincers. These and other instruments were used to make persons speak; and again, when one spoke too much, or said what became unpleasant, a gag secured silence. In addition to the torture inflicted by such articles as we have enumerated, suspected criminals were not unfrequently put in the stocks and jugs, whipped at a "cart tail," made to stand bare-headed and bare-footed before the public, or exposed in sackcloth at a church door or the market cross, to be gazed at, laughed at, and sometimes to be pelted by onlookers, rendered cruel and superstitious by their rulers and spiritual advisers.

All things have an end. Examinations by torture were declared illegal in this country in 1628, yet, notwithstanding such a declaration, examinations under torment were resorted to in 1640. As an instance of the danger of torturing a criminal, not to speak of its inhumanity, we notice the case of John Felton, accused of assaulting the Duke of Buckingham in the year last above mentioned. On the Bishop of London proposing to put Felton on the rack with the view of obtaining from him the names of his associates, the criminal replied, "If it must be so, I know not whom I may accuse in the extremity of pain--Bishop Laud, or perhaps any lord at this board." But we return to our proper subject.

An appalling story of an English witch comes down to us from the ninth century. The Berkly witch was rich and gay, living, to all appearance, a life of pleasure; but, having sold herself to the devil, a sad day of reckoning came at last. Before her death she called on the monks and nuns of a monastery, to whom she confessed that she had entered into a compact with Satan, who would, after her death, snatch away body and soul, unless prevented by means she explained. According to directions, her body was sewed into a stag's skin, and placed in a stone coffin, strongly secured with an iron chain. If the holy men and women, she said, could prevent the devil for three days from getting her, he could not after that time injure either her body or spirit. Faithfully did the monks and nuns watch over the witch's dead body, protected as far as iron, stone, and lead could do. On the first two nights minor demons kept up a loud howling. On the third night the monastery swarmed with more powerful demons, one of whom proved so strong and terrible that he shook the sacred edifice to its foundation. In spite of all the precautions taken, the big fiend burst into the church, went straight to the witch's coffin, and commanded her to follow him. With faltering tongue the dead woman said she could not stir, as she was chained down. A slight twist of his hand broke the chain into two pieces. Slowly the corpse rose; and the devil dragged his prey to the door, where stood a horse breathing fire. Away went horse, devil, and witch down to the infernal abode.

King Edward II. of England and two of his favourites had an attempt made on their lives by persons who sought the assistance of Master John of Nottingham, a famous necromancer. John agreed, for a money consideration, to assist them. He made wax images, representing his Majesty and the other gentlemen intended for death. The necromancer, his assistant, and twenty-seven Coventry men were tried for the foul offence, but escaped punishment, the evidence against them proving insufficient to warrant a conviction.

Ursley Kempe *alias* Gray, an English witch, killed many of her near neighbours. If her own statement could be relied on, she possessed four imps. Two of them had power to kill, but the other two could do no more than punish men and beasts with lameness. Other witches in the neighbourhood where Ursley lived controlled imps that wrought mischief on all sides, until they became a terror to the country.

Annis Herd had six little spirits like blackbirds, and six resembling cows, though not larger than rats.

About the beginning of the seventeenth century a grievous affliction befell the Earl and Countess of Rutland's family. Their eldest son died; their second son was seized with severe sickness; and their daughter, Lady Catherine, suffered from a severe malady. Witchcraft lay at the root of the whole matter. Johan Flower, a widow, and her two daughters, Philip and Margaret, were the suspected witches. They were brought before a magistrate. Philip stated that the evils referred to had been brought on the Earl's family by her mother and sister, because the latter, a servant at the castle, had been dismissed. Margaret, by desire of her mother, stole the eldest son's right-hand glove and carried it home. The mother, who had an imp or evil spirit like a cat, rubbed the glove on the cat's back, ordering it to go and kill Lord Henry (the eldest son); and it set off to perform the devilish work assigned it. That the deed might be the more quickly performed, Johan put the glove into boiling water, pricked it with pins, and buried it. Lord Henry died.

A glove of Lord Francis (the second son) was operated on in a similar manner; but, his life not being desired, he sickened only. Lady Catherine's malady was caused by a process similar to that which killed one of her brothers and brought her other brother nigh death's door. Philip admitted she had an imp like a white rat, which made Thomas Simpson love her. Margaret had two spirits, to whom she had sold herself, soul and body. Johan's spirits told her she would neither be burned nor hanged--a prediction verified; for she died from some unknown cause on the way to prison. The two daughters suffered the extreme penalty of the law.

Edmund Robinson, a boy about eleven years of age, living at Pendle in 1632, told his friends remarkable stories about witches. One day two greyhounds with golden collars came to him, and, because they would not chase a hare that happened to pass, he tied the dogs to a bush, and began to beat them. While the work of castigation proceeded, one of the hounds became like the wife of a man named Dickenson, living in the neighbourhood, and the other hound turned into the shape of a little boy. The woman beseeched Robinson not to tell she was a witch. Little Edmund imprudently said he would not keep the secret, whereupon she transformed the boy that had appeared as a greyhound into a white horse. Dickenson's wife took Edmund, and mounted the horse with him. Before they had ridden more than a quarter of a mile they came to a new house, where threescore persons were assembled at a splendid entertainment. Ample supplies came down by six visitors pulling as many ropes. By this operation smoking-hot joints, lumps of butter, and milk in abundance fell into basins placed under the ropes. Little Edmund ran away, but before he reached his father's house a boy with cloven feet attacked him most unmercifully, cutting his face and ears. What the result would have been none can tell, had not two horsemen come forward and rescued Edmund from the evil spirit. The case being reported to Charles I., he instructed one of his bishops to make special inquiry into the matter. The bishop did not credit the boy's statement, so the king ordered the liberation of several women identified by the boy as having been concerned in the witch proceedings at the new house.

At one time a band of Essex witches, numbering not less than thirteen, killed people, cattle, and horses, caused sickness, destroyed milk, beer, and batches of bread by their wicked arts, and sent their imps to burn dwelling houses, barns, and corn.

The witches of Northamptonshire were famous in their day and generation. Agnes Brown and Johan Vaughan were grievously implicated. They, out of revenge against Mrs. Belcher for insulting Johan, Agnes Brown's daughter, griped and gnawed the lady's body, and put her mouth awry. Mrs. Belcher's brother, Alexander, went to the witches' house to draw their blood, and thereby counteract their enchantments. He repeatedly struck at them, but some unseen power warded off the blows. He returned home without performing the task he undertook, and without doing his sister any good. Naturally enough, Agnes Brown and Johan were offended at the attempted outrage; and they, by their witchcraft, laid the young man on a bed of sickness. The witches were apprehended and lodged in Northampton gaol. Hither did Mrs. Belcher and her brother proceed, to draw blood of the witches. They succeeded in performing the operation, which we presume was done by cutting them above the mouth; for if the blood is not spilled "above the breath" in a case of this kind, the sanguinary deed is of no avail. The afflicted man and woman found relief for a short space of time. Scarcely, however, had they left the prison than their pains returned with double torment. That was not all. As they drove along in a coach, a man and woman, riding on a black horse, suddenly appeared. The sight was taken as an omen of mischief; and so it happened; for the horses of Mrs. Belcher and her brother fell down dead on the road.

Once upon a time, when the Earl of Essex and his army were marching through Newbury, they saw a woman crossing a river on a narrow plank, and otherwise conducting herself, so as to make them conclude she was a witch. The soldiers caught her, and, by desire of their captain, two of them shot at her. With loud laughter and derision, she caught the bullets in her hands and threw them back. One daring fellow went close to the woman and discharged his carbine at her breast, but the bullet rebounded without taking effect. Another soldier tried to cut her down with his sword, but his arm lost its power. All efforts to kill her proved abortive, until blood was drawn from above the witch's temples, and then she fell by a pistol shot under her ear.

Anne Bodenham, an English witch, told fortunes, kept imps, and held intercourse with the devil. She could raise storms, and kill and cure at pleasure. There was a law-plea between Richard Goddard and Mr. Mason, his son-in-law. Anne Styles went to inquire at Anne Bodenham how the law-suit would be decided. Bodenham made a circle on the floor with her staff, and then placed a book, a green glass, and a pan of coals, within the circle. Suddenly a high wind rose, which made the house shake; and five puny devils resembling ragged boys entered the circle, followed by Boden-ham's dog and cat. Boys, dog, and cat danced round the pan of coals. After deep thought, the woman took up her book and read part of it, then she threw white seeds to the spirits, which they picked up. Dancing commenced again, and again the woman Bodenham read her book. At last she went out at the back door, followed by her sprites; and the wind, which kept blowing a furious blast all the time, ceased. Alone the witch returned, and told the messenger how the law-suit would terminate.

At another time Anne Styles went, by order of Mrs. Goddard, to learn from Bodenham where a quantity of poison, concealed by the lady's two step-daughters, could be found. The witch went through all the ceremonies formerly performed, and the sprites acted their parts. One of the boys, however, on this occasion turned into a snake, and afterwards into a dog. Herbs that caused a noisome smell were burned, the book was again consulted, and a glass produced, in which Styles saw Mrs. Goddard's bed-chamber, and the poison concealed below a pillow. To punish the young ladies for their diabolical intention, Anne Bodenham sent Mrs. Goddard powdered leaves and the parings of her finger nails, to operate injuriously on their stomachs and brains. The witch offered to carry Anne Styles through the air to London--an offer that was not accepted. Bodenham often changed herself into the form of a black cat of enormous size. The witch had a tame toad that she constantly kept in a small bag, suspended from her neck. She could say the Creed backwards as well as forwards. She was condemned to death, and died impenitent, refusing to listen to psalm-singing or prayers.

Glasgow, like other towns, did not lack witches and warlocks, nor did it permit its burning faggots to be extinguished. The fury against such members of society may be judged of when it is known that repentance stools, pillars, and jugs were made, and whips prepared for ordinary church offenders--when it is known that scolding women were stuck up in jugs and branks in the most public places of Glasgow--when it is known that holy men and women were burned alive there for adhering to the principles of the Reformation--when it is known that men and women were imprisoned and whipped every day during the kirk-session's pleasure, for offences now considered venial--when it is known that, for a breach of the seventh commandment, some were carted through the streets, whipped, and thereafter banished from the town; that others, for a violation of the said commandment, were fined and ordained to stand at the cross with "fast bands of iron about their craigs, and papers on their foreheads, bareheaded, and without cloaks or plaids;" and that others again, for similar offences, were carted through the town, and lowered by means of a pulley from the Glasgow Bridge and ducked in the Clyde.

In 1649 the session requested all who knew any acts of witchcraft or sorcery against witches and warlocks in Glasgow to intimate the same to the ministers and magistrates, that the offenders might be proceeded against with rigour. As a proof that "the work goes bonnily on" (as Mr. David Dickson, professor of divinity, said on seeing Sir Walter Rollock, Sir Philip Nisbet, and Ogilvie of Inverquharty led to execution in 1645), we mention that, so frequent were the prosecutions against witches and warlocks in Glasgow, that the magistrates, in 1698, considered it expedient to bargain with the jailor for the keep of witches and warlocks imprisoned in the tolbooth by order of the Lords Commissioners of Justiciary.

Paisley would appear to have been a western centre for witches. In fact, if tradition and written history can be relied on, Renfrew, with Paisley for its capital, suffered more from witchcraft than almost any other county in Scotland. Mr. D. Semple informs us that, so recently as 1697, six poor creatures were convicted of this crime before the regality of Paisley, and were "worrit" and burned to death on the Gallows Green. So audacious were those in league with Satan, that they assailed men in high position as well as those in low degree. John P---- and others were indicted in 1692 for slandering, calumniating, reproaching, and taking away the good name of John Adams, late bailie of Paisley, and others; and for drinking the devil's health. Being found guilty, they were ordered "to go to the stair-foot of Bailie Adams, and confess they scandalised; and if not, to be taken to the mercatt cross of Paisley, with a paper on their breast, bearing these words in great letters: 'We stand here for scandalising,' etc. They all obeyed but Janet Fife, on whom the sentence was executed." Mr. Hector, sheriff-clerk of Renfrewshire, from whose work on the peculiar trials of his county we are quoting, remarks, "If this wholesome treatment was more carried out, we would have fewer long tongues."

CHAPTER LXIV.

Paying Blackmail to Witches--Breach of Contract with a   Witch--Demon of Tedworth--Mysterious Drum--A   Persecuted Family prayed for--Unaccountable Sounds and   Sights--Satan's Audible Responses--Drummer found   guilty of Sorcery--Raising Storms--A Wizard in   Cromwell's Army--Florence Newton--Aldermen's Children   bewitched to Death--Man kissed to Death in Youghal Prison--Witch unable to say the Lord's Prayer--Julian   Cox, an old Taunton Witch--Woman in shape of a   Hare--Bewitched Cattle--Mode of discovering a   Witch--Selling a Soul to the Devil--Witch Executed--A   Song of the Seventeenth Century.

In the seventeenth century it was not uncommon for people in England to secure themselves against witchcraft after the manner Lowland Scotchmen protected themselves from Highland robbers--by paying "blackmail." In 1612 John Davice, a Lancashire man, agreed to give a dangerous witch, residing near him, a quantity of meal annually, on condition that she would not bewitch him or his. She adhered to her part of the contract, but Davice, like a foolish fellow, ceased to implement his part of it. The covenant being broken, he was no longer safe, and she bewitched him to death.

Many have heard of the Demon of Tedworth, in the county of Wilts, in the year 1661. Mr. John Mompesson, of Tedworth, hearing a drum beaten one day, inquired what it meant. The bailiff told him that the people had for some days been troubled with an idle drummer, who demanded money from them. On learning this, Mr. Mompesson sent for the man, and, on his coming, commanded him to lay aside his drum. At the same time the gentleman directed the constable to carry the disturber of the peace before a magistrate, in order to have him punished. The fellow begged earnestly to have his drum, but it was not thought advisable to let him have it; therefore it was kept in Mr. Mompesson's house.

About a month after the drummer's apprehension, Mr. Mompesson's family were sadly annoyed by violent knocking and drumming--at times apparently in the house, and at other times seemingly on the house-top. This disturbance continued for weeks without much change, but then the annoyance became unbearable. An offensive smell pervaded the house; boards danced through rooms and passages by day; and at night, drumming was heard for hours together in the apartment where the drum lay.

To administer comfort, if not to afford protection, to the family, the minister and divers pious neighbours came to the house to pray. The clergyman knelt down at a bed-side, but soon rose again, to avoid being injured by shoes and other missiles thrown at him. Singing was sometimes heard, blue lights were seen, doors closed and opened with a bang ten times in as many minutes, although no one could be seen near them. During the time of a more than ordinary alarm, when many people were present, a gentleman said, "Satan, if the drummer set thee to work, give three knocks, and no more." Three knocks immediately followed. For further trial, the gentleman said, "If the drummer has instructed thee, Satan, to molest this innocent family, give five knocks, and no more, to-night." Five knocks were given in response, which were the last knockings heard before next day.

One morning Mr. Mompesson, seeing a quantity of wood in a corner of the house, discharged a pistol at the sticks, as he thought a person lay concealed under them. On their being removed, no one could be seen, but a pool of blood met the eye. For a whole year the family suffered by the wicked arts of the vagabond drummer. For his malicious doings he was tried at the Salisbury assizes. On the evidence of the parish minister, and of other intelligent witnesses, he was found guilty of sorcery, and condemned to transportation. It is reported that, on the voyage to the penal settlements, he alarmed the sailors and endangered the ship, by raising storms which almost engulphed the vessel. The drummer told a few confidential companions that he had served in Cromwell's army with another soldier, a well-known wizard, who instructed him in the magical art.

Florence Newton was committed to Youghal prison the same year (1661) for witchcraft. The mayor of Youghal, in giving evidence against her, said there were three aldermen, whose children had been bewitched to death by the accused kissing the little ones. The indictment also contain a charge against her for bewitching David Jones to death, by kissing his hand through the prison grating. It appears that Jones and Francis Besely were watching Newton one night in the prison, to see if she had any familiars resorting to her. David Jones told the prisoner that he had heard she could not say the Lord's Prayer, to which she replied that she could. They found, however, that she could not repeat it. David tried to instruct her; but, all he could do, she would not utter the words, "Forgive us our trespasses." Seemingly grateful for his assistance, she asked him to come near her, that she might kiss his hand. He stretched out his hand, and she kissed it through a window protected with iron bars. Subsequently Jones told deponent that ever since the old hag kissed his hand he felt ill. At times he imagined she was pulling his arm. The court found Newton guilty of witchcraft, and she fell a victim to the popular superstition of her time.

Julian Cox, aged seventy years, was indicted at Taunton summer assizes in the year 1663, before Judge Archer, for witchcraft practised upon a young maid. The evidence against her was divided into two heads: first, to prove her habit and repute a witch; secondly, to prove her guilty of the witchcraft mentioned in the indictment.

The first witness, a huntsman, swore that, while out with a pack of hounds to hunt a hare, not far from Julian Cox's house, he started one. The dogs chased the creature very close, so that it was fain to take shelter in a bush. He ran to protect the hare from being torn; and great was his surprise to find that, in place of a quadruped, there lay Julian Cox, panting for want of breath.

A farmer said she had caused his cattle to run mad. Some of the animals killed themselves by striking their heads against trees; and that nearly every one of his herd died, either through their own violence, or by a disease evidently brought on by witchcraft. To discover the witch, he cut off the bewitched animals' ears and burned them, an infallible process for bringing the offender to light. While those animal organs were consuming in the fire, Julian Cox came raging into the house, asserting she was being abused without cause. He once saw her flying through a window of her house in her own proper likeness.

In her declaration before a justice of the peace, Cox admitted that the devil often tempted her to be a witch. One evening there came riding on broom-sticks three persons--a witch, a wizard who had been hanged years before, and a black man. The last-mentioned tempted her to give him her soul; but, though he offered great rewards, she did not yield--no, not for a moment.

Judge Archer told the jury he had heard a witch could not repeat that petition in the Lord's Prayer, "Lead us not into temptation;" and having this opportunity, he would try whether any reliance could be placed in the report. He then asked the prisoner whether she could say the Lord's Prayer. She declared she could, and went over it readily enough, except the part thereof just quoted. Several chances were given her to complete the prayer, but she could not finish it without mistakes. The jury found her guilty of witchcraft, and she was executed a few days afterwards without confessing her sins.

As an example of how the people's minds were filled with superstition, even in their merry moments, we give the following popular English song of the seventeenth century, as sung by Robin Goodfellow to the fairies:

"Round about, little ones, quicke and nimble;
In and out, wheele about, run, hope, and amble;
Joyne your hands louingly; well done, muisition:
Mirth keepeth one in health like a physicion.
Elues, vrchins, goblins all, and little fairyes
That doe filch, blacke, and pinch maydes of the dairyes,
Make a ring in this grasse with your quick measures:
Tom shall play and I'le sing for all your pleasures.

Pinch and Patch, Gill and Grim,
Gae you together;
For you change your shapes
Like to the weather:
Sib and Tib, Licks and Lull,
You all have trickes too:
Little Tom Thumb that pipes,
Shall goe betwixt you;
Tom, tickle up thy pipes
Till they be weary;

I will laugh ho, ho, hoh,
And make me merry.
  Make a ring on this grasse
  With your quicke measures:
  Tom shall play and I will sing
  For all your pleasures.

The moone shines faire and bright,
And the owle hollows:
Mortals now take their rests
Upon their pillows:
The bats around likewise,
And the night rauen,
Which doth use for to call
Men to death's hauen.
Now the mice peep abroad,
And the cats take them;
Now doe young wenches sleepe,
Till their dreams wake them.
  Make a ring on the grasse
  With your quicke measures:
  Tom shall play, I will sing,
  For all your pleasures."

CHAPTER LXV.

Elizabeth Style's Confession--Signing a Covenant with Blood--Alice Duke, Anne Bishop, and Mary Penny--Somerset Witches--Witch Oil--Power to injure Men and Cattle--Elizabeth Style sentenced to Death--Running backwards round a Church--Compact with Satan--More Mischief--Richard Hathaway's Accusation against Sarah Morduck--Women hunted in the Streets by a Mob--A Judge's Opinion of Witchcraft--Supposed Sufferer from Witchcraft prayed for in the Church, and a Subscription raised for him--Richard Hathaway convicted of falsely accusing a Woman of Witchcraft--Witch and Stolen Plate--Man Bewitched--Charm for Sore Eyes--Young Woman Bewitched--Flames issuing from a Bewitched Person's Mouth--Tormenting a Witch--Jane Wenham's Witchcrafts and Trial--The last Persons who suffered in England for Witchcraft--Long List of Persons who suffered as Witches.

Elizabeth Style, of Stoke Trister, Somersetshire, was accused, in the year 1664, by divers persons of witchcraft. She confessed before Robert Hunt, Esquire, a justice of the peace for the county, that the devil, ten years before that time, had appeared to her as a handsome young man, offered her money, said she would live gay, and have all the pleasures of the world for twelve years, if she would with her blood sign a document, binding herself to obey his laws, and give her soul over to him. She agreed to do as requested; whereupon he pricked the fourth finger of her right hand, and with a few drops of blood that issued from the wound she signed the engagement.

When she desired to do harm, Satan gave her power according to their agreement. About a month before her examination she desired him to torment Elizabeth Hall by thrusting thorns into her flesh--a request he promised to comply with. She declared that, not long before her apprehension, she, Alice Duke, Anne Bishop, and Mary Penny met the devil at night, in a common near Trister Gate. Their meeting terminated with dancing and feasting.

Similar meetings subsequently took place. Before Style and her companion witches started to midnight meetings, they anointed their foreheads with an oil given them by a spirit. They were then carried swiftly through the air. Sometimes they were present at the meetings in body, but more frequently in spirit only. The devil gave them power to injure men and cattle, either by a touch or curse. Style gave the names of many men and women in the neighbourhood who attended the meetings. The meetings being ended, the devil suddenly vanished or burnt himself in flames, and the people went home, singing "Merry we meet, merry we meet, and merry we part."

The poor miserable woman was tried before a jury of her countrymen, and found guilty of witchcraft. Sentence of death was passed on her, but she escaped punishment by the hands of an ordinary executioner, for before the day fixed for her execution she died in prison.

Alice Duke, a confederate of Elizabeth Style, being brought before Mr. Hunt for examination on a charge of witchcraft, stated that she and Anne Bishop went to the churchyard at night, and stepped backward round the church three times. In their first round they met a man in black clothes, who returned with them. In the second round they met a big black toad, which leapt into deponent's apron. As they went round the third time they met a rat, that vanished into air. Like many more witches entering into a compact with Satan, she could have her wishes and revenge. If she cursed any person or thing with "a pox," evil happened the object of her hatred.

Witches were found in every part of Somerset in the seventeenth century. Hundreds of them were brought to trial; but as their reported doings, confessions, and punishments were in all essential particulars the same as those of Elizabeth Style and Alice Duke, they are unimportant here.

Richard Hathaway appeared before Lord Chief Justice Holt at the Guildford assizes in 1701, to support a charge of witchcraft against Sarah Morduck. Hathaway frequently vomited pins in great numbers, pieces of tin, nails, and small stones. He foamed at the mouth, and barked like a dog; sometimes he felt a burning sensation, and not unfrequently lay as if dead. Being convinced that Sarah Morduck caused his troubles, he scratched her "above the breath," to draw blood from her. Subsequent to this operation he recovered, and remained well for six weeks. All his afflictions returned, and the suspected witch was scratched a second time. To escape her tormentors at Southwark, she went to London; but, her fame preceding or following her, she was hunted in the streets by an infuriated mob. Hathaway pursued the unhappy woman to the great metropolis, and took her before Sir Thomas Lane, a judge who regarded witchcraft in a different light to that which the Lord Chief Justice did. Sir Thomas ordered her to be stripped, to ascertain whether she had any witch-marks; and Hathaway, still suffering, scratched her for the third time. Sarah Morduck was committed to prison as a dangerous witch. Her supposed victim, Hathaway, became an object of prayer in the churches, and subscriptions were raised to defray his charges at the assizes. In July Sarah Morduck was brought, as already stated, before Lord Chief Justice Holt, but escaped with her life, for no other reason than that the judge did not believe in witchcraft. Hathaway's conduct being inquired into, he was brought to trial, when it was ascertained that his sayings about being bewitched were false. He was therefore sentenced, by the same judge that had liberated Sarah Morduck, to imprisonment for a year, and to stand in the pillory three times as a cheat and liar.

Sending a witch to catch a witch or thief occasionally had its beneficial results. On the communion service having been stolen from a church, a wise man instructed the church-wardens how to discover the thief. They did as directed, and, true enough, the thief hastened to give himself up to justice; and, what proved better, he restored the stolen plate. One man having a child sorely afflicted with boils, consulted a wizard. By direction of the cunning man, a portion of the child's hair was cut off and thrown into the fire. This had the effect of compelling a witch to hasten to the house and confess that she had in reality brought trouble on the child. The father scratched the witch "above the breath," and the sufferer recovered.

Jane Stretton, a young woman twenty years of age, was bewitched in 1669, and consequently suffered much by flax, hair, thread, and pins gathering in her throat. Still more strange, red-hot flames issued from her mouth. A wise man's wife was suspected of bringing about the calamity. Various means were resorted to with the view of establishing her guilt. Sympathising neighbours were consulted, and one of them suggested a method that proved effectual. Foam was collected from Jane's mouth and chin, and thrown into the fire, as a charm to injure her tormentor. We are assured the expedient succeeded admirably. While the foam hissed in the flames, the witch, compelled by the operation, came into the house to confess that she alone had caused the young woman's distemper.

One of the last persons generally supposed to have been condemned to death in England for witchcraft was Jane Wenham, residing in Walkerne, a village in Hertford. For years her neighbours suspected her to be a witch. In 1712 she was tried before one of the legal tribunals, and condemned on evidence of a singular nature. It appears that she went to Matthew Gibson, a servant to John Chapman, and asked for a pennyworth of straw. He refused to give her any, and she went away muttering threats against him. Soon thereafter Gibson became like an insane man, and ran three miles along the highway, asking every one he met for a pennyworth of straw. Then he gathered all the straws he could find by the roadside and put them into his shirt, which he used as a sack. Gibson's master met Jane, and called her a witch. Offended at such an imputation, she brought Mr. Chapman before Sir Herbert Chauncey, a magistrate, on the charge of defaming her character. The magistrate recommended the pursuer and defender to submit the case to the Rev. Mr. Gardiner, that the dispute might be settled quietly. To the parson they accordingly went; and he awarded Jane one shilling of damages. The decision did not please Jane; and out of revenge, it was subsequently alleged, she bewitched the minister's servant-maid, Anne Thorne. As soon as the suspected witch had left the parsonage, the maid felt a giddiness in her head, which impelled her to run away through fields and over fences, notwithstanding her having a very sore knee. On her way she met a little old woman, who asked her where she was going. To this inquiry Anne replied, "I am going to Cromer for sticks." The little woman said it seemed unnecessary to go so far, and pointed out an oak-tree close at hand where she could get them. The little woman vanished like a spirit, and Anne returned home, in a partial state of nudity, with a quantity of sticks wrapped in her gown and apron. Mrs. Gardiner, who, like the minister, her husband, believed in witchcraft, on hearing the girl's tale, said she would burn the witch; and, suiting the action to the words, threw the sticks into the fire. The charm had the desired effect; for immediately Jane Wenham came in, and made a false statement touching the cause of her call. That did not, however, deceive the people at the parsonage, who were convinced the burning of the sticks had made her come, whether she would or not. She was apprehended on suspicion, and put to the test. The minister asked her to repeat the Lord's Prayer, but she could not say it. This being regarded as presumptive evidence of guilt, Wenham's persecutors brought her to trial. Three clergymen and thirteen other witnesses gave evidence in the case. Proof was adduced that she had by witchcraft killed cattle, taken the power from men's bodies, destroyed people's substance, turned divers persons into a state of insanity, and by her curses and evil eye had killed a child.

Witnesses also swore that she had on various occasions assumed the form of a cat. The jury found Wenham guilty, and the judge condemned her to death, but, like a humane Christian, he applied and obtained a pardon for the culprit.

We now come to the last victims who suffered in England for the alleged crime of witchcraft. One Mrs. Hicks, and her little daughter nine years of age, were executed on the scaffold at Huntingdon in 1716, for the suppositious offences of raising storms and selling their souls to the devil.

With the judicial murder of this unfortunate mother and her innocent daughter we close a long list of tragedies which disgraced England for hundreds of years--which exhibits the ignorance and violence of past ages. Dr. Sprenger estimates that nine million persons have been burned or otherwise put to death as witches during the Christian epoch. For such a dreadful waste of life Catholics and Protestants were equally guilty. Any one who raised his voice on behalf of the proscribed class, ran the risk of himself being accused of sorcery, or at least of heresy. At last, in 1563, J. Weier, a physician in Germany, spoke boldly against the belief in witchcraft. Twenty years later, Reginald Scot, as already stated, wrote and spoke, not against witches, but against the absurdity of believing that such persons existed.

Happily, no longer can hysterical girls and malicious individuals give false evidence in a court of law touching the feigned crime of witchcraft; no longer can the witch-finder exert his skill; no longer can judges and jury condemn to the flames or scaffold suspected witches and wizards; and no longer can an ignorant people listen to the despairing cries--cries which neither evoked pity nor secured mercy--of victims of superstition expiring amidst blazing faggots. But yet superstition lingers amongst us, as we shall show under the head "Superstition in the Nineteenth Century."

CHAPTER LXVI.

Scotchmen and Englishmen in America--Superstition in   the Back Settle-ments--Witchcraft in New England--Rev.   Cotton Mather's View of Witchcraft--Judges and   Witnesses overawed by Witches--Men and Beasts   bewitched--Bewitched Persons prayed for--Preternatural   Diseases beyond Physicians' Skill--Trial of Susan   Martin--Absurd Evidence--Belief in the Existence of Witchcraft--Witchcraft in Sweden--Commission of   Inquiry appointed--The Devil's Tyranny--Deluded   Children--Day of Humiliation appointed on account of   Witchcraft--Threescore and Ten Witches in a   Village--Children engaged in Witchery put to   Death--How Witches were conveyed from place to   place--Girl healed by the Devil--The Devil bound with   an Iron Chain--An Angel's Warning Voice--Angel keeping   Children from Wickedness--Witches on a Min-ister's   Head--Witch assaulting another Minister--Witches'   Imps--Butter of Witches--The Devil described--How   Witches are punished--Horse burned on account of being   supposed to be an Agent of Satan.

When Scotchmen and Englishmen went out first to inhabit America, they did not forget the superstitions of their native land. A belief in charms, incantations, and all kinds of witchcraft prevailed among the earlier settlers of the United States and Canada. From sire to son, and from mother to daughter, a belief in mysterious agen-cies has come down to the existing inhabitants of the transatlantic States. It may be that the inhab-itants of large cities in the West have forgotten the traditions of their ancestors respecting things supernatural, but every observant American traveller knows that the burning embers of superstition have not expired in the back settlements of that vast country. Trials of persons accused of witchcraft were not unfrequent in New England in the seventeenth century. The Rev. Cotton Mather has writ-ten an account of proceedings connected with such cases, but want of space prevents us following him at great length. He says:

"We have now, with horror, seen the discovery of a
great witchcraft. An army of devils has broken in upon
this place, which is the centre, and, after a sort,
the first-born of our English settlements; and the
houses of the good people there are filled with the
doleful shrieks of their children and servants

tormented by invisible hands, with tortures altogether preternatural. After the mischiefs there endeavoured, and since in part conquered, the terrible plague of evil angels hath made its progress into some other places, where other persons have in like manner been diabolically handled.

"These, our poor afflicted neighbours, quickly, after they become infected and infested with these demons, arrive to a capacity of discerning those which they conceive the shapes of their troubles; and notwithstanding the great and just suspicion that the demons might impose the shape of innocent persons in their spectral exhibitions of the sufferers, (which may perhaps prove no small part of the witch-plot in the issue), yet many of the persons thus represented being examined, several of them have been convicted of a very damnable witchcraft: yea, more than one, twenty have confessed that they have signed unto a book which the devil showed them, and engaged in his hellish design, of bewitching and ruining our lands.

"We know not, at least I know not, how far the delusions of Satan may be interwoven into some circumstances of the confessions; but one would think all the rules of understanding human affairs are at an end, if after so many most voluntary, harmonious confessions, made by intelligent persons of all ages, in sundry towns, at several times, we must not believe the main strokes wherein those confessions agree; especially when we have a thousand preternatural things every day before our eyes, wherein the confessors do acknowledge their concernment, and give demonstration of their being so concerned. If the devils now can strike the minds of men with any poisons of so fine a composition and operation that scores of innocent people shall unite in the confessions of a crime which we see actually committed, it is a thing prodigious, beyond the wonders of the former ages, and it threatens not less than a sort of dissolution upon the world.

"Now, by these confessions 'tis agreed that the devil
has made a dreadful knot of witches in the country,
and by the help of witches has dreadfully increased
the knot; that these witches have driven a trade of
commissioning their confederate spirits to do all
sorts of mischiefs to their neighbours. Whereupon
there have ensued such mischievous consequences upon
the bodies and estates of the neighbourhood as could
not otherwise be accounted for."

Human beings were not always the only victims of superstition in olden times, for we have
information of dumb animals suffering on account of it being thought they were active agents of
Satan. The Inquisition in Portugal in 1601, in its sanguinary infatuation, condemned to the flames,
for being possessed of the devil, a horse belonging to an Englishman, who had taught it to perform
uncommonly clever tricks. And the poor animal was publicly burned at Lisbon. Instances are also on
record of swine being burned, under the suspicion that they, too, were helpers of the devil.

Through sorcery, Mr. Mather thought witnesses were occasionally prevented from giving evidence in courts of justice against witches, and even judges were sometimes so overawed by the culprits' looks that they could not discharge their duties with firmness. A witch could, by a cast of her
evil eye, strike people to the ground, and by the same visual organ kill cattle. Men and beasts were
also bewitched into madness. To such an extent, we are told, were people tormented by witches
in New England, that the Church appointed days of prayer on behalf of afflicted persons. And so
peculiar were diseases, that the physicians declared their patients' troubles were preternatural. That
being so, a little ingenuity, strengthened with spite, enabled the afflicted or the afflicted's friends to
trace the disorder to the malevolence of a certain witch or witches.

In the trial of Susan Martin, in 1692, among other absurdities of circumstantial evidence relied
on, was that her skirts were not draggled when out on a wet day, while the clothes of other women
travelling with her were bespattered and clotted with mud.

Writers of no mean order, including clergymen, believed in the existence of witches, ghosts,
and goblins, and boldly defended the proceedings in New England against the victims put to death
for their alleged diabolical deeds through the agency of Satan.

Witchcraft spread alarm over Sweden in the seventeenth century. The news of particular acts
of witchcraft coming to the king's ear, his Majesty appointed commissioners to inquire into the matter. From a public register of 1669 and 1670, we ascertain that the commission, consisting of clergymen and laymen, were instructed to visit Mobra and inquire into frightful proceedings there. The
commissioners met at the parson's house to hear complaints. Both the minister and people of fashion
complained, with tears in their eyes, of the miserable condition they were in, from the calamity of
witchcraft. They gave the commissioners strange instances of the devil's tyranny among them--how,

by the help of witches, he had drawn hundreds of children to him; how he had been seen going in visible shape through the country; how he had wrought upon the poorer people, by presenting them with meat and drink. The inhabitants begged earnestly, yet in the most respectful manner,

"The Lords Commissioners to root out this hellish crew, that rest and quietness might be regained; and the rather, because the children who used to be carried away in the district of Elfdale, since some witches had been burnt there, remained unmolested."

An elaborate report of the peculiar proceedings says:--

"That day," *i.e.* the 13th of August, "the last humiliation-day instituted by authority for removing of this judgment, the commissioners went to church, where there appeared a considerable assembly.... Two sermons were preached, in which the miserable case of those people, that suffered themselves to be deluded by the devil, was laid open....

"Public worship being over, all the people of the town were called together to the parson's house; nearly three thousand of them attended.

"Next day the commissioners met again, consulting how they might withstand this dangerous flood. After long deliberation, they resolved to execute such as the matter of fact could be proved upon. Examination being made, there were discovered no less than threescore and ten witches in the village. Three and twenty of whom, freely confessing their crimes, were condemned to die. The rest pleading not guilty, were sent to Fabluna, where most of them were afterwards executed.

"Fifteen children, who likewise confessed they were engaged in the witchery, died as the rest; six and thirty youths, between nine and sixteen years of age, who had been less guilty, were forced to run the gauntlet; twenty more, who had no great inclination, yet had been seduced to those hellish enterprises, because they were very young, were condemned to be lashed with rods upon their hands for three Sundays together at the church door; and the aforesaid six and thirty were also doomed to be lashed this way once a week for a whole year together. The number of the seduced children was about three hundred.

"Several of the witches were asked how they were able to carry so many children with them; and they answered, that they came into the chamber where the children lay, laid hold of them, and asked them whether they would go to a feast with them? to which some answered yes, others no; yet they were all forced to go. They only gave the children a shirt, a coat, and a doublet, which was either red or blue, and so they did set them upon a beast of the devil's providing, and then they rid away.

"The children confessed the same thing; and some added, that because they had very fine clothes put upon them, they were very willing to go.

"A little girl of Elfdale confessed that, on naming the name of Jesus as she was carried away, she fell suddenly upon the ground, and got a great hole in her side, which the devil presently healed up again, and away he carried her; and to this day the girl confessed she had exceeding great pain in her side.

"The children said they had seen sometimes a very great devil like a dragon, with fire round about him, and bound with an iron chain....

"Some of the children talked much of a white angel, which used to forbid them to do what the devil bade them do, and told them that those doings would not last long: what had been done was permitted because of the wickedness of the people, and the carrying away of the children should be made manifest. And they added, that this white angel would place himself

sometimes at the door betwixt the witches and the
children; and when they came to Blockula, their
meeting-place, he pulled the children back, but the
witches went in.

"The minister of Elfdale declared that one night the
witches were, to his thinking, upon the crown of his
head, and that from thence he had a long continued
pain of the head.

"One of the witches confessed that the devil had sent
her to torment the minister, and that she was ordered
to use a nail and strike it into his head, but it
would not enter very deep and hence came the headache.

"The minister said also that one night he felt a pain
as if he were torn with an instrument, and when he
wakened he heard somebody scratching and scraping at
the window, but could see nobody. And one of the
witches confessed that she was the person that did it,
being sent by the devil.

"The minister of Mobra declared also that one night
one of the witches came into his house, and did so
violently take him by the throat that he thought he
should have been choked; and waking, he saw the person
that did it, but could not know her; and that for some
weeks he was not able to speak, or perform divine
service.

"They confessed also that the devil gave them a beast
about the bigness and shape of a young cat, which they
called a carrier; and that he gave them a bird too, as
big as a raven, but white. And these two creatures
they could send anywhere; and wherever they came, they
took away all sorts of victuals they could
get--butter, cheese, milk, bacon, and all sorts of
seeds, whatever they found, and carried it to the
witch. What the bird brought, they kept for
themselves; but what the carrier brought, they

reserved for the devil....

"They added, likewise, that these carriers filled themselves so full sometimes that they were forced to spue by the way, which spueing was found in gardens where colworts grew, and not far from the houses of witches. It was of a yellow colour like gold, and was called butter of witches.

"The Lords Commissioners were very earnest, and took great pains to persuade the witches to show some of their tricks, but to no purpose; for they unanimously said that, since they had confessed, they found that all their witchcraft was gone, and that the devil appeared to them very terrible, with claws on his hands and feet, and with horns on his head, and a long tail behind, and showed them a pit burning with a hand put out; but the devil did thrust the person down again with an iron fork, and suggested to the witches, that if they continued in their confession, he would deal with them in the same manner."

CHAPTER LXVII.

Superstition in France--Pope John XXII. celebrated in   the History of Sorcery and Magic--A Bishop skinned   alive and torn by Horses for Witchcraft--King Philippe   and Superstition--Springs poisoned by Lepers and   Jews--Extracting Teeth without Pain--A Dentist   strangled by a Demon--Berne Witch--Charmed   Ointment--Sorcerers in Navarre--Demoniacal   Operations--Voice in the Air--Witch Flying--Witches   meeting their Deserts--Maria Renata's Witchcrafts--Nuns possessed of Devils--Promise of Life   by Satan--End of Renata--Jeanne D'Arc--Credulity of   France and England--Fairies of Domremi--Charmed   Tree--Sparkling Spring--Mandrakes--Jacques D'Arc and   his Wife--Jeanne D'Arc in Childhood--Converse with   Spirits and Angels--France under Tyranny--Jeanne's   Heavenly Mission communicated to the Dauphin--Maid at the head of Troops--Her Achievements--Siege of   Orleans--Great Victories--Dauphin Crowned--Jeanne's   Desire to retire into Private Life--Opposition to her   Retirement--The Maid's Feats of Valour--Heroine   Betrayed--Charmed Sword--Jeanne's Surrender--King's   Ingratitude--Great Rejoicing at the Maid's Downfall--Attempt to Escape--Trial and   Condemnation--Maid Burned--A white Dove rising from   her Ashes--Imitators--Unreliable Reports.

France, like her neighbouring nations, entertained strong opinions in regard to superstition; and so did the high dignitaries of Rome. Pope John XXII. is celebrated in the history of sorcery and magic. He believed that sorcery had been resorted to to procure his untimely death, soon after his accession to the Papacy, by the Bishop of Chahors, the Pope's native place. The bishop being brought before the College of Cardinals, was, after deposition from his holy office, delivered to the secular powers in Avignon to receive punishment. A cruel fate awaited him; the unfortunate bishop being first skinned alive, next torn by horses, and then burned. Pope John continued to persecute persons suspected of sorcery, and many an unhappy creature suffered at his suggestion.

In the spring of 1321 King Philippe summoned the States-General to meet at Poictiers, and proceeded in person to Poitou to hold his court there. Soon after the assembly of the Estates, information was given to the king that the lepers, of whom there were many in the place, had entered into a conspiracy to poison and bewitch the springs throughout Aquitaine, in order to kill the Christians, or reduce them to the same state of loathsome disease as they themselves suffered. Some who were arrested admitted, under torture, the accusation. The king became so greatly alarmed that he fled from Poitou, after giving orders to arrest and imprison all the lepers in France. Multitudes of them were condemned and burned; still the king thirsted for more blood. Jews were also accused of aiding to poison and bewitch the wells. At Chinon upwards of one hundred Jews suffered the extreme penalty of the law for such groundless crimes. After a show of trial, and trumped-up charges equally false, many more Jews and lepers were put to death in Paris.

Dentists will be surprised to learn that in bygone days none but those acquainted with occult science were supposed capable of extracting teeth without pain. In the seventeenth century an astrologer in France, who sold talismans and extracted teeth without pain, was strangled in bed by a demon.

A woman, executed at Berne, stated she belonged to a sect who had sworn eternal subjection to the devil, and that she knew how to prepare a decoction which, when swallowed by any one, would convert the novice into a witch equal in knowledge and power to the older members of her fraternity.

Here is a case exhibiting the power of charmed ointment. In the year 1527 a band of one hundred and fifty sorcerers, says Llorente, greatly disturbed Navarre. The sect held "Sabbath" orgies, where demons were adored, and transformations of witches and wizards took place, after anointing themselves with a compound made from the grease of reptiles. One witch, on condition of receiving a pardon, agreed to show the demoniacal operations gone through at the "Sabbath" meetings. Provided with a box of witch ointment, she ascended a high tower, accompanied by a commissioner of the royal council. In the sight of a vast concourse of people, she applied the ointment to various parts of her person. Having done this, she exclaimed in a loud voice, "Are you there?" From the air a voice answered, "Yes, I am here." The woman then descended the tower to its centre, crawling down the outside of the wall on her hands and feet. Suddenly she flew away, and vanished out of sight beyond the horizon. Her one hundred and forty-nine companions were brought to trial, and met their deserts.

Maria Renata, sub-prioress of a convent at Unterzell, proved to be a witch. She tormented the nuns at night, and, to assist her in the black art, she kept a considerable number of cats. General alarm prevailed; five of the nuns became possessed of devils. Renata avowed to her confessor that she was a witch, that she had often been carried bodily to witch Sabbaths, and presented to the prince of darkness. Her name appeared in a black book, and she consented to be the devil's property. In return, she received the promise of life for seventy years. After trial by the civil judges, they condemned Renata to the flames; but at the appointed time of execution, by way of showing a little mercy, her head was struck off before the flames kindled around her body. This tragedy took place in the year 1749--strange to say, in the seventy-first year of Renata's age.

We next give a more extraordinary story illustrative of superstitious sentiments in France, viz. the world-wide one of Jeanne D'Arc (sometimes called Johan of Arc, the Maid of Orleans), who fell a victim to the credulity prevalent in that country and in England. The small village of Domremi is a retired spot, where popular superstitions have been almost religiously preserved. Fairies were believed to frequent the neighbourhood of Domremi. Near to it stood a large ancient beech-tree, known as the charmed tree of Bourlemont, supposed to be a favourite haunt of elves. Beneath the spreading boughs gushed a sparkling fountain, of which people drank to preserve them from fevers. Witches went thither at night to dance with the fairies. Young men and maidens also resorted to the spot, to dance round the tree and fountain. Garlands were made there, and presented as offerings to our lady of Domremi. The priests of the village said mass once a year over the fountain, to strengthen its healing qualities. Under a hazel-tree, not far from the charmed tree, grew mandrakes, one of which never failed to add wealth and domestic happiness to any person who possessed it.

In the village lived a labouring man, named Jacques D'Arc, who, with his wife, the villagers looked upon with respect. They had several children, boys and girls. The youngest daughter, named Jeanne, was born in the year 1410. At childhood she assumed a reserved and pensive disposition, and often sought solitude within the village church. Having but a limited education, the superstitions of her time were implicitly believed in by her. In addition to dancing round the charmed tree and fountain with other young maidens, she often went there alone. She grew up to be an attractive young woman, of peculiar mind. Subject to fits or trances, she became prostrated by them; and she had, according to her own account, converse with angels and the spirits of dead saints.

At an early period of life Jeanne D'Arc received the impression that providence intended her to achieve great feats in behalf of her country. More than once she exclaimed, "Nobody but me can recover the kingdom of France!" At this time, it should be observed, France groaned under the tyranny of contending factions; and so low had the Dauphin sunk, that not a single place remained in his power except Orleans; and even it the English closely besieged. After various unsuccessful attempts, the Maid obtained permission to communicate her heavenly mission to the Dauphin. Assuming male attire and warlike equipments, including a white banner, she placed herself at the head of the French troops, who, through her example, became inspired with new enthusiasm. On the 29th April 1429 she threw herself, with supplies of provisions, into Orleans. Soon after arriving there she attacked Fort St. Loup, which she carried, while wielding a sword that had lain more than a century in a knight's tomb behind the altar of St. Catherine at Fierbois. In an assault on the English, Jeanne received a severe wound on the neck, from which a large quantity of blood flowed; but she said it was not blood, but glory, that streamed out. The siege of Orleans being raised on 8th May, Jeanne D'Arc carried the news to the Dauphin, and entreated him to come and be crowned at Rheims, then in possession of the English. The siege of Gergeau was next undertaken. Jeanne boldly went into the ditch, standard in hand, at a part most vigorously defended. The soldiers followed, and soon the town fell by the courageous woman's hands. She next took possession of Auxerre, Troyes, and Chalons, thus opening for the Dauphin the road to Rheims. Thither he proceeded, and on 17th July was crowned. Jeanne D'Arc (or the Maid of Orleans, as she is now called) assisted at the ceremony. The Maid having accomplished, so far, the object of her mission, wished to return home; but, seeing her presence inspired great confidence in the army, the king, and others of influence, opposed her departure. She therefore stuck to her post of military leader. She accompanied the king to Crepi, Senlis, and Paris. In the siege of Compeigne, in the year 1430, Jeanne made a sally, at the head of a hundred men, over the bridge, and twice repulsed the besiegers. The king's troops were surrounded, yet, after performing feats of valour, the Maid disengaged her company, who re-entered the town. The heroine remained in the rear to facilitate the retreat, and, when she wished to enter the town, the gates were shut. She again charged her pursuers, but finding herself unsupported she exclaimed, "I am betrayed!" It turned out as supposed: the shutting of the gates while Jeanne remained exposed to danger did not take place through accident. Jealousy and treachery were at work: her pretended friends had conspired to bring her bright career to a speedy end. Many brave soldiers fell under the Maid's charmed sword; but as one sword and a single hand could not mow down a whole army, she surrendered to Lionel Vasture of Vendome, who gave her up to John of Luxembourg. The latter nobleman basely sold Jeanne to her enemies--the English--for ten thousand livres; and, what appeared most cruel, the king did not attempt to redeem the heroine, to whom he and his kingdom owed much.

The ingratitude of Charles VII. has remained a blot on his memory. Even those who refuse to admit that Jeanne D'Arc possessed supernatural powers, regard his conduct with abhorrence. On Jeanne being made prisoner, the English rejoiced exceedingly. The Duke of Bedford thought it proper to disgrace her, in order to reanimate the courage of his countrymen. In Paris, the authorities, to evince their joy at her downfall, ordered salvoes of artillery to be fired. A *te deum* was sung in the church of Notre Dame; and preachers returned thanks to the Most High, for his mercy in bringing to an end the influence of such a wicked sorceress.

Jeanne, in an effort to escape from a high tower (her place of confinement), cast herself from its summit to the ground, yet, strange to say, sustained little injury. To guard against another attempt to gain liberty, iron chains were put round her legs and body. A court of French bishops met to try the Maid. The charge embraced seventy articles of impeachment. Questions were asked concerning politics; her belief in and intercourse with fairies; her favourite spiritual visitants, St. Catherine and St. Margaret; the devices of her banner; and the sacred sword.

A formula of sentence, after fifteen separate examinations, was read, declaring her guilty of apostasy, sorcery, etc., and setting forth that, lest the culprit should corrupt others, she should be cast out of the church, and delivered to the temporal authorities, praying them to deal mildly and humanely with her, and to rest satisfied with the death of her body. Burning the body only, the ecclesiastics considered mild treatment. Had they delivered their victim to Satan, loaded with the fearful curses contained in the greater excommunication, who can tell when her guilt would be expiated? As the secular powers were merely instruments of the ecclesiastical authorities, sentence of death by burning against the Maid of Orleans soon became an accomplished fact. Fastened to a stake, without much delay, the flames consumed her fair form, at the age of nineteen years. To the very last she believed in the reality of her visions, and intercourse with the spirits of departed saints. Her dying agonies were witnessed by a pitying crowd, who separated to proclaim abroad, that at the moment her breath went out a pure white dove rose from the pile and soared up to heaven.

Subsequent to this heroine's death several women emerged from obscurity, and feigned to be inspired in the same way as Jeanne D'Arc had been. Two young maids residing near Paris pretended that her mantle had fallen on them. The clergy interfered. The young women were apprehended, tried, and declared guilty of holding communication with evil spirits. One of them recanted, and thereby saved her life; the other remained firm, and perished at the stake.

After the real or unreal execution of Jeanne D'Arc, the report became current that she was alive, and playing a conspicuous part in society at a considerable distance from the scene of her triumphs and degradation. Some would have it that she escaped punishment through the interference of her admirers; but the general belief remained, that she really suffered in terms of her sentence. Another report represents the Maid's persecutors as being overtaken by more than ordinary misfortunes in their estate, in addition to suffering the torments of accusing consciences.

SUPERSTITION IN THE NINETEENTH CENTURY.
CHAPTER LXVIII.

Generality of Superstition--The Church and Superstition--St. Mourie--People forbidden to resort to the island Innis Maree--Various Modes of Superstition--Charms--Lucky and Unlucky Times--A Tinker's Curse and a Gipsy's Warning--Sailors' and Fishermen's Delusions--Spitting on one's Loof--Weddings, Funerals, and Baptisms--Spae Wives--May Dew--Holy-days--Kirk-session Records--Fort-William Fisherman--Dipping in Fountains--Lochmanur--Holy Well of Kilvullen--Well of Craiguck--Superstition in the Highlands--Warlock Willox--Superstition in Dundee.

Notwithstanding the progress of religion, science, and education generally so called, superstition prevails in this and other countries to an extent scarcely credible, and certainly not creditable to the leaders of public opinion. In every town and country, in every village and hamlet, yea, in every domestic circle, a belief in the supernatural has a place. Although the time has gone by for the burning of witches, and though the human mind is less disturbed by the thoughts of ghosts and Satan in corporeal shape than in past centuries, nevertheless man has not been able to rise altogether above the notion that there are such mortal creatures as witches and warlocks, and such immortal visible visitants to our sublunary world as spirits and the devil. Not only is there a general belief in the existence of ghosts, but we have people asserting that they possess the faculty of making spirits of the dead answer them at pleasure. Learned men (men in high position) have written lengthy arguments in favour of the spiritual theory.

Signs and omens are observed, faith in miracles have not died out, charms are not considered valueless, curses and evil wishes make a large proportion of our population tremble, dreams are believed in. Indeed nearly all, if not all, the various aspects and phases of superstition of the sixteenth, seventeenth, and eighteenth centuries are, to a certain extent, believed in in the nineteenth century. We make no mere random statement, but are stating facts falling under our own notice and that of reliable witnesses.

Fear of the supernatural is confirmed by the dread one has of passing a graveyard at night. Among the English, Scotch, and Irish people the tales of their forefathers are remembered. Who has forgotten his nursery tales? Who does not remember the stories of aged friends as they sat round the winter fire? We have somewhere read of our nursery tales under eight heads. First, of a hero waging successful war with monsters; (2nd), of a neglected individual mysteriously raised into position, like "Cinderella;" (3rd), of one thrown into a magic trance, like the "Sleeping Beauty;" or (4th) of a person overpowered by a monster, as in the case of "Little Red Riding Hood." "Blue Beard," says the writer from whom we have just quoted, is a specimen of a group of tales, in which (5th) the hero or heroine is forbidden to do something, but disobeys. "Beauty and the Beast" and "The White Cat" are examples of a large group in which (6th) a brilliant being is transformed, by means of a spell, into the form of a lower animal. A number of stories, such as "Fortunatus and his Companions," turn upon (7th) the possession of magic implements or spells. The concluding group consists (8th) of moral tales. But these eight groups are far too few to supply examples of either ancient or modern superstition. Hahn endeavoured to group the folk-tales of Europe under forty heads, and Baring Gould has followed his example. In every corner of Christendom some form of kelpie, sprite, troll, gnome, imp, or demon has a place in the mind of the people, much the same as in Pagan times.

Those who have turned their attention to archaeology are in a position to corroborate what is here advanced. No doubt, modern superstition, in its various forms, is the result of ancient delusion in regard to religion and moral rectitude. To overlook or neglect the prescribed formula in regard to blessing and cursing, was certain to bring its own punishment. Superstition is believed in by persons accounted neither irreligious nor desperately profane. Church dignitaries, once foremost in the persecution of reputed witches, found it necessary to change their front. Everything bordering on witchcraft, devil worship, or such like, met with ecclesiastical censure. Let the inhabitants of Applecross say why they and their forefathers sacrificed to St. Mourie, their patron saint, at certain seasons; and let the Synod of Glenelg and the Presbytery of Lochcarron say why they considered it necessary to forbid the people resorting to the island Innis Maree on 25th August. And let those reverend bodies say whether certain stones are not consulted as to future events--whether oblations are not left on hills--and whether a species of adoration is not paid to wells.

Why is the mountain ash, or rowan tree, seen growing in almost every garden, when not another tree adorns the landscape or shelters the family dwelling? Why are the caudal appendages of the cottar's cow and calf adorned with red thread? and wherefore are horse-shoes nailed to stable-doors, ships' masts, and buried under thresholds? What parish or district has not its haunted house and "white lady?" In what quarter do not the young fear to pass ruined castles after sundown? And have we not everywhere a confessed belief in lucky and unlucky times and circumstances, and admitted presentiments of evil?

The tinker's curse and the gipsy's warning are prophetically regarded. In the north of Scotland there is a class of lay preachers, or catechists, known as the "Men," who lay claim to prophetic talent; yea, there are among them enthusiasts, who pretend they possess keys equal in efficacy to those of St. Peter. At the seaside, among the sailors and fishermen, strong indications of superstition are observable. Buyers and sellers, especially cattle dealers and hucksters, daily evince their adherence to the credulity of their progenitors, by spitting on the first money received by them in the morning, and preferring to deal first with persons reputed to have good luck. Athletes (particularly boxers and wrestlers) spit into their loofs before commencing a combat, thinking that by so doing they are more likely to prevail.

At wedding-parties, baptisms, and funerals we have seen numerous forms of superstition displayed. First, the bride's dress must consist of certain fabrics, while the flowers with which her person is adorned must not include hated sprigs, repellers of love, or such as attract evil spirits. All know the custom, if not the value, of throwing slippers, rice, etc. after a newly-wedded pair; and the ceremony of breaking a cake over a bride's head as she first enters her husband's house is not forgotten. Who has not eaten the "child's cheese," and been forbidden to depart from the infantile home before drinking the young one's health, on every occasion the nursery was entered before the christening. Maidens dream, as often as they have the chance, on "children's cheese" and brides' cakes, in order to obtain glimpses in their slumbers of future love and matrimony.

Tea in abundance has been infused to supply the necessary material for the spae-wife to read her cups. Coins and jewellery, deposited with the fortune-teller to enable him or her to discover the fortune of the owners, have too often failed to be restored to the lawful owners. Servant-girls can tell how often they and their employers have been plundered by fortune-tellers in the guise of beggars and pedlars.

May-dew has not lost its virtue; the carrying of fire round houses, fields, and boats are still supposed to drive away witches and evil spirits; and diseases are supposed to be capable of cure by means of charms.

Superstitious families are less terrified at thunder and lightning than at the ticking of the death-watch (*anobium tesselatum*), whose noise is supposed to prognosticate an early death in the household. With little less fear are the crowing of cocks, the lowing of cattle, and the howling of dogs at night listened to. The passing of a sharp-edged or pointed instrument from one lover to another is continued to be looked upon with anything but favour, as such articles, even pins, divide affection. If an angler step over his fishing-rod, he will have indifferent piscatory sport. It is a good sign for swallows to build their nests at one's windows; but if a person destroy a swallow's nest, or kill any of those birds of passage, he should prepare for misfortunes. Unusually dark-coloured magpies flying about a house, betokens grief to the inmates. When the palm of one's hand itches, money may be looked for; when the sole of the foot itches, prepare for a long journey.

Of particular festive and holy-days we have more than once taken notice, and pointed out how they were observed. Well, we have Christmas, Hallow-e'en, Good Friday, observed with something resembling the fashion of olden times. The evergreens, kail-stocks, pan-cakes, and buns have the same significations as they had in generations past. To break a Good Friday bun between two persons, is accepted as a pledge of friendship. Many superstitious persons keep a Good Friday bun throughout the year, to secure good fortune, prevent fires, and keep disease away.

At a recent meeting of the British Archaeological Association, Mr. H. Syer Cuming, F.S.A., said it was only a few years since he saw a woman drink a little grated cross-bun in water, to cure a sore throat, and that, at the time he was speaking, twenty stale cross-buns, strung on a cord, were suspended as a festoon above the door of an apartment at Brixton Hill, to scare away evil spirits. Fortunately, those who adopt such precautions do so now without fear of punishment. No doubt the Church of Rome interdicts her adherents from eating flesh on Fridays and other prescribed times, but the laws are changed since the seventeenth century. An extract from the kirk-session records of Dunfermline for 1640-89 will show the ecclesiastical law of that period:--

> "21 December 1641.--That day John Smart, flesher,
> being convict for selling a carkeis of beefe, and
> hav^g pott on a rost at hes fire ye last fasting day,
> is ordainit to pay 8 mks., qhlk. he payit. And William
> Anderson in knockes for bring^g a hamelading of y^e
> s^d carkeis of beefe ye fast day, is ordainit to pay
> 30s., q^r of he payit 24s."

Of the magical properties of May dew little is now known, compared with the knowledge of former times. Our grandmothers firmly believed that three applications of it at the beginning of May preserved the complexion in brilliant bloom for a year; consequently they were up and out long before sunrise, to wash their faces in the charmed moisture. There is still much value in the recipe, which is, however, applicable to all the dewy-morning months. It was not only on the brightness of the cheek that May dew was believed to have a marvellous effect, but many physical ailments were amenable to its virtues. It is related that the people about Launceston say that a child weak in the back may be cured by being drawn through the wet grass thrice on the mornings of the 1st, 2nd, and 3rd of May. Swellings in the neck are similarly cured; but the dew in such cases should, if the patient is a man, be sought on the grave of the last young woman buried, and if a woman, on that of the last young man interred.

These May-day practices are not confined to England. The medicinal and cosmetic properties of spring rain and May dew appear to have been at one time universally credited. In fact, water, in whatever shape--dew, rain, river--when associated with spring, was invested with a sort of divine enchantment in the popular mind. The heavy dew which brightened and refreshed the young and tender green of all growing things was holy and hallowing. Running water shared in the same veneration.

In some parts of Russia, at the present day, the girls go into the water up to the girdle on May-day, or, if the streams be still frozen, they dance about a hole broken in the ice, and sing a welcome to the "beautiful spring." The sick are carried down to the banks of a river and sprinkled with water, which has received a healing power from the new season. Cattle are driven afield at early dawn through the May dew, and the young people roll about in it where it lies thickest.

Not many years ago a fisherman near Fort William purchased a set of nets, to enable him to prosecute the herring fishing. He toiled all night without catching any fish. Dispirited, he returned home in the morning to his anxious wife, who was expecting to receive a heavy haul. On learning her husband had been so unfortunate while their neighbours had been successful, she suspected the nets were bewitched, and therefore procured consecrated water wherewith to sprinkle them. The experiment proved successful beyond expectation: every morning the fisherman went to sea he returned with so many fish that his circumstances were considerably improved.

Holy water is kept, in certain localities in the north, for sprinkling on the sea to still the waves in case of a storm. Holy oil, we are assured, is equally efficacious. We have seen a lady turning her chair three times round, to secure luck at cards.

Dipping in a fountain or lake in Scotland for the purpose of healing diseases, is a matter of frequent occurrence. In the beginning of August (old style), between midnight and early morning, may be seen the impotent, the halt, and the lunatic immersing themselves, or being immersed by their friends, in Lochmanur, Sutherlandshire, in the full expectation that benefit to mind and body will be secured by the operation. One who has witnessed the strange scenes within the last ten years, *i.e.* since 1870, gives the following graphic account of the superstitious actions he beheld:--

> "The hour was between midnight and one o'clock in the
> morning, and the scene was absurd beyond belief,
> though not without a touch of weird interest, imparted
> by the darkness of the night and the superstitious
> faith of the people. The lame, the old, and young were
> waiting for an immersion in Lochmanur or Lochmonaire.
> About fifty persons were present near one spot, and
> other parts of the loch were similarly occupied. About
> twelve stripped and walked into the loch, performing
> their ablutions three times. Those who were not able
> to act for themselves were assisted, some of them
> being led willingly and others by force, for there
> were cases of each kind. One young woman, strictly
> guarded, was an object of great pity. She raved in a
> distressing manner, repeating religious phrases, some
> of which were very earnest and pathetic. She prayed
> her guardians not to immerse her, saying that it was
> not a communion occasion, and asking if they could
> call this righteousness or faithfulness. No male, so
> far as I could see, denuded himself for a plunge.
> These gatherings take place twice a year, and are
> known far and near to such as put belief in the spell.
> But the climax of absurdity is in paying the loch in
> sterling coin."

Another writer says he has seen even more than fifty dipping in this loch in one night. A third eye-witness never saw more than two or three of a night venturing into the loch; but many more, he adds, were present to see and be seen. And there are persons who have declared they derived benefit from bathing in it. The late Rev. D. Mackenzie, minister at Farr, who often denounces from the pulpit the superstitious practice of dipping in the loch, says, in his description of it in the *New Statistical Account of Scotland*: "Numbers from Sutherland, Caithness, Ross-shire, and even from Inverness and Orkney, come to this far-famed loch."

The holy well of Kilvullen, on the Irish coast, is as good as Lochmanur. Every year, in the month of August, there are high festivals held there. The water has a wonderful repute for healing qualities. It has worked miraculous cures ever since the great saint of Kilvullen flourished in the parish. The inhabitants have vague though reverential notions of the date of St. Kilvullen's existence. That he was of foreign extraction would appear to be proven, some way or other, through a boulder lying on the beach, on which, it is stated, the blessed Kilvullen travelled here direct from Rome, with a commission from the Pope to convert the Irish. To wriggle under a cavity in this stone and come out on the other side, is an infallible remedy for lumbago.

There is a mountain not far distant from Kilvullen with a gap in it, supposed to have been made by a single bite of the devil. There is scarcely an eminence in Ireland out of which the demon has not devoured a bit. Travellers are shown the devil's bites, the devil's gaps, and the devil's punch-bowls, over nearly every part of the country.

Dr. Arthur Mitchell, while lecturing on Scottish superstition, said: "The adoration of wells continues in certain aspects to the present day, from John-o'-Groat's to the Mull of Galloway. I visited-a well at Craiguck, in the parish of Avoch, Ross-shire, some years ago, and found numerous offerings fastened to a tree beside it; and of at least a dozen wells in Scotland the same thing is more or less true. An anxious loving mother would bring a sick child to such a well at early morning on the 1st May, bathe the child, then cause the little one to drop an offering into the well--usually a pebble, but sometimes a small coin. Then a bit of the child's dress was attached to a bush or tree growing on the side of the well. These visits were paid in a spirit of earnestness and faith, and were kept more or less secret. Some of the wells have names of Christian saints attached to them; but I never knew of a case in which the saint was in any way recognised or prayed to. There is reason to believe these wells were the objects of adoration before the country was christianised, and that such adoration was a survival of the earlier practice to which Seneca and Pliny referred."

However much the custom of seeking health by bathing or dipping in lakes, or drinking from certain springs, may be deplored, it is tolerable compared with the superstitious belief that prevails, of epilepsy being cured by the affected person drinking water out of a suicide's skull, or by tasting or touching the blood of a murderer.

A gentleman, writing lately from Fort William, says:--"It is a mistake to suppose that superstition is entirely extinct in the Highlands, or that it is confined to old women alone. It was only the other day a certain spinster in Lochaber, who has reached the shady side of sixty, owned a cow. Up to last week the cow was a model one in every sense of the term, but last week it showed sure signs of the effect of the 'evil eye.' The symptoms were chiefly deficiency in quantity and quality of milk. A consistory of old women was soon called, and, among a host of other queer contrivances, they had recourse to one--commendable chiefly for its simplicity, and also for its complete success. It was no other than smearing the brute all over with soot and salt! As this was done for the purpose of spoiling the beauty of the beast, it may be better guessed than described how completely it answered the purpose."

Another gentleman, writing from Grantown, assures us that "One night in 1878, two men, one of whom was blind, entered the village of Grantown and inquired as to the nearest route to Tom-intoul. They came from a parish north of Inverness, and the object of their long journey was to visit a representative of the family of the warlock Willox, with a view to overturn some bad luck which had beset the course in life of the younger of the two. The attempt to dissuade them from proceeding further on their foolish errand was fruitless. Their faces had been set on the journey, and they were sternly resolved to accomplish it at all hazards. They pressed on their way, the blind man leaning on the arm of his companion, though night was on the point of falling. The matter pressed heavily on the younger, and it was in vain he tried to conceal his thoughts, being either 'crazed with care or crossed in hopeless love.'"

We have not learned how the travellers succeeded, but this we know, that members of the Willox family have been supposed for generations to profess knowledge of the occult science. Those of the nineteenth century, to whom the hidden secrets of their fathers have been imparted, eke out a livelihood by cultivating a small patch of land in a mountainous district, and vending nostrums for the cure of diseases in man and beast, and selling charms to counteract witchcraft. Persons have been known to travel more than a hundred miles to consult a Willox. That a wide-spread belief exists of this family's mystical powers, is manifest from the number of people seeking their advice. Further, the warlocks of untainted Willox blood not only direct attention to the healing art and the means of outwitting witches, but they aid in discovering lost and stolen property.

In 1871 a little boy in Dundee was afflicted with a sore upon his right leg. Medical skill proved of no avail, and the parents began to fear the boy would be rendered helpless for life. One day, how-ever, an old Irish woman saw the boy, and, on ascertaining the nature of his disease, declared that she could by means of the "gold-touch" heal the sore. She asked for and obtained the marriage ring of the invalid's mother. With the ring the strange woman rubbed three times round the sore. She performed the same operation next day, and on the next again. On the fourth day no mark of a sore could be discovered. No doubt remained on the parents' and neighbours' minds that the operator was a white witch, possessed of valuable charms.

CHAPTER LXIX.

Ghost at Sea--Tragical Event--Ghosts in   Edinburgh--Fear of Ghosts in Glasgow--Fortune-telling--Choice of Lovers, how   decided--A handsome Dowry--Old Irish Story--How a   Ghost settled a Land Question--A Highland Prophecy   respecting the Argyll Family--Gipsies and   Superstition--Yetholm Gipsies--Episode in a Police   Court--Curses--Superstition among   Fishermen--Superstition among Seamen--Providing for   the Dead--A Warning--Blood Stains--Various   Superstitions--Hallow-e'en at Balmoral--Faith in   Dreams, Signs, Omens, Predictions, and   Warnings--Self-accusing Catalogue--Reflections on the   Memories of our Ancestors.

A strange story is told in connection with the report of the murder at sea on board the barque "Pontiac," of Liverpool, by Jean Moyatos, a Greek sailor, in custody in Edinburgh a few years ago. We do not know whether the particulars we are about to relate came out in the investigation, but undoubtedly they had a strong bearing on the case, and made it probable, that but for the hallucination of one of the crew--not the Greek sailor--the murder would not have taken place.

Five days after the "Pontiac" left Callao, Jean Moyatos murdered one of his fellow-seamen, and stabbed another in such a dangerous manner that his life was despaired of. Two nights before the fatal occurrence the mate of the "Pontiac" was standing near the man at the helm, no other person being on the quarter-deck at the time, when the latter in great terror called out, "What is that near the cabin door?" The mate replied that he saw nothing, and looked about to see if any one was near, but failed to discover any person. The steersman then, much terrified, said the figure he saw was that of a strange-looking man, of ghostly appearance, and almost immediately afterwards exclaimed, "There he is again, standing at the cabin window!" The mate, though in view of the place referred to, saw no figure near it, nor at any other part of the quarter-deck, though he looked round and round. Next day the report went from one to the other that a ghost was on board, which filled some of the sailors with alarm, while others made a jest of it. Next night a boy (a stowaway) was so dreadfully alarmed in his bunk by something he saw or felt (we do not know which), that he cried out so loudly as to waken all the seamen in bed. The boy was sure it was the ghost seen the previous night that had frightened him; and others of more mature years were inclined to think so too. Perhaps more than one-half of those on board believed that something supernatural was in the ship, and that some calamity would soon happen. But there were two at least on board who did not believe the ghost stories, and these were the man subsequently murdered, and his companion who was stabbed. The former joked with the boy about the ghost, and said he would have his knife well sharpened and ready for the ghost if it appeared the next night. He would give it a stab and "chuck" it overboard. The latter joined in the joke, saying he also would help "to do for the ghost;" and others said they would have letters ready for the ghost to carry to their friends in the other world. Jean Moyatos overheard what was said as to stabbing and throwing overboard; and in consequence of his imperfect knowledge of the English language, and having previously supposed there was a combination against him, thought the threats were made against him, and therefore resolved to protect himself. A few hours after the jesting we have briefly explained took place, he stabbed the two men who principally carried on the jest, with the fatal result known. The murder, as might be expected, filled every one on board with horror; and the terror of the sailors who believed there was a ghost on board became overwhelming. At night, whether in bed or on watch on deck, they had great dread, it being heightened by reports that strange noises were heard below. Not even at the end of the voyage had the fear been overcome; for, after the ship lay moored in the docks of Leith, two of the crew who had agreed to sleep on board became so frightened, after their companions were paid off, that they refused to remain in the vessel at night.

Jean Moyatos, on being brought to trial before the High Court of Justiciary, was found to be insane; and therefore the Court ordered him to be confined in a lunatic asylum during Her Majesty's pleasure.

A circumstance, freely spoken of within the past few years, has given rise to a rumour that ghosts frequent the neighbourhood of the Dean Cemetery, Edinburgh. The story is, that about three o'clock one morning a private watchman named Clark (employed to look after a block of buildings at Bell's Mills, Water of Leith) and his friend the constable on the beat, were surprised, in the midst of a friendly talk, by a tall figure--which, at least to their startled eyes, seemed to be in white--clearing a wall and alighting on the ground close beside them. It darted along the road towards the Dean Cemetery. As it ran, the two men heard, or thought they heard, a clinking sound like that made by a horse with a loose shoe. Too much frightened to watch the movements of their visitor, Clark and his companion took to their heels, nor thought of halting until they were a considerable distance from the locality. Clark refused to return to his post, and some difficulty was even experienced in getting the constable to look upon the matter from a business point of view.

Whether the same ghost or not we cannot tell, but not long ago many in Edinburgh became startled at rumours of a ghost being seen in various parts of Edinburgh. On a Saturday night the movements of a ghost caused great excitement in the Fountainbridge district, particularly at Murdoch Terrace, Bainfield, where a large crowd collected. On the ghost being observed, five men, armed with bludgeons, pursued it till it reached the Dalry Cemetery, where it jumped over the wall, and was not seen again. Bodies of men formed themselves into a detective force, to lie in wait at different places for the apparition. It was gravely alleged that the ghost made its appearance in varied attire--sometimes in black, sometimes in white, and occasionally with the addition of horns. One dark night a cabman, driving through the Grange, and looking about him with great fear, and trembling for the appearance of this irrepressible "Spring-heel Jack," suddenly heard a loud noise over his head, and the next instant something descended with such force on his shoulders as to send his pipe flying over the splashboard, and himself nearly after it.

The alarm excited in the weak-minded and ignorant can scarcely be credited. We know of one case where a cab-driver, who was ordered to go at an early hour in the morning to a house in the suburbs to convey a lady and gentleman from an evening party, positively refused to go, through sheer terror of encountering "Jack," as the ghost was named, preferring rather to risk losing his situation. It is said that the girls employed in factories in the vicinity of the Canal would not venture to their work till it was fairly daylight, and even then they went in a body. Several policemen asserted that they had seen the ghost. The stories about the ghost created such an impression on the minds of many young people residing within a wide radius of the haunted district, that they would not venture out after dark.

Glasgow, as recently as 1878, had its ghost also, or supposed it had. The residents in the Northern District of that city were thrown into a state of excitement, hardly to be credited in enlightened times. One night it was whispered that the school at the corner of Stirling Street and Milton Street had become the abode of a horde of warlocks, whose cantrips were equalled only by the antics cut by their demoniacal ancestors in "Alloway's Auld Haunted Kirk." It was seriously averred by dozens of persons that they had actually witnessed the hobgoblins in the enjoyment of their fiendish fun. In a brief space of time the whole neighbourhood turned out to see the terrible visitants that had come among them. Frequently as many as from four to six thousand people--the large majority of whom were children in groups of threes and fours, clinging to each other's hands, and evidently in mortal terror of being suddenly spirited away no one knew where--assembled to catch a glimpse of the mysterious cause of the commotion. To such a height did the excitement grow, that one night the authorities stationed no fewer than nine policemen round the school, for the purpose of restoring order. On the following night "the ghost," as it was now called, still uncaught, and gliding as noiselessly and swiftly through the deserted rooms as on the first night of its appearance, frightening the souls and raising the hair of all who believed in it, and the authorities, being suspicious of mischief on the part of some one concealed on the premises, sent two detectives into the attics of the building, for the purpose of arresting the apparition should it stalk in their direction and prove to be made of flesh and blood. After waiting several hours the officers relinquished their watching, and left the school to its ghostly occupant. All sorts of theories were propounded to account for the unearthly sights that were witnessed through the windows of the building, but it turned out that a very innocent combination of circumstances had caused all the excitement. It was believed that the reflection from a set of mirrors in the house opposite, falling upon a series of thickly-glazed maps hanging upon the school wall, had produced the appearances which served to create so great a sensation.

We have seen there was neither ghost nor goblin in the city of St. Mungo, but we have also seen from the above incident that time has not enabled us to cast off altogether the fetters of superstition.

Cunning, duplicity, and falsehood are associated with fortune-telling. An instance in exemplification is within our recollection. Not far from the junction of the Gadie and Urie with the

Don, in Aberdeenshire, dwelt a rich farmer. His only daughter possessed rare natural charms, gifts, and graces. She could spin, sew, manage the dairy, sing with a voice equal to that of the mavis or blackbird, while her heart was as tender as that of any other sighing maiden. Two lovers sought her hand--one rich, the other poor. The poor man she declared to be her choice, but the purse-proud father declared his firlot of silver money, his twelve cows, and as many calves, his sheep and oxen, intended as his daughter's dower, would never enrich a pennyless man without houses and lands. So he said; yet he changed his mind through the influence of a fortune-teller, hired to tell what pleased her employers best. In presence of father and mother the sibyl professed to see, first, in her cup a splendid mansion, with wealth in great store, cattle, and fields of waving corn, then gradual decline of riches, until the young lady, her husband, and six or eight children, were seen living in a little hut in great poverty.

On hearing such an evil prophecy, the interpreter desired to cast the cup again, to ascertain whether the Fates were resolved to adhere to their former announced decree. Father and mother leaned back in their chairs, giving utterance to disquieting thoughts. Through various incantations the gods were propitiated. A second cup disclosed a small beginning for the daughter and her husband, but a grand ending. To prove which prediction was the correct one, the fortune-teller had recourse to the egg and lead tests--pouring the white of an egg and boiling lead into water, and watching the fantastic figures produced. Every fresh trial terminated in favour of the poor wooer. Father and mother changed their minds; the daughter almost leaped for joy; two fond hearts were united, and the promised dower was not kept back. For many years the young couple throve, and at last died, in peace and possession of plenty, leaving an honourable name, likely to descend to future generations.

The immediately preceding anecdote reminds us of an old Irish story bearing on the land question, and showing how agrarian difficulties were settled in ancient times, without recourse to assassination.

One night in 1662, one Francis Taverner, while riding home near Drumbridge, observed two horsemen pass him silently. Not even the treading of the horses' feet could be heard, and presently a third horseman appeared in the likeness of James Haddock, formerly a farmer at Malone, where he died five years previously. Mr. Taverner asked the spectre rider number three (for in reality the three riders were apparitions) why he appeared to him. To this the ghost replied, that if he would ride his (the ghost's) way he would inform him. Mr. Taverner refused to go any other way than that which led to his own home. Man and ghost parted company; but no sooner had they done so than a dreadful storm arose, in the midst of which hideous screeches rose above the gale. Mr. Taverner and his horse were sensible of some evil influence being near them; and they continued in a state of semi-stupor until cock-crowing. Chanticleer's clarion notes seemed to work a charm; for as they wakened the morn, all became calm--placid as an inland lake unrippled by the wind.

Next night an apparition in the likeness of James Haddock appeared again to Mr. Taverner, and bade him go to Eleanor Welsh, wife of one Davis, but formerly the spouse of James Haddock, by whom she had an only son, to whom Haddock had by will given a lease of a farm, but of which the son was deprived by Davis. "Tell her," said the ghost, "that it is the will of your former husband that our son should be righted in the lease." Through some infatuation, the man disregarded the instructions of the apparition, and for his neglect he was haunted and threatened by the apparition in several forms.

So uneasy did Mr. Taverner feel, that he left his mountain home and went to Belfast. Thither the ghost followed him, and again threatened to tear him in pieces unless he delivered the message. He therefore went to Lord Chichester, owner of the farm, and with tears in his eyes related the whole story. Dr. Lewis Downs, a minister in Belfast, hearing the relation, at first questioned the lawfulness of obeying a spirit, but, on mature consideration, and having respect to the injured son's interest, not only thought the message should be delivered, but agreed to accompany Taverner to Davis's house to hear it communicated.

Dr. Taylor, bishop of Down, Connor, and Dromore, after strictly examining Taverner anent the whole matter, expressed his belief in the realness of the apparition. No doubt the medium of communication suffered much mental torture, and great excitement prevailed in the north of Ireland; but, however, to use a hackneyed phrase, "All's well that ends well." The apparition's mission to earth was fulfilled; for the young man's wrongs were redressed, and he remained for many years in secure possession of his father's lands.

An old Highland prophecy respecting the Argyll family has been brought to mind by the marriage of the Marquis of Lorn, heir apparent to the dukedom, with a princess of England. It was foretold that all the glories of the Campbell family would be renewed in the first chief who in the colour of his locks approached nearest to that of the great Jan Roy Cean (Red John the Great), Duke of Argyll. Nature has performed her part in the person of the noble Marquis, and fate is not likely to allow the prophecy to remain unfulfilled.

Gipsies have always been associated with superstition. In their tents, and elsewhere, the women belonging to that class are professed fortune-tellers. We have heard them in all parts of Scotland and England telling fortunes, and seen people trembling at their curses, and witnessed others highly elated at their blessings and favourable predictions. In far-back times the leaders of the gipsies were chosen as their chiefs in consequence of this acknowledged power of divination and enchantment; they were therefore regarded not as kings or princes, but as prophets or magicians.

At Yetholm the gipsies have an idea that it is unlucky to have unbaptized children in their houses. Women of that village sell dreaming powders, by sleeping on which for a certain number of nights the sleepers are privileged to see their future partners in life.

As an instance in the belief of unholy prayers, we give an episode in the Leith police court in 1878. A woman named Allan was charged with assaulting a man because he had ill-used one of her boys. She was a person of wild passions, and upbraided the man with divers acts of cruelty to her children. Bursting out into loud cursing, she reminded the man that, eight years previously, she had, in consequence of him kicking her orphan child, prayed that neither he nor his wife should have children; "and you know," she exclaimed, "my prayers have been answered!" The woman professed to believe her unholy prayers had hindered the subjects of her wrath from having offspring. The man quailed under the termagant's piercing eye, and trembled at the renewed curses.

At the same court, a few years ago, it transpired that two women in the fishing village of Newhaven had a quarrel, during which one of them cursed the other and "salted her," *i.e.* threw salt at her. To cast salt with an evil intent after one, is as unlucky, in the estimation of fishermen and their wives, as it is to tell a fisherwoman that a hare's foot is in her creel, or to mention "Brounger" or the name of a four-footed beast at sea.

A few sceptical friends, not believing all they had heard regarding the superstitious notions of fishermen, were advised to put a young pig among some fishermen's lines on board of a boat at Newhaven pier. The trick being performed, and discovered before the boat put to sea, both pig and lines were tossed overboard, to the spoiling of a whole day's fishing.

A boat's crew recently left Newhaven pier for the oyster dredging in the Firth of Forth. One of the crew, a young lad, who had been at a circus in Edinburgh the previous evening, happened, while giving an account of what he had seen, to say "horse." No sooner had the hated word been uttered, than his companions assailed him in a most unmerciful manner. His disregard of the tradition of his fathers put an end to the fishing, it not being considered prudent by the men to prosecute their calling any more that day. In these superstitions, fishermen are following the examples of the ancients. It will be remembered the names of the Furies, Kings, etc. were not to be named, and that there were birds and beasts of ill omen.

Fishermen have an aversion to go to sea in a boat from which a man has been drowned, and they are opposed to the breaking up of an old boat. This last-mentioned superstition continues to prevail, and it accounts for so many useless crafts being seen at fishing towns unnecessarily occupying much valuable ground, as in olden times, and as mentioned by us under "Signs, Omens, and Warnings," at page 399. At the Tweed, fishermen still (1879) have a belief in the power of fairies to affect the fisheries. It is the custom not only to impregnate nets with salt, but also to throw part of that commodity into the water, to blind the mischievous elves, who are said to prevent fish being caught. The salting process was carried on at Coldstream very recently, with a result highly satisfactory to the operators, if not to others.

A ship captain has informed us that, when a young man, he incurred the displeasure of an old seaman, with whom he sailed in one of the old trading smacks between Leith and London. On refreshments being served out, according to custom, one day, he (our informant) handed a jug of beer to the old sailor through the steps of a ladder. For this act the aged salt swore at him, and called him an unlucky lubber, while at the same time he dealt him a severe blow on the face.

Another captain of a vessel trading between Leith and London has told us of a singular passage he had thirty years ago. To oblige a friend, he agreed to convey a hare to another friend in the English metropolis. A fair wind carried the vessel past the Bass Rock, but then a storm sprang up, which kept the ship tossing about for days without reaching the English coast. An old sailor declared their retarded progress was due to the hare being on board. By consent of all the crew, the hare found a place overboard, and then the wind became so favourable that the ship made a quick run to the Thames.

A gentleman in Edinburgh told us recently he had frequently seen burning candles beside a corpse at mid-day, while at the same time a small plate or saucer with salt rested on the corpse's breast, and every one who looked on the body had to put his hand on the inanimate brow. He further told us he had seen a priest of the Roman Catholic Church put a half-crown into the mouth of a corpse at Portobello, to represent, we presume, the obolus exacted by Charon for ferrying the shades of the buried dead across the under-world rivers.

In Ireland, at a period not remote, an opinion prevailed that the spirit of a dead person went about deceased's former home for a month. During that length of time a fire was always kept burning in the house, and a jug of water stood in deceased's chamber, so that his spirit might refresh itself. At the month's end a clergyman, by means of prayer, put the spirit to rest.

Within the last decade (we think in 1872) a highly respectable family in the county of Edinburgh was greatly alarmed by a pheasant flying through their dining-room window, killing itself on the spot, and breaking a large pane of plate glass. To the family the event came as a warning of early calamity. Next day a messenger announced that a worthy doctor of divinity, a dear family friend, had died the previous night.

We hear occasionally of the impossibility of wiping out the traces of flagrant crimes. The blood of Rizzio, shed on the floor of Holyrood Palace, in presence of Queen Mary, has defied the rubbing of years to wipe it away. There the blood stains remain a wonder to the thousands who visit Scotland's royal palace. At a time almost forgotten, a good man was hurled from a window of Torwood Castle, not far from the field of Bannockburn. His blood stained the grass on which the body fell, and since that time the herbage there is mixed with red blades of grass and red clover.

A Saturday's flitting is followed by a short sitting. No one should take possession of a new house before throwing coals and salt into it. No important undertaking should be commenced on Friday or Saturday, nor yet at the end of a year. "Berchta spoils flax found unspun the last day of the year." A shooting star falling near a house, foretells an early death in that dwelling.

Old flint arrow-heads are worn as charms, under the belief that they were the points of elfin arrows. If a lady be wise, she will not have two tea-spoons in her saucer at the same time. If a young lady desire to know how many sweethearts she has, let her pull her fingers, and the number will be equal to the cracks heard. In fact we have nearly as many signs, omens, charms, and freits as our forefathers had. We have legendary lore concerning the supernatural, we have mythological fables, forecasts, fatalities, our spell-bound individuals, our fey persons, and those who have had glamour cast into their eyes. None of us are likely to forget the New Year, Christmas, St. Valentine's Day, Beltane, Hallow-e'en, and many other high days, which come to us, month after month, with their peculiar rites and ceremonies. Even Queen Victoria, with a desire to please, takes pleasure in observing Hallow-e'en at her Highland residence.

In 1876 Hallow-e'en was celebrated at Balmoral Castle with unusual ceremony, in presence of Her Majesty, the Princess Beatrice, the ladies and gentlemen of the royal household, and a large gathering of the tenantry and servants on the estates of Balmoral and Invergeldie. The leading features of the celebration were a torchlight procession, the lighting of large bonfires, and the burning in effigy of witches and warlocks. Upwards of 150 torchbearers assembled at the castle as darkness set in, and separated into two parties, one band proceeding to Invergeldie, and the other remaining at Balmoral. The order was given to light the torches at a quarter before six o'clock, and shortly after that hour the Queen and the Princess Beatrice drove to Invergeldie, followed by the Balmoral party of torchbearers. The two parties then united and returned in procession to the front of Balmoral Castle, where all were grouped round a large bonfire, which blazed and crackled merrily, the Queen's pipers playing the while. Refreshments were then served to all, and dancing was engaged in to the strains of the bagpipes. When the fun was at its height, there suddenly appeared from the rear of the castle a grotesque figure, representing a witch, with a train of followers dressed like sprites, who appeared terrified at the monster fire blazing, and danced and gesticulated in all fashions; then followed a warlock of demoniacal shape, who was succeeded by another warlock drawing a car, on which was seated a witch, surrounded by other figures in the guise of demons. The unearthly visitors having marched several times round the burning pile, the principal figure was taken from the car and tossed into the flames amid weird shrieks and howls, the burning of blue lights, and a display of crackers and other fireworks. The health of her Majesty the Queen was then pledged and drunk with Highland honours by the assembled hundreds; the health of the Princess Beatrice was also received with enthusiasm. Dancing was then resumed, and was carried on till a late hour at night. The scene was very picturesque, Lochnagar and other mountains in the neighbourhood being covered with snow. Although the wind blew piercingly cold from the north, her Majesty and the Princess remained a considerable time, viewing the sports with evident interest.

As to giving up faith in dreams, signs, omens, predictions, and warnings, some people would nearly as soon give up their belief in the Bible. Then add to these a belief in ghosts, and we have a catalogue before us so self-accusing that we dare not cast serious reflections on the memories of our ancestors.

CHAPTER LXX.

Lizzie M'Gill, the Fifeshire Spaewife--Fortune-telling--Predicting a Storm at Sea--Servants alarmed thereby--Prediction Fulfilled--Adam Donald, an Aberdeenshire Prophet--Adam supposed to have been a Changeling--A Careless Mother--Adam as a Linguist--His Predictions and Cures--His Marriage--Valuable Charm--The Wise Woman of Kincardineshire--The Recruiting Sergeant--High-spirited Lady wooed and won--Lucky Lightfoot, the Spaewife--Charmed Ring and its Effects--Elopement and Marriage--An Enraged Father--Life in America--Sergeant Campbell's Death--Second Marriage--Literary Talents--Strong-minded Women.

In the spring of 1866, Eliza M'Gill, who resided near a romantic church in the Presbytery of St. Andrews, died at the advanced age of ninety-three years. For a long period almost every one, far and near, knew her as a spaewife of no ordinary knowledge. Lizzie (the name usually given her) could scarcely be called an impostor, for she appeared to have sincere faith in her profession. Often she exclaimed with solemn fervency, "The gift I hae is fae aboon, an' what He gies daurna be hidit." It was common for coy damsels and staid matrons to wend their way to Lizzie's cot about twilight, to have their fortunes spaed. About ten years before her death, when the prospects of the herring fishing were discouraging in the extreme, a buxom young woman, belonging to Pittenweem or St. Monance, repaired one evening to Carnbee to consult Lizzie. The damsel went with a heavy countenance, but she returned radiant with smiles, for the wise woman had said, "That altho' it was to be an awfu' puir draw, yet her folk was to hae a grand haul next e'enin'." And, true to the old wife's prediction, the crew in which she interested herself returned with a splendid prize from the fishing ground, followed, of course, with an increase of fame to the prophetess. On another occasion Lizzie was no less fortunate in the result foretold. A fisher-wife in the former place had received a sovereign from her husband, which, in the hurry of the moment, she had placed on the bedside. Going shortly afterwards to remove it, what was her consternation to find that the gold piece was gone! The most diligent search and inquiry were instituted after the lost treasure, but all to no purpose. In the extremity of her distress the poor woman thought of the "witch o' Carnbee," and, adjusting her cap, was soon on her journey thither. Lizzie's words fell on her troubled spirit like oil on the stormy sea; for she was told that, in the course of a day or two, the sovereign would be again in her possession. And so it proved: on drawing her husband's sea boots from under the bed, the coin fell from the toe of one of them.

On one occasion, a cheap trip by the steamer "Xantho" from Anstruther to Leith being advertised, many of the labouring classes, with their friends, arranged to visit Leith and Edinburgh. Unfortunately, however, the trip was to take place when the farmers of the district were very busy with the sowing of the turnips, and when, of course, their people were needed for that work. For the purpose, it is said, of keeping the men at home, a rumour circulated over the East Neuk, to the effect that the steamer and all on board were to perish in a fearful gale. The servants were so greatly alarmed by the prediction of Lizzie (it was she who spread the report), that they resolved to remain at home. The most remarkable feature of the affair is, that on the day in question a violent gale arose, which prevented the steamer returning to Anstruther until next morning. The non-arrival of the boat, as may be inferred, was the cause of the liveliest alarm to the friends of those on board, and an old worthy was heard to exclaim with respect to the prediction: "I dinna believe in sic things mysel', but, some way or ither, they aye come true." Lizzie's father and her whole family are said to have been highly respectable. Her truant and impulsive disposition led her, however, into conduct and habits that deprived her of the respect and help of her friends; and necessity at length appears to have constrained her to act the part of a fortune-teller, which she is known to have practised with success more than half a century.

Adam Donald, the prophet of Bethelnie, a contemporary of Lizzie M'Gill, stood high in Aberdeenshire as a seer. From his peculiar appearance in early life, grave doubts existed as to whether he was actually the offspring of his reputed parents, or whether he had not been substituted by the fairies for a lovely boy, the son of a worthy pair who believed not in the existence of witches or fairies.

One day the mother went out, leaving the child well in his cradle, and on returning, about an hour afterwards, she found a cold, marble-like infant, that never throve, never smiled, but, on the contrary, cried from morning to night, and from night till morning. On hearing of the changed infant, people flocked to witness the sudden alteration which had taken place in Mr. and Mrs. Donald's child. One knowing dame thought she understood the whole matter. The fairies were the wicked beings that had done all the mischief; and that they were permitted to do so, arose entirely through the parents' carelessness or ignorance. "Would it be believed," said the dame when speaking of the extraordinary circumstance, "that the simple mother went out, leaving her child alone, uncrossed, without a charm about its person, and without a horse-shoe being nailed on the threshold or behind the door, or a piece of rowan-tree at the door or window or in the cradle?" The friend to whom the reflections were made shook her head, while she replied, "Ay, ay, unbelieving generation; they will be burning the Bible some day soon."

Adam grew up, and became a wonderful being. From his ability to tell secrets past and future, and his power to effect cures, he became known as the "prophet of Bethelnie." Owing to a distorted state of body, he could not engage in robust employment to obtain a subsistence. He therefore, to amuse himself, read such books as his parents' stinted means could afford. Though it was supposed he could scarcely read English, he carefully collected many curious books in French, Latin, Greek, Italian, and Spanish. He often retired to an old churchyard and church in ruins, near his residence, to hold converse (so he said) with spirits of the dead, which informed him of things unknown to ordinary men.

When property went amissing, the owner repaired to the "prophet;" when cattle died, he named the witch who had killed them; and when any one became sick, Adam Donald supplied a remedy either by charms or herbs. Every Sunday, for many years, people of all classes crowded to consult him either as a necromancer or physician. His fee seldom exceeded sixpence for each consultation, yet he lived in comparative comfort.

When far advanced in life, miserable-looking object though the "prophet" remained, he prevailed on one of the handsomest girls of his neighbourhood to marry him. This matrimonial alliance helped to strengthen the supposition that Adam possessed more than human power.

The prophet of Bethelnie, although he had offspring, went to his long home without instructing a successor in the secret art he for many years followed with pecuniary advantage. He saved his reputation by preserving silence. If the following anecdote be true, there can be little doubt that the prophet assisted to restore decaying nature by the use of amulets or charms.

An old woman, whose eyes had become dim by reason of years, purchased a charm from the prophet, which Adam assured her would revive her sight to its former clearness. On the charm-- hieroglyphics traced on parchment--being suspended from the neck, it proved effectual. In a short time the old woman could thread a small needle, and see to pick up a pin from the floor. A female neighbour, with impaired sight, hearing of the cure, begged the charm from the lucky owner, but she would not part with it. All the favour the applicant could obtain was permission to copy the hieroglyphics on paper. The copy thus obtained and worn by the second patient brightened up her eyes also. Adam's medicines excited love, and his charms secured affection.

Fifty or sixty years ago Kincardineshire had its wise women. At the time referred to, a recruiting sergeant (whom we shall call Donald Campbell), equally devoted to his sovereign and the fair sex, made a favourable impression on the inhabitants of a small town fifteen or twenty miles from Aberdeen. The parish minister, the parochial teacher, and the doctor had something favourable to say of the sergeant. Nurses and other servant-maids could see nothing but the sergeant's red-coat; and it was whispered that even the young ladies smiled on him. Indeed that must have been so, for we are told that every one welcomed the Highlander: even the little children ran to meet him; and how heartily he did kiss them, but whether for their own sakes or the love he bore to their nurses, sisters, or aunts, none could tell. This, however, is certain: he did not encourage the shoemaker's sister, the tailor's daughter, nor the buxom widow who presided at the little inn. His affections were concentrated on a lady whom one could scarcely expect to yield her heart to such a humble son of Mars. The fair one was no less a personage than the daughter of Captain B---- of U----, a lady well known for miles around for her courage and love of out-door sports. Few could manage a high-spirited horse better than Rose Bloomer (by this name we introduce the young lady to our readers), or clear a fence with greater ease. And as for the fishing-rod and fowling-piece, she could handle them as dexterously as any disciple of Isaac Walton or of Nimrod could desire. True, she was not what is generally termed a beauty: her features, though not coarse, were scarcely those a sculptor or a painter would desire to have before him while completing his "Venus" for the next fine-art exhibition. In her short stout figure and determined look were indications of a strong-minded woman. Miss Bloomer, having lost her mother in early life, and her father being devoted to the chase, pedestrianism, and other athletic sports congenial to most country gentlemen, the young lady, his only child, had ample scope for indulging her inclinations.

Sergeant Campbell greatly admired Miss Bloomer's dexterity. Often did he watch her guidance of a high-mettled steed, now urging it to its utmost speed, and then reining in the impatient animal. The sergeant, we have said, greatly admired Miss Bloomer's dexterity; but, what is more, he resolved to secure her hand in marriage. Plan after plan, laid with the view of obtaining an introduction, failed. The lady frequently passed him without deigning to cast her eyes on his red-coat. Why should she? Was he not a poor soldier? and was she not a match for the best young gentleman in the county? These and like questions occurred to Campbell, and more than once made him almost despair of securing the lady's affections. Again and again his drooping spirits revived; his pertinacity had no bounds. What could not be secured, thought he, by ordinary means, might be obtained by extraordinary measures.

Sergeant Campbell, learned in the superstitions of his native land, believed them with a child-like faith. He had heard of Lucky Lightfoot, the spaewife; and to her he went for assistance. The old woman, on hearing the sergeant's tale, requested him to leave with her a gold ring he was wearing--a request he complied with. A few days afterwards the woman returned the soldier his ring, now charmed, with instructions to endeavour to get Miss Bloomer to wear it, though but for a few minutes.

In her frequent rambles along the banks of a meandering stream, the beauties of which Arthur Johnstone had celebrated in Latin verse, and regarding which Thomas the Rhymer had uttered prophecies, Campbell, unnoticed, followed Miss Bloomer, in the hope that fortune would favour him some day. She botanized, fished, and shot, unheeding her secret admirer. One day, to his delight, he observed her coming along a footpath, and resolved to drop the ring, in the hope that she would pick it up. Having left it in a conspicuous place, he retired into a thicket to watch the result. The lady, seeing the ring, took it up, examined it, and having no pocket or purse, put it on one of her fingers, and, as fate would have it, on the fourth finger of the left hand--the finger the Greeks discovered, from anatomy, had a little highly sensitive nerve going straight from it to the heart. "Now," thought he, "she is mine. I shall follow her, and ask whether she has found my ring;" but before he could muster courage to carry his resolution into effect, Miss Bloomer disappeared.

With the view of discovering the owner, she continued to wear the ring. Unexpectedly, Fred and Georgina Hopper, her cousins, while driving past, stopped to take dinner, and to them she showed the ring. Fred, who was an inveterate joker, made it the subject of several jests, all of which Miss Bloomer bore with good humour; but when Miss Hopper suggested that the ring might belong to some mean person, and hinted that it was an act of impropriety to wear it, the blood rushed to Miss Bloomer's cheeks; and she clenched her little fist, but for what purpose did not transpire.

In the evening the cousins drove away, leaving Miss Bloomer in anything but a pleasant mood. Evidently the charm had commenced to take effect, or Miss Hopper's remarks had disturbed the young lady's equanimity.

Still wearing the ring, Miss Bloomer retired to rest, or rather to bed, for during the night she was restless, tossing from side to side like one in delirium. One, two, three struck on the old clock, and still sleep did not come to soothe her disturbed brain. Whether in a sleeping or waking state she could not tell, but a regiment of armed men, with the recruiting sergeant at their head, seemed to pass before her, while in the distance there appeared ships at anchor in a large commodious bay. At four o'clock the lady stood at her window admiring the beautiful scenery. Retiring again to rest, she fell asleep, and did not waken before her accustomed time of rising.

After breakfast Miss Bloomer went out, as usual, to follow the bent of her mind. She had not gone far, before Sergeant Campbell approached her in a most respectful manner, and inquired if she had found a ring the previous day. It was scarcely necessary for her to return an answer, because there before him, on her ungloved hand, the ring appeared. As she handed it to him, an indescribable sensation ran through her whole frame. They entered into conversation; and how long they walked and chatted together, and what were the subjects of their conversation, we shall not pause to mention: sufficient to say that, before they parted, an early meeting was arranged. In due time, and quickly after each other, other meetings took place.

In course of time, old dames hinted that if the lady continued to keep tryst in the romantic secluded spots of her father's domains with such a fine-looking soldier as Campbell, she would provoke the goddess supposed to preside over love affairs, and most likely entitle herself to a rush-ring only on her wedding-day, instead of the customary gold one. But the evil prophetesses were wrong for once. Seldom did a recruiting party forward more stalwart soldiers to headquarters than Sergeant Campbell and his subordinates did. Indeed he owed much of his success to Miss Bloomer's exertions. She proved a valuable assistant; for, through her persuasion, a large number of young men on her father's estate were induced to enlist, and leave the homes of their youth for ever.

Happy days of single bliss cannot last for ever. Before three short months had passed, Sergeant Campbell and Miss Bloomer observed more than once the finger of scorn pointed at them. Threats were made by the parents of certain young men who had enlisted, to make known the conduct of the young lady and her lover to Captain Bloomer. What was to be done? Miss Bloomer's reputation was at stake, and the sergeant's life endangered, as will afterwards appear.

The betrothed pair (by this time Sergeant Campbell and Miss Bloomer were engaged to be married) perceived the necessity of acting promptly, and therefore they resolved to elope. An obstacle, however, stood in the way of their doing so immediately. If the sergeant abandoned his station, he would be pursued, arrested, and dealt with as a deserter. Miss Bloomer, equal to the occasion, resolved to "buy him off."

The discharge from the army being obtained, and the indispensable arrangements for a long journey completed, the sergeant and his true love secretly departed for Aberdeen, where they were united for better and worse--not by a clergyman, but by a magistrate, before whom they went and declared themselves to be husband and wife--a ceremony as binding by the law of Scotland as if there had been regular proclamation of banns, according to custom, in the parish church, and they had been married by an ordained minister. In place of a new marriage ring being placed on the bride's finger by the gallant sergeant, he, at her request, put on the charmed ring, the magical power of which she confessed could not be resisted.

Having shown the effect of Lucky Lightfoot's subtle art, we might take leave of the subject; but as the career of Mrs. Campbell (Mr. Campbell did not survive long) is peculiarly interesting, particularly in connection with a class that has created no small stir on both sides of the Atlantic, we shall pursue our narrative a little further.

The newly married couple, not considering themselves safe from pursuit in the Granite City, posted south, and reached the Clyde in less than twenty-four hours, where they secured a passage on board a vessel bound for America.

As soon as Captain Bloomer heard of his daughter's elopement, his rage could not be restrained. Arming himself with a brace of pistols, and mounting his fleetest steed (and a valuable stud he had), he rode in pursuit, stopping not before he reached Aberdeen. Not finding the fugitives there, he hastened to Edinburgh, with the twofold object of bringing back his daughter and shooting her companion in flight. After diligent inquiry in the city, he obtained what he considered reliable information that they had proceeded in the direction of the Borders, to be married at Gretna Green, a village celebrated as a place where many distinguished and obscure persons have been married by a blacksmith. As the reader already knows, the offended father went in the wrong direction.

Months passed before the captain's equanimity became restored; but time, the alleviator of sorrow and best soother of a turbulent spirit, brought a favourable change.

Mr. and Mrs. Campbell arrived safe in America, the land of their adoption, with little more means than sufficient to provide for their immediate wants. After love's first fever ended, calm reflection followed. Romance disappeared before the stern realities of life. Friends they had few, relations none, in the wild wide expanse of America. Mrs. Campbell became home-sick: the scenes of her father's mansion, and everything pleasant connected with the estate, rose before her mind's eye. Above all, she constantly thought of her father with more than half regret at the rash act she had been guilty of. Then she did what most young ladies would do under similar circumstances--wrote to her father asking forgiveness. Before Captain Bloomer received the letter, the last spark of anger in his breast had given place to paternal anxiety. Left alone without wife or child, gladly would he have welcomed her home, had not prudential reasons rendered it necessary to keep father and daughter separate. Her letter gave great satisfaction; and he resolved to assist her and her husband. Through an English friend, a sufficient amount was remitted to America, to enable Mr. Campbell to purchase an estate. The young couple settled down comfortably in an improving locality, with every prospect of comfort and happiness.

Before the fifth winter of Mr. and Mrs. Campbell's married life had passed, Mr. Campbell died, leaving his wife alone (they had no issue) in a far distant country. Mrs. Campbell returned to Scotland, and took up her residence in Edinburgh for a few years. Again a brave defender of his country led the lady to the hymeneal altar. The union proved an unhappy one: Mrs. Smith (this, though a common name, is the cognomen by which she will now be known) separated from her husband, and sailed once more for America. Preferring town life to solitude in the forest, Mrs. Smith settled down (if such could be said of one possessed of bustling active habits like hers) in the greatest city of the United States. To augment an income rendered small through the misfortune and death of her father, she became a journalist. Her papers were favourably received, being pointed and piquant. Her talents were chiefly directed to the support of women's rights; and she became a leader of the class of strong-minded women, still seeking to assert their rights in politics, science, and art.

CHAPTER LXXI.

Superstition at Chelmsford--Woman   Bewitched--Fortune-telling Quack--
Old   Zadkiel--Incantation in Somerset--Turning the Bible   and Key--Woman
assuming the form of a Hare--Woman   ruling the Stars--Young Women De-
ceived--Superstition   in London--Generality of Superstition--A   Prediction--
How to preserve Children from   Disease--Dreams Fulfilled--Virtue of Holly and
Ivy in   Worcestershire and Herefordshire--Legend concerning   the Tichborne
Family--Romantic Divorce Case.

A case tried at Chelmsford, on the Home Circuit, in 1864, affords a curious proof how much antique superstition still lingers amongst the English peasantry. For twenty years before 1863 there had been living in one of the Essex villages an old man, deaf and dumb, who enjoyed the reputation of a wizard or fortune-teller. He was eighty years of age, and the singularities of his manner and appearance contributed to the impression he made on the rustic mind. The better sort of people treated the old man with a kindness due rather to his calamities than to his profession, while the more sceptical of the rabble who did not fear him, seem to have amused themselves occasionally at his expense.

Dummey had been at the village of Ridgewell, near Hedingham, in the summer of 1863, where there was a beer-house, the landlady of which was one Emma Smith. The old magician wanted to sleep in the beer-house instead of returning to his own hut, but Emma Smith refused to give him leave. He gesticulated menacingly in his own fashion with his stick, and went his way angrily. Soon after this Emma became ill. The image of Dummey rose before her mind, and she pronounced herself "bewitched."

After long misery, she went forth to seek the old man, found him at the "Swan," a public-house near his own den, and tried to persuade him to return with her, that his presence might break the spell which hung over her. She repeatedly offered him three sovereigns as payment for this service; but neither money nor words could move him. Meanwhile the news spread that a woman who had been bewitched by old Dummey was at the "Swan," and a crowd assembled and pulled the unlucky wizard about, so that he fell once or twice on the ground. Smith took an active part in the assault; and after the "Swan" was closed, she was seen beating him and tearing his clothes. Fear for herself--fear of his supernatural gifts--were both merged in the stronger feeling of rage; and at last she, assisted by one Stammers, a carpenter, pushed the old man into a brook. He died at Halsted poorhouse from the effects of the ill-usage. Emma Smith and Stammers were sentenced to six months hard labour for their share in this outrage--the judge excusing the leniency of the punishment on the ground of the woman's state of mental excitement, and of the man's having pulled Dummey out of the water when the ducking seemed likely to produce death.

Only a few years ago an example of superstition in England came prominently before a public court of justice. It appears that in the neighbourhood of South Molton, North Devon, an old man aged eighty-six, living at Westdown, near Barnstaple, was charged with "using certain subtle craft, means, or device by palmistry and otherwise, to deceive and impose on certain of her Majesty's subjects." For some time a woman named Elizabeth Saunders, then residing in an adjacent hamlet, had been ill. Doctors' remedies failed, and her husband sent for the old man named Harper, generally called the "White Witch," but who called himself an herbalist. He went to the house of the woman, and gave her four or five iron rods in succession, with which she tapped a piece of iron held by her in the other hand while in bed. At the ends of the rods were the names of planets, such as Jupiter and Mercury. He asked the age of the woman and the hour she was born, saying he wanted to find out under what planet she came into the world. He gave her some bitters to take, but she died a few days afterwards. The defence was that the rods and piece of metal were a rude method of using electricity, by which means the defendant had effected many cures; but no explanation was given as to the meaning of the names of the planets. It was stated that the "White Witch" charged the woman 25s. for his services. Several witnesses, called for the defence, said they had been cured of complaints in the legs and arms by the defendant's magic rods when nobody else could cure them. The Bench sentenced him to a month's imprisonment.

A case of witchcraft came recently to our knowledge from Stonehouse. Ann Bond, a professed herbalist, stood charged before a bench of justice with having obtained L1 by means of a subtle device. Mary Ann Pike said her sister, Mrs. Summers, having a bad leg, had been advised to let the prisoner see it. Bond, after looking at the limb, declared that it was not an affliction by God. She went away, and afterwards returned with some cards. These she arranged, and, after looking at them, said her sister was so ill-wished that her face would be drawn to her toes, and that she would die at the age of thirty-seven. Mrs. Summers asked the prisoner if she could do her any good. Bond replied, "Yes; if you come at once under my demand; my usual price is 25s., but I'll do it for L1." Deponent lent her sister a sovereign to give to the woman. Bond turned up a bottle, and said to witness, "There is one dark woman, and a tall woman, doing your sister injury; the circle was not laid intentionally for her, but for her husband." The prisoner was convicted and punished. She had formerly been imprisoned for a similar offence.

In 1878, at a meeting of the guardians of the Coventry Union, an inmate named Arnold, *alias* "Old Zadkiel," a professor of astrology, was the subject of inquiry. A letter had been addressed to him by a lady at Dorchester, anxious to learn "what planet she was born under, and the position of her future husband." She forwarded a number of postage stamps. There was another letter from a lady at Leamington, asking Arnold to keep an appointment with her, to "read her destiny." The astrologer formerly lived in Coventry, and carried on an extensive trade until he was sent to Warwick gaol, which he left for the workhouse. He was cautioned by the Board. "Old Zadkiel," taking offence, left the workhouse, saying he "should resume his astrology" and the "ruling of the planets."

Not long ago a well-to-do farmer near Ilchester, in Somerset, had the misfortune to have several of his cattle taken away by disease. A veterinary surgeon who was consulted, thought the remainder of the herd were in a fair way of recovery; the farmer, however, insisted that he and his cows had been "overlooked," and immediately sought out a "wise woman" residing in an adjacent town. Acting upon the advice of the old hag, the farmer returned home, and encircled with a faggot the last bullock that died, ignited the pile, and burnt the carcase, an incantation being pronounced over the burning beast. The remainder of the herd became well, and their recovery was attributed by the farmer and his simple-minded neighbours, not to the skill of the veterinary surgeon, but to the success of the weird ceremonial prescribed by the fortune-teller.

A remarkable case of credulity came before Ludlow police court, in January of this year (1879). Mary A. Collier was summoned under the local bye-laws for using abusive language to Elizabeth Oliver. Both parties, it transpired, lived in Lower Gouldford; and a sheet having been lost off a garden line, with a view to discover the thief, the superstitious practice of "turning the key and the Bible" was resorted to. Complainant said Collier met her in the street, and said the Bible had been turned down for Jones' yard, Martha Cad's yard, and Burnsnell's yard, and when Mrs. Oliver's name was mentioned, "the Bible fled out of their hands." The Bible was then turned to see if the sheet was stolen during the day or night, and Mrs. Collier then called her "a daring daylight thief." Mrs. Collier informed the Court that "the key turned for Mrs. Oliver and no one else, and the words in the Bible were for her." Mrs. Oliver said the sheet had been found under the snow. The Bench dismissed the case, and said such gross superstition was more like a relic of the past, and would not have believed that such a thing existed in this advanced age.

In the village of East Knighton, Dorsetshire, in the year above mentioned, a remarkable case reached the public ears. In a cottage dwelt a woman named Kerley and her daughter, a girl of about eighteen years, supposed to be bewitched. It was positively stated that they had been thrown out of the cottage into the street, although neither window nor door was open, and heavy articles of furniture were sent flying about in all directions.

An old woman called Burt was named as the cause of all the mischief, and she was declared to have assumed the form of a hare, to have been chased by the neighbours, and then to have sat up and looked defiantly at them. It is positively believed that until blood is drawn from the witch the manifestations will not cease.

We must confess that superstition is stripped of its romance by prosaic courts and stern judges. A case tried at Newbury quarter-sessions is fresh in the memory of many. Maria Giles, *alias* "The Ranter," well known as the "Newbury Cunning Woman," was tried on the charge of having obtained sums of money from two women living at villages in a wild district in North Hants, by falsely pretending she had the power to recover some goods they had lost. The women travelled twelve miles to consult the prisoner. She went through some absurd proceedings, and pretended she saw in a glass the parties who had taken the goods. Prisoner had practised witchcraft for many years. She professed to rule the stars, and said that if the nights were clear and fine she would be able to recover the goods sooner. The jury returned a verdict of guilty, and sentenced her to five years penal servitude.

The proceedings of a professional fortune-teller formed the subject of investigation by the mayor and other magistrates of Newbury in 1871. A widow named Maria Moss had been pretending to tell the fortune of divers persons, particularly young women, whom she had induced to go to her house. The principal witnesses called were Alice Prior and Maria Low, two young women, who proved that the prisoner had promised to tell their fortunes. Her practice had been to produce a pack of cards, which she placed upon the table, and told each girl to cut them into three parts. In one case she said she saw "London," and told Prior that she would get a good situation there, and be married to a widower. She represented to Low that she would also have an excellent situation in London, and be married to a gentleman with plenty of money. She induced the girls to obtain goods from tradesmen in the town and bring them to her house, and the girls also removed wearing apparel from their own homes and deposited the same with the prisoner, who promised to send the goods after the girls had arrived in the metropolis. However, the mother of Low discovered that clothes had been taken away from her house, and the intended journey of the girls was of course prevented. The Bench dealt with the case under the Vagrant Act, and sentenced the woman to fourteen days in Reading gaol.

In the beginning of 1879 a photographer named Henry, of Cooper's Road, Old Kent Road, London, was charged at the Southwark police court with obtaining money by false pretences. The prisoner issued an advertisement, offering for eighteen stamps to send to unmarried persons photographs of their future wives or husbands, and for twenty-four stamps a bottle of magnetic scent, or Spanish love scent, which were described, the first as "so fascinating in its effects as to make true love run smooth," and the other as "delicious, and captivating the senses," so that "no young lady or gentleman need pine in single blessedness." Several witnesses stated that they had answered these advertisements; and numbers of letters--some from Australia, China, and other places abroad, relating to them--were found at the defendant's house. It appeared that he had been carrying on a very successful fraud for some time. The magistrate sentenced the prisoner, under the Vagrant Act, to three months hard labour.

Four men were charged at the Marylebone police court, London, in 1871, with telling fortunes. They had a place in that district, in which the police found a magic mirror, cards, nativities, planetary schemes, and all the paraphernalia of fortune-telling imposition. On the police going to the house, they found no fewer than thirty or forty young women in a waiting-room, each having paid a fee. A book was found in which were entries of the dupes in each week, the numbers varying from 89 to 662. The prisoners were sentenced to three months hard labour.

Liverpool, Birmingham, Manchester, London, and nearly all the other cities, towns, and country districts of England continue to have their fortune-tellers and reputed witches and ghosts. There are still many believers in the prophecies of Mother Shipton, but none believe more implicitly in her sayings than the labouring classes of Somerset. Recently a report, put in circulation in the neighbourhood of Ham Hill, made them think a great catastrophe was about to occur in that particular locality. Mother Shipton had predicted that Ham Hill, one of the great stone quarries of Somerset and a prominent feature in the landscape for many miles, would be swallowed up on Good Friday. The collapse of this immense hill was to ensue from a terrible earthquake, the effect of which would be felt especially in that part of Somersetshire. One result of this belief was that persons left the neighbourhood temporarily in order to escape the disaster. Other people removed their household goods from shelves and cupboards, in order that they might not be thrown down by the upheaval of the earth; and in some cases, we are told, people delayed planting and cultivating their gardens. The residents who believed in the predicted event said that Yeovil would also be visited at the same time by a great and disastrous flood. One case was that of a man who delayed planting his garden with potatoes because he believed there would be a terrible frost, and that the River Thames would be covered with ice. This he connected in some way with the Ham Hill affair. Amongst the labouring classes considerable alarm existed, and Good Friday was looked forward to with no little amount of anxiety in that part of Somerset.

Good Friday came and passed without any untoward event. Yet that is not enough to dispel the faith in Mother Shipton's prediction. She is not at fault. Some blundering calculator made a mistake as to time, and the people of Somerset are yet to have their great catastrophe.

A curious superstitious custom is observed in the Isle of Man. Mothers believe their children may be preserved from disease by placing them in the hopper of a water flour-mill while the wheel makes three revolutions. On a Sunday not long since a number of children were taken to the Grena-by mill, in the parish of Malew, three miles from Castletown, in order to be subjected to the "charm" we have mentioned. Two hoppers of the mill were crammed full of children, and, as soon as they were settled, the miller caused the wheel to revolve three times, the parents of the children being present at the time. In order to be efficacious, the ceremony must be gone through at a time when the ministers of the district are preaching in their pulpits. For this reason, about noon on Sundays is generally the time chosen for the performance of this curious rite.

At an inquest lately held in London on the body of a woman aged eighty-two years, the evidence showed that the woman's death resulted from injury to the head, caused by a fall from her chair. One of the witnesses told the coroner that he believed the time had come for the woman to die. His reason for that opinion was, that she had dreamed, a fortnight before her death, that she had a fall, and cut open her head, and was likely to die in consequence.

An awful fulfilment of a dream took place at a calico-printing establishment at Sunnyside. A clerk in the work remarked to one of the machine printers that he was glad to see him at his employment; the printer asked his reason for his congratulations, when the clerk observed that during the previous night he (the clerk) had dreamed that he (the printer) had, while at his work, dropped down dead. The printer replied, in a jocular way, "You see you were mistaken, for I am alive yet." The printer being in his usual health and spirits, no further notice was taken of the matter; but singularly, at three o'clock in the afternoon of the same day, while attending to his duties at his machine, he dropped down dead without the least warning.

This year (1879) the Deal magistrates sentenced a man named George Wylds to two months imprisonment for refusing to proceed to sea in the barque "Umzinto," on a voyage from London to Port Natal. The man told the magistrate that he was satisfied with the ship, officers, and food, but he had had a dream that the ship would be lost, and would not go to sea in her for any amount of money. Once before he had a dream that a vessel in which he was sailing would be lost, and it was lost.

It is worth recording that in many parishes of Worcestershire and Herefordshire the holly and ivy that have adorned churches at Christmas-time are much esteemed and cherished.

If a small branch of holly, with the berries upon it, is taken home and hung up in the house, it is considered sure to bring a lucky year. A little of this church ivy given to sheep is considered likely to make them bring forth two lambs a-piece. The evergreens that were hung up in the house must, however, all be burned, except the mistletoe bough, which should be kept throughout the year; and it generally is in farmhouses, as, according to old people, it prevented any bad effect from the evil eye, and fiends and hobgoblins were scared away by it, as stated in this verse of an old sagacious adviser:

> "On Candlemas eve kindle the fire, and then
> Before sunset let every leaf it bren;
> But the mistletoe must hang agen
>   Till Christmas next return;
> This must be kept, wherewith to tend
> The Christmas bough, and house defend,
> For where it's safely kept, the fiend
>   Can do no mischief there."

Some country churches in Worcestershire and Herefordshire are still usually decked with sprigs of yew at Easter, and boughs of fragrant fresh-leaved birch at Whitsuntide; and a sprig of yew thus consecrated, when taken and kept in the house, is deemed a preservative from the influence or entrance of any malignant spirits. In like manner, a branch of the birch is honoured by being placed on or over the kneading-trough; for, thus placed, it is considered to be a sure antidote against heavy bread.

A celebrated case, in which the pursuer, newly returned from Australia, sought to establish, in the Court of Common Pleas (we think in 1871 or 1872), his claim to the ancient baronetcy of Tichborne, recalls to mind a legend current in the Tichborne family for many generations relative to the "Tichborne Dole." The house of Tichborne dates the possession of its right to the manor of Tichborne, near Winchester, as far back as two centuries before the Norman Conquest.

About the middle of the twelfth century the then head of the family married Mabel, only daughter and heiress of Sir Ralph de Lamerston, of Lamerston, in the Isle of Wight, by which he acquired considerable estates in that part of England, in addition to his own possessions in Hampshire. After many years of wedded happiness, during which the Lady Mabel became celebrated for her kindness and care of the poor, and death approaching, she besought her husband to grant her the means of leaving behind her a charitable bequest, in the shape of a *dole*, or measure of bread, to be distributed annually, on the 25th of March (the Feast of the Annunciation of the Blessed Virgin Mary), to all needy and indigent people who should apply for it at the hall door. The said bread was to be the produce of a certain piece of ground containing an area of fifteen acres, and of known value; but should the applicants be greater in number than the measures produced, twopence in money was to be given as the *dole*.

Lady Mabel's husband was induced to consent to his wife's request, only on condition of her being able to crawl or walk round the piece of ground demanded--a condition of apparent impracticability, from the fact of her having been bedridden for many years previous; and this task was to be performed while a certain brand, or billet of wood, was burning on the fire in the hall at Tichborne. The dame, nothing daunted, ordered her attendants to carry her to the place she had selected, where, being set down, she seemed to receive a renovation of strength, and, to the surprise of admiring onlookers, she succeeded in crawling round several rich and goodly acres within the required time. The field which was the scene of Lady Mabel's extraordinary feat retains the name of "Crawls" to the present day.

On the task being completed, the lady was re-conveyed to her chamber, and, summoning the family to her bed-side, she proceeded in a most solemn manner to deliver a prophecy respecting the future inheritors of Tichborne--predicting its prosperity as long as the annual *dole* existed, and leaving her malediction on any of her descendants who should discontinue or divert it, and declaring that, when such event should happen, *the old house would fall, the family would become extinct from the failure of heirs-male*, and that--as a final warning of the approach of their decay--a generation would appear of *seven sons*, followed immediately by one with *seven daughters and no sons*.

The *dole* continued to be regularly given from the time of Henry II. to 1799, when Sir Henry Tichborne discontinued it. Then began the fulfilment of Lady Mabel's prediction. In 1803, four years after the cessation of the gift, a portion of the house fell, and the remainder was pulled down. Sir Henry, the seventh baronet of the name of Tichborne, who had abolished the *dole*, had *seven sons*. Sir Henry, the eighth baronet, and eldest of the seven sons, married Anne, daughter of Sir Thomas Burke, Bart., of Marble Hill, and by her had *seven daughters*. Sir Henry died leaving no sons.

In 1826 Sir Henry's second brother, Edward, who eventually became the ninth baronet, having inherited the extensive property of Miss Elizabeth Doughty of Snarford Hall, was obliged, by the terms of her will, to drop the name of Tichborne and assume that of Doughty, thus fulfilling, in some measure, that part of Lady Mabel's prediction which foretold that the name would become extinct. Sir Edward Doughty married in 1827, and had an only son, who died before he attained the age of six years. Sir Edward's brother James, who eventually became the tenth baronet, married, and had two sons--Roger Charles, who was supposed to have been lost at sea off the coast of South America in the spring of 1854 (the claimant of the baronetcy from Australia called himself the said Roger); and Alfred Joseph, the eleventh baronet, whose son Henry--a posthumous child, born in 1866--is now in possession of the title and estates.

When the only son of Mr. Edward Doughty (subsequently the ninth baronet) died, the hitherto singular fulfilment of Lady Mabel's prediction struck him so forcibly that he besought his elder brother, Sir Henry Joseph, to restore the ancient *dole*, which he agreed to do; and it was again distributed, with certain restrictions, in flour, confining it to the poor of the parish of Tichborne; and in this manner it continues to be distributed to the present day.

Whether the resumption of Lady Mabel's gift may prove sufficient to ward off the fatal prediction, *time alone will show*. The male race is supposed to depend upon the life of a single heir in his minority.

This *cause celebre*, one of the most important disposed of this century, not only ended, in the claimant's defeat, but in his conviction for perjury and attempted fraud--a fraud which, if successful, would have secured him estates worth between L20,000 and L30,000 a year.

A romantic divorce case came before the High Court of Justice in England in 1876, in which the superstitious element was strongly blended. The proprietor of an extensive estate asked for a divorce from his wife, belonging to the gipsy tribe. The petitioner became interested in a family of gipsies, who were in the habit of pitching their tents on his ground. He visited their encampment, and became familiar with them. The member of the company who most excited the petitioner's attention was a daughter, by name Esmeralda, whose charms ultimately captivated the petitioner, and they were married in Norway in June 1874. The co-respondent, stated to be an Oxford man, and who also interested himself in the welfare of the gipsy race, seemed to have made the acquaintance of the parties some time after the marriage. The lady became enamoured of the Oxford gentleman. She went with him to Bristol, and after that the petitioner did not see his wife for some time. The husband received a letter from his wife stating that she was ready to be reconciled to him. They accordingly came together, and his wife suggested to him that they were both bewitched, and she stated that in order to have such bewitchment removed she would go to the Gussoree Gorge, a fabled deity in the Roman Camp, who had the power to dispel the bewitchment and restore the parties to their *status quo*. They did go to this famed astrologer, Gussoree Gorge, who turned out to be none other than the co-respondent, with whom Esmeralda was afterwards found living as his wife in Edinburgh.

The petitioner, on being examined, said the respondent complained of being bewitched, and went to Cardiff to consult the wise men of the tribe. On another occasion she went again to consult the Gussoree Gorge, or wise man, and brought back two letters from the astrologer. It occurred to witness that they were in the co-respondent's handwriting. He, on receipt of another letter after his wife left him again, went to Edinburgh, where he found her. She threw herself on her knees and craved forgiveness. He promised to forgive her. She asked to go home at once, but there was a difficulty about the train. That night they slept at Melrose, and in the morning she said she had had a dream that her lover whom she had left in Edinburgh had committed suicide. Witness agreed to allow her to go to Edinburgh, it being understood she should immediately return. She never did so, and witness did not see her again until the 31st of January.

Here the romance and superstition end. The petitioner became a wiser and sadder man. Esmeralda lived to repent of her folly, and so did the Oxford man of learning.

CHAPTER LXXII.

Spiritualism--Spiritualism not a new   Delusion--Phantoms at a *Seance*--Juggling of a   Medium--Unsuccessful Effort at a Vulgar   Deception--Spiritualists exposed--A Medium's Deception   discovered--Foolish Exhibitions--Russian Peasants and   their House Spirits--Spirits' Care over Persons and   Property--Death, Pestilence, War, and other Evils   foretold by Spirits--A Suggestion.

Much might be written concerning spiritualism (already alluded to in these pages); but really the subject deserves little attention, further than that it might be worth serious consideration whether the class of persons who lay claim to the power of raising the dead, and of being able to command responses from spirits, should not be prosecuted as rogues and cheats. Spiritualists cannot even pretend they have discovered anything new. We have repeatedly, particularly under the head "Laws against and Trials of Witches," shown that deceitful girls and old crones could perform all the sleight-of-hand and delusions practised by modern spiritualists.

Spiritualists have grossly imposed upon credulous persons; and others, without much consideration, attend *seance* after *seance*, for no other reason than that the manifestations displayed by the tricksters have become the grand arcana of fashion. The phantoms raised at a *seance* are in proportion to the gloom surrounding the audience. It cannot be doubted by men of penetration, that spiritualism, in its birth and maturity, is associated with sordidness and wickedness. At best, the spiritual operations are childish, or at least they fall short of the tricks of a Chinese juggler.

One gentleman, writing of the spiritualistic movement in 1871, says:--

"A new movement on behalf of spiritualism has sprung up in the metropolis, and Miss Kate Fox, Rochester, United States, in whose family the phenomena were first discovered, is now in England on a propagandist mission. I was invited last night to meet Miss Fox, but owing to a cold the lady was unable to come. A celebrated medium was, however, present, as were some half-dozen ladies and gentlemen well known in society--one of the latter being a sergeant-at-law, and a judge accustomed to sift evidence and determine the difference between truth and falsehood. The *seance* was not, however, productive of anything very strange. The only curious manifestation occurred with a lath about two feet long and a quarter of an inch thick, which most certainly rose off the table apparently of its own accord, and at one time seemed disposed to walk about the room, but didn't. Two glass ornaments, filled with flowers, were also attracted towards each other, and subsequently parted company though no hands were near them. The great anticipated incident of the evening was, however, a failure. A Morse writing telegraphic machine had been prepared, and it was hoped that the lever would be worked with spirit hands, but, after waiting two hours, no indication was given of any movement, and the experiment was abandoned in despair."

The well-known Walter Thornbury relates as follows his experience at a spiritual *seance*:--

"I went up into a stuffy parlour and found about fourteen people, hot, nervous, and evidently uncomfortable. They were staring at some weird-looking pictures. On a long table were several speaking-trumpets, formed of stiff brown and gilt paper. Some of the visitors took up these, talked hollowly through them, and laughed with uneasy scepticism. There were two ladies, several young men who looked like clerks, a bluff man from Liverpool, and a dwarf. Presently Messrs. A. and C. (two coarse-looking young men) entered, seated us round the table, and requested us to join hands. The gas was then turned down, and the *seance* began. A. was at the end of the table, facing C. at the other. There was at first a good deal of half-hysterical laughing and nervous talking, and shy or bold voices from here and there in the dark. The bluff Liverpool man objected to joining hands--he had been to successful *seances*, where hands were not joined. Mr. A. said that joining hands often improved 'the conditions.' One did not know what was passing behind one, or what was coming. So even the boldest of us 'held his breath for a time.' All at once Mr. C., at the further end from me, began to gurgle and groan like a person in an epileptic fit. Some one cried, 'Turn up the gas.' It was done, and we beheld the medium with his head twisted like a young laocoon in the folds of a red tablecloth. He disentangled himself with a disturbed, suffering air. The spirits were upon us, though why they should stifle their interpreter I could not quite see. The sceptics smiled sardonically. I suspected the lady in nankeen colour next me, and the dwarf and people immediately round both mediums. A female voice tremulously suggested that singing might 'improve the conditions;' on which Mr. C. struck up 'Power of Love Enchanting' in maudlin spiritualistic words. Things looked dull. All at once we were hailed by one of the most tremendous gruff bass voices that ever hailed a man-of-war. John King, the favourite spirit of Mr. A., had appeared with a grumbling announcement of his presence. 'Who is this John King?' inquired the Liverpool man, who, if he was a confederate, acted peculiarly well. 'He lived about three hundred years ago,' said some one in the dark. 'Then he must have fought with the Armada,' suggested the Liverpool representative. Mr. A. leaped at the suggestion, and replied, 'It is supposed he did.' On John King again growling that there he was and what did they want, a sceptic opposite me exclaimed in the true dramatic manner, 'Rest, rest, perturbed spirit,' which so enraged John King (whom the lady in buff next me whispered 'had been a notorious pirate') that he bellowed in his ear, 'You seem very fond of Shakspere.' A few minutes after there were sounds of violent blows, and several sceptics were struck on the head by John King's speaking-trumpet; a sofa cushion was flung at me, and something else was thrown at the gentleman from Liverpool. A sceptic who had said that any ventriloquist could imitate a deep voice, got rapped violently on the head, and John King bellowed at the same time, 'Is that ventriloquism?' A man near me said he thought he felt a cold breeze passing over his hands, and a cold finger touch his. One thing I could not help observing: this was, that the missiles hurled at sceptics came in a slanting line from where Mr. A. sat. I also noticed that a singular creaking of the medium's chair usually preceded any utterances of John King. The lady in nankeen now began, in a wheedling, coaxing voice, to beg 'Kate' to appear. Kate is Mr. A.'s second 'familiar,' and he described her to us as a short person with dark ringlets, and wearing a blue robe fastened by a girdle--facts which seemed to deeply interest the lady in nankeen. Presently a little whiffling voice announced Kate, who, however, only said something about 'Jenny Jones, of Hampstead,' and then withdrew. To Kate Mr. A. assumed a gallant, lover-like manner; to John King an air of half-amused defiance. By-and-bye two stones were thrown violently upon the table, but no one expressed any audible alarm. Still the room was hot and stifling, the darkness affected the coolest imagination, and straining one's eyes and ears for spiritual manifestations produced a not unnatural feeling of uneasiness in the mind. Sometimes I fancied the table jerked or reared a little, sometimes I thought I heard animals' feet pattering up and down the table. It is on such workings of the imagination that spiritualists, and especially the professional mediums, trade. No more voices coming, Mr. A. proposed our changing places to 'improve the conditions'--that is to say, to re-pack the confederates, and still more isolate the sceptics; but no result came. A grosser and more unsuccessful effort at a vulgar deception I never saw; and I only ask whether it is just to prosecute poor women for getting a few shillings by telling servants' fortunes, and leave professional spiritualists like Messrs. A. and C. unprosecuted? If pretending to evoke the dead and predict death for hire is not obtaining money under false pretences, what is?"

For a short time the spiritualists created a considerable sensation, but their prosperity did not long continue. Mr. W. Irving Bishop, an American gentleman, who came to Great Britain recommended by Dr. Carpenter and other members of the Royal Society, exposed the phenomena attributed to the influence of spirits, in the Windsor Hotel, Edinburgh, in January 1879.

There was a distinguished company present, including Principal Sir Alexander Grant, Lord Curriehill, Archbishop Strain, and a number of the University professors. A committee of four gentlemen having been chosen to watch the proceedings, Mr. Bishop gave an exposure of the galvanometer test, accepted by a number of scientific men in London as conclusive proof of the *bona fides* of spirit manifestations. Mr. Bishop next gave an illustration of the theory of "unconscious cerebration." Archbishop Strain, having written on a slip of paper a number of figures and the name of a deceased person, took in his left hand the end of a long wire. Mr. Bishop, taking the other, recited the numerals from 1 to 9, and stopped at the figures in one of the papers. Afterwards he recited the alphabet in the same manner, stopping at the letters in the name on the same slip. The figures 6952 were found to be those which had been written. The archbishop stated before the paper was opened that he did not himself remember the figures he had put down, and that he had never mentioned what they were to any one. Mr. Bishop explained that he detected the figures when naming them, from the unconscious action of the archbishop's mind on his nervous system as it affected the wire. In the same way he informed the archbishop correctly that the name of a deceased person written in the enclosed piece of paper was Sir Walter Scott. Mr. Bishop also furnished illustrations of the manner in which sounds were produced from instruments of music, and bells rung by persons tied with their hands and legs to seats, and how, even in that situation, he could put a ring upon a handkerchief placed round his neck--a feat which had been considered impossible by one fastened as he was, without the loosing of the knots of the cords with which he was bound. His last exposure was the Katie King mystery, the calling of 'material spirits' from the other world, and exhibiting them in the room. This performance puzzled the audience as much as any of the others while it proceeded, and the explanation given of it was as amusing as it turned out to be ingenious.

Another spiritualist exposure recently created a sensation in "spiritualistic circles," by the detection of a medium fraud in Portland, Maine, United States. Doctors Gerrish and Greene, of Portland, were instrumental in bringing about the issue. The medium in question was a female, who, after hiding herself behind a screen in the corner of her parlour, was enabled to send out "spirits" for the inspection of her select audiences. Attired in the ordinary way, she would allow her skirts to be pinned to the floor; and while she was seated upon a stool, the lower portion of the screen being some distance from the floor, the audience were invited to satisfy themselves that the medium did not move from her position. Dr. Greene, on one occasion, while the so-called spirit was moving around, asked it to shake hands. This request being granted, he firmly grasped the hand, and found the spirit to be the medium herself, who struggled in a very unbecoming way to free herself. While Dr. Greene thus secured the medium, Dr. Gerrish quickly drew the screen aside, and discovered the apparel of the lady in a heap at the foot of her stool, and still pinned to the floor. The trick was then shown to consist in wearing under-garments, with which she could emerge from her external apparel with ease, and, to all outside appearance, without any disturbance.

To our mind, the most foolish of all foolish exhibitions is that at which one has the presumption to stand before an intelligent audience and declare his ability to call one from the dead for his or their amusement. But if we can by any great stretch of imagination suppose that Englishmen and Americans have succeeded in opening up a communication between them and spirits, they are still far behind the Russian peasants, who have their house spirits, who are of considerable use. These spirits take persons, houses, cattle, and chattels of every description under their care. They are heard wailing before a death. One of them rouses the inmates of a house if fire or robbery be threatened. Pestilence and war are foretold by such spirits lamenting in the meadows. Here we have useful spirits, worth having--not like our ones, capable of communicating only by means of knocks and through showmen. If spirits can do no more for living men than they have done, they may remain away, and let the showman medium return to honest labour, or be sent to seek knowledge and truth within the walls of a prison or in a house of correction.

CHAPTER LXXIII.

Superstition in Roman Catholic Countries--Miracle-working Images, Winking Madonnas and Apparitions--Image paying Homage to the Virgin Mary--St. Dominic--Madonnas at Trastevere--Girl carrying the Sacred Stigmata of the Passion--Miraculous Cures--The Virgin Mary appearing to Children--Superstitious Ceremony at Dieppe--Blessing the Neva--Lady offering up her Life to save the Pope--A Legend--Superstitious Belief of Napoleon's Mother--Trust in Amulets--Zulu Superstition--Witchcraft forbidden under Treaty of Peace with Great Britain--Eating Fetish--Superstition among the Ashantees--Endeavour to prevent the Advance of the British Army--Shah of Persia's Talismans--Bathing Fair--Indian Princes consulting Fortune-tellers--The Queen of Hearts--Procuring Rain in India--Superstition in America--Mysterious Lights at St. Lawrence--Superstitious Artists--Hogarth's last Picture, "The End of all Things."

In Roman Catholic countries superstition frequently culminates in miracle-working images, winking madonnas, and apparitions resembling the Virgin Mary. For not a few delusions the priests and nuns are responsible. We are not speaking without authority. The Very Rev. Father A. Vincent Jandel, General of the Dominican Order, addressed from Rome a circular letter in 1870 to all the provincials of his order, giving an account of what he considered a wonderful occurrence that took place at Soriano, in Calabria. There is at Soriano a celebrated Sanctuary of St. Dominic, and in the church an ancient image of that saint, life-size, carved in wood, held in high veneration. On the 15th of September of that year, which is its festa, another image of wood is carried processionally with much pomp. Thirty persons, who had remained after the conclusion of the solemnity to pray before the ancient image, suddenly perceived it to move, as if alive. It came forward, then retreated, and turned towards the image of the Virgin of the Holy Rosary. The cry of "St. Dominic! St. Dominic! A miracle! a miracle!" burst from every lip. The wonderful news sped like lightning through the town. Men and women left their occupations to crowd to the sanctuary; and soon no fewer than two thousand persons had witnessed the strange movements, which continued for about an hour and a half, amidst prayers, tears, and acclamations.

To the great joy of the monks of the Holy Trinity, in 1871, two madonnas, in an obscure, out-of-the-way church of St. Grisogono, in Trastevere, melted multitudes to tears by the miraculous movements and expressions of their eyes. The most remarkable in its exercises was an oil painting in the interior of the church. To such a height did the excitement reach amongst the crowd privileged to witness it, that the friars judged it prudent to bring its performances to a close by removing it from the church, and shutting it up in a press in the convent. The second madonna is a fresco in the open piazza as one approaches the church and convent. It is a recent painting, of life-size, with eyes lowered on the spectators looking at it from below, in such a manner that the movements of the pupils (if movements there be) should be very sensible. The madonna is but one of three figures on the fresco. On her right is John the Baptist in the dress of the monks of the establishment, and on the left Pio Nono as Pontiff. This madonna began to move its eyes as soon as its companion was locked up, and the wonder lasted for many days.

In the same year (1871) the Rev. Father Ubald sent a letter to a colleague, the following passages of which were quoted in the *Bulletin Religieux* of Versailles:--"I arrive from Belgium; this time I have seen Louise Lateau. I do not know whether you ever heard of her, but at present the name is in everybody's mouth in Belgium and Northern France. Louise Lateau is a girl of 21, who carries the sacred stigmata of the Passion, and every week on Friday is in a state of profound ecstacy. Dr. Lefevre, professor of medicine at the University of Louvain, has published a medical examination, in which he says: 'The flow of blood begins in the night (from Thursday to Friday generally), between midnight and one o'clock.' It took place for the first time on the 24th April 1868, by her losing blood on the left side of her chest. On the Friday following, hemorrhage was observed at the same place, and, moreover, blood oozed out from the top or instep of the foot. On the third Friday--viz. the 8th May--blood came out at the left side and from the feet during the night. Towards nine in the morning blood rushed out copiously from both hands, back and palm. Finally, on the 27th September, a percolation of blood also set in on the forehead, as if the young girl had been crowned with thorns. Since then the marvellous phenomenon never missed a Friday, except once or twice. Doctors affirm that Louise thus loses from five to ten ounces of blood every Friday. In spite of this, and albeit she has not taken food for the last six months, she has, I assure you, quite ruddy cheeks (*teint vermeil*), and seems to enjoy capital health (*sante florissant*)."

The correspondent of the Paris Ultramontane paper *L'Univers* wrote from the Lourdes in 1876: "I have just been witness of a marvel, of which I hasten to send you an account. Several other miracles have taken place within the last couple of days, but I have said nothing about them, as they did not come under my own observation. However, I can assure you of the accuracy of the following statement:--Madeleine Lansereau, aged 33 years, broke one of her legs about 19 years ago, and became lame, her left leg being fearfully twisted. She came to Lourdes with the pilgrimage from Picardy, and was radically cured at the moment the Papal Nuncio sent to crown the Holy Virgin was saying the paternoster in the mass he was celebrating in the grotto. She told the crowd that, having walked into the little pool, a lively internal emotion took possession of her, and she cried out, 'I am cured! I am cured!' Her companions wept with joy and admiration at the miracle. When they asked her what she had done for that great grace, her simple reply was, 'I have prayed to St. Radogonde and St. Joseph, but especially to the Holy Virgin, and now I am cured.' While she was speaking, the Bishop of Poictiers came and said, 'Madeleine, thank the Holy Virgin fervently.'"

The Rev. Canon Tandy, D.D., writing from St. Paul's Convent, Birmingham, in 1871, to a reverend brother, informs him, in pious phraseology, that two nuns had been suddenly cured of serious disorders of long standing by drinking a bottle of water from Lourdes. In acknowledgment of the favours shown by our Lady of Lourdes, the *Te Deum* was recited.

A deaf and dumb girl from Blois was made whole at Lourdes a few years ago by the Virgin Mary.

Not long since the Bishop of Laval wrote a pastoral letter on the subject of the miraculous appearance of the Virgin to four children in a village in Mayence, and was so convinced of the reality of the fact that he decided to erect a chapel in honour of Mary on the ground upon which she had condescended to appear.

Recently there might be seen emerging from a church at Dieppe, on a Saturday morning, a religious procession, headed by a person carrying a silver processional cross, and accompanied by choristers singing penitential psalms, proceeding to the eastern pier of the harbour to perform a curious Roman Catholic ceremony. Taking up a position beside the rolling water, the priests prayed for the success of the fishing, then said a paternoster, while the people knelt; then a priest, dipping a brush in holy water (which was carried in a swinging silver vase), sprinkled three times the salt water of the ocean with the holy fluid, making the sign of the cross with the brush at the words, *Seo sibera nos a malo*. Then came a collect of repose for the souls of the dead whose bodies had not been recovered from the depths of the sea; and, all being over, the priests, with the choristers, people, and cross-bearers, returned, chanting their psalms to the church, where the high mass of the festival of St. Luke was celebrated.

This ceremony at Dieppe reminds one of the well-known annual ceremony in Russia, of blessing the Neva in presence of the Czar and other members of the Imperial Family; but, as the performance has been described by numerous writers, we shall not further refer to it.

The Marquis of Segur, a zealous Catholic, relates that, in 1866, when the Pope was seriously ill, Mdlle. Leautard, a lady of Marseilles, resolved to offer up her life in place of his Holiness, and sought his permission to do so. The Pope, after long silence, placed his hand on her head, and said, "Go, my daughter, and do what the Spirit of God has suggested to you." Next day, on receiving the consecrated wafer, the lady fervently expressed her desire to die, and was immediately seized with a sharp pain, which carried her off three days afterwards. The Pope, on hearing of her death, exclaimed, "So soon accepted!" The Marquis believes this sacrifice accounted for the Pope's prolonged life.

A Hohenzollern legend was brought to mind in Germany through a serious illness of the Emperor, who, however, fortunately recovered, and continues to adorn his exalted position. The legend runs thus:--

Many years ago there was a Hohenzollern Princess (a widow with two children), who fell in love with a foreign Prince--rich, handsome, and brave. She sent him a proposition of marriage; but the Prince declined her suit, explaining that "four eyes" stood between him and acceptance. He referred to his parents, whose consent he could not obtain. But the Princess understood him to refer to the four eyes of her two children--to his unwillingness, in fact, to become a stepfather. So she suffocated the infant obstacles, and wrote to her lover that the way was clear. He was stricken with horror at the cruel deed, and died cursing her bloodthirsty rashness. The Princess, in her turn, became overwhelmed with remorse. After lingering a day or two in indescribable anguish, she too died, and was buried under the old castle at Berlin; but not to rest quietly in her unhappy grave. At rare intervals she appears at midnight, clad in white, gliding, ghost like, about the castle; and the apparition always forebodes the death of some member of the Hohenzollern family. The white lady has been seen, we are assured, three times within about a year--once just before the death of Prince Albrecht; again, to announce the end of Prince Adalbert; and the last time while Queen Elizabeth lay on her deathbed.

We have shown that the great Napoleon Bonaparte was superstitious in the highest degree; and so was his mother before him. Both believed in fate or destiny. She was surrounded by luxury and pomp; but her solicitude about her son, and the belief that his glory could not last, rendered her miserable. The divorce of Josephine, the retreat from Russia, the exile to Elba, the final overthrow at Waterloo, and the banishment to St. Helena, were heavy blows; but she was prepared for them. While the sun of the Emperor's fortunes blazed in the zenith, she shivered under the shadow of her fear; and her fear proved prophetic. She witnessed the downfall of every one of her children; but she bore her adversity with dignity and resignation, and died in her eighty-seventh year.

Indeed not only were Napoleon and his mother superstitious, but the whole Bonaparte family were believers in fate. Napoleon III. says in his will, "With regard to my son" (the late Prince Imperial, who perished at the hands of Zulus), "let him keep, as a talisman, the seal attached to my watch." True to the traditions of his family, the young Prince put trust in amulets. When the Prince's body was discovered (here we have a double case of superstition), it lay stripped of all its clothing, but there were left with the body a locket and a gold amulet, admittedly the seal bequeathed to him by his Imperial father, as the Zulus were afraid they were charms--articles they stand in great dread of.

Thinking of Prince Napoleon's untimely death, brings the Zulu character to remembrance. Among the Zulus a belief prevails that kindly and angry spirits hover around them--the former endeavouring to do them good; the latter trying to do them harm. Zulus also believe in divine smoke, witchcraft, and dreams. Whenever a charge of witchcraft is made against any one, no mercy is shown him. Such an accusation affords a pretext to a king or chief for getting rid of an obnoxious person and acquiring his substance. The Inyanga, like our witch-finder of old, has no difficulty in bringing home guilt to the unfortunate accused. A Zulu judge, before pronouncing sentence, pretends that he consults the divine oracles of his nation. When a Zulu sneezes he says, "I am blessed, and the ancestral spirit is with me." So he praises the family manes, and ends by asking blessings, such as cattle and wives.

In September 1879 official news came from Sir Garnet Wolseley that King Cetewayo had been captured, that the Zulu war had come to an end, and that the following were among the terms of peace, signed by the chiefs of Zululand: "I will not tolerate the employment of witch doctors, or the practice known as smelling out, or any practices of witchcraft."

Not unfrequently the representatives of Great Britain, in concluding peace with heathen nations, have, as in the case of the Zulus, to respect the superstitious notions of the people they have to deal with, so as to make the agreement more binding in the minds of the heathen contracting parties.

On one occasion the Ashantees put up a fetish to stop the advance of the British army. It consisted of a kid transfixed through the throat and heart, and staked to the ground; six cooking-pots, inverted, were stuck on stakes round the kid, and, a few feet from it, another kid was found buried: this, according to Ashantee custom, had been buried alive. A similar fetish had been put up at a river near Moinsey to stop the British troops. The advancing army found almost every turn of the road to Coomassie strewn with fetish documents. Near Fommanah nearly every tree had a white rag fastened to it as a charm. On the King hearing of the British victory, he went to pour libation to the spirits of his ancestors, and to ask their assistance against the enemies of his country.

The Shah of Persia has numerous talismans, exceeding two hundred in number. We give details of four of them. One is a gold star, supposed to have been possessed by the legendary Rustem. It is called Merzoum, and has the reputation of making conspirators immediately confess. When the Shah's brother was accused of treason some time since, the star was shown him, and, terrified and overcome by remorse, he avowed his iniquities. His confession was, of course, attributed to its efficacy. He was banished. The next important talisman is a cube of amber, which, we are told, fell from heaven in Mohammed's time. It is supposed to render the Shah invulnerable, and he wears it about his neck. Another is a little box of gold, set in emeralds, and blessed by the Prophet. It renders the Royal Family invisible as long as they are celibates. Another is a diamond set in one of the Shah's scimitars, which renders its possessor invincible; and there is also a dagger with the same property, but it is ordained that those who use it shall perish by it. It is therefore carefully kept shut up in a sandal-wood box, on which is engraved a verse of the Koran.

As of old, superstition prevails all over India. Semi-religious ceremonies are gone through in seasons of drought, to procure rain. At other times means are taken to propitiate the gods, to subdue enemies, and to secure good fortune to individuals, households, and communities. There are Indian princes who regularly consult their fortune-tellers regarding public and private affairs.

A curious bathing fair was held at Ajudhia, in Oude, in February 1878. When a peculiar conjunction of the planets takes place (which occurs only once in eighty years), the natives rush in crowds to the river, as they believe that if they manage to bathe and go through certain ceremonies in four minutes and a half, they will obtain the remission of their own sins and those of millions of their ancestors. On this occasion the rush to the river turned out so great that numbers were trodden under foot, and sixty-five persons lost their lives.

The mysterious lights in the Gulf of St. Lawrence, which are believed by mariners to be warnings of great tempests and shipwreck, were unusually brilliant in 1878. It is said to be a fact, established by the experience of a century, that when these lights blaze brightly in the summer nights, the phenomena are invariably followed by great storms. They give the appearance to spectators on the shore of a ship on fire. The fire itself seems to consist of blue and yellow flames, now dancing high above the water, and then flickering, paling, and dying out, only to spring up again with fresh brilliancy. If a boat approaches, it flits away, moving further out, and is pursued in vain. The lights are plainly visible from the shore from midnight until two in the morning. They appear to come from the sea shoreward, and at dawn retire gradually, and are lost in the morning mist. Paradis, the French pilot, who took charge of the British Fleet under Admiral Sir Hovenden Walker when it sailed up the St. Lawrence to seize Quebec in 1711, declared he saw one of these lights before that armada was shattered by a dreadful gale on the 22d of August. The light, he said, danced before his vessel all the way up the gulf. Every great wreck that has taken place there since Sir Hovenden Walker's calamity has been preceded, if tradition is to be believed, by these mysterious lights, and they have thus warned the mariner of fatal storms.

In July last (1879) a woman, known as the Queen of Hearts, who had attained the age of one hundred years, and who had been known for three quarters of a century as a fortune-teller, died in Vienna. Apparently gifted with the faculty of prescience, intimately acquainted with the shuffling of cards, deeply learned in the lore of the prophetic lines traced by the graver of Fate upon human hands and feet, this lady devoted her days to the unravelling of the tangled secrets of the future, charging those whose curiosity prompted them to pry into the regions of the unknown, five ducats per revelation. As many of the leading ladies of the Austrian aristocracy were among her clients, and the accuracy of her forecasts having earned for her a mighty reputation throughout the realms of the Hapsburgs, she contrived to amass a handsome fortune. "Herz-Dame" was a person of extraordinary acumen, and a physiognomist of the highest order. Her sources of private information were numerous, and her ramifications are believed to have permeated every class of Austrian society.

A comparatively recent instance of superstition in America is that of an old Indian woman being suspected of witchcraft, and stoned to death in Pine Nut Valley, Nevada; and in another part of the world, far separated from America, a similar act of superstition was committed, in which a human creature fell a victim to the gross delusions of her neighbours. We refer to a case of witch-burning in Russia. In October 1879 seventeen peasants were tried for burning to death a supposed witch, who resided near Nijni-Novgorod. Of the accused persons, fourteen were acquitted, and three sentenced to church penances--sentences which, if rigorously carried out, will not be easily borne.

A Leipsic writer gives an account of a number of superstitious artists, some of which are very curious. Tietjens, for instance, believed that the person would speedily die who shook hands with her over the threshold at parting; Rachel thought she gained her greatest successes immediately after she had met a funeral; Bellini would not permit a new work to be brought out if on the day announced he was first greeted by a man, and "La Somnambula" was several times thus postponed; Meyerbeer regularly washed his hands before beginning an overture; and a noted *tragedienne* never plays unless she has a white mouse in her bosom.

But these eccentricities can hardly compare with the strange belief and doings of Hogarth, the celebrated painter and engraver, particularly towards the close of his long life. A few months before he was seized with the malady which cut him off, he commenced his "End of all Things." A few of his intimate friends looked upon his picture as prophetic; and so he seemed to regard it himself. The artist worked with diligence, seemingly with an apprehension that he would not live to complete the piece. Finish it, however, he did in a masterly style, grouping everything that could denote the end of all things. Prominent were a broken bottle, an old broom, a bow unstrung, the butt-end of an old musket, a crown tumbled in pieces, towers in ruins, the moon in her wane, the map of the globe burning, Ph[oe]bus and his horses dead in the clouds, a vessel wrecked, Time with his hour-glass and scythe broken, a tobacco-pipe in his mouth, the last puff of smoke going out; a play-book, with *Exeunt Omnes* on one of the open pages; an empty purse, and a statute of bankruptcy taken out against nature.

"So far so good," said Hogarth. "Nothing remains but this,"--taking his pencil and dashing off the similitude of a painter's palette broken. "FINIS!" exclaimed the artist; "*the deed is done*--ALL IS OVER." Hogarth never handled pencil again, and within a month of the completion of this picture he was no more.

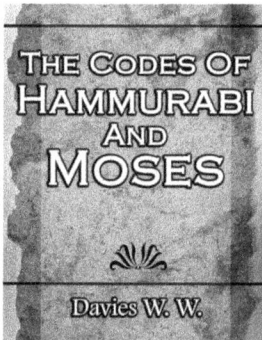

The Codes Of Hammurabi And Moses
W. W. Davies

QTY

The discovery of the Hammurabi Code is one of the greatest achievements of archaeology, and is of paramount interest, not only to the student of the Bible, but also to all those interested in ancient history...

Religion **ISBN:** *1-59462-338-4* **Pages:132**
MSRP $12.95

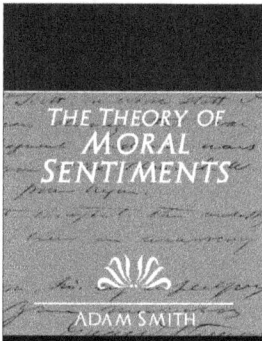

The Theory of Moral Sentiments
Adam Smith

QTY

This work from 1749. contains original theories of conscience amd moral judgment and it is the foundation for systemof morals.

Philosophy **ISBN:** *1-59462-777-0* **Pages:536**
MSRP $19.95

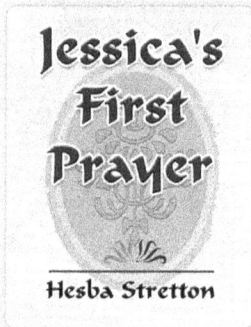

Jessica's First Prayer
Hesba Stretton

QTY

In a screened and secluded corner of one of the many railway-bridges which span the streets of London there could be seen a few years ago, from five o'clock every morning until half past eight, a tidily set-out coffee-stall, consisting of a trestle and board, upon which stood two large tin cans, with a small fire of charcoal burning under each so as to keep the coffee boiling during the early hours of the morning when the work-people were thronging into the city on their way to their daily toil...

Pages:84

Childrens **ISBN:** *1-59462-373-2* *MSRP $9.95*

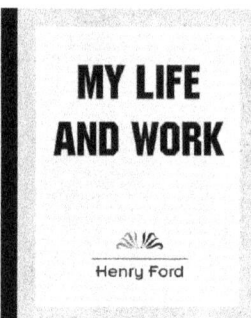

My Life and Work
Henry Ford

QTY

Henry Ford revolutionized the world with his implementation of mass production for the Model T automobile. Gain valuable business insight into his life and work with his own auto-biography... "We have only started on our development of our country we have not as yet, with all our talk of wonderful progress, done more than scratch the surface. The progress has been wonderful enough but..."

Pages:300

Biographies/ **ISBN:** *1-59462-198-5* *MSRP $21.95*

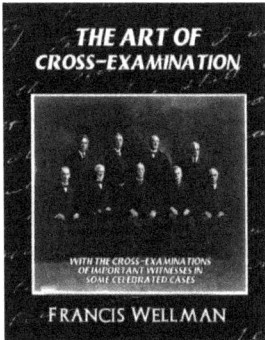

The Art of Cross-Examination
Francis Wellman

QTY

I presume it is the experience of every author, after his first book is published upon an important subject, to be almost overwhelmed with a wealth of ideas and illustrations which could readily have been included in his book, and which to his own mind, at least, seem to make a second edition inevitable. Such certainly was the case with me; and when the first edition had reached its sixth impression in five months, I rejoiced to learn that it seemed to my publishers that the book had met with a sufficiently favorable reception to justify a second and considerably enlarged edition. ...

Reference   ISBN: *1-59462-647-2*   Pages:412   MSRP *$19.95*

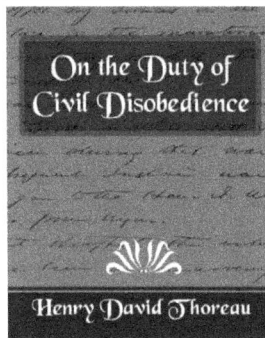

On the Duty of Civil Disobedience
Henry David Thoreau

QTY

Thoreau wrote his famous essay, On the Duty of Civil Disobedience, as a protest against an unjust but popular war and the immoral but popular institution of slave-owning. He did more than write—he declined to pay his taxes, and was hauled off to gaol in consequence. Who can say how much this refusal of his hastened the end of the war and of slavery ?

Law   ISBN: *1-59462-747-9*   Pages:48   MSRP *$7.45*

Dream Psychology Psychoanalysis for Beginners
Sigmund Freud

QTY

Sigmund Freud, born Sigismund Schlomo Freud (May 6, 1856 - September 23, 1939), was a Jewish-Austrian neurologist and psychiatrist who co-founded the psychoanalytic school of psychology. Freud is best known for his theories of the unconscious mind, especially involving the mechanism of repression; his redefinition of sexual desire as mobile and directed towards a wide variety of objects; and his therapeutic techniques, especially his understanding of transference in the therapeutic relationship and the presumed value of dreams as sources of insight into unconscious desires.

Psychology   ISBN: *1-59462-905-6*   Pages:196   MSRP *$15.45*

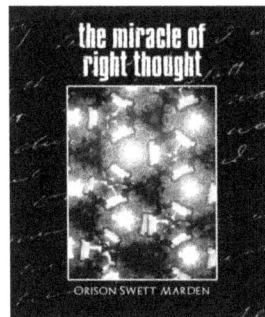

The Miracle of Right Thought
Orison Swett Marden

QTY

Believe with all of your heart that you will do what you were made to do. When the mind has once formed the habit of holding cheerful, happy, prosperous pictures, it will not be easy to form the opposite habit. It does not matter how improbable or how far away this realization may see, or how dark the prospects may be, if we visualize them as best we can, as vividly as possible, hold tenaciously to them and vigorously struggle to attain them, they will gradually become actualized, realized in the life. But a desire, a longing without endeavor, a yearning abandoned or held indifferently will vanish without realization.

Self Help   ISBN: *1-59462-644-8*   Pages:360   MSRP *$25.45*

www.bookjungle.com *email: sales@bookjungle.com fax: 630-214-0564 mail: Book Jungle PO Box 2226 Champaign, IL 61825*

QTY

☐	**The Rosicrucian Cosmo-Conception Mystic Christianity** by *Max Heindel* — ISBN: *1-59462-188-8* **$38.95** *The Rosicrucian Cosmo-conception is not dogmatic, neither does it appeal to any other authority than the reason of the student. It is: not controversial, but is: sent forth in the, hope that it may help to clear...* — New Age/Religion Pages 646
☐	**Abandonment To Divine Providence** by *Jean-Pierre de Caussade* — ISBN: *1-59462-228-0* **$25.95** *"The Rev. Jean Pierre de Caussade was one of the most remarkable spiritual writers of the Society of Jesus in France in the 18th Century. His death took place at Toulouse in 1751. His works have gone through many editions and have been republished...* — Inspirational/Religion Pages 400
☐	**Mental Chemistry** by *Charles Haanel* — ISBN: *1-59462-192-6* **$23.95** *Mental Chemistry allows the change of material conditions by combining and appropriately utilizing the power of the mind. Much like applied chemistry creates something new and unique out of careful combinations of chemicals the mastery of mental chemistry...* — New Age Pages 354
☐	**The Letters of Robert Browning and Elizabeth Barret Barrett 1845-1846 vol II** — ISBN: *1-59462-193-4* **$35.95** by *Robert Browning* and *Elizabeth Barrett* — Biographies Pages 596
☐	**Gleanings In Genesis (volume I)** by *Arthur W. Pink* — ISBN: *1-59462-130-6* **$27.45** *Appropriately has Genesis been termed "the seed plot of the Bible" for in it we have, in germ form, almost all of the great doctrines which are afterwards fully developed in the books of Scripture which follow...* — Religion/Inspirational Pages 420
☐	**The Master Key** by *L. W. de Laurence* — ISBN: *1-59462-001-6* **$30.95** *In no branch of human knowledge has there been a more lively increase of the spirit of research during the past few years than in the study of Psychology, Concentration and Mental Discipline. The requests for authentic lessons in Thought Control, Mental Discipline and...* — New Age/Business Pages 422
☐	**The Lesser Key Of Solomon Goetia** by *L. W. de Laurence* — ISBN: *1-59462-092-X* **$9.95** *This translation of the first book of the "Lemegton" which is now for the first time made accessible to students of Talismanic Magic was done, after careful collation and edition, from numerous Ancient Manuscripts in Hebrew, Latin, and French...* — New Age/Occult Pages 92
☐	**Rubaiyat Of Omar Khayyam** by *Edward Fitzgerald* — ISBN: *1-59462-332-5* **$13.95** *Edward Fitzgerald, whom the world has already learned, in spite of his own efforts to remain within the shadow of anonymity, to look upon as one of the rarest poets of the century, was born at Bredfield, in Suffolk, on the 31st of March, 1809. He was the third son of John Purcell...* — Music Pages 172
☐	**Ancient Law** by *Henry Maine* — ISBN: *1-59462-128-4* **$29.95** *The chief object of the following pages is to indicate some of the earliest ideas of mankind, as they are reflected in Ancient Law, and to point out the relation of those ideas to modern thought.* — Religion/History Pages 452
☐	**Far-Away Stories** by *William J. Locke* — ISBN: *1-59462-129-2* **$19.45** *"Good wine needs no bush, but a collection of mixed vintages does. And this book is just such a collection. Some of the stories I do not want to remain buried for ever in the museum files of dead magazine-numbers an author's not unpardonable vanity..."* — Fiction Pages 272
☐	**Life of David Crockett** by *David Crockett* — ISBN: *1-59462-250-7* **$27.45** *"Colonel David Crockett was one of the most remarkable men of the times in which he lived. Born in humble life, but gifted with a strong will, an indomitable courage, and unremitting perseverance...* — Biographies/New Age Pages 424
☐	**Lip-Reading** by *Edward Nitchie* — ISBN: *1-59462-206-X* **$25.95** *Edward B. Nitchie, founder of the New York School for the Hard of Hearing, now the Nitchie School of Lip-Reading, Inc, wrote "LIP-READING Principles and Practice". The development and perfecting of this meritorious work on lip-reading was an undertaking...* — How-to Pages 400
☐	**A Handbook of Suggestive Therapeutics, Applied Hypnotism, Psychic Science** — ISBN: *1-59462-214-0* **$24.95** by *Henry Munro* — Health/New Age/Health/Self-help Pages 376
☐	**A Doll's House: and Two Other Plays** by *Henrik Ibsen* — ISBN: *1-59462-112-8* **$19.95** *Henrik Ibsen created this classic when in revolutionary 1848 Rome. Introducing some striking concepts in playwriting for the realist genre, this play has been studied the world over.* — Fiction/Classics/Plays 308
☐	**The Light of Asia** by *sir Edwin Arnold* — ISBN: *1-59462-204-3* **$13.95** *In this poetic masterpiece, Edwin Arnold describes the life and teachings of Buddha. The man who was to become known as Buddha to the world was born as Prince Gautama of India but he rejected the worldly riches and abandoned the reigns of power when...* — Religion/History/Biographies Pages 170
☐	**The Complete Works of Guy de Maupassant** by *Guy de Maupassant* — ISBN: *1-59462-157-8* **$16.95** *"For days and days, nights and nights, I had dreamed of that first kiss which was to consecrate our engagement, and I knew not on what spot I should put my lips..."* — Fiction/Classics Pages 240
☐	**The Art of Cross-Examination** by *Francis L. Wellman* — ISBN: *1-59462-309-0* **$26.95** *Written by a renowned trial lawyer, Wellman imparts his experience and uses case studies to explain how to use psychology to extract desired information through questioning.* — How-to/Science/Reference Pages 408
☐	**Answered or Unanswered?** by *Louisa Vaughan* — ISBN: *1-59462-248-5* **$10.95** *Miracles of Faith in China* — Religion Pages 112
☐	**The Edinburgh Lectures on Mental Science (1909)** by *Thomas* — ISBN: *1-59462-008-3* **$11.95** *This book contains the substance of a course of lectures recently given by the writer in the Queen Street Hall, Edinburgh. Its purpose is to indicate the Natural Principles governing the relation between Mental Action and Material Conditions...* — New Age/Psychology Pages 148
☐	**Ayesha** by *H. Rider Haggard* — ISBN: *1-59462-301-5* **$24.95** *Verily and indeed it is the unexpected that happens! Probably if there was one person upon the earth from whom the Editor of this, and of a certain previous history, did not expect to hear again...* — Classics Pages 380
☐	**Ayala's Angel** by *Anthony Trollope* — ISBN: *1-59462-352-X* **$29.95** *The two girls were both pretty, but Lucy who was twenty-one who supposed to be simple and comparatively unattractive, whereas Ayala was credited, as her Bombwhat romantic name might show, with poetic charm and a taste for romance. Ayala when her father died was nineteen...* — Fiction Pages 484
☐	**The American Commonwealth** by *James Bryce* — ISBN: *1-59462-286-8* **$34.45** *An interpretation of American democratic political theory. It examines political mechanics and society from the perspective of Scotsman James Bryce* — Politics Pages 572
☐	**Stories of the Pilgrims** by *Margaret P. Pumphrey* — ISBN: *1-59462-116-0* **$17.95** *This book explores pilgrims religious oppression in England as well as their escape to Holland and eventual crossing to America on the Mayflower, and their early days in New England...* — History Pages 268

QTY

The Fasting Cure *by Sinclair Upton* ISBN: *1-59462-222-1* **$13.95**
In the Cosmopolitan Magazine for May, 1910, and in the Contemporary Review (London) for April, 1910, I published an article dealing with my experiences in fasting. I have written a great many magazine articles, but never one which attracted so much attention... New Age/Self Help/Health Pages 164

Hebrew Astrology *by Sepharial* ISBN: *1-59462-308-2* **$13.45**
In these days of advanced thinking it is a matter of common observation that we have left many of the old landmarks behind and that we are now pressing forward to greater heights and to a wider horizon than that which represented the mind-content of our progenitors... Astrology Pages 144

Thought Vibration or The Law of Attraction in the Thought World ISBN: *1-59462-127-6* **$12.95**
by William Walker Atkinson Psychology/Religion Pages 144

Optimism *by Helen Keller* ISBN: *1-59462-108-X* **$15.95**
Helen Keller was blind, deaf, and mute since 19 months old, yet famously learned how to overcome these handicaps, communicate with the world, and spread her lectures promoting optimism. An inspiring read for everyone... Biographies/Inspirational Pages 84

Sara Crewe *by Frances Burnett* ISBN: *1-59462-360-0* **$9.45**
In the first place, Miss Minchin lived in London. Her home was a large, dull, tall one, in a large, dull square, where all the houses were alike, and all the sparrows were alike, and where all the door-knockers made the same heavy sound... Childrens/Classic Pages 88

The Autobiography of Benjamin Franklin *by Benjamin Franklin* ISBN: *1-59462-135-7* **$24.95**
The Autobiography of Benjamin Franklin has probably been more extensively read than any other American historical work, and no other book of its kind has had such ups and downs of fortune. Franklin lived for many years in England, where he was agent... Biographies/History Pages 332

Name	
Email	
Telephone	
Address	
City, State ZIP	

☐ **Credit Card** ☐ **Check / Money Order**

Credit Card Number	
Expiration Date	
Signature	

Please Mail to: Book Jungle
PO Box 2226
Champaign, IL 61825
or Fax to: 630-214-0564

ORDERING INFORMATION

web: *www.bookjungle.com*
email: *sales@bookjungle.com*
fax: *630-214-0564*
mail: *Book Jungle PO Box 2226 Champaign, IL 61825*
or PayPal *to sales@bookjungle.com*

Please contact us for bulk discounts

DIRECT-ORDER TERMS

**20% Discount if You Order
Two or More Books**
Free Domestic Shipping!
Accepted: Master Card, Visa,
Discover, American Express

www.ingramcontent.com/pod-product-compliance
Lightning Source LLC
Chambersburg PA
CBHW080602270326
41928CB00016B/2903